# Technology Integration Advancements in Distributed Systems and Computing

Nik Bessis
*University of Derby, UK & University of Bedfordshire, UK*

**Information Science**
**REFERENCE**

| | |
|---|---|
| Managing Director: | Lindsay Johnston |
| Senior Editorial Director: | Heather Probst |
| Book Production Manager: | Sean Woznicki |
| Development Manager: | Joel Gamon |
| Development Editor: | Heather Probst |
| Acquisitions Editor: | Erika Gallagher |
| Typesetter: | Lisandro Gonzalez |
| Cover Design: | Nick Newcomer, Lisandro Gonzalez |

Published in the United States of America by
Information Science Reference (an imprint of IGI Global)
701 E. Chocolate Avenue
Hershey PA 17033
Tel: 717-533-8845
Fax: 717-533-8661
E-mail: cust@igi-global.com
Web site: http://www.igi-global.com

Library of Congress Cataloging-in-Publication Data

Technology integration advancements in distributed systems and computing / Nik
Bessis, editor.
     p. cm.
  Includes bibliographical references and index.
  Summary: "This book offers a vital compendium of research and developments within the field of distributed computing, giving case studies, frameworks, architectures, and best practices for academics and practitioners alike"--Provided by publisher.
  ISBN 978-1-4666-0906-8 (hardcover) -- ISBN 978-1-4666-0907-5 (ebook) -- ISBN 978-1-4666-0908-2 (print & perpetual access) 1. Electronic data processing--Distributed processing. I. Bessis, Nik, 1967-
  QA76.9.D5T43 2012
  004'.36--dc23
                                2011052646

British Cataloguing in Publication Data
A Cataloguing in Publication record for this book is available from the British Library.

All work contributed to this book is new, previously-unpublished material. The views expressed in this book are those of the authors, but not necessarily of the publisher.

Hala Skaf-Molli, *University of Henri Poincaré, France*
Rob Smith, *Newcastle University, UK*
George Spanoudakis, *City University, UK*
Konstantinos Tserpes, *National Technical University of Athens, Greece*
Scott Turner, *University of Northampton, UK*
Hossana Twinomurinzi, *University of Pretoria, South Africa*
Steven Warburton, *King's College London, UK*

# Table of Contents

## Section 1
## Advanced Integration Methods and Services

*Xia Zhao, University of Bedfordshire, UK*
*Tao Wang, University of Bedfordshire, UK*
*Enjie Liu, University of Bedfordshire, UK*
*Gordon J. Clapworthy, University of Bedfordshire, UK*

*Sana Sellami, LIRIS, National Institute of Applied Science of Lyon, France*
*Aïcha-Nabila Benharkat, LIRIS, National Institute of Applied Science of Lyon, France*
*Youssef Amghar, LIRIS, National Institute of Applied Science of Lyon, France*

*Ghalem Belalem, University of Oran, Es Senia, Algeria*
*Naima Belayachi, University of Oran, Es Senia, Algeria*
*Radjaa Behidji, University of Oran, Es Senia, Algeria*
*Belabbes Yagoubi, University of Oran, Es Senia, Algeria*

*Ye Huang, University of Fribourg, Switzerland*
*Amos Brocco, University of Fribourg, Switzerland*
*Michele Courant, University of Fribourg, Switzerland*
*Beat Hirsbrunne, University of Fribourg, Switzerland*
*Pierre Kuonen, University of Applied Sciences of Western Switzerland, Switzerland*

### Section 2
### State-of-the-Art Middleware Technologies and Architectures

## Section 3
## High Performance Distributed Systems and Applications

# Detailed Table of Contents

## Section 1
## Advanced Integration Methods and Services

### Chapter 1

    *Xia Zhao, University of Bedfordshire, UK*

    *Tao Wang, University of Bedfordshire, UK*

    *Enjie Liu, University of Bedfordshire, UK*

    *Gordon J. Clapworthy, University of Bedfordshire, UK*

Distributed information systems are growing rapidly in response to the improvement of computer hardware and software and this is matched by the evolution of the technologies involved. This paper focuses mainly on Web Services technology and discusses related technical issues including availability, performance and composition. It also introduces Grid, agents and Semantic Web technologies that can work together with Web Services to serve different business goals.

### Chapter 2

    *Sana Sellami, LIRIS, National Institute of Applied Science of Lyon, France*

    *Aïcha-Nabila Benharkat, LIRIS, National Institute of Applied Science of Lyon, France*

    *Youssef Amghar, LIRIS, National Institute of Applied Science of Lyon, France*

With the development and the use of a large variety of DB schemas and ontologies, in many domains (e.g. semantic web, digital libraries, life science, etc), matching techniques are called to overcome the challenge of aligning and reconciling these different interrelated representations. Matching field is becoming a very attractive research topic. In this paper, the authors are interested in studying scalable matching problem. The authors survey the approaches and tools of large scale matching, when a large number of schemas/ontologies and attributes are involved. They attempt to cover a variety of techniques for schema matching called Pair-wise and Holistic. One can acknowledge that this domain is on top of effervescence and scalable matching needs many more advances. Therefore, they propose our scalable schema matching methodology that deals with the creation of a hybrid approach combining these techniques. Their architecture includes a pre-matching approach based on XML schemas decomposition.

As shown by their experiments, their proposed methodology has been evaluated and implementing in a PLASMA (Platform for LArge Scale MAtching) prototype.

Ghalem Belalem, University of Oran, Es Senia, Algeria

Naima Belayachi, University of Oran, Es Senia, Algeria

Radjaa Behidji, University of Oran, Es Senia, Algeria

Belabbes Yagoubi, University of Oran, Es Senia, Algeria

Data grids are current solutions to the needs of large scale systems and provide a set of different geographically distributed resources. Their goal is to offer an important capacity of parallel calculation, ensure a data effective and rapid access, improve the availability, and tolerate the breakdowns. In such systems, however, these advantages are possible only by using the replication technique. The use of this technique raises the problem of maintaining consistency of replicas of the same data set. In order to guarantee replica set reliability, it is necessary to have high coherence. This fact, however, penalizes performance. In this paper, the authors propose studying balancing influence on replica quality. For this reason, a service of hybrid consistency management is developed, which combines the pessimistic and optimistic approaches and is extended by a load balancing service to improve service quality. This service is articulated on a hierarchical model with two levels.

Ye Huang, University of Fribourg, Switzerland

Amos Brocco, University of Fribourg, Switzerland

Michele Courant, University of Fribourg, Switzerland

Beat Hirsbrunne, University of Fribourg, Switzerland

Pierre Kuonen, University of Applied Sciences of Western Switzerland, Switzerland

This work presents the design and architecture of a decentralized grid scheduler named MaGate, which is developed within the SmartGRID project and focuses on grid scheduler interoperation. The MaGate scheduler is modular structured, and emphasizes the functionality, procedure and policy of delegating local unsuited jobs to appropriate remote MaGates within the same grid system. To avoid an isolated solution, web services and several existing and emerging grid standards are adopted, as well as a series of interfaces to both publish MaGate capabilities and integrate functionalities from external grid components. Meanwhile, a specific swarm intelligence solution is employed as a critical complementary service for MaGate to maintain an optimized peer-to-peer overlay that supports efficient resource discovery. Regarding evaluation, the effectiveness brought by job sharing within a physically connected grid community with the use of the MaGate has been illustrated by means of experiments on communities of different scale, and under various scenarios.

Ankur Gupta, Model Institute of Engineering and Technology, India

Lalit K. Awasthi, National Institute of Technology, India

P2P networks have caught the imagination of the research community and application developers with their sheer scalability and fault-tolerance characteristics. However, only content-sharing applications based on the P2P concept have reached the desired level of maturity. The potential of the P2P concept for designing the next-generation of real-world distributed applications can be realized only if a comprehensive framework quantifying the performance related aspects of all classes of P2P applications is available. Researchers have proposed some QoS (Quality-of-Service) parameters for content-sharing P2P applications based on response time and delay, but these do not cover the gamut of application domains that the P2P concept is applicable to. Hence, this research paper proposes an early QoS framework covering various classes of P2P applications; content distribution, distributed computing and communication and collaboration. Early results from the prototype implementation of the Peer Enterprises framework (a cross-organizational P2P collaborative application) are used as a basis for formulation of the QoS parameters. The individual performance measures which comprise the QoS framework are also discussed in detail along with some thoughts on how these can be complied with. The proposed framework would hopefully lead to quantifiable Service-Level Agreements for a variety of peer-to-peer services and applications.

## Chapter 6

*Theodora Varvarigou, National Technical University of Athens, Greece*
*Konstantinos Tserpes, National Technical University of Athens, Greece*
*Dimosthenis Kyriazis, National Technical University of Athens, Greece*
*Fabrizio Silvestri, Italian National Research Council, Italy*
*Nikolaos Psimogiannos, University of the Aegean, Greece*

This article deals with the problem of quality provisioning in business service-oriented environments, examining the resource selection process as an initial matching of the provided to the demanded QoS. It investigates how the application and resource characteristics affect the provided level of QoS, a relationship that intuitively exists but has not yet being mapped. To do so, it focuses on identifying the application and resource parameters that affect the customer-defined QoS parameters. The article realistically centres upon modeling a data mining application and simple PC nodes in order to study how they affect response times. It moves on, by proving the existence of these specific relations and maps them using simple artificial neural networks so as to be able to wrap them in a single mechanism for resource selection based on customer QoS requirements and real time provider QoS capabilities.

### Section 2
### State-of-the-Art Middleware Technologies and Architectures

## Chapter 7

*Pierre Kuonen, University of Applied Sciences of Western Switzerland, Switzerland*
*Marie-Christine Sawley, Swiss Federal Institute of Technology Zurich, Switzerland*

Foresight in HPC is not merely a question of when Petaflop, or Exa- applications will be available. A much deeper view is fundamental for understanding the accompanying driving forces –both present and future-, and for making important choices based on the most relevant criteria. The SOS workshop series established in 1997 aims at bringing together once a year scientists and industries from all over the world to discuss and to envision the future of HPC technologies. These meetings have proved invaluable for discussing the state of the art and for anticipating future major developments in the field. We propose here a brief review of the history of HPC since the foundation of SOS and of the impact of the major trends and possible disruptions envisioned for the next five years.

There is considerable interest in achieving a 1000 fold increase in supercomputing power in the next decade, but the challenges are formidable. In this paper, the authors discuss some of the driving science and security applications that require Exascale computing (a million, trillion operations per second). Key architectural challenges include power, memory, interconnection networks and resilience. The paper summarizes ongoing research aimed at overcoming these hurdles. Topics of interest are architecture aware and scalable algorithms, system simulation, 3D integration, new approaches to system-directed resilience and new benchmarks. Although significant progress is being made, a broader international program is needed.

In a recent acquisition by DOE/NNSA several large capacity computing clusters called TLCC have been installed at the DOE labs: SNL, LANL and LLNL. TLCC architecture with ccNUMA, multi-socket, multi-core nodes, and InfiniBand interconnect, is representative of the trend in HPC architectures. This paper examines application performance on TLCC contrasting them with Red Storm/Cray XT4. TLCC and Red Storm share similar AMD processors and memory DIMMs. Red Storm however has single socket nodes and custom interconnect. Micro-benchmarks and performance analysis tools help understand the causes for the observed performance differences. Control of processor and memory affinity on TLCC with the numactl utility is shown to result in significant performance gains and is essential to attenuate the detrimental impact of OS interference and cache-coherency overhead. While previous studies have investigated impact of affinity control mostly in the context of small SMP systems, the focus of this paper is on highly parallel MPI applications.

As high-performance computing moves to the petascale and beyond, a number of algorithmic and software challenges need to be addressed. This paper reviews the main performance-limiting factors in today's high-performance computing software and outlines a possible new programming paradigm to address them. The proposed paradigm is based on abstract parallel data structures and operations that encapsulate much of the complexity of an application, but still make communication overhead explicit. The authors argue that all numerical simulations can be formulated in terms of the presented abstractions, which thus define an abstract semantic specification language for parallel numerical simulations. Simulations defined in this language can automatically be translated to source code containing the appropriate calls to a middleware that implements the underlying abstractions. Finally, the structure and functionality of such a middleware are outlined while demonstrating its feasibility on the example of the parallel particle-mesh library (PPM).

**Chapter 11**

Curtis L. Janssen, Sandia National Laboratories, USA

Helgi Adalsteinsson, Sandia National Laboratories, USA

Scott Cranford, Sandia National Laboratories, USA

Joseph P. Kenny, Sandia National Laboratories, USA

Ali Pinar, Sandia National Laboratories, USA

David A. Evensky, Sandia National Laboratories, USA

Jackson Mayo, Sandia National Laboratories, USA

Efficient design of hardware and software for large-scale parallel execution requires detailed understanding of the interactions between the application, computer, and network. The authors have developed a macro-scale simulator (SST/macro) that permits the coarse-grained study of distributed-memory applications. In the presented work, applications using the Message Passing Interface (MPI) are simulated; however, the simulator is designed to allow inclusion of other programming models. The simulator is driven from either a trace file or a skeleton application. Trace files can be either a standard format (Open Trace Format) or a more detailed custom format (DUMPI). The simulator architecture is modular, allowing it to easily be extended with additional network models, trace file formats, and more detailed processor models. This paper describes the design of the simulator, provides performance results, and presents studies showing how application performance is affected by machine characteristics.

**Chapter 12**

James L. Tomkins, Sandia National Laboratories, USA

Ron Brightwell, Sandia National Laboratories, USA

William J. Camp, Sandia National Laboratories, USA

Sudip Dosanjh, Sandia National Laboratories, USA

Suzanne M. Kelly, Sandia National Laboratories, USA

Paul T. Lin, Sandia National Laboratories, USA

Courtenay T. Vaughan, Sandia National Laboratories USA

John Levesque, Cray Inc., USA

Vinod Tipparaju, Oak Ridge National Laboratory, USA

The Red Storm architecture, which was conceived by Sandia National Laboratories and implemented by Cray, Inc., has become the basis for most successful line of commercial supercomputers in history. The success of the Red Storm architecture is due largely to the ability to effectively and efficiently solve a wide range of science and engineering problems. The Cray XT series of machines that embody the Red Storm architecture have allowed for unprecedented scaling and performance of parallel applications spanning many areas of scientific computing. This paper describes the fundamental characteristics of the architecture and its implementation that have enabled this success, even through successive generations of hardware and software.

The conjugation of High Performance Computing (HPC) and Grid paradigm with applications based on commercial software is one among the major challenges of today e-Infrastructures. Several research communities from either industry or academia need to run high parallel applications based on licensed software over hundreds of CPU cores; a satisfactory fulfillment of such requests is one of the keys for the penetration of this computing paradigm into the industry world and sustainability of Grid infrastructures. This problem has been tackled in the context of the PI2S2 project that created a regional e-Infrastructure in Sicily, the first in Italy over a regional area. Present paper will describe the features added in order to integrate an HPC facility into the PI2S2 Grid infrastructure, the adoption of the InifiniBand low-latency net connection, the gLite middleware extended to support MPI/MPI2 jobs, the newly developed license server and the specific scheduling policy adopted. Moreover, it will show the results of some relevant use cases belonging to Computer Fluid-Dynamics (Fluent, OpenFOAM), Chemistry (GAMESS), Astro-Physics (Flash) and Bio-Informatics (ClustalW)).

**Section 3**
**High Performance Distributed Systems and Applications**

This article describes new security solutions for Grid middleware, and specifically faces the issues related to the management of users' and servers' credentials, together with storing and secure data transmission in the Grid. Our work, built on Grid Security Infrastructure (GSI), provides new capabilities (i.e. smart card Grid access, and strong security file storage XML-based) to be used on top of different Grid middlewares, with a low level of changes. This work is currently implemented on gLite and accomplishes the access to Grid resources in a uniform and transparent way. These improvements enable the Grid computing toward the new processing model known as business services.

## Chapter 15

*Eleana Asimakopoulou, University of Bedfordshire, UK*

*Chimay J Anumba, Loughborough University, UK*

*Dino Bouchlaghem, The Pennsylvania State University, USA*

The emergency management community is working toward developments associated with the reduction of losses in lives, property and the environment caused by natural disasters. However, several limitations with the particular collaborative nature of current Information and Communication Technology (ICT) in use have been reported. In particular, how emergency management stakeholders within an ICT environment can bring together all their resources in a collaborative and timely manner so as to improve the effectiveness and efficiency of emergency response tasks. With this in mind, the authors describe the Grid-Aware Emergency Response Model (G-AERM) to make the best of functionality offered by emerging ICT to support intelligence in decision making toward a more effective and efficient emergency response management.

## Chapter 16

*Nik Bessis, University of Bedfordshire, UK*

*Antony Brown, University of Bedfordshire, UK*

*Eleana Asimakopoulou, University of Bedfordshire, UK*

Much work is under way within the Grid technology community on issues associated with the development of services fostering the integration and exploitation of multiple autonomous, distributed data sources through a seamless and flexible virtualized interface. These developments involve fluid and dynamic, ad hoc based interactions between dispersed service providers and consumers. However, several obstacles arise in the design and implementation of such services. In this article, the authors examine a notable obstacle, namely how to keep service consumers informed of relevant changes about data committed in multiple and distributed service provider levels, and most importantly, when these changes can affect others' well-being. To achieve this, the authors use aggregated case scenarios to demonstrate the need for a data-Grid push service in a disaster management situation. In this regard, the article describes in detail the service architecture, as well as its mathematical analysis for keeping interested stakeholders informed automatically about relevant and critical data changes.

## Chapter 17

*Yu Fang, Tongji University, China*

*Dong Liang Zhang, Tongji University, China*

*Chun Gang Yan, Tongji University, China*

*Hong Zhong Chen, Tongji University, China*

*Changjun Jiang, Tongji University, China*

Traffic information service plays an important role in one's daily life. However, traffic information processing is very complicated because of its dynamic, cooperative and distributed features. This paper presents the Service and Monitoring Oriented Traffic Information Grid. In this system, it is a remarkable characteristic to provide real-time, dynamic information services for travelers and traffic managers by grid technology. The system provides travelers with services of optimized route scheme, bus arrival prediction based on real-time route status, and route status forecast. For traffic managers, the system can provide vehicle tracing, traffic monitoring, history data analysis, and decision making on traffic control strategy. In this regard, key research includes large multi-source traffic data integration, route status forecast, and optimum dynamic travel scheme implementation based on massive GPS data.

**Chapter 18**

*Ondrej Habala, The Slovak Academy of Sciences, Slovakia*
*Martin Šeleng, The Slovak Academy of Sciences, Slovakia*
*Viet Tran, The Slovak Academy of Sciences, Slovakia*
*Branislav Šimo, The Slovak Academy of Sciences, Slovakia*
*Ladislav Hluchý, The Slovak Academy of Sciences, Slovakia*

The project Advanced Data Mining and Integration Research for Europe (ADMIRE) is designing new methods and tools for comfortable mining and integration of large, distributed data sets. One of the prospective application domains for such methods and tools is the environmental applications domain, which often uses various data sets from different vendors where data mining is becoming increasingly popular and more computer power becomes available. The authors present a set of experimental environmental scenarios, and the application of ADMIRE technology in these scenarios. The scenarios try to predict meteorological and hydrological phenomena which currently cannot or are not predicted by using data mining of distributed data sets from several providers in Slovakia. The scenarios have been designed by environmental experts and apart from being used as the testing grounds for the ADMIRE technology; results are of particular interest to experts who have designed them.

**Chapter 19**

*Genoveffa (Jeni) Giambona, University of Reading, UK*
*David W. Birchall, University of Reading, UK*

Small and medium-sized enterprises (SMEs) create a dynamic and successful European economy. Existing skill deficiencies in sales, management and administrative staff are adversely affecting competitiveness in almost a third of those small firms surveyed (Bolden, 2001, 2007). Additionally, attending face-to-face and classroom-based development courses is problematic for time-poor SME managers. Thanks to the development of new technologies online learning is becoming commonplace due to wireless and mobile devices, together with the Internet boom, are providing the infrastructure necessary to support the development of new learning forms. Collaborative learning, especially as represented by an action learning approach, would seem ideal for SME managers. But can collaborative learning be adopted as a blanket approach in the case of SME managers? Or should one first take into account the contextual influences on learning, networking and collaboration?

As the use of instructional video is becoming a key component of e-learning, there is an increasing need for a distributed system which supports collaborative video annotation and organization. In this paper, the authors construct a distributed environment on the top of NaradaBrokering to support collaborative operations on video material when users are located in different places. The concept of video annotation is enriched, making it a powerful media to improve the instructional video organizing and viewing. With panorama based and interpolation based methods, all related users can annotate or organize videos simultaneously. With these annotations, a video organization structure is consequently built through linking them with other video clips or annotations. Finally, an informal user study was conducted and result shows that this system improves the efficiency of video organizing and viewing and enhances user's participating into the design process with good user experience.

It has been widely recognized that bibliographic information plays an increasingly important role for scientific research. Peer-to-peer (P2P) networks provide an effective environment for people belonging to a community to share various resources on the Internet. This paper presents OBIRE, an ontology based P2P network for bibliographic information retrieval. For a user query, OBIRE computes the degree of matches to indicate the similarity of a published record to the query. When searching for information, users can incorporate their domain knowledge into their queries which guides OBIRE to discover the bibliographic records that are of most interest of users. In addition, fuzzy logic based user recommendations are used to compute the trustiness of a set of keywords used by a bibliographic record which assists users in selecting bibliographic records. OBIRE is evaluated from the aspects of precision and recall, and experimental results show the effectiveness of OBIRE in bibliographic information retrieval.

# Preface

Distributed systems and technologies have been the subject of intense research for many years. Clearly, this is not a new subject, yet it continues to be very vibrant. This is mainly due to the fact that many concerns have been encountered, as most of the technologies are very often heterogeneous and geographically distributed. Notably enough, technologies are in fact meant to be used by several communities of users, which are also geographically distributed. Hence, the ability to make technologies interoperable remains a crucial factor for the development of several types of society systems. Clearly, one of the challenges for such facilitation is that of technologies integration, which aims to provide seamless and flexible access to multiple autonomous, distributed, and heterogeneous resources.

On the other hand, the volume of data being currently created and digitized is growing at an unprecedented rate. The efficient and effective mining of useful information from high volume data sets is becoming an increasing scientific challenge: what is currently known as the "big data" challenge.

While a wealth of data processing techniques have been proposed, traditionally these algorithms can only be deployed on single computers utilizing limited computing resources for data processing. Thus, the combination of large dataset size, geographic distribution of users and resources, and computationally intensive analysis results in complex and stringent performance demands that, until recently, have not been satisfied by any existing computational and data management infrastructure. However, a rapid development of novel distributed computing paradigms have been emerged including but not limited to peer-to-peer (P2P), service oriented, Grid and Cloud computing and other, next generation technologies. These computing paradigms can utilize various resources over the Internet for solving data and computationally intensive problems in an efficient way. Implementation of data processing algorithms and systems in high-performance distributed computing environments is thus becoming crucial to ensure system scalability as data continues to grow inexorably in size and complexity.

Even though the advantages of these types of evolutionary research are continually acknowledged, it is only recently that the need to appreciate its applicability into the real world of the information society has been realized. During the last decade, scientists have almost exclusively used these for their own research and development purposes, but lately the focus is clearly shifting to more interdisciplinary application domains that are closer to everyday life. These can provide people from different organizations and locations with the opportunity for resource (hardware, instrumentation, software, application, and data) level integration as a means to help assist diverse disciplines' progression.

In turn, these distributed systems' integration pushes typical application developments and involves application areas in Web dynamic data integration such as resource, process and workflow integration, and management for science-to-science, science-to-business, business-to-business, business-to-customer, or customer-to-customer integration. Hence, these paradigms have an increased focus on the integration of distributed systems, resources, and technologies, which are available within and across various collaborative communities or organizations. As such, the size and complexity of integrating and applying cutting-edge distributed technologies are enormous and thus, there is a particular need to acknowledge research undertaken as a means to broaden the applicability and scope of the current body of knowledge in the area.

The maturation of the field, together with these new issues raised by the continuous and diversified challenges in the underlying technology and application domains, require a central focus in the area. The goal of the Technology Integration Advancements in Distributed Systems and Computing book is to provide such a focus for the presentation and dissemination of new research results about the development and integration of applicable distributed systems and technologies.

## THE PURPOSE OF THE BOOK

The book aims to demonstrate a network of excellence in effectively and efficiently integrating distributed related resources using a variety of advanced computational methods and technologies. Its mission is to introduce, and thus, to highlight a feasible and applicable arrangement within business and other organizational e-infrastructures.

It also deepens its focus by highlighting strengths, weaknesses, opportunities, and threats when these are deployed within a real-world organizational setting. Contributions in this book pay particular attention to presenting topics that are diverse in scale and complexity, as well as written by and for a technical minded audience.

More importantly, the goal of the book is to prompt and foster further development for best practices in identifying opportunities and thus, it provides an excellent source for future applicable directions and technology innovative adoptions in the society.

## WHO SHOULD READ THIS BOOK?

The content of the book offers state-of-the-art information and references for research work undertaken in the challenging area of advanced integration technologies and distributed computing including resource discovery and scheduling; service oriented architectures; Web and Grid services; high performance data processing and high performance computing middleware and architectures. With this in mind, the book offers an excellent source for the technical audience and the computer science minded scholar. Thus, the book should be of particular interest for the following people.

First, it is of interest to researchers and doctoral students who are fully engaging in the area of distributed computing, distributed data technologies, and integration technologies. The book should be also a very useful reference for all researchers and doctoral students working in the broader fields of high performance computing, applicable computational technologies, distributed computing, service oriented architectures, Web services, collaborative technologies, agent intelligence, and data mining.

Second, the book should be useful to academics and mainly postgraduate students engaging in research informed teaching and/ or learning in the aforementioned emerging technologies fields. The view here is that the book can serve as a good reference offering a solid understanding of the integration and distributed computing subject area.

Third, the book is a great resource for professionals including computing specialists, practitioners, managers, and consultants who may be interested in identifying ways and thus, applying a number of well defined and/or applicable cutting edge techniques and processes within the aforementioned domain areas.

## BOOK ORGANIZATION AND OVERVIEW

Twenty-one self-contained chapters, each authored by experts in the area, are included in this book. The book is organized into three sections according to the thematic topic of each chapter. Having said that, it is quite possible that a chapter in one section may also address issues covered in other sections.

### Section 1: Advanced Integration Methods and Services

This section includes six chapters. It introduces both principles and advancements in various integration technologies, methods, and services for delivering high quality of service in several environments that are supported from Web Services, peer-to-peer, service oriented, and Grid architectures. While these stand as a state-of-the-art reference, some chapters present scenarios and approaches on how these methods and techniques could be further improved. As such, they underpin future development and implementation of relevant services.

In Chapter 1 – Web Services in Distributed Information Systems: Availability, Performance and Composition – authors focus on Web services technology and discusses related technical issues including availability, performance and composition. It also introduces Grid, agents, and Semantic Web technologies that can work together with Web services to serve different business goals.

In Chapter 2 – Towards a more Scalable Schema Matching: A Novel Approach – authors are interested in studying scalable matching problem. They survey the approaches and tools of large scale matching, when a large number of schemas/ ontologies and attributes are involved. They attempt to cover a variety of techniques for schema matching, and as such, they propose a scalable schema matching methodology that deals with the creation of a hybrid approach combining these techniques. Their architecture includes a pre-matching approach based on XML schemas decomposition and as shown by their experiments, the proposed methodology has been evaluated and implementing in a PLASMA (Platform for LArge Scale MAtching) prototype.

In Chapter 3 – Load Balancing to Increase the Consistency of Replicas in Data Grids – authors discuss that data grids are current solutions to the needs of large scale systems. In such systems, advantages are possible only by using the replication technique. In order to guarantee replica set reliability, it is necessary to have high coherence. This fact, however, penalizes performance. In this chapter, the authors propose studying balancing influence on replica quality. For this reason, a service of hybrid consistency management is developed, which combines the pessimistic and optimistic approaches and is extended by a load balancing service to improve service quality. This service is articulated on a hierarchical model with two levels.

In Chapter 4 – MaGate: An Interoperable, Decentralized and Modular High-level Grid Scheduler – authors present the design and architecture of a decentralized grid scheduler, named MaGate, which is developed within the SmartGRID project and focuses on Grid scheduler interoperation. The MaGate scheduler is modular structured, and emphasizes the functionality, procedure and policy of delegating local unsuited jobs to appropriate remote MaGates within the same grid system. In addition, a specific swarm intelligence solution is employed as a critical complementary service for MaGate to maintain an optimized peer-to-peer overlay that supports efficient resource discovery. Finally, several experiments on communities of different scale, and under various scenarios are offered.

In Chapter 5 – Towards a Quality of Service Framework for Peer-to-Peer Applications – authors discuss that the potential of the Peer-to-Peer (P2P) concept for designing the next-generation of real-world distributed applications can be realized only if a comprehensive framework quantifying the performance related aspects of all classes of P2P applications is available. In this chapter, authors propose an early Quality of Service (QoS) framework covering various classes of P2P applications; content distribution, distributed computing and communication and collaboration. Early results from the prototype implementation of the Peer Enterprises framework (a cross-organizational P2P collaborative application) are used as a basis for formulation of the QoS parameters. The individual performance measures, which comprise the QoS framework, are also discussed in detail along with some thoughts on how these can be complied with.

In Chapter 6 – A Study on the Effect of Application and Resource Characteristics on the QoS in Service Provisioning Environments – authors deal with the problem of quality provisioning in business service-oriented environments by examining the resource selection process as an initial matching of the provided to the demanded Quality of Service (QoS). The chapter realistically centres upon modeling a data mining application and simple PC nodes in order to study how they affect response times. It moves on, by proving the existence of these specific relations and maps them using simple artificial neural networks so as to be able to wrap them in a single mechanism for resource selection based on customer QoS requirements and real time provider QoS capabilities.

## Section 2: State-of-the-Art Middleware Technologies and Architectures

This section includes seven chapters. The content of this section is particularly valuable to those whose interest resides within the area of high performance computational technologies and architectures. While it stands as a state-of-the-art reference it also provides forthcoming real-world advances in the area.

In Chapter 7 – The Crystal Ball in HPC Has Never Been More Exciting, nor More Important – authors detail that foresight in High Performance Computing (HPC) is not merely a question of when Petaflop, or Exa- applications will be available. A much deeper view is fundamental for understanding the accompanying driving forces, both presently and in the future, and for making important choices based on the most relevant criteria. In this chapter, authors propose a brief review of the history of HPC since the foundation of SOS and of the impact of the major trends and possible disruptions envisioned for the next five years.

In Chapter 8 – On The Path to Exascale – authors refer to that there is considerable interest in achieving a 1000 fold increase in supercomputing power in the next decade, but the challenges are formidable. This chapter discusses some of the driving science and security applications that require Exascale computing (a million, trillion operations per second). The chapter summarizes ongoing research aimed at overcoming these hurdles. Topics of interest are architecture aware and scalable algorithms, system simulation, 3D integration, new approaches to system-directed resilience, and new benchmarks.

In Chapter 9 – Application Performance on the Tri-Lab Linux Capacity Cluster (TLCC) – authors discuss that in a recent acquisition by DOE/NNSA several large capacity computing clusters called TLCC have been installed at the DOE labs: SNL, LANL, and LLNL. TLCC architecture with ccNUMA, multi-socket, multi-core nodes, and InfiniBand interconnect, is representative of the trend in High Performance

Computing (HPC) architectures. This chapter examines application performance on TLCC contrasting them with Red Storm/Cray XT4. Micro-benchmarks and performance analysis tools help understand the causes for the observed performance differences. Control of processor and memory affinity on TLCC with the NUMACTL utility is shown to result in significant performance gains. While previous studies have investigated impact of affinity control mostly in the context of small SMP systems, the focus in this chapter is on highly parallel Message Passing Interface (MPI) applications.

In Chapter 10 – Abstractions and Middleware for Petascale Computing and Beyond – authors describe that as high-performance computing moves to the petascale and beyond, a number of algorithmic and software challenges need to be addressed. Authors review the main performance-limiting factors in today's High Performance Computing (HPC) software and outline a possible new programming paradigm to address them. The proposed paradigm is based on abstract parallel data structures and operations that encapsulate much of the complexity of an application, but still make communication overhead explicit. Finally, the chapter outlines the structure and functionality of such a middleware and demonstrates its feasibility on the example of the parallel particle-mesh library (PPM).

In Chapter 11 – A Simulator for Large-scale Parallel Computer Architectures – authors explain that efficient design of hardware and software for large-scale parallel execution requires detailed understanding of the interactions between the application, computer, and network. Authors have developed a macro-scale simulator (SST/macro) that permits the coarse-grained study of distributed-memory applications. In the present work, applications using the Message Passing Interface (MPI) are simulated; however, the simulator is designed to allow inclusion of other programming models. Authors describe the design of the simulator, provide performance results, and present studies showing how application performance is affected by machine characteristics.

In Chapter 12 – The Red Storm Architecture and Early Experiences with Multi-Core Processors – authors explain that the Red Storm architecture, which was conceived by Sandia National Laboratories and implemented by Cray, Inc., has become the basis for most successful line of commercial supercomputers in history. In this chapter, authors describe the fundamental characteristics of the architecture and its implementation that have enabled this success, even through successive generations of hardware and software.

In Chapter 13 – The Sicilian Grid Infrastructure for High Performance Computing – authors discuss that the conjugation of High Performance Computing (HPC) and Grid paradigm with applications based on commercial software is one among the major challenges of today e-Infrastructures. Several research communities from either industry or academia need to run high parallel applications based on licensed software over hundreds of CPU cores; a satisfactory fulfillment of such requests is one of the keys for the penetration of this computing paradigm into the industry world and sustainability of Grid infrastructures. This problem has been tackled in the context of the PI2S2 project that created a regional e-Infrastructure in Sicily, the first in Italy over a regional area. Moreover, it shows the results of some relevant use cases belonging to Computer Fluid-Dynamics (Fluent, OpenFOAM), Chemistry (GAMESS), Astro-Physics (Flash), and Bio-Informatics (ClustalW).

## Section 3: High Performance Distributed Systems and Applications

This section includes eight chapters. This section goes beyond and builds upon current theory and practice, providing cutting edge and visionary real-world directions on how distributed computing and integration technologies are and could be used in the near future to the benefit of various settings.

In Chapter 14 – Credential Management Enforcement and Secure Data Storage in gLite – authors describe new security solutions for Grid middleware, and specifically faces the issues related to the management of users' and servers' credentials, together with storing and secure data transmission in the Grid. The work is built on Grid Security Infrastructure (GSI) and it provides new capabilities (i.e. smart card Grid access, and strong security file storage XML-based) to be used on top of different Grid middleware, with a low level of changes. This work presented in this chapter is currently implemented on gLite and accomplishes the access to Grid resources in a uniform and transparent way.

In Chapter 15 – A Grid-Aware Emergency Response Model (G-AERM) for Disaster Management – authors concern with the emergency management community that is working towards developments associated with the reduction of losses in lives, property, and the environment caused by natural disasters. With this in mind, the chapter goes on to propose the Grid-Aware Emergency Response Model (G-AERM) and describe on how to make the best of functionality offered by emerging ICT to support intelligence in decision making towards a more effective and efficient emergency response management.

In Chapter 16 – A Mathematical Analysis of a Disaster Management Data-Grid Push Service – authors refer to that several obstacles arise in the design and implementation of data Grid services. In this chapter, authors are particularly interested in a notable obstacle, namely how to keep service consumers informed of relevant changes about data committed in multiple and distributed service provider levels, and most importantly, when these changes can affect others well-being. With this in mind, the chapter - via the use of relevant case scenarios – describes in detail the service architecture, as well as its mathematical analysis for keeping interested stakeholders informed automatically about relevant and critical data changes.

In Chapter 17 – Service and Management Oriented Traffic Information Grid – authors presents a real-time, dynamic information services provision for travelers and traffic managers by using Grid technology. The system provides travelers with services of optimized route scheme, bus arrival prediction based on real-time route status, and route status forecast. For traffic managers, the system can provide vehicle tracing, traffic monitoring, history data analysis, and decision making on traffic control strategy. In this regard, the chapter explores key research such as large multi-source traffic data integration, route status forecast, and optimum dynamic travel scheme implementation based on massive GPS data.

In Chapter 18 – Mining Environmental Data in the ADMIRE Project Using New Advanced Methods and Tools – authors present the EU funded project Advanced Data Mining and Integration Research for Europe (ADMIRE), that is about designing new methods and tools for comfortable mining and integration of large, distributed data sets. The authors present a set of experimental environmental scenarios, and the application of ADMIRE technology in these scenarios. The scenarios try to predict meteorological and hydrological phenomena which currently cannot or are not predicted by using data mining of distributed data sets from several providers in Slovakia.

In Chapter 19 – Collaborative e-Learning and ICT Tools to Develop SME Managers: An Italian Case – authors focus on face-to-face and classroom-based development courses that is problematic for time-poor SME managers. Authors describe that collaborative learning, especially as represented by an action learning approach, would seem ideal for SME managers. But can collaborative learning be adopted as a blanket approach in the case of SME managers? Or should we first take into account what the contextual influences on learning, networking, and collaboration are?

In Chapter 20 – Sketch Based Video Annotation and Organization System in Distributed Teaching Environment – authors explain that as the use of instructional video is becoming a key component of e-learning, there is an increasing need for a distributed system that supports collaborative video annotation and organization. In this chapter, the authors construct a distributed environment on the top of NaradaBrokering to support collaborative operations on video material when users are located in different places. Finally, an informal user study was conducted and results show that the system improves the efficiency of video organizing and viewing and enhances user's participating into the design process with good user experience.

In Chapter 21 – OBIRE: Ontology Based Bibliographic Information Retrieval in P2P Networks – authors discuss that it has been widely recognized that bibliographic information plays an increasingly important role for scientific research. The chapter presents Ontology Based Bibliographic Information Retrieval (OBIRE) that is an ontology based Peer-to-Peer (P2P) network for bibliographic information retrieval. OBIRE is evaluated from the aspects of precision and recall, and experimental results show the effectiveness of OBIRE in bibliographic information retrieval.

*Nik Bessis*
*University of Derby, UK & University of Bedfordshire, UK*

# Acknowledgment

It is my great pleasure to comment on the hard work and support of many people who have been involved in the development of this book. It is always a major undertaking but most importantly, a great encouragement and somehow a reward and an honor when seeing the enthusiasm and eagerness of people willing to advance their discipline by taking the commitment to share their experiences, ideas, and visions towards the evolvement of collaboration like the achievement of this book. Without their support the book could not have been satisfactory completed.

First and foremost, I wish to thank all the authors who, as distinguished scientists despite busy schedules, devoted so much of their time preparing and writing their works, and responding to numerous comments and suggestions made from the reviewers, and myself. I trust this collection of chapters will offer a solid overview of current thinking on these areas and it is expected that the book will be a valuable source of stimulation and inspiration to all those who have or will have an interest in these fields.

I wish to gratefully acknowledge that I was fortunate to work closely with an outstanding team at IGI Global. Specifically and with no particular order, I wish to thank Erika Gallagher, Heather Probst, Joel Gamon, and Jan Travers who were everything someone should expect from a publisher: professional, efficient, and a delight to work with. Thanks are also extended to all those at IGI Global who have taken care with managing the design and the timely production of this book. The editor wishes to apologize to anyone whom they have forgotten.

Finally, I am deeply indebted to my family for their love, patience, and support throughout this rewarding experience.

*Nik Bessis*
*University of Derby, UK & University of Bedfordshire, UK*

# Section 1
# Advanced Integration Methods and Services

# Chapter 1
# Web Services in Distributed Information Systems:
## Availability, Performance and Composition

**Xia Zhao**
*University of Bedfordshire, UK*

**Tao Wang**
*University of Bedfordshire, UK*

**Enjie Liu**
*University of Bedfordshire, UK*

**Gordon J. Clapworthy**
*University of Bedfordshire, UK*

## ABSTRACT

*Distributed information systems are growing rapidly in response to the improvement of computer hardware and software and this is matched by the evolution of the technologies involved. This chapter focuses mainly on Web Services technology and discusses related technical issues including availability, performance and composition. It also introduces Grid, agents and Semantic Web technologies that can work together with Web Services to serve different business goals.*

## INTRODUCTION

Distributed information systems are becoming more popular as a result of improvements in computer hardware and software, and there is a commensurate rise in the use of the associated technologies. Because of the increasing desire for business-to-business (B2B) communication and integration, technologies such as Service-Oriented

Computing (SOC), Semantic Web, Grid, Agents/Multi-agents, peer-to-peer, etc., are receiving a high level of interest nowadays.

As a part of distributed information systems, web information systems play an important role in the modern, ubiquitous Internet world and the applicability of Web Services as a particular implementation of SOC has been widely recognized for current B2B integration (e.g. e-commerce, e-government and e-healthcare).

DOI: 10.4018/978-1-4666-0906-8.ch001

However, building all aspects of Web Services comprehensively needs further improvement, for instance, Quality of Service (QoS) has yet to be properly addressed. Likewise, the detection of service availability to achieve self-healing in the invocation process, service reuse, how best to define atomic services, and service composition are all issues that urgently require more research.

Meanwhile, it should be noted that Web Services play only a partial role in evolving distributed information systems. With the development of future computer hardware, software and business requirements, many other technologies will probably emerge that will serve particular business goals better. Therefore, much recent research has been focusing not only on individual technologies in distributed systems, but also on the possibility of combining currently available technologies to improve business outcomes.

In this chapter, we concentrate mainly on Web Services and technical issues associated with current Web Services standards, but we also give a brief overview of three other distributed technologies, namely Grid, agents and Semantic Web, which can work with Web Services. Thus, it concentrates initially on the background of services in distributed information systems, then it introduces Grid, agent and Semantic Web technologies. After that, the chapter discusses several technical aspects of Web Services in current distributed information systems, in particular, general Web Service availability and performance issues and the possibility of combining agent technology and Web Services to provide improved understanding of service availability. We then introduce JSON (JavaScript Object Notation), which may provide an alternative to current approaches that will deliver better Web Service Performance and discuss service composition, illustrating it with an implementation from the EU Living Human Digital Library (LHDL) project.

## WEB SERVICES AND RELATED TECHNOLOGIES IN DISTRIBUTED INFORMATION SYSTEMS

Internet applications are developed and hosted by many different organizations, and customers from all over the world access them via the Internet from their desktops, or possibly from hand-held devices, such as a PDA or mobile phone. Originally, Internet applications referred to activities such as web browsing, FTP, and email. More recently, they have also included more advanced applications that are generally referred to as services. These mirror our real-world business activities in the cyber world.

Let us take a ticket-booking system as an example. The processes may include: the initial search for the right ticket, using criteria such as price, timing, etc; the actual booking, which will include some form of payment process which itself may involve authentication processes such as a credit check by the credit-card company; then various forms of after-sales service, such as notifications a few days before travel, etc. In the real world, all the services may be provided by different specialist companies and achieved by human interaction, using their knowledge and intelligence. In the cyber world, these actions are achieved by so-called software services. To avoid continually having to rebuild services, there has been a trend towards using "atomic" services as building blocks from which to construct more complex services.

In open distributed systems, independent components cooperate with each other in order to achieve a goal. Apart from SOC, Grid technology and agent technology are the most widely used technologies for developing distributed systems. In this chapter, the authors do not offer a syntactic classification of the technologies, but rather, discuss the problem from a developer's standpoint.

## Web Services

Web Services are emerging as a promising technology for building distributed applications. A Web Service is a software system that is designed to support interoperable machine-to-machine interaction over a network. As one instantiation of Service-Oriented Architecture (SOA), they have the property of being loosely-coupled, open-standard, language- and platform-independent. "Loosely-coupled" implies that service providers can modify backend functions while retaining the same interface to clients; the core service functions are encapsulated and remain transparent to clients. "Open-standard" ensures the viability of collaboration and integration with other services. Language and platform independence enables services to be developed in any language and deployed on any platform.

### Technical issues in Web Services

The following lists some technical issues in Web Services, some of which will be the main focus of this chapter.

- *Defining and Building Atomic Services:* An atomic service generally solves an individual, specific problem. The granularity of what are chosen as atomic services has to be defined carefully. If an atomic service is too complicated, it may not be easy to employ it in a variety of applications, so it becomes less useful. It may also mean that similar atomic services, differing only in a few subtle ways, may have to be created to cover the range of possible circumstances, which will result in a large library of atomic services being established.

On the other hand, if atomic services are kept very simple, then composing even fairly straightforward tasks requires the use of many atomic services, which makes their creation tedious and time consuming. There is no general guideline for identifying the appropriate level of granularity. One should definitely seek the opinion of domain experts on how to split tasks – the breakdown of a task into its components should correlate closely with the "internal" description that a user familiar with the domain would see as natural.

- *Cooperation Between Services:* By combining atomic services, one can create more complicated services. This should be a design goal for future Web Services development as it provides the possibility of using existing services to reduce development time and of providing greater transparency and efficiency for users.

- *Service Availability and Performance:* Service availability and performance are two factors in the Web Services QoS (Quality of Service) model. (Lee et al., 2003) categorized the Web Service QoS into 12 aspects: performance, reliability, scalability, robustness, exception handling, accuracy, integrity, accessibility, availability, interoperability and security. In general, a high-quality service implies that it is secure and has high availability, high throughput, rapid response, execution and transmission, and low round-trip delay.

## Grid

The Grid concept (Foster & Kesselman, 1998; Foster, Kesselman & Tuecke, 2001) is encapsulated by 'coordinated resource sharing and problem solving in a dynamic, multi-institutional virtual organization'. IBM defines a Grid in a more commercial way as 'a standards-based application/resource-sharing architecture that makes it possible for heterogeneous systems and applications to share, compute and store resources transparently' (Clabby Analytics, 2004).

Grid has evolved through several phases. It began as a means of sharing computing resources;

then, as an extension, data sharing was added, and some special devices such as scientific instruments and medical equipment were included. The marriage of the first generation of Grid with Web technology led to generic Grid services.

Later, the focus moved to knowledge sharing and led to collaboration between organizations while retaining the security requirements of each. The knowledge Grid facilitates data mining across the Internet and requires techniques for abstracting heterogeneous data, creating metadata, publishing, discovering and describing data in the Grid.

With the maturity of SOA and Web Services technologies, the Grid Community has begun to combine them and build a Grid infrastructure. The emergence of the Open Grid Services Architecture (OGSA) (http://www.globus.org/ogsa/) is an example that represents an evolution towards a Grid system architecture based on Web services concepts and technologies. OGSA is a community standard with multiple implementations. It provides a framework, and the users can define a wide range of interoperable, portable services.

## Agents

Multi-agent systems evolved from a need for knowledge-aware, distributed, problem-solving mechanisms. According to Jennings (2001), agents have the following characteristics:

- *Problem Solvers:* By clearly identifying problem-solving entities with well-defined boundaries and interfaces;
- *Proactive:* By being both reactive (able to respond in a timely fashion to changes in their environment) and proactive (able to opportunistically adopt goals and take the initiative);
- *Goal-oriented:* They are designed to fulfill a specific role;
- *Context-aware:* They are situated (embedded) in a particular environment over which they have partial control and absorb-

ability, they receive inputs related to the state of their environment through sensors and they act on the environment through effectors;
- *Autonomous:* They have control over both their internal state and their own behavior.

Some toolkits, frameworks and libraries are based on agent technology. Some frameworks allow developers to define their own architecture and inter-relationships between the agents, for example, JADE (Java Agent Development Framework) (http://jade.tilab.com/) provides a communication architecture for the agents with good debugging functions. Camacho, Aler, Castro & Molina (2002) have compared some of these platforms.

Research into agents has focused on providing formal proofs to proof-of-concept demonstrators and provided only limited, pragmatic support in terms of systems, software and tools. In contrast, according to Payne (2008), research into Web Services has focused on the user community, resulting in pragmatic, bottom-up enabling technology that readily facilities the robust construction of service-oriented systems. Much of the focus of Web Services research has been on developing declarative descriptions that application developers can share and that their tools can use to construct and develop large-scale distributed software.

Foster, Jennings & Kesselman (2004) describe Grid and agents as 'brain meets brawn' –historically, the Grid community has focused on 'brawn' (the infrastructure and tools for sharing within dynamic and geographically distributed virtual organizations), while agents have been associated with 'brain' (the development of concepts, methodologies and algorithms for autonomous problem solvers). They share some common interests such as a robust infrastructure and autonomous and flexible behaviors and becoming mutually stronger when allied.

## Semantic Web

One aim of introducing Web Services is to achieve machine-to-machine communication. With the basic Web Services technologies, this can be achieved at a certain level such as invocation between service requesters and service providers, but many other forms of communication, such as service discovery, service selection and service composition, cannot be accomplished efficiently and dynamically. With the development of Semantic Web technologies, such as ontologies, semantics can be used in conjunction with Web Services to offer better services.

Knowledge discovery is a key issue in distributed systems. Take service discovery in the Web Service world as an example – there may be many services that can solve a particular problem on the Internet, but how does one find them? Or, if someone has developed such a service, how can they let other people know about it? Further, as a customer, how can I tell which of the various available services is better than the others? These needs are very familiar to us in the real world and to resolve them, we read reviews, receive 'word of mouth' opinion, etc. The question is, how can we achieve this in the cyber world?

Web Services within the basic SOA concept can solve some of these problems. For example, service providers hide functionalities through service interfaces and publish machine-readable descriptions of their services in publicly accessible registries. Service consumers discover these services by querying the registry and bind to the selected services dynamically.

The Semantic Web has made further strides towards solving this problem. It is an evolution of the World Wide Web in which information is machine processable (rather than being only human oriented), thus permitting browsers or other software agents to find, share and combine information for us more easily.

Data and the relationships among the data are well understood by the machines that process them. This allows the machines to do more than simply display the requested web pages to the user; software will be able to analyze and process metadata – data about the data – to find the best pages to display to a particular user or to deliver to another machine.

Data that is generally hidden away in HTML files is often useful in some contexts, but not in others. The majority of data on the Web is in this form at the moment, which makes it difficult to use on a large scale, because there is no global system for publishing data in such a way that it can be easily processed by anyone.

The main problem with the use of standards for Web Service description (e.g. WSDL) and publishing (e.g. in this case, a semantic broker) is that the syntactic definitions used in these descriptions do not completely describe the capacity of a service and cannot be understood by software programs. It requires a human to interpret the meaning of inputs, outputs and applicable constraints as well as the context in which the services can be used.

Semantic Web Services (SWS) research aims to automate the development of Web-Service-based applications through Semantic Web technology. By providing formal representations based on ontologies, we can facilitate the machine interpretation of Web Service description. Thus, a business organization can view a Semantic Web Service as the basic mechanism for integrating data and processes across applications on the Web.

## WEB SERVICE AVAILABILITY

The term "*availability*" indicates whether a service is ready to respond immediately to a request, or not (Erradi, Padmanabhuni & Varadharajan, 2006). This is useful for some busy and popular services within a system – for example, a consumer would like to use a fast service, but too many requests for the same service will cause a reduction in throughput and performance on the server. The current consensus seems to be, first, to try to ensure that all services are available, then try to improve the performance of the services.

From its definition, Web Services, the most popular middleware, consists of SOAP, WSDL and UDDI. The UDDI specification V3 (Adam, 2005) does not provide query APIs with associated QoS information. A typical process from a service consumer will be: consumer query in UDDI, construct the request and receive the response. All of these processes are encoded in XML. From within, Web Services can be considered as XML-message based, with the messages having 3 classifications: query, request and response.

## Stateless and Context-Unaware Web Services

An atomic Web Service is used for specific tasks and can be seen as a stateless and context-unaware process. There are two states for a service, namely active and asleep. An available service has two requirements: it is ready immediately for a request, and a service consumer can receive the correct response within the necessary time. If a service cannot perform a specific task in the required time, it can be seen as unavailable.

Services providers register and publish a service as an interface, at which point the service is in the sleep state. It is activated only when it receives a request; after execution, the service will return to the sleep state. The service has no knowledge about its context – we call this *context-unaware*. The context includes factors that can affect the service QoS, such as network QoS, container throughput, hardware throughput and execution time.

## Heavyweight ESB Framework for Service Availability

To increase service availability, services can be distributed to different service containers and then use a QoS meter to manage access control, request filtering and request scheduling. For example, Erradi, Padmanabhuni & Varadharajan (2006) suggest a Web-Services DiffServ Framework by adding a request classifier, request dispatcher and QoS manager. This kind of framework is a prototype of the Enterprise Service Bus (ESB) (Chappell, 2004 – services are published as endpoints, all requests are filtered and scheduled as the QoS requires.

ESB frameworks are generally characterized as 'heavyweight' – complex, centralized and difficult. Complex indicates that they are hard to configure or install. Furthermore, many additional libraries are required within the products. As a result, it is very easy to get exceptions because of version-control issues. Centralized implies that an ESB product tries to gather all functions such as routing, inter-change protocol, service monitoring, security, and so on – it is constructing a 'super' link between distributed objects. It is found that users generally have to receive training before they can use it effectively.

ESB frameworks improve the availability of atomic Web Service, but they do not solve the problems of stateless and context-unawareness. In another words, ESB frameworks have not addressed the root of the problem.

## Lightweight and Context-Aware Agents for Availability

According to Payne (2008), many systems assume prior knowledge of the context and, hence, focus on a specific problem. For example, a service provider gives a fixed value to a service's execution time, but this value will obviously be different depending upon whether a single request or one hundred separate requests have just arrived. Moreover, when we consider the various factors contributing to possible network delay, the response time can vary substantially. If both the service provider and the service consumer use the fixed value without any dynamic environmental consideration, when many requests come simultaneously, service consumers may find that the service is not as available as expected.

As mentioned earlier, agents have a knowledge of context and the ability to monitor changes to the context – "*Agents are embedded in a particular environment over which they have partial control and observe-ability. They receive inputs related to the state of their environment through effectors*" (Payne, 2008, p12-14). This context-monitoring ability is also what the service needs.

Likewise, agents are autonomous as "*they have control both over their internal state and over their own behaviour*" (Payne, 2008. p12-14). As noted above, an atomic service performs a specific task by accepting a request and returning a response. If the throughput is fixed, more requests mean slow execution and the service will crash if the request exceeds the throughput. Providing a capacity for autonomy on a stateless service will be helpful for service execution. Moreover, agents have knowledge about new agents, which can be used to conduct requests to several services performing same function.

Suppose we map a service with an agent into a pair named Agent-ServiceX which has the characteristics of both the agent and the service. The Agent-ServiceX will be context-aware and autonomous and will have knowledge of other services. For instance, within the Jade agent platform, services can be used for specific tasks, service agents can be used as service monitors and directory agents can be used to filter and schedule requests. The agent system will not only perform a similar function to ESB frameworks but will also provide QoS information based on the changing context, rather than fixed values set up by the service providers.

## WEB SERVICE PERFORMANCE

The term "*performance*" associated with a Web Service represents how quickly the service can be completed or how rapidly the user can obtain the result (Lee, Jeon, Lee, Jeong & Park, 2003).

For each individual service, let $T_{total}$ be the time between the client sending the request with parameters and receiving a response with the result, so

$$T_{total} = T_{request} + T_{response} + T_{exec} + T_{serialization} + T_{RTD}$$
(1)

where $T_{request}$ is the transmission time for the request, $T_{response}$ is the transmission time for the response, $T_{exec}$ is the execution time for the service, $T_{serialization}$ is the serialization time for the service and $T_{RTD}$ is the round-trip delay for the process. Serialization and deserialization are coupled; here, serialization time means the time for serialization and deserialization.

The transmission time for request and response can be calculated as:

$$T_{request} = \frac{L_{request}}{R} \; ; \; T_{response} = \frac{L_{response}}{R},$$

where $L_{request}$ is the length of the request message, $L_{response}$ is the length of the response message, and the R is the transmission rate.

Then, Equation 1 can be reformatted as:

$$T_{total} = \frac{L_{request}}{R} + \frac{L_{response}}{R} + T_{exec} + T_{serialization} + T_{RTD}$$
(2)

so it is clear that the time of a service is effected by length of request, length of response, transmission rate, execution time, serialization time and round-trip delay.

Execution time is based on the software throughput and hardware configuration. Routing delay and transmission rate are decided by the network QoS. Execution time and network QoS are outside the consideration of this chapter. Suppose the transmission rate and round-trip delay are of fixed value, the time of a service is decided by the request and response length, the request and response delivery and serialization. In another words, the performance of a service is decided by the message length, serialization and message transmission.

## Factors Affecting Web Service Performance

In this section, we discuss three main factors that affect Web Service performance.

## XML

XML is designed for data storage and transmission. It uses plaintext as tags, so platforms that can process plaintext can also process XML; in another words, XML can be used on any platform. This made it attractive for use in SOAP.

Reducing the volume of data to be transmitted will clearly reduce the transmission time. Unfortunately, plaintext formatted xml with repeated labels makes the file much bigger than the user may expect. The website of SoapUI (www.soapui. org), a leading tool for Web Service testing, shows that a SOAP request of "hello world" is almost 280 bytes, and the SOAP response would be 350 Bytes. Menasce (2002) shows that XML's way of representing data usually results in files of substantially greater size (on average, 400% larger) than representations of the same data in binary.

## HTTP

HTTP (Hypertext Transfer Protocol) is used for SOAP as it will not be blocked by a firewall. Assuming that the transmission rate and round-trip delay are of fixed value, an efficient method for message delivery would be helpful. This efficiency has three requirements: once and exactly once delivery; message arrival in the right sequence; and message arrival in the exact form.

A single delivery can be used to ensure accurate response and no repeat request. If a response message exceeds the maximum segment size of the TCP protocol, a message is divided into several packages, and all the packets should arrive in the correct sequence and in the exact form.

HTTP uses the Best Effort QoS (Quality of Service) model, which means that it will perform a FIFS (First In First Service) policy to transform all data packets without filtering. Thus, packages sent by HTTP have no guarantee on the order of the arriving packets and no guarantee of packets being delivered to the destination. If there is no bandwidth available, the packets are simply discarded.

## SOAP

SOAP (Simple Object Access Protocol) defines a set of serialization rules for encoding data in XML and all data is serialized as elements – all the data transmitted by SOAP are encoded in repeated tags.

From Equation 2, we know that, to reduce transmission time, serialization should try to use less time and decrease the length of the message. But SOAP goes the other way because SOAP defines a complex format for a message, with repeated element tags. It is time-consuming to encapsulate information into a SOAP envelope and retrieve information from a SOAP envelope. In effect, SOAP uses more bytes to express repeated tags which results in longer messages.

## Possible Solution for Atomic Service Performance

## Using JSON instead of XML

According to RFC 4627 (Crockford, 2006), JSON (JavaScript Object Notation) is an open, text-based data-exchange format. Like XML, it is human-readable, platform independent and enjoys a wide availability of implementations (Aziz & Mitchell,

2007). Furthermore, it provides mechanisms for data serialization and deserialization.

In contrast to the document-oriented XML, JSON is data-oriented. Without repeated element tags, a message encoded with JSON will use fewer bytes than when encoded with XML and will thus be transmitted faster. The decrease in message length is a strong reason to adopt JSON for service communication protocol, because serialization and deserialization occur in both sides of the service consumer and the service container. JSON has its own method for data serialization and deserialization and, as far as we know, there are no documents comparing the serialization performance of JSON and SOAP. Thus, further investigations should be performed to obtain detailed information concerning possible performance improvements.

## WEB SERVICE COMPOSITION

Individual services, which provide a single specific functionality, are referred to as atomic services. Traditionally, only atomic services are available, so complex functionality has to be achieved by a series of service invocations via service requesters, as shown in Figure 1.

However, if one is regularly performing the same complex task, continually having to invoke several services successively makes this approach time consuming and error prone. By use of service composition, the same task can be achieved by assembling existing atomic services, possibly

from different service providers, into a composite service. For example, consider a travel booking scenario, which may include a series of tasks such as booking flights and trains, booking hotels and purchasing travel insurance. There may be various services for flight booking, accommodation booking and travel insurance purchase available from different service providers. A travel agent may offer a composite Web Service that integrates all of these services together to create customized functions – the composite service will handle all of the coordination among the atomic services involved. Thereafter, service requesters can directly invoke the new composite services without having to worry about the internal coordination changes, as shown in Figure 2.

Composition is an important aspect of Service-Oriented Architecture (SOA). The composite service usually performs functions including coordination, monitoring, conformance and Quality of Service (QoS) composition (Papazoglou, 2003).

- Coordination refers to the execution of the control and data flow of the component services and the output of the composition. A typical example is defining a workflow process and applying a workflow engine for the run-time execution of the whole process.
- Monitoring can be event based, which allows the composite service to publish the events subscribed from the component ser-

*Figure 1. Service request of a series of atomic services*

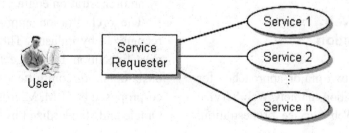

*Figure 2. Service request with a composite service*

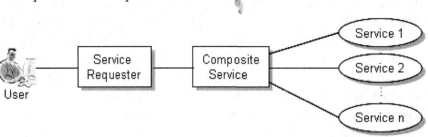

vices; this may include filtering, correlating, and so on.

- Conformance ensures that the constraints among component services are properly imposed and that the integrity of the composite service is achieved by appropriate service parameter matching and data fusion.
- QoS Composition includes the overall cost, performance, privacy, security, scalability, reliability, etc., of the composite service.

Compared with traditional approaches, Web Service composition brings the following benefits.

- *Prompting reusability:* The composite Web Service is built from existing autonomous Web Services, and since the composition is a new Web Service, it can itself be reused either directly or as part of a new composition.
- *Transparency:* Assembling a commonly used flow of services into a single service by using composition can significantly reduce the complexity for requesters who wish to access an extended series of services on a regular basis.

## Approaches to Web Service Composition

Currently, there are two major approaches for Web Service composition, namely Web Service choreography and Web Service orchestration.

Some groups also apply semantic technologies to enhance the composition process.

In this chapter, we mainly focus on the basic approaches of choreography and orchestration. The distinctive difference between these two methods is that orchestration describes a process flow between services that are controlled by a single party; whereas choreography refers to a more collaborative interaction between the parties involved and tracks the sequence of messages among them in which no single party truly owns the conversation (Peltz, 2003).

## Orchestration

Service orchestration refers to a process in which one party acts as a coordinator in relation to other services. The coordinator may receive a message from one service and make decisions based on the messages such as changing the content of the data, then invoking another service. The orchestration model addresses the local internal communications among data and control flow. It is usually used within one organization, in which constraints on the services are not viewed globally. The orchestration process is also known as an *executable process* as it is intended to be executed by an orchestration engine.

The orchestration approach has been well recognized by industry. The Web Service Business Execution Language (WS-BPEL) (www.oasis-open.org/committees/wsbpel/), which is co-proposed by IBM, Microsoft, BEA, SUN and Oracle and standardized by OASIS, is the main workflow standard for Web Service orchestration. WS-BPEL is an executable language and most supporting development environments offer process execution engines.

## Choreography

In service choreography, there is no coordinating party – all participants are treated equally in achieving the composition goal. It is a more decentralized form of processing which is based on rules known to each service. It captures interactions from a global perspective and does not present any internal communications among the participants that do not appear in the global interactions. Therefore, choreography is commonly used in the inter-organization environment.

Choreography addresses the agreements among the interaction participants. Although its interactions include both data and control flow of the communication, from the global point of view, it focuses more on the constitution of composition conformance.

Further into standards, the Web Service Choreography Definition Language (WS-CDL) (www.w3.org/TR/2004/WD-ws-cdl-10-20041217/), which is defined by the W3C, describes Web Service collaborations among cooperating participants. WS-CDL is the current *de facto* standard for Web Service choreography. It is based on metamodel and XML syntax and is non-executable.

## Combining Choreography and Orchestration

As mentioned earlier, choreography and orchestration are two service composition approaches that concentrate on different perspectives of interaction, namely global and local. However, they are supposed to work together to form the complete service composition, and the standard language WS-CDL can also be used in conjunction with WS-BPEL. In fact, several research initiatives have already explored approaches to combining WS-CDL and WS-BPEL.

The TrustCoM project proposes an approach for automated derivation of the executable business process from choreographies in virtual organizations (Weber, Haller & Mulle, 2008). The approach is mainly based on an XML tree query. The CDL2BPEL algorithm is introduced, which consists of 5 main steps: a) reading a source document; b) generating an object tree for the source document; c) performing validation; d) performing transformation on the tree; e) serializing the resulting object trees to a set of documents in the target language. A Knowledge Base (KB) is introduced in CDL2BPEL; it stores CDL patterns and their respective BPEL replacements and is used to record the information gap between WS-CDL and WS-BPEL. This approach allows the re-use of the choreography patterns and achieves automated WS-CDL to WS-BPEL generation. However, it is simply based on the XML syntax transformation and no validations are mentioned on global constraints.

Mendling & Hafner (2007) implemented a proof-concept mapping between BPEL and WS-CDL for inter-organizational workflows. They adopted the concept of Model Driven Architecture (MDA). Mapping between WS-CDL and WS-BPEL is implemented in XSLT and can be supported in both directions. A wscdl2bpel.xslt is already implemented. The transformation algorithm is defined according to the WS-CDL XML tag elements. This approach achieves bilateral mapping between WS-BPEL and WS-CDL and offers tool support for automated generation of BPEL stubs. However, it does not provide validation on the BPEL stubs generated or formalization to handle complex workflows. As far as we know, the backward mapping, from WS-BPEL to WS-CDL, has not yet been implemented.

Since both WS-CDL and WS-BPEL can be represented in graphs using UML or similar technologies, another approach worth considering is to apply graph transformation theory to transform between WS-CDL and WS-BPEL. Triple Graph Grammar (TGG) (Königs, 2005) may provide a good method to achieve this. In

TGG, models can be defined and transformed in either direction, which makes it possible to perform transformations from WS-CDL to WS-BPEL and back again. TGG can synchronize and maintain the correspondence of the two models, which helps to achieve composition conformance during transformation. In addition, TGG supports working incrementally, which would allow a complex transformation process to be completed step by step. However, further research has to be performed to evaluate this idea.

## AN EXAMPLE: WEB SERVICE COMPOSTION AT ORCHESTRATION LEVEL

In this section, we describe, from the orchestration perspective, a proof-concept Web Service composition example that was implemented in the EU LHDL (Living Human Digital Library) project. In the context of this chapter, the details of the background of the project and the implementation of the atomic services used in composition are not important. However, more information can be found in Zhao, Liu, Clapworthy, Quadrani, Testi & Viceconti (2008) and Zhao, Liu & Clapworthy (2008).

Instead of simply giving the end users the existing WS-BPEL designers, we implemented a web-based tool that allows users to compose the services available in the LHDL project in an easy and intuitive way. Compared to existing WS-BPEL designers such as Active BPEL Designer and Oracle Business Process Manager, our composition tool has the following benefits for the project:

- *End-user Oriented:* The tool hides the complexity of the WS-BPEL process from the end-users, adopts subsets of the WS-BPEL language and gives users a straightforward sequence composition designer;

- *Dynamic Service Composition:* It automatically generates BPEL processes based on the end-users' configuration inputs and deploys the BPEL process in the ActiveBPEL Engine Community Edition (www.active-vos.com/community-open-source.php) on the fly; no extra manual deployment is required to make the process executable on the execution engine.

This framework simulates the data flow combinations and generates a .bpel file that represents the composition process. Figure 3 illustrates an example composition process (*extractisosurface-*

*Figure 3. An example of BPEL Workflow for service composition*

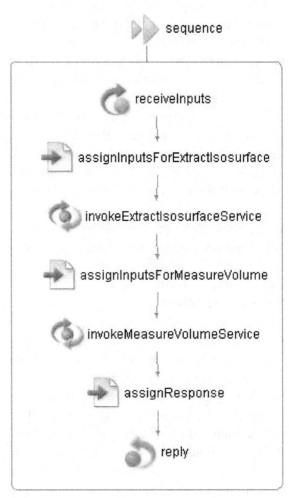

*measurevolume*) by invoking and combining two existing Web Services.

The process is organized into a sequence with the *receive* activity waiting for an inbound message from outside and the *reply* activity transmitting an outbound message back to the requester. A series of *assign* and *invoke* activities take inputs from *receive*, invoke each service, then pass the response to *reply*.

The current composition framework consists of four main components (see Figure 4):

- *Composition Designer:* A web-based rich application client for composition sequence configuration;
- *Workflow Generator:* This accepts and validates the user's configuration and generates a composite service;
- *Workflow Engine:* This acts as a platform for deploying the newly generated composite service;
- *Policy Descriptions:* These are XML files used by the generator to validate composition configurations.

As seen in Figure 5, the Composition Designer interface is much simpler and more intuitive than

a standard BPEL designer. In the screen shot, the left-hand tree structure displays the available atomic services, which are categorized as *Import*, *Modification*, *Measurement*, *Preview* and *Export* in the LHDL project. The main data grid on the right regulates the composition in the sequence structure. To create a composite service, users first drag and drop services from the service list into the composition sequence, then submit the configuration together with a predefined service name to the generator.

The generator handles the complexities of validating the data flow, creating the composition process and deploying the newly generated service. It accepts the user's configuration inputs and dynamically generates a BPEL process file, a WSDL (Web Service Description Language) file and a process deployment description file.

When all the workflow files have been generated, the workflow generator automatically deploys the process on a workflow engine – an ActiveBPEL Engine in our case. A service metadata file is also generated through the workflow generator, which enables end-users to directly publish the newly created service in the service repository.

*Figure 4. The framework of the LHDL Web service composition*

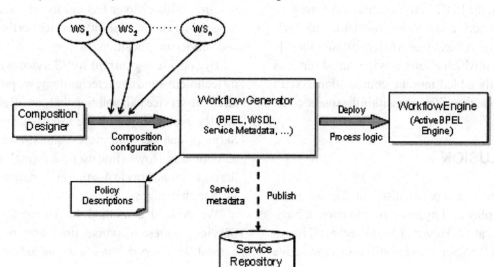

*Figure 5. A screen shot of the LHDL Web service composition tool*

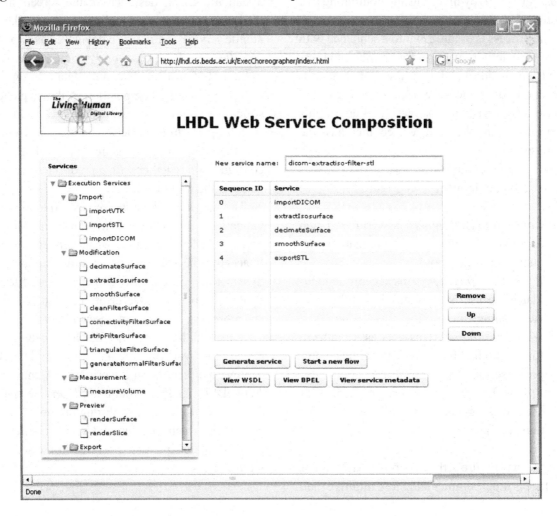

Within the LHDL project, this workflow generator is generic and scalable from the developer's perspective. An external XML configuration file is provided which allows newly created services to be easily added into the composition system without much modification within the source code.

## CONCLUSION

Web Services, as a part of distributed information systems, play an important role in current business integration. However, many technical issues related to Web Services are still subject to active research. This chapter has discussed three main aspects: service availability, service performance and service composition.

By considering current Web Service availability techniques and agent technology, we proposed an agent-service pair solution that can offer better service availability – by the use of agents, Web Services can become more context-aware and autonomous. How to find useful information from the context and how to use this information would further challenges.

We defined a method for calculating Web Service request-response time and reviewed current Web Service standards, including XML,

HTTP and SOAP. JSON has been proposed in this chapter as an alternative to XML to achieve better service performance.

We discussed issues relating to Web Service composition including the key concepts, common choreography and orchestration approaches, and possible combinations between them. A graph transformation idea was proposed to transform between choreography and orchestration. Moreover, the chapter gave a Web Service composition example that has been implemented in the LHDL project.

Furthermore, the chapter discussed some other technologies distributed information systems including Grid, Agents and Semantic Web. All these technologies can be applied together with Web Services to serve different distributed business goals. The chapter gave an example of using agents with services to solve the Web Service availability problem.

# REFERENCES

Adam, C. (2005). *From Web Services to SOA and everything in between: The journey begins.* Retrieved March 20, 2009, from http://www.webservices.org

Aziz, A., & Mitchell, S. (2007). *An introduction to JavaScript Object Notation (JSON) in JavaScript and .NET.* Retrieved March 20, 2009, from http://msdn.microsoft.com/ en-us/library/bb299886.aspx

Camacho, D., Aler, R., Castro, C., & Molina, J. M. (2002). Performance evaluation of ZEUS, JADE, and SkeletonAgent framework. *2002 IEEE Systems, Man, and Cybernetics Conference, 4*(6). IEEE.

Chappell, D. (2004). *Enterprise Service Bus.* USA: O'Reilly Press.

Clabby Analytics. (2004). *The grid report.* Retrieved July 3, 2008, from http://www-03.ibm.com/grid/pdf/ Clabby_Grid_Report_2004_Edition.pdf

Crockford, D. (2006). *RFC 4627, The application/json media type for JavaScript Object Notation (JSON).* Retrieved March 20, 2009, from http://www.faqs.org/ftp/rfc/ pdf/rfc4627.txt.pdf

Erradi, A., Padmanabhuni, S., & Varadharajan, N. (2006). Differential QoS support in Web Services management. *IEEE Intentional Conference on Web Services* (pp. 781-788). Chicago: IEEE Computer Society.

Foster, I., Jennings, N., & Kesselman, C. (2004). Brian meets brawn: Why grid and agents need each other. *3rd International Joint Conference on Autonomous Agent and Multi-agent Systems (AAMAS'04)* (pp. 8-15). New York: ACM Press.

Foster, I., & Kesselman, C. (Eds.). (2000). *The grid: Blueprint for a new computing infrastructure.* San Francisco: Morgan Kaufmann Publishers.

Foster, I., Kesselman, C., & Tuecke, S. (2001). The anatomy of the grid: Enabling scalable virtual organizations. *The International Journal of Supercomputer Applications, 15*(3), 200–222. doi:10.1177/109434200101500302

Jennings, N. R. (2001). An agent-based approach for building complex software systems. *Communications of the ACM, 44*(4), 35–41. doi:10.1145/367211.367250

Konigs, A. (2005). Model transformation with triple graph grammars. *Model Transformations in Practice Workshop, Part of ACM/IEEE 8th International Conference on Model Driven Engineering Languages and Systems (MoDELS 2005)*, Jamaica.

Lee, K., Jeon, J., Lee, W., Jeong, S., & Park, S. (2003). *QoS for Web Services: Requirements and possible approaches*. Retrieved March 20, 2009, from W3C: http://www.w3c.or.kr/ kr-office/ TR/2003/ws-qos/

McLaughlin, B. (2002). *Building Java enterprise applications*. O'Reilly Press.

Menasce, D. A. (2002). QoS issues in Web Services. *IEEE Internet Computing, 6*(6), 72–75. doi:10.1109/MIC.2002.1067740

Mendling, J., & Hafner, M. (2007). From WS-CDL choreography to BPEL process orchestration. *Journal of Enterprise Information Management, 21*(5), 525–542. doi:10.1108/17410390810904274

Papazoglou, M. P. (2003). Service-oriented computing: Concepts, characteristics and directions. *4th International Conference on Web Information Systems Engineering (WISE 2003)* (pp. 3-12). Rome: IEEE Computer Society.

Payne, T. R. (2008). Web Services from an Agent perspective. *IEEE Intelligent Systems, 23*(2), 12–14. doi:10.1109/MIS.2008.37

Peltz, C. (2003). Web Services orchestration and choreography. *Web Services Journal, 03*(07), 30–35.

Weber, I., Haller, J., & Mulle, J. A. (2008). Automated derivation of executable business processes from choreographies in virtual organisations. *International Journal of Business Process Integration and Management, 3*(2), 85–95. doi:10.1504/ IJBPIM.2008.020972

Zhao, X., Liu, E., & Clapworthy, G. J. (2008). Service-oriented digital libraries: A Web Services approach. *3rd International Conference on Internet and Web Applications and Services (ICIW2008)* (pp. 608-613). Athens: IEEE Computer Society.

Zhao, X., Liu, E., Clapworthy, G. J., Quadrani, P., Testi, D., & Viceconti, M. *(2008). Using Web Services for distributed medical visualisation.* 5th Intenational Conference on Medical Visualisation (MediVis08) *(pp. 57-62). London: IEEE Computer Society.*

*This work was previously published in International Journal of Distributed Systems and Technologies, Volume 1, Issue 1, edited by Nik Bessis, pp. 1-16, copyright 2010 by IGI Publishing (an imprint of IGI Global).*

# Chapter 2
# Towards a More Scalable Schema Matching:
## A Novel Approach

**Sana Sellami**
*LIRIS, National Institute of Applied Science of Lyon, France*

**Aïcha-Nabila Benharkat**
*LIRIS, National Institute of Applied Science of Lyon, France*

**Youssef Amghar**
*LIRIS, National Institute of Applied Science of Lyon, France*

## ABSTRACT

*With the development and the use of a large variety of DB schemas and ontologies, in many domains (e.g. semantic web, digital libraries, life science, etc), matching techniques are called to overcome the challenge of aligning and reconciling these different interrelated representations. Matching field is becoming a very attractive research topic. In this chapter, the authors are interested in studying scalable matching problem. The authors survey the approaches and tools of large scale matching, when a large number of schemas/ontologies and attributes are involved. They attempt to cover a variety of techniques for schema matching called Pair-wise and Holistic. One can acknowledge that this domain is on top of effervescence and scalable matching needs many more advances. Therefore, they propose our scalable schema matching methodology that deals with the creation of a hybrid approach combining these techniques. Their architecture includes a pre-matching approach based on XML schemas decomposition. As shown by their experiments, their proposed methodology has been evaluated and implementing in a PLASMA (Platform for LArge Scale MAtching) prototype.*

DOI: 10.4018/978-1-4666-0906-8.ch002

# 1 INTRODUCTION

Nowadays, the Information Technology domains (semantic web, deep web, e-business, digital libraries, life science, biology, etc) abound with a large variety of DB schemas, XML schemas or ontologies stored in many heterogeneous databases and information sources. One can observe commonly in e-business applications for example schemas with several thousand elements and expressed in different formats. Thereby, a hard problem has been brought up: solving the semantic heterogeneity in the large and perform the integration of such heterogeneous collections of schemas and ontologies. Matching techniques are solutions to automatically find correspondences between these schemas/ontologies in order to allow their integration in information systems. More precisely, matching is an operation that takes as input (e.g XML schemas, ontologies, relational database schemas) and returns the semantic similarity values of their elements. Even if matching has found considerable interest in both research and practice "in the small", it still represents a laborious process "in the large". The standard approaches trying to match the complete input schemas often leads to shading off performance. Various schema matching systems have been developed to solve the problem semi-automatically. Since schema matching is a semi-automatic task, efficient implementations are required to support interactive user feedback. In this context, scalable matching becomes a hard problem to be solved.

A number of approaches and principles (Rahm& Bernstein, 2001, Shvaiko & Euzenat, 2005, Do & all, 2002) have been developed for matching small or medium schemas and ontologies (50-100 components), whereas in practice, real world schemas/ ontologies are voluminous (hundred or thousand components). In consequence, matching algorithms are facing up to more complicated contexts. As a result, many problems can appear, for example: performance decreasing when the matching algorithms deal with large

schemas/ontologies, their complexity becomes consequently exponential, increasing human effort and poor quality of matching results is observed.

In this context, a major challenge that is still largely to be tackled is to scale up semantic matching according to two facets: a large number of schemas to be aligned or matched and very large schemas. While the former is primarily addressed in the database area, the latter has been addressed by researchers in schema and ontology matching. Based on this observation, we propose a new scalable methodology for schema matching. Our methodology supports ii) a hybrid approach trying to address the two facets based on the combination of pair-wise and holistic strategies and is deployed in three phases (pre-matching, matching and post-matching; ii) a decomposition strategy to divide large. XML schemas into small ones using tree mining technique. Our methodology has been evaluated and implementing in PLASMA (Platform for LArge Scale MAtching) prototype specifically developed to this aim.

The chapter is organized as follows. Section 2 reviews related works. In section 3, we describe in detail our methodology for scalable schema matching. Section 4 presents experimental evaluation results. Finally, we conclude and discuss future works.

# 2 RELATED WORKS

In this section, we discuss the proposed solutions in the literature of the large scale matching problems. This issue has been tackled in holistic and pair-wise matching approaches, using different strategies e.g fragmentation, clustering, statistical, etc. We describe in the following section these different strategies and review the scalable matching tools.

## 2.1 Pair-Wise Matching

Being a central process for several research topics like data integration, data transformation, schema evolution, etc, schema and ontology matching has attracted much attention by research community. The matching has been approached mainly by finding pair-wise attribute correspondences, to construct an integrated schema for two sources. Several pair-wise matching approaches and tools over schemas and ontologies have been developed.

## 2.1.1 Pair-Wise Matching Strategies

We present the main strategies dealing with scalability problem. These strategies represent an effective attempt to resolve large scale schema/ontology matching problem. The used techniques aim at reducing the dimension of the matching problem:

- *Fragment based strategy (Rahm & all, 2004):* This is a divide and conquer approach which decomposes a large matching problem into smaller sub-problems by matching at the level of schema fragments. The fragment can be a schema, or sub-schema that represents parts of a schema which can be separately instantiated, or shared that is identified by a node with multiple parents. Fragmentation is achieved in two matching steps: The first step is the fragments identification of the two schemas that are sufficiently similar and the second step is to match similar fragments. This approach has been implemented in COMA++ (Aumueller & all, 2005) matching tool. The fragment-based approach represents an effective solution to treat large schemas.

- *Extraction of common structures (Lu & Wang, 2005):* The main goal of this approach is to extract a disjoint set of the largest approximate common substructures between two trees. This set of common structures represents the most likely matches between substructures in the two schemas. However, this approach has not been implemented yet.

- *Clustered schema matching strategy (Smiljanic & all, 2006):* This is a technique for improving the efficiency of schema matching by means of clustering. In this approach, matching is achieved between a small schema and a schema repository. The clustering is introduced after the generation of matching elements. Clustering is then used to quickly identify regions in the schema repository which are likely to include good matchings for the smaller schema. The clustered schema matching is achieved by the clustering algorithm K-means (Xu & Wunsch, 2005). The authors choose an adaptation of the k-means clustering algorithm. Bellflower system implements this technique. However this approach does not improve the matcher's performance and does not evaluate the quality of cluster and consequently the loss of good matchings risk.

- *Partitioning strategy:* (Hu & Qu, 2006) introduced this strategy as a method for partition-based block matching that is appropriate to large class hierarchies. Large class hierarchies are one of the most common kinds of large-scale ontologies. The two large class hierarchies are partitioned, based on both structural affinities and linguistic similarities, into small blocks respectively. The matching process is then achieved between blocks by combining the two kinds of relatedness found via predefined anchors and virtual documents between them. The partitioning process is realized based on ROCK (Robust Clustering Using Links) algorithm (Xu & Wunsch, 2005). However, this approach is not completely applicable to large ontologies and it partitions two large class hierarchies separately without considering the correspondences between them. In addition, it only assumes matchings between classes, thus it is not a general solution for ontology matching. To cope with large ontologies matching, (Hu & all, 2008) then propose a partitioning-based approach to address the block matching problem. This approach considers both linguistic and structural characteristics of domain entities based on virtual documents for the relatedness measure. Partitioning ontologies is achieved by a hierarchical bisection algorithm to provide block mappings.

- *Modularization strategy:* (Wang & all, 2006) propose this approach to deal with large and complex ontologies. The authors propose a Modularization-based Ontology Matching approach (MOM). This is a divide-and-conquer strategy which decomposes a large matching problem into smaller sub-problems by matching at the level of ontology modules. This approach includes sub-steps for large ontology partitioning, finding similar modules, module matching and result combination. This method uses the $\varepsilon$ -connection (Grau & all, 2005) to transform the input ontology into an $\varepsilon$ -connection with the largest possible number of connected knowledge bases.

## 2.1.2 Pair-Wise Matching Tools

- *COMA++* is a composite matching tool that has been developed by (Aumueller & all, 2005). It supports matching of large real world schemas as well as ontologies using different match strategies (e.g fragmentation). It implements an extensible library of matching algorithms including more than 15 matchers exploiting different kinds of schema (e.g. simple string matchers (Affix, Trigram, EditDistance, etc), reuse oriented matchers, combined matchers) and auxiliary information. It provides a graphical interface that allows the user to interact, match two schemas or ontologies and evaluate match algorithms.

- *PROTOPLASM* (A PROTOtype PLAtform for Schema Matching) is a matching tool (Bernstein &all, 2004) that implements a simplified version of Cupid (Madhavan & all., 2001) and Similarity Flooding (Melnik & all, 2002) algorithms to match the schemas. PROTOPLASM supports numerous operators for computing, aggregating, and filtering similarity matrices. By using a script language, it provides the flexibility for defining and customizing the work flow of the match operators. This tool has been integrated with a prototype version of Microsoft Biztalk Mapper, a visual programming tool for generating XML-to-XML mappings.

- *Bellflower* is a prototype System that implements clustered schema matching approach proposed by (Smiljanic & all, 2006). Bellflower uses a schema repository built by randomly selecting XML schemas available on the Internet. Matching is achieved one personal schema and a repository of schemas with only comparing the element names.

- *Falcon-Ao* (Hu & all, 2008) is an ontology matching system to enable interoperability between Web applications using different but related ontologies expressed in RDFS or OWL. Falcon-Ao implements a partitioning-based approach to divide large ontologies into smaller ones and uses a library of matchers: V-Doc to discover linguistic alignment between entities in ontologies, I-Sub based on string comparison technique and GMO that is an iterative structural matcher which uses RDF Bipartite graphs and computes structural similarities. Falcon-AO provides a graphical user interface (GUI) to make it easily accessible to users.

- *Malasco* (Matching large scale ontologies) (Paulheim, 2008) is an ontology matching system which serves as a framework for reusing existing, non-scalable matching systems on large scale ontologies. It implements a partitioning approach to divide input ontologies into smaller partitions.

- *QOM* (Quick Ontology Matching) (Ehrig & Staab, 2004) is a semi-automatic mapping tool between two ontologies. The ontologies are represented on RDF. QOM avoids the complete pair-wise comparison in favour of top-down strategy. It improves then the quality of mappings and represents a way to trade off between effectiveness and efficiency. It shows better quality results than approaches within the same complexity class.

- *ONTOBUILDER* (Roitman & Gal, 2006) is a generic tool for extraction, consolidating, matching and authoring ontologies. OntoBuilder accepts two ontologies as input, candidate ontology and target ontology. It attempts to match each attribute in the target ontology with an attribute in the candidate ontology. OntoBuilder supports an array of matching algorithms and can be used as a framework for developing new schema matchers which can be plugged-in and used via GUI or as an API. OntoBuilder contains also several matching algorithms, that can match concepts (terms) by their data types, constraints on value assignment, and above all, the sequencing of concepts within forms (termed precedence), capturing sequence semantics that reflect business rules.

## 2.2 Holistic Matching

Traditional schema matching research has been found by pair-wise approach. Recently, holistic schema matching has received much attention due to its efficiency in exploring the contextual information and scalability. Holistic matching matches multiple schemas at the same time to find attribute correspondences among all the schemas

at once. These schemas are usually extracted from web query interfaces in the deep Web. The deep Web refers to World Wide Web content not indexed by search engines. The data sources in the deep Web are structured and accessible only via dynamic queries instead of static URL links.

### 2.2.1 Holistic Matching Strategies

A lot of current approaches of holistic schema matching tackle a large amount of web interfaces in order to discover semantic correspondences between their attributes. We describe the most important strategies proposed in the literature and we highlight the used techniques to improve holistic matching process.

- *Statistical Strategy:* This approach has been introduced in (He & all, 2004; He & all, 2003) with MGS (for hypothesis modeling, generation, and selection) and a DCM (Dual Correlation Mining) framework. It is based on the observation that co-occurrence patterns across schemas often reveal the complex relationships of attributes. However, these approaches suffer from noisy data. The works suggested in (Chen & all, 2005; He & all, 2006) outperform (He & all, 2004; He & all, 2003) by adding sampling and voting techniques, which are inspired by bagging predictors. Specifically, this approach creates a set of matchers, by randomizing input schemas into many independently down sampled trials, executing the same matcher on each trial and then aggregating their ranked results by taking majority voting.

- *Clustering Based Approach:* This approach has been presented in (Pei & all, 2006). First, schemas are clustered according to their contextual similarity. Second, attributes of the schemas that are in the same schema cluster are clustered in turn to find attribute correspondences between these schemas. Third, attributes are clustered across different schema clusters using statistical information gleaned from the existing attribute clusters to find attribute correspondences between more schemas. The K-means algorithm has been used in these three clustering tasks and a resampling method has been proposed to extract stable attributes from a collection of data.

## 2.2.2 Holistic Matching Tools

- *MGS* (for hypothesis Modeling, Generation, and Selection) *and DCM* (Dual Correlation Mining) (He & all, 2004; He & all, 2003): The MGS is a holistic framework for global evaluation, building upon the hypothesis of the existence of a hidden schema model that probabilistically generates the schemas we observed. This evaluation estimates all possible "models," where a model expresses all attributes matchings. Nevertheless, this framework does not take into consideration complex mappings. DCM (Dual Correlation Mining) framework has been proposed for local evaluation, based on the observation that co-occurrence patterns across schemas often reveal the complex relationships of attributes. These frameworks are based on the statistical approaches extracted from data mining domain and are implemented in the *MetaQuerier* system.

- *PSM* (Parallel Schema Matching) *and HSM* (Holistic Schema Matching) (Su & all, 2006) are implementations of holistic matching to find matching attributes across a set of Web database schemas of the same domain. HSM integrates two steps: matching score calculation that measures the probability of two attributes to be synonym, grouping score calculation that estimates whether two attributes are grouping attributes. PSM form parallel schemas by comparing two schemas and deleting their common attributes. HSM and PSM are purely based on the occurrence patterns of attributes and do not exploit the linguistic similarity between names and types.

- *WISE-Integrator* (He & all, 2005) is an automatic search interface and integration tool. To identify matching attributes between web search interfaces, Wise-integrator applies three levels of schema information: attribute names, field specification and attribute values and patterns. It uses clustering techniques to improve the accuracy of attribute matching. First, all search interfaces belong to the same domain and attributes are clustered based on exact matches of attributes names/values. Second, further clustering is performed based on approximate matches and meta-information matches. When all potentially matching attributes are clustered together, the global attribute for each group of such attributes is generated.

## 2.3 Optimization Techniques

Most of the proposed matching large schemas or ontologies approaches integrate optimization techniques (e.g clustering, sampling, etc). We classify some of the widely used optimization techniques in four categories: Machine learning techniques, Description logics, heuristic algorithms and statistical algorithms.

- *Machine learning techniques* are supported by unsupervised classification, bagging predictors techniques, genetic algorithms, dynamic programming. Unsupervised classification may be hierarchical or partitional. These clustering algorithms are commonly used in several matching approaches to group matching results. Hierarchical algorithms (Xu & Wunsch, 2005) classify data into a hierarchical structure according to the proximity matrix. The results are usually represented by a dendrogram. Among hierarchical algorithms we can mention ROCK (Robust Clustering Using Links) that employs the similarity/proximity between a pair of data when merging clusters. HAC (Hierarchical Agglomerative Clustering), which is Bottom-up hierarchical clustering that treats each document as a singleton cluster at the outset and then successively merge (or agglomerate) pairs of clusters until all clusters have been merged into a single cluster that contains all documents. While partitional clustering algorithms divide data objects into some pre specified number of clusters without the hierarchical structure. K-means is the most used clustering algorithm. The main idea of K-means is to assign each point to the cluster whose center (also called centroid) is nearest. Genetic Algorithms (GA) (Berkovsky & all, 2005), on the other hand, are search techniques used in computing exact or approximate solutions for optimization and search problems. Genetic algorithms are categorized as global search heuristics. They are a particular class of evolutionary algorithms (also known as evolutionary computation) that use techniques inspired by evolutionary biology such as inheritance, mutation, selection, etc.

- *Description logics methods* like $\varepsilon$-Connections (Grau & all, 2005) are defined as a combination of other logical formalisms. They were defined as a way to go beyond the expressivity of each of the component logics, while preserving the decidability of the reasoning services in the combination.
- *Heuristic algorithms* such B&B (Branch and bound) are also used to search the complete space of solutions for a given problem for the best solution. It is the most widely

used tool for solving large scale NP-hard combinatorial optimization problems.

- *Statistical Algorithms* are also available to further improve matching quality; examples include resampling (Bootstrap, cross-validation), sampling methods, chi-square $X^2$, correlation and voting techniques.

## 2.4 Summary and Discussion

### 2.4.1 Classification of Matching Strategies

In this section, we classify the previous described approaches in (Figure 1) according to the optimization techniques that have been used in the literature.

Figure 1 can be read from two points of view: In the top down view, we present different input schemas and ontologies occurring in both holistic and pair-wise approaches. In the bottom up view, we can base the classification on strategies (Fragmentation, clustering, modularization, partitioning and statistical) related to the optimization techniques. We classify several widely used optimization techniques in four categories: Machine learning techniques, Description logics, heuristic algorithms and statistical algorithms.

### 2.4.2 Matching Tools Comparison

Figure 2 presents a comparison of large scale matching tools. We have compared tools based on different criteria: the input, the resulted output, the use of auxiliary resources, the implemented strategies and tools availability. We can notice from this table the major differences between pair-wise and holistic tools. First, pair-wise tools (e.g COMA++, Flacon-Ao, QoM, etc) take two large schemas/ontologies as input and produce a matching between their elements that correspond semantically to each other. While, holistic tools (e.g DCM, PSM, Wise-Integrator) are not applied on ontologies and perform matching between

*Figure 1. Classification of large scale matching approaches*

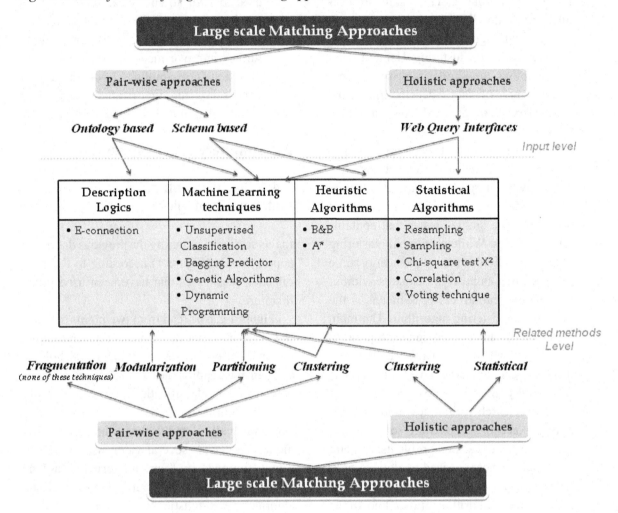

many small web query interfaces and finds all matching at once. Then none of these existing tools cope with large and numerous schemas, ontologies and query interfaces at the same time. Second, all tools implementing holistic approaches do not employ any semantic resource to help the correspondences determination process. Third, the majority of the described matching tools implement different strategies: Fragmentation, partitioning and modularization strategies are based on the decomposition of schemas or ontologies into small fragments. Statistical strategies are more based on the probability of occurrence attributes and clus-

tering is based on the linguistic affinities between attributes. All these strategies aim at improving the performance of large scale matching. However, only the work proposed by (Rahm & all, 2004) in schema matching, addresses and implements the fragmentation of XML schemas. But fragmentation has been applied only on two schemas and is based on the characteristics of schemas. These characteristics are determined during the parsing of schemas. Moreover, this approach needs the help of GUI and human input to choose the fragment type. Then the major limit is that this approach does not identify automatically the most pertinent

*Figure 2. Large scale matching tools comparison*

| Tools | Input | Input Characteristics | Output | Auxiliary Resources | Strategies | Tools availability |
|---|---|---|---|---|---|---|
| COMA++ | Relational schemas, XSD, XDR, OWL | 2 large schemas/ ontologies | Mappings | Auxiliary thesauri, Alignment reuse repository of structures | Fragmentation Reused oriented approach | Yes |
| PROTOPLASM | Relational schemas, XML, ODMG | 2 large schemas | Mappings | WordNet | None | No |
| Bellflower | XSD | A small schema And a repository Of schemas | Matchings | None | Clustering | No |
| Falcon-AO | RDF, OWL | 2 large ontologies | Alignment (RDF/XML Formats) | None | Partitioning | Yes |
| Malasco | RDF | 2 large ontologies | Alignment | None | Partitioning | No |
| QOM | RDF, OWL | 2 large ontologies | Alignment | Thesauri | None | No |
| ONTOBUILDER | RDF | 2 large ontologies | Mediated ontology | None | None | Yes |
| MGS and DCM | Web query interface | Several small Interfaces | Mappings | None | Statistical (Correlation Mining) | No |
| PSM and HSM | Web query interface | Several small Interfaces | Mappings | None | Statistical (Correlation Mining) | No |
| Wise Integrator | Web query interface | Several small Interfaces | Integrated Schema | None | Clustering | No |

and similar fragments, depending on the schemas characteristics. Finally, most of these tools are not available as a demo. Some of them are not implemented yet and do not provide a graphical user interface. This unavailability makes difficult their evaluation against real world schemas or ontologies to determine their performance and the quality of matching results produced.

# 3. SCALABLE MATCHING METHODOLOGY IN PLASMA

Based on the previous described observations, we propose a scalable matching methodology that includes the following features:

- *Scalability:* Most of the proposed matching tools suffer from handling large and several schemas and ontologies. Real

*Figure 3. Scalable matching methodology in PLASMA*

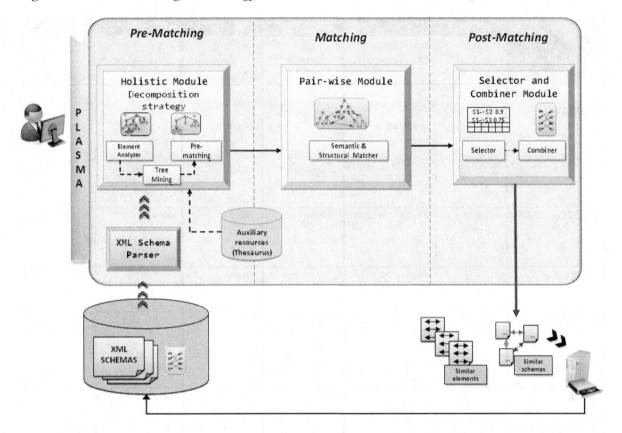

problems in specific application contexts require scalable solutions as a first priority. Our methodology is able to provide such capability.

- *Combining holistic and pair-wise approaches:* The combination of holistic and pair-wise matchers analyzes schemas/elements under different aspects, resulting in a more stable and accurate similarity for heterogeneous schemas.

- *Using optimization techniques and strategies:* If the described strategies have dealt with fragmentation approach in pair-wise context on one hand and statistical approach in holistic context on the other, we propose a decomposition approach able to divide large and numerous schemas in a statistical manner at the same time.

- *External resources:* We assess that it is essential to employ some auxiliary semantic information to identify finer matching and to deal with the lack of background knowledge in matching tasks. It is also the way to obtain semantic mappings between different schemas.

Figure 3 illustrates the three phases (pre-matching, matching and post-matching) of our methodology.

We present in the following sub-sections a description of each phase. The pre-matching phase is the most important one.

## 3.1 Pre-Matching Phase

This phase represents a pretreatment of voluminous schemas. The input is a set of large schemas

*Figure 4. Example of type reference constraint*

```
<xsd:schema xmlns:xsd="http://www.w3.org/2001/XMLSchema">
    <xsd:element name="purchaseOrder" type="PurchaseOrderType"/>
    <xsd:complexType name="PurchaseOrderType">
        <xsd:sequence>
            <xsd:element name="shipTo" type="USAddress"/>
            <xsd:element name="billTo" type="USAddress"/>
        </xsd:sequence>
    </xsd:complexType>
    <xsd:complexType name="USAddress">
        <xsd:sequence>
            <xsd:element name="name" type="xsd:string"/>
            <xsd:element name="street" type="xsd:string"/>
            <xsd:element name="city" type="xsd:string"/>
            <xsd:element name="state" type="xsd:string"/>
            <xsd:element name="zip" type="xsd:decimal"/>
        </xsd:sequence>
    </xsd:complexType>
</xsd:schema>
```

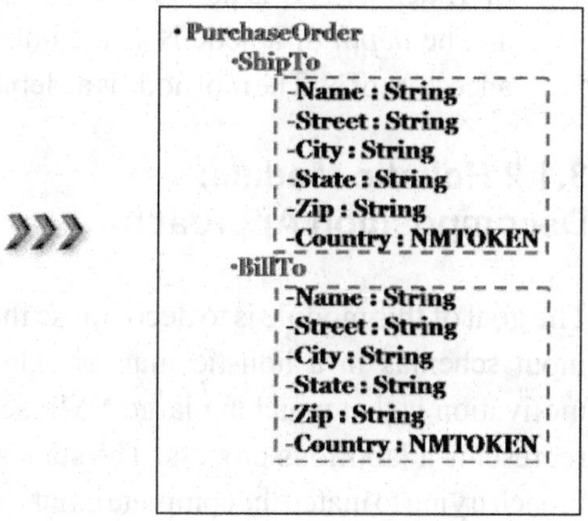

```
• PurchaseOrder
  -ShipTo
    -Name : String
    -Street : String
    -City : String
    -State : String
    -Zip : String
    -Country : NMTOKEN
  -BillTo
    -Name : String
    -Street : String
    -City : String
    -State : String
    -Zip : String
    -Country : NMTOKEN
```

that are analyzed and parsed. The holistic module addresses the issue that the schemas from the same domain may share similar and common sub schemas. We adapt data mining techniques like tree mining algorithm to find frequent sub schemas in a set of schemas. Moreover, we use semantic resources like WordNet thesaurus to exploit synonyms. The interest of this phase is to decompose large XML schemas before matching and to find, at the same time, the linguistic similarity of sub-parts of these schemas.

### 3.1.1 XML trees: From Schemas to Trees

In this initial phase, we model an XML schema as a tree. Modeling real world XML schemas represent a difficult exercise because they contain different referential constraints. In fact, there are many shared XML schema components (elements, attributes, types) that are referenced in several places. There are two types of references in XML schema: data type reference and name reference. For example, in XSD, global elements and attributes are created by declarations that appear as the children of the schema element. Once declared, a

global element or attribute can be referenced in one or more declarations using the "ref" attribute. The ref attribute of element allows referring to previously declared elements. To cope with these constraints, we duplicate the segment which they refer to resolve their multiple contexts as shown in Figure 4. We notice that referential constraints are important for schema matching. Most of the previous matching systems focused on schemas without referential elements.

An XML schema is then modeled as a labeled unordered rooted tree. Each element or attribute of the schema is translated into a node. The child elements and attributes are translated into children of the element node. The names of elements and attributes represent the labels of the nodes.

We present the formal definition of basic XML tree concept.

*Definition 1 (XML Tree):* T= (r, N, E, Ø) is a labeled unordered rooted tree, where r is the root, N is a set of nodes (elements or attributes), E is the set of edges, and Ø is a labeling application Ø: N→ L assigning a label (element name) to each node of the tree, where L is the set of labels of nodes.

*Definition 2 (Tree size and depth):* T= (r, N, E, Ø) is a labeled unordered rooted tree. The *size* of T, denoted |T| is the number of nodes in T. The *depth* of a node N is the number of ancestors of N. The root node is at depth zero.

## 3.1.2 Holistic Module: Decomposition Approach

The goal of this module is to decompose the large input schemas in a holistic manner. The main motivation is that matching large XML schemas represents a laborious process. The standard approach trying to match the complete input schemas will often lead to performance problems. In this context, we propose an XML schema decomposition approach. Our method uses tree mining techniques to identify common structures between and within XML schemas. Tree mining is a classical data mining problem which has received lots of efforts these last years. Many efficient algorithms have been proposed to process huge amount of data. As illustrated in Figure 5, our proposed approach is composed of three phases: (1) converting XML schemas in trees, (2) identifying and mining frequent sub-trees, (3) Finding relevant frequent sub-trees. This approach can lead to reduce the workload of schema matchers.

Our approach is based on the following observations and assumptions: a) Schemas at large scale are numerous, various and voluminous, b) Schemas in the same domain contain the same domain concepts, and c) In one schema, several sub-schemas are redundant.

We discuss in this section the different phases of decomposition approach.

### 3.1.2.1 Analyzing XML Schemas

In this first phase, we parse the element names and gather them into sequences of tokens. A tokenizer identifies punctuation (e.g PARTY_ID→ <Party, ID>), special symbols, etc. We use WorldNet thesaurus to find synonym elements. This analysis allows the identification of the most relevant elements in the next step. These elements are then mapped into integer representation to make faster the mining process. This representation considers the linguistic and synonym similarities between the elements and represents the input of tree mining algorithm. The linguistic similar elements are mapped into the same integer representation.

*Figure 5. XML Schema decomposition approach*

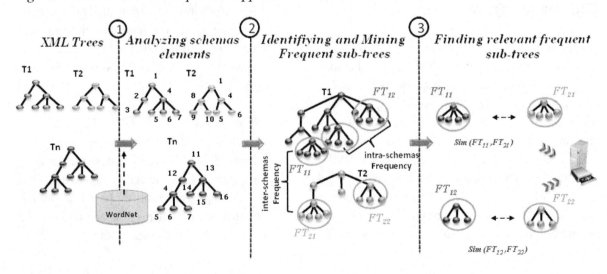

### 3.1.2.2 Identifying and Mining Frequent Sub-Trees

The main goal of this phase is to decompose the input schemas into smaller ones. To this end, we identify and extract the common sub-structures from XML schemas belonging to the same domain. We propose to use tree mining techniques to identify these common structures. More precisely, we adapt the algorithm proposed by (Termier & all, 2004) with making distinction between two sub-structures: inter and intra schemas structures and finding automatically the most relevant frequent sub-trees.

- We call Inter-schemas the common structures between different XML schemas. They represent an important source of structural and semantic information
- We call Intra-schemas the frequent structures within an XML schema. Identifying such structures plays a key role for decomposition.

We describe in this phase the way in which the tree mining algorithms can be effectively used for detecting the common structures from XML schemas.

*Problem Statement:* Tree mining is a classical pattern mining problem (an important class of data mining problem) which aims at discovering automatically sub-trees that appear frequently in a set of trees. The problem of discovering frequent XML sub-trees can be defined as follows:

*Frequent tree mining:* Given a set of trees F (also called the forest) and a user defined threshold $\sigma$, the problem is to find all the sub-trees *included* at least $\sigma$ times in F. The solutions are called the frequent trees of F w.r.t. $\sigma$.

*Definition 3 (Tree Inclusion):* Let $T_1 = (r_1, N_1, E_1, \emptyset_1)$ and $T_2 = (r_2, N_2, E_2, \emptyset_2)$ two labeled unordered trees. $T_1$ is included into $T_2$ (noted $T_1 \subseteq T_2$) if there exists an injective

mapping $M: N_1 \rightarrow N_2$ that satisfies the following rules:

$R_1:$ M preserves the labels: $\forall u \in N_1, \emptyset_1 (u) = \emptyset_2 (M(u)) (\emptyset: N \rightarrow L$ is an application that assigns a label to each node).

$R_2:$ M preserves the parent (a) and ancestor relationship (b):

(a) $\forall u, v \in N_1, (u, v) \in E_1 \Leftrightarrow (M(u), M(v)) \in E_2$

(b) $\forall u, v \in N_1$ si $(u, v) \in E_1 \Leftrightarrow (M(u), M(v)) \in E_2^+$

We consider the tree inclusion as shown in Figure 6:

$T_1 = (r_1, N_1, E_1, \emptyset_1)$ and $T_2 = (r_2, N_2, E_2, \emptyset_2)$ are two trees.

$T_1 \subseteq T_2$ means That:

$R_1:$ For $u \in N_1 \mid \emptyset_1 (u) = $ Contact $\Rightarrow \emptyset_1 (u) = \emptyset_2 (M (u)) = $ Contact

$R_2:$ For $u, v \in N_1 \mid (u, v) \in E_1 \Leftrightarrow (M(u), M(v)) \in E_2^+$

The frequency is computed using the notion of *frequency support*. The support of a tree X is noted *Support(*X,F). The basic definitions of these concepts are listed as follows:

*Definition 4 (Frequency support):* Let F = $\{T_1, T_2, \ldots T_n\}$ be a set of trees (or forest).

The *frequency Support* of a tree X noted *Support*(X,F) is defined as:

$$Support(X,F) = \sum_{i=1}^{n} intra\text{-}support(X,T_i)$$

Where *intra-support*(X, $T_i$) is the number of occurrence of X in $T_i$. Note that this support definition considers both intra and inter-schemas.

*Definition 5 (Frequent tree):* A tree X is said to be frequent in a forest F w.r.t. a minimum support threshold $\sigma$ iff Support(X,F) $\geq \sigma$.

The set of all frequent trees of a forest is noted FT = $\{FT_1, FT_2, \ldots, FT_j\}$ and $FT_i = \{FT_{i1}, FT_{i2},$

*Figure 6. Example of tree inclusion*

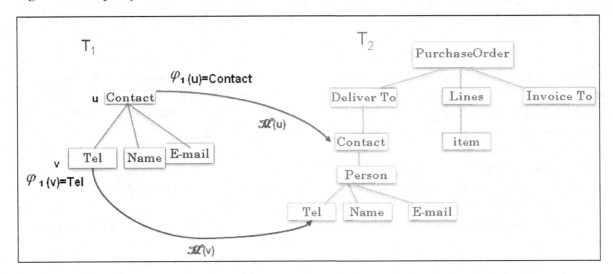

..., FT$_{in}$} that represent the set of elements in the frequent tree FT$_i$.

Figure 7 illustrates an example of mining frequent sub-trees in a forest F= {T$_1$, T$_2$, T$_3$}. For a threshold =2, the result of mining algorithm is 6 frequent sub-trees FT= {FT$_1$, FT$_2$, FT$_3$, FT$_4$, FT$_5$, FT$_6$}. The sub-trees FT$_1$, FT$_2$ are intra-frequent in T$_1$ and T$_3$, respectively. FT$_3$ and FT$_4$ are common to T$_3$ and T$_1$. FT$_6$ is common to all the trees T$_1$, T$_2$ and T$_3$. For example, the intra-support of FT$_2$ in T$_2$ and T$_3$ is respectively 2 and 2. Consequently, Support (FT$_2$, F) = 4.

### 3.1.2.3 Relevant Frequent Trees Calculus

The focus of this phase is to identify the sub-schemas candidates for matching. This aims at reducing match effort by only matching relevant parts from the other schemas. These sub-schemas are then selected for matching.

This pre-matching phase (Figure 8) includes two main steps:

A.    Selection of maximal sub-trees

The goal of this operation is to find the maximal frequent trees (*FT$_{max}$*) (Def. 6) to avoid redundant calculation between the same nodes. Our approach pruned out all the minimal ones (*FT$_{min}$*) (see Def. 7).

*Definition 6 (Maximal frequent sub-tree):* A frequent sub-tree is said to be maximal (*FT$_{max}$*) $\Leftrightarrow \exists\ FT\ /\ FT \subseteq FT_{max}$

*Definition 7 (Minimal frequent sub-tree):* A frequent sub-tree is said to be minimal (*FT$_{min}$*) $\Leftrightarrow \neg\exists\ FT \subseteq FT_{min}\ /\ FT$ is a frequent sub-tree.

B.    Finding similar sub-trees

The goal of this step is to identify the most similar sub-trees (*FT$_{Sim}$*) for matching. This is done in two phases

B.1) Testing the linguistic similarity between element sub-trees to find the most related nodes:

The objective is to find similar nodes between the frequent sub-trees. This similarity (*Sim$_{edit}$*) is done with the use of edit distance function (Cohen &all, 2003).

*Figure 7. Example of frequent tree mining*

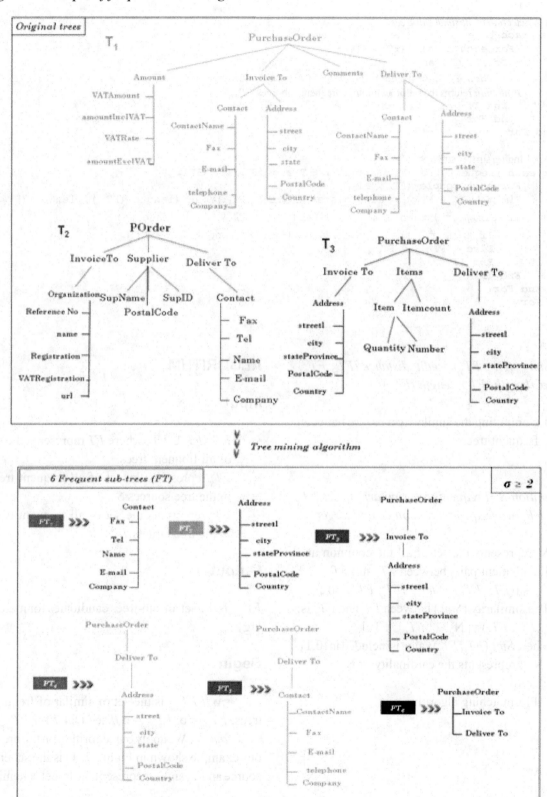

*Figure 8. Description of Pre-matching algorithm*

```
    1.   Selection of maximal sub-trees
For each tree T
        For each couple (FTᵢ, FTⱼ) ∈ FT
            If FTᵢ ⊆ T and FTⱼ ⊆ T
                Then FTmin ← Find_min (FTᵢ, FTⱼ) and FTmax = FT - FTmin
        // Find_min returns the set of all minimal frequent sub-trees FTmin
            End If
            End For
    End For

    2.   Finding similar sub-trees
For each frequent tree FTₛ ∈ S and FT_T ∈ T and (FTₛ,FT_T) ∈ FTmax
        For each couple (FTsi, FTTj)
        Simedit (FTsi, FTTj) = edit_distance (FTsi, FTTj)/max (length (FTsi), length (FTTj))
            If Simedit ≠ 0 then Sims(FTₛ,FT_T)= |Nc|/|FTₛ ∪ FT_T| //see Def.8
                If Sims ≠ 0 then FTsim= FTsim ∪ {FTₛ, FTT)and FTcand = FTsim
                Else    FTcand = FTmax
                End If
            End If
        End For
    End For
End For
 End
```

$$Sim_{edit}\ (FT_{si},\ FT_{Tj}) = edit\_distance\ (FT_{si},\ FT_{Tj})\ /\ max\ (length\ (FT_{si}),\ length\ (FT_{Tj}))$$

B.2)  Computing the similarity measure between frequent trees:

*Definition 8 (Frequent tree similarity). Let $FT_S$ and $FT_T$ two frequent trees source and target*

$N_c$ represents the set of all the common and similar element pairs between $FT_S$ and $FT_T$:

$N_c = \{(FT_{si}, FT_{Tj}) \mid Sim_{edit} (FT_{si}, FT_{Tj}) \neq 0 \}$

The similarity ($Sim_s$) between $FT_s$ and $FT_T$ is:

$Sim_s (FT_S, FT_T) = | N_c | / | FT_s \cup FT_T |$

where $Sim_s(FT_S, FT_T)$ value is included in [0,1].
$| N_c |$: represents the cardinality of $N_c$

c)    Pre-matching algorithm

## ALGORITHM

### Input

- $FT = FT_s \cup FT_T$ where $FT$ represents the set of all frequent trees.
- $FT_S$ represents the set of all frequent trees in the tree sources $S$
- $FT_T$ represents the set of all frequent trees in the tree targets $T$

### Output

$FT_{cand}$ is the set all sub-trees candidates for matching

### Begin

$FT_{Sim} = \emptyset$ // $FT_{Sim}$ is the set of similar of frequent trees, $FT_{min} = \emptyset$, $FT_{cand} = \emptyset$ // see Def.7 for $FT_{min}$

*Example:* We apply our algorithm on the previous example shown in Figure 7. $T_1$ is the schema source and $T_2$ and $T_3$ represent the target schemas.

*Figure 9. Short description of EXSMAL algorithm*

```
Input: FT_S, FT_T: two XML sub-schemas source and target

Ouput: set of triplets < FT_si , FT_Tj, Vsim>
            With      FT_si  , an element of  FT_S,
                      FT_Tj  , an element of  FT_T
                      Vsim    the similarity value between FT_si and    FT_Tj

Begin
Matching (FT_S, FT_T)
 {
For each pair of elements < FT_si,FT_Tj>,
    Compute {
                 Basic similarity value
                 Structural similarity value
                 Pair-wise element similarity value
                 }
Filter: eliminate the element pairs having their Vsim below an acceptation threshold
value
}
                                                          End
```

$FT_1 \subseteq FT_5$, $FT_2 \subseteq FT_3$ and $FT_2 \subseteq FT_4$, then $FT_{max} = \{FT_3, FT_4, FT_5 \text{ and } FT_6\}$ that represents the set of the maximal frequent sub-trees. All these sub-trees are included in $T_1$ and are consequently the sub-tree sources.

We calculate then the similarity between the maximal frequent sub-trees. For example, the similarity calculus gives:

For $FT_3$, $\in T_1$ and $FT_4$, $\in T_3$, $Sim_s(FT_3, FT_4)$= 7/ 16= 0.43

For $FT_3$, $\in T_1$ and $FT_6$, $\in T_2$ and $T_3$, $Sim_s(FT_3, FT_6)$= 2/ 16= 0.125

For $FT_4$, $\in T_1$ and $FT_4$, $\in T_3$, $Sim_s(FT_4, FT_4)$= 16/ 16= 1

All the maximal frequent sub-trees are similar, then $FT_{cand} = FT_{max} = \{FT_3, FT_4, FT_5 \text{ and } FT_6\}$

## 3.2 Matching phase

In this phase, the resulted sub-schemas of the decomposition approach are selected for matching. Then matching large schemas is reduced to the matching of much smaller ones. For every pair of schemas of $FT_{cand}$ set, we apply our matching algorithm called EXSMAL (Chukmol & all, 2005) to discover semantic and structural correspondences between elements of pairs of schemas (Figure 9). Our algorithm considers the element types, descriptions (basic similarity) and structural similarities. Structural similarity is very important because, the same element may appear in many different contexts, for example, DeliverTo.Address and BillTo.Address which should be differentiated for a correct matching.

## EXSMAL Algorithm

## 3.3 Post-Matching phase

The main goal of this phase is to *aggregate* the different similarity values found by the matcher EXSMAL and the thesaurus WordNet, to *select* the best correspondences between elements and to *combine* these similarities in order to derive the similarity between the input schemas.

### 3.3.1 Selector step

The objective of this step is to find the best correspondences between schema elements by applying a filter to determine the most plausible ones. This filter consists of eliminating all the pairs of

*Table 1. Characteristics of the Input schemas set*

| Domain | Number of schemas | Smallest/Largest schema size (K bytes) | Smallest/Largest schema size (number of elements) | Min/ Max depth |
|---|---|---|---|---|
| XCBL | 40 | 22 / 1130 K bytes | 22 / 7090 | 4 /18 |
| OAGIS | 100 | 30 / 227 k bytes | 28 / 4480 | 5 / 13 |

elements with the pair wise element similarity value below the threshold value given by the user (0≤threshold≤1).

### 3.3.2 Combiner Step

In this step, we combine the match similarities resulted from the previous step into a single similarity value to determine the similarity between the different input schemas. This similarity value depends on the similarity between the frequent sub-schemas.

*Frequent sub-schemas similarity:* This similarity *sim_freqschemas* is determined by dividing the sum of the similarity values of all frequent sub-schema elements $FT_{Si}$ and $FT_{Tj}$ of $FT_{cand}$ set by the total number of elements, $|FT_S| + |FT_T|$.

$$Sim\_freqschemas\ (FT_S,\ FT_T) = \sum_{i=1}^{|FTSi|} \sum_{j=1}^{|FT\,Tj|} sim$$

$(FT_{Si},\ FT_{Tj})\ /\ (|FT_S| + |FT_T|)$

Where *sim* $(FT_{Si},\ FT_{Tj})$ represents the similarity of frequent sub-schemas elements:

*sim* $(FT_{Si},\ FT_{Tj})$ = *coeff_ling* * *sim_ling* $(FT_{Si},\ FT_{Tj})$ +*coeff_struct* **sim_struct* $(FT_{Si},\ FT_{Tj})$.

Where *sim_ling* $(FT_{Si},\ FT_{Tj})$ and *sim_struct* $(FT_{Si},\ FT_{Tj})$ represent respectively the linguistic and structural similarities between elements. The linguistic similarity considers the similarity of names, determined by edit distance function, types and description. The structural similarity considers the context of the elements (parent, ancestor, child, sibling and leaf).

*Schemas similarity:* The similarity *Sim_schemas (S, T)* between two schemas S (source) and T (target) is obtained by summing up all the frequent

sub-schema similarities by the total number of sub-trees |FT|.

*Sim_schemas (S, T)* = $\sum$ *Sim_freqschemas* $(FT_S,\ FT_T)\ /\ |FT|$.

Where FT is the set of all frequent trees source $FT_S$ and target $FT_T$ between S and T.

## 4. EVALUATION

We conducted our experiments on real world XML schemas (XCBL and OAGIS). XCBL (XML Common Business Library) is a set of XML schemas for business-to-business e-commerce. The standard OAGIS (Open Application Group Inc.) represents a set of business process schemas.

*Experimental Environment:* Our experiments were conducted on a Windows machine with a 2.80GHz Intel Pentium and 2Go RAM.

Table 1 summarizes the major characteristics of the schema collection used in experiments.

The main goal of our experiments is to show that our proposed methodology improves large scale matching in terms of schemas parsing, schema decomposition and matching.

### 4.1. Parsing XML Schema Evaluation

We have evaluated the time elapsed in loading and parsing XML schema by our parser implemented within PLASMA and compared in the same conditions with the time elapsed by COMA++. This experience was done on medium schemas with 245 elements (≈154ko), large schemas with 630 elements (≈330ko) and very large with 3800 elements (≈950ko). Parsing schemas depends naturally on elements number and on files size.

*Figure 10. Parsing XML schemas by PLASMA and COMA++*

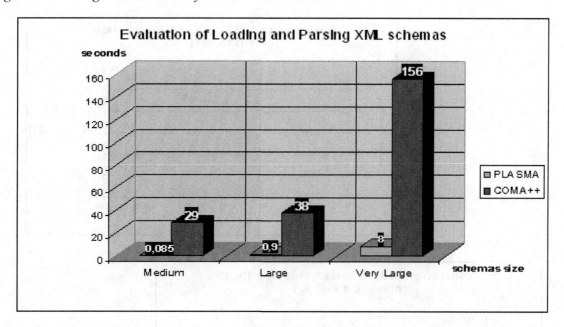

Figure 10 illustrates these results showing clearly a better performance of the PLASMA parser.

## 4.2 Experimental Results

Our experimentations show that the most of schemas share inter and intra-schemas structures (Figure 11 a). We have observed that our approach highly depends on the schemas origin and domain. For example, we have noticed an important rate of inter-schemas structures for the schemas issued from the same sub-domains (e.g. Order.xsd, Order-Confirmation.xsd, OrderConfirmationResponse. xsd, OrderRequest.xsd, OrderResponse.xsd). Moreover, schemas from different sub-domains like XCBL and OAGIS schemas need a linguistic treatment before applying decomposition approach. These schemas share similar elements describing the same content but are not identical. Then, we use WordNet thesaurus to find semantic relations between elements.

We evaluate also the variation of decomposition rate according to the threshold $\sigma$. We have observed that the decomposition rate of schemas highly depends on the threshold value. Results indicate that the more the threshold is low, the more the decomposition is important. An example of this variation is shown in Figure 11 (a) and (b).

## Definition 9 (Decomposition Rate of a Schema)

The decomposition rate of a schema T takes into consideration the size of schemas, the size of discovered frequent trees and their supports:

$$D_T = \left( \sum_{i=1}^{n} |FT_i| * intra\text{-}support (FT_i, T) \right) / |T_i|$$

Where $|T_i|$: represents the *size* of the original schema. The *size* of schemas is equal to the number of nodes.

$|FT_i|$: represents the size of the frequent trees.
n is the number of frequent trees.

We have also evaluated the execution times of our matcher on large schemas after having performed the pre-matching process. We have

*Figure 11 (a) (b). Variation of decomposition rate according to the threshold*

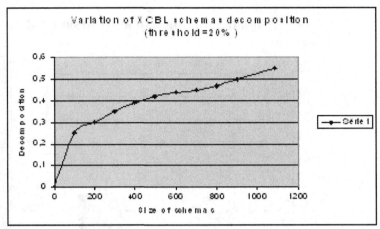

(a)

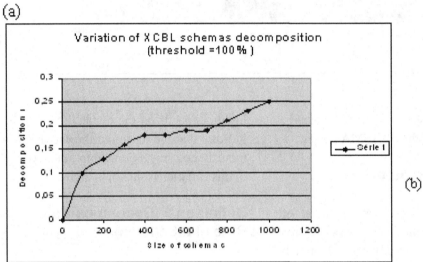

(b)

*Figure 12. Execution times of decomposition approach*

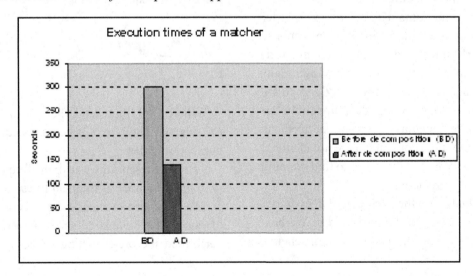

*Figure 13. Screenshot of PLASMA Graphical user interface*

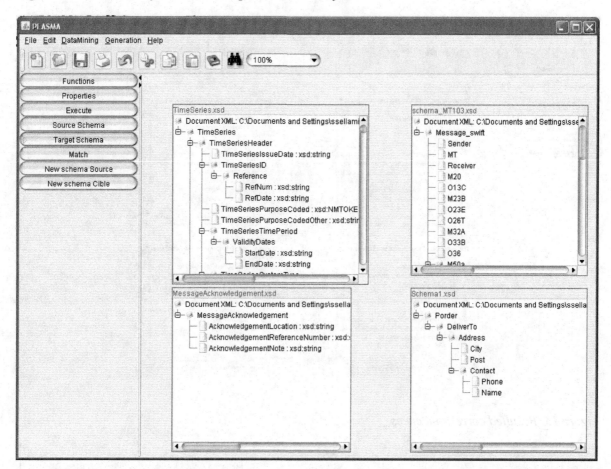

observed that using our approach, matcher's execution is more efficient. For example, Figure 12 illustrates the execution times of two OAGIS large schemas (having 356 and 192 elements) matching before (BD) and after decomposition (AD). We notice then that our approach improves execution time of schema matcher. Note that, in our experimentations, the execution time of the tree mining algorithm is only few seconds (0.007656 s).

### 4.3 PLASMA Prototype

We have implemented our proposed methodology in PLASMA (Platform for LArge Scale MAtching) platform. PLASMA represents our scalable

tool for automatically matching elements / attributes residing in multiple schemas that address similar domains. PLASMA provides a Graphical user Interface that accepts the drag and drop of schemas and allows the user to load and view different XML schemas (Figure 13). Matching in PLASMA between frequent sub-trees (in red) is achieved with EXSMAL algorithm as shown in Figure 14 and Figure 15.

### 5. CONCLUSION AND FUTURE WORKS

This chapter presented a novel approach for scalable schema matching. We have achieved a

*Figure 14. Matching frequent sub-schemas in PLASMA*

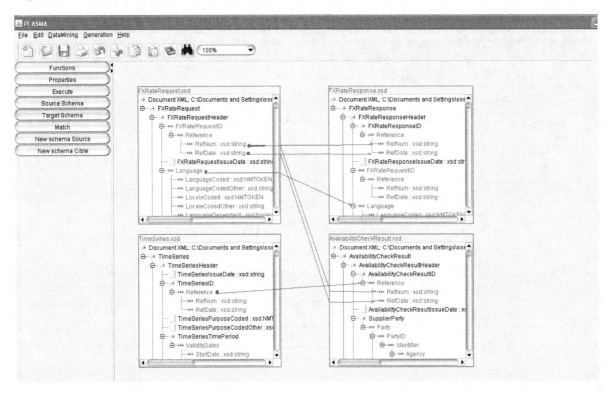

*Figure 15. Resulted correspondences*

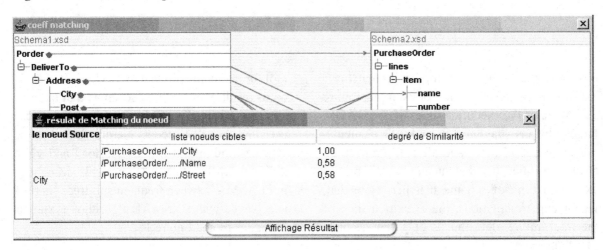

state of the art study covering existing matching approaches and tools. We have summarized this survey with listing some important issues and research trends for matching techniques at large scale. Based on the existing research, we have proposed a scalable matching methodology including three phases (pre-matching, matching and post-matching). Our architecture takes as input numerous and voluminous XML schemas and produces matching between them. We have proposed a decomposition approach as a first attempt to reduce large scale matching problem. Our approach identifies common structures between and within XML schemas and attempts to decompose these input schemas. One can notice that most of the previous matching systems focused on schemas without referential elements while our system deals with this aspects of real world schemas.

We have especially described the way in which the tree mining algorithms can be effectively used for detecting common structures from XML schemas describing same domains and our adaptation of this technique with proposing a pre-matching algorithm to find the most pertinent frequent substructures. This algorithm identifies the maximal and the most similar frequent sub-structures which represent the candidates for matching.

Our experiments confirm an improvement of the execution times performance of schema parsing, mining and matching.

To resume, matching at large scale requires deep domain knowledge: characteristics and representations of data, user's needs, time performance, etc. There is no matching system that can tackle completely all of the problems mentioned in this study. Existing approaches resort to different techniques: machine learning techniques, heuristic algorithms, statistical algorithms, etc.

We intend in the future to complete the implementation quality modules of our architecture. We plan to do further experiments with real large scale XML schemas.

## ACKNOWLEDGMENT

Special thanks to Alexandre Termier, associate professor at the university Joseph Fourier (Grenoble, France) for providing the sources of Dryade mining Algorithm.

## REFERENCES

Aumueller, D., Do, H. H., Massmann, S., & Rahm, E. (2005). Schema and ontology matching with coma++. In *Acm sigmod* (pp. 906-908).

Berkovsky, S., Eytani, Y., & Gal, A. (2005, September 19-22). Measuring the Relative Performance of Schema Matchers. In *Proceedings of the 2005 IEEE/WIC/ACM International Conference on Web Intelligence* (WI'05) (pp. 366-371), Compiegne, France.

Bernstein, P. A., Melnik, S., Petropoulos, M., & Quix, C. (2004). Industrial-Strength Schema Matching. In *ACM SIGMOD Record* (pp. 38-43).

Chen-Chan Chang, K., He, B., & Zhang, Z. (2005). Toward Large Scale Integration: Building a MetaQuerier over Databases on the Web. In *Proceedings of the Second Conference on Innovative Data Systems Research* (CIDR) Asilomar, Ca. (pp. 44-55).

Chukmol, U., Rifaieh, R., & Benharkat, A. (2005). EXSMAL: EDI/XML semi-automatic Schema Matching Algorithm. In the *7th International IEEE Conference on E-Commerce Technology (CEC)* (pp. 422-425).

Cohen, W., Ravikumar, P., & Fienberg, S. E. (2003) A Comparison of String Distance Metrics for Name-Matching Tasks. In: Proceedings of *IJCAI-03 Workshop on Information Integration on the Web* (pp. 73-78).

Do, H. H., Melnik, S., & Rahm, E. (2002). Comparison of schema Matching Evaluations. In *GI-Workshop Web and Databases.* (pp 221-237), Erfurt, Germany.

Ehrig, M., & Staab, S. (2004). QOM-Quick Ontology Mapping. In *Proceedings of the Third International Semantic Web Conference (ISWC)* (pp. 683-697).Hiroshima, Japan.

Grau, B. C., Parsia, B., Sirin, E., & Kalyanpur, A. (2005). Automatic Partitioning of OWL Ontologies Using $\varepsilon$ -Connections. In *Proceedings of the International Workshop on Description Logics (DL),* Edinburgh, Scotland, UK.

He, B., & Chen-chuan Chang, K.(2006). Automatic Complex Schema Matching Across Web Query Interfaces: A Correlation Mining Approach. In *ACM Transactions on Database Systems (TODS)* (pp. 346-395). New York: ACM Press.

He, B., & Chen-Chan Chang, K. (2003). Statistical Schema Matching across Web Query Interfaces. In Proceedings of the *ACM SIGMOD International Conference on Management of Data* (pp. 217-228), San Diego, California.

He, B., Chen-Chan Chang, K., & Han, J. (2004). Discovering complex matchings across Web Query Interfaces: A Correlation Mining Approach. In Proceedings of the *Tenth ACM SIGKDD International Conference on Knowledge Discovery and Data Mining (KDD)* (pp. 148-157). New York, NY: ACM Press.

He, H., Meng, W., Yu, C., & Wu, Z. (2005). WISE-Integrator: A System for Extracting and Integrating Complex Web Search Interfaces of the Deep Web. In *Proceedings of the 31st International Conference on Very Large Data Bases (VLDB)* (pp. 1314-1317), Trondheim, Norway.

Hu, W., & Qu, Y. (2006). Block Matching for Ontologies. In Proceedings of the *5th International Semantic Web Conference (ISWC).* (pp. 300-313), Athens, GA, USA.

Hu, W., Zhao, Y., & Qu, Y. (2008). Matching large ontologies: A divide-and-conquer approach. *Journal of Data Knowledge Engineering, 67,* 140–160. doi:10.1016/j.datak.2008.06.003

Lu, J., Wang, S., & Wang, J. (2005). An experiment on the Matching and Reuse of XML Schemas. In Proceedings of the *5th International Conference on Web engineering (ICWE)* (pp. 273-284), Sydney, Australia.

Madhavan, J., Bernstein, P. A., & Rahm, E. (2001, September 11-14). Generic schema matching with cupid. In *Proceedings of 27th International Conference on Very Large Data Bases* (pp. 49-58), Roma, Italy.

Melnik, S., Garcia-Molina, G., & Rahm, E. (2002). Imilarity Flooding: A Versatile Graph Matching Algorithm and Its Application to Schema Matching. In *Proceedings of the 18th International Conference on Data Engineering* (pp. 117-128), San Jose, CA.

Pei, J., Hong, J., & Bell, D. A. (2006a). A Novel Clustering-based Approach to Schema Matching. In Proceedings of the 4th *International Conference on Advances in Information Systems (ADVIS)* (pp. 60-69), Izmir, Turkey.

Rahm, E., & Bernstein, P. A. (2001). A survey of approaches to automatic schema matching. In *The International Journal on Very Large Data Bases.*

Rahm, E., Do, H. H., & Maßmann, S. (2004). Matching Large XML Schemas. In *SIGMOD Record* (pp. 26-31). New York, NY: ACM Press.

Roitman, H., & Gal, A. (2006). Ontobuilder: Fully automatic extraction and consolidation of ontologies from web sources using sequence semantics. In *EDBT workshops* (pp. 573-576).

Shvaiko, P., & Euzenat, J. (2005). A Survey of Schema-based Matching approaches. *Journal on Data Semantics IV, 3730,* 146–171. doi:10.1007/11603412_5

Smiljanic, M., Keulen, M., & Jonker, W. (2006). Using Element Clustering to Increase the Efficiency of XML Schema Matching. In *Proceedings of the 22nd International Conference on Data Engineering Workshops (ICDE Workshops).*

Su, W., Wang, J., & Lochovsky, F. (2006). Holistic Query Interface Matching using Parallel Schema Matching. In *Proceedings of the 22nd International Conference on Data Engineering (ICDE),* Atlanta, GA.

Termier, A., Rousset, M.-A., & Sebag, M. (2004). DRYADE: a new approach for discovering closed frequent trees in heterogeneous tree databases. In *Proceedings of the 4th IEEE International Conference on Data Mining* (ICDM) (pp. 543-546).

Wang, C., Hong, M., Pei, J., Zhou, H., Wang, W., & Shi, B. (2004). Efficient Pattern-Growth methods for Frequent Tree Pattern Mining. In *8th Pacific-Asia Conference,on Advances in Knowledge Discovery and Data Mining* (PAKDD). LNCS, 3056, (pp. 441-451), Springer, Sydney, Australia.

Wang, Z., Wang, Y., Zhang, S., Shen, G., & Du, T. (2006). Matching Large Scale Ontology Effectively. In Proceedings of the *First Asian Semantic Web Conference (ASWC)* (pp. 99-106), Beijing, China.

Xu, R., & Wunsch, D. (2005). Survey of Clustering Algorithms. *Neural Networks, IEEE Transactions* (pp. 645-678).

*This work was previously published in International Journal of Distributed Systems and Technologies, Volume 1, Issue 1, edited by Nik Bessis, pp. 17-39, copyright 2010 by IGI Publishing (an imprint of IGI Global).*

# Chapter 3
# Load Balancing to Increase the Consistency of Replicas in Data Grids

**Ghalem Belalem**
*University of Oran, Es Senia, Algeria*

**Naima Belayachi**
*University of Oran, Es Senia, Algeria*

**Radjaa Behidji**
*University of Oran, Es Senia, Algeria*

**Belabbes Yagoubi**
*University of Oran, Es Senia, Algeria*

## ABSTRACT

*Data grids are current solutions to the needs of large scale systems and provide a set of different geographically distributed resources. Their goal is to offer an important capacity of parallel calculation, ensure a data effective and rapid access, improve the availability, and tolerate the breakdowns. In such systems, however, these advantages are possible only by using the replication technique. The use of this technique raises the problem of maintaining consistency of replicas of the same data set. In order to guarantee replica set reliability, it is necessary to have high coherence. This fact, however, penalizes performance. In this chapter, the authors propose studying balancing influence on replica quality. For this reason, a service of hybrid consistency management is developed, which combines the pessimistic and optimistic approaches and is extended by a load balancing service to improve service quality. This service is articulated on a hierarchical model with two levels.*

DOI: 10.4018/978-1-4666-0906-8.ch003

## INTRODUCTION

Both computer system and network development has enabled large data set creation.

Most often, these data sets are replicated in multiple copies. This replication can meet different objectives: availability, performance, fault tolerance, etc. Unfortunately the more you reply, the more differences emerge and the more one is subject to inappropriate behaviour, and poor quality consequently. Broadly speaking,

we can say that despite all its advantages, replication raises some problems (Gray et al., 1996) such as: (i) The choice of the entity to be replicated, (ii) Degree of replication, (iii) Replica placement (Belalem & Slimani, 2007; Xu et al., 2002), (iv) Replica choice which aims to select the best replica in terms of consistency (Ranganathan & Foster, 2001), (v) The problem of replica consistency, which deals with synchronization of multiple data copies updates in order to have a completely coherent view (Saito & Shapiro, 2005). However, ensuring replica set reliability requires high consistency, a fact which can degrade performance. By contrast, good performance necessitates consistency loosening, which penalizes reliability (Belalem & Slimani, 2007).

In this chapter, our proposal is to extend service management consistency by a load balancing sub-service to improve the service quality (QoS) in Data Grid (Foster & Kesselmann, 2004). The proposed approach is based on a hierarchical model with two levels.

The main purpose is maintaining the system coherence on a large scale system while maintaining acceptable performance.

## CONSISTENCY MANAGEMENT APPROACHES

The Consistency is a relation which defines the degree of similarity between copies of a distributed entities. In the ideal case, this relation characterizes copies which have identical behaviors. Although in the real cases, even when the copies evolve in a different way, consistency defines the threshold of dissimilarity authorized between these copies. We hope of a consistency protocol which ensures the execution of the operations of users, the mutual consistency of copies in accordance with a behavior defined by a model of coherence. The consistency protocol gives an ideal view as if there is only one user and only one copy of the data in the system. Replica consistency management can be achieved, either synchronously, using the so-called pessimistic algorithms, or asynchronously, deploying optimistic ones (Belalem & Slimani, 2007; Saito & Shapiro, 2005). Fundamental tussles between pessimistic and optimistic approach are those related to scalability and security. The execution of pessimistic consistency assures that any change in one replica is atomically notified to all other replicas. Therefore, there is an inherent guarantee that all replicas will have the same data all the time, making this approach indispensable in the mission of critical and sensitive applications like the distributed banking application. On the other hand, the optimistic approach is employed for applications (large scale systems, mobile environments and system weakly coupled), which evolves rapidly in terms of response time for example. So that we can say that, the pessimistic approach is interested in consistency more than availability, while the optimistic approach supports the availability more than the consistency (Belalem & Slimani, 2007; Saito & Shapiro, 2005).

### Techniques of Pessimistic Consistency

The technique of pessimistic consistency is interesting, since it guarantees a data consistency all the time. This approach gives users an illusion of having a single, highly available copy of data. However, the guarantee of the total maintenance of consistency involves a high communication cost (Pacitti et al., 1999; Yu & Vahdat 2001). The pessimistic algorithms (Saito & Shapiro 2005) prohibit the access to a replica unless it is updating. The advantage of the pessimistic approach is to avoid the problems involved in the reconciliation. A basic protocol, called RAWA (Read Any Write All) (Zhoun et al., 2004) consists in obtaining an exclusive bolt on all the copies before to effect a writing (respectively reading) on one of the copies. The availability of the readings is improved with protocol ROWA (Read Once Write All) (Goel et al., 2005). The readings lock and access only one copy, while the write access mode continues to lock and modify all the copies. Nevertheless, this protocol is blocking in the event of breakdowns. An alternative ROWAA (Read Once Write All Available) (Kemme, 2000; Zhoun et al., 2004) adapts this protocol to the cases of crashes by locking only the available copies. When a copy covers its availability, it must initially synchronize itself to execute the remaining updates. Another strategy of replication is proposed by the vote protocol family by Quorum (Amir & Wool, 1998; Rodrigues & Raynal, 2003). The transactions are sent to a group of copies which vote (to decide which update is the most recent, writing or reading). These strategies are adapted to cases of unavailability of frequent nodes. Moreover, if a reproduction is inalienable (i.e., the cause is node failure), it can prevent other reproductions from being temporarily consulted until the failure of node is detected. Several characteristics for pessimistic approach, we can be summerized these as follows (Belalem & Slimani, 2007; Saito & Shapiro, 2005):

- Quality of Service (QoS) is very well, in pessimistic consistency;
- Very badly adapted to uncertain and unsteady environments (i.e., the mobile environments and data grid) with high rate of changes. But it performs well in local area networks, in which latencies are small and failures uncommon;

- It cannot bear the updating cost when the degree of replication is very high.

## Techniques of Optimistic Consistency

The techniques based on optimistic consistency promise higher availability and performance, but let replicas temporarily diverge and users see inconsistent data (Saito & Shapiro, 2005). Also means the optimistic strategy allow users to reach any copy for the reading or the writing operations, even when there are breakdowns of network or when some copies are unavailable. It scales well in the front of a high number of replicas (Saito & Shapiro, 2005). This also means that the approach can lead to replica inconsistency. On the other hand, the approach requires a follow-up phase to detect and then correct divergences between replicas by converging them toward a coherent state. Although this approach does not guarantee a high consistency with respect to the pessimistic one. One can also indicate some characteristics of the optimistic approach like (Belalem & Slimani, 2007; Kuenning et al., 1998; Saito & Shapiro, 2005):

- Optimistic consistency improve availability, applications make progress even when network links and sites are unreliable;
- It is well adapted to the large scale systems, because it's require little synchronization among replicas, and mobile environments;
- In optimistic consistency, QoS is not very signifiant. Often it attached factor degree of quality. Because the states of copies can be temporarily mutually contradictory;
- An update can be applied to one copy without being synchronically applied to other copies, and there will can be even a substantial time since the application of an update in a copy until the propagation of the update to other copies. The concurrent updates with the various copies can cause

*Figure 1. Main steps of the proposed approach*

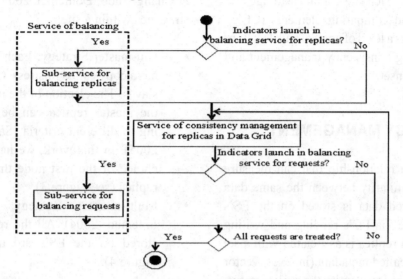

conflicts. For example, in a system distributed of the reservation of the airline company, the use of optimistic coherence, two copies cannot accept a reservation for the same seat (Belalem & Slimani, 2007).

## THE PROPOSED APPROACH

In order to improve the customer service quality starting from the processing of queries on repli-

cas, we have designed a consistency management service from a combination of optimistic and pessimistic approaches. This service is extended by a load balancing module (see Figure 1). The main objective of the service is that it allows to study and measure load balancing influence on replica quality.

In our work, we consider a grid as a tree forest at two levels (see Figure 2) (Belalem & Slimani, 2007), level 0 consists of a set of sites that make

*Figure 2. Hierarchical model used*

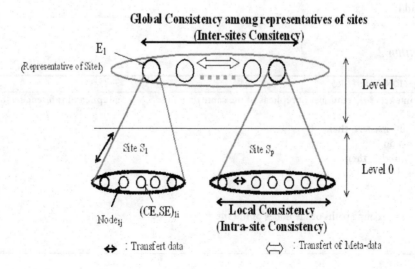

up the grid where each site contains storage elements (ES's) and computing elements (CE's), Level 1 represents a level of control and decision-making regarding consistency management and load balancing onset.

## CONSISTENCY MANAGEMENT

Consistency is a relationship that can measure the degree of similarity between the same data copies. Replicated data is stored on the ES's and is accessible via EC's reading and writing operations. Each replica is associated with a set of information, called metadata (indexes, vector version ...) and used to identify the replica status. Each replica of a given site in a version vector with a size equal to the number of that data replicas on this site. In consistency management (Chang & Chang, 2006; Domenici, 2004), there are two strategies within a site:

- Uni-master Strategy: Each replicated data has a copy called mistress. Other copies are slaves. The election of the node containing the master replica can be made according to different criteria (Saito & Shapiro, 2005). In this work, we have adopted the choice of the first node that contains the replica (see Figure 3).
- Multi-masters Strategy (Garmany & Freeman, 2004): All the replicas that are stored on the ES's are mistresses (See Figure 4).

*Figure 3. Algorithm 1*

---
**Algorithm 1** ELECTION-MASTER

**Require:** $j$, $m_i$: integer /* $m_i$ : number of nodes in $site_i$; $j$ : index node in the $site_j$ */
1:  **if** Strategy = Uni-master **then**
2:      **while** ( $j \mathbin{\text{i}} m_i$ ) **do**
3:          **if** replica $\in node_j$ **then**
4:              master $\longleftarrow node_j$
5:              $j \longleftarrow m_i$ /* to exit the while loop */
6:          **end if**
7:          $j \longleftarrow j + 1$
8:      **end while**
9:  **end if**

---

*Figure 4. Algorithm 2*

---
**Algorithm 2** ELECTION-MASTERS

**Require:** $j,y$, $n_i$: integer /* $n_i$ : number of replicas of the same data in $site_i$, $y$ : a replica of reference $y$ to the site, $j$ : index node in the site */
1:  **if** Strategy = Multi-masters **then**
2:      **while** ( $y \mathbin{\text{i}} n_i$ ) **do**
3:          **if** replica $\in node_j$ **then**
4:              master $[y] \longleftarrow node_j$
5:              $y \longleftarrow y + 1$
6:          **end if**
7:          $j \longleftarrow j + 1$ /* routing paths of the nodes of the site */
8:      **end while**
9:  **end if**

---

*Figure 5. Activity diagram for local consistency management*

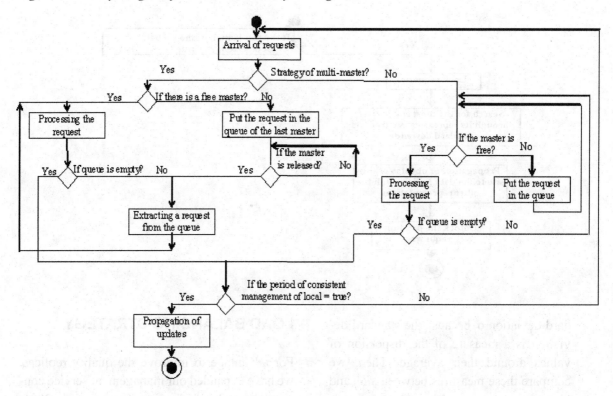

## A. Local Consistency

Consistency which is local or intra-site allows to converge the replicas of the same object to a local reference replica. In our application we have used an optimistic approach (Barreto & Ferreira, 2004). The main steps of the local coherence are illustrated in Figure 5.

## B. Local Consistency

This sub-service is responsible for inter-site consistency. Each site cooperates with other sites via representatives which communicate with one another. In our work, we have opted for the pessimistic approach, Figure 6 describes the key steps of the global consistency service.

Consistency Management in the overall level is triggered periodically to compare the version vectors (different sizes) of each site (Barreto &

Ferreira, 2004), we calculate the standard deviation of conflict and the rate of divergence:

- The sum $S$ of the vector version $Vct$ of the node containing the responsible replica of data $d$:

$$S = \sum_{x=1}^{n_i^d} Vct\left[x\right]$$ Where: $n_i^d$ : number od replicas of the data $d$ in the $site_i$

- The average of the vector $Vct$: $\overline{Vct} = S / n_i^d$
  ∘ The standard deviation $\sigma_i$ for this vector:

$$\sigma_i = \sqrt{(1 / n_i^d)\sum_{x=1}^{n_i^d}(Vct\left[x\right] - \overline{Vct})^2}$$

- At regular intervals, each representative of data $d$ in $site_i$ calculates the rate $nb_i^{div}$ stan-

*Figure 6. Activity diagram for management of global consistency*

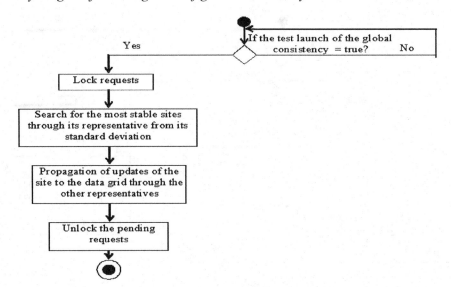

dard deviation $\sigma_i$ because the standard deviation is a measure of the dispersion of values around their average. Then, we compare these measures between *site*$_i$ and *site*$_j$: $\sigma_{ij} = \sigma_i - \sigma_j$

- The rate of divergence between *site*$_i$ and *site*$_j$:

$$\tau_{ij} = \frac{nb_i^{div} + nb_j^{div}}{n_i^d + n_j^d}$$

Where $nb_i^{div}$ number of divergences of replicas for data *d* in *site*$_i$ and $nb_j^{div}$ number of divergences of replicas for data *d* in *site*$_j$;

In the presence of such a situation, if $\sigma_i$ is over $\sigma_j$ then the *site*$_i$ is said to be in crisis otherwise *site*$_j$ is said in crisis. To address this problem we look among all the grid sites that have a standard deviation minimal to propagate updates to other sites because plus the standard deviation is small, the more replicas are close to the average, this means that the site is stable.

## LOAD BALANCING STRATEGY

For advantage to improve the quality replicas, we have expanded our management service consistency module balancing (Surana et al., 2006; Watts & Taylor, 1998). In this study, we want to measure the influence of this module balancing consistency between replicas in the data grid. We have defined two balancing strategies, that of requests and that of replicas. The following figure (see Figure 7) illustrates the decomposition in balancing service.

## A. Replica Balancing

According to the model used, we propose one load balancing level for replicas: Inter-sites. The indicators which we have chosen for replica balancing management sub-service are developed in Table 1.

Design of sub-service of balancing of replicas is composed of three main steps:

1. Phase of collection of information: The manager starts by collecting the following information:

*Figure 7. Load balancing strategy*

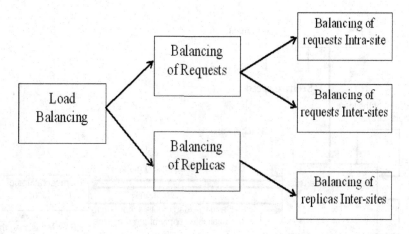

*Table 1. Calculated measures in replica balancing*

| Measures | Definition |
|---|---|
| $n_i^d$ | Number of replicas of the same data $d$ in the $site_i$ |
| $nbT\_rep^d$ | Total of replicas of the same data $d$ in Data Grid |
| $nb\_req_i^d$ | Number of queries that access the same data $d$ in the $site_i$ |
| $nbT\_req^d$ | Total number of queries that access the same data $d$ in Data Grid |
| $\zeta_i^d$ | The rate of requests accessing the same data $d$ in the $site_i$ $$= \frac{nb\_req_i^d}{nbT\_req^d} * 100$$ |
| $nb\_necessary\_rep_i^d$ | Number of replicas necessary depending on the number of requests of the $site_i$ $$= \frac{\zeta_i^d * nbT\_rep^d}{100}$$ |
| $\omega_i^d$ | $$= \frac{n_i^d}{nb\_necessary\_rep_i^d}$$ |
| $\mu$ | The threshold of imbalance replicas |

a.   The number of replicas of data $d$ of its site;

b.   The full number of replicas of data $d$ of data grid;

c.   The number of requests of data $d$ of its site;

d.   The total number of requests of data $d$ in the data grid.

*Figure 8. Collaboration diagram for the management of request balancing*

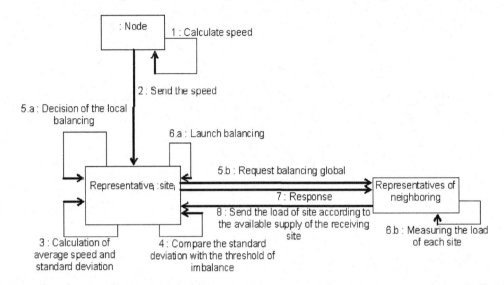

2.    Phase of treatment: The manager calculates:
a.    The rate of requests of data *d* in its site;
b.    The necessary number of replicas according to the number of requests of the site;
c.    The report $\omega$ (See Table 1).
3.    Phase Decision making: During this stage, the site manager decides the opportunity to start load balancing for replicas.

## B. Request Balancing

The management of the request balancing service, intra and inter-sites, can be represented by the collaboration diagram as follows (Figure 8).

In accordance with the hierarchical structure of the proposed model, we distinguish two load balancing levels of requests: Intra-site and Inter-sites. The indicators which we have chosen for sub-service of request balancing management are developed in Table 2.

The request *Demand* is the number of requests to be transferred from one node to another. One first calculates the difference between the average speed of *site*$_i$ and speed of *node*$_j$ appointed $d_{ij} = \overline{V}_i - V_{ij}$.

This difference is equal to the ratio between the number of queries which are not addressed by the total number of queries

$$(d_{ij} = nbr\_req\_not\_traitees_{ij} / nbr\_req\_total_{ij}),$$

from Subtracting this demand, the number of complaints not dealt with, and we write:

$$nbr\_req\_not\_traitees_{ij} = d_{ij} * nbr\_req\_total_{ij} = Demand_{ij}$$
;

The offer is the number of queries that the node can receive while remaining balanced. It first calculates the difference between the speed of *node*$_k$ and the average speed of *site*$_i$. This difference is called $\beta_{ik} = V_{ik} - \overline{V}_i$. This difference represents the ratio between the number of queries which are not addressed by the total number of queries

$$(\beta_{ik} = nbr\_req\_not\_traitees_{ik} / nbr\_req\_total_{ik})$$

From this formula, it is deduced that the offer is equal to the number of untreated queries

$$nbr\_req\_not\_traitees_{ik} = \beta_{ik} * nbr\_req\_total_{ik} = Offer_{ik}$$

*Table 2. Calculated measures in request balancing*

| Measures | Definition |
|---|---|
| $m_i$ | The number of nodes in the $site_i$ |
| $V_{ij}$ | The speed of $node_j$ owned $site_i$ $= nbr\_req\_traitees_{ij} / nbr\_req\_total_{ij}$ |
| $\overline{V_i}$ | The average speed of $site_i = \dfrac{1}{m_i} \sum_{j=1}^{m_i} V_{ij}$ |
| $\sigma_i$ | standard deviation of the $site_i = \sqrt{\dfrac{1}{m_i} \sum_{j=1}^{m_i} (V_{ij} - \overline{V_i})^2}$ |
| $R_{size}$ | The size of the request |
| bdp | Bandwidth intersites |
| $TT_{ij}$ | Tansfer time of request of $site_i$ to $site_j$ |
| $Demand_{ij}$ | Number of requests to transfer $node_j$ of $site_i$ |
| $Offer_{ik}$ | Number of requests to receive the $node_k$ of $site_i$ |
| NR | List of recipients node |
| NS | List of sources nodes |
| $\overline{\omega}$ | The threshold of hope |
| $\lambda$ | The threshold of the imbalance |

This sub-service can run a local balancing (intra-site balancing), ie within a site, if this balance can not be satisfactory, the sub-service triggers a balance between the grid sites (inter-site balancing).

## B.1. Intra-Site Balancing

In the case of intra-site balancing, three stages can be also used:

1. Estimate of the Site Load: This stage defines the mechanisms of load measurement and of communication. Knowing the number of site

nodes like their respective capacities; each manager estimates the site capacities with which it is associated by carrying out the following actions: Considering the requests more or less of the same size, we propose like load index, the speed of treatment requests. We consider the average speed of the site starting from the information received periodically by its nodes. This measurement allows to give us a sight on dispersion of speeds of the nodes. We have chosen to calculate the standard deviation to measure the extent of the variations between the average velocity of the site and speeds of its nodes. Each node sends the load information to its associated manager.

2.  Decision Making: During this stage, the site manager decides the opportunity to start a local load balancing. For that, it carries out the following actions:

    ◦   The site load state: we can say that a site is in a state of balance when this variation is relatively weak. That means that the speed of each node converges towards the average speed of its site;

    ◦   State of balance: In practice, it is a question of defining a threshold of balance, to leave we can say that the standard deviation tends towards zero and thus the site is in state of balance. Thus, we can write: If ($\alpha < \lambda$) then the site is balance if not it site is in a state of imbalance.

    ◦   The Site Partitioning: When a site is imbalance, we can consider it release of an operation of request balancing. To determine if a site node is in a suitable state to take part in a transfer of requests like source or like receiver, we divide the site into two groups of Nodes:

        i.   Overloaded nodes (sources);
        ii.  Undercharged nodes (receivers).

This classification depends on the difference between the speed of each node and that of its site.

3.  Transfer of requests: To carry an operation of request balancing, we propose the following heuristics:

    ◦   To calculate the request (*Demand*), i.e., the number of necessary requests to be transferred by an overloaded node;

    ◦   To calculate the offer (*Offre (Supply)*), i.e., the number of requests to be received.

We can distinguish three types of undercharged nodes:

A.  The nodes which never receives requests, and in this case Offrer can have any number of requests;

B.  The nodes which treated all their requests Offre can have any many requests;

C.  The nodes which have treated requests and untreated requests In this case, if the offer is not able to satisfy the request sufficiently, it is not recommended to start a local balancing. To measure the offer compared to ask, If (*Tenders>Demand*) then to start local balancing If not to start global balancing.

## B.2. Inter-Sites Balancing

In inter-sites balancing, three stages can be also used:

A.  Estimate of the site load;
B.  Decision making;
C.  Request transfer.

If a manager fails to balance its load locally, it estimates its charge compared to its vicinity. In the case of an imbalance, the manager decides to transfer his requests towards under charged closest sites (pertaining to its vicinity). In addition to the collection of information of his neighbors' load, the site manager must take account of communication costs induced by possible request transfer.

## THE METRICS USED

In order to evaluate our approach with optimistic and hybrid approaches of consistency management (Belalem & Slimani, 2007; Kuenning et al., 1998), we have used three metrics that can be classified into categories of measures: the first category to measure performance and the second for the quality of the replicas.

### A. *Performance Measurement*

The study of system performance is usually estimated by its speed to meet a user request. Most often, this speed is measured by response time made to process a request from a client. The response time of a request represents the time during which this request has been processed, i.e., its waiting time and execution time:

$$The\_average\_response\_time = (\sum response\_time\_of\_request)/number\_request$$

### B. *Measuring Service Quality*

We have used two types of metrics to measure the service quality in the replication system.

- *Average divergence:* We recall that two replicas of the same data expressed different if their vectors are different versions of a component. By using this metric, we try to mount the dispersion of replicas of the same data at any given time on the grid:

$$Average\_divergence = Number\_of\_divergence / Number\_of\_sites$$

*Average Conflict:* One of the major problems encountered in the propagation phase of updates concerning the conflict detection. The control and resolution of this phenomenon is essential for managing consistency. Starting from the conflict, we can propose another metric. The latter is the average of conflicts to calculate the average per site of conflict for a given period.

$$Average\_Conflict = Number\_of\_Conflicts / Number\_of\_sites$$

## EXPERIMENTAL RESULTS

Simulations have been carried out to be experimented with four approaches: Optimistic approach, Optimistic approach with balancing, Hybrid approach and Hybrid approach with balancing. Several series of simulations have been run. We choose for this chapter to vary the number of requests from clients to study and measure the differences, conflicts and time response of aftershocks in the approaches with and without balancing. For this simulation, we have chosen 5 sites, 30 knots per site, 100 replicas, and we have made the requests vary from 20 to 80 in steps of 20.

*Figure 9. Average number of divergences*

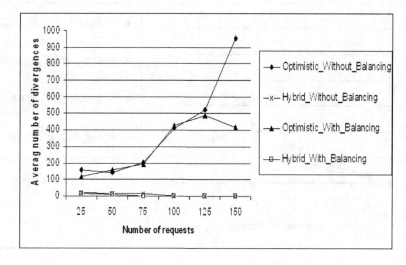

*Figure 10. Average number of divergences for Hybrid Approach*

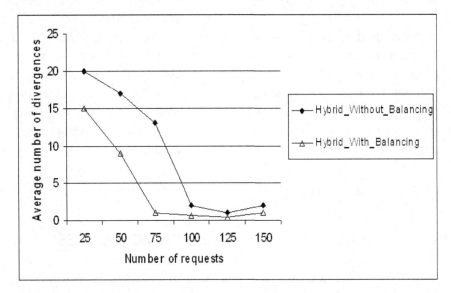

In Figure 9, we have measured the number of differences of four approaches. We note the balancing influence in reducing the number of divergences.

In this figure, we cannot see the curves approach hybrid, Figure 10 clearly shows this approach with and without balancing. We summarize that balancing can improve the replica quality.

Figure 11 shows the variation of the average number of conflicts between replicas compared to the number of requests. We can show from this figure that the balance has a strong influence on the conflict. So balancing reduces the average

*Figure 11. Average number of conflicts*

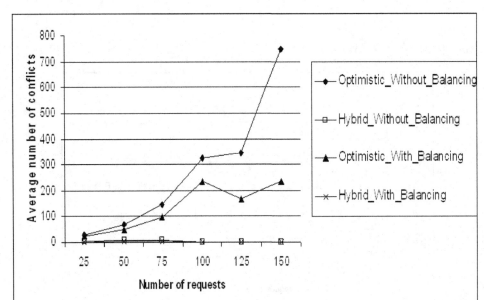

*Figure 12. Average response time for Hybrid approach*

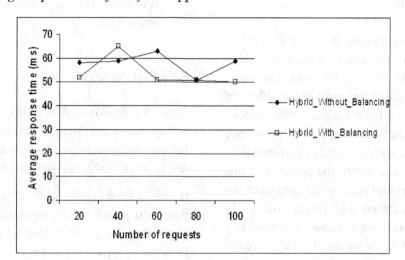

number of conflicts, which impact directly is on replica quality.

Figure 12 lets you view and compare the response time of the hybrid approach with and without balancing.

We note that from 60 requests the response time of the hybrid approach with balance decreases as the balancing approach without. The result is encouraging because we can see that

during the simulation of the application balance, you have fewer conflicts and disagreements which means better service to customers.

In Figure 13, we measured the behavior of the average number of differences by varying the number of sites. We can see from the curves in this figure, the use of balancing brings a positive influence on quality replicas.

*Figure 13. Average number of divergences in number of sites*

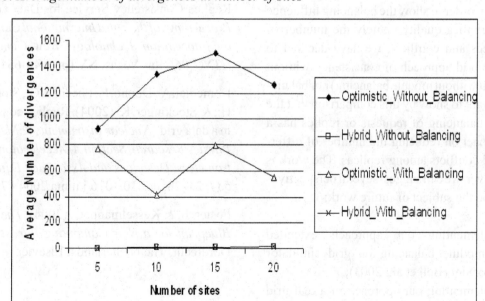

## CONCLUSION

The replication technique is widely used for data management in distributed systems and grids to ensure availability and fault-tolerance. However, the use of this technique raises the problem of replica consistency maintaining. Unfortunately, to ensure the replica consistency, you must have high consistency, with a degraded performance.

It is in this issue where the purpose of this study occurs. The aim is to see the impact of the balancing character on the replica quality. To meet this goal, we have achieved a consistency management service based on a hybrid approach (based on optimistic and pessimistic approaches) and enriched by a load balancing module to maintain the system consistency by ensuring a good performance in terms of average response time. This is by taking into account communication costs induced by the request transfer during a global balancing (inter-sites). The proposed approach is designed for a hierarchical model with two levels (Belalem & Slimani, 2007). It is under implementation on a Java platform. To evaluate our proposal, we have used three metrics to know the response time, the average number of conflicts and the average number of inconsistencies among replicas. In order to show the balancing influence over the replica quality namely the number of divergences and conflicts, we have decided to test the hybrid approach of consistency without balancing (without module balancing) nor balancing. We want to show by this comparison that the factor of balancing of requests or replies has a direct impact on reducing the number of differences and conflicts among replicas. The work is far from over, we can suggest several perspectives that can be the subject of future work:

- Implementing our approach extended by module balancing on grid simulator OptorSim (Bell et al., 2003);
- Implementing our approach in a real grid as GLOBUS;

- Improving this approach to tolerate faults in the grid.

## REFERENCES

Amir, Y., & Wool, A. (1998). Optimal availability quorum systems: Theory and Practice. *Information Processing Letters*, 65(5), 223–228. doi:10.1016/S0020-0190(98)00017-9

Barreto, J., & Ferreira, P. (2004). *Optimistic consistency with version vector weighted voting* (Tech. Rep. No. RT/004/2004). Lisboa, Portugal: Distributed Systems Group.

Belalem, G., & Slimani, Y. (2007). A Hybrid Approach to Replica Management in Data Grids. *International Journal of Web and Grid Services*, 3(1), 2–16. doi:10.1504/IJWGS.2007.012634

Bell, W. H., Cameron, G. D., Capozza, L., Millar, A. P., Stockinger, K., & Zini, F. (2003). Optorsim: A grid simulator for studying dynamic data replication strategies. *International Journal of High Performance Computing Applications*, 17(4), 403–416. doi:10.1177/10943420030174005

Chang, R.-S., & Chang, J.-S. (2006). Adaptable Replica Consistency Service for Data Grids. In *Proceedings of the Third International Conference on Information Technology: New Generations (ITNG'06)*, Las Vegas, NV (pp. 646-651).

Domenici, A., Donno, F., Pucciani, G., Stockinger, H., & Stockinger, K. (2004). Replica consistency in a data grid. *Nuclear Instruments & Methods in Physics Research. Section A, Accelerators, Spectrometers, Detectors and Associated Equipment*, 534, 24–28. doi:10.1016/j.nima.2004.07.052

Foster, I., & Kesselmann, C. (2004). *The Grid 2: Blueprint for a New Computing Infrastructure*. Dordrecht, The Netherlands: Elsevier.

Garmany, J., & Freeman, R. (2004). Multi-master replication conflict avoidance and resolution. *Select Journal, independent Oracle Users Group, 11*(4), 9-15.

Goel, S., Sharda, H., & Taniar, D. (2005). Replica Synchronisation in Grid Database. *Int. Journal Web and Grid Services, 1*(1), 87–115. doi:10.1504/IJWGS.2005.007551

Gray, J., Helland, P., O'Neil, P. E., & Shasha, D. (1996). The Dangers of Replication and a Solution. In *Proceedings of the 1996 ACM SIGMOD International Conference on Management of Data*, Montreal, Quebec (pp. 173-182).

Kemme, B. (2000). *Database Replication for Clusters of Workstations*. Unpublished doctoral dissertation, Swiss Federal Institute of Technology Zurich, Germany.

Kuenning, G. H., Bagrodia, R., Gay, R. G., Popek, G. J., Reiher, P. L., & Wang, A.-I. (1998). Measuring the Quality of Service of Optimistic Replication. In *Proceedings of the Workshops on Object-Oriented Technology (ECOOP '98)*, Brussels, Belgium (pp. 319-320).

Pacitti, E., Minet, P., & Simon, E. (1999). Fast Algorithms for Maintaining Replica Consistency in Lazy Master Replicated Databases. In *Proceedings of the Int. Conf. on Very Large Databases*, Edinburgh, UK.

Ranganathan, K., & Foster, I. (2001). Identifying dynamic replication strategies for a high performance data grid. In *Proceedings of the Grid: Second International Workshop, 2242*, 75–86.

Rodrigues, L., & Raynal, M. (2003). Atomic Broadcast in Asynchronous Crash-Recovery Distributed Systems and its use in Quorum-Based Replication. *IEEE Transactions on Knowledge and Data Engineering, 15*(5), 1206–1217. doi:10.1109/TKDE.2003.1232273

Saito, Y., & Shapiro, M. (2005). Optimistic Replication. *ACM Computing Surveys, 37*(1), 42–81. doi:10.1145/1057977.1057980

Surana, S., Godfrey, B., Lakshminarayanan, K., Karp, R., & Stoica, I. (2006). Load balancing in dynamic structured peer-to-peer systems. *Performance Evaluation, 63*(3), 217–240. doi:10.1016/j.peva.2005.01.003

Watts, J., & Taylor, S. (1998). A practical approach to dynamic load balancing. *IEEE Transactions on Parallel and Distributed Systems, 9*(3), 235–248. doi:10.1109/71.674316

Xu, J., Li, B., & Lee, D. (2002). Placement Problems for Transparent Data Replication Proxy Services. *IEEE Journal on Selected Areas in Communications, 20*(7), 1383–1398. doi:10.1109/JSAC.2002.802068

Yu, H., & Vahdat, A. (2001). The Costs and Limits of Availability for Replicated Services. In *Proceedings of the Eighteenth ACM Symposium on Operating Systems Principles (SOSP '01)* (pp. 29-42). New York: ACM.

Zhoun, W., Wang, L., & Jia, W. (2004). An Analysis of Update Ordering in Distributed replication systems. *Future Generation Computer Systems, 20*(4), 565–590. doi:10.1016/S0167-739X(03)00174-2

*This work was previously published in International Journal of Distributed Systems and Technologies, Volume 1, Issue 4, edited by Nik Bessis, pp. 42-57, copyright 2010 by IGI Publishing (an imprint of IGI Global).*

# Chapter 4

# MaGate:
## An Interoperable, Decentralized and Modular High–Level Grid Scheduler

**Ye Huang**
*University of Fribourg, Switzerland*

**Amos Brocco**
*University of Fribourg, Switzerland*

**Michele Courant**
*University of Fribourg, Switzerland*

**Beat Hirsbrunne**
*University of Fribourg, Switzerland*

**Pierre Kuonen**
*University of Applied Sciences of Western Switzerland, Switzerland*

## ABSTRACT

*This work presents the design and architecture of a decentralized grid scheduler named MaGate, which is developed within the SmartGRID project and focuses on grid scheduler interoperation. The MaGate scheduler is modular structured, and emphasizes the functionality, procedure and policy of delegating local unsuited jobs to appropriate remote MaGates within the same grid system. To avoid an isolated solution, web services and several existing and emerging grid standards are adopted, as well as a series of interfaces to both publish MaGate capabilities and integrate functionalities from external grid components. Meanwhile, a specific swarm intelligence solution is employed as a critical complementary service for MaGate to maintain an optimized peer-to-peer overlay that supports efficient resource discovery. Regarding evaluation, the effectiveness brought by job sharing within a physically connected grid community with the use of the MaGate has been illustrated by means of experiments on communities of different scale, and under various scenarios.*

DOI: 10.4018/978-1-4666-0906-8.ch004

# INTRODUCTION

The grid scheduling service, also known as super-scheduling (Schopf, 2003), is defined as "scheduling job across grid resources such as computational clusters, parallel supercomputers, desktop machines that belong to different administrative domains". It is a crucial component for grid computing infrastructures because it determines the effectiveness and efficiency of a grid system by identifying, characterizing, discovering, selecting, and allocating the resources that are best suited for a particular job.

Grid scheduling is a critical but complex task. The heterogeneous and distributed nature of grid systems imposes additional constraints on scheduling services, such as lack of remote resource control, or incomplete overall knowledge of the grid system.

Besides the theoretical issues, the realities of grid scheduler design and implementation have made things even more complicated. Existing grid schedulers typically depend on (or are completely integrated in) some particular grid middleware. Therefore, it is a nontrivial task to migrate a grid scheduler from one middleware to another, or to exchange messages between schedulers, or to delegate jobs between different types of scheduler. Grid schedulers designed upon various middlewares respectively can be regarded as a set of heterogeneous grid schedulers.

The contribution of this chapter is the design of a decentralized modular high-level grid scheduler named MaGate. The MaGate scheduler dedicates to improve the rate of successfully executed jobs submitted to the same grid community, by means of interacting with each other and delegating jobs amongst all participating nodes of the community. In other words, the MaGate schedulers are driven to co-operated with each other, to provide intelligent scheduling for the scope of serving the grid community as a whole, not just for a single grid node individually.

To achieve the purpose mentioned above, the MaGate scheduler emphasizes on several relevant issues: (i) the approach of discovering remote resources dynamically and efficiently; (ii) the community policy of determining jobs to delegate remotely, and acceptation of arrived remote jobs; (iii) the platform independent communication protocol to facilitate the interaction between different MaGate schedulers on heterogenous nodes; (iv) the negotiation procedure to tackle various job delegation scenarios flexibly, i.e., job delegation accept/reject/conditional reject, job delegation proxy and forwarding, etc.

The MaGate is being developed within the SmartGRID project (Huang, Brocco, Kuonen, Courant, & Hirsbrunner, 2008), which aims at improving the efficiency of existing grids through a modular, layered architecture: the Smart Resource Management Layer (SRML) to support grid scheduling, and the Smart Signaling Layer (SSL) to provide resource discovery. Furthermore, communication between layers is mediated by means of the Datawarehouse Interface (DWI).

The Smart Resource Management Layer (SRML) is comprised of a set of MaGates. Each MaGate is composed of a set of loosely coupled modules, in order to tackle several critical issues raised by grid scheduling, such as:

- Standard-compliant interaction between different grid schedulers. In order to guarantee the interoperability, extensibility and reusability of MaGates, all input and output communication protocols and data formats are designed to be based on existing and emerging standards, especially for job representation, resource modeling, resource capabilities advertisement, and negotiation agreement management.
- Dynamic resource discovery. It is fundamentally important to be able to efficiently discover resources in a dynamic network. Our work tackles this issue by using a self-structured peer-to-peer overlay net-

work, constructed and maintained using ant colony algorithms, whose intrinsic design, adaptiveness and robustness provide an optimal platform for resource discovery and monitoring mechanisms.

- Infrastructure independent job allocation and management. Infrastructure independency is a nontrivial issue, and the main difficulty lies on the semantics. To overcome such a problem requires either to find a common denominator to hide the infrastructure differences, or to develop separate adaptors for each diverse infrastructure respectively. In order to minimize the work related with this issue, and to provide interoperability and reusability, MaGate relies on the unified interfaces provided by standardized specifications, to achieve infrastructure independent job allocation and management.
- Platform independent interface to external grid services. Presently, the grid community has realized the importance of standardizing grid solutions, and developed many relevant specifications and libraries, to facilitate grid development with web services technologies. MaGate follows this philosophy, and provides a series of web services based interfaces both to obtain external functionalities from other grid services, and to advertise its own reusable capabilities to external users also.

The remainder of the chapter is organized as follows: related work on grid schedulers, the grid standards and resource discovery is introduced in next section. Derivation and purpose of the MaGate is illustrated in section SmartGRID, followed by a detailed MaGate description in section MaGate Architecture. Section Reference Experimental Results discusses the experiment configuration and corresponding results. Finally, section Conclusions and future work presents some insights to future development.

# RELATED WORK

## Grid Schedulers

Considering the important role of grid scheduling, many approaches on this topic have been proposed. Between the most known works, the Meta-Scheduling Service (MSS) (Waldrich, Wieder, & Ziegler, 2006) is a middleware-independent grid scheduler designed with prdefined policies and currently implemented on the Unicore USite architecture. The GridWay (Huedo, Montero, & Llorente, 2005) is also a well-known highlevel scheduler from the Globus Toolkit (Foster & Kesselman, 1997) that provides abundant features, such as adaptive scheduling and adaptive execution, within a modular structure. In order to avoid scheduling selfcompetition, GridWay only allows one scheduler to manage each virtual organization. Additionally, other grid scheduling solutions, such as Moab Grid Suite (Moab Grid Suite, 2009) and Community Scheduler Framework (CSF) (Xiaohui, Zhaohui, Shutao, Chang, & Huizhen, 2006), have been developed in collaboration with the industry.

Besides the existing implementations, general scheduler structures, such as the Scheduling Instance (Tonellotto, Wieder, & Yahyapour, 2005), have also been proposed to give a design cornerstone for future grid schedulers.

Current grid schedulers are set up to bridge the gap between grid applications and various pre-existing local resource management systems. Combined with a general lack of grid infrastructure information, two constraints have emerged regarding grid schedulers: (a) the scope of grid system is assumed to be known a-priori, (b) no horizontal interaction between grid schedulers is considered.

To overcome the dilemmas mentioned above, with respect to existing grid scheduling systems, MaGate is designed to be a decentralized grid schedule that emphasizes on grid scheduler interoperation, and complemented by a dynamic resource discovery approach on decentralized network. In order to share the jobs submitted from a local MaGate to other MaGates within the same grid community, a set of community scheduling relevant parameters are evaluated and discussed to address various job delegation scenarios between different MaGates.

## Existing and Emerging Standard Specifications

The experiences of the grid community so far have shown that the realization of an ideally single interconnected, interoperating computation ecosystem is difficult. Instead, many different grids for specific usage scenarios have appeared. In order to achieve the promised unified computation environment and being widely adopted by the e-science and industry community, standardized technologies in many fields are being developed, and some of them have established their importance through time.

In particular, the Job Submission Description Language (JSDL) (Anjomshoaa et al., 2005) is known as a XML-based language specifically for describing computational grid jobs submission and their resource requirement. WS-Agreement (Andrieux et al., 2004) works as a platform independent protocol for advertising capabilities of services, and making agreement between service providers and consumers.

Meanwhile, both Simple API For Grid Application (SAGA) (Goodale et al., 2006) and Distributed Resource Management Application API (DRMAA) (Troger, Rajic, Haas, & Domagalski, 2007) dedicate to provide API specification to cover the functionalities of submitting, controlling, and monitoring jobs on local resource management systems.

The aforementioned specifications facilitate either the interoperation amongst grid components, or the interaction between grid components and local resource management systems. All such scenarios are critical for MaGate.

## Resource Discovery in Distributed Systems

Resource discovery mechanisms are a vital fundamental part of grid computing, not only because they affect the efficiency of discovering appropriate resources for job execution, but also because their architecture influence the logical topology of grid resources. Concerning the ecosystem of MaGate, resources distributed on a decentralized peer-to-peer (P2P) based network have to discover dynamically.

At present, proposals of discovering resources on P2P topology have gained significant momentum and being generally categorized into structured and unstructured systems. Structured systems, such as Distributed Hash Tables (DHTs), offer deterministic query search results within logarithmic bounds on network complexity, which means that a look-up operation will be successful within a predefined time bound. Unstructured systems (Ripeanu & Foster, 2001) don't put any constraints on the structure of network and data distribution. Normally, a query flooding protocol is adopted to process look-up requests: this might have series drawbacks, such as high communication overhead and non scalability.

In an attempt to remedy the issues of unstructured overlay, self-structured solutions have been proposed. In contrast to structured approaches, self-structured systems reorganize existing unstructured topologies by adding and removing logical links between nodes (Ripeanu, Iamnitchi, Foster, & Rogers, 2007; Shen, 2004; Schmid & Wattenhofer, 2007). Our work addresses the problem of decentralized resource discovery by using a self-structured overlay topology maintained with help of a bioinspired algorithm that borrows ideas from the swarm intelligence and ant colony optimization. Swarm intelligence (Bonabeau, Dorigo, & Theraulaz, 1999) is a branch of artificial intelligence that focuses on algorithms inspired by the collaborative behavior of swarms of insects. Such bioinspired solutions have already been successfully applied to several network routing problems (Schoonderwoerd, Holland, Bruten, & Rothkrantz, 1997; Di Caro & Dorigo, 1998), as well as for resource discovery in unstructured networks (Michlmayr, 2006). More generally, swarm algorithms exhibit an inherent decentralized design, which helps their implementation in fully distributed systems.

## SMARTGRID

SmartGRID is a generic and modular framework that supports intelligent and interoperable grid resource management using swarm intelligence algorithms. SmartGRID is structured as a loosely coupled architecture, which is comprised of two layers and one internal interface, as shown in Figure 1.

Smart Resource Management Layer (SRML). SRML is responsible for grid level dynamic scheduling and interoperation serving grid applications with dynamically discovered computing resources. SRML is composed of all the engaged MaGates schedulers. Each participating MaGate is expected to delegate jobs that are submitted through local MaGate but can not fit the local resource, titled local unsuited jobs, to

discovered remote MaGates; inversely, each MaGate is also expected to accept job delegation requests from other MaGates within the same community, if the delegation requirements match local MaGate's community policy and current working status. A detailed description of MaGate is presented in section MaGate Architecture.

The Smart Signaling Layer (SSL). SSL represents the interface from and to the network of the SmartGRID framework, and provides information about the availability of resources on other nodes, as well as their status. The SSL hides the complexity and instability of the underlying network by offering reliable services based on distributed ant algorithms. Ants are defined as lightweight mobile agents traveling across the network, collecting information on each visited node. A middleware named Solenopsis (Brocco, Hirsbrunner, & Courant, 2007) is developed to run each ant node, providing an environment for the execution of ant colony algorithms, specially the BlåtAnt collaborative ant algorithm (Brocco, Frapolli, & Hirsbrunner, 2008, 2009).

The Data Warehouse Interface (DWI). The DWI acts as a loosely coupled communication channel, which is used to mediate the data exchange between SRML and SSL without exposing technical implementation details of either layer.

*Figure 1. SmartGRID architecture overview*

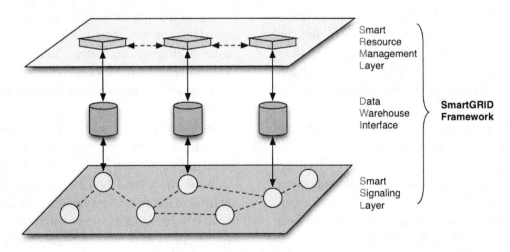

*Figure 2. MaGate modular architecture*

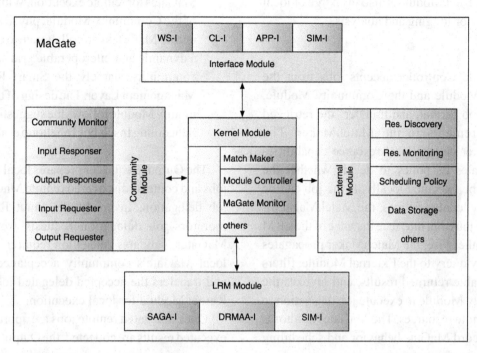

The DWI is comprised of a series of distributed data storages that store both persistent and cached grid information concerning network infrastructure, resource status, grid scheduling request/response, strategy parameters, SmartGRID specific events, etc.

## MAGATE ARCHITECTURE

As mentioned before, the MaGate scheduler dedicates to improve the rate of successfully executed jobs submitted to the scope of entire grid community, by means of interacting with each other and delegating jobs amongst all participating MaGates of the same community, using various community policies. Besides, a set of other relevant issues are also targeted, such as utilizing dynamic resource discovery service and open structured for cooperating with external grid components. In order to address different purposes within an uniform and loosely coupled architecture, the MaGate is modular designed,

as illustrated in Figure 2: (a) the Kernel Module is responsible for MaGate self-management and addressing of internal events; (b) the Community Module tackles the interoperation with external schedulers; (c) the LRM Module performs job allocation and management on Local Resource Management systems (LRM); (d) the External Module interacts with external grid services for additional functionalities; (e) the Interface Module manages the interface for accepting job submission from various local invokers, and delivers the results back. A detailed description of each individual module of MaGate is given in the following subsections.

### Modules

*Kernel Module:* The Kernel Module is responsible for MaGate self-management, which disposes internal events, provides local scheduling decisions, and connects other modules to work as a whole. Additionally, the Kernel Module is also in charge of local behavior logging and analysis.

The Module Controller accepts jobs from the Interface Module and the Community Module, validates job format, and transfers the retrieved job requirements to the MatchMaker. The MatchMaker checks local resource capabilities and evaluates its policy to decide whether the job could be executed locally. If the job can be fulfilled by local resources, the MatchMaker allocates the job to an interface instance of the LRM Module; otherwise, the MatchMaker propagates a discovery query to the External Module, filters out unsuitable returned results, and invokes the Community Module to execute job delegation to proper remote resources. The MaGate Monitor is used to record MaGate behavior and scheduling history for statistic purposes.

*Interface Module:* The Interface Module is responsible for accepting job submissions from MaGate local invokers, including grid users and high level grid applications. MaGate's local available functionalities are also published through the Interface Module.

The CL-I provides a command line based interface for the interacting with the MaGate, which accepts parameter based job local submissions, and delivers the results back. Besides, both APP-I and WS-I offer the alternative approaches to grid applications and web services based invokers respectively.

The MaGate prototype within a simulation environment, the SIM-I is provided to accept submission of simulated grid jobs.

*Community Module:* The Community Module is a mandatory component of MaGate. It acts as a connector that both accepts jobs from remote MaGates for local execution, and delegates local unsuited jobs to other

MaGates for remote execution. With the help of the Community Module, physically connected MaGates can collaborate to construct a dynamic and interoperable grid scheduler community, namely the Smart Resource Management Layer. The design of the Community Module follows the suggestion of the Scheduling Instance (Tonellotto et al., 2005).

The Output Requester prepares local unsuited jobs and contacts discovered remote MaGates for job delegation. Inversely, the Input Requester monitors job delegation requests from other MaGates, validates delegation requirements and local MaGate's community acceptance policy, and transfers the accepted delegated jobs to the Kernel Module for local execution.

Once delegated remote jobs are approved and executed results are collected, the Output Responser is used to construct corresponding responses and send them back to the delegation initiators. Inversely, the Input Responser is used to monitor the incoming delegation response messages from other MaGates.

The Community Monitor maintains a known neighborhood list, and periodically contacts each remote MaGate from the list to obtain a replica of their node status, including node workload, node neighborhood list, etc. Furthermore, more remote MaGates could be proactively discovered and complemented by the External Module. In this case, each MaGate has a partial view of the entire grid scheduler community, titled the MaGate Community, which helps to achieve exchanging of work, load balancing and failure recovery within the scope of this known community.

*LRM Module:* The LRM Module empowers MaGate to utilize grid infrastructure, such as local resources management systems, to allocate the accepted jobs for local execution, monitor the execution status, and retrieve results back. As mentioned before, instead of direct support to too many existing facilities, the LRM Module provides several interfaces to support local resource management systems through standardized API-based specifications, such as SAGA-I (Goodale et al., 2006) for "Simple API For Grid Application (SAGA)", and DRMAA-I (Troger et al., 2007) for "Distributed Resource Management Application API (DRMAA)". Meanwhile, in order to validate MaGate simulation based prototype, the SIM-I, which simulates resource management systems, is also provided to execute accepted simulated jobs.

*External Module:* The External Module offers a plug-in mechanism for MaGate. It works as a multi-functional outlet that helps to strengthen the MaGate by integrating appropriate external grid services, components, algorithms and strategies. Since developing grid services using web services has gained significant momentum recently, the service interfaces exposed by the External Module are web services compliant.

The Resource Discovery connects MaGate to an external grid resource discovery service for obtaining information of remote resources. It is a critical component for MaGate to validate the idea of scheduler community. The Resource Monitoring empowers MaGate to monitor the change of re- mote resource status. The Scheduling Policy offers a parameter-based approach for adopting external scheduling algorithms, which follow the uniform I/O parameter schema and developed by other organizations. The Data Storage facilitates MaGate to preserve its data into external storage facilities.

## Reference Scenario

To make the MaGate scheduler fulfil the purpose of serving grid community as a whole, each newly established MaGate must be connected to a resource discovery service, which is able to discovery remote MaGates from an existing community. Meanwhile, each MaGate of the community is required to publish their public capability profile using a specific key-value format, which is supposed to be discovered and monitored by resource discovery services from other MaGates during the lifecycle. Additionally, if an individual MaGate wishes to contribute its local resources, the LRM Module must be utilized to mediate the communication between the MaGate and the local resource management system.

The Interface Module receives job submissions from the exposed interfaces, and transfers the validated jobs to the Kernel Module. Scheduling algorithms are launched by the Kernel Module to evaluate the job requirements. If the local resource could satisfy the job requirements, the jobs are transferred to the LRM Module for local execution; if not, the Community Module is invoked, to either looks up appropriate remote resources from its local cached neighbors list, or propagates resource searching queries based on job requirements, and transfers such queries to the interconnected external resource discovery services through the External Module. At a later stage, the discovered information regarding remote resources is used by the Community Module to initialize job delegation requests respectively. As soon as one delegation request is accepted by a remote MaGate, the Community Module delegates the corresponding job, leaving a callback address for getting results back. If all delegation requests of an individual job have been rejected, it is then the responsibility of the Community Module to decide whether renegotiation iteration should be issued later, with modified delegation parameters. Such decisions are made regarding the utilized community policies by different MaGates.

Inversely, once the Community Module of a MaGate has received job delegation requests from other remote MaGates, acceptance decisions are also made depending on the adopted community policies, such as the length limit of MaGate's Community Input Queue, which is used to preserve the accepted but unprocessed delegated remote jobs.

Noteworthy that the Kernel Module is able to addresses the job requests both from local users and from other connected remote MaGates.

## Reference Implementation

The current reference implementation of MaGate is simulation based (Huang, Brocco, Courant, Hirsbrunner, & Kuonen, 2009). The implemented MaGate simulator is based on GridSim (Buyya & Murshed, 2002) and Alea (Klusacek, Matyska, & Rudova, 2008).

For both the Interface Module and the LRM Module, the SIM-I interfaces have been implemented to allocate simulated jobs to simulated resources. The interaction between the MaGate and existing local schedulers/middlewares is not mentioned at current stage. Regarding the job allocation on local resource has been out of the main interest of the MaGate, external grid components, such as SAGA (Goodale et al., 2006) and DRMAA (Troger et al., 2007), will be evaluated to facilitate this work in our future implementation.

For the External Module, according to the ecosystem of MaGate, Smart Signaling Layer (SSL) is adopted as the default external service for both Resource Discovery and Resource Monitoring.

For the Community Module, a socket based implementation has shown that the scheduler interaction is functionally ready. Meanwhile, different job delegation related factors, such as resource discovery policies and community scheduling policies (e.g., delegation negotiation/renegotiation policy, delegation acceptance policy), have been evaluated respectively. Regarding the future work, a web services based communication service is being developed to achieve the infrastructure independent scheduler interoperation; additional, an algorithm to integrate diverse community policies and automate the negotiation/renegotiation procedure is under the development.

For the Kernel Module, the Module Controller is implemented to dispose MaGate internal events, and interact with simulation environment. The MaGate Monitor is used to record event history from simulated infrastructure and produce logged data for statistic analysis. A benchmarked "First Come First Service" algorithm is adopted by the Match Maker for making local scheduling decision. Meanwhile, algorithm "Easy Backfilling", which is used for comparison purpose, is under the development.

The reference implementation is used to do the reference experiment, which is discussed as follows:

## Reference Experimental Results

The reference experiment is evaluated to prove a functional ready MaGate prototype, which is able to address different scheduling related events using a uniform modular architecture. Specially, the capability of scheduler interoperation and work sharing within the interconnected community is emphasized to facilitate the improvement of our criterion: the Rate of successfully executed Jobs from the entire grid Community (RJC). The RJC is adopted as the judgement of experiment results to prove the functional effectiveness brought by the design of job delegation on an interoperable MaGate community. We try to maximize this value because it presents the capability and effectiveness of disposing local unsuited jobs on remote nodes from the scope of grid community. The disadvantages of using the RJC as the only criterion are that both the overall resource throughput and the network load of transferring resource discovery requests are missing currently, which will be considered and measured in our future work.

## Reference Models

Although grid systems vary widely depending on the usage scenarios, one of the typical example of a computational grid is still the execution of computational intensive batch jobs on collaborative computers. Several models retrieved from this scenario are used in our experiment, and represented as follows:

*Machine Model*: The machine refers to the Massive Parallel Processor Systems (MPP), which are comprised of several Process Elements (PE) connected via fast interconnections. Each process element is a single processing system with local CPU and memory, using spacesharing policy and running jobs exclusively. All process elements of the same MPP share the same operating system.

*Site Model:* The site stands for the grid participators who contribute their computational resources and share their jobs in a grid system. Each site is comprised of several machines, has its own resource management system and local policies. The resources between different sites are heterogeneous. Cluster(s) of a single affiliation is a typical site.

*Node Model:* The node is a group of sites, managed by a single MaGate scheduler. The grid community is comprised of different nodes, each participating node has the possibility to discover another node, and interacts with each other.

*Job Model:* The job concerns computationally intensive batch jobs submitted by users continuously through time. Each job is comprised of several parameters, including requested run time, requested number of PE, requested type of operating system, etc. Both sequential and parallel jobs are simulated for execution upon a single machine with sufficient number of PEs, job migration and pre-emption are not supported currently.

## Experimental Scenarios

Once a MaGate with local resource exists and being connected to grid community, it is assumed to be discoverable by resource discovery services from other MaGates. The interesting thing is that various parameters can be utilized to generate community scheduling policies with different cost and benefit. Considering each individual user might have his/her own judgment on the cost and benefit, an automatic mechanism that is capable of generating user customized community scheduling policies dynamically will bring great flexibility and adaptability in our future work.

In current experiment, various scenario parameters have been demonstrated as follows, and utilized to compose diverse policies for determining job delegation across grid communities with different size.

- The Local means that each MaGate is configured to work alone, no job delegation to remote MaGates is allowed. In this case, all the local unsuited jobs submitted on each MaGate will be simply suppressed and considered as failed.

- The Neighbor means that each MaGate is allowed to look up appropriate remote MaGates from its direct neighborhood list, and delegate the local unsuited jobs to the discovered remote MaGates. The direct neighborhood list of each MaGate is kept up-to-date by its resource discovery service, depending on the network connection between the local MaGate and the remote MaGate.

- The Search means that each MaGate is able to propagate and submit job requirement based queries to the grid community, in order to discover appropriate remote MaGates for accepting the local unsuited jobs. The interval time between the query submission and result obtention plays an important role because it represents user's endurable delay to get the discovered results back. In our experiment, for example, the Search100 illustrates once a query has been submitted to the grid community, 100 milliseconds are allowed to wait and get the discovered results back.

- The Nego represents the maximal number of negotiation allowed to achieve a single job delegation. For example, the Nego1 means that each to delegate job is allowed to be negotiated with a set of appropriate remote MaGates for one time; while the Nego10 means that the host MaGate is able to retry a single job delegation for maximally ten times, with same or different parameters.
- The Queue stands for the length limit of the Community Input Queue. Each time the host MaGate approves a job delegation request, the accepted but unprocessed remote job will be preserved in the Community Input Queue until the job is processed and sent back to the delegation initiator. In our experiment, for example, the Queue5 presents that the host MaGate is able to manage at most five accepted but unprocessed remote jobs, as long as the length limit is reached, the subsequent delegation requests to the host MaGate will be rejected.

## Simulation Configuration

Both job and machine parameters are either constants, or randomly generated according to a uniform distribution.

- Number of locally submitted jobs on each MaGate: 100.
- Job arrival time: [0-12 hours].
- Job estimated execution time: 1000s.
- Job estimated MIPS: 1000.
- Number of PEs required by each individual job: [1-5].
- Number of sites per MaGate: 1.
- Number of machines per site: 1.
- Number of PEs per machine: [64-128].
- MIPS of each PE: 1000.
- Size of the Direct Neighborhood List: 6.

- Number of times for negotiation/re-negotiation: [1, 3].
- Length of the Community Input Queue: [5, 10].
- Types of operating system required by job: [Linux, Windows, Mac].
- Types of machine operating system: [Linux, Windows, Mac].

In order to obtain stable values, each scenario results were averaged from 10 repeated iterations. The experiments are performed upon an Intel Core Duo 2.2GHz machine, with 2GB RAM.

## DISCUSSION

All the scenarios tested in the reference experiment are comprised of several parameters mentioned above. For example, the scenario Search250-Nego3-Queue5-57.1% stands for that the host MaGate is using community search policy, with 250 millisecond interval waiting time, to discover remote MaGates for job delegation; the maximal times of negotiation allowed for each single delegation is three, remote MaGates's length limit of the Community Input Queue is five, and the obtained RJC has reached 57.1%.

The RJC of a 10-MaGate community is shown in Figure 3. As expected, for scenario Local, because no job delegation to community is allowed, all submitted local unsuited jobs are suppressed till end of the simulation. Regarding each MaGate manages one site with a single operating system, and the jobs submitted by its local users vary their operating system requirements from a uniform three-option distribution, only 1/3 of the locally submitted jobs can be satisfied by the local resource. Simultaneously, considering the choices of operating system, which are owned by all sites within the grid community, fall into the same distribution as job requirement, it is expected that for each individual local unsuited job, 1/3

*Figure 3. Community of 10 MaGates*

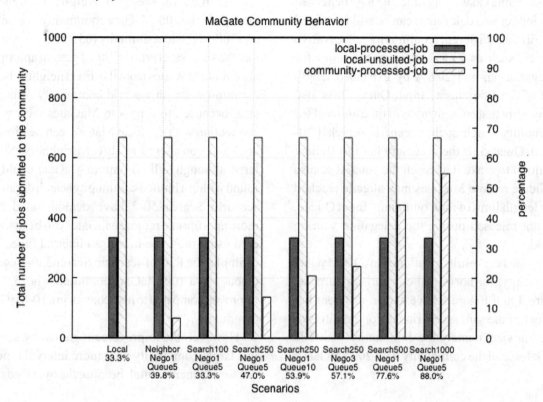

MaGates of the entire grid community have, in average, the expected capabilities to accept them.

Furthermore, illustrated by scenario Neighbor-Nego1-Queue5 from the 10-MaGate community, involved MaGates are allowed to delegate local unsuited jobs to the grid community by looking up proper remote MaGates from their direct neighborhood list, which are constructed and kept up-to-date by the interconnected resource discovery services. It is evident that, from the point of view of the grid community, some MaGates have found appropriate neighbors, and additional 6.55% jobs were accomplished due to the achieved delegations.

An alternative approach of seeking remote MaGates for job delegation is sending resource discovery queries to the grid community. It is to be expected that if appropriate re- mote MaGates exist, being connected within the same community, represented properly and approved to be public

available by their community policies, the corresponding queries will be matched within enough interval waiting time. As presented in Figure 3, a short waiting time (Search100-Nego1- Queue5 allows 100ms) for getting the results from the community search leads to no delegations achieved because the adopted resource discovery solution could not find expected resources from the community within such a limited du- ration. However, if more time is allowed, as shown by scenario Search250-Nego1-Queue5 and Search500-Nego1- Queue5, useful discovered remote MaGates start to appear, and the RJC benefited from job remote delegation can be improved by 13.7% and 44.3% respectively. The more interval time between query submission and result obtention is allowed, the better RJC becomes.

Meanwhile, results illustrated by scenario Search250-Nego1-Queue10 and Search250-Nego3-Queue5 has demonstrated that even within the same interval waiting time, the RJC benefited from job remote delegation can be still improved by utilizing different community cooperative policies, such as 23.8% by increased times for re-negotiation, and 20.6% by expanded length limit of the Community Input Queue. It is also noteworthy that enough interval time allowed for community search, such as scenario Search1000-Nego1-Queue5, is the necessary but insufficient condition to make RJC reach the 100%, because candidate remote MaGates may already reached their length limit of the Community Input Queue, and not released during the delegation waiting period.

Besides the results mentioned in a 10-MaGate community, for horizontal comparison purpose, Figure 4 and Figure 5 have shown different behaviors of the same scenarios in communities of different size, namely the community with 100 MaGates, and the community with 200 MaGates.

The RJC of scenario Neighbors-Nego1-Queue5 in the 100-MaGate community (48.66%) and 200-MaGate community (63.13%) has shown that the successful probability of getting appropriate remote MaGates from the direct neighborhood list improves within a grid community of larger size, because more remote MaGates with good connection with the local MaGate can be discovered and considered as direct neighbors. Similarly, although still no remote MaGate could be found within a limited community search duration, scenario Search250-* have demonstrated that more appropriate remote MaGates can be discovered using the same increased interval time. For example, the RJC of scenario Search250-Nego1-Queue5 in a 100-MaGate community is 25.47% improved compared to his behavior in a 10-MaGate community.

However, the improvement gained by search in a larger community with more interval time is not simply incremental, because the overload dis-

*Figure 4. Community of 100 MaGates*

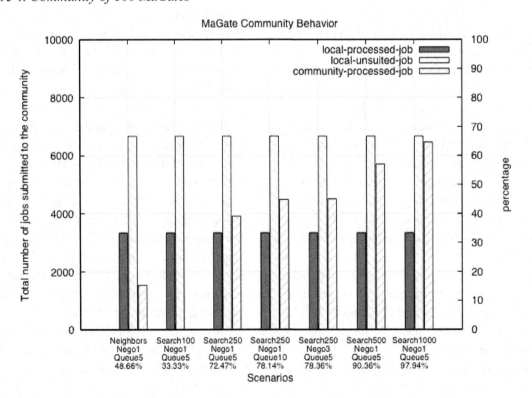

*Figure 5. Community of 200 MaGates*

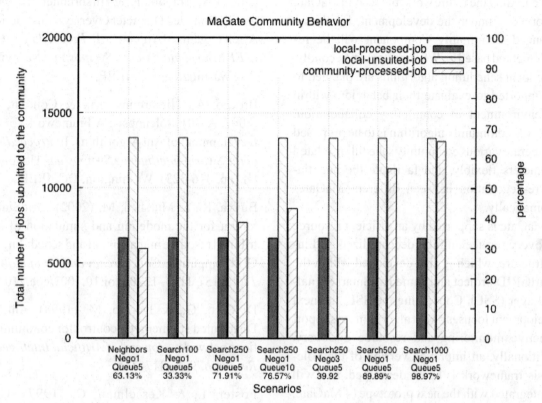

tributed resource discovery service has limited the number of discovered remote MaGates. Specially, as shown in scenario Search250-Nego3-Queue5 in a 200-MaGate community, the RJC benefited from job remote delegation has dropped to 6.62% because too many resource discovery queries almost halt the adopted ant-based resource discovery service. In this case, how to balance the cooperation between different factors to achieve an effectiveness and efficient job delegation procedure will be an interesting issue in our future work.

## CONCLUSION AND FURTHER WORK

This chapter presented the design of an interoperable, de- centralized and modular high-level grid scheduler named MaGate. The MaGate scheduler dedicates to improve the rate of successfully executed jobs submitted to the same grid com-

munity, by means of interacting with each other and delegating jobs amongst all participating nodes of the community. In other words, the MaGate schedulers are driven to cooperate with each other, to provide intelligent scheduling for the scope of serving the grid community as a whole, not just for a single grid node.

Currently, both design and the first prototype of MaGate have been completed. Together with the adopted resource discovery service, the reference experiment results have proven a functional ready MaGate scheduler, which is able to address different scheduling related events using a uniformed modular architecture. Specially, the capability of scheduler interoperation and work sharing within the inter- connected community is emphasized, and various community scheduling related parameters have been evaluated to illustrate the effectiveness brought by sharing local unsuited jobs within an interoperable and collaborative grid community.

Regarding the future work, the second MaGate prototype is under the development. Firstly, an advanced Community Component will be re-implemented based on WS-* protocols. Secondly, more local scheduling algorithms are planned to be supported to evaluate their behaviors within the environment of community collaboration. Finally, a community algorithm is to be proposed to integrate various community scheduling related parameters flexibly, and facilitate the negotiation/re-negotiation between different MaGates automatically.

MaGate is supported by an efficient resource discovery service on fully decentralized grid infrastructure, which is also developed within the SmartGRID project and named as Smart Signaling Layer (SSL). Concerning the SSL, the next development focuses on ant algorithms to support proactive monitoring and resource discovery. Additionally, an improved version of the Solenopsis framework is being developed, and will be integrated with the next prototype of MaGate.

# REFERENCES

Andrieux, A., Czajkowski, K., Dan, A., Keahey, K., Ludwig, H., & Pruyne, J. (2004). *Web Services Agreement Specification (WS-Agreement) (Tech. Rep.)*. Muncie, IN: Open Grid Forum.

Anjomshoaa, A., Brisard, F., Drescher, M., Fellows, D., Ly, A., & Mc-Gough, S. (2005). *Job submission description language (JSDL) specification (Tech. Rep.)*. Muncie, IN: Open Grid Forum.

Bonabeau, E., Dorigo, M., & Theraulaz, G. (1999). *Swarm intelligence: from natural to artificial systems*. New York: Oxford University Press.

Brocco, A., Frapolli, F., & Hirsbrunner, B. (2008, September). BlatAnt: Bounding Networks' Diameter with a Collaborative Distributed Algorithm. In *Proceedings of the Sixth International Conference on Ant Colony Optimization and Swarm Intelligence*, Bruxelles, Belgium. New York: Springer.

Brocco, A., Frapolli, F., & Hirsbrunner, B. (2009, April). Bounded Diameter Overlay Construction: A Self Organized Approach. In *Proceedings of the IEEE Swarm Intelligence Symposium*, Nashville, TN. Washington, DC: IEEE.

Brocco, A., Hirsbrunner, B., & Courant, M. (2007, April). Solenopsis: A Framework for the Development of Ant Algorithms. In *Proceedings of the Swarm Intelligence Symposium*, Honolulu, HI (pp. 316-323). Washington, DC: IEEE.

Buyya, R., & Murshed, M. (2002). GridSim: a toolkit for the modeling and simulation of distributed resource management and scheduling for Grid computing. *Concurrency and Computation*, *14*(13-15), 1175–1220. doi:10.1002/cpe.710

Di Caro, G., & Dorigo, M. (1998). AntNet: Distributed stigmergetic control for communications networks. *Journal of Artificial Intelligence Research*, *9*(2), 317–365.

Foster, I., & Kesselman, C. (1997). Globus: a Metacomputing Infrastructure Toolkit. *International Journal of High Performance Computing Applications*, *11*(2), 115. doi:10.1177/109434209701100205

Goodale, T., Jha, S., Kaiser, H., Kielmann, T., Kleijer, P., & Laszewski, G., von, et al. (2006). SAGA: A Simple API for Grid Applications. High-level application programming on the Grid. *Computational Methods in Science and Technology*, *12*(1), 7–20.

Huang, Y., Brocco, A., Courant, M., Hirsbrunner, B., & Kuonen, P. (2009). MaGate Simulator: a simulation environment for a decentralized grid scheduler. In *Proceedings of the International Conference on Advanced Parallel Processing Technologies (APPT'09)*, Rapperswil, Switzerland. New York: Springer.

Huang, Y., Brocco, A., Kuonen, P., Courant, M., & Hirsbrunner, B. (2008). SmartGRID: A Fully Decentralized Grid Schedul-ing Framework Supported by Swarm Intelligence. In *Proceedings of the Seventh International Conference on Grid and Cooperative Computing (GCC '08)*, China (LNCS 4967pp. 160-168). Washington, DC: IEEE Computer Society.

Michlmayr, E. (2006). Ant Algorithms for Search in Unstructured Peer-to-Peer Networks. In *Proceedings of the 22nd International Conference on Data Engineering Workshops (ICDE2006)* (p. 142). Washington, DC: IEEE Computer Society.

Moab Grid Suite. (2009). *Cluster Resource Inc*. Retrieved from http://www.clusterresources.com/pages/products/moab-grid- suite.php

Ripeanu, M., & Foster, I. (2001). Peer-to-peer architecture case study: Gnutella network. In *Proceedings of the First Conference on Peer-to-peer Computing*, Sweden (pp. 99-100). Washington, DC: IEEE Computer Press.

Ripeanu, M., Iamnitchi, A., Foster, I., & Rogers, A. (2007). *In Search of Simplicity: A Self-Organizing Group Communication Overlay* (Tech. Rep. No. TR-2007-05). Vancouver, Canada: University of British Columbia.

Schmid, S., & Wattenhofer, R. (2007). Structuring Unstructured Peer-to-Pee Networks. In *Proceedings of the 14th Annual IEEE International Conference on High Performance Computing (HiPC)*, Goa, India. Washington, DC: IEEE Press.

Schoonderwoerd, R., Holland, O., Bruten, J., & Rothkrantz, L. (1997). Ant-based load balancing in telecommunications networks. *Adaptive Behavior, 5*(2), 169. doi:10.1177/105971239700500203

Schopf, J. (2003). *Ten actions when superscheduling: A grid scheduling architecture*. Paper presented at the Workshop on Scheduling Architecture, Tokyo.

Shen, K. (2004). Structure management for scalable overlay service construction. In *Proceedings of the First Symposium on Networked Systems Design and Implementation (NSDI'04)* (pp. 21-21). Berkeley, CA: USENIX Association.

Tonellotto, N., Wieder, P., & Yahyapour, R. (2005). A proposal for a generic grid scheduling architecture. In *Proceedings of the Integrated Research in Grid Computing Workshop*, Greece (pp. 337-346). New York: Springer.

Troger, P., Rajic, H., Haas, A., & Domagalski, P. (2007). Standardization of an API for Distributed Resource Management Systems. In *Proceedings of the Seventh IEEE International Symposium on Cluster Computing and the Grid (CCGRID '07)* (pp. 619-626). Washington, DC: IEEE Computer Society.

Waldrich, O., Wieder, P., & Ziegler, W. (2006). A meta-scheduling service for co-allocating arbitrary types of resources. *Lecture Notes in Computer Science, 3911*, 782. doi:10.1007/11752578_94

Xiaohui, W., Zhaohui, D., Shutao, Y., Chang, H., & Huizhen, L. (2006). CSF4: A WSRF compliant meta-scheduler. In *Proceedings of the 2006 World Congress in Computer Science, Computer Engineering, and Applied Computing (GCA)* (Vol. 6, pp. 61-67). Las Vegas, NV: Bentham Science.

*This work was previously published in International Journal of Distributed Systems and Technologies, Volume 1, Issue 3, edited by Nik Bessis, pp. 24-39, copyright 2010 by IGI Publishing (an imprint of IGI Global).*

# Chapter 5
# Toward a Quality-of-Service Framework for Peer-to-Peer Applications

**Ankur Gupta**
*Model Institute of Engineering and Technology, India*

**Lalit K. Awasthi**
*National Institute of Technology, India*

## ABSTRACT

*P2P networks have caught the imagination of the research community and application developers with their sheer scalability and fault-tolerance characteristics. However, only content-sharing applications based on the P2P concept have reached the desired level of maturity. The potential of the P2P concept for designing the next-generation of real-world distributed applications can be realized only if a comprehensive framework quantifying the performance related aspects of all classes of P2P applications is available. Researchers have proposed some QoS (Quality-of-Service) parameters for content-sharing P2P applications based on response time and delay, but these do not cover the gamut of application domains that the P2P concept is applicable to. Hence, this chapter proposes an early QoS framework covering various classes of P2P applications; content distribution, distributed computing and communication and collaboration. Early results from the prototype implementation of the Peer Enterprises framework (a cross-organizational P2P collaborative application) are used as a basis for formulation of the QoS parameters. The individual performance measures which comprise the QoS framework are also discussed in detail along with some thoughts on how these can be complied with. The proposed framework would hopefully lead to quantifiable Service-Level Agreements for a variety of peer-to-peer services and applications.*

## INTRODUCTION

P2P networks have traditionally been considered too transient in nature to perform useful computations for real-world applications, leave aside the formulation of a viable QoS framework.

The only mature application that P2P networks successfully cater to, are those related to content sharing, where the sheer scale of P2P networks along with strategies for content-caching and replication enable content to be located and downloaded in a time-bound manner. Gummadi

DOI: 10.4018/978-1-4666-0906-8.ch005

et al. (2003), made an early attempt at analyzing the P2P content sharing workloads, quantifying the impact of content locality on query performance and bandwidth savings. Since, then some QoS parameters for P2P applications have been proposed, but they have been limited to content-sharing applications. Specifically, QoS parameters have been proposed for:

1.  Guaranteed content location and retrieval (if it exists) – Query Success
2.  Time-bound content location and retrieval - Query Performance
3.  Correct content retrieval – Content Quality
4.  Video Streaming and Multicasting – Delay, Bandwidth and Jitter

However, the P2P concept has wide applicability in various application domains and the scale and fault-tolerant nature of P2P networks can be exploited to ensure that some useful work gets done even with the transience of participating peers. To quantify the extent of useful work performed and the expected performance a minimal and generic QoS framework needs to be established.

This chapter uses the preliminary experimental results from the implementation of the Peer Enterprises (PE) framework (a cross-organizational peer-to-peer framework encompassing content search, distributed computation, communication, remote storage and services deployment) and uses these experimental results to establish a minimal QoS framework for such P2P applications. Many of the proposed QoS parameters are applicable to P2P applications offering a subset of the features provided by the PE framework.

## BACKGROUND

P2P applications can broadly be classified (Milojicic et al., 2002) into the following categories based on their functionality:

A.  Content Distribution
B.  Distributed Computation
C.  Communication and Collaboration

Table 1 summarizes the application categories, application characteristics and examples of some well-known P2P applications.

As can be seen from the table, most of the real-world applications based on the P2P concept are freeware for content sharing or communication or those operating within a federated domain. Hence, QoS is not a major requirement for such applications. Hence, research on QoS for P2P networks remains in a nascent stage barring establishment of a few parameters related to content search. A new class of P2P applications integrating content, computation and communication and specialized services – the Peer Enterprises (PE) framework has been proposed by Gupta and Awasthi (2007). The PE framework has the potential to enable new cross-organizational service and business models. Hence, a detailed QoS model if available for such applications would facilitate their deployment and ensure viability. To ensure that P2P applications in general become more pervasive and can progress beyond file-sharing applications, a minimal QoS framework, based on specific quantifiable and non-quantifiable parameters must be established. Such a framework shall provide the much needed guidelines for P2P application designers and developers to cater to the QoS parameters and help meet application performance requirements effectively. Research on QoS pertaining to P2P systems has focused on the following areas:

A.  Content Search;
B.  QoS-aware Routing;
C.  Content Delivery/Video Streaming; and
D.  Use of P2P concepts in Grid Computing/ Service-Oriented Architectures

*Table 1. Summary of various categories of P2P applications*

| P2P Application Category | Application Characteristics | Popular Examples |
|---|---|---|
| Content Distribution | • Peers are either organized into structured overlay topologies or unstructured overlay topologies.<br>• Query response times on structured topologies are bounded; no such guarantees on unstructured topologies.<br>• Content is hashed and indexed and indexes distributed throughout the P2P network for increased scalability and ease of location.<br>• Content is cached as it passes through individual peers and is also actively replicated to improve redundancy and search performance.<br>• Other optimizations like query hop count and Time-to-Live (TTL) parameters are used to improve performance.<br>• Schemes such as content-based routing (routing-decision based on probability of content location), random-parallel walks (queries executed in parallel), range queries (locating items in a range rather than single items) and Hierarchical Distributed Hash Tables (HDHT for improving routing latency) have been proposed to improve content search and download efficiency.<br>• New class of systems focuses on media-streaming applications like P2P TV. Here focus is on creating high-bandwidth end-to-end routing paths between the source and destination peers to ensure uninterrupted streaming through schemes such as adaptation and peer selection. | KaZaa, Bit-Torrent, Cool-streaming, LimeWire, P2P TV. |
| Distributed Computation | • Jobs are offloaded to remote peers to be executed.<br>• Node-transience is biggest hurdle in these schemes.<br>• Need centralized coordination for parallel execution of job fragments.<br>• Need redundancy; execution of job at multiple peers to ensure completion.<br>• Not very performant by nature.<br>• Very difficult to quantify performance parameters unless some simplifying assumptions are made.<br>• Exisiting applications operate within federated domains and assume little or no transience. | SETI@HOME, G2-P2P, Condor, Avaki, CompuP2P, P3. |
| Communication/Collaboration | • Chatting and file sharing between known users has been around for the longest time.<br>• Biggest challenge is to ensure that a viable communication channel exists between communicating peers, even with node transience (similar to media-streaming). | Instant Messenger, Jabber, TerraNet, OceanStore, Facebook, Groove, JXTA. |

# RELATED WORK

A good discussion on QoS pertaining to content management for P2P file-sharing applications is provided by Meo and Milan (2008), wherein a QoS policy at individual peers works out the best content management strategy for ensuring high-availability of content and its assured retrieval. Using a Markovian model it works out which content should be retained by a peer and which should be discarded to improve the overall probability of query satisfaction. AGnuS or Altruistic Gnutella Server (Hughes et al., 2004) is an adaptation based strategy to improve the load-balancing and hence file-serving capacity of the Gnutella (http://rfc-gnutella.sourceforge.net/) file sharing P2P network. It relies on caching, load-balancing, content-based routing and file-filtering to improve the query response times of each peer. Recently a novel QoS preserving strategy which spans multiple CDNs (Content Delivery Networks) has been proposed (Pathan & Buyya, 2009). This scheme allows proprietary CDNs to negotiate Service Level Agreements with each other allowing excess queries to be offloaded to peer CDNs such that the user perceived performance is not impacted and QoS is met. Although this scheme is similar to the PE framework in terms of cross-domain interactions it focuses only on content delivery.

QoS-aware routing for P2P Networks (Linnolahti, 2004) also attempts to speed up content location and delivery, but focuses on the path selection problem. QRON (Li & Mohapatra, 2004) (QoS Routing for Overlay Networks) relies on a network of overlay brokers which exchange information to construct QoS-satisfied overlay paths for routing. QoS is preserved by load balancing the traffic amongst the brokers. Rajashekhar et al. (2006) propose a probabilistic QoS model for routing in wireless P2P networks, which computes the best-possible paths in terms of reliability and capacity while also reducing the number of hops. The paths are computed in $O\ (MH)$ time, where M is the number of edges examined and H is the diameter of the P2P network.

A strategy for video streaming which aims to satisfy QoS parameters by creating and maintaining a high-performance overlay structure through peer selection is presented by Liang and Nahrstedt (2006). Here peers are selected on the basis of their bandwidth and performance characteristics to create a routing path which can satisfy the QoS for content distribution or video streaming. QCast (Cai & Lin, 2008) is an example of a DHT-based multi-casting strategy which complies with QoS parameters for multi-media streaming. Participating peers first organize themselves into a distribution tree according to their buffer sizes and bandwidths to create and end-to-end distribution path for streaming. This approach attempts to optimize the delay and reduce the packet loss. The issue of ensuring QoS for media streaming in the face of rapidly changing network topology and communication channels is addressed by Nemati and Takizawa (2008). The strategy selects multiple sources which can meet the QoS requirements of the receiver. As the QoS from a particular source drops below a certain threshold, another source steps in to ensure QoS compliance.

Hardly any QoS parameters have been proposed for P2P applications involving distributed computation, simply because frequent node-transience makes the task of distributed computa-tion extremely challenging in a P2P environment. This is especially true for applications on the open internet. SETI@HOME (http://setiathome.berkeley.edu) remains the only real-world distributed computing P2P application utilizing the compute power of millions of PCs connected to the internet. For a more viable computing model researchers have focused on federated P2P systems (those which operate within a domain, say an organization) and successful examples like G2-P2P (Kelly & Mason, 2005), Condor (http://www.cs.wisc.edu/condor), Avaki (http://www.avaki.com), CompuP2P (Gupta et al., 2006) and P3 (Shudo et al., 2005) etc. do exist for such systems. However, these applications make overly-simplifying assumptions regarding P2P networks, including little or no node transience/failure. Also, these applications make no mention of Quality-of-Service for distributed computation performed.

Some researchers have attempted an amalgamation of P2P and Grid environments by utilizing some aspects of the P2P concept for service discovery and provisioning. Stefano et al. (2009) present a P2P-based grid service discovery mechanism which relies on flooding discovery queries through neighboring peers to locate services in an optimal manner. This is done by having each peer maintain a service cache, which maintains an index of services. Zhu et al (2008) propose a QoS-aware architecture for grid information service based on structured P2P systems. It utilizes a DHT-based P2P network to index information on resource/service availability in a distributed manner. This helps in locating services in a more efficient manner over traditional centralized grids. A different take on QoS for P2P applications is provided by Bocciarelli et al (2007) and Gao et al. (2006) wherein a P2P-based QoS-complaint framework for discovery of SOA (Service-Oriented Architecture) applications is presented. These strategies aim towards faster discovery of peer services by avoiding low-bandwidth links and network latencies by the use of registries for discovery of services.

However, such attempts focus on QoS parameters involving some aspects of P2P grids and are not comprehensive to say the least. Moreover, QoS models for P2P applications which do not involve the use of centralized elements for load-balancing, fault-tolerance, task migration etc. is non-existent to the best of our knowledge. Hence, proposing a QoS model for pure P2P applications' involving distributed computing and communication is venturing into unchartered territory.

## THE PEER ENTERPRISES FRAMEWORK

The Peer Enterprises (PE) (Gupta & Awasthi, 2007) framework is a multi-level hybrid P2P network, enabling cross-organizational P2P interactions involving distributed computation, content sharing, communication and collaboration, besides specialized services provided by peer organizations. A prototype has been implemented using JXTA (Juxtapose http://www.sun.com.jxta), a set of JAVA APIs facilitating creation, maintenance and services deployment over P2P networks. Several aspects of the PE framework have already been researched and its viability established. The PE framework provides features such as security via a Containment-Based Security Model (Gupta & Awasthi, 2008) and fault-tolerance via the Neighbor Selection and Ranking (NSR) algorithm (Gupta & Awasthi, 2007) to ensure that useful computations can be performed while ensuring complete security of the deployed application as well as the peer hosting remote work. Other real-world applications such as IndNet (Gupta & Awasthi, in press), a P2P community network connecting the various stakeholders in the Indian Academia and the IT Industry and PArch (Gupta and Awasthi, in press), a P2P based cross-organizational application for E-mail archival, that build on the PE concept have also been proposed. Such applications have not been proposed in literature earlier. Figure 1 provides a high-level schematic

of the PE framework detailing the various mechanisms/operations involved, i.e., registration with nodal agency, resource aggregation, contract negotiation, resource exchange, containment-based security model, fault-tolerance mechanism, audit trails etc. Peer Enterprises interact through designated Edge Peers whose main responsibility is to aggregate the peer resources for a particular organization and negotiate the best possible contract with another edge peer. A single edge peer can enter into contracts with multiple other edge peers, leading to the creation of a hierarchical, multi–level P2P network.

Broadly, the edge peer is responsible for the following:

- *Aggregation of peer resources* in its Home Peer Network (HPN). Peers advertise the resources they offer – information, storage or empty CPU cycles for remote work, to the edge peer, which aggregates the resources into a single enterprise resource advertisement.
- *Negotiation of contract* with other edge peers on the resources provided by peers in its home network and the resources expected. Once the contract has been agreed upon, peers from both the enterprises interact independently as in a pure P2P system.
- *Information/Relationship Management* by broadcasting any changes in the status of the negotiated relationship with another enterprise, within its HPN. It also updates the counterpart edge peer with any changes in the status of peers in its HPN. After successful negotiation edge peers also exchange seed files containing references to well-known peers from their respective HPN's. This helps the home peers in establishing direct connections with the away peers and utilizing their resources. If peers report any malicious activity from counterpart peers, the edge peer can terminate the contract unilaterally. In the normal scenar-

*Figure 1. High-level schematic of the Peer Enterprises Framework*

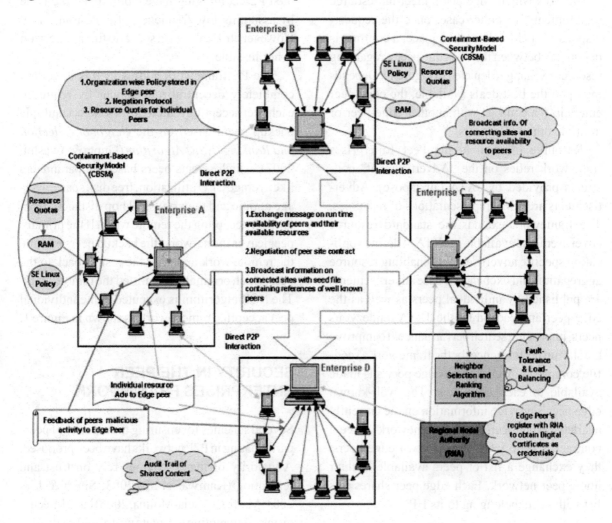

io, contract termination occurs after elapse of the configured hours of availability of the peer enterprise.

## RESOURCE LOCATION

Enterprises which wish to join the Peer Enterprises P2P network must create a P2P network within the enterprise i.e. the Home Peer Network (HPN) (Figure 1) and designate an edge-peer. All other peers send an advertisement of their resources – percentage idle CPU, free disk space usage, average uptime, available hardware/software plat-

forms etc. to the edge peer, which consolidates the resources available within the enterprise in a single aggregated enterprise resource advertisement. Moreover, the edge-peer also accepts requests for specific resources from the peers in its local P2P network which it also consolidates. The edge peer participates in a second P2P network, comprising the edge-peers from all enterprises participating in the Peer-Enterprises framework. The edge peer then either responds to requests for specific resources or broadcasts the requests from its local Home Peer Network onto the second P2P network comprising edge peers. Once an "expression of interest" is received by the advertising edge peer, it evaluates which edge peers meet its resource requirements. In either case, once the request-response matching has taken place, a contract is negotiated between the two edge peers, regarding resource exchange (depicted in Figure 1). Depending upon the best deals available, the edge-peer enters into a contract with another edge-peer or multiple other edge peers.

Resource location in the Peer Enterprises framework relies on the "Advertisement" constructs provided by JXTA (Juxtapose). Advertisements are XML representations of resources. The framework extends the standard resource advertisements available in JXTA to define application specific advertisements enabling resource aggregation and exchange. These advertisements are published by individual peers as well as the edge peer and cached by the JXTA rendezvous peers, improving search performance. To improve the startup performance for the framework a seed-file comprising well-known edge peer's is made available to each edge peer. The well-known edge peer's provide information on the currently available edge peer's in the framework. Once a contract is negotiated between two edge peers, they exchange a list of peers available in their home peer network. Each edge peer shares this list with peers belonging to its HPN.

## FAULT-TOLERANCE FOR THE DEPLOYED APPLICATIONS

Within the PE framework, ensuring fault-tolerance of deployed P2P applications is a major requirement. Since, peers are free to join and leave the HPN at will; the framework needs to ensure that the remote work gets completed even if the peer executing the remote work leaves the network. Thus, the framework needs to provide for task migration and ensuring remote work completion in the face of heavy node transience. Similar frameworks like G2-P2P (Kelly & Mason, 2005) and CompuP2P (Gupta et al., 2006) for distrib-

uted P2P computing have sidestepped the issue by assuming low frequency of node-transience. However, in a real-world scenario this assumption is not feasible.

The PE framework addresses this issue in a completely decentralized manner by requiring each peer accepting remote work to select multiple backup peers based on the *Neighbor Selection and Ranking (NSR) Algorithm* (Gupta & Awasthi, 2007), which selects peers based on parameters like average CPU utilization, free disk space, average uptime and their physical hop distances from the peer accepting the remote work. If the primary peer leaves the network, the backup peers execute the remote work and send the results back to the peer which originally submitted the remote work. The NSR algorithm is executed at the individual peer accepting remote work as shown in Figure 1.

## SECURITY IN THE PEER ENTERPRISES FRAMEWORK

Several schemes for ensuring the security of peers participating in P2P networks have been proposed. A majority of these schemes rely on trust and reputation (Kamwar et al., 2003; Singh & Liu, 2003; Marti & Garcia-Molina, 2006) based mechanisms in attempting to isolate un-trusted/malicious peers from the rest of the peer network. However, such schemes require computing trust values for each peer interaction and then communicating the computed values to all peers in the network. The computational overheads required for such schemes render them ineffective when trying to ensure bullet-proof security for participating peers. Other schemes incorporating elements of access control (Park et al., 2007), authentication/authorization (Gupta et al., 2008) and security policies (Gaspary et al., 2007) have also been proposed. Many of these schemes rely on introducing centralized security servers in an otherwise decentralized P2P environment. This introduces a single-point-of-failure in the P2P network, besides constituting a performance bottleneck. Also, in resource-exchanging P2P environments, once the remote code is resident on the host-peer these approaches are silent on containing the potential damage that can occur. What is really needed is to secure individual peers while dealing with un-trusted peers and reduce or mitigate the impact of hosting malicious remote code.

The PE Framework handles this issue by moving the onus of security to the individual peers. The framework thus employs a Containment Based Security Model (Gupta & Awasthi, 2008) at each peer (Figure 1), which creates specialized security compartments and utilizes fine-grained privileges provided by Secure Linux (http://www.nsa.gov/selinux/info/docs.cfm) to restrict the damage that a malicious remote task can cause. It also introduces run-time monitoring of the remote-code resident on the host peer and terminates the application on detection of any malicious activity. Thus, it can host un-trusted and even hostile remote applications without requiring any additional message exchanges for trust computations or introducing centralized servers to manage identities or perform authentication. The next step in the evolution of such applications is to be able to provide minimum performance guarantees so that new business/economic models covering of cross-organizational interactions can be developed.

## EXPERIMENTAL SETUP

A basic prototype encompassing the major functionality envisioned by the Peer Enterprises concept has been implemented on JAVA 1.6.0_07 and JXTA v2.5. The prototype supports the following operations:

A.  Aggregation of available peer resources at edge peer
B.  Negotiation of contract between edge peers

C.  Implementation of query issuing/handling interface supporting content, resource and user queries
D.  Content search and exchange between peers
E.  Submission of jobs for remote execution at other peers and return of processed results
F.  Chat interface for interacting with other peers.
G.  Storing content/data remotely in encrypted and compressed form.

The prototype has been successfully deployed across two organizations in Jammu city (Jammu and Kashmir State in India) located 12 kilometers and 5 routing hops apart. Both organizations are connected to the internet by 1 Mbps leased line provided by the same service provider. The PE software was installed on 50 peers in each organization for testing purposes with the 50 peers forming a JXTA-based P2P network in each organization. The experimental setup serves to establish that the framework works as intended and to assess the potential overheads associated with remote operations such as job execution and content/resource queries. The following tests were conducted on the experimental setup: query-response performance, content search and download performance, remote job execution performance, peer transience impact, failover performance, peer security analysis, message load analysis and peer load analysis to shed light on the various functional aspects of the framework. Peer's join and leave the network randomly. The results obtained were used as a basis to formulate a QoS model for the framework, which can be easily extended to generic P2P systems.

## A QOS MODEL FOR P2P APPLICATIONS

This section provides an indicative QoS model for P2P applications in general, providing details of specific aspects related to the Peer Enterprises

*Figure 2. A generic QoS model for p2p applications*

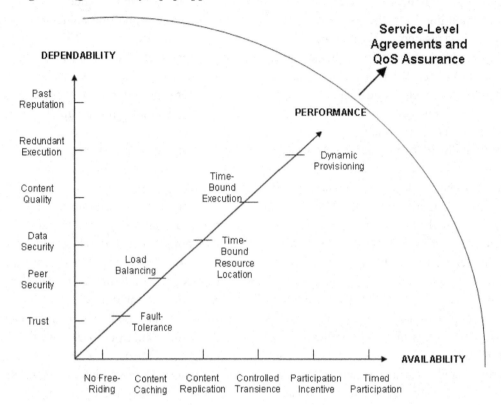

framework. Figure 2 provides details of the proposed QoS framework. The QoS model for the PE framework includes 3 major elements:

A. Availability of Resources
B. Dependability of Resources
C. Performance of the Deployed Applications

Clearly, performance of any P2P application can emerge only if the underlying compute resources are available and dependably so. Hence, any move towards providing quality assurances or entering into Service-Level-Agreements (SLAs) with other peers or organizations, is feasibly only if basic assurances regarding the general availability of resources and their dependability can be secured.

The following sections discuss individual parameters which comprise the QoS Model and how compliance with each parameter can be ensured:

## AVAILABILITY OF RESOURCES

Availability of resources is the basic assumption on which any QoS model is based on since resources need to be available and accessible before any meaningful interaction can commence. Since, node transience is a feature of P2P networks, availability cannot be assumed and it must be provided for. The proposed QoS model identifies the following parameters which can directly impact resource availability:

A. *No Free-Riding*: Typically as peers join the P2P network it becomes increasingly scaleable as bandwidth and resources get added to the entire network. Free-riding drastically reduces the resource availability in a P2P network, since peers utilize the resources of other peers without offering anything in return. Hence, to ensure a high-degree of resource availability, free-riding needs to be eliminated entirely, unless the interaction model supports it (say a pay-per-use model, which allows peers to use other peer resources for a financial consideration). The PE framework ensures this by requiring peers to first advertise their resources before they can even join the P2P network. Also, the middleware is fairly autonomous, i.e., it accepts remote work and shares content if a query is received without user permission or intervention, provided the peer's resources are available. Thus, the user cannot prevent the peer resources from being contributed/utilized if the peer is active in the PE framework.

B.  *Content-Caching*: Content/Resource location is a significant aspect of any P2P application, since the required resource must be located before it can be used. The P2P application must be able to guarantee that if a resource exists in the network it should be locatable. Caching has been widely employed to improve the search performance of P2P networks. The PE framework does not need to provide any explicit support for content-caching, since it is already done at the JXTA level. Each resource advertisement is cached at individual peers or at the defined *Rendezvous* peers (http://www.sun.com/jxta). Peers chose to either have remote advertisements stored in their local cache or access the rendezvous peers for the same. Rendezvous peers propagate the query only amongst themselves to prevent needless broadcasts and to speed up resource/content location.

C.  *Content-Replication:* To overcome node-transience and still ensure that the shared content is available requires that content be made available redundantly throughout the network. This is also needed to avoid swamping the peer hosting the desired content with download requests, thus improving

scalability. As content is shared throughout the network, it gets redundantly stored at different peers. The content sharing application on each peer in the PE framework automatically scans the dedicated shared content directory while handling content search queries and ensures that the newly downloaded content too gets shared. This approach is referred to as passive replication.

D.  *Controlled Transience:* No P2P application can guarantee service levels in the face of adhoc node transience. Hence, peers should remain in the P2P network for a sufficient length of time to enable useful interactions. This would also help in reducing transience to manageable levels. The PE framework envisages that organizations would enter into contracts with other organizations during periods of low network usage (say after 8 pm). During this time peers can generally be expected to be online and available for remote work processing. Such an assumption cannot be made for peers on the open internet and hence such applications need to experiment with requiring peers to be available for a minimum amount of time before they can access resources or offering incentives for peers to participate in the network for longer durations.

E.  *Participation Incentive:* Several schemes have previously proposed the use of incentives, both monetary and in terms of greater privileges for resource usage in return for offering their resources for longer periods and have been shown to be pretty effective. Hence, incentives are known to work well in P2P environments. The better the incentives, greater is the resource contribution/availability and greater is the amount of useful processing made possible. Within the PE framework an organization can have a variety of incentives to participate –to grow business by collaborating with other organizations, to access specialized compute resources in other organizations, to improve its resource utilization and Return on Investment (RoI). An individual peer may participate to – increase technical skills and improve professionally, work on joint projects, seek useful information and access required resources.

F.  *Timed Participation:* Apart from the above mentioned parameters one of the main strategies for improving the availability of participating peers is to ensure that peers participate in the P2P network for a fixed time if possible allowing resources to be utilized to the maximum. The PE framework achieves this by factoring in time-zone differences between two organizations. Thus, one organization utilizes the resources of another organization when its resources are idle or near idle, greatly improving the availability in reduced transience levels. Also, the application traffic generated does not overload the organization's network at that time.

## DEPENDABILITY OF RESOURCES

Simple availability of a resource does not imply that it can be utilized effectively. A malicious peer can propagate a wide-variety of security attacks. Remote work could potentially cause damage to the host peer besides compromising confidential information. Hence, QoS without dependable resources is definitely not realizable. The following factors contribute to resource dependability:

A.  *Trust:* A resource is dependable if it can be trusted. However, building trust in P2P applications is far from trivial. The sheer scale of P2P networks introduces immense overheads in trust computation and communication of trust values to other peers. Within the Peer Enterprises framework organizations can chose to go in for either trusted or non-trusted interactions. In case of trusted

interactions organizations are required to register with a trusted authority and obtain digitally signed credentials to establish its identity. These credentials are provided by each peer during its interactions with other peers. In case of non-trusted interactions, the PE framework provides fool-proof security to the host peer via the Containment-Based Security Model to enable it to host untrusted or hostile applications.

B.  *Peer Security:* A peer's security is of paramount importance, since P2P applications present many vulnerabilities from a security perspective. A peer could download malware, viruses or spyware as part of downloaded content. Malicious remote code can also cause severe damage to the host peer. An insecure peer can only adversely impact QoS. Thus, ensuring security is vital to building a quality assurance strategy. The PE framework utilizes the access-control features of SE Linux to provide bullet-proof security for peers by clearly defining what a remote user or remote application can or cannot access on the host peer. It also monitors the run-time behavior of the remote code and terminates it if it indulges in malicious activity or violates pre-defined thresholds on resource usage quotas.

C.  *Data Security:* The security of data stored on each peer has traditionally been secured by the use of encryption, but this introduces some centralized elements into the network and affects scalability. The PE framework ensures data security in three ways (Gupta and Awasthi, in press):

    ◦   By generating an audit trail of peer interactions to prevent intended data theft

    ◦   By having sensitive content digitally signed and introducing checks in the middleware preventing sharing of signed content and

- ◦ Sand-boxing of file-sharing application so that it cannot access any data outside the shared content directory it is supposed to access.

D. *Content Quality:* A peer's dependability is directly related to the quality of content that it provides in response to queries. Not only should the content be what the user is looking for, but it should also be free of viruses or malware which could impact the security of other peers. Within the PE framework peers report the malicious behavior of other peers to their edge peer which then terminates the contract. All peers within an organization can also be expected to have an enterprise strength anti-virus package installed which screens all downloaded content to cover any eventuality. The SE linux security policies further secure the peer against any malicious content which may get downloaded. Thus, providing bad content quality causes an enterprise's contract to be terminated by the counterpart enterprise.

E. *Redundant Execution:* To further improve dependability, a peer can transfer the remote job to be processed by multiple peers belonging to other organizations, so that the job gets completed even with node transience. The PE framework provides for backup peers to execute the remote job if the primary peer leaves the network. There are no centralized elements to coordinate remote job execution and peers are directly responsible for ensuring that a remote job gets completed. Redundant execution is also employed by SETI@HOME to cover for node transience and is an acceptable strategy for P2P-based distributed computing applications.

F. *Past Reputation:* Past reputation is a good indicator of the confidence that can be reposed in a peer. Reputation also needs to be aggregated from peer's which have had past interactions with the peer in question and this introduces the same challenges as in trust-based schemes. The PE framework does not employ a reputation-based mechanism since groups of malicious peers can exaggerate the reputation of a peer, allowing it to indulge in malicious activities.

## APPLICATION PERFORMANCE

From available and dependable peer resources emerges quantifiable performance and some viable performance assurances can be provided. With dependable peer's being available for some minimum time and with controlled transience thrown in, bounds can be provided on application performance in such an environment. The following performance parameters seem feasible based on experimental results obtained from deploying the Peer Enterprises prototype across two organizations:

A. *Fault-Tolerance:* QoS is feasible if a confidence level to the degree of fault-tolerance can be assigned. This is established by executing fault-tolerance scenarios for an application with varying degrees of node transience. The PE framework relies on the NSR algorithm to achieve fault-tolerance for deployed cycle-stealing P2P applications. Based on simulation results and testing of the prototype a confidence level of 90% is achieved with up to 50% churn in the network i.e. the strategy ensures survival of check-pointing data 90% of the time with 50% of the nodes either joining or leaving the network with equal probability. Confidence levels for different environments and for different classes of applications shall need to be worked out on a case-to-case basis. Figure 3 and Figure 4 provide the success percentage for the P4P strategy in the face of 50% node transience for shrink (nodes only leave the network) and churn (nodes

*Figure 3. Fault-tolerance success percentage in face of 50% node transience (shrink analysis)*

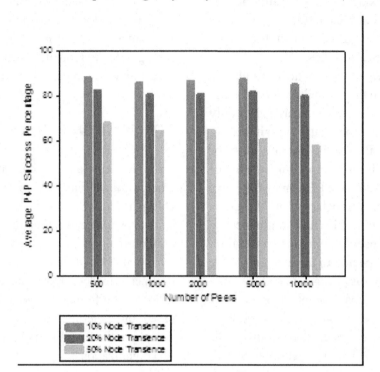

*Figure 4. Fault-tolerance success percentage in face of 50% node transience (churn analysis)*

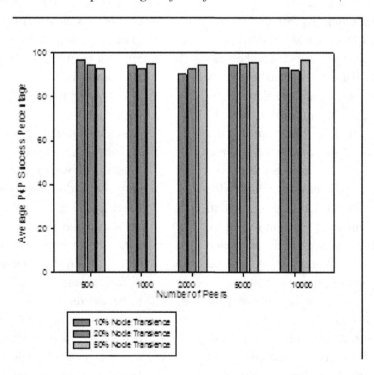

both join and leave the network) analysis for varying topology sizes respectively.

It can be seen that even with 50% nodes leaving the network, the P4P strategy ensures survival of check-pointing data for 60% of the test cases. With the more realistic churn analysis being employed the success percentage goes up considerably to 90%. Another important measure is to determine the ideal check-pointing interval for deployed applications. This is done by finding the job completion rates for remote jobs with varying execution times in the face of varying degrees of node transience. Clearly smaller jobs have a better probability of completion in case of node transience than larger jobs. In this scenario, it is better to schedule larger jobs on peers with greater average availability times. Figure 5 provides the average job failure rates for different jobs in the face of varying degree of node transience. Clearly jobs with durations of 20 and 30 minutes are the worst affected when node tran-

sience increases. With 50% node transience, jobs with 30 minutes duration fail for 35% of the times. Failure rates for jobs up to 10 minutes duration increase linearly with the degree of node transience. Hence, a check-pointing interval of 8-10 minutes should be ideal for deployed applications.

Node transience also impacts the query success rate. Figure 6 provides the query failure rates for varying degrees of node transience for unique and random file search queries. The query success rate is also directly related to whether the content has been looked up previously. This causes another copy of the content to be available due to the passive replication employed in the PE framework, thus increasing chance of query success. This explains why there is a greater probability of unique queries failing due to node transience than random queries, since content would be more widely available at multiple peers in the latter case. It can be seen from the result that over 33% of queries for unique files fail when 50% of peers leave the network while only 21% of the queries

*Figure 5. Failure rate for remote jobs for varying degree of node transience*

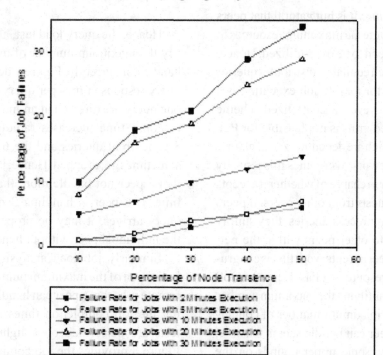

*Figure 6. Query failures as a result of varying degree of node transience*

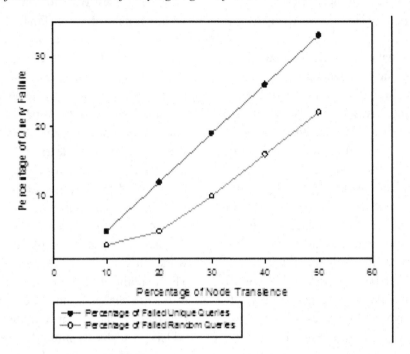

for random files fail in the same scenario. Thus, queries for popular files have a greater chance of being successful in the face of node transience.

B. *Load-Balancing:* It is but natural that peers which contribute the maximum resources to the network tend to be over-utilized. Hence, a scheme which equitably distributes queries and requests for remote job execution is a necessity. However, a centralized scheme as in dedicated grids is not feasible for P2P networks, which are decentralized in nature. The PE framework overcomes this issue by making a peer in charge of whether it accepts or rejects requests from other peers. If peers do not wish to process queries, they simply propagate it to other peers within the network. Each peer accepts work that is congruent with the resources it has. Hence, a QoS parameter quantifying the maximum number of queries or maximum number of concurrent jobs a peer can handle seems feasible. Consequently, some upper bounds on the percentage of failed queries/jobs can be

worked out based on further testing. If the number of failed requests crosses this parameter the SLA may be deemed to be violated.

Hence, the query load test, allows us to quantify the maximum number of queries a peer can handle concurrently. Figure 7 details the average query response times per query when more than one query are directed at an individual peer. The response time increases rapidly for more than 3 concurrent queries and the 6th and 7th queries sometimes got dropped. Hence, it is recommended that a peer not handle more than 3 queries at a time. If a peer is handling 3 queries and a 4th query arrives, it may be propagated further by the individual peer without handling it.

Similarly job load analysis provides us an indication of the maximum number of concurrent remote jobs that a peer can handle without affecting the job completion times significantly. All tests are performed on a lightly loaded CPU. Figure 8 provides the job completion times as a function of concurrent remote jobs running on an

*Figure 7. Query response times for concurrent queries on a single peer*

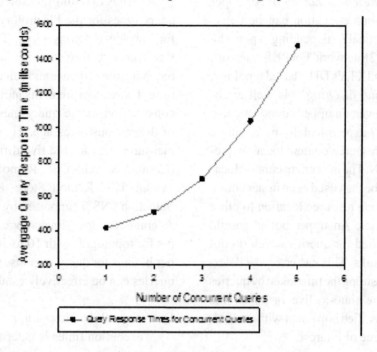

*Figure 8. Job completion times for concurrent jobs on a single peer*

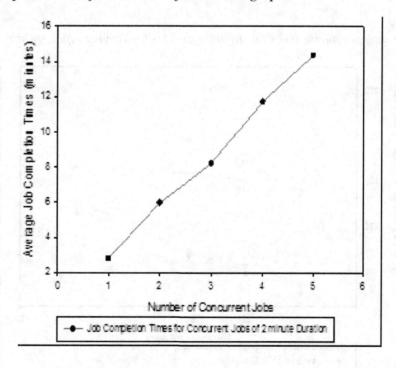

individual peer. With 5 active remote jobs on a peer the individual job completion time goes up nearly 7 times. Hence, it is recommended that a peer not accept more than 3 concurrent jobs pro-

vided it is lightly loaded. Also, when jobs are large or job deadlines are involved then a single job may be accepted at a time to ensure compliance.

C. *Time-Bound Resource Location:* An upper bound on resource-location can be determined theoretically depending upon the nature of the P2P network. For PE framework which utilizes JXTA's DHT-based topology, an upper bound of *O(logN)* is well established. Moreover, an upper bound can also be determined experimentally by issuing a multitude of resource/content location queries in the HPN. The maximum content location time can be then used as an upper bound for guaranteeing resource location to other peer enterprises. An upper bound should also be specified for queries which do not return any results. This can easily be determined by measuring the time taken by queries to expend the time-to-live or reach the maximum specified hop count without finding the resource of interest.

A variety of timing measurements for different query types for the PE prototype were obtained for varying topology sizes. The measurements were taken before issuing the query and after receiving the response and calculating the elapsed time. These measurements include time taken for construction of the query message and parsing of the response message. Figure 9 provides the measurements for the five different query types (Content Search "CS", Remote Job "RJ", User Search "US", Remote Store "RS" and Neighbor Selection "NS") supported by the PE prototype. Average response times range from 325 to 1250 ms for topologies with 10 to 50 peers. Thus, upper bounds for query response times for different queries can be effectively established.

D. *Time-Bound Execution:* An upper bound on execution times is determined by having a variety of remote jobs execute in failover scenarios. The average failover times are

*Figure 9. Average query-response times for different queries for varying topology size*

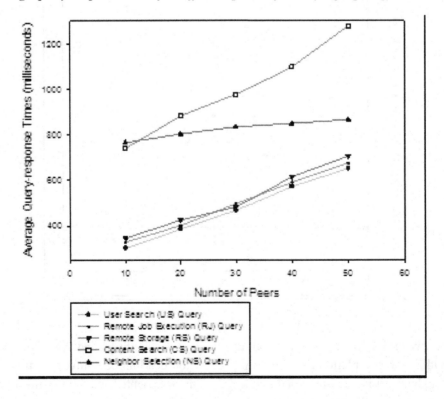

measured and the overheads added to normal job execution times to arrive at a figure. For multiple failovers before job completion, the overall execution time increases further. Thus, a job's committed execution time could be the normal execution time plus the overheads involved in two failover scenarios and this can be expected to hold in 90% of the cases since the confidence level for fault-tolerance provided by the P4P approach is 90%. Within the PE framework execution overheads in the range of 12-150% were observed in failover scenarios for jobs with different execution times. Hence, a commitment for time-bound execution can definitely be provided with some degree of confidence.

The failover scenario is implemented in a simple manner. Each peer implements a listener which gets invoked by the JXTA Rendezvous Service, each time a peer joins/leaves the network. If the backup peer (selected via NSR algorithm)

receives an event indicating that the primary peer has left the network it executes the remote job already available locally and sends back the results to the peer which originally submitted the remote work. In this case the additional time taken is just the time of job execution and time taken to transfer the results back to the peer. Figure 10 provides details of the average failover time (387 to 408 ms) from the primary peer to the backup peer, defined as the elapsed time between the primary peer leaving the network to the beginning of the execution of the remote job on the backup peer for varying topology sizes.

Figure 11 provides the overheads involved in remote job execution in various failover scenarios for jobs with 0.5, 1, 2, 5 and 10 minutes execution times. With multiple peers leaving the network before completion of the remote work, the failover time increases drastically since the task needs to be migrated. Also, for larger jobs the overall impact on remote execution times in failover scenarios as a percentage of the actual

*Figure 10. Average failover time for remote job execution (primary to backup peer)*

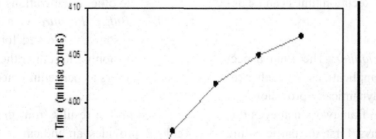

*Figure 11. Local vs. remote job execution times (failover scenario)*

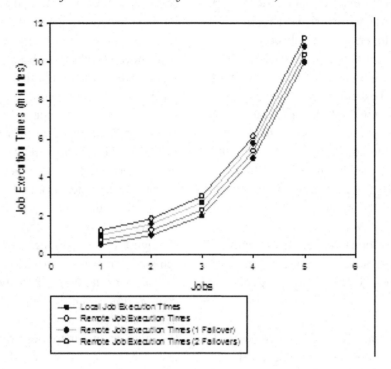

job execution time is less than that for smaller jobs.

Thus, given the job characteristics, average failover times and overheads involved in remote execution in failover scenarios an effective upper bound on remote job execution times can be determined.

E.  *Dynamic Provisioning:* The final aspect of QoS for P2P applications is whether resources can be dynamically provisioned if required. The PE framework achieves this in a couple of ways. First, the participating organization may not commit all its available resources in a contract and could keep some resources in reserve to cater to dynamic provisioning. Second, an organization could enter into multiple contracts and could utilize peer resources belonging to another organization if one organization is unable to meet its resource requirements. Broadly, an organization can divide the total available resources into three categories as depicted in Figure 12.

i.   *Home Resources:* a percentage of resources reserved for applications deployed within the HPN.
ii.  *Away Resources:* a percentage of resources reserved for peers belonging to other organizations.
iii. *Buffer Resources:* a percentage of resources reserved for dynamic provisioning for either the home or away peers as per requirement.

Based on the results from the PE prototype Table 2 provides an indicative Service Level Agreement encompassing various QoS parameters:

The SLA's have not been completely validated and more efforts shall be required in this area. However based on initial experimental results these SLA's seem reasonable in a P2P environment. The proposed QoS model and indicative SLA's can be adapted to work at the level of an organization or an individual peer and can vary according to the service model.

*Figure 12. Resource allocation strategy catering to dynamic provisioning of peer resources*

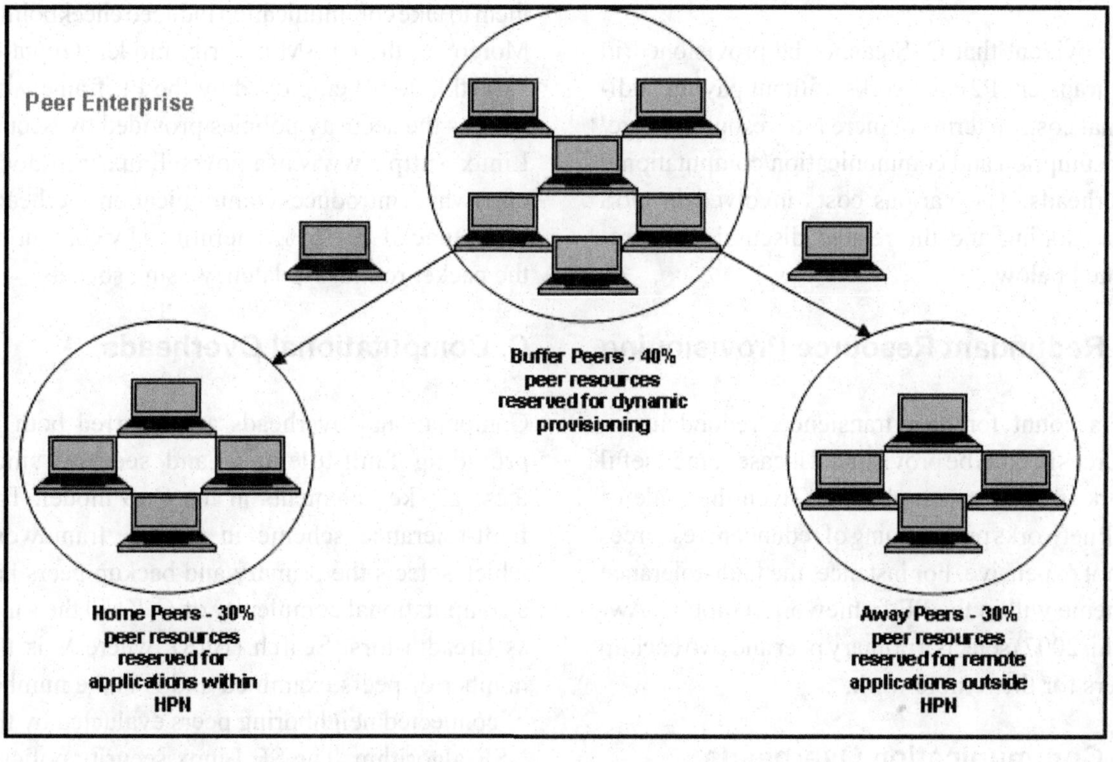

*Table 2. An organization's indicative Service Level Agreement (SLA)*

```
<SLA: Service Level Agreement >
<Contract_Info ="Classification of Relationship">
<Contract _Type value="Exclusive" description ="Can be Exclusive/Shared"/>
</Interaction_Type value="Provider" description="Resource Exchange/Provider/Consumer">
<Max_Contracts value = "3" description="Maximum number of contracts"/>
</Contract _Info >
<Availability_Time ="Time of Operation">
<Start_Time value="10" unit ="pm" description ="Start time of resource availability"/>
<Duration value = "6" unit="hours" description="Duration of resource availability"/>
</Availability_Time >
<Search Latency ="Search Related Assurance">
<Search _Time value="1" unit="seconds" description ="Avg. time to search content/resource"/>
<Turnaround_Time value="2" unit="seconds description ="Max time to search"/>
</Search Latency>
<Fault_Tolerance ="Extent of Fault_Tolerance Service Provided">
<Backup_Peers value="3" description ="Number of backup peers selected for each peer"/>
<Confidence_Interval value= "90" unit="%" description="Promised 90% success rate"/>
</Fault _Tolerance >
<Job_Execution = "Job-Execution related QoS">
<Max_Jobs value="2" description ="Max number of concurrent jobs on a peer"/>
<Delay value= "25" unit="%" description="Maximum 25% delay in job-execution"/>
<Confidence_Interval value= "80" unit="%" description="Promised 80% compliance"/>
</Job_Execution>
<Dynamic_Provisioning = "Assurances for on-demand resource-availability">
<Service_Provided value="Yes" description ="Yes/No"/>
<Extra _Resources value= "10" unit="%" description = "Additional 10% peers available"/>
<Confidence_Interval value= "90" unit="%" description="Promised 90% compliance"/>
</Dynamic_Provisioning>
</SLA: Service Level Agreement>
```

## THE COST OF QOS PROVISIONING

It is evident that QoS cannot be provisioned in the transient P2P networks without paying additional costs in terms of increased resource usage/consumption and communication/computational overheads. The various costs involved in QoS provisioning and the related discussion is presented below:

## A. Redundant Resource Provisioning

To account for peer transience, redundant resources need to be provisioned incase some useful work is to be accomplished. Given the scale of P2P networks provisioning of redundant resources is not expensive. For instance, the fault-tolerance scheme within the PE framework (Gupta & Awasthi, 2007) selects a primary peer and two backup peers for the remote work.

## B. Communication Overheads

To ensure QoS, communication overheads are involved in selecting backup peers, redundant transmissions of messages to backup peers, task migrations etc. Combined with the usual P2P broadcasts, query propagations and content flows, it can cause P2P traffic to reach alarming proportions. The PE framework counters this in two ways: first it allows the hours of operation to be specified (typically during lean traffic periods) and second by allowing organizations residing in different time-zones to utilize each others resources during periods of little or no activity. It is also possible to specify resource usage quotas at individual peers which control the number of network connections that a peer can establish and the quantum of network traffic that it generates, thus controlling traffic to some extent. For instance, the fault-tolerance scheme (Gupta & Awasthi, 2007) within the PE framework incurs a message exchange overhead of two messages per message received by the primary peer executing the remote work, since it relays the message

redundantly to the two backup peers to enable them to take communication induced checkpoints. Moreover, the CBSM security model (Gupta & Awasthi, 2008) employed by the PE framework utilizes the security policies provided by Secure Linux (http://www.nsa.gov/selinux/info/docs.cfm) which introduces communication overheads to the tune of 10-15%, determined by computing the packet round-trip latency using sockets.

## C. Computational Overheads

Computational overheads are incurred both in providing fault-tolerance and security since these are key elements in the QoS model. The fault-tolerance scheme in the PE framework which selects the primary and backup peers has a computational complexity of $O(V+E)$ the same as Breadth-First Search (BFS), where V is the number of peers examined and E is the number of connected neighboring peers evaluated by the NSR algorithm. The SE Linux security policies which control access to critical system resources introduces computational overheads around 11% on average to each operation by the remote work. This compares favorably to similar policy-based security mechanisms (Gaspary et al., 2007) which introduce computational and communication overheads ranging from 35-55%.

The costs discussed above would also need to be incurred in any distributed system such as grids or client/server systems and would depend upon the criticality of the deployed application. More critical the application, more the costs incurred in ensuring fault-tolerance, load-balancing and application uptime. However, the rate of failure/transience of participating peers is much more in P2P networks and hence the costs involved are that much higher. However, the sheer scale of P2P networks allows application developers the luxury of utilizing additional resources in ensuring application uptime and QoS provisioning. Security vulnerabilities of P2P networks are a major disadvantage and the main hurdle in their widespread deployment beyond content sharing applications. Hence, the 11% average overhead as obtained in our test setup in ensuring security of individual peers is completely justified.

## CONCLUSION

Although a lot more testing and benchmarking would need to be carried out before a real-world QoS model for P2P applications involving content sharing, communication and distributed computing becomes a reality, the preliminary results from the PE framework and the scenario in which it is employed, throw some positive indications that by controlling some aspects of the adhoc nature of P2P networks some degree of confidence can be assigned to meeting key performance parameters. Future work shall involve validation of the QoS parameters and experimentation with various SLAs in different deployment scenarios leading to performance characterization and enforcement of SLAs in the Peer Enterprises framework. It is hoped that this early model will invite further work and validation and a formal QoS framework and Service-Level Agreements for P2P applications in general shall become a reality in the near future.

## REFERENCES

*Avaki Corporation Home Page*. Retrieved September 3, 2009, from http://www.avaki.com

*BitTorrent Home Page*. (n.d.). Retrieved August 21, 2009, from http://www.bittorrent.com/

Bocciarelli, P., D'Ambrogio, A., & Angelaccio, M. (2007). QShare: QoS-Enabled Description and Discovery of Services in SOA-Based P2P Applications. In *Proceedings of the 16th IEEE International Workshop on Enabling Technologies: Infrastructures for Collaborative Enterprises* (pp. 159-166). Washington, DC: IEEE Press.

Cai, Z., & Lin, X. (2008). QCast: A QoS-Aware Peer-to-Peer Streaming System with DHT-Based Multicast. *Lecture Notes in Computer Science*, *5036*, 287–295. doi:10.1007/978-3-540-68083-3_29

*Condor Project Home Page*. (n.d.). Retrieved August 24, 2009, from http://www.cs.wisc.edu/condor/

*CoolStreaming Home Page*. (n.d.). Retrieved September 15, 2009 from http://www.coolstreaming.us

Di Stefano, A., Morana, G., & Zito, D. (2009). P2P Strategy for QoS Discovery and SLA Negotiation in Grid Environment. *Future Generation Computer Systems*, *25*(8), 862–875. doi:10.1016/j.future.2009.03.001

*Facebook Home Page*. (n.d.). Retrieved August 28, 2009, from http://www.facebook.com

Gao, X., Yu, Z., & Shin, Y. (2006). The Lagrangian Algorithm Implement of QoS-Aware Service Composition on P2P Networks. In *Proceedings of the IEEE Asia-Pacific Conference on Services Computing* (pp. 356-361). Washington, DC: IEEE Press.

Gaspary, L. P., Barcellos, M. P., Detsch, A., & Antunes, R. S. (2007). Flexible Security in Peer-to-Peer Applications: Enabling New Opportunities Beyond File Sharing. *Computer Networks*, *51*(17), 4797–4815. doi:10.1016/j.comnet.2007.07.005

*Gnutella Protocol Specification*. (n.d.). Retrieved September 1, 2009, from http://rfc-gnutella.sourceforge.net/

*Groove HomePage*. Retrieved September 5, 2009, from http://office.microsoft.com/ en-us/groove/FX100487641033.aspx

Gummadi, K. P., Dunn, R. J., Saroiu, S., Gribble, S. D., Levy, H. M., & Zahorjan, J. (2003). Measurement, Modeling and Analysis of Peer-to-Peer File-sharing Workload. *ACM SIGOPS Operating Systems Review*, *37*(5), 314–329. doi:10.1145/1165389.945475

Gupta, A., & Awasthi, L. K. (2007). Peer Enterprises: Possibilities, Challenges and Some Ideas Towards Their Realization. *Lecture Notes in Computer Science, 4806*(2), 1011–1020. doi:10.1007/978-3-540-76890-6_27

Gupta, A., & Awasthi, L. K. (2007). P4P: Ensuring Fault Tolerance for Cycle-Stealing P2P Applications. In *Proceedings of the International Conference on Grid Computing and Applications* (pp. 151-155). Las Vegas, NV: CSREA Press.

Gupta, A., & Awasthi, L. K. (2008). Secure Thyself: Securing Individual Peers in Collaborative Peer-to-Peer Environments. In *Proceedings of the International Conference on Grid Computing and Applications* (pp. 140-146). Las Vegas, NV: CSREA Press.

Gupta, A., & Awasthi, L. K. (in press). IndNet: towards a peer-to-peer community network connecting the information technology industry and academia in India. *International Journal of Networking and Virtual Organizations.*

Gupta, A., & Awasthi, L. K. (in press). PArch: A Cross-Organizational Peer-to-Peer Framework Supporting Aggregation and Exchange of Storage for Efficient Email Archival. *International Journal of Business Information Systems.*

Gupta, R., Manion, T. R., Rao, R. T., & Singhal, S. K. (2008). Peer-to-Peer Authentication and Authorization. *United States Patent: 7350074.*

Gupta, R., Sekhri, V., & Somani, A. K. (2006). CompuP2P: An Architecture for Internet Computing Using Peer-to-Peer Networks. *IEEE Transactions on Parallel and Distributed Systems, 17*(11), 1306–1320. doi:10.1109/TPDS.2006.149

Hughes, D., Warren, I., & Coulson, G. (2004). Improving QoS for Peer-to-Peer Applications Through Adaptation. In *Proceedings of the IEEE International Workshop on Future Trends in Distributed Computing Systems* (pp. 178-183). Washington, DC: IEEE Press.

*Instant Messenger Home Page.* (n.d.). Retrieved September 10, 2009, from http://www.aim.com

*Jabber Home Page.* (n.d.). Retrieved September 7, 2009, from http://www.jabber.org

*JXTA HomePage.* (n.d.). Retrieved August 29, 2009, from http://www.sun.com/jxta

Kamwar, S. D., Schlosser, M. T., & Garcia-Molina, H. (2003). The EigenTrust Algorithm for Reputation Management in P2P Networks. In *Proceedings of the 12th International Conference on World Wide Web* (pp. 640-651).

KaZaA Home Page. (n.d.). Retrieved September 5, 2009, from http://www.kazaa.com/us/index.htm

Kelly, W., & Mason, R. (2005). G2-P2P: A Fully Decentralized Fault-Tolerant Cycle Stealing Framework. In *Proceedings of the Australian Workshop on Grid Computing and e-Research* (pp. 33-39).

Li, Z., & Mohapatra, P. (2004). QRON: QoS-Aware Routing in Overlay Networks. *IEEE Journal on Selected Areas in Communications, 22*(1), 29–40. doi:10.1109/JSAC.2003.818782

Liang, J., & Nahrstedt, K. (2006). RandPeer: Membership Management for QoS Sensitive Peer-to-Peer Applications. In *Proceedings of the 25th IEEE International Conference on Computer Communications* (pp. 1-10). Washington, DC: IEEE Press.

*LimeWire Home Page.* (n.d.). Retrieved September 7, 2009, from http://www.limewire.com

Linnolahti, J. (2004). QoS Routing for P2P Networking (HUT T-110.551). *Seminar on Internetworking.*

*LiveStation Home Page.* (n.d.). Retrieved August 28, 2009, from http://www.livestation.com

Marti, S., & Garcia-Molina, H. (2006). Taxonomy of Trust: Categorizing P2P Reputation Systems. *Computer Networks, Special Issue on Trust and Reputation in Peer-to-Peer Systems, 50*(4), 472–484.

Meo, M., & Milan, F. (2008). QoS Content Management for P2P file-sharing applications. *Future Generation Computer Systems, 24*(3), 213–221. doi:10.1016/j.future.2007.07.002

Milojicic, D., Kalogeraki, V., Lukose, R. M., Nagaraja, K., Pruyne, J., Richard, B., et al. (2002). *Peer-to-peer Computing* (Tech. Rep. No. HPL-2002-57 20020315). HP Labs Research Library, Technical Publications Department.

Nemati, A. G., & Takizawa, M. (2008). Application Level QoS for Multi-Media Peer-to-Peer Networks. *In Proceedings of the International Conference on Advanced Information Networking and Applications* (pp. 319-324).

*OceanStore Home Page.* (n.d.). Retrieved September 2, 2009, from http://oceanstore.cs.berkeley.edu/

Park, J. S., An, G., & Chandra, D. (2007). Trusted P2P Computing Environments With Role-Based Access Control. *Information Security, IET, 1*(1), 27–35. doi:10.1049/iet-ifs:20060084

Pathan, M., & Buyya, R. (2009). Architecture and performance models for QoS-driven effective peering of content delivery networks. *Multiagent and Grid Systems, 5*(2), 165–195.

Rajasekhar, S., Khalil, I., & Tari, Z. (2006). Probabilistic QoS Routing in WiFi P2P Networks. In *Proceedings of the 20th International Conference on Advanced Information Networking and Applications* (pp. 811-816).

*Secure Linux Home Page.* (n.d.). Retrieved September 15, 2009, from http://www.nsa.gov/research/ selinux/index.shtml

SETI@Home Project Home Page. (n.d.). Retrieved August 28, 2009, from http://setiathome.berkeley.edu

Shudo, K., Tanaka, Y., & Sekiguchi, S. (2005). P3: P2P-Based Middleware Enabling Transfer and Aggregation of Computational Resources. In *Proceedings of the IEEE International Symposium on Cluster Computing and the Grid* (pp. 259-266). Washington, DC: IEEE Press.

Singh, A., & Liu, L. (2003). TrustMe: Anonymous Management of Trust Relationships in Decentralized P2P Systems. In *Proceedings of the Third International Conference on Peer-to-Peer Computing* (pp. 142-149). Washington, DC: IEEE Press.

*TerraNet Home Page.* (n.d.) Retrieved August 29, 2009, from http://www.terranet.se

*TVU Networks Home Page.* Retrieved August 25, 2009, from http://www.tvunetworks.com

Zhu, X., Luo, J., & Song, A. (2008). A Grid Information Services Architecture Based on Structured P2P Systems. *Lecture Notes in Computer Science, 5236,* 374–383. doi:10.1007/978-3-540-92719-8_34

*This work was previously published in International Journal of Distributed Systems and Technologies, Volume 1, Issue 3, edited by Nik Bessis, pp. 1-23, copyright 2010 by IGI Publishing (an imprint of IGI Global).*

# Chapter 6
# A Study on the Effect of Application and Resource Characteristics on the QoS in Service Provisioning Environments

**Theodora Varvarigou**
*National Technical University of Athens, Greece*

**Konstantinos Tserpes**
*National Technical University of Athens, Greece*

**Dimosthenis Kyriazis**
*National Technical University of Athens, Greece*

**Fabrizio Silvestri**
*Italian National Research Council, Italy*

**Nikolaos Psimogiannos**
*University of the Aegean, Greece*

## ABSTRACT

*This chapter deals with the problem of quality provisioning in business service-oriented environments, examining the resource selection process as an initial matching of the provided to the demanded QoS. It investigates how the application and resource characteristics affect the provided level of QoS, a relationship that intuitively exists but has not yet being mapped. To do so, it focuses on identifying the application and resource parameters that affect the customer-defined QoS parameters. The chapter realistically centres upon modeling a data mining application and simple PC nodes in order to study how they affect response times. It moves on, by proving the existence of these specific relations and maps them using simple artificial neural networks so as to be able to wrap them in a single mechanism for resource selection based on customer QoS requirements and real time provider QoS capabilities.*

DOI: 10.4018/978-1-4666-0906-8.ch006

## INTRODUCTION

The matching of available resources to application instances is considered a fundamental problem in distributed computing, even in its current cornerstone, that is cloud computing. Cloud computing enables the virtualization of infrastructure capabilities that are delivered as a service to the customer. Even though this virtualization layer usually hides other abstraction layers, set up for serving interoperability and/or dynamic service provisioning such as Grid middlewares, distributed operating systems and distributed applications, they all end up in an actual resource infrastructure with several interconnected computing, storage, network and perhaps other types of resources. The conclusion is that the infrastructure (or service) provider will always want to manage the resources' usage so as to support the application requirements in an optimal way.

This optimization aims at improving the rate of the revenue for service provision/offered quality of the service. However, quality of service (QoS) and specifically the provided level of quality, is affected by various parameters which are related to the application (i.e. security, accessibility, availability and reliability), the resources (i.e. availability, reliability, throughput and utilization) as well as to the customer-defined requirements (i.e. cost and time). It is usually possible for the service provider to "play" with the application and resource parameters in order to satisfy the customer-defined ones. So, apart from the matching of applications to resources, the service provider has to also make sure that this matching will satisfy the customer's QoS requirements.

Service providers will always apply a scheme for load balancing however mapping the actual service provisioning level to the quality requirements of the customer is an issue that still needs to be investigated. The reason is that the problem requires to be examined by both the resource capabilities and the application requirements point of view. A supercomputing node may not be

adequate to run the simplest algorithm efficiently if the data generated and consumed are huge, if the network support is inadequate or if the current load simply does not permit it.

What is needed, is for the service provider to identify the current (real time) resource characteristics and map them to the application characteristics so as to satisfy QoS requirements. For example, in a 3D rendering application service, a service provider would have to ensure that the processor that will undertake the task to render 100 frames will be able to do so in 3 seconds because the customer demands imply that (implicitly or explicitly). Nonetheless, using such a mapping mechanism would make sense only before applying the provider's business models because this would require the incorporation of market parameters together with the QoS parameters and market parameters are extremely variable. A first mapping of quality demand to quality provision would work as a pre-selection phase for the resources that are capable to fulfil the SLA conditions.

In this chapter, we investigate the correlation of application and resource characteristics and how it affects the provided quality. Intuitively, we understand that there are sets of parameters that represent these characteristics and we try to examine what is their relation. Thus, we create a simple modeling scheme for describing in a unique way the resource and the application characteristics with regards to the QoS. We put our assumption to the test, by focusing on a data-mining application deployed on a Grid middleware which poses computational, storage and network challenges. Our tests lead to the development of a model that provides solid indications to a service provider of how this mapping can take place in the service provisioning environment using neural networks. The purpose of this model is not to constitute a readily exploitable mechanism but to evaluate the assumptions made in an already-deployed environment. Having stated that, our model is designed in a way to reduce assumptions, to simplify the understanding of the results and to deliver evidence that such a mapping can be implemented by a more sophisticated mechanism that will still be based on the proposed model.

The document is structured as such: The following section (State of the Art) gives the state of the art in application and resource modeling, providing examples of indicative works using neural networks; it also explains how our work progress the state of the art. The Section entitled Application Modeling, explains what application modeling means and how we can apply it specifically in a data mining application. The following section (Resource Modeling), presents the respective modeling method for resources and specifically for a typical PC architecture. The next Section is providing proof that our modeling methods are correct using actual measurements and concluding in capturing the relationships between data mining parameters and response time and resource parameters and response time, setting the foundations for building a mechanism for resource selection. Finally, in the Appendix we incorporate some indicative results from our evaluation measurements.

## STATE-OF-THE-ART

There are various approaches for mechanisms that aim to model the service performance and estimate the resources needed to fulfil specific QoS requirements. For example the Network Weather Service (NWS) (Wolski, 1999) measures resource information, processor and network loads, and predicts the future resources, while other works (e.g. Strube, 2008) focus on analysing the source code of an application in order to perform a simulation and prediction of its performance. Moreover, there are a number of approaches that conduct performance estimation using analytical models. Analytical models use simple algebraic expressions that enable the characterization of the performance and other QoS features of SOIs.

The predictions obtained by characterisation are less accurate; however they provide a quick estimation of the impact of various parameters. Such examples on analytical models that cover a range of applications including large scale engineering simulations, multi-user environments and transaction processing are presented in (Floros, 1999; Meacham, 1998; Risse, 2001). Based on the analytical models the application-specific load models can be derived. These models can be used to compare tasks prior to making scheduling decisions about the selection of the machine on which the service will be executed. The accuracy of performance predictions obtained by this technique was illustrated in several case studies drawn from the domain of mechanical simulations (Hey, 2005). The advantage of analytical approach is that it provides simple mathematical expressions that include the key parameters governing the performance of the application, however in the case of commercial software codes, the source code for the application is not available for instrumentation and all analytical models have therefore to be derived from benchmarking the application. Moreover, it is almost impossible to obtain high accuracy for arbitrary inputs from a single model of a complex industrial application.

Besides the analytical modes, neuro-fuzzy models can also be used for performance estimation - it was studied in the framework of the COPE project (COPE). The experience with hand-tuned performance modeling has shown that this approach requires a substantial knowledge of the governing parameters and the relationship between them if we wish to derive accurate mathematical models. The neuro-fuzzy technique offers a more promising approach since it provides learning capability and also higher accuracy. It is also important to mention that no detailed knowledge of the application is required in order to generate prediction models.

Furthermore, Queuing Network approaches have been used for many years for modeling distributed systems. These models for the simplest cases can be evaluated analytically and by using simulations. Although the analytical models provide quick results, however they are applicable only for the analysis of simplest cases. An example of this approach is described in (Kraiss, 2001) where an M/G/1 model was used for the performance evaluation of a message passing system. Extending Queuing Networks with parameters representing application terms is an intensive research area (Petriu, 2000; Woodside, C. M., 2006). For example, in the TAPAS (TAPAS) project an approach that enables to generate queuing models directly from the UML specification was studied.

A framework for incorporating QoS in Grid applications is discussed in (Benkner, 2006). In this article, a performance model to estimate the response time and a pricing model for determining the price of a job execution are used. In order to determine whether the client's QoS constraints can be fulfilled, for each QoS parameter a corresponding model has to be in place. This work follows analytical modeling approaches, the drawbacks of which were described previously. The importance of considering QoS requirements is also illustrated in Marculescu's work (2001) and (2004). In these works, Stochastic Automata Networks (SANs) are used for application modeling in order to conclude to which services shall be selected to meet the aforementioned QoS requirements. Literature (Chen, 2007) proposes a two step analysis for multi-tier applications in order to decompose the SLAs into low level objectives. In the first step, a resource demand estimation scheme is implemented through a profiling process. Profiling creates detailed resource profiles of each component in the application. A resource profile captures the demand of each transaction type at that resource, through historical data or benchmarking. Regression analysis is then applied to the data, to derive the per transaction-type resource demands. The resulting resource profile for the application is then stored in a repository, while analytical models are used afterwards.

Another interesting work is presented in (Lee, 2006). The application, whose performance must be estimated, is run under a strict reservation of resources in order to determine if the given set of reservation parameters satisfies the time constraints for execution. If this is not the case, then these parameters are altered accordingly. The main disadvantage of this methodology is the fact that there is a need for many test executions for every application instance. A code analyzing process that allows for the simulation of system performance is described in (He, 2006). It models the application by a parameter-driven Conditional Data Flow Graph (CDFG) and the hardware (HW) architecture by a configurable HW graph. The execution cost of each task block in the application CDFG is modelled by user-configurable parameters, which allows highly flexible performance estimation. However, this implementation needs the source code in order to provide the CDFG. Similar to the above, authors in (Hasselmeyer, 2006), discuss a scheme that uses information about potential pre-calculated complexities or former business transactions. A Knowledge Database stores information about the system requirements for the different complexities, depending on experiences made by running similar jobs in the past, while the Complexity Database stores previous calculated complexities of jobs. The main problem with this implementation lies in the cases where no similar execution has occurred in the past, or the complexity of the algorithm is unknown. Using the source code to analyse an application in terms of performance is also proposed in (Jarvis, 2006), in which the PACE (Performance Analysis and Characterization Environment) toolkit is presented. The system works by characterizing the application and the underlying hardware on which the application is to be run, and combining the resulting models to derive predictive execution data.

The approach we introduce in this chapter advances the field of research in estimating which resources have to be selected in order to meet specific application requirements by performing an initial estimation with the use of a Neural Network without requiring the source code to be available. It does so by identifying the parameters that model a data mining application characteristics that relate to the QoS. And it does the respective modeling for the resource characteristics, considering a typical PC architecture as a resource. In sequel, the research focuses on validating these models and mapping their relationship to the response time QoS parameter. In this way it establishes a mechanism for estimating the response time of resources for a given dataset when running the data mining application, that can be further used for resource selection according to response time requirements and current infrastructure load. All these are presented below.

## APPLICATION MODELING

The problem that is tried to be resolved in this Section is to identify those application parameters that are affecting the quality of the service providing the application. In this way we can conclude to a set or vector of parameters that characterize uniquely the application effect on provided quality. In other words we are trying to map the function that connects applications to QoS for a reference resource as presented in the equation below:

$$y = f\left(x_1, x_2, \ldots, x_n\right)$$

where y is the QoS parameter(s) in question and are the application parameters.

However, it was considered more realistic to target this modeling in specific applications and QoS parameters. So, in the effort to demonstrate that there is a method to model applications so as to provide the associating QoS parameters, the authors dealt with e-business applications. Examples stated in (Wikipedia) are Internal business systems, Enterprise communication and collaboration, e-commerce. An attempt to model any type of applications by addressing them one by one is a-priori rendered impossible. Instead an analytical method is employed which shows that there is a general way to model applications and proving how they are associated to QoS parameters (and the way that this is happening) without loss of generality.

When comparing e-business applications with traditional IT applications several differences can be found. Since e-business has a highly dynamic nature the applications designed for this kind of environment should be developed and adapted very quickly to these changes. For e-business applications security is an important issue. Internet is currently insecure, for this reason e-business applications have to provide sophisticated security mechanisms both for protecting the application itself and for ensuring the data managed. Traditional applications were often based on one single technology (i.e. CASEs, ERPs, etc.). In e-business often many different modules developed using different tools and technologies must be integrated and must be able to interoperate among them. Performance is another very important point. The worldwide availability of e-business services within the Internet enables access to a large, potentially unlimited, customer base. Additionally, the volume of the customer base can grow rapidly. Therefore, e-business applications have to be extremely scalable and their articulate nature fits fully to the service oriented environment profile.

Thinking about e-business applications on service provisioning environments the first thing coming to one's attention is that, due to the large number of resources that can be used in order to run an application, one may need to select the resources best fitting with the application requirements. In order to do so it may need to model an application performance in a way independent from the particular resource on which it runs. Algorithmic complexity theory tries to model the performance of an algorithm on the characteristics of the data on which it is applied to. E.g. knowing in advance the cost of a comparison operation in a sorting algorithm for a given architecture, the computation of the actual cost of the sort operation is enabled. Unfortunately, a quite large number of e-business applications involve a number of operations on datasets that depend on the distribution of elements inside the dataset itself. The case of data mining applications will be employed as case study. Data mining is commonly defined as the activity of discovering non-trivial information hidden in databases.

Typically, data mining tasks involve costly operations on datasets that are usually stored on disk. For example, Market Basket Analysis (MBA) (Han, 2006) is a popular data mining task that aims to find interesting correlations within a database that stores customers' purchases. Since the complexity of typical MBA algorithms depend on the number of correlations found, the higher the correlation within the items of a dataset is, the greater the cost of executing MBA algorithms on it.

The obvious question is: "Why Data Mining?" As said before, data mining applications can be seen as a good example of application mixing both CPU intensive operations and data intensive ones. Moreover the performance requirements do not only depend on the characteristic of the application but also on the dataset it will be ran on. Furthermore, in order to rapidly obtain results usually distributed/parallel programming techniques are needed thus making a service oriented infrastructure a suitable platform for this kind of application.

Several works have been directed toward discovering the complexity and the performance of data mining applications (e.g. Bradford & Fortes, 1998; Czezowski & Christen, 2002; Vazhkudai, 2002). In just a few cases this have been possible in the traditional (i.e. complexity-theory oriented) way, for the remaining cases only an empirical evaluation of the cost has been possible.

## Data Mining Modeling

Most of the complexity of common data mining tasks is concerned with the unknown amount of information contained in the data being mined. The more patterns and correlations are contained within such data, the more resources are needed to extract them. This is also confirmed by the fact that, in general, there is not a single best algorithm for a given data mining task on any possible kind of input dataset. Rather, in order to achieve good performances, strategies and optimizations have to be adopted according to the dataset specific characteristics. For example one typical distinction in transactional databases is between sparse and dense datasets. In this document, the Frequent Set Counting (FST) (Perego, 2001) is considered as a case study for data mining algorithms. This study proposes a list of statistical properties of transactional datasets that allows for a characterization of the dataset complexity. It is shown how such characterization can be used in many fields, from performance prediction to optimization.

Before describing the features adopted let us define briefly what is a transactional dataset. Let $I$ be a set of items, $t$ be a subset of $I$ called transaction, $i$ be a subset of $I$ called itemset. Let $D$ be a list of transactions called dataset. The support for an itemset $i$ is defined as the number of transactions containing $i$.

The following example should clarify the definitions given above.

Let I be the set $\{a,b,c,d\}$, let $D = \{\{a\},\{a,c\}, \{b,c,d\},\{a,b,c\},\{b,c\},\{d\}\}$. The element "a" is an item, the set $\{a,c\}$ is an itemset, the support of the itemset $\{b,c\}$ is three since it appears in three different transactions of $D$ – i.e. {b,c,d}, {c,b,c}, and {b,c}.

It is understood that there are several parameters that could be used to describe a dataset. However, in our investigation we considered DCI as an algorithm for solving the Frequent Set Counting (FSC) problem. Through a trial and error process we ended up with a list of parameters that characterize the algorithm's performance. The full analysis of the application is out of the scope of this chapter therefore we focus on the selected parameters which are analyzed below:

- Total number of transactions, i.e. the number of elements contained within the dataset D;
- Total number of items, i.e. the cardinality of the dataset I;
- Average length of transactions:

$$\overline{l} = \frac{1}{|D|} \sum_{l_i \in D} |l_i|$$

Average support of items:

$$\overline{s} = \frac{1}{|I|} \sum_{i \in I} \text{supp}(i)$$

Variance of the support:

$$s^2 = \frac{1}{(|I| - 1)} \sum_{i \in I} \left(\text{supp}(i) - \overline{s}\right)^2$$

K-th order empirical entropy of the dataset computed for a given support level:

$$H_k(s) = -\sum_{i=1}^{\binom{|I|}{k}} \left\langle \text{supp}(i) > s \right\rangle \left[ \frac{\text{supp}(i)}{\binom{|I|}{k}} \log \left( \frac{\text{supp}(i)}{\binom{|I|}{k}} \right) \right]$$

where s is a support level, i is the *i-th k*-itemset, *<P>* evaluate to 1 if and only if P is true. The intuitive idea behind this equation is that of considering the information containing a transaction source. Only frequent itemsets (i.e. those verifying *<supp(i) > s>*) are selected, thus considering the minimum support threshold influence on the problem complexity: the lower the minimum support, the harder the mining process;

- K-th order logarithmic inverted support:

where the symbols have the same meaning with those used for $H_k$.

In summary the modeling we are trying to achieve can be denoted by a function $y = f\left(x_1, x_2, x_3, x_4, x_5, x_6, x_7, x_8, x_9\right)$, where y is the output QoS parameter (in this case response time) and the rest of the definitions can be found in the following table (Table 1).

Later on, in the Evaluation section, we show that since function f exists, then the abovementioned parameters affect directly the QoS level.

## RESOURCE MODELING

Each service oriented environment such as a Grid system has a number of available resources that identify uniquely its capability to deliver QoS. We claim that the characteristics of these resources can be measured by some corresponding parameters, forming a vector that it is representative of the performance capabilities of a resource at a specific time (given that the load of the resource plays a significant role in its performance). To draw an analogy with the previous section we denote the modeling that we attempt to do here as:

$$y = f\left(x_1, x_2, \ldots, x_n\right)$$

As a first step, we investigated the way in which we can model the resources. We have

*Table 1. Data mining parameters used to uniquely model a dataset*

| Total number of Transactions | $x_1$ |
|---|---|
| Total number of items | $x_2$ |
| Average length of transactions | $x_3$ |
| Average support of items | $x_4$ |
| Variance of the support | $x_5$ |
| 1th order normalized entropy | $x_6$ |
| 2nd order normalized entropy | $x_7$ |
| 1st order normalized LIS | $x_8$ |
| 2nd order normalized LIS | $x_9$ |

chosen performance analysis because, clearly, the results of a resource's performance analysis are characterizing the resource in a unique way and intuitively there is a direct relationship between resource characteristics and the QoS parameters.

In an ideal case the resource model needs to be application independent which compels us to examine the resource from various perspectives, thus, the list of parameters in interest is the most comprehensive possible. The more exhaustive the list is, the more applications can be addressed by the model, because for each application there might be a different set of resource parameters that affect the QoS. Furthermore, we need to be aware of performance details related to the basic components of a typical computer architecture (CPU, memory, hard disks, video and sound card, network card, etc) in order to broaden the scope of our study as much as possible.

In order to achieve these, we studied several related works on performance analysis and surveyed various benchmarking tools. The resource parameters that we are interested can be extracted in the form of a feature vector using each one (or a set) of the abovementioned tools. From our survey we concluded that there is a set of resource performance characteristics that are of particular interest and which are giving a clear view of the resource's model. Unlike application modeling where a reference resource needs to be

considered, this is not the case for resource modeling. However, when the modeling is happening in real time, the application needs to be considered as well as a specific QoS parameter that these resource parameters affect. It is later proved that this set of parameters is connected to the provided QoS parameters through a function $y = f\left(x_1, x_2, ..., x_{21}\right)$ where $y$ is the QoS parameter (e.g. response time) and the $x_i$ are presented below (Table 2).

This set of parameters has been set up more based on intuition, experience and observation. Therefore, we put the model to the test, evaluating its performance in a legacy Grid system running a data mining application. The results of this evaluation are presented in the following section.

## Evaluation

In this section we attempt to evaluate the above-mentioned modeling. In practice, we desire to show that the selected parameters that were selected as indicative to characterize the application and the resources do affect the level of the provided QoS and that there is an actual relationship between them that once identified, will lead in the efficient mapping of applications and resources.

The evaluation takes place in two steps: we first evaluate the application model and then the resource model against a pre-determined QoS aspect, that is, time. What is attempted is to identify that there is a function that when is fed with the (application or resource) parameters will yield the response time in a reference resource or a reference application (fixed resource or application parameters) respectively.

$$y = f\left(Grid\ node\ params\right) = response\ time$$

$$y = f\left(dataset\ params\right) = response\ time$$

*Table 2. Resource-specific parameters used to uniquely model a resource from a QoS perspective*

| | |
|---|---|
| Million Floating Operations per second | $x_1$ |
| Bus clock | $x_2$ |
| Cache average I/O bandwidth | $x_3$ |
| Memory average I/O bandwidth | $x_4$ |
| Disk average I/O bandwidth | $x_5$ |
| Send communication bandwidth | $x_6$ |
| Send communication latency | $x_7$ |
| Receive communication bandwidth | $x_8$ |
| Receive communication latency | $x_9$ |
| Minimum Free Memory | $x_{10}$ |
| Minimum Free Disk Space | $x_{11}$ |
| Queue time interval | $x_{12}$ |
| SMP (number of processors) | $x_{13}$ |
| Cache total | $x_{14}$ |
| Minimum Free Video Memory | $x_{15}$ |
| Maximum Resolution/vert. refresh rate | $x_{16}$ |
| Color depth | $x_{17}$ |
| Sound Card Maximum Standard Sampling Bits | $x_{18}$ |
| Sound Card Maximum Standard Sampling Rate | $x_{19}$ |
| Probability of Errors | $x_{20}$ |
| Mean Time Between Errors = error free sec | $x_{21}$ |

We now need to justify why this evaluation takes place in two separate steps rather than one and why time was selected among the other customer-defined QoS parameters.

First of all, evaluating a mixed model, that is, a case where both the sets of parameters are involved in the equation would be ideal but this would be a very risky undertaking considering the complexity of the problem

$$\left( f\left( dataset\ params, response\ time \right) = Grid\ node\ params \right)$$

We needed realistic solutions and thus we ended up in isolating the problem into two separate problems that were easier to be resolved and didn't complicate the problem any further.

This was also the reason for which we focused on response time of the data mining algorithm in the datasets. We needed not to over-complicate the problem and we needed to focus in a QoS parameter that could be easily measured.

At this point it is important to mention that the abovementioned assumptions (splitting the problem into two different ones and using time as a QoS parameter) may narrowed the scope of the experiment but did not reduced the value of the results. The separation of the problem provides more credibility in the result that we obtained and the use of time showed that it is feasible to run the model having a different QoS parameter as target, of course using a different set of input parameters.

The evaluation included the identification of the abovementioned function: a) running the data mining algorithms in a number of datasets in a reference machine in the application modeling case and b) running the data mining algorithm for one dataset in a number of resources. In both cases, we monitored the response time and trained an artificial neural network (ANN) that is able to estimate the response time for new input samples. In this way, we concluded to two response time prediction mechanisms that put together, they give an application-resource mapping model. When the response time is estimated for a specific dataset, then the resources are ranked according to their current capability to run the data mining algorithm for the reference dataset. This gives an indication of which resource should be used. The mechanisms because of their simplicity pose no serious overhead in the QoS parameter estimation which is important due to the real-time limitations.

Having stated these, one could claim that only the one estimation mechanism would suffice if we could identify which resource or dataset is closer to the respective reference ones by comparing the parameters vectors. In this way we could, for example, estimate the response time for a dataset and if the customer requirements were for smaller times to define a new comparison operation in order to see which resource will provide smaller response times for that dataset by applying the comparison operation to the reference one. However, this would not make any sense, as it is not always clear how each parameter is contributing to changing each QoS aspect (e.g. how the combination of two resource parameters affect the response time). In other words, we cannot identify what kind of comparison is required and perhaps this is a work of another research effort.

Finally, the used infrastructure consisted of eight PCs each one consisting a Grid node/site running GRIA middleware (Surridge, 2005; GRIA) basic application services and exposing the data mining application in a service front end. Also, the middleware was configured so as to allow us to run the experiment in an unmanaged mode (without using SLAs) so as to be able to examine each resource independently of the application service. The specifications of the nodes are presented in the following table (Table 3).

The reason we selected the Grid nodes for our experiments rather than isolated computers, is to simulate the load conditions in a service provisioning environment and to take advantage of the fact that in these environments applications and resources are discrete.

In what follows we describe in detail the evaluation procedure for each model using neural networks technologies.

## Artificial Neural Network Set Up

In each of the two cases a simple feed-forward-structured network was used for the evaluation process and the objective was to train it in order to predict the response times. In that type of neu-ral networks, signals flow from inputs, forward through any hidden units, eventually reaching the output units. Such a structure has a stable behavior and can model functions of almost arbitrary complexity, with the number of layers, and the number of units in each layer, determining the function complexity (Ping).

Among the supervised and unsupervised training types the first one was selected, while the training algorithm that was used was back-propagation as it has lower memory requirements than most algorithms, and usually reaches an acceptable error level quite quickly, although it can then be very slow to converge properly on an error minimum. The architecture that has been used included one hidden layer in both cases.

The number of input, hidden and output units is always defined by the problem. In our case the empirical rule was used which dictates to use one hidden layer, with the number of units equal to half the sum of the number of input and output units. By the result of this procedure the specific configuration proved to be sufficient. More details about the number of neurons and the full architecture can be seen in Table 4.

The transfer functions for the input and the hidden layers were sigmoid while the output layer transfer function was set to be linear. The goal was to minimize the Mean Square Error (MSE) of the output so as to reach a specific value ($10^{-5}$, $10^{-3}$ in respective cases), while the minimum gradient was set in both cases to $10^{-10}$.

For the training and evaluation process, two sets of data were used for each modeling method. The one set comprised the training set and was used for the training of the ANNs while the other was the evaluation set. Both sets contained data

*Table 3. Specifications of the Grid nodes*

| CPU | Memory | Disk Capacity | Network | Operation System |
|---|---|---|---|---|
| x86 Intel P4 3GHz | 1GB RAM | 80GB HDD | 1Gbps LAN | LINUX Ubuntu |

*Table 4. Number of neurons per layer in each of the modeling evaluation cases*

|  | Input Layer | Hidden Layer | Output Layer |
|---|---|---|---|
| Application Modeling | 10-to-5 fully connected | 5-to-1 fully connected | 1 neuron |
| Resource Modeling | 22-to-11 fully connected | 11-to-1 fully connected | 1 neuron |

derived from real-time benchmarking. In the first case we were monitoring the response times per application instance (per dataset) and in the second, per resource type.

The training and evaluation sets' data were normalized in the interval [-1 1]. This was a direct consequence of the fact that the scalability of the values of the elements was extremely high and as a result the deviation of the minimum and maximum values was great. The intermediate element values do not help in scaling the input vector normally. Instead, they are closer to the minimum rather than the maximum, forming peaks in both cases. Normalizing the data (subtracting the mean and dividing by the standard deviation) ensures that the distance measure accords equal weight to each variable.

Finally, the emulation and training of the ANN has been implemented on Matlab Version 7.0.1, in a commodity of the shelf comprised of an Intel Pentium® M 1.76GHz processor, 1GB SDRAM memory and 80GB hard disk.

The results of this process are presented below.

## Data Mining Application Modeling Evaluation

The correlation between the application properties and the response time of the application has to be based on strong foundations (Palmerini, 2004). In order to provide some strong evidence, demonstrative results should be produced. For that, the application was tested in a real-life environment and the produced results were used for evaluation of the role that those selected properties play in the execution.

First, a number of indicative datasets was chosen in order to execute them in a selected resource that played the role of the reference machine. That resource was not part of the Grid system but an isolated machine that was used solely for that purpose. We ended up with using an obsolete PC in order to make sure that this would run the data mining algorithms without the interference of other tasks and users. That PC was composed of an Intel Xeon 2GHz processor, 1GB of main memory, and an Ultra-ATA 60GB disk.

From the datasets considered (connect-4 dense dataset, which contains many frequent itemsets also for high support thresholds) we extracted the features described in the application modeling section. In order to do so, we simply modified a popular frequent set mining algorithm known in literature, that is, Direct Count & Intersect (DCI) (Orlando, 2002). The algorithm just stopped at the second iteration giving in output the number of frequent items found in the first and second iteration. These figures have been subsequently used to compute the four Entropy and LIS values. It is important to keep under control the computational cost of extracting such measures. The evaluation of $H_1$ and $LIS_1$ only involves single items frequencies, therefore a single dataset scan is required while the amount of memory is of $O(\#items)$. To evaluate $H_2$ and $LIS_2$ it is necessary to know the pair frequencies, which implies a further dataset scan or, if enough memory is available - $O(\#items_2)$ - everything can be evaluated in the first scan. In Figure 5 in the Appendix, the full datasets' details are presented as well as the corresponding computing times for an indicative amount of datasets (not all samples are included for readability purposes). The values of comput-

*Figure 1. Training attempt without normalizing the data. The training stops when the minimum gradient is reached (The Mean Square Error value, remains steadily in ~$10^8$)*

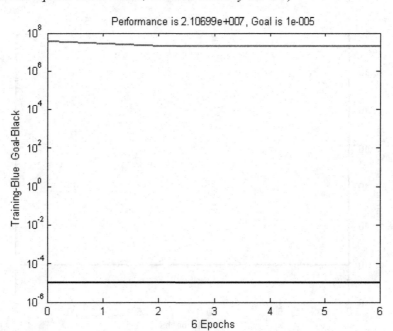

ing time, marked as "-", imply that the mining algorithm could not end its computations on that dataset for that support threshold. Those values were replaced with the value 9999 that is relatively much greater than any dataset's computing time.

Then, we trained an Artificial Neural Network (ANN) in order to predict the response time, by feeding the input with the extracted values that part of them are presented in Figure 5 (Appendix). The total number of the samples used as a training set was 300 with a set of 20 datasets being used for evaluation purposes.

The goal that was indented to be met was to minimize the Mean Square Error (MSE) of the output so as to reach the value 10-5, while the minimum gradient was set to $10^{-10}$.

The last feature vector of each dataset's training set was not fed directly in the ANN during the training process but was held for evaluation purposes instead. When the training process finished (given the MSE criterion), the sets used for evaluation, where also used for training so

as to increase the amount of the training feature vectors to the maximum available. Obviously, the last column labeled "Computing Time" comprised the output of the training set or the target vector.

In the case where no normalizing is taking place the training concludes after 6 epochs because the minimum gradient is reached ($10^{-10}$) while the MSE is steadily set to roughly 108 (Figure 1).

However, the result after the normalization of the data is much more satisfactory. The training concluded successfully in 24 epochs as can be seen in the following figure (Figure 2).

As described above, a set of feature vectors was not used for training purposes but instead for evaluation purposes. The results after the successful training were satisfactory as the ANN managed to predict successfully the computing time for each one of the feature vectors. In the following figure we present the 6 expected values in contrast to the 6 predicted values (Figure 3).

As can be seen the greatest deviation is of order of magnitude of 0.0648 while the smallest

*Figure 2. The MSE evolution during the training process. The black line symbolizes the goal while the blue line the training progress.*

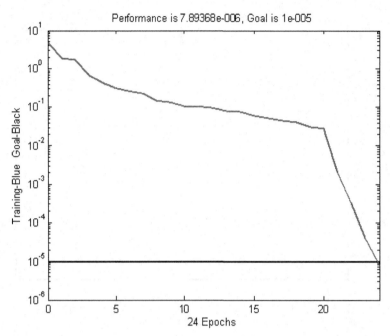

*Figure 3. The red "plus" ('+') represent the expected computing times while the blue ones the Neural Network output*

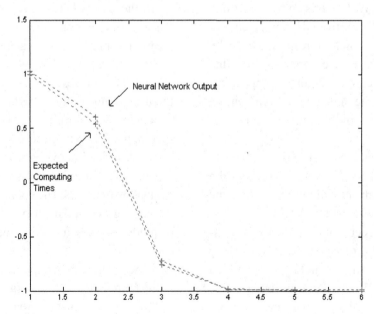

*Figure 4. Convergence of the training curve*

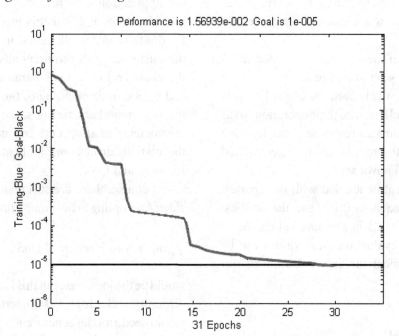

is of 0.0098 (absolute values). These values are sufficient in order to consider the prediction successful given the amount of datasets we had in our disposal.

## Resource Modeling Evaluation

The experiment procedure was analogous to the one presented in the Section above. It included the collection of test cases in order to train the artificial neural network and evaluate the results. For that purpose, the Grid nodes in our disposal were benchmarked as isolated resources because the obtained parameters should characterize uniquely the specific resource.

In the Section above we presented a number of parameters that seemed to affect the response time of the data mining algorithm based on literature, experience and observation. Of course the list cannot be exhaustive but it is certainly adequate to provide a first indication of the relation of the resource characteristics and the response time of data mining algorithms. In order to cover future experimentation with other applications as well,

we also included parameters that seemed irrelevant to data mining (e.g. sound card details). These parameters did not affect the current experiment as counting them in or removing them would make no difference.

For the measurements we employed a commonly used benchmarking tool in our legacy system. The outcome of the benchmarking was for a specific time of measurement depicted in Figure 6 in the Appendix (only for five out of the eight nodes and only for one measurement for readability purposes). Each time we needed to calculate the resources' current performance (in relation to data mining response times), we needed to run such benchmarks to acquire the real-time information.

The exact number of the resources' sampling that comprised the testing set (the number of the set of parameters equals the number of feature vectors used for training purposes) was 20 for each resource (Grid node) while another 5 samplings for each resource were used for evaluation purposes. All in all, our training set comprised of 160 input vectors, while our evaluation set of 40.

For each one of the training sets, a corresponding response time was extracted for a specific reference dataset.

The training of the network concluded in 31 epochs as can be seen in Figure 4.

The next step was to feed the evaluation sets in the network and simulate their operation, so as to receive the estimated response times for each resource. Then, the results had to be compared with the already known set.

The experiment concluded with the greatest deviation being equal to 0.156 and the smallest being equal to 0.0023 in absolute values. As in the data mining evaluation these values can be considered sufficient for the evaluation of our experiment.

## CONCLUSION

The value of this chapter lies mainly to the fact that it provides evidence that the relationship between applications and resources with QoS exists. This is of high importance when one considers modern heterogeneous and distributed service provisioning environments that are all the rage at these times. In a business service provisioning environment such as a Grid, a SOI or a more advanced internet version of them, that is, a Cloud, services can be seen as a combination of an application and a resource that may be totally disperse from both an administrative and a physical point of view. When this distinction is not clear (and this has appeared in the past due to the use of inflexible architectures), services are discreet combinations of applications on resources and QoS provisioning is dealt through service selection processes that in turn are coupled to discreet offer negotiation types, etc. In modern service-oriented architectures it is understood that quality of service is affected by the application characteristics, the resource characteristics and of course market parameters.

In such a complex environment, we presented that it is possible for a service provider to model the application and resource influence to the provided QoS and that this model can be used for doing resource allocation in order to satisfy the customer QoS requirements. By observing the changes in the QoS parameter in question and a good understanding of the application and the resource characteristics, we can isolate the parameters that affect QoS and use them to model the relationship between application and QoS and resource and QoS.

Of course, there are still many things to consider: Attempting to fully map a function of the type

$$f\left( app\ params, required\ QoS \right)\ = res\ params$$

would be the ideal case but this is a task of extreme difficulty and a high risk undertaking. First, we would need a model generic enough to cover all the applications and a respective one for all resources. Second, this function would yield a very complex relationship between the application parameters and the resource parameters, as it is very unlikely that there is a one-on-one relationship or that the function $f$ is a linear. Because of these reasons, we focused on realistic goals that will set the foundations for further research. We focused on data mining because we regard it as indicative of a great set of currently used applications (e-business) and specific resource types. We attempted to model the applications and resources by first making sure, through observation, that there is a relationship between the modeling parameters and the QoS. We focused on a single QoS parameter, that is response time, because it is easily measured and a common QoS demand to the majority of the provided services. However, we made sure that replication of the chapter outcomes will be easy for other cases. One can easily replace the resource or application parameters with the ones related to his own case. Also, one can reproduce the ANN training building his own mechanism, for other parameters than response time as long as he has conducted the appropriate measurements.

In the evaluation phase, considering the extent that our training samples were adequate for such an undertaking, the evaluation of the ANN operation implies that there is a dependence of the response time of a data mining service and the dataset and resource parameters. Of course we do not consider network latencies for the final delivery of the result to the service consumer. The abovementioned dependency has been mapped and in can be used as a mechanism for resource selection using response time predictions as an arbitrator. The cost of the prediction cannot be regarded as a serious overhead in the whole process because of low calculation times, especially when compared to the data mining algorithm execution times for real datasets.

## REFERENCES

Benkner, S., & Engelbrecht, G. (2006). A Generic QoS Infrastructure for Grid Web Services. *AICT-ICIW: Proceedings of the Advanced Int'l Conference on Telecommunications and Int'l Conference on Internet and Web Applications and Services* (p. 141). Washington, DC: IEEE Computer Society

Bradford, J. P., & Fortes, J. (1998). Performance and memory access characterization of data mining applications. *WWC: Proceedings of the Workload Characterization: Methodology and Case Studies* (p. 49). Washington, DC: IEEE Computer Society.

Chen, Y., Iyer, S., Liu, X., Milojicic, D., & Sahai, A. (2007). SLA Decomposition: Translating Service Level Objectives to System Level Thresholds. *International Conference on Autonomic Computing: Proceedings of the Fourth International Conference on Autonomic Computing* (p. 3). Washington, DC: IEEE Computer Society.

COPE. Corporate-Scale Resources Context-Sensitive Performance Modeling, EPSRC Project GR/L59610/01.

Czezowski, A., & Christen, P. (2002). *Performance Analysis of KDD Applications using Hardware Event Counters*. Retrieved May 15, 2009, from http://datamining.anu.edu.au/ talks/2002/cap2002-kdd.ps.gz

Floros, N., Meacham, K., Papay, J., & Surridge, M. (1999). Predictive Resource Management for Unitary Meta-Applications. *Future Generation Computer Systems, 15*(5-6), 723–734. doi:10.1016/S0167-739X(99)00022-9

GRIA. Grid Resources for Industrial Applications. Retrieved May 15, 2009, from www.gria.org

Han, J., & Kamber, M. (2006). *Data Mining: Concepts and Techniques*. Morgan Kaufmann

Hasselmeyer, P., Koller, B., Schubert, L., & Wieder, P. (2006). Towards SLA-Supported Resource Management. *Lecture Notes in Computer Science: Vol. 4208 High Performance Computer Communications*, 743–752.

He, Z., Peng, C., & Mok, A. (2006). A Performance Estimation Tool for Video Applications. *RTAS Proceedings of the 12th IEEE Real-Time and Embedded Technology and Applications Symposium* (pp. 267-276). Washington, DC: IEEE Computer Society.

Hey, T., Papay, J., & Surridge, M. (2005). The Role of Performance Engineering Techniques in the Context of the Grid. *Concurrency and Computation: Practice and Experience, 17*(2-4).), 297-316.

Jarvis, S. A., Spooner, D. P., Keung, H. N., Cao, J., Saini, S., & Nudd, G. R. (2006). Performance prediction and its use in parallel and distributed computing systems. *Future Generation Computer Systems, 22*(7), 745–754. doi:10.1016/j.future.2006.02.008

Kraiss, A., Schoen, F., Weikum, G., & Deppisch, U. (2001) Towards response time guarantees for e-service middleware, In C. Jensen, C., et al. (Eds.), *Extending Database Technology: Vol. 2287 Archive Proceedings of the 8th International Conference on Extending Database Technology: Advances in Database Technology* (pp. 58–63), London, UK: Springer-Verlag.

Lee, J. W., & Asanovic, K. (2006). METERG: Measurement-Based End-to-End Performance Estimation Technique in QoS-Capable Multi-processors. *RTAS Proceedings of the 12th IEEE Real-Time and Embedded Technology and Applications Symposium* (pp. 135-147). Washington, DC: IEEE Computer Society.

Marculescu, R., & Nandi, A. (2001). Probabilistic application modeling for system-level performance analysis. In W. Nebel, W., & A. Jerraya, A., (Eds.), *Design, Automation, and Test in Europe: Proceedings of the conference on Design, automation and test in Europe* (pp. 572–579). Piscataway, NJ: IEEE Press

Marculescu, R., Pedram, M., & Henkel, J. (2004) Distributed Multimedia System Design: A Holistic Perspective., *Design, Automation, and Test in Europe: Vol. 2 Proceedings of the conference on Design, automation and test in Europe* (pp. 21342). Washington, DC: IEEE Computer Society.

Meacham, K., Floros, N., & Surridge, M. (1998). Industrial Stochastic Simulations on a European Meta-Computer. In Pritchard, D., & Reeve, J.S., (Eds.), *Lecture Notes In Computer Science: Vol. 1470 Proceedings of the 4th International Euro-Par Conference on Parallel Processing* (pp. 1131-1139). London, UK: Springer-Verlag

Orlando, S., Palmerini, P., Perego, R., & Silvestri, F. (2002). Adaptive and Resource-Aware Mining of Frequent Itemsets. *ICDM: Proceedings of the 2002 IEEE International Conference on Data Mining* (pp. 338-345). Washington, DC: IEEE Computer Society.

Palmerini, P., Orlando, S., & Perego, R. (2004). Statistical Properties of Transactional Databases. *Symposium on Applied Computing: Proceedings of the 2004 ACM symposium on Applied computing* (pp. 515-519). New York: ACM

Perego, R., Orlando, S., & Palmerini, P. (2001). Enhancing the Apriori Algorithm for Frequent Set Counting. In G. Goos, J. Hartmanis, & J. van Leeuwen (Eds.). ), *Lecture Notes In Computer Science: Vol. 2114 Proceedings of Third International Conference on Data Warehousing and Knowledge Discovery* (pp 71-82). Springer Berlin / Heidelberg

Petriu, D., Amer, H., Majumdar, S., & Abdull-Fatah, I. (2000) Using analytic models for predicting middleware performance., In M. Woodside, M. et al. (Ed.), *Workshop on Software and Performance: Proceedings of the 2nd international workshop on Software and performance* (pp. 189-194), New York: ACM Ping, W. An Introduction to Artificial Neural Networks. Lecture Notes. Retrieved May 15, 2009, from http://www.physiol.net/study/resource/pdf/An%20Introduction%20to%20Artificial%20Neural%20Networks.ppt

Risse, T., Wombacher, A., Surridge, M., Taylor, S., & Aberer, K. (2001). Online Scheduling in Distributed Message Converter Systems. In Gonzalez, T., (Ed.), *Parallel and distributed computing and systems: proceedings of the IASTED international conference* (pp. 177-184), California: ACTA Press.

Strube, A., Rexachs, D., & Luque, E. (2008). Software probes: Towards a quick method for machine characterization and application performance prediction. *Proceedings of the 2008 International Symposium on Parallel and Distributed Computing* (pp. 23-30). Washington, DC: IEEE Computer Society

Surridge, M., Taylor, S., De Roure, D., & Zaluska, E. (2005). Experiences with GRIA-Industrial Applications on a Web Services Grid. In *E-SCIENCE: Proceedings of the First International Conference on e-Science and Grid Computing* (pp. 98-105). Washington, DC: IEEE Computer Society. TAPAS, Trusted and QoS-Aware Provision of Application Services. Retrieved May 15, 2009, from http://tapas.sourceforge.net

Vazhkudai, S., Schopf, J. M., & Foster, I. (2002). Predicting the performance of wide area data transfers. *Proceedings of the 16th International Parallel and Distributed Processing Symposium* (pp. 34-43). Washington, DC: IEEE Computer Society. Wikipedia. *Subsets of e-business applications*. Retrieved May 15, 2009, from http://en.wikipedia.org/wiki/E-business#Subsets

Wolski, R., Spring, N., & Hayes, J. (1999). The Network Weather Service: A Distributed Resource Performance Forecasting Service for Metacomputing. *Future Generation Computer Systems, 15*(5-6), 757–768. doi:10.1016/S0167-739X(99)00025-4

Woodside, C. M., & Menascé, D. A. (2006). Guest Editors' Introduction: Application-Level QoS. *IEEE Internet Computing, 10*(3), 13–15. doi:10.1109/MIC.2006.49

## APPENDIX (Figure 5 and Figure 6)

*Figure 5. Collected data from the sample datasets. The values in the left remain blank for readability purposes, however it is sufficient to mention that they remain constant as the support threshold is altered to a number of distinct values*

| Dataset | Total number of Transactions | Total number of items | Average length of transactions | Average support of items | Variance of the support | Support Threshold | 1th order normalized entropy | 2nd order normalized entropy | 1st order normalized LIS | 2nd order normalized LIS | Computing Time |
|---|---|---|---|---|---|---|---|---|---|---|---|
| accidents | 340183 | 468 | 33,8079 | 24574,5 | 3,90586E+09 | | | | | | |
| | | | | | | 0 | 0,731177 | 0,41606 | 0,560772 | 1 | - |
| | | | | | | 0,05 | 0,668302 | 0,310363 | 0,0280085 | 0,198655 | 7700 |
| | | | | | | 0,1 | 0,600973 | 0,246904 | 0,0150041 | 0,154194 | 1179,75 |
| | | | | | | 0,2 | 0,499806 | 0,173207 | 0,00609597 | 0,113301 | 114,62 |
| | | | | | | 0,5 | 0,336703 | 0,0838063 | 0,00109184 | 0,0426965 | 11,86 |
| | | | | | | 0,9 | 0,0835467 | 0,00565686 | 1,60208E-05 | 0,00467384 | 10,61 |
| chess | 3196 | 75 | 37 | 1576,69 | 1209420 | | | | | | |
| | | | | | | 0 | 0,932864 | 0,510328 | 0,15979 | 0,999281 | - |
| | | | | | | 0,05 | 0,924428 | 0,494991 | 0,0919015 | 0,323483 | - |
| | | | | | | 0,1 | 0,912131 | 0,476221 | 0,0688002 | 0,212555 | - |
| | | | | | | 0,2 | 0,878432 | 0,432588 | 0,0456134 | 0,176141 | - |
| | | | | | | 0,5 | 0,710426 | 0,269599 | 0,0143806 | 0,0483476 | 7,59 |
| | | | | | | 0,9 | 0,286794 | 0,0444496 | 0,000724783 | 0,00962904 | 0,13 |
| mushroom | 8124 | 119 | 23 | 1570,18 | 3727000 | | | | | | |
| | | | | | | 0 | 0,862593 | 0,49262 | 0,306558 | 0,769017 | - |
| | | | | | | 0,05 | 0,817147 | 0,414603 | 0,103431 | 0,293965 | 17,9 |
| | | | | | | 0,1 | 0,756701 | 0,329659 | 0,0603347 | 0,221827 | 2,89 |
| | | | | | | 0,2 | 0,670894 | 0,2215 | 0,0365694 | 0,171881 | 1,07 |
| | | | | | | 0,5 | 0,293327 | 0,0429071 | 0,00429881 | 0,0631926 | 0,2 |
| | | | | | | 0,9 | 0,111565 | 0,00582825 | 0,000123808 | 0,00596116 | 0,18 |
| pumsb | 49046 | 2113 | 74 | 1717,65 | 44371600 | | | | | | |
| | | | | | | 0 | 0,694433 | 0,397598 | 0,631012 | 1 | - |
| | | | | | | 0,05 | 0,584075 | 0,286707 | 0,00989888 | 0,232194 | - |
| | | | | | | 0,1 | 0,552314 | 0,257133 | 0,00556881 | 0,208895 | - |
| | | | | | | 0,2 | 0,514406 | 0,219366 | 0,00350955 | 0,146159 | - |
| | | | | | | 0,5 | 0,324581 | 0,0842213 | 0,000620705 | 0,0576024 | 1814,92 |
| | | | | | | 0,9 | 0,147319 | 0,0159841 | 3,54708E-05 | 0,00691143 | 7,88 |
| pumsb_star | 49046 | 2088 | 50,4821 | 1185,8 | 20920400 | | | | | | |
| | | | | | | 0 | 0,703527 | 0,400579 | 0,638498 | 1 | - |
| | | | | | | 0,05 | 0,548635 | 0,235267 | 0,00994824 | 232194 | - |
| | | | | | | 0,1 | 0,504569 | 0,195682 | 0,00556632 | 0,208948 | - |
| | | | | | | 0,2 | 0,452333 | 0,145257 | 0,00348241 | 0,132347 | - |
| | | | | | | 0,5 | 0,193617 | 0,013978 | 0,000558972 | 0,0547527 | 7,11 |
| | | | | | | 0,9 | 0 | 0 | 0 | 0 | 2,99 |
| retail | 88162 | 16470 | 10,3058 | 55,1655 | 322746 | | | | | | |
| | | | | | | 0 | 0,804335 | 0,492162 | 0,784911 | 0,999998 | - |
| | | | | | | 0,05 | 0,0551246 | 0,00270939 | 5,08705E-05 | 0,172453 | 1,26 |
| | | | | | | 0,1 | 0,0524307 | 0,00186516 | 3,49737E-05 | 0,17038 | 1,26 |
| | | | | | | 0,2 | 0,031249 | 0,000835189 | 6,88931E-06 | 0,0972163 | 1,25 |
| | | | | | | 0,5 | 0,0165809 | 0 | 2,95262E-06 | 0 | 1,25 |
| | | | | | | 0,9 | 0 | 0 | 0 | 0 | 1,18 |
| T10I4D100K | 100000 | 870 | 10,1023 | 1161.18 | 1266130 | | | | | | |
| | | | | | | 0 | 0,940332 | 0,482939 | 0,434275 | 0,997671 | - |
| | | | | | | 0,05 | 0,0452423 | 0 | 0,00280915 | 0 | 1,22 |
| | | | | | | 0,1 | 0 | 0 | 0 | 0 | 1,13 |
| | | | | | | 0,2 | 0 | 0 | 0 | 0 | 1,13 |
| | | | | | | 0,5 | 0 | 0 | 0 | 0 | 1,13 |
| | | | | | | 0,9 | 0 | 0 | 0 | 0 | 1,13 |
| T40I10D100K | 100000 | 942 | 39,6051 | 4204,36 | 15289100 | | | | | | |
| | | | | | | 0 | 0,94391 | 0,494097 | 0,321382 | 0,960683 | - |
| | | | | | | 0,05 | 0,587354 | 0,000429413 | 0,0694802 | 0,248029 | 5,58 |
| | | | | | | 0,1 | 0,231026 | 0 | 0,0153332 | 0 | 4,52 |
| | | | | | | 0,2 | 0,0218824 | 0 | 0,000679233 | 0 | 4,34 |
| | | | | | | 0,5 | 0 | 0 | 0 | 0 | 4,18 |
| | | | | | | 0,9 | 0 | 0 | 0 | 0 | 4,21 |

*Figure 6. Values of the parameters for 5 resources at the time of measurement*

| Parameter description | Parameter value range | Resource 1 | Resource 2 | Resource 3 | Resource 4 | Resource 5 |
|---|---|---|---|---|---|---|
| Million Floating Operations per second | (MFLOPs) | 2483 | 2146 | 9262 | 13726 | 10104 |
| Bus clock | (MHz) | 400 | 333 | 800 | 400 | 400 |
| Cache average I/O bandwidth | (Mbytes/second) | 3538 | 3477 | 9271 | 9957 | 10258 |
| Memory average I/O bandwidth | (Mbytes/second) | 1729 | 1840 | 2937 | 2937 | 5091 |
| Disk average I/O bandwidth | (Kbytes/second) | 24 | 19 | 29 | 31 | 29 |
| Send communication bandwidth | (Kbytes/second) | 8940 | 534 | 8934 | 8910 | 8840 |
| Send communication latency | (µs) | 400 | 489 | 400 | 400 | 400 |
| Receive communication bandwidth | (Kbytes/second) | 9123 | 535 | 9012 | 9024 | 8996 |
| Receive communication latency | (µs) | 400 | 470 | 400 | 400 | 400 |
| Minimum Free Memory | (Mbytes) | 496 | 393 | 693 | 693 | 504 |
| Minimum Free Disk Space | (Kbytes) | 37 | 80 | 120 | 120 | 120 |
| Queue time interval | (seconds) | 0,03 | 0,023 | 0,029 | 0,024 | 0,025 |
| SMP (number of processors): | number | 1 | 1 | 1 | 1 | 1 |
| Cache total | (Mbytes) | 1 | 0,25 | 1 | 0,5 | 1 |
| Minimum Free Video Memory | (Mbytes) | 14 | 32 | 32 | 32 | 32 |
| Maximum Resolution/vert. refresh rate | (Pixels x Hertz) | 0,786432 | 1,6 | 1,6 | 1,6 | 1,6 |
| Color depth | (Bits) | 32 | 32 | 32 | 32 | 32 |
| Sound Card Maximum Standard Sampling Bits | (Bits) | 16 | 24 | 24 | 24 | 24 |
| Sound Card Maximum Standard Sampling Rate | (KHz) | 96 | 192 | 192 | 192 | 192 |
| Mean Time Between Errors = error free sec | (seconds) | 100.000 | 118000 | 118000 | 100000 | 100000 |

*This work was previously published in International Journal of Distributed Systems and Technologies, Volume 1, Issue 1, edited by Nik Bessis, pp. 55-75, copyright 2010 by IGI Publishing (an imprint of IGI Global).*

# Section 2
# State-of-the-Art Middleware Technologies and Architectures

# Chapter 7
# The Crystal Ball in HPC has Never Been More Exciting, nor More Important

**Pierre Kuonen**
*University of Applied Sciences of Western Switzerland, Switzerland*

**Marie-Christine Sawley**
*Swiss Federal Institute of Technology Zurich, Switzerland*

## INTRODUCTION

Foresight in HPC is not merely a question of when Petaflop, or Exa- applications will be available. A much deeper view is fundamental for understanding the accompanying driving forces –both present and future-, and for making important choices based on the most relevant criteria. The SOS workshop series established in 1997 aims at bringing together once a year scientists and industries from all over the world to discuss and to envision the future of HPC technologies. These meetings have proved invaluable for discussing the state of the art and for anticipating future major developments in the field.

We propose here a brief review of the history of HPC since the foundation of SOS and of the impact of the major trends and possible disruptions envisioned for the next five years.

DOI: 10.4018/978-1-4666-0906-8.ch007

## A BRIEF REVIEW OF THE PREVIOUS DECADE

### 1997-2002: The Hope of Home Made HPC Machines

The origin of the SOS workshop series has to be found in 1997. Until then, HPC had been dominated by twenty years of vector computing. At the time, Massively Parallel Processing (MPP) model emerged as the driving force for the decade which was starting. Back in those days, the MPP model was incarnated by two tendencies: the CRAY T3E, which was holding strong positions in the Top500 with six machines, and the HPC cluster made of "commodity processors": Number One was the ASCI Red system at Sandia Labs which had just conquered the Teraflops blue ribbon. That machine still holds today the record of longevity as Number One with seven nominations, from June 97 until November 01: an unusually long time, revealing the difficulties many vendors encountered and how hard the transition had been.

Scientists and engineers from Sandia Lab, Oak Ridge and EPFL sat together during summer 1997 as they were seeking for the most suitable technologies, interconnect, topologies and solutions needed for building their next HPC cluster using commoditized computing elements. The idea was to benchmark their respective solution and as much as possible contribute to the cross fertilization for the next generation systems. The following editions of the workshop provided excellent opportunities for focusing on software development, programming models and parallel compilers, as well as on the effort of writing codes that could help solving leading edge science problems.

## 2002-2005: The Era of the Ecosystem

The announcement of the Japanese Earth Simulator, the first non-US Number one of the Top500 marked a new chapter: with a Linpack rate of 41 Tflops, this highly efficient machine was able to run a real, complete application at 35 Tflops. At the same time, we could observe that the number and quality of computational scientists developing community software had grown significantly and that these new groups used entry level clusters to access the arena. In return, they expected their software to be able to scale on a larger machine, as similar as possible to that on which they had been using while developing the code. The Top10 has since shown an aggregation around two or three driving solutions, slightly differing replica of mainstream architectures. New problematic emerged with the massive increase of number of components: individual failures or data corruptions, impacting the correct execution of a task. This gave rise to new areas of research in Computer Science such as fault tolerance and resilience.

This decade was characterized by what was in those years coined as the "Ecosystem" a fertile environment on different parts of which the scientific tasks are shipped according to performance, production campaigns or development phases. In spite of its admirable achievement, the Earth Simulator was scarce of an irrigation system and of vast soil where new applications can be rooted and nurtured. This relative isolation played certainly a role in keeping the segment of vector computer narrow and which has dwindled then.

## 2005-2009: The Manycore Era; in the Meantime, MPP Systems Came Back

By 2004, mainstream HPC was solidly anchored around the MPP and cluster architecture. Fine grain, granular parallel MPP have taken a large portion of the top end market with the strong presence of both Blue Gene and Cray XT systems in enviable positions. Computing elements started to be packed at a growing density, with the emergence of blades first, and multicore solutions made their entry with ITANIUM2 and POWER4 in 2001. Today, the canonical machine is built around 4 cores, soon to go up to 6 or 8. The difficulty of programming these multi-core systems can be really steep: programming models and algorithms have yet to take full advantage of the multiplication of the computing cores without paying a too high price to memory wall problem or data locality.

## TODAY'S SITUATION

As of today two systems have crossed the psychological barrier of the Petaflop systems: Roadrunner –AMD Opteron accelerated by IBM PowerXCell- at LLNL and Jaguar –CRAY XT5- at ORNL. Psychological, because there are no real difference between an application running at 0.99 PF and one at 1.01, except for the large satisfaction of changing the prefix! Major problematic and significant steps forward happen in conjunction to major changes in paradigma of HPC. But changes can be delusive in this area as they can be quiet when influenced by the base of the "ecosystem", as it happened with the Beowulf revolution.

As of mid-2009, the bulk of HPC systems –below the Top50- is made of quad-core Xeon-Linux, MPI and Infiniband as interconnect. Vendors are striving to propose new solutions based on many cores less prone to performance degradations due memory bandwidth limitations – a revitalization of IA64 or vector features for codes that need that sort of performance.

A number of pioneering groups are trying to use GPU as accelerators. Its is interesting to note that this device was conceived originally to procure a more realistic rendering visual capacity used in video games by simulating the physics of the object: texture, reflection, crash deformation…; a welcome, albeit unexpected, cross-fertilization. We will see if this interest persists, as it can provide a number of alternative solutions for highly specific tasks making the best use of its extreme data parallelism capacity, but is hard to program. Again, its capacity to interact with vast ecosystem in the medium term will determine its future.

In Europe, the establishment of the PRACE consortium will undoubtedly open a period of relative stability for software developers around 2 or 3 architecture families. There will be the need to capitalize on large investments provided by public funding to this end –between 0.5 and 1 billion Euros-, this will play its role in the stabilization around this handful of architectures for 5 to 7 years. In Japan, the final architecture of the Kei Soku Keisanki system has become unclear following the withdrawal of NEC and Hitachi from the project in May 2009, but news need to be followed as Japan industry and scientists have proven they can do extremely well once the focus and ultimate goal has been chosen.

## WHAT ABOUT THE FUTURE?

Two major facts will greatly impact development of HPC technologies during the next decade. First on the point of view of hardware it is largely recognized in the HPC community that currently used technologies will not allow to scale up to the exaflops ($10^{18}$ floating points operations per second). Second, today and future applications will be more and more multi-science and heterogeneous compared to traditional today applications based on the "flat parallel" programming model as generated by domain decomposition approach and the MPI programming model. As applications become more "multi-science", they will also rely more and more on combination of both advanced simulation models and use of extremely large set of complex data coming from experiments or observations; this will require new programming model paradigms, better algorithms for iterative solvers and innovative ways to regulate the workflow between the different components. To oversimplify, the combination of powerful numerical models –as used for example by weather forecasters-, and of extremely performing tools for analyzing mass of data collected by observation or experimentations - such as the LHC- will give the key for solving future challenges in major areas of science. Technology developments catering for the Top end will be driven by this extremely powerful interaction, at the crossroad between modelling and data analysis.

In addition we can remark that the effort of code development will be significantly supported in the 7th Call of FP7 of the European Research framework due for the end of 2009, confirming the fact that software and algorithms will be major part of the infrastructure. Significant and new driving forces may be emerging.

Through computer modelling and simulation there are unprecedented opportunities in the next decade to tackle important problems that are orders-of-magnitude more complex than those that can be investigated today. Multi-simulation-based research has indeed become a new branch of knowledge creation, combining the best of scientific theory, computer science and applied mathematics that allow us to explore and understand complex systems behaviour with minimum intrusion.

## CONCLUSION

In this last twelve years, the HPC community learnt much about over expectations, about the reality of what technology can bring but even more importantly, learnt about its own inner strengths. HPC, numerical simulation and data analysis have become essential to all areas of science. Observing past developments gives us the chance to glance into the future: architectures may be specialized, but they have to be interconnected with all the other parts of the value chain; codes need to be developed on mainstream systems –canonical department server as it is known in the academic world- in order to be enriched with new science and shared; finally, the highest value is to be found in people's mind and ultimately, in the software (both application and computer science development) where generations of PhD students and scientists deposit their scientific knowledge. Literacy in IT architecture, simulation or analysis has become essential for young scientists and will play a major role in their professional life; the education they are receiving will shape the HPC world in which they will be evolving. HPC will continue to be driven by time or cost critical missions, leading edge science and by the forefront in computer science and technology; but its capacity to absorb and digest the value of data from previous massive simulations, experimentations and observations will determine the success.

Therefore, the strong dialog between computer scientists, computational scientists and vendors will be key for addressing those challenges. The first community innovates in compilers, OS, computer architecture and software stacks; the second takes such new features and creates numerical algorithms at the forefront of sciences, making significant progresses in their field; the last produces extremely powerful prototype and benefits of a formidable test bed for its newest technology. In this view, the SOS workshops series will remain a major place for allowing scientists and industries to discuss and delineate the future of HPC.

Scientists who introduced their work during the last SOS workshops present five papers in this edition. They represent well the topics discussed during these workshops and offer a good insight about major problematic that will affect us in the near future: exascale software including HPC software stack, leadership class architecture at the origin of a successful product, application performance and simulation of a complete HPC architecture.

For more information on the SOS workshop series please consult: http://gridgroup.hefr.ch/sos

# Chapter 8
# On the Path to Exascale

**Ken Alvin**
*Sandia National Laboratories, USA*

**Brian Barrett**
*Sandia National Laboratories, USA*

**Ron Brightwell**
*Sandia National Laboratories, USA*

**Sudip Dosanjh**
*Sandia National Laboratories, USA*

**Al Geist**
*Oak Ridge National Laboratory, USA*

**Scott Hemmert**
*Sandia National Laboratories, USA*

**Michael Heroux**
*Sandia National Laboratories, USA*

**Doug Kothe**
*Oak Ridge National Laboratory, USA*

**Richard Murphy**
*Sandia National Laboratories, USA*

**Jeff Nichols**
*Oak Ridge National Laboratory, USA*

**Ron Oldfield**
*Sandia National Laboratories, USA*

**Arun Rodrigues**
*Sandia National Laboratories, USA*

**Jeffrey S. Vetter**
*Oak Ridge National Laboratory, USA*

## ABSTRACT

*There is considerable interest in achieving a 1000 fold increase in supercomputing power in the next decade, but the challenges are formidable. In this chapter, the authors discuss some of the driving science and security applications that require Exascale computing (a million, trillion operations per second). Key architectural challenges include power, memory, interconnection networks and resilience. The chapter summarizes ongoing research aimed at overcoming these hurdles. Topics of interest are architecture aware and scalable algorithms, system simulation, 3D integration, new approaches to system-directed resilience and new benchmarks. Although significant progress is being made, a broader international program is needed.*

DOI: 10.4018/978-1-4666-0906-8.ch008

# INTRODUCTION

In 1997 Intel's ASCI Red broke the Teraflops barrier, achieving over 1 trillion floating point operations per second (Heermann, 1998). Last year both IBM's Roadrunner and Cray's Jaguar system surpassed 1 PetaFLOPS or 1,000 TeraFLOPS (Feldman, 2008). The next factor of 1000 improvement in supercomputing performance (Exascale) will be even more challenging. The primary driver for the architectural change underway is that clock speeds are increasingly constrained by power and cooling limits. All of the major chip manufactures are moving to multi-core architectures, which results in the addition of hierarchical parallelism to supercomputers. Oak Ridge National Laboratory's Cray Jaguar system has 18,688 nodes, each comprised of two quad core AMD Opterons. Roadrunner is a one of a kind supercomputer composed of 6480 dual core AMD Opterons, each connected to two IBM PowerXCell 8i processors, which are similar to the processor used in Sony's Playstation 3 (Kahle, 2005). Both of these systems demonstrate that the transition to multi-core is already a key design challenge for supercomputer architectures.

The memory wall is defined as the mismatch between CPU and memory performance (latency, chip I/O capabilities, etc.), and will continue to plague processor design. Today's applications are primarily limited by data movement, represented by the statement "FLOPS are free" (Shiva, 2005). Power budgets continue to increase, which will result in power requirements in excess of 100 MW if existing Petascale design methodologies are used for an Exascale system. It is unlikely that such a system would be built unless power demands can be decreased significantly. Additionally, resilience will limit the availability of such systems. The current method for recovering from faults is check-pointing – at various times during a calculation a restart file is written to disk. Given weak scaling, I/O bandwidth requirements scale with the memory size and inversely with the mean time between interrupts (which decreases with increasing parts counts). Since Exascale will require millions of nodes, the mean time between interrupts will decrease and check-pointing will become an impractical mechanism for fault recovery.

These challenges require new approaches to applications, algorithms, system software, and computer architecture, which has been noted by the numerous workshops and reports devoted to the problem (Kogge et al., 2008; Simon et al., 2007). The remainder of the chapter discusses science and security applications that require Exascale computing, architectural challenges, and ongoing work aimed at overcoming some of these obstacles.

# APPLICATIONS

Scientific computing is essential to the advancement of numerous fields of study. Never before have we been able to accurately anticipate, analyze, and plan for complex events that have not occurred—from the operation of a reactor running at 100 million degrees to future changes in climate. Combined with the more traditional approaches of theory and experiment, scientific computing provides a profound tool for insight as we look at complex systems containing billions of components.

# SCIENCE

Key areas of scientific research, including materials science, Earth science, energy assurance, fundamental science, biology and medicine, engineering design, and security can benefit from continued growth in high performance computing (to Exascale and beyond). Table 1 summarizes scientific opportunities that can be enabled by Exascale computing, key application areas, and the goals and associated benefits.

The system and application-wide advances required to reach Exascale are not inevitable, and require a fundamental rethinking across all aspects of High Performance Computing (HPC).

## MATERIAL SCIENCE

Materials science drivers, objectives, and impacts that are enabled by Exascale leadership platforms have been identified in Table 2 (Department of Energy, 2007).

## EARTH SCIENCE

Earth science and climate change research will focus on two principal activities in the decade ahead:

- *Mitigation:* Evaluating strategies and informing policy decisions for climate stabilization; and

- *Adaptation:* Preparing for committed climate change with decadal forecasts and region impacts.

Simulations of 100–1,000 years will be typical for mitigation activities, while shorter simulations of 10–100 years will be used for adaptation. Each set of simulations must be predictive and quantifiable in order to reliably inform policy makers. The requirements for computing can be tied to these activities and goals, as shown in Table 1. For example, estimates call for compute factors $10^{10}$–$10^{12}$ greater than those available today to meet goals for spatial resolution, model completeness, simulation times, and breadth and depth of ensembles and scenarios.

Climate models are currently more reliable at short times scales and long, asymptotic scales. Since many of the questions to be answered are targeted in the 20–50 year range, the ability of models to provide reliable forecasts will be challenged.

*Table 1. The promise of exascale computing*

| Opportunity | Key application areas | Goal and benefit |
|---|---|---|
| Materials science | Nanoscale science; material lifecycles, response and failure; and manufacturing | Design, characterize, and manufacture materials, down to the nanoscale, tailored and optimized for specific applications |
| Earth science | Weather, carbon management, climate change mitigation and adaptation, environment | Understand the complex biogeochemical cycles that underpin global ecosystems and control the sustainability of life on Earth |
| Energy assurance | Fossil, fusion, combustion, nuclear fuel cycle, chemical catalysis, renewables (wind, solar, hydro), bioenergy, energy efficiency, energy storage and transmission, transportation, buildings | Attain, without costly disruption, the energy required for economically viable, and environmentally benign ways to satisfy residential, commercial, and transportation requirements |
| Fundamental science | High energy physics, nuclear physics, astrophysics, accelerator physics | Decipher and comprehend the core laws governing the universe and unravel its origins |
| Biology and medicine | Proteomics, drug design, systems biology | Understand connections from individual proteins through whole cells into ecosystems and environments |
| National security | Disaster management, homeland security, defense systems, public policy | Analyze, design, stress-test, and optimize critical systems such as communications, homeland security, and defense systems; understand and uncover human behavioral systems underlying asymmetric operation environments |
| Engineering design | Industrial and manufacturing processes | Design, deploy, and operate safe and economical structures, machines, processes, and systems with reduced concept-to-deployment time |

*Table 2. Select materials science drivers for leadership applicatoins at exascale*

| Application area | Science driver | Science objective | Impact |
|---|---|---|---|
| Nanoscale science | First principles design of increasingly complex materials with specific, targeted properties | Understand and use isolated nanostructures to design materials made out of nano-building blocks | Smart materials for nanoelectronics, photo voltaics, information technology, and medicine |
| | Predictive description of microscopic behavior of water to understand systems in aqueous environments | Perform molecular dynamics with forces found with Quantum Monte Carlo computations | Detailed understanding of the structure of water—fundamental understanding of biological systems. |
| | Understand synthesis of alloy nanoparticles with potential impact for design of new catalysts | Define the thermodynamics of compositions of alloy nanoparticles | Magnetic data storage Economically viable ethanol production Energy storage via structural transitions in nanoparticles |
| | Physics of strongly correlated electron materials | Explain the fundamental mechanism of high-temperature superconductivity, including materials specificity and inhomogeneities | New materials for practical applications in oxide electronics and next-generation power transmission |

The Earth Science community has also done well in articulating what it believes to be attainable biogeochemical objectives over the next decade (Department of Energy, 2007):

- Integrated models and measurements of biogeochemical cycles;
- Development of next-generation ecological models; and
- Better theory for and quantification of uncertainty.

Climate science opportunities at the Exascale are abundant (Hack and Bierly, 2007):

- Decadal prediction on regional scales (accuracy in global models);
- Climate extremes (heat waves, drought, floods, synoptic events, etc.);
- Climate variability (low-frequency variability);
- Water cycle (particularly in the tropics);
- Human-induced impacts on carbon cycle;
- Sea-level rise (melting of the Greenland and Antarctic ice sheets); and
- Abrupt climate change.

The rate limiters above are decadal prediction, abrupt climate change, and climate variability.

## SECURITY

Nuclear weapons provide an application driver for high performance computing and advanced simulation in the security. The complexity of nuclear weapons design, certification and assessment requires a combination of the most advanced computational and experimental science, even during the era of underground nuclear testing. Presently, under the nuclear testing moratorium and the U.S. Stockpile Stewardship Program (SSP), advanced computational simulation has come to play a significant and foundational role in stewardship of the U.S. nuclear stockpile, as led by the Department of Energy's Advanced Simulation and Computing Program (ASC)

The most significant application needs for Exascale simulation are the assessment and certification of nuclear explosive package performance, full system safety, and weapon survivability in nuclear environments. These simulations involve highly coupled, nonlinear multi-physics with three-dimensional features, multi-scale phenomena, and inherent variability in materials and manufacturing processes. By the end of the first decade of ASC, it was possible to move from two-dimensional to three-dimensional nuclear performance simulations with "standard" mesh resolutions and calibrated physics. This required achieving the goal of 100 tera-flops of integrated hardware and software capability. It is now estimated that, to replace existing ad-hoc physics models, we must increase average mesh spacing in each spatial dimension by an order of magnitude, incorporate more sophisticated, multi-scale model-based physics, and quantify uncertainties in those physical models. The increase in spatial resolution increases computational needs by at least a factor of 1000, while improved physics models are estimated to increase computational needs by an additional factor of 100. Finally, the costs of estimating uncertainties can be expected to results in suites of computations, ranging from 100s to 1000s of realizations of the uncertain system parameters. This final class of computational demand may not directly multiply the previous contributions, with the development of more sophisticated sampling and model reduction techniques. However, even conservative estimates of needed model evaluations increases computational needs by a least an additional order of magnitude.

Additionally, we see emerging application areas in Informatics, where the goal is to examine very large data sets (from direct observation or the output of simulations) to ask new questions, form hypotheses, or generate new understanding. These emerging Informatics applications show significantly more difficult data movement properties than do traditional 3D Physics applications, and represent a critical challenge for the Exascale era.

## ARCHITECTURAL CHALLENGES

The architectural challenges for reaching Exascale are dominated by power, memory, interconnection networks, and resilience. There are also significant software challenges including the need for new programming models, latency and bandwidth tolerant techniques, fault-tolerant methods, and algorithms that are scalable to millions and perhaps billions of threads (see the discussion of architecture aware algorithms under ongoing research).

### Power

Power is the dominant constraint for Exascale computing. Already, current installations consume tens of megawatts. Many large organizations have relocated their datacenters to areas providing cheap electricity. Though shrinking feature size helps to alleviate these requirements, high-end HPC machines have outpaced Moore's law, resulting in an upward trend in power requirements. The sheer scale of a machine performing one exa-operation per second (i.e., $10^{18}$ operations/second) means that if individual operations each require a single picojoule (1 pJ=$10^{-12}$ J) of energy, a total of one megawatt of power will be required.

Extrapolating current power consumption trends into the Exascale timeframe (2018 for the purposes of this chapter) yields startling trends. It is estimated that in the 2018 time frame a single floating point operation will require 10 pJ of energy (Kogge et al., 2008). This assumes the operands are already present at the floating point unit and does not include moving the data to or from a register file. Using the Cacti 5.1 tool (Thoziyoor et al., 2008), and extrapolating to the 18nm technology node, a 32K L1 cache would consume 31 pJ and a 512K L2 96 pJ per access. In addition to floating point and cache access, a processor core must also perform instruction fetch and decode, integer operations for bookkeeping and data management, and drive its control path. This can require substantial power. A MIPS64 5Kc processor, designed for low power consumption still consumes 490 pJ per cycle at 90nm (MIPS Technologies, Inc., 2007). A 32-bit ARM11 processor consumes 180 pJ/bit at 130nm. Adjusting to 64bit and assuming a linear extrapolation, these processor cores would require 50-90pJ/cycle in an 18nm process.

Based on HPC workload analysis (Murphy et al., 2009) and the above estimates, we consider two possible cases of instruction mix and cache performance to calculate processor power consumption (see Table 3) to be 118-125 pJ per average operation. For an Exa-op machine, this would become 118-125 MW.

DRAM requirements for an Exascale machine will also be large. In 2018 it is estimated that DRAM density will be 16GB/chip (ITRS, 2007). 300 Petabytes of DRAM storage would require 18 to 21 million chips depending on ECC. If we assume DRAM chip power to be at 260-450mW – based on current chips (Micron technology, 2007) and assuming a drop to 1.0V – an Exascale memory system would require 5.5-9.5MW. Again, this assumes an extrapolation of current technologies, which will likely not provide sufficient bandwidth to future massively multi-core processors.

Network requirements are discussed in more detail as part of the discussion of Architectural Challenges. If we assume 8,192 to 32,768 routers, each capable of routing 77.8 Tb/sec and 128K-512K 1.2Tb/sec network endpoints, we have a unidirectional system bandwidth of 790.9 to 3,163.8 Pb/sec. Current long distance electrical interconnect can operate at 30 pJ/bit (bidirectional) (Kogge et al., 2008). It should be quite feasible to reach 10 pJ/bit by 2018, resulting in a total network power of 4.0-15.6MW

This results in a total system power of 79.3 to 142.0 MW (See Table 4). It should be noted that this does not include archival storage, cooling, a RAS monitoring system, the internal router power and many other necessary system components.

From 2007 to 1987 commercial power rates ranged from 9.2-12.0 cents per KWH in real 2008 dollars (DOE, 2007). Thus, one Watt-year costs $0.80 to $1.05, or one megawatt-year is $800,000 to $1,050,000. This would mean that a conventionally constructed Exascale machine would cost between $63.4 million and $149.1 million a year simply to keep powered. Again, this ignores cooling, power conversion, and other probably inefficiencies. Clearly, power will become a limiting factor in designing an Exascale machine.

## Memory

Data movement has been the dominant performance bottleneck for all electronic computer systems since their invention in the mid 1940s. Today's HPC systems are no different (Murphy, 2007; Murphy & Kogge, 2007). As discussed in the Power and Packaging Section, data movement, particularly "far" remote accesses will dominate the power requirements for all levels of the memory hierarchy. Within a node, analysis of applications shows that even for scientific codes, most of the instructions executed are not floating point, but memory and integer instructions, and that most of the integer instructions are computing memory addresses (See Figure 1). Furthermore, today's dominant MPP architecture does a poor job of exposing the memory hierarchy beyond a single node to fine-grain data access. While Partitioned Global Address Space (PGAS) mechanisms in software and hardware may exist in modern supercomputers, these mechanisms provide very little capability to do anything other than copy

*Table 3. HPC workload characteristics and processor power*

| % FP instructions | % Load/Store | L1 Hit Rate | Energy/op |
|---|---|---|---|
| 10% | 50% | 90% | 69.8 pJ |
| 5% | 60% | 80% | 116.9 pJ |

*Table 4. Total system power requirements*

|  | Low (MW) | High (MW) |
|---|---|---|
| Processor | 69.8 | 116.9 |
| DRAM Memory | 5.5 | 9.5 |
| Network | 4.0 | 15.6 |
| **Total** | **79.3** | **142.0** |

data throughout the system. Worse, most node-to-node copies must be performed in a coarse grained fashion, creating bursty communication patterns and forcing the programmer to explicitly manage copies (even in a PGAS environment).

Fundamental technology imbalances between processor and memory systems, combined with large memory footprints required by many applications typically produce low Instruction Per Cycle (IPC) measures on modern processors, often significantly less than one. This inefficiency is primarily dominated by a lack of concurrency and overabundance of latency in modern memory systems (Murphy, 2007). Creating a more balanced system is one of the key challenges in reducing power to enable Exascale machines.

Finally, while mechanisms for synchronization, atomic operations, and transactions may exist in small-scale cache coherent environments, there are no lightweight analogues to these mechanisms available on MPPs. Performing operation at a distance, minimizing unnecessary data copies, and enabling fine-grained operation will be required to optimize both power and performance.

Figure 2 summarizes the results of Murphy and Kogge (2007), and measures three key data movement and memory access pattern properties for applications: the Spatial Locality (or use of data "near" data already used in memory), the Temporal Locality (or resuse of already used data), and unique data set size normalized over an instruction interval (represented by the relative size of the points on the graph). The application space can be thought of as consisting of two classes: first, Physics Applications, which are the core of traditional HPC; and second, Informatics Applications that represent increasingly important new codes. Whereas Physics applications are generally simulations, have a 3D spatial decomposition, and are computing floating point results, the Informatics applications tend to be unstructured, integer oriented, and are used to form hypotheses from large data sets (either sensor data or the results of simulations).

There are two key points that increase the challenges of data movement on an Exascale system. First, the Informatics applications are much more data movement oriented than the Physics applications. For a comparable data set

*Figure 1. Instruction characterization and use of a portfolio of department of energy applications*

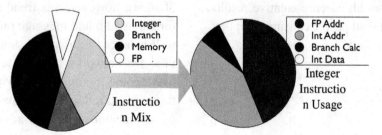

*Figure 2. Application Temporal Locality, Spatial Locality, and Data Set Size (adapted from Murphy & Kogge (2007))*

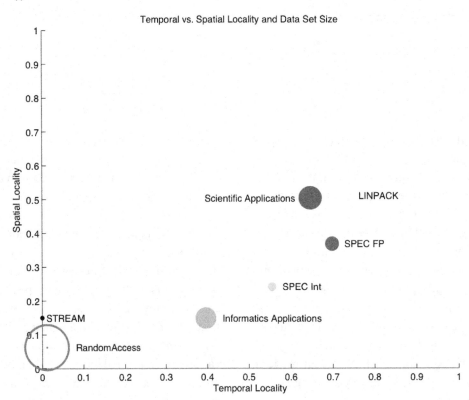

size, they exhibit only 61% of the temporal locality and 30% of the spatial locality. And second, neither application set is well represented by the benchmark suites used to tune the performance of machines. LINPACK has an extremely small data set and much more temporal locality than the typical Physics code it is meant to represent (and looks nothing like an informatics code), and neither SPEC benchmark suite (Int or FP) is representative of anything, despite the fact that SPEC typically dominates CPU design optimizations. An environment where the critical measures of success are demonstrably unrepresentative, results inevitably in additional power consumption that we can no longer afford.

## Interconnection Networks

One of the critical challenges for Exascale computing will be providing sufficient interconnect performance to facilitate application performance and scaling. Traditionally, three primary metrics have been used to characterize interconnection networks: bandwidth, latency and message rate. All of these metrics have seen slowing performance gains in the last several years, and, going forward, latency is unlikely to improve much given the physical limitations (i.e., speed of light); however, this trend must be reversed for bandwidth and message rate if we are to see well balanced Exascale systems. It will also be vital for networks to provide mechanisms for overlapping communication with computation, as this tends to reduce the bandwidth requirements for applications that take advantage of it. This implies that providing independent progress and high message rate in the network hardware and software will become increasingly important. However, in the Exascale timeframe, two other characteristics will jump to the forefront: power and resilience. The main challenge of Exascale networks will be in providing sufficient interconnect performance while maintaining reasonable power and resilience.

To illustrate the power problem with respect to bandwidth, consider an Exascale machine that maintains the system balance found in the Cray XT4 system. The XT4 configuration considered here has a network byte per FLOP ratio of 0.25 and a memory bandwidth to network bandwidth ratio of 3:1. We assume that both of these ratios are maintained, but believe that the memory to network bandwidth ratio is generally more important, as it typically drives on-node performance for most of our applications. The analysis is topology agnostic, but assumes a direct network where 1/4 of the switch bandwidth is used for host connections, while the remaining 3/4 is used to build the network topology. This ratio is consistent with those used in recently developed network topologies, such as dragonfly (Kim, 2008) and flattened butterfly (Kim, 2007).

If these requirements are projected forward to the Exascale, then total bidirectional node bandwidth becomes 250 PB/s. It is generally felt that the use of direct to package optics and WDM (wave division multiplexing) will readily lead to 10 pJ (Kogge, 2008) per bit transmission energy requirements[1], and a similar amount of energy required to move the data through the internal switch logic. This leads to a total power requirement for this example Exascale interconnect of 100 MW (including NIC and switch power) – which is an unreasonable number for even the largest, contemporary computer data center.

There are two approaches to reducing the interconnect power requirements: reduce the application bandwidth requirements and/or reduce the energy per bit transferred. We believe pursu-

ing both of these opportunities will be crucial. First, we note that there are ways to improve the efficiency with which the network performance can be utilized. For example, our applications have generally run slower on a per core basis on a Cray XT5 system than on an XT4 system. The difference between these two systems is that the FLOP rate and memory bandwidth of an XT5 node is roughly twice that of an XT4, while the network performance remained constant. However, we believe much of the application performance could be recovered by facilitating higher message rate and true independent progress in the network. These features would allow the applications to be modified to overlap computation and communication. Enabling these capabilities will require research into both NIC architecture and the network stack software. Enabling computation/communication overlap could allow us to reduce the bandwidth requirements by a factor of 2 or more, depending on the application. However, the cost may be the requirement for more memory bandwidth to provide enough memory performance to complete both activities simultaneously. A factor of 2 reduction would bring the network power requirements to 50MW and further reductions may be possible based on application requirements. Part of the challenge of Exascale will be in understanding the application requirements so that the system can be properly balanced without wasting energy.

Further reductions can be found in fundamental device technologies. It has been suggested (Kogge, 2008) that data transmission energy could be reduced to 2 pJ/bit. However, substantial research investment will need to be made to reach this goal. A similar research effort will be required to reduce the energy consumption of the core switch, which could include fundamental circuit research and/or optical switching technology. A 5X power reduction in both of these areas would lower the interconnect power requirements to 10MW, which is finally in a reasonable range.

We feel the primary challenge to building reasonably balanced Exascale systems will be power consumption, though reliability will also be an important area to consider. Current trends will not lead us to viable interconnect options and substantial investment in various research areas will be necessary. These include, but are not limited to: fundamental device technologies, particularly in the field of silicon photonics; mechanisms to provide high message throughput and true independent progress; applications; and network topologies to take advantage of advances in these areas.

## Resilience

As massively parallel processing (MPP) systems continue to grow in size, complexity, and component count, the ability of applications to endure failures and make effective use of increasing computational power is rapidly decreasing. The average time that the largest platforms can run without incurring a failure fatal to a full-system application was once measured in weeks. That time is now being measured in hours, and, barring any change to current practices, it will soon be measured in minutes. A recent study led by Sandia concluded that, as systems grow beyond 100 thousand components, a combination of factors lead to a situation where more than half of the available computational resources will be wasted (Oldfield, 2006). Figure 3 shows the minimum checkpoint overhead as a percentage of the overall execution time. This calculation is overly optimistic because it assumes data transfers at theoretical network and storage rates, and that the application writes a checkpoint at the "optimal" checkpoint period (Daly, 2006). In practice, these overheads will be worse. In the remainder of this section, we discuss the issues related to application resilience for Exascale systems and outline potential solutions.

In some cases faults are automatically detected and corrected by hardware and system software. For uncorrectable errors, resilience on Massively Parallel Processing (MPP) systems has traditionally been the responsibility of the ap-

plication, with the primary tool being application-directed checkpoints to secondary storage. There are several reasons that this approach will not be sufficient in the near future.

For nearly all systems, secondary storage comes in the form of disk system that is accessible by each computing element, typically through a parallel file system. Writing checkpoint data from tens of thousands of processes in a parallel application simultaneously places great strain on the parallel file system in terms of both performance and reliability. The parallel file system and the underlying disk components are arguably the most fragile pieces of software and hardware in any system. Depending on the most unreliable part of a system to ensure application resilience is disconcerting. Currently, the only method of increasing I/O performance is to add more disks, which in turn increases the likelihood of a disk failure. As the amount of checkpoint data increases with system size, disk-based parallel file systems will not be sufficient.

In addition, the hardware components from which systems are composed are becoming more fragile. In an effort to continue to increase performance and lower energy costs, hardware components are becoming more susceptible and sensitive to uncorrectable errors. For example, reducing the feature size of an integrated circuit to increase the number of processing elements per area also increases the probability of errors stemming from naturally occurring radiation sources, such as cosmic rays. While the probability of such errors can be extremely low for commodity components for mass consumer markets, the massive scale at which these parts are used in large parallel computing systems increases the probability of error to a statistical certainty. Current methods of using MPP systems are not sufficient to deal with an environment where there is at least one failed component throughout the lifetime of the application.

*Figure 3. Approximations of checkpoint overheads for HPC systems*

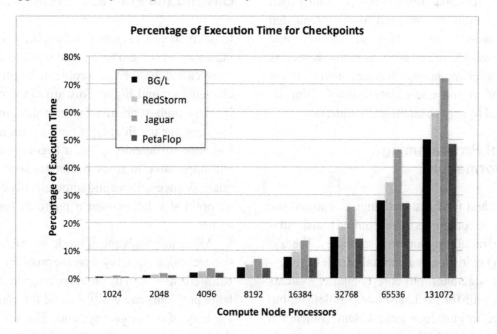

## ONGOING RESEARCH

This section summarizes ongoing research within the DOE Institute for Advanced Architecture aimed at overcoming some of the challenges discussed in the previous section. A key strategy is to co-evolve architectures and algorithms as we strive to reach Exascale computing. Key facets of this work are the development of:

1. Architectural-aware and highly scalable algorithms;
2. Simulation tools to quantify the impact of architectural changes on algorithms and applications, to guide the development of future supercomputers, and to identify algorithm bottlenecks and hence aid in the development of new methods;
3. 3D-Packaging techniques to reduce power consumption and increase memory bandwidth;
4. New approaches to enable resilience; and
5. New benchmarks that better characterize HPC applications.

Each of these is discussed in turn in the following sections.

## Architecture Aware Algorithms and Scalability

For many years, science and engineering application developers have enjoyed a stable programming environment in the context of standard programming languages and message passing on a nearly homogeneous network of serial processors. However, the path to Exascale computing poses several new challenges to application developers. Exascale performance will require the use of multi-core nodes such that MPI-only will not be sufficient. Furthermore, optimal node performance will be challenged by reduced memory bandwidth per core, the need for SIMD expressions and underdeveloped programming environments.

Although there is much that hardware and system software developers can do to aid application performance on new systems, more than ever before scalable algorithms and implementations will need to be architecture-aware and be developed for scalability. It is especially important that algorithms be designed and implemented with knowledge of the node architecture, and that new modeling and analysis methods such as time-parallel methods, advanced mathematical optimization and uncertainty quantification be cultivated to expose additional parallelism.

## Parallel Programming Transformation

The first and foremost challenge to optimal use of Exascale computers is the required transformation of parallel programming strategies. There is mounting evidence that optimal parallel applications for scalable multi-core computer systems will rely on MPI for inter-node parallelism, but will need to introduce large-volume functional parallelism and SIMD vectorization to effectively use the multi-core node. Vectorization is the job of the compiler, with a limited help from the programmer via pragmas and directives, so the real issue is that presently there is no obvious parallel programming model for implementing the middle layer of parallelism. Current standards such as OpenMP, Pthreads and UPC are not designed for multi-core nodes. CUDA, RapidMind and related products target multi-core nodes but are proprietary. OpenCL is an emerging standard but is not really a user-oriented interface, and will likely not provide optimal performance (e.g., in comparison to CUDA on GPUs).

However, even without an emerging programming model for multi-core, there is a vast amount of work required to prepare existing applications for multi-core nodes. Two major tasks are reducing bandwidth requirements as much as possible, primarily by introducing the use of mixed precision, storing data in 32-bit arrays wherever possible; and rewriting low-level kernels as stateless functions with large enough granularity to keep a SIMD core busy, and small enough that there is a large volume of simultaneous function calls to execute.

## Beyond the Forward Problem

In many areas of science and engineering, solving a single problem with given input conditions, often called the forward problem, is sufficiently challenging, and higher forward problem fidelity is the highest priority for scalable computing. However, as the fidelity of the forward problem becomes sufficiently good, it becomes possible and imperative to study parameter sensitivities, quantify uncertainties and automatically compute an optimal solution over a range of parameter values.

All of these advanced modeling and simulation techniques quickly increase problem size and parallelism—often by orders of magnitude—and large problems can easily exceed the computing capacity of our largest systems. The simplest of these approaches are "black box" in nature and do not require a true Peta/Exascale system (instead requiring a cluster of Tera/Petascale systems). However, more advanced methods (often called embedded methods) rely on a tightly coupled aggregation of forward problems and require a true Peta/Exascale system. The challenge with embedded methods is that they require the transformation of an application into a "subroutine" because embedded methods need to call the forward solve as a function. Most applications were not designed with this mindset, so this transformation will be challenging. Furthermore, many of these approaches assume a smoothly varying nonlinear function, which is often not the case in practice. Some functions are inherently nonsmooth. Others are implemented in such a way that function evaluations involve table lookups, or ad hoc evaluation techniques. Such functions can often be rewritten to improve smoothness.

An additional dimension of potential parallelism is in time. Traditionally, we have restricted our parallelism to spatial dimensions, but there are promising new algorithms that can extract parallelism by considering multiple time steps simultaneously. Such approaches can greatly improve parallel execution, especially in situations where the spatial resolution cannot be practically increased, either due to stability constraints or sufficient spatial resolution.

## Robust Multi-Precision Algorithms

Floating point computation has always been faster for single precision (SP) data and computation than for double precision (DP). However, presently, SP computations are even more attractive because bandwidth-intensive calculations can severely limit effective core use on a multi-core node. Figure 4 shows the impact of SP vs. DP for an implicit finite element mini-applications called MiniFE on the Intel Nehalem and AMD Barcelona processors. Use of SP is not only faster

than DP on a single core, but also allows much more effective use of additional cores.

Using preconditioned iterative methods as an example, new basic kernels such as pre-conditioners for multi-core processors must support multiple scalar data types, including single and double precision. These kernels will enable the use of mixed precision algorithms and multi-core processors. They will provide the foundation for optimal pre-conditioners on scalable multi-core systems. In addition, we will need production quality metrics of condition estimates, and accuracy and precision estimates that can help determine the required precision for storing a given data object and the required precision for a given computational step.

*Figure 4. Single precision (SP) vs. Double precision (DP) performance for a finite element mini-applications. Nehalem performance from 4 to 8 cores goes up by 50% for SP, 15% for DP. SP is nearly twice as fast as DP at 8 cores.*

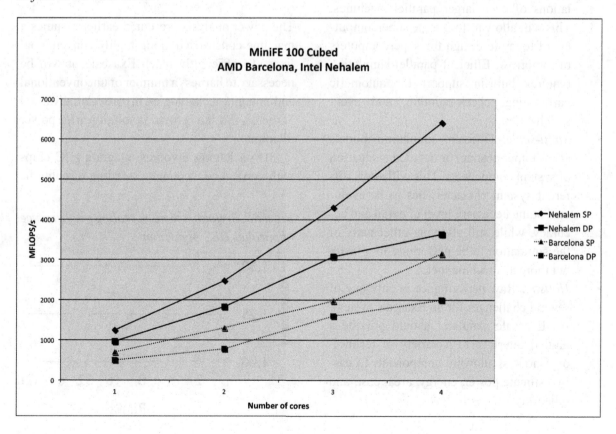

## Simulation

To reach the goal of Exascale, it will be necessary to make substantial leaps in a number of technologies and architectures. Unfortunately, it will not always be practical to construct prototype systems of sufficient size to fully evaluate the impact of these new technologies at scale. Therefore we will have to rely on simulation to guide many design decisions. Currently, the architecture community lacks the tools needed for such evaluations.

To meet this need, we are constructing a simulation environment for simulating large-scale HPC systems. The Structural Simulation Toolkit (SST) will allow parallel simulation of machines at multiple levels of detail (from cycle-accurate instruction-based to message-driven simulation). It will incorporate models for processors, memory, and network subsystems. Some key features:

- *Scalable Parallel Simulation:* The simulation framework allows large parallel simulations of even larger parallel machines. This will allow us to use the supercomputers of today to design the supercomputers of tomorrow. Efficient parallel simulation requires built-in support for automatic partitioning, check-pointing, and event serialization.
- *Multi-scale:* Different simulation models allow either abstract or detailed evaluation of system components. This will allow different system characteristics to be evaluated at the necessary level of detail and accuracy, while still allowing other parts of the simulation to be performed in a faster but more abstract manner.
- *Holistic:* Raw performance is only one of several challenges for an Exascale system. An Exascale simulator should provide a unified interface to a variety of technology models, allowing components to easily estimate power, energy, area, cost, and reliability.

Currently, Sandia has completed a serial implementation of the SST. This version has been used to explore interconnect (Hemmert et al., 2007) and perform application analysis (Rupnow, et all, 2006). Currently, Sandia is expanding the serial SST into a parallel version. Already, we have constructed a parallel core that demonstrates many of these features and have integrated basic processor and network models and a detailed memory model (Jacob, 2009) into the framework. Preliminary scaling studies of the (See Figure 5) conservative distance-based parallel discrete event simulation algorithm under a variety of levels of detail indicate good scaling characteristics. A consortium of other academic and laboratory partners has formed to continue to improve this core and add new components. We are actively soliciting input from potential users and partners on the structure and requirements of this simulation toolkit.

## 3D Packaging

The power analysis presented earlier assumes a machine constructed along highly conventional lines. To efficiently reach Exascale, it will be necessary to harness a number of unconventional and emerging technologies. In particular, advanced 3D packaging may provide a solution to the power dilemma.

3D packaging involves integrating IC chips with vertical connections extending through the

*Figure 5. Preliminary weak scaling performance of parallel DES Algortihm*

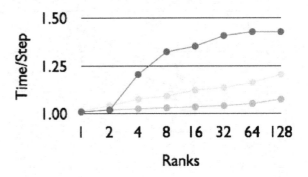

substrate of one chip to connect the next. These connections through the silicon, or Through-Silicon Vias (TSVs) allow information to be moved from one chip to another with very little power – 1-11 fJ/bit (Kogge et al., 2008). TSVs may be used to allow close connections between a processor, DRAM, and network chips.

Currently, a DDR3 DRAM chip consumes 400mW-450mW, with about 180-200 mW of that used for communication across the memory bus to the processor. A stacked DRAM would only require about 10 fJ/bit to drive a Through-Silicon Via, or only a single mW to reach a similar bandwidth as the DDR3. This would save 40-50% of the DRAM's power. Additionally, with more signal lines to access the DRAM it will be possible to reduce the number of bits charged in each DRAM activation from the 8K bits per device in current DRAMs to only the 512 needed to fill a cacheline. This could save another 15-20%. Total savings would then be on the order of 55% to 70%, or $2.4M to $7.0M a year.

The processor could also benefit from close integration with memory. Currently, I/O across the memory bus can account for 10-15% of a processor's energy (Laudon, 2007). This could be reduced substantially with the use of TSVs instead of power-hungry bus-based communication. Additionally, the proximity of stacked memory could make it possible to remove the L2 cache from processors, reducing the size of the clock tree and saving an additional 10-20%. Total savings of 20-35% would translate into $11.2 to $43.0M a year.

Lastly, the network could be improved by enabling silicon photonic interconnect. By using optical instead of electrical signaling, silicon photonic networks have the potential to reduce network power requirements to 0.2 to 1.5 pJ/bit (Kogge et al., 2008; Watts, 2009). However, to function effectively, they require extremely low capacitance connections between the optical devices and the communicating processor. 3D TSV integration could provide the necessary connec-

tions. This would reduce the network power to .01 to 2.34 MW a savings of $1.3 to $16.4M per year.

Additionally, 3D packaging may reduce the cost of systems by allowing more efficient integration of silicon pieces fabricated in heterogeneous processes and by amortizing packaging costs.

Using an IC Cost estimation tool (ICKnowledge LLC, 2009) and current prices for DRAM (DRAM Exchange, 2009), it is possible to estimate the production cost for known good die for various devices (See Table 5). From this it can be seen that not all ICs are equal. The cost of a DRAM die may be as low a penny per $mm^2$, while a processor may be over ten times this, due to the extra layers of metal and more exotic materials and processes required. While it is beneficial to integrate processing and memory in close proximity, doing this on the same die would either be wasteful (running a simple DRAM part through a processor fab line) or detrimental to performance (implementing a processor in a DRAM fab process). With 3D integration, it is possible to choose the fabrication line which best suits each intended device and still provide tight integration with other dissimilar devices.

Package and post-package test of processors can account for 50% or more of their total gross cost. The cost per pin (including test, packaging yield, redistribution layers, etc…) can be 2-4 cents. Additionally, each pin requires more that complexity be added to the socket, and a new trace on the board. Though 3D integration introduces new difficulties and cost into the cost packaging stage it may reduce overall cost by amortizing the cost of a package over several chips and by replacing expensive pins with inexpensive VIAs.

In summary, advanced packaging will have to be a critical part of any Exascale strategy. The prohibitive cost of powering an Exascale system can be reduced to more manageable levels ($48.5M to $82M/year) by allowing tighter integration of processor, memory, and interconnect.

*Table 5. Estimated die production costs*

| Device | Date | Size (mm²) | Good Die Cost ($) | G.D. Cost/mm² | Packaging Cost |
|--------|------|-----------|-------------------|---------------|----------------|
| DRAM 1Gb | June 17 | 45-90 | 1.07-1.63 | $.01-$.03 | 18% |
| Core Duo 45nm | 09Q1 | 143 | $13.50 | $.094 | 46% |
| Nehalem 45nm | 09Q1 | 263 | $36.80 | $.140 | 47% |
| Barcelona 65nm | 07Q4 | 285 | $41.92 | $.147 | 54% |

## Approaches to Resilience

In order to reduce the amount of data that needs to be preserved and managed, we are developing runtime support for high-reliability data storage and retrieval. By developing runtime system capabilities that provide user-requested high-reliability for a given data object, algorithm and application developers can make known to the system the critical subset of data needed by a computation.

In addition, we are exploring the ability for a user to declare a computational scope that needs to be free from soft data errors and/or computation errors. This approach allows the programmer to explicitly communicate the performance/reliability tradeoff to the system. These mechanisms would be used in the development of resilient iterative Krylov methods. By using flexible variants of these methods, and careful formulations of orthogonalization steps, we believe that we can still have reliable iterative results with only a fraction of the total data and computation.

From a system software perspective, we are investigating system-directed checkpointing strategies and transparent redundant computation. The goal of system-directed checkpointing is to provide efficient, application-transparent resilience through coordinated use of system resources. To efficiently quiesce and checkpoint a large-scale application not only requires cooperation among the individual processes, it also requires integration and cooperation with shared services like the network, scheduler, and storage system. This approach will have to deal with messages in transit, in-progress file system operations, and interactions

with various other shared services. We expect to leverage the simplicity of a lightweight kernel environment and an integrated RAS system to reduce the complexity and increase the performance of extracting application state. For transparent redundant computation, we are providing the ability for an MPI application to run extra processes on a set of redundant nodes and automatically switch to using these extra processes should a failure be encountered. Our current approach is to provide this capability entirely at the application layer using MPI, in order to be as portable as possible.

We are also actively engaged in real-time statistical analysis of monitored systems (Brandt, 2009) as well as detailed analysis of system log files (Oliner, 2007). This work provides a critical foundation for understanding the root cause of failures and could ultimately lead to mathematical models that enable prediction for certain types of system faults.

## Improved Benchmarks

Production-quality science and engineering applications are typically large, complicated and full-featured software products. As a result, they tend to be challenging to port to new computer platforms and require a well-trained user to do so. Although benchmarking of these applications on new platforms is an essential part of the design and implementation of a new computer system, the scope of this benchmarking is necessarily limited by the complexity of the software product, not to mention its demand for a full scope of system features that are only available after a new computer system reaches its near-production capabilities.

Characteristics that impact performance should be understood as early as possible in the analysis and design of new computers. Furthermore, it is often the case that there are multiple ways to design and implement the algorithms used in an application, and the choice can have a dramatic impact on application performance.

To address these needs, our recent work in application performance analysis takes advantage of two important properties of many applications: Although an application may have one million or more source lines of code, performance is often dominated by a very small subset of lines; and, for the remaining code, these applications often contain many physics models that are mathematically distinct but have very similar performance characteristics.

To exploit the properties listed above, we have developed a growing collection of mini-applications (called *miniapps*). Miniapps take advantage of the above two application properties by encapsulating only the most important computational operations and consolidating physics capabilities that have the same performance profiles. The large-scale application developer, who is tasked with developing the miniapp, guides the decisions, resulting in a code that is a small fraction of the original application size, yet still captures the primary performance behavior.

There are many benchmarking efforts for scientific computing. The Top 500 High Performance Linpack (HPL) and the HPC Challenge benchmark suite are among the most popular. In addition, full-scale applications are often used for performance analysis, but usually on near-production systems. Between these two extremes there is a middle ground for small, self-contained programs that, like benchmarks, contain the performance-intensive computations of a large-scale application, but are large enough to also contain the context of those computations. The

NAS Parallel Benchmarks fall into this category and have been commonly used, as have the compact or synthetic applications developed as part of the Department of Defense High Performance Computing Modernization Program. SWEEP3D also fits this category.

The Mantevo project (Heroux et al., 2009) has developed several miniapps that are available via the GNU Lesser General Public License (LGPL) and downloadable from the Mantevo website. The miniapps include implicit finite elements (MiniFE), molecular dynamics (MiniMD), contact detection (phdMesh) and electrical circuits (MiniXyce). The following sections discuss MiniFE and MiniMD.

## MiniFE: Implicit Finite Elements

Many engineering applications require the implicit solution of a nonlinear system of equations where the vast majority of time--as problem size increases--is spent in some variation of a conjugate gradient solver. As a result, any miniapp focusing on this area will necessarily have a conjugate gradient solver as the dominant computational kernel.

MiniFE (also known as HPCCG) is a miniapp that mimics the finite element generation, assembly and solution for an unstructured grid problem. The physical domain is a 3D box with configurable dimensions and a structured discretization (which is treated as unstructured). The domain is decomposed using a recursive coordinate bisection (RCB) approach and the elements are simple hexahedra. The problem is linear and the resulting matrix is symmetric, so a standard conjugate gradient algorithm is used with a general sparse matrix data format and no preconditioning.

This simple code—which is not intended to be a true physics problem—is sufficiently realistic for performance purposes. Furthermore, it contains approximately 1,500 lines of C++ code.

## MiniMD: Molecular Dynamics

The MiniMD application is miniature version of the molecular dynamics (MD) application LAMMPS (LAMMPS 2009). The source for MiniMD is less than 3,000 lines of C++ code. Like LAMMPS, MiniMD uses spatial decomposition MD, where individual processors in a cluster own subsets of the simulation box. And like LAMMPS, MiniMD enables users to specify a problem size, atom density, temperature, timestep size, number of timesteps to perform, and particle interaction cutoff distance. But compared to LAMMPS, MiniMD's feature set is extremely limited, and only one type of pair interaction (Lennard-Jones) is available. No long-range electrostatics or molecular force field features are available. Inclusion of such features is unnecessary for testing basic MD and would have made MiniMD much bigger, more complicated, and harder to port to novel hardware. The current version of LAMMPS includes over 130,000 lines of code in hundreds of files, nineteen optional packages, over one hundred different commands, and over five hundred pages of documentation. Such a large and complicated code is not ideally suited for answering certain performance questions or for tinkering by non-MD-experts.

A rewrite of a full application code base would be a daunting task, but a complete rewrite of a miniapp to test a new idea can be achieved fairly quickly. We have used MiniFE, MiniMD and the other Mantevo miniapps to test numerous software performance questions and ideas. Explorations included changing from double to single precision to investigate how much performance would improve. We have also developed performance models that provide a mathematical description of performance. For example, MiniMD has been used to test the scaling performance of the spatial decomposition algorithm as the number of processors increased towards infinity. It was found that the fraction of time spent on computation did not approach unity (the fraction of time spent on communication did not approach zero). This finding demonstrated a limitation of the spatial decomposition algorithm for performing MD (MiniMD, 2009).

## CONCLUSION

There is currently considerable interest in Exascale computing. This chapter discussed several application drivers, technological challenges and ongoing research aimed at overcoming some of these hurdles. However, a collaborative international effort will be needed to overcome all the key research challenges.

## REFERENCES

Brandt, J., Gentile, A., & Mayo, J. P'ebay, P., Roe, D., Thompson, D., & Wong, M. (2009). Methodologies for advance warning of compute cluster problems via statistical analysis: a case study. In *Proceedings of the 2009 workshop on Resiliency in high performance (Resilience '09)* (pages 7-14). New York: ACM.

Brown, J. L., Goudy, S., Heroux, M. A., Huang, S. S., & Wen, Z. (2006). An evolutionary path towards virtual shared memory with random access. In *Proceedings of the eighteenth annual ACM symposium on Parallelism in algorithms and architectures (SPAA '06)* (page 117). New York: ACM.

Daly, J. (2006). A Higher Order Estimate of the Optimum Checkpoint Interval for Restart Dumps. *Future Generation Computer Systems*, 303–312.

Department Of Energy. (2007). Annual Energy Review 2007. *Energy Information Administration*. Retrieved June 16, 2009 from www.dramexchange.com

Department of Energy. (2007). *Modeling and Simulation at the Exascale for Energy and the Environment*. Washington, DC: Office of Science. Retrieved from http://www.mcs.anl.gov/~insley/E3/E3-draft-2007-08-09.pdf

Exchange, D. R. A. M. (2009). Retrieved June 16, 2009 from http://www.dramexchange.com

Feldman, M. (2008). ORNL's "Jaguar" Leaps Past Petaflop. *HPCWire*. Retrieved July 5, 2009 from http://www.hpcwire.com/blogs/ ORNLs_Jaguar_Leaps_Past_Petaflop_34282109.html

Hack, J., & Bierly, E. (2007, November 6-7). *Computational and Informational Technology Rate Limiters to the Advancement of Climate Change Science*. Paper presented to the DOE Advanced Scientific Computing Research Advisory Committee. Retrieved from http://www.sc.doe.gov/ascr/ ASCAC/presentationpage1107.html

Heermann, P. (1998). Production Visualization for the ASCI One TeraFLOPS machine. In *Proceedings of the Visualization, 98*, 459–462.

Hemmert, S., Underwood, K., & Rodrigues, A. (2007). An Architecture to Perform NIC Based MPI Matching. In *Proceedings of the 2006 International Conference on Cluster Computing (Cluster 2007)*.

Heroux, M. (2003). *Trilinos Home Page*. Retrieved from http://trilinos.sandia.gov

Heroux, M. (2009). *Mantevo Home Page*. Retrieved from http://software.sandia.gov/mantevo

Heroux, M., et al. (2009). Improving Application Performance via Mini-applications (Tech. Rep. No. SAND2009-5574). Sandia National Laboratories, USA.

ICKnowledge LLC. (2009, June). *IC Cost Model 0904a*.

ITRS International Roadmap Committee. (2007). *International Technology Roadmap for Semiconductors*.

Jacob, B. (2009). DRAMSim: University of Maryland Memory-System Simulation Framework. *University of Maryland Memory-Systems Research*. Retrieved June 19, 2009 from http://www.ece.umd.edu/dramsim/#version2

Kahle, J. (2005). The Cell Processor Architecture. In *Proceedings of the 38th Annual IEEE/ACM International Symposium or Microarchitcture*. Washington, DC: IEEE Computer Society.

Keiter, E. R., Mei, T., Russo, T. V., Rankin, E. L., Pawlowski, R. P., Schiek, R. L., et al. (2008). *Xyce Parallel Electronic Simulator: Users' Guide, Version 4.1* (Tech. Rep. No. SAND2008-6461). Sandia National Laboratories, USA.

Keyes, D., Kritz, A., & Tang, W. (2007, November). *Fusion Simulation Project (FSP): Workshop Report*. Paper presented at the DOE Advanced Scientific Computing Research Advisory Committee (ASCAC) meeting.

Kim, J., Dally, W. J., & Abts, D. (2007). Flattened butterfly: a cost-efficient topology for high-radix networks. In *Proceedings of the 34th Annual International Symposium on Computer Architecture* (pp.126-137).

Kim, J., Dally, W. J., Scott, S., & Abts, D. (2008). Technolgy-driven, highly-scalable, Dragonfly topology. In *Proceedings of the 35th Annual International Symposium on Computer Architecture* (pp.77-88).

Kogge, P. (2008). *ExaScale Computing Study: Technology Challenges in Achieving Exascale Systems (Tech. Rep.)*. Notre Dame, IN: University of Notre Dame, Department of Computer Science.

Laudon, J. (2007). *UltraSPARC T1: A 32-threaded CMP for Servers*. Paper presented at the Berkeley CMP.

Mann, R. (2007, September). *BioEnergy Science Center: A DOE Bioenergy Research Center*. Paper presented at the 2007 Fall Creek Falls Workshop, Nashville, Tennessee. Retrieved from http://www.iter.org

Micron technology. (2007). *Calculating Memory System Power for DDR3*. Boisie, ID.

Molecular Dynamics Simulator, L. A. M. M. P. S. (2009). Retrieved from http://lammps.sandia.gov/index.html

Murphy, R., Rodrigues, A., Kogge, P., & Underwood, K. (2009). *The Implications of Working Set Analysis on Supercomputing Memory Hierarchy Design*. Paper presented at the International Conference on Supercomputing, Cambridge, UK.

Murphy, R. C. (2007, September 27-29). On the Effects of Memory Latency and Bandwidth on Supercomputer Application Performance. In *Proceedings Of the IEEE Internaional Symposium on Workload Characterization 2007 (IISWC07)*.

Murphy, R. C., & Kogge, P. M. (2007, July). On the Memory Access Patterns of Supercomputer Applications: Benchmark Selection and Its Implications. *IEEE Transactions on Computers*, 56(7), 937–945. doi:10.1109/TC.2007.1039

Numrich, R. W., & Heroux, M. A. (2009). A performance model with a fixed point for a molecular dynamics kernel. In *Proceedings International Supercomputing Conference '09*.

Oldfield, R. A., Arunagiri, S., Teller, P. J., Seelam, S., Riesen, R., Varela, M. R., & Roth, P. C. (2007, September). Modeling the impact of checkpoints on next-generation systems. In *Proceedings of the 24th IEEE Conference on Mass Storage Systems and Technologies*, San Diego, CA.

Oliner, A., & Stearley, J. (2007, June). What supercomputers say: A study of five system logs. In *Proceedings of the 37th Annual IEEE/IFIP International Conference on Dependable Systems and Networks*, Edinburgh, UK (pp. 575-584). Washington, DC: IEEE Computer Society Press.

Qthreads. (2009). *Sandia National Laboratories: Qthreads*. Retrieved from http://www.cs.sandia.gov/qthreads

Rupnow, K., Rodrigues, A., Underwood, K., & Compton, K. (2006). Scientific Applications vs. SPEC-FP: A Comparison of Program Behavior. In *Proceedings of the International Conference on Supercomputing*.

Shiva, S. (2005). *Advanced Computer Architectures* (p. 7). Boca Raton, FL: CRC Press.

Simon, H., Zacharia, T., Stevens, R., et al. (2007). *Modeling and Simulation at the Exascale for Energy and the Environment* (Tech. Rep.). Department of Energy. Retrieved from http://www.sc.doe.gov/ascr/ ProgramDocuments/TownHall.pdf

MIPS Technologies, Inc. (2007). *MIPS64® 5Kc® Processor Core Data Sheet*.

Thoziyoor, S., Ahn, J. H., Muralimanohar, N., & Jouppi, N. (2008). *Cacti 5.1*. HP Labs.

Watts, M. (2009). *Microphotonic Circuits, Networks, and Sensors*. Center For Integrated Photonic Systems Annual Meeting: Massachusetts Institute of Technology.

Weigand, G. (2007, November). *Energy Assurance and High Performance Computing*. Paper presented at Supercomputing 2007 ORNL booth.

## ENDNOTE

[1] It should be noted that WDM increases the energy requirements per bit, but will be necessary to keep the cable count to a reasonable level.

*This work was previously published in International Journal of Distributed Systems and Technologies, Volume 1, Issue 2, edited by Nik Bessis, pp. 1-22, copyright 2010 by IGI Publishing (an imprint of IGI Global).*

# Chapter 9
# Application Performance on the Tri–Lab Linux Capacity Cluster –TLCC

**Mahesh Rajan**
*Sandia National Laboratory, USA*

**Douglas Doerfler**
*Sandia National Laboratory, USA*

**Courtenay T. Vaughan**
*Sandia National Laboratory, USA*

**Marcus Epperson**
*Sandia National Laboratory, USA*

**Jeff Ogden**
*Sandia National Laboratory, USA*

## ABSTRACT

*In a recent acquisition by DOE/NNSA several large capacity computing clusters called TLCC have been installed at the DOE labs: SNL, LANL and LLNL. TLCC architecture with ccNUMA, multi-socket, multi-core nodes, and InfiniBand interconnect, is representative of the trend in HPC architectures. This chapter examines application performance on TLCC contrasting them with Red Storm/Cray XT4. TLCC and Red Storm share similar AMD processors and memory DIMMs. Red Storm however has single socket nodes and custom interconnect. Micro-benchmarks and performance analysis tools help understand the causes for the observed performance differences. Control of processor and memory affinity on TLCC with the numactl utility is shown to result in significant performance gains and is essential to attenuate the detrimental impact of OS interference and cache-coherency overhead. While previous studies have investigated impact of affinity control mostly in the context of small SMP systems, the focus of this chapter is on highly parallel MPI applications.*

DOI: 10.4018/978-1-4666-0906-8.ch009

## INTRODUCTION

This chapter investigates application performance on the Tri-lab Linux Capacity Cluster (TLCC) using a variety of applications and compute kernels. This is motivated by the size of the NNSA's Advanced Simulation and Computing (ASC) TLCC program, the initial procurement of which consisted of 21 "Scalable Units" (SUs) spread out over eight clusters: three for Lawrence Livermore (8 SU, 2 SU, and 1 SU systems), two for Los Alamos (two 4 SU systems), and three for Sandia (three 2 SU systems, one of which will be housed at Sandia Livermore). The systems were designed around a single hardware design point, called a "Scalable Unit" (SU) to minimize costs. Multiple clusters of varying sizes are in service based on the scalable unit module.

Each SU consists of 144 four-socket, quad-core AMD Opteron (Barcelona) nodes, using 4x DDR InfiniBand as the high speed interconnect. Each node has 32 GB of 667 MHz DDR2 memory resulting in 8GB per processor socket. The systems also use a common software stack, based on the ASC Program Tripod Operating System Software (TOSS), a Tri-Lab packaging of the CHAOS/SLURM environment that has been in production on systems for several years (https://computing.llnl.gov/linux/projects.html#chaos). The basic elements of TOSS consist of Red Hat Enterprise Linux (RHEL5U2), the OpenFabrics Enterprise Distribution InfiniBand stack, MVAPICH and Open-MPI, and the MOAB/SLURM resource manager.

A common set of FORTRAN, C and C++ development tools are also provided. The site-specific software components include the parallel file system as well as the RAS and system monitoring software.

This chapter examines application performance on TLCC and contrasts them with Red Storm/Cray XT4 performance. Comparisons of TLCC performance, to the partition of Red Storm with quad-core single socket nodes, are useful because of the processor and memory DIMM similarities. This is fortuitous as it provides a unique opportunity to evaluate the impact of node memory architecture, node interconnect architecture, and the operating system on performance. However differences in MPI libraries and possible choices of compiler must also be considered. While processor speed for both is 2.2 GHz, the Red Storm quad-core nodes have 800 MHz DDR2 DIMMs, a higher memory speed than on the TLCC with 667 MHz DIMMs. However, a smaller development system called Red Storm Qualification system (RSQUAL) with 667 MHz memory DIMMs has been employed for a few closer comparisons to TLCC.

This effort led to the following findings that are of interest in extracting the best performance from systems like TLCC, with multi-socket NUMA nodes. It further provides analysis of possible limitations to scaling of such clusters through the comparisons to Red Storm.

1.  Control of processor and memory affinity with the *numactl* utility can result in significant performance gains. While previous studies have investigated impact of affinity control mostly in the context of small SMP systems, the focus here is MPI applications, the predominant programming model for all of our applications.

2.  Simple memory performance benchmarks help to explain the loss of performance of the TLCC NUMA node. Coherency enforcement overheads on the sixteen cores of the quad-socket node are investigated through memory latency and bandwidth benchmarks. Data was collected on a specially configured TLCC node with two sockets populated (two of the processors taken out), and also on both Red Storm and RSQUAL single socket nodes.

3.  Operating system interference leading to thread migration or application process interruptions are known performance inhibi-

tors. This is particularly true with loosely synchronous applications that use frequent synchronizations through MPI global operations (Petrini, Kerbyson, & Pakin, 2003). Such applications are shown to benefit from enforcing processor and memory affinity settings.

4. For quite a number of applications, TLCC node architecture proved adequate for typical capacity computing job sizes.

5. For memory bandwidth intensive applications, using all the 16 cores on a TLCC node can lead to 20% to 50% loss of performance as compared to Red Storm. The higher the bytes to FLOPS ratio of the computational kernel, the larger the performance difference.

6. No significant improvements in scaling were observed while using fewer (e.g., 15) MPI processes per node as opposed to 16 MPI processes per node (using all the cores). This is in contrast to some of the experiences with early HPC systems built with SMP nodes.

7. The MVAPICH MPI library provides better collective performance than the OpenMPI library. Using MVAPICH made for significant gains in performance at 512 cores or larger for some applications.

8. The benefit of affinity settings for MPI processes on TLCC's performance is directly related to the intensity of memory accesses in the application. The use of *numactl* increases performance by eliminating the performance penalty associated with cache coherency overheads and fewer remote socket memory accesses, and, eliminating task migration and subsequent non-local memory accesses. This is illustrated by a detailed analysis of a mini-application, a memory access intensive computation utilizing a sparse matrix-vector multiply kernel. The node level processing speed imbalance due to memory contention and non-local memory access destroy the needed near synchronous arrival at the subsequent global operation. This behavior is similar to the impact of OS noise on applications and global operations first reported by Petrini, Kerbyson, and Pakin (2003).

In the following sections, we provide a description of the TLCC and Red Storm architectures, a short description of benchmarks and applications, and provide analysis of the performance differences observed.

## SYSTEM ARCHITECTURE OVERVIEW

### A. TLCC Architecture

The SNL TLCC cluster has 38 teraFLOPS peak performance. It is built with 2 scalable units (SU) for a total of 272 compute nodes with 16 cores per node for a total of 4352 processor cores. Each scalable unit is nominally constructed with 144 nodes (136 compute, 1 login, 1 management, 6 gateway). The node utilizes a SuperMicro H8QM8-2 motherboard as shown in Figure 1. The node has four AMD Opteron 8300 Barcelona quad-core processors clocked at 2.2 GHz. The quad-socket node has independent 667 MHz DDR2 DIMMS for each socket as shown in the figure. The total node memory is 32 GB giving the compute nodes a total memory of 9.2 TB. The nodes are connected with 24-port InfiniBand 4x DDR switches with 12 second level switches that connect the 2 SUs and forming a single fully connected fat-tree. The InfiniBand HCAs are the Mellanox ConnectX 4x DDR cards. The Tri-Lab developed operating system called TOSS and resource manager MOAB/SLURM make up the principle cluster OS suite. Intel, PGI, GNU compilers and math libraries together with OpenMPI and MVAPICH MPI libraries form the programming environment. Performance analysis tools Open|Speedshop and

*Figure 1. Quad-socket TLCC node*

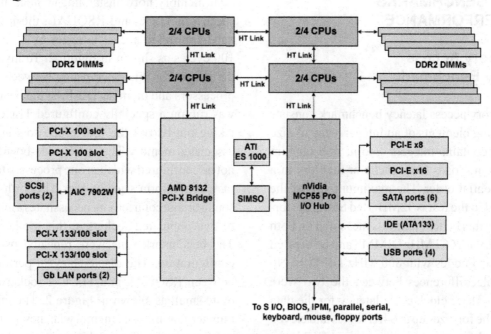

**SuperMicro H8QM8-2 Motherboard**

SCALASCA have been recently installed on the system.

## B. Red Storm Architecture

To facilitate the comparison of performance to the Red Storm/XT4 at Sandia National Laboratories in Albuquerque, we provide a brief description below. Red Storm currently is a heterogeneous system made up of 6240 2.2GHz AMD Opteron-Budapest quad-core nodes and 6720 2.4GHz AMD Opteron-280 dual-core nodes for a total of 12,960 compute nodes. The Budapest quad-core processor developed by AMD for single socket servers with 64KB data and 64KB instruction per core of L1 cache, 512K per core of L2 cache and a shared 2MB L3 cache mirrors the TLCC AMD Barcelona processor cache sizes. The most significant technical difference between the Budapest and Barcelona chips is that Budapest processors use AMD's HyperTransport 3 technology while the Barcelona processors utilize HyperTransport 2.

The Budapest Opteron is functionally equivalent to the Barcelona Opteron differing with it in the number of HyperTransport links and the logic for the NUMA. The dual core nodes have 4GB of DDR-400 RAM memory and the quad-core node have 8GB of DDR2-800 RAM memory. The DDR2 memory provides a peak memory of 12.8GB/s while the older DDR-400 has a bandwidth 6.4GB/s. The theoretical peak performance of the Red Storm is 284 teraFLOPS. Nodes are interconnected with the Cray SeaStar network. The network is a 27x20x24 mesh topology with a peak bidirectional link bandwidth of 9.6 GB/s. The nearest neighbor node to node latency is specified to be 2 µsec, with 4.8 µsec measured MPI latency. The compute nodes run the Catamount lightweight kernel. The I/O and administrative nodes run a modified version of SuSE Linux. Additional details of Red Storm can be found in these references (Camp & Tomkins, 2002), (Brightwell et al., 2006).

## MICRO BENCHMARKS AND PERFORMANCE

### A. Memory Access Latency Benchmark

The memory access latency benchmark consists of accessing elements of an integer array of size n, which contains integers 1 to n, in a random order forcing loads from cache or memory in a non-sequential order. The maximum size of the array used in the test is 32MB. Red Storm performance for this benchmark was measured on both RSQUAL with 667 MHz DIMMS and on the Red Storm Quad nodes with 800 MHz DIMMS. No appreciable differences between the two were observed. Three clock cycle latency for the data on L1 cache for sizes up to 64KB bytes and eleven cycles for the data in L2 cache up to 512KB bytes were observed for both TLCC and Red Storm. Thirty two cycles' latency on Red Storm and fifty six cycle latency on TLCC were measured for data in the L3 cache for sizes up to 2MB. However once the data access occurs from the

main memory, notwithstanding identical memory speeds on TLCC and RSQUAL, the RSQUAL quad-core node access is faster by as much as 100 cycles as shown in Figure 2. To investigate the reason for this discrepancy between similar processors and memory DIMMs, the benchmark was run on a specially configured TLCC node, taking out two of the four processors and their associated memory. The TLCC node-boards could not be configured with just one processor to better match Red Storm's quad-nodes. The north-bridge, south-bridge connectivity necessitates a minimum of two populated sockets in this mother board. The benchmark runs were repeated using this configuration. The discrepancy in performance between RSQUAL and TLCC 2 socket node is quite small as shown in Figure 2. The other parameter that impacts memory latency is the TLB page size. The TLCC cluster is operated with a nominal 4KB page size while the Red Storm default page size at job launch is 2MB. These set of test results clearly demonstrate the substantial cache coherency overhead of the TLCC node.

*Figure 2. Memory access latency*

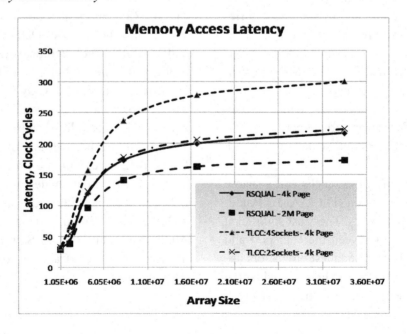

## B. Memory Bandwidth Benchmark – STREAMS

The MPI version of the STREAMS bandwidth test was used to measure the memory bandwidth on an RSQUAL node, a TLCC node and a Red Storm Quad-core node. The PGI compiler flags chosen were the same (-O3 –fastsse) on these platforms. Although higher bandwidth may result with more optimal compiler flags it does not impact the comparisons. The single MPI task memory bandwidth test shows that the Red Storm quad-core node has about 30% better performance than TLCC as shown in Figure 3. To investigate the cause of this discrepancy between similar processors and memory DIMMs, as in the case of the latency test, the test was run on the specially configured TLCC node taking out two of the four processors and their associated memory. The considerable coherency overhead on the TLCC node leads to the lower bandwidth. Figure 3 illustrates this through the improved performance measured on the 2 socket TLCC node. The remaining divergence is due to

page size differences. Red Storm has a default 2MB page size and TLCC 4KB page size.

On the Red Storm quad-core node two MPI ranks saturate the node. Similarly on TLCC two STREAM ranks saturate a single socket. For a STREAMS test of two or more MPI ranks the process placement on TLCC was explicitly controlled via "*numactl* –physcpubind= --membind=" flags. At eight MPI tasks the memory access is saturated and no increase in memory bandwidth is observed on the TLCC node with additional threads. This impacts applications requesting sixteen MPI tasks per node on TLCC. However it must be mentioned that the AMD Opteron with its independent memory subsystem for each socket scales quite nicely in comparison to other frontside bus based multi-core architectures.

## C. MPI Ping-Pong Benchmark

Figure 4 shows the performance of a simple inter-node ping-pong test. Red Storm achieves a peak uni-directional bandwidth of 1.7 GB/s while TLCC

*Figure 3. Streams triad memory bandwidth (MB/sec)*

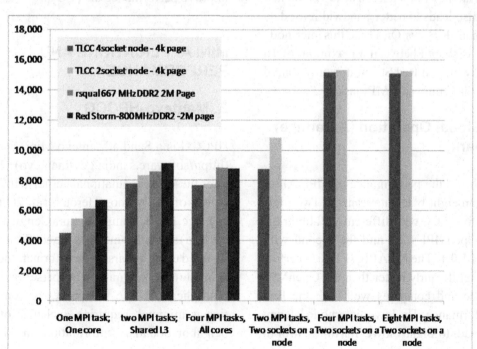

*Figure 4. Ping-Pong internode bandwidth (MB/sec)*

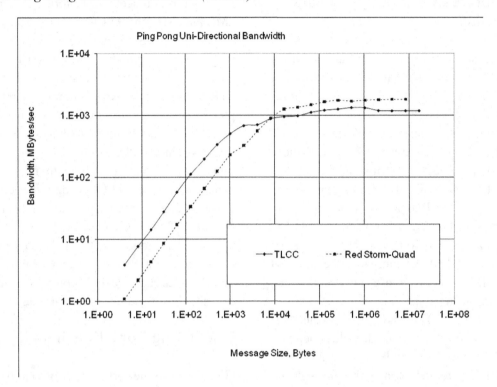

shows a performance of 1.2GB/s. The InfiniBand internode latency on TLCC is 2 μsec while the Red Storm latency is 4.8 μsec. The lower latency on TLCC also leads to better bandwidth for data sizes less than 5K Bytes. On TLCC this inter-node bandwidth is shared between a maximum of 16 MPI tasks, while on Red Storm it is only shared between a maximum of 4 MPI tasks.

### D. MPI Global Operation (Allreduce) Benchmark

Figure 5 shows the performance of MPI_Allreduce with an eight byte data transfer. Two plots are shown for TLCC with different MPI libraries: one with OpenMPI 1.2.3 and the second with MVAPICH 1.0.1. The MVAPICH TLCC performance is significantly better than the OpenMPI performance and compares well with the Red Storm performance. The lower internode latency on TLCC leads to slightly lower run times. In both

cases all cores on each node were used for this benchmark. Affinity settings did not significantly improve performance on TLCC.

### MINI APPLICATIONS AND PERFORMANCE

### A. Mantevo-HPCCG

HPCCG is a Sandia Mantevo Mini-Application (http://software.sandia.gov/mantevo) that captures the key computational kernel in the implicit solvers of the Trillinos (Heroux et al., 2006) solver package. HPCCG implements a Conjugate Gradient (CG) algorithm in which the coefficient matrix is stored using a sparse matrix format. Most of the compute time is dominated by sparse matrix-vector multiplication. The interprocessor communication is minimal, requiring exchange of nearest neighbor boundary information, in addition to

*Figure 5. MPI global allreduce time (msecs)*

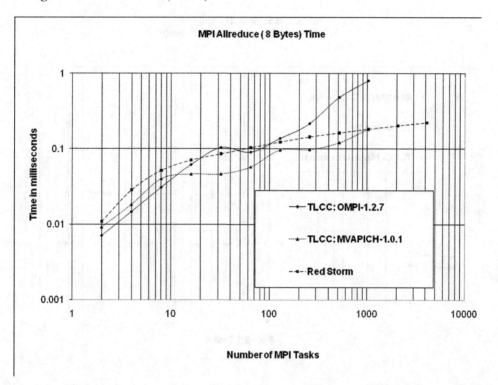

global MPI_Allreduce operations required for the scalar computations in the CG algorithm. Weak scaling studies, assigning identical computational load to each MPI task, have been carried out. Figure 6 shows the total wall time as a function of the number of MPI tasks for each system. This mini-application clearly brings out the impact of memory architecture on application scaling. We can see that for the quad-core Red Storm node, the jump from two to four MPI tasks degrades performance by 41% due to memory contention. Once the best performance within a node is achieved, the weak scaling curve is near perfect (flat). For the quad-socket, quad-core TLCC node, we see that from 1 to 2 MPI tasks we get perfect scaling (no contention for memory), 37% degradation in performance from 2 to 4 MPI tasks and an additional 44% loss in going from 8 to 16 MPI tasks on a node. Using multiple nodes on TLCC, and assigning an MPI task to every core on each node, shows subsequent perfect weak scaling,

when memory and processor affinity are forced with the *numactl* utility. This mini-application also nicely brings out the destructive impact of OS imposed thread migration as evident by looking at the scaling curve for TLCC when no *numactl* is used (TLCC-16ppn plot). Nearly a five-fold loss of performance is possible when no affinity control is used.

## B. Mantevo-phdMesh

Contact detection has been a performance-critical algorithm for parallel explicit dynamics simulation codes for over a decade. The parallel heterogeneous dynamic mesh (phdMesh) is a library in Trilinos (Heroux et al., 2006) that provides an in-memory mesh and field database for parallel, heterogeneous, dynamic, unstructured meshes. This library includes a parallel implementation of an oct-tree geometric proximity detection algorithm with state-of-the-practice $N*log(N)$

*Figure 6. HPCCG weak scaling performance*

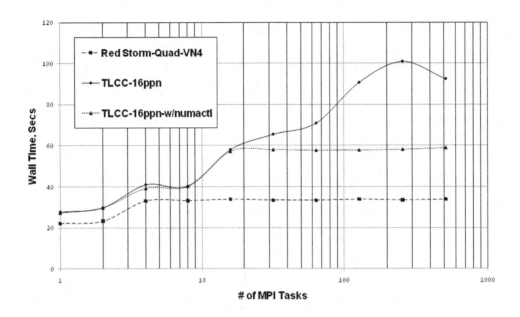

complexity. The phdMesh library and oct-tree geometric search algorithm are integrated to form a parallel geometric proximity search mini-application.

The weak scaling study for this mini-application uses a grid of simple counter-rotating gears, as shown in Figure 7. Gear configurations of 4x3x1, 4x3x2, 4x3x4, 4x6x4, etc., were set up to run on 2,4,8,16, etc., processors respectively. In other words, the number of gears along the X,Y,Z axes were scaled so as to create an approximate weak scaling input, while maintaining a reasonable aspect ratio. The basic 4x3x1 configuration has 5952 surface-facets (N) and the surface-facets for

*Figure 7. phdMesh test case: grid of counter-rotating gears*

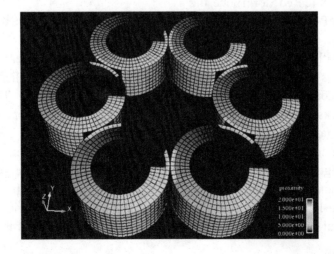

the others scale accordingly. When the application is executed, the run times for different execution regimes, such as Meshing, Rebalance, and Search/step, etc., are tabulated on output. The performance characteristic of principal interest is the oct-tree geometric search proximity detection execution time for the rolling surface-facets of these gears.

Figure 8 presents the weak scaling characteristics observed by plotting the Search/step wall time in seconds, against the number of MPI Tasks. The best scaling performance is observed on Red Storm. This is essentially due to its superior communication architecture. It is illustrative to compare this performance against algorithmically predicted $N*log(N)$ performance as shown in the 'ideal scaling' dotted curve. This curve is computed taking as the basis the two MPI task, dual-core Red Storm time. From comparing the slope of the Red Storm performance curves shown to the ideal, it can be concluded that the Red Storm's performance is very good. The jump from 128 to 256 is input related as the aspect ratio along X in

changing from 8x12x8 to 16x12x8. However the plot seems to indicate a similar $N*log(N)$ behavior beyond 256. For less than 16 MPI tasks the better performance on TLCC is due to faster shared memory MPI performance within the node. However, for 32 or more MPI tasks, the slower TLCC network and contention among the MPI tasks increases the run time by 50%. Beyond 128 tasks on the run time of TLCC is not logarithmic. The reason for this behavior is yet to be investigated. These examples are illustrative of the usefulness of this mini-application in understanding architectural balance issues, particularly when scaling complexity models are available.

## APPLICATIONS PERFORMANCE

### A. SIERRA/Presto

Presto is a Lagrangian, three-dimensional explicit, transient dynamics code for the analysis of

*Figure 8. phdMesh weak scaling performance*

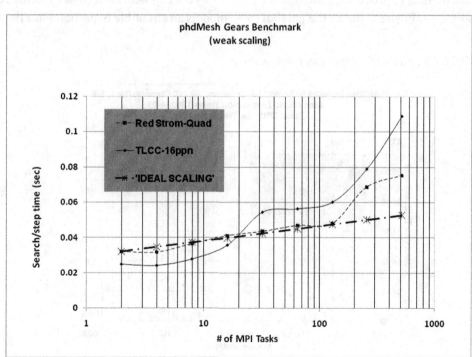

solids subjected to large, suddenly applied loads (Koteras & Gullerud, 2003). Presto is designed for problems with large deformations, nonlinear material behavior and contact. There is a versatile element library incorporating both continuum and structural elements. The contact algorithm is supplied by ACME (Brown et al., 2001). The contact algorithm detects contacts that occur between elements in the deforming mesh and prevents those elements from interpenetrating each other. This is done on a decomposition of just the surface elements of the mesh. The contact algorithm is communication intensive and can change as the problem progresses.

The analysis used in this investigation is the Brick Walls problem consisting of two sets of two brick walls colliding with each other. It is a weak scaling investigation where each processor is assigned 80 bricks. Each brick is discretized with 4x4x8 elements, for a total of 10240 elements per processor. Each brick is located on one processor so the only communication for the finite element portion of the code is for the determination of the length of the next time step. As the problem grows with the number of processors, the contact problem also grows. Figure 9 shows the parallel

performance of Presto on this problem. The contact portion of the calculation, however, involves communication in several phases. First, a small amount of information is communicated to allow for the calculation of the new decomposition. Then the face information for the surface elements needs to be redistributed to the new decomposition. After contact detection is performed, a smaller amount of information representing the forces on the nodes is communicated back to the original decomposition. The resulting communication pattern is not well structured and can involve the sending of a large number of small messages to processors that may not be nearby. The rapid increase in run time on TLCC is suspected to be a consequence of the contact algorithm's sensitivity to message injection rate and demand on unstructured communication in the network. This application is most demanding on the communication infrastructure among all tested.

## B. LAMMPS

LAMMPS (http://lammps.sandia.gov/index. html) is a classical molecular dynamics code that models an ensemble of particles in a liquid, solid,

*Figure 9. SIERRA/Presto walls collision performance*

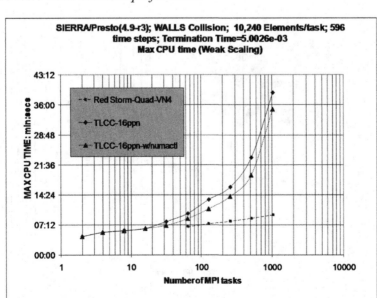

or gaseous state. It can model atomic, polymeric, biological, metallic, granular, and coarse-grained systems using a variety of force fields and boundary conditions. LAMMPS runs efficiently on single-processor desktop or laptop machines, but is designed for parallel computers. It will run on any parallel machine that compiles C++ and supports the MPI message-passing library. This includes distributed- or shared-memory parallel machines and Beowulf-style clusters. LAMMPS can model systems with only a few particles up to millions or billions.

The current version of LAMMPS is written in C++. In the most general sense, LAMMPS integrates Newton's equations of motion for collections of atoms, molecules, or macroscopic particles that interact via short- or long-range forces with a variety of initial and/or boundary conditions. For computational efficiency LAMMPS uses neighbor lists to keep track of nearby particles. The lists are optimized for systems with particles that are repulsive at short distances, so that the local density of particles never becomes too large. On parallel machines, LAMMPS uses spatial-decomposition techniques to partition the simulation domain into small 3D sub-domains, one of which is assigned to each processor. Processors communicate and store "ghost" atom information for atoms that border their sub-domain. The simulation used in this study is a strong scaling analysis with the RhodoSpin benchmark. The run time to compute the dynamics of the atomic fluid with 32,000 atoms for 100 time steps is measured. The execution time is shown in Figure 10. This LAMMPS benchmark is not memory intensive and does not show significant difference in performance when memory and processor affinity are forced. Red Storm scales well even beyond 64 tasks although the balance of computation to communication is steadily decreased for this strong scaling test. Instrumentation data is being collected using performance tools to understand why TLCC does not scale beyond 64 MPI tasks.

## C. DSMC/ICARUS

The Direct Simulation Monte Carlo (DSMC) method is a proven method for simulating noncontinuum gas flows because continuum methods break down where particles move in ballistic

*Figure 10. LAMMPS RhodoSpin strong scaling performance*

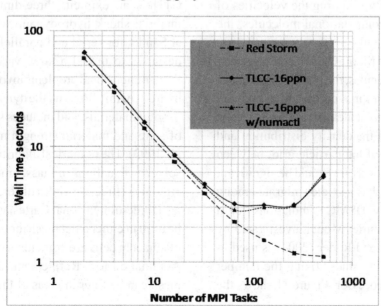

*Figure 11. DSMC ICARUS – fourier model performance*

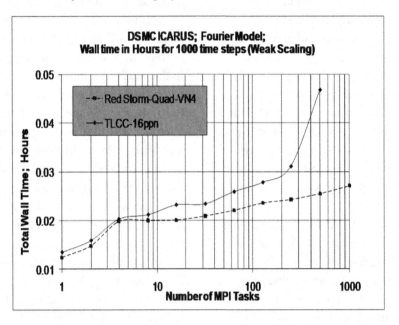

trajectories with mean free path larger than cell dimensions, often because the device is small (micro- or nano-technology) or the fluid is at very low pressure as in plasma or upper atmosphere. Unlike most flow-simulation methods, DSMC uses computational molecules ("simulators") that mimic real molecules by moving through space, reflecting from solid boundaries, and colliding with one another. By sampling the velocities of large numbers of computational molecules, the gas flow is determined.

Since DSMC is a Monte Carlo technique using computational molecules, the phases of computation corresponding to movement, reflection and collision of the molecules parallelizes easily. However, based on the density distribution and the decomposition of the particle grid, between stages of computations, there could be significant messaging overhead as particles migrate among the cells. Unsteady DSMC simulations for a two-dimensional Fourier Model investigated by Gallis, Torczynski, and Rader (2004) is used to set up a weak scaling study, fixing the number of simulators per processor. Figure 11 shows the

wall clock time for a thousand time steps. The rapid increase in TLCC run time beyond 256 MPI tasks is suspected to be OS noise related. Additional instrumentation data is being collected to understand this better.

## D. CTH

CTH is an explicit, three-dimensional, multi-material shock hydrodynamics code developed at Sandia for serial and parallel computers. It is designed to model a large variety of two- and three-dimensional problems involving high-speed hydrodynamic flow and the dynamic deformation of solid materials, and includes several equations of state and material strength models (Hertel et al., 1993). The numerical algorithms used in CTH solve the equations of mass, momentum, and energy in an Eulerian finite difference formulation on a three-dimensional Cartesian mesh. CTH can be used in either a flat mesh mode where the faces of adjacent cells are coincident or in a mode with Automatic Mesh Refinement (AMR) where the mesh can be finer in areas of the problem where there is more activity. We will be using the code in a flat mesh mode for this study.

The shaped-charge model consists of a cylindrical container filled with high explosive and capped with a copper liner. When the explosive is detonated from the center of the back of the container, the liner collapses and forms a jet. The problem is run in quarter symmetry and includes a target material.

By using the code in flat mesh mode, the communication patterns are fairly simple and fixed for the entire calculation. The problem space is a rectilinear grid of cells where each processor has a rectilinear sub grid of cells. The processors' domains are also arranged in a grid so that if two processors' domains meet at a face, they share the entire face. Quantities are exchanged at regular intervals across these faces, so each processor exchanges information with up to six other processors in the domain. These messages occur several times per time step and are fairly large since a face can consist of several thousand cells with each cell containing forty quantities. For this simulation, there are processors that

communicate with six other processors once the number of processors in the simulation reaches 128. There are also a few global communications to determine quantities such as the length of the next time step.

Figure 12 shows the weak scaling performance with a large number (90x216x90) of cells per MPI task. This model does not fit within the memory of a TLCC node when we assign one task to each core. The scaling study was run with 8 MPI tasks per node (8ppn).

The performance of TLCC was quite impressive when compared to the Red Storm quad-core. This was particularly true when memory and processor affinity were forced. Detailed analysis of these results with performance analysis tools is in progress. The benefit of *numactl* as previously discussed in other examples is similarly related to the memory access intensity. The faster run time is thought to be due to a combination of better cache utilization and a faster messaging. For tasks within a TLCC NUMA node the predominant nearest neighbor communications seems to execute faster.

*Figure 12.CTH Shape Charge Model Performance*

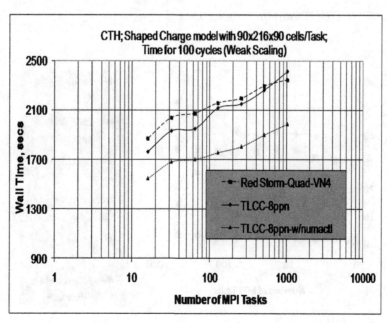

## OPERATING SYSTEM IMPACT

### A. Processor and Memory Affinity With 8-ppn on TLCC

The HPCCG mini-app discussed in Section IV-A is used to further investigate the impact of not controlling memory affinity at run time. The same scaling study was run using only 8 (referred to as *8ppn)* of the 16 cores on each node (with a pair per socket). Before this study, it was anticipated that affinity control through *numactl* would not be beneficial because upon leaving 8 free cores on each node, the OS would be less prone to migrate the MPI tasks. However, as seen in Figure 13, there is still a penalty when *numactl* is not used. For example, on a 256 task job the run time without affinity control takes almost twice as long. This mini-application nicely brings out the destructive impact of thread migration that the OS seems to impose. All of the increase in run time is directly recorded as the increase in time for the DDOT function, a scalar computation at the end of each sparse matrix-vector calculations. The function DDOT has a local dot product computation followed by a global MPI Allreduce operation. The plot shows a nice correlation between the increases in total run time (average over the processors) to the maximum measured time in Allreduce. Even with identical loads, some tasks lag due to memory contention during the memory intensive sparse matrix-vector computations. This leads to staggered arrival at the subsequent global operation in DDOT. This effect may be accentuated when the OS scheduler migrates the MPI tasks not only to another core on the same socket, but also to a different core on another socket.

This is in contrast to the common experience in the early days of HPC systems built with SMP nodes, where the recommended workaround of using fewer MPI tasks than the maximum number of processing elements on a node was often used. So the interesting conclusion that emerges is that the detrimental impact of the OS is most severe in applications that are strongly memory bound. In this context, affinity control is seen to be essential to improve the delivered performance and throughput of such clusters.

*Figure 13. HPCCG Total, DDOT, allreduce times, secs*

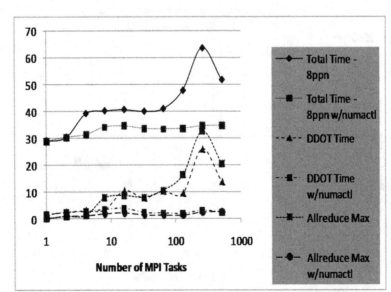

*Table 1. Affinity impact on message bandwidth*

| NUM MPI TASKS | 64 | 256 | 1024 |
|---|---|---|---|
| w/numactl MAX | 88 | 91 | 97 |
| no/numactl MAX | 87 | 96 | 96 |
| w/numactl MIN | 74 | 55 | 29 |
| no/numactl MIN | 74 | 49 | 26 |
| w/numactl AVG | 79 | 78 | 65 |
| no/numactl AVG | 79 | 74 | 66 |

## B. CBENCH Rotate Ping-Pong Test

The Rotate ping-pong test in the benchmark suite cbench (http://sourceforge.net/projects/cbench) was used to investigate the effect of *numactl* on message rates on TLCC.

Table 1 shows the results using all the 16 cores on each node for every configuration. While a small benefit with affinity control is seen, it is not as striking as seen with the applications discussed previously. These results help us understand the elements of computation in a parallel application that are impacted by *numactl*.

## C. POP – Ocean Modeling Code

The POP Ocean Modeling code has often been used to look at the impact of operating system noise on application scalability (Ferreira et al., 2008). A 500 MPI task parallel run with a global ocean grid of 3600x2400 was timed on both the Red Storm and the TLCC with and without *numactl* and using all cores on a node. The Red Storm run time was measured at 614 seconds. The run time on TLCC was measured at 960 seconds without *numactl*, and 731 seconds with *numactl*. This 23% performance gain is another example of a large production application that benefits from processor and memory affinity settings.

## DISCUSSIONS AND SUMMARY

We have looked at the performance of a number of micro benchmarks, mini-applications and real applications on a HPC architecture with multi-core and multi-socket nodes. In this chapter we have shown that control of processor and memory affinity can result in significant performance gains of MPI parallel applications. Operating system interference leading to thread migration, or application process interruptions, are known performance inhibitors. This is particularly true for loosely synchronous applications that use frequent synchronizations through MPI global operations. Forcing affinity, rather than leaving some of the cores unloaded with application threads on each node, leads to the desired improvements in parallel scaling. Comparison of TLCC to Red Storm brings out the substantial coherency enforcement overhead observed with multi-core, multi-socket node architecture. Some analyses explaining the performance differences between the two systems have been presented. We are in the process of obtaining quantitative data from performance analysis tools to shed further insights into the impact of the contrasting hardware and software characteristics associated with the application performances discussed in this chapter.

## ACKNOWLEDGMENT

This work was supported in part by the U.S. Department of Energy. Sandia is a multiprogramming laboratory operated by Sandia Corporation, a Lockheed Martin Company, for the United States National Nuclear Security Administration and the Department of Energy under contract DE-AC04-94AL85000.

# REFERENCES

Brightwell, R., Hudson, T., Pedretti, K., & Underwood, K. D. (2006). SeaStar Interconnect: Balanced Bandwidth for Scalable Performance. *IEEE Micro, 26*(2).

Brown, K. H., Summers, R. M., Glass, M. W., Gullerud, A. S., Heinstein, M. W., & Jones, R. E. (2001). *ACME Algorithms for Contact in a Multiphysics Environment API Version 1.0* (Sand Report SAND2001-3318).

Camp, W. J., & Tomkins, J. L. (2002). Thor'sHammer: The First Version of the Red Storm MPP Architecture. In *Proceedings of the Supercomputing 2002 Conf. High Performance Networking and Computing*.

Ferreira, K., Brightwell, R., & Bridges, P. (2008). *Characterizing Application Sensitivity to OS Interference Using Kernel-Level Noise Injection*. Paper presented at the International Conference for High Performance Computing, Networking, Storage, and Analysis (SC'08), Austin, TX.

Gallis, M. A., Torczynski, J. R., & Rader, D. J. (2004). Molecular gas dynamics observations of Chapman-Enskog behavior and departures there from in nonequilibrium gases. *Physical Review E: Statistical, Nonlinear, and Soft Matter Physics, 69*, 042201. doi:10.1103/PhysRevE.69.042201

Heroux, M. A., Bartlett, R. A., & Howle, V. E. (2005). An overview of the Trilinos project. *ACM Transactions on Mathematical Software, 31*(3), 397–423. doi:10.1145/1089014.1089021

Hertel, E. S., Jr., Bell, R. L., Elrick, M. G., Farnsworth, A. V., Kerley, G. I., McGlaun, J. M., et al. (1993). CTH: A Software Family for Multi-Dimensional Shock Physics Analysis. In *Proceedings of the 19th International Symposium on Shock Waves 1, 274ff*, Université de Provence, Provence, France.

Koteras, R., & Gullerud, A. S. (2003, April). *Presto User's Guide Version 1.05* (JSand Report SAND2003-1089).

Petrini, F., Kerbyson, D., & Pakin, S. (2003). *The Case of the Missing Supercomputer Performance: Achieving Optimal performance on the 8,192 Processors of ASCI Q*. Washington, DC: IEEE.

*This work was previously published in International Journal of Distributed Systems and Technologies, Volume 1, Issue 2, edited by Nik Bessis, pp. 23-39, copyright 2010 by IGI Publishing (an imprint of IGI Global).*

# Chapter 10
# Abstractions and Middleware for Petascale Computing and Beyond

**Ivo F. Sbalzarini**
*ETH Zurich, Switzerland*

## ABSTRACT

*As high-performance computing moves to the petascale and beyond, a number of algorithmic and software challenges need to be addressed. This chapter reviews the main performance-limiting factors in today's high-performance computing software and outlines a possible new programming paradigm to address them. The proposed paradigm is based on abstract parallel data structures and operations that encapsulate much of the complexity of an application, but still make communication overhead explicit. The authors argue that all numerical simulations can be formulated in terms of the presented abstractions, which thus define an abstract semantic specification language for parallel numerical simulations. Simulations defined in this language can automatically be translated to source code containing the appropriate calls to a middleware that implements the underlying abstractions. Finally, the structure and functionality of such a middleware are outlined while demonstrating its feasibility on the example of the parallel particle-mesh library (PPM).*

## INTRODUCTION

Numerical simulations are well established as the third pillar of science, alongside theory and experiments. As numerical methods become more powerful, and more data and knowledge become available about complex real-world systems, the simulations become increasingly elaborate. The availability of parallel high-performance comput-

ing (HPC) systems has enabled simulations with unprecedented numbers of degrees of freedom. The corresponding simulation codes are mostly tightly coupled, which means that the different processors of the HPC machine need to exchange data (communicate) several times while solving a problem, and not only at the beginning and the end of the simulation. Minimizing the communication overhead is thus key to parallel efficiency. In this chapter we propose a novel abstraction layer that

DOI: 10.4018/978-1-4666-0906-8.ch010

provides the proper level of granularity to address some of the software challenges the field is facing as we move beyond petascale systems. We focus on tightly coupled simulations as they occur in classical HPC applications in, e.g., material science, fluid dynamics, astrophysics, or computational chemistry, and in emerging user fields such as biology, finance, or social science.

Despite the proliferation of HPC applications to new areas of science, programming and using HPC machines is becoming increasingly difficult. As the performance of single processors has stopped increasing, speedup can only be achieved through parallelism. There is no more "free speedup" for legacy codes. In addition, memory capacity is growing faster than memory bandwidth (aggravated by the fact that several processor cores are sharing a memory bus), such that accessing memory becomes increasingly expensive compared to compute operations. Presently, it takes about one to two orders of magnitude longer to access the main memory than to perform a floating-point multiplication[1]. In GPUs and other emerging heterogeneous cores this ratio is even higher. Efficient codes should thus minimize memory access counts rather than operation counts. This presents challenges to both the traditional HPC user fields as well as the emerging fields. In traditional fields, well-tested and efficient codes have existed for several decades. These codes are usually large and of limited parallel scalability. They have to be ported to heterogeneous multi-core HPC systems or re-written altogether. For emerging users in biology or social science, there is a high entry hurdle into HPC since parallel programming is notoriously difficult, requires experience, and takes a long time. The predominantly used message-passing paradigm resembles "communication assembly language" with every single point-to-point communication explicitly coded by the programmer. Together, these developments cause several growing gaps in parallel HPC:

1.  *The performance gap:* the actual sustained performance of scientific simulation codes is a decreasing fraction of the theoretical peak-performance of the hardware,

2.  *The knowledge gap:* efficient use of HPC resources requires more and more specialized knowledge and is restricted to a smaller and smaller community,

3.  *The reliability gap:* as machines contain more and more processor cores, the mean-time between failure drops below the typical runtime of a simulation, and

4.  *The data gap:* storing, accessing, and analyzing the peta-bytes of data generated by large simulations or experiments (such as those in astronomy or particle physics) becomes increasingly difficult.

Since the advent of multi-core CPUs, some of these gaps even exist on the single-processor level. Portable, generic scientific software libraries such as GSL or "numerical recipes" are about one order of magnitude slower than vendor-provided, machine-specific libraries such as Intel's IPP/MKL. This is mainly due to the fact that the latter are explicitly optimized and often contain hand-tuned assembly language code for the performance-critical sections, which, however, limits their portability. Moreover, as memory is becoming more expensive than processor cores, the available memory per core decreases, causing bottlenecks due to memory contention when independent heavy-weight processes (such as MPI processes) are running on the different cores (Sbalzarini, Walther, & Bergdorf et al., 2006). Simulations are increasingly memory limited and often use only as many cores per processor as are needed to saturate the memory bandwidth, disabling the rest of the cores or reducing their clock frequency (Gruber & Keller, 2009). In order to maximize the number of usable cores, multi-core parallelism thus has to account for coordinated memory access and be able to profit from shared caches.

In high-end HPC systems, the situation is proportionally worse. Current petascale systems contain around 130 000 processor cores of potentially different architectures, such as the mixture of Opteron and Cell processors used in the Roadrunner system at Los Alamos. These cores are connected by a hierarchy of communication layers of different speeds and operate on data that are stored in memory systems with at least 4 levels of hierarchy (registers, L1 cache, L2 cache, main memory). The different cores on the same processor (chip) have a very fast interconnect and additionally benefit from shared L2 cache and shared main memory. The different chips in the same compute node are connected on the next level of the hierarchy and may still share the main memory, but no cache. The various compute nodes of the machine are finally connected by a network of a certain, again potentially hierarchical, topology. This hardware complexity is expected to increase even more as we move toward exaflop systems. Exaflop systems are expected around 2020 (talk by J. Dongarra at ISC Dresden, 2008) and could well have tens of millions of heterogeneous cores.

Addressing the above-mentioned gaps in these HPC systems requires novel programming paradigms and novel algorithms (Asanovic et al., 2006), the availability of which will be the decisive factor determining the utility of future supercomputers. These programming paradigms should emphasize the hierarchical organization and access cost of the memory and the interconnect, but should be independent of the number of processing elements. In addition, they should be application-independent, portable, and easy to learn and use. One strategy is to introduce an additional layer of abstraction between the computer system and the programmer. This layer should provide a transparent view of the machine, independent of the number and architecture of the processors, such that it will not be necessary for the user to write "communication assembly language". One could then implement scalable, memory-aware algorithms on top of this abstrac-

tion layer. While this idea has already proven useful in areas such as numerical linear algebra (ScaLAPACK, PETSc ...), it remains un-extended to other simulation paradigms, including agent-based models, particle methods, tree codes, etc.

In this chapter, we propose a layer of abstract parallel data types and operations. Their intermediate granularity makes the parallel semantics of the program explicit while still hiding the individual communication operations. Each abstraction defines an encapsulated functionality that can be efficiently implemented as a module of a middleware or a run-time system, thus effectively hiding the hardware complexity from the scientific programmer and reducing the knowledge gap. As a result, the parallel efficiency of scientific simulations based on middleware often surpasses that of hand-parallelized codes (Sbalzarini, Walther, & Bergdorf et al., 2006; Voronenko, 2008). In addition, the abstractions presented here naturally define a language in which the semantics of a parallel simulation program can be expressed. This enables automatic generation of fine-tuned code and ensures portability across machine architectures. Ultimately, we envision a paradigm where the simulation program is specified in an abstract language, which is then automatically translated to source code containing the appropriate calls to the run-time system that implements the abstractions. These implementations can then afford to be platform-specific and auto-tuned. We believe that such a programming paradigm would increase the performance, efficiency, portability, and reliability of large-scale parallel simulations, reduce code development time, and enable a larger community of scientists to benefit from the power of supercomputing.

## ABSTRACTIONS AND THEIR IMPLEMENTATION

Data and operation abstractions are a powerful concept to encapsulate complexity at various levels and to address the challenges outlined. Their purpose is to introduce transparent layers between the application programmer and the hardware of the machine in order to achieve code portability and ease of use. The price one pays for this is a loss of flexibility and generality. Using an abstraction, such as the message passing interface (MPI), necessarily restricts the types of operations one is able to perform to those defined in the abstraction layer. This loss of flexibility is controlled by the granularity (level of detail) of the abstraction layer. The more coarse-grained an abstraction, the less flexible it is, but the easier to use. For scientific computing, it is critically important to develop abstractions at the right granularity. We argue that they do not necessarily diminish the performance of application codes. In practice, simulations that are implemented on top of abstractions are often even more efficient than hand-written, machine-specific codes (Sbalzarini, Walther, & Bergdorf et al., 2006; Voronenko, 2008). This can be explained by the abstraction layer reducing the knowledge gap. By depriving the user of some of the flexibility and complexity of the underlying system, it becomes much harder for the average programmer to write inefficient code.

We propose an abstraction layer that is based on simple parallel data structures and operations that encapsulate computation and communication separately and allow semantic specification of large-scale distributed HPC applications.

## Abstractions

Scientific simulations involve discretizing space and time. We posit that most discretizations on parallel computers can be described in terms of topologies, particles, meshes, connections, interactions, and mappings. We define a topology as a (not necessarily disjoint) decomposition of the computational domain into sub-domains and the assignment of these sub-domains onto processors. Particles are computational elements that are characterized by their position in the computational domain and an arbitrary number of associated properties or methods. Meshes are structured (Cartesian) computational grids, and connections are linker objects between particles that allow grouping them. Interactions are multi-threaded compute operations that can be executed on a set of particles, mesh nodes, and/or connections. Lastly, mappings are communication operations that move particle data, mesh data, or connection data between processors. We define a processor as the collection of all cores that operate on the same memory address space. Processors support multi-threading and can possibly be distributed across several chips.

The abstractions defined here provide an intermediate level of granularity. They are coarse-grained enough to be easy to use and to hide individual point-to-point communications, and they are fine-grained enough such that all of Colella's original 7 dwarfs (Colella, 2004) can be composed from them. These dwarfs are self-contained numerical kernels that constitute the building blocks of today's numerical simulations. The original 7 dwarfs are: dense linear algebra (e.g., BLAS), sparse linear algebra (e.g., OSKI), spectral methods (e.g., FFT), N-body methods (e.g. particle methods or fast multi-poles), structured grid methods (e.g. finite differences or lattice Boltzmann), unstructured grid methods (e.g., finite elements or finite volumes), and MapReduce (e.g., Monte Carlo). Six additional dwarfs have been added to also cover application areas such as databases, machine learning, computer graphics, or embedded computing. We now discuss the proposed abstractions in more detail.

*Topologies* are created by applying a domain decomposition algorithm and a load balancing (processor assignment) algorithm to the computational domain and, possibly, the initial distribution of particles, connections, and/or meshes. They establish a correspondence between the computational elements (particles, mesh nodes, connections) and individual processors of the machine. Topologies are dynamically created and destroyed at run-time and several topologies can exist concurrently in order to, e.g., allow for optimal load balance when particles and mesh nodes are unequally distributed. Each topology comprises a set of cuboidal sub-domains that have halo layers on exactly half of their surfaces (Sbalzarini, Walther, & Bergdorf et al., 2006) in order to allow for symmetric communication with neighboring sub-domains and local evaluation of finite-cutoff interactions (see below). Symmetric communication significantly reduces the memory and communication overhead. Typically, the number of sub-domains is much larger than the number of available processors in order to achieve sufficient granularity for load balancing and re-balancing (see Figure 1). Assigning more than one sub-domain per processor comes at no additional cost, as outlined below. Since several topologies may be defined, this allows for implementation of parallel tree codes or Barnes-Hut algorithms using a hierarchy of topologies that correspond to the different levels of the tree (Sbalzarini, Walther, & Polasek et al., 2006).

*Mappings* encapsulate the communication between processors. There are four basic mapping types that the user can invoke: global, local, ghost-get, and ghost-put. A global mapping involves a potentially all-to-all communication between the processors and can be used to distribute data according to a certain topology or switch from one topology to another. In a local mapping, processors only communicate with their neighbors, defined as those other processors that are assigned sub-domains adjacent to any of the sub-domains of the current processor. Local mappings can be used when particles have moved across processor boundaries or to adjust load balance. Two ghost mappings are provided to operate on the halo layers. The ghost-get mapping populates the halo layers of all sub-domains with copies ("ghosts") of the computational elements from the neighboring processors so they are available for the local evaluation of interactions. At intra-processor sub-domain boundaries, no additional memory or communication is required since the ghost elements are, in this case, identical to the correspond-

*Figure 1. Example of a topology. The computational domain (bounding rectangle) is subdivided into 9311 cuboidal sub-domains (small rectangles) that are distributed onto 64 processors (patches of different gray level). Each processor is assigned a connected set of multiple sub-domains in order to provide sufficient granularity for load-balancing and shared-memory parallelism within each processor. The inter-processor boundaries are optimized to minimize the overall communication volume.*

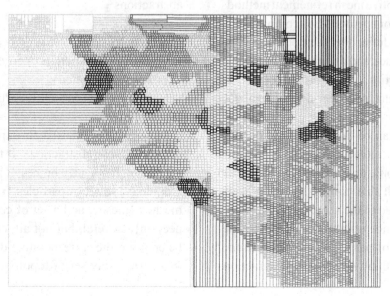

ing real elements, and they are in the same memory address space. The ghost-put mapping is available to send back ghost contributions from the halo layer of the current processor to the corresponding real elements on neighboring processors. This allows computing symmetric interactions that involve ghosts and performing particle–to–mesh and mesh–to–particle interpolations locally per sub-domain. The mapping abstractions internally keep track of the correspondence between ghost elements and real elements such that no bookkeeping is required from the user program. Mappings also internally determine a communication schedule such that a near-minimal number of communication operations are required and no conflicts occur. For global mappings this can be done using rings or trees. For local mappings, graph-based methods can be used, such as minimum edge coloring (or rather: an approximate solution to it). Besides their correctness, we can also require mappings to be tolerant to single-processor hardware failures. With appropriate support from the run-time system (see below), this can be implemented entirely inside the mapping routines since they encapsulate all communication.

*Meshes* are defined by their resolution. Each topology can have several meshes associated with it. This allows for implementation of multi-grid algorithms or adaptive mesh refinement methods.

*Particles* are connectivity-free computational elements that are defined by their position in the computational space and an arbitrary number of additional properties. These properties can be methods, scalar data, or higher-dimensional data of any type.

*Connections* can be used to link particles in order to define, e.g., molecular bonds, unstructured grids, triangulations, or graphs. They constrain the topology such that connected particles are preferably assigned to the same processor.

*Interactions* encapsulate local compute operations on a set of particles, mesh nodes, and/ or connections within a sub-domain. Interactions

therefore do not involve any communication, but can still be distributed over multiple cores of the same processor by multi-threading. In most applications, interactions amount to evaluating pair-wise kernels between elements within a certain cutoff radius. Computing particle–particle interactions allows implementing particle-based simulations or agent-based models. Mesh–mesh interactions account for purely mesh-based operations such as finite differences or FFTs. Finally, particle–mesh interactions are available to implement interpolation schemes, remeshing, or particle-in-cell methods by specifying pairwise interaction kernels between mesh nodes and particles. Since all interactions are local to a sub-domain, they might constrain the types of topologies that can be used. FFTs, for example, require topologies with pencil domain decomposition, where all mesh nodes along at least one spatial direction are in the same memory space. Such constraints are, however, easily accounted for since several topologies can exist concurrently. When computing interactions between particles without connectivity information, the interaction routine can transparently build and use internal cell lists (Hockney & Eastwood, 1988) or Verlet lists (Verlet, 1967) for fast neighbor search within the given cutoff radius.

In summary, we define the following data abstractions:

- Topology (sub-domain, processor assignment)
- Particle(position, properties)
- Mesh(resolution)
- Connection(particle1, particle2)

Any simulation is then expressed in terms of sets of these abstractions. It thus comprises a set (denoted by curly braces "{}") of topologies {topology}, a set of particles {particle}, a set of meshes {mesh}, and a set of connections {connection}. Several, but not all, of these sets may be empty if the corresponding data types are not used. An empty set of topologies, for example, provides for sequential single-processor simulations. On these abstract parallel data types, the following operations are defined:

- Mapping(type, {particle} or mesh or {connection}, topology)
- Interaction({particle} or {connection} or {mesh} or {particle, mesh}, cutoff)
- Create topology(computational domain, {particle, mesh, connection}, domain decomposition algorithm, processor assignment algorithm)

By choosing different domain decomposition and processor assignment algorithms, one can include problem-specific prior knowledge.

When using these abstractions, models from all four realms can be simulated: continuous-deterministic, continuous-stochastic, discrete-deterministic, and discrete-stochastic. The classical numerical simulation methods for these four model types include mesh-based and mesh-free discretization schemes for PDEs, sampling-based schemes such as Monte Carlo, interacting particle systems, agent-based simulations, molecular dynamics, discrete element methods, and discrete-event simulations. All of these methods can be phrased in terms of particles, meshes, connections, interactions, mappings, and topologies.

Mappings are pure communication operations and interactions are pure compute operations. This makes it possible to assess the communication overhead of a simulation already in its abstract specification since computation and communication are not interleaved. The abstractions naturally define a language in which parallel simulations can be specified. As an example, a simple parallel molecular dynamics simulation could be specified as follows in Box 1.

In this example, the topology t1 is created based on the possibly inhomogeneous distribution of atoms and bonds using a recursive orthogonal bisection (ROB) domain decomposition and a processor assignment that minimizes the edge cut in the communication graph. If the molecular dynamics simulation also includes long-range interactions such as electrostatics, the cutoff becomes too large for direct particle–particle interactions. In this case, the simulation is more efficient when solving the corresponding Poisson equation

*Box 1.*

```
read or create {particle} (atoms), {connection} (bonds)
t1 = create topology(computational domain, {particle, connection}, ROB,
minEdgeCut) mapping(global, {particle}, t1)
mapping(global, {connection}, t1)
for time-step = 1,..., T do
mapping(ghost-get, {particle}, t1)
mapping(ghost-get, {connection}, t1)
# non-bonded interactions
interaction({particle}, cutoff)
# bond interactions
interaction({connection}, cutoff)
update the positions and properties in {particle}
mapping(partial, {particle})
mapping(partial, {connection})
end
```

on a mesh using FFTs or multi-grid methods. In order to use FFTs in three dimensions, we define a mesh of resolution h and three additional topologies before the time loop:

```
m1 = mesh(h)
t2 = create topology(computational
domain, {m1}, x-pencil, minEdgeCut)
t3 = create topology(computational
domain, {m1}, y-pencil, minEdgeCut)
t4 = create topology(computational
domain, {m1}, z-pencil, minEdgeCut)
```

Each of these topologies uses a load-balanced pencil decomposition of the mesh m1 where the sub-domains extend throughout the entire computational domain in one direction. Inside the time loop (before updating the particle positions and properties), an FFT can then be computed in parallel as shown in Box 2.

Using three additional interactions to interpolate {particle} to m1, solve the Poisson equation in frequency space (cutoff = 0), and interpolate the result back onto the particles completes the solver. The global mappings required by the FFT can be avoided by solving the Poisson equation using a multi-grid method. Then, only the topology t1 is needed, but with several meshes of different resolution defined on it: m1 = mesh(h), m2 = mesh(h/2), ...

*Box 2.*

```
mapping(global, m1, t2)
# compute the FFT in x direction
interaction({m1}, Lx)
mapping(global, m1, t3)
# compute the FFT in y direction
interaction({m1}, Ly)
mapping(global, m1, t4)
# compute the FFT in z direction
interaction({m1}, Lz)
mapping(global, m1, t1)
```

## Implementation

The abstractions defined above can directly be implemented in a run-time system or middleware as platform-specifically tuned software modules. Depending on the granularity of the underlying abstractions, different levels of encapsulation can be realized. On the lowest level, libraries that implement the MPI standard (Message Passing Interface Forum, 2008) provide abstractions for point-to-point and collective communication operations by encapsulating the communication stacks of the operating system. Adaptive MPI (AMPI) supports dynamic load balancing and multi-threading at this level of the run-time system (Huang, Lawlor, & Kale, 2004). On an intermediate level, more coarse-grained abstractions can be implemented. Examples include the ASTRID programming environment that transparently parallelizes structured-grid finite-element and finite-volume simulations (Bonomi et al., 1989) or the parallel scalable I/O libraries PASSION (Thakur, Bordawekar, Choudhary, Ponnusamy, & Singh, 1994) and ROMIO (Thakur, Gropp, & Lusk, 1999) (now part of the MPI 2.1 standard). On the highest level of abstraction, entire numerical methods can be encapsulated using the abstraction of dwarfs. This includes libraries such as FFTW, ScaLAPACK, PETSc, or the PARTI run-time library for Monte Carlo simulations (Moon & Saltz, 1994).

The abstractions outlined in this chapter are implemented on the intermediate level. Support for topology creation entails dynamic partitioning of the data and operations onto the available processors, and support for mappings can include communication scheduling and mechanisms of fault-tolerance. This is inspired by libraries such as the parallel utilities library PUL (Chapple & Clarke, 1994), which provides domain decomposition methods, data communication, and parallel file I/O for purely mesh-based simulations.

These implementations can afford to be machine-specific since portability is ensured on the level of the abstract specification language. Optimized implementations of the abstractions can thus fully benefit from language and compiler support, as well as from auto-tuning code generators.

*Language support* includes programming languages that are aware of (and provide some control over) the hardware memory hierarchy and that can make data dependencies explicit in order to allow streaming or SIMD vectorization by the compiler. An example of the former is the Sequoia language (Fatahalian et al., 2006), which exposes the memory hierarchy and allows controlled memory-aware programming. Examples for the latter include array programming languages such as APL, HPF, and Co-Array Fortran (included in Fortran, 2008). An interesting early example is the Vectoral programming language that was developed by Alan Wray in 1978 to provide language-level SIMD parallelism on the Illiac IV computer (Wray, 1988). In addition, some languages have a notion of MIMD/SPMD parallelism. Meta-languages such as Linda (Carriero & Gelernter, 1989), however, suffer from a loss of computational efficiency (Turkiyyah, Reed, & Yang, 1996). This is avoided in compiled parallel languages such as Unified Parallel C (UPC Consortium, 2005) or the object-oriented parallel language Charm++ (Kale, Bohm, Mendes, Wilmarth, & Zheng, 2007).

*Compiler support* exploits the data distribution and dependencies made explicit by the programming language. Currently, however, it is almost impossible for compilers to automatically extract the parallel semantics of a program and use them for high-level optimizations. A promising approach for message-passing codes, where every communication operation is explicitly specified, is the generalization of data-flow graphs to parallel data-flow graphs (Bronevetsky, 2009).

*Automatic code generators* such as SPIRAL (Püschel et al., 2005; Voronenko, 2008) can be used to tune the middleware implementations of the abstractions to specific hardware platforms. Such auto-tuned code often outperforms hand-written

code (Voronenko, 2008). This is mainly because elegant, human-readable code is not always the fastest code possible. Code generators that can handle vectorization (SIMD) or shared-memory parallelism (MIMD) could be used to implement the individual abstractions on multi-core processors. This, however, relies on the availability of accurate performance prediction tools or models that allow the code generator to evaluate different options and choose the one that is best suited for a specific machine architecture. Accurate parameterization of the effective hardware performance and of the resource needs of the various code optimization options can help choose the right one, abstracting from the very details of the hardware (Gruber & Keller, 2009). Given the time and space complexity of an algorithm and several measured run-time parameters, such models predict the expected execution time of the algorithm on a given machine. One example of a performance prediction model is the extended $\Gamma-\kappa$ model. In this model, the parameter $\Gamma$ quantifies how communication-limited the distributed-memory part of an applications is and $\kappa$ distinguishes memory-limited multi-threaded application parts from CPU-time-limited ones (Gruber & Keller, 2009). This allows accurate prediction of the parallel scalability of an application, and an informed choice of the algorithms and hardware resources to be used. Application of such models is, however, currently hindered by unpredictable run-time influences from the hardware: caches, look-ahead logics, network routing, and dynamic over-clocking (e.g., in Intel's Nehalem architecture).

Once the implementations are available in a middleware or run-time system, it is conceivable that the semantic description of a parallel numerical simulation, formulated in terms of abstractions, is automatically translated to source code containing the appropriate calls to the run-time system or middleware that implements the abstractions.

## RUN-TIME SYSTEM STRUCTURE

We outline the structure and functionality of a run-time system that supports implementations of the abstractions defined above. In order to implement interaction operations with multiple levels of parallelism (mixed multi-processing/multi-threading), as well as self-optimizing and fault-tolerant mappings, the run-time system has to provide:

1.  A multi-level parallelization layer that is aware of the communication/memory hierarchy,
2.  A hardware-aware communication scheduler and dynamic load balancer, and
3.  A fault-tolerant communication layer.

*Multi-level parallelism* is frequently implemented using nested OpenMP or MPI-2 threads. In the context of the presented abstractions, shared-memory threads are used within individual interaction and mapping modules, whereas each processor runs a separate distributed-memory message-passing process. The parallelization layer can also internally probe, at run-time, the network topology and the memory hierarchy of the machine and make this information available to the communication scheduler and the load balancer.

The *hardware-aware communication scheduler and load balancer* uses this information to optimize the communication schedule through graph algorithms. Approximately solving the minimum edge-coloring problem (Vizing, 1964) on the graph of required (from the application software) communications provides near-optimal schedules with a +1 error bound (Djordjevic & Tosic, 1996; Durand, Jain, & Tseytlin, 2003). Bandwidth, latency, and distance between the processors (according to the network's hardware topology) can be accounted for by weights on the edges of the graph (Bhatele & Kale, 2008). The load balancer can use the measured run-time parameters in a performance prediction model

in order to decide which part of an application should run on cores of which architecture, or to dynamically migrate processes to better-suited parts of the machine (Gruber & Keller, 2009). Among cores of the same architecture, processor assignment can be based on graph partitioning algorithms (Karypis & Kumar, 1998a, 1998b). There, each node of the graph corresponds to a work package (such as a sub-domain) and each edge corresponds to a required communication between work packages. Every node is attributed a weight reflecting the computational cost of that work package, and every edge has a weight that represents the communication volume. The nodes are then partitioned onto the processors of the machine such that the variance of computational costs across processors and the total edge-cut are minimized. In this step, the relative speeds of the processors, their architecture (in a heterogeneous machine), and their proximity relations in the machine interconnect can be accounted for by using, for example, parameterized descriptions (Gruber & Keller, 2009). This ensures that every work package runs in its "optimal" hardware environment. In the framework of the proposed abstractions, this can be done at the level of topologies for the multi-processing parts of an application, and at the level of interactions for the multi-threaded parts.

A *fault-tolerant communication layer* becomes important when machines grow large enough such that the mean time between hardware failures is less than the average run-time of a simulation. In a machine with 1 million processors, at least one node is expected to fail every 30 minutes. While the mean-time between failures can be increased by about a factor of 2 if all unused cores and machine parts are dynamically powered down and the clock frequency is adjusted to the application needs (Gruber & Keller, 2009), fault tolerance remains an issue. Mostly, it is addressed by checkpointing (Elnozahy, Alvisi, Wang, & Johnson, 2002), which means that the data of the simulation are periodically copied from the main memory of the computer to hard disks. If one of the nodes fails, the whole simulation program halts and restarts from the most recent checkpoint by recovering the data from disk. While global checkpointing does not scale to large systems, local recovery protocols have an overhead that is independent of the number of processors. In the simplest local scheme, checkpoint files are written to the scratch disks of the individual compute nodes with a copy onto the neighboring node. The constant overhead of local checkpointing can be reduced if the communication layer of the run-time system includes mechanisms of fault tolerance. This has been implemented in the Converse run-time system (Kale, Bhandarkar, Jagathesan, Krishnan, & Yelon, 1996) for Charm++ and AMPI, and the fault-tolerant HARNESS run-time system (Beck et al., 1999; Angskun, Fagg, Bosilca, Pjesivac-Grbovic, & Dongarra, 2006). Based on such run-time systems, fault-tolerant message-passing libraries have been implemented. Examples include the fault-tolerant FT-MPI (Fagg et al., 2004), which is implemented based on HARNESS, and AMPI (Huang, 2004) as implemented based on Converse. Other fault-tolerance techniques include direct (possibly asynchronous) use of communication sockets, message logging (Elnozahy et al., 2002), and in-memory data redundancy (Zheng, Shi, & Kale, 2004).

## A FEASIBILITY STUDY: THE PARALLEL PARTICLE-MESH LIBRARY (PPM)

The PPM library (Sbalzarini, Walther, & Bergdorf et al., 2006; Sbalzarini, Walther, & Polasek et al., 2006) was a first attempt to implement the abstractions outlined in this chapter in a transparent, portable middleware. The overall goal is to provide a processor-independent, data-transparent programming model for distributed-memory computers and to completely hide MPI from the application programmer. In PPM, this has been done for tightly coupled parallel numerical simulations

that are formulated in the framework of hybrid particle-mesh methods. PPM is a middleware in the sense described here, introducing an additional, transparent layer between infrastructure libraries such as MPI, Metis (Karypis & Kumar, 1998a, 1998b), and FFTW and the user's simulation programs. This is schematically depicted in Figure 2 and has made it possible to implement scalable parallel simulations without having to know MPI, which immediately renders supercomputing accessible to a larger user community. Since PPM limits the flexibility of the application programmer to hybrid particle-mesh methods described using the abstractions defined above, even inexperienced programmers can implement simulations that outperform state-of-the-art hand-parallelized codes (see Sbalzarini, Walther, & Bergdorf et al., 2006 for examples).

The PPM library is independent of specific applications. The library design goals include ease of use, efficient parallel scalability in both CPU time and memory requirements, and SIMD vectorization of all major loops. PPM implements encapsulated modules for the abstractions defined above and provides the adaptive domain decomposition, dynamic load balancing, and communication scheduling methods required to create topologies and mappings based on a specific data (particle or mesh) distribution at run time. Communication scheduling is done using an approximate solution of the minimum edge-coloring problem (Vizing, 1964). The SAR heuristic (Moon & Saltz, 1994) is used to decide when to re-decompose a problem in order to achieve a good trade-off between the cost of domain decomposition and arising load imbalance from particle motion. All of this is done transparently in the background, without participation of the user program. For further details about the PPM library architecture, the reader is referred to the original publication (Sbalzarini, Walther, & Bergdorf et al., 2006).

Supplementing the library core functionalities, PPM also includes frequently used numerical

*Figure 2. The parallel particle mesh (PPM) library is a transparent middleware layer between system-specific low-level libraries (MPI, METIS, FFTW) and the user's parallel simulation programs. It provides a run-time environment that implements abstract parallel data structures and operations in encapsulated software modules. The simulation codes are then specified in terms of these abstractions (see main text for details).*

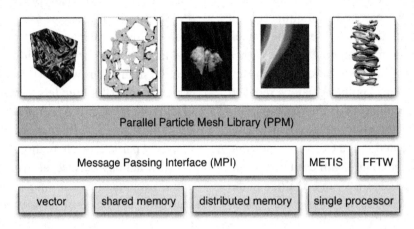

solvers, such as multi-grid and FFT Poisson solvers, multi-stage ODE integrators, fast multipole methods (Greengard & Gropp, 1990), and fast marching methods (Sethian, 1999) as well as group marching methods (Kim, 2001) for level sets. These numerical modules can be interpreted as dwarfs that are implemented using the data and operation abstractions provided by the PPM library core. In addition, PPM also provides transparent parallel file I/O.

The efficiency, scalability, and ease of use of PPM have been demonstrated in a number of past applications as summarized in Table 1. In all of these past applications, the PPM-based simulation codes outperformed the corresponding state-of-the-art hand-written codes in wall-clock time, parallel efficiency, or both (Sbalzarini, Walther, & Bergdorf et al., 2006). Also, it is interesting to note that the PPM codes were implemented in short time even without using automatic code generation. The molecular dynamics code was, for example, implemented in less than 3 months by a first-year PhD student with no prior experience in parallel programming or in using PPM. This implementation outperformed (by more than

a factor of 2) an existing handcrafted molecular dynamics code that was developed over 6 years by the same group. It completed one time step of an 8 million-atom simulation in 0.25 seconds at 63% parallel efficiency on 256 processors (see Table 1). The discrete element simulation (Walther & Sbalzarini, 2009) was implemented in less than 2 days by two of the PPM developers who are acquainted with the middleware. Discrete element methods (DEM) are particularly hard to parallelize due to the dynamically changing contact lists and the need to integrate contact deformations over time. The PPM-based simulation code sustained 40% parallel efficiency on 192 processors of a standard Ethernet-Linux cluster (Table 1). The simulation used 122 million fully resolved visco-elastic spheres, constituting the largest DEM simulation done thus far.

The remeshed smoothed particle hydrodynamics (SPH) simulation in Table 1 used 268 million particles transparently distributed onto 128 processors of the Cray XT4 computer at the Swiss National Supercomputing Centre (CSCS) to simulate the fluid dynamics of a compressible vortex ring (Sbalzarini, Walther, & Bergdorf et

*Table 1. Weak scaling results from past applications using the PPM library*

| Application | # particles | # proc. | Machine | Parallel efficiency | Reference |
|---|---|---|---|---|---|
| smoothed particle hydrodynamics of compressible flow | $268 \times 10^6$ | 128 | Cray XT4 | 91% | (Sbalzarini, Walther, & Bergdorf et al., 2006) |
| vortex method for incompressible flow (using the PPM-based multi-grid Poisson solver) | $268 \times 10^6$ | 512 | IBM p690 | 76% | (Sbalzarini, Walther, & Bergdorf et al., 2006) |
| particle strength exchange for diffusion in a complex biological geometry (Sbalzarini, Mezzacasa, Helenius, & Koumoutsakos, 2005; Sbalzarini, Hayer, Helenius, & Koumoutsakos, 2006) | $10^9$ | 242 | IBM p690 | 84% | (Sbalzarini, Walther, & Bergdorf et al., 2006) |
| molecular dynamics of Lennard-Jones atoms | $8 \times 10^6$ | 256 | IBM p690 | 63% (0.25 s/ time step) | unpublished |
| discrete element method for granular flow | $122 \times 10^6$ | 192 | AMD Opteron Linux cluster, Gigabit Ethernet | 40% | (Walther & Sbalzarini, 2009) |
| vortex method for incompressible turbulent flow | $6.5 \times 10^9$ | 16 384 | IBM BG/L | 62% | (Chatelain et al., 2008a; Chatelain et al., 2008b) |

al., 2006). The simulation sustained 91% parallel efficiency (weak scaling) on 128 processors. This compares well to the 85% efficiency achieved by the GADGET SPH code of the Max-Planck Institute for Astrophysics on 32 processors. The same PPM-based SPH code was later also used to simulate a self-propelled swimmer with an immersed-boundary SPH. Using 13 million particles, the code took 70 seconds per time step on a Linux cluster with 32 AMD Opteron 2.2 GHz processors (Hieber & Koumoutsakos, 2008).

Vortex methods are hybrid particle-mesh methods to simulate incompressible fluids. In contrast to SPH, the incompressibility constraint requires the solution of a Poisson equation at every time step. This introduces long-range interactions that require global mappings, hence increasing the communication overhead of the parallel simulation. Together with the larger number of processors needed, this leads to lower parallel efficiencies compared to SPH simulations. The PPM-based vortex method code used in Table 1 nevertheless sustained 76% parallel efficiency on 512 processors for 268 million particles (Sbalzarini, Walther,

& Bergdorf et al., 2006). A further optimized and adapted version of this code was later used on 16384 processors of an IBM BG/L for a vortex method simulation using 6.5 billion particles at 62% parallel efficiency (Chatelain et al., 2008a; Chatelain et al., 2008b).

In complex-shaped geometries, the adaptive domain decomposition and load-balancing methods of the PPM library become important. This has been tested in particle simulations of diffusion in the endoplasmic reticulum, a complex tubular network in biological cells (Sbalzarini, Mezzacasa, Helenius, & Koumoutsakos, 2005; Sbalzarini, Hayer, Helenius, & Koumoutsakos, 2006). The simulations used up to 1 billion particles distributed onto up to 242 processors of the IBM p690 computer at CSCS. The weak-scaling efficiency was better than 84% in all cases, demonstrating the scalability of automatic, transparent data distribution using the abstractions presented above (Sbalzarini, Walther, & Bergdorf et al., 2006).

In summary, the PPM library has demonstrated the feasibility and viability of a processor-independent, data-transparent parallel programming model for hybrid particle-mesh simulations. The model was based on a preliminary version of the abstractions presented above.

## CONCLUSION

As computing is becoming an integral part of many sciences and the models become more complex, HPC is an indispensable catalyst of progress as its use proliferates. However, the complexity of such large hardware systems and the architecture of modern (heterogeneous) multi-core processors have led to several gaps, of which the knowledge gap is arguably the most important one. Efficient use of HPC machines and their availability to emerging user fields depends on new programming paradigms and algorithms. Some of the resources must thus be invested in computer science research and education. It is widely accepted that an additional layer of abstraction, which hides the hardware complexity and exposes a programming model that is independent of the number and architecture of processors, is one possible solution.

We have introduced data and operation abstractions that provide intermediate granularity and disentangle computation from communication, enabling automatic analysis and optimization. These abstractions also define a language in which the parallel semantics of simulations can be expressed, and they define encapsulated functionalities that can be implemented as architecture-specifically optimized modules of a middleware or run-time system. In the future, these implementations could be constructed and optimized using auto-tuning code generators, provided the necessary performance prediction tools are available. It is also possible to construct "simulation compilers" that automatically translate an abstract definition of a simulation to the proper sequence of middleware calls. This would have several benefits: (a) the abstract definition is independent of the number of processors, ensuring portability and ease of use; (b) the implementations of the individual abstractions (i.e., the modules of the middleware) can be tuned to the machine architecture, thus transparently optimizing hardware use; (c) implementing a parallel simulation is reduced to writing its abstract definition, thus greatly reducing code development time and the knowledge gap; (d) if better algorithms become available they only have to be implemented in the middleware, immediately benefitting all simulations without changing their abstract descriptions.

The presented abstractions are deliberately kept simple, encapsulating simple and regular data structures such as particles and meshes. This is motivated by our expectation that simple data structures tend to scale better to larger numbers of processors, which seems to be confirmed by the experiences made with the PPM library. In particular, operation counts lose importance compared to memory access and communication (latency) counts. Several efficient single-processor algorithms use trees or graphs, which might not parallelize well and tend to be memory limited. Instead of using a complex surface triangulation on a large distributed system, for example, it might be favorable to use a simple Cartesian mesh with an embedded boundary method.

In summary, the abstractions and middleware presented in this chapter provide a starting point that has already led to highly scalable and easy-to-implement parallel simulations (Sbalzarini, Walther, & Bergdorf et al., 2006). At this stage, however, there are more open questions (and research opportunities!) than solutions. Even though many bits and pieces exist in all areas (abstractions, languages, compilers, middleware, tools), they are yet to be combined in a programming model that is independent of the number of processors and their architecture. In this venture, care must be taken that the abstractions are general enough not to "over-fit" the present-day multi-core architectures. Abstractions should be sufficiently independent of the hardware and based on theoretical compute models. This will help prevent today's simulations from becoming tomorrow's legacy codes.

## ACKNOWLEDGMENT

I am deeply grateful to Prof. Dr. Jens H. Walther (DTU, Copenhagen, Denmark) for his initiative and vision to start the PPM project as well as for countless discussions on parallel programming and joint programming sessions. I also thank Prof. Dr. Petros Koumoutsakos (ETH Zurich, Switzerland), in whose group the PPM project started and is still on going, as well as all contributors to the PPM library, in particular Dr. Michael Bergdorf (D. E. Shaw Research, New York, USA) and Prof. Dr. Philippe Chatelain (Université Catholique de Louvain, Belgium). Special thanks also to Prof. Dr. Ralf Gruber (EPFL, Switzerland), Dr. Greg Bronevetsky (LLNL, USA), Prof. Dr. Jens H. Walther (DTU, Copenhagen, Denmark), Rajesh Ramaswamy (ETH Zurich, Switzerland), and Justin Park (ETH Zurich, Switzerland) for proofreading the manuscript and providing valuable feedback and suggestions. We thank the Swiss National Supercomputing Centre (CSCS) for dedicated access to their HPC systems.

## REFERENCES

Angskun, T., Fagg, G. E., Bosilca, G., Pjesivac-Grbovic, J., & Dongarra, J. J. (2006). Scalable fault tolerant protocol for parallel runtime environments. In *Proceedings of the Euro PVM/MPI* (p. ICL-UT-06-12).

Asanovic, K., Bodik, R., Catanzaro, B. C., Gebis, J. J., Husbands, P., Keutzer, K., et al. (2006). *The landscape of parallel computing research: A view from Berkeley* (Tech. Rep. No. UCB/EECS-2006-183). University of California at Berkeley, Berkeley, CA.

Beck, M., Dongarra, J. J., Fagg, G. E., Geist, G. A., Gray, P., & Kohl, J. (1999). HARNESS: A next generation distributed virtual machine. *Future Generation Computer Systems*, *15*, 571–582. doi:10.1016/S0167-739X(99)00010-2

Bhatele, A., & Kale, L. V. (2008). Application-specific topology-aware mapping for three dimensional topologies. In *Proceedings of the IEEE international symposium on parallel and distributed processing* (pp. 1-8).

Bonomi, E., Flück, M., George, P., Gruber, R., Herbin, R., & Perronnet, A. (1989). Astrid: Structured finite element and finite volume programs adapted to parallel vectorcomputers. *Computer Physics Reports*, *11*, 81–116. doi:10.1016/0167-7977(89)90019-1

Bronevetsky, G. (2009). Communication-sensitive static dataflow for parallel message passing applications. In *Proceedings of the International symposium on code generation and optimization (CGO)* (pp. 1-12).

Carriero, N., & Gelernter, D. (1989). Linda in context. *Communications of the ACM*, *32*(4), 444–458. doi:10.1145/63334.63337

Chapple, S. R., & Clarke, L. J. (1994). The parallel utilities library. In *Proceedings of the IEEE scalable parallel libraries conference* (pp. 21-30).

Chatelain, P., Curioni, A., Bergdorf, M., Rossinelli, D., Andreoni, W., & Koumoutsakos, P. (2008a). Billion vortex particle direct numerical simulations of aircraft wakes. *Computer Methods in Applied Mechanics and Engineering*, *197*, 1296–1304. doi:10.1016/j.cma.2007.11.016

Chatelain, P., Curioni, A., Bergdorf, M., Rossinelli, D., Andreoni, W., & Koumoutsakos, P. (2008b). *Vortex methods for massively parallel computer architectures, LNCS, 5336*, 479–489.

Colella, P. (2004). *Defining software requirements for scientific computing.* Presentation slides.

Consortium, U. P. C. (2005). *UPC language specifications* (Vol. 2) (Tech Rep. No. LBNL-59208). Berkeley, California: Lawrence Berkeley National Laboratory.

Djordjevic, G. L., & Tosic, M. B. (1996). A heuristic for scheduling task graphs with communication delays onto multiprocessors. *Parallel Computing, 22,* 1197–1214. doi:10.1016/S0167-8191(96)00041-5

Durand, D., Jain, R., & Tseytlin, D. (2003). Parallel I/O scheduling using randomized, distributed edge coloring algorithms. *Journal of Parallel and Distributed Computing, 63,* 611–618. doi:10.1016/S0743-7315(03)00015-7

Elnozahy, E. N. M., Alvisi, L., Wang, Y.-M., & Johnson, D. B. (2002). A survey of rollback-recovery protocols in message-passing systems. *ACM Computing Surveys, 34*(3), 375–408. doi:10.1145/568522.568525

Fagg, G. E., Gabriel, E., Bosilca, G., Angskun, T., Chen, Z., Pjesivac-Grbovic, J., et al. (2004). Extending the MPI specification for process fault tolerance on high performance computing systems. In *Proceedings of the international supercomputing conference (ISC2004).*

Fatahalian, K., Knight, T. J., Houston, M., Erez, M., Horn, D. R., Leem, L., et al. (2006). Sequoia: Programming the memory hierarchy. In *Proceedings of the SC06 conference on high performance networking and computing* (p. 83). Washington, DC: ACM/IEEE.

Greengard, L., & Gropp, W. D. (1990). A parallel version of the fast multipole method. *Computers & Mathematics with Applications (Oxford, England), 20*(7), 63–71. doi:10.1016/0898-1221(90)90349-O

Gruber, R., & Keller, V. (2009). *HPC @ GreenIT.* Berlin, Germany: Springer.

Hieber, S. E., & Koumoutsakos, P. (2008). An immersed boundary method for smoothed particle hydrodynamics of self-propelled swimmers. *Journal of Computational Physics, 227,* 8636–8654. doi:10.1016/j.jcp.2008.06.017

Hockney, R. W., & Eastwood, J. W. (1988). *Computer simulation using particles.* London: Institute of Physics Publishing.

Huang, C. (2004). *System support for checkpoint/restart of Charm++ and AMPI applications.* Unpublished Master thesis, University of Illinois, Illinois.

Huang, C., Lawlor, O., & Kale, L. V. (2004). *Adaptive MPI, LNCS, 2958,* 306–322.

Kale, L. V., Bhandarkar, M., Jagathesan, N., Krishnan, S., & Yelon, J. (1996). Converse: an interoperable framework for parallel programming. In *Proceedings of the IEEE international parallel processing symposium (IPPS)* (pp. 212-217).

Kale, L. V., Bohm, E., Mendes, C. L., Wilmarth, T., & Zheng, G. (2007). Programming Petascale Applications with Charm++ and AMPI. In *Proceedings of the Petascale computing: Algorithms and applications.* New York: CRC Press.

Karypis, G., & Kumar, V. (1998a). A fast and high quality multilevel scheme for partitioning irregular graphs. *SIAM Journal on Scientific Computing, 20*(1), 359–392. doi:10.1137/S1064827595287997

Karypis, G., & Kumar, V. (1998b). Multilevel k-way partitioning scheme for irregular graphs. *Journal of Parallel and Distributed Computing, 48,* 96–129. doi:10.1006/jpdc.1997.1404

Kim, S. (2001). An O(N) level set method for Eikonal equations. *SIAM Journal on Scientific Computing, 22*(6), 2178–2193. doi:10.1137/S1064827500367130

Message Passing Interface Forum. (2008). *MPI: A message-passing interface standard, version 2.1.* Stuttgart, Germany: High-Performance Computing Center Stuttgart.

Moon, B., & Saltz, J. (1994). Adaptive runtime support for direct simulation Monte Carlo methods on distributed memory architectures. In *Proceedings of the IEEE scalable high-performance computing conference* (pp. 176–183). Washington, DC: IEEE.

Püschel, M., Moura, J. M. F., Johnson, J. R., Padua, D., Veloso, M. M., & Singer, B. W. (2005). SPIRAL: Code generation for DSP transforms. *Proceedings of the IEEE, 93*(2), 232–275. doi:10.1109/JPROC.2004.840306

Sbalzarini, I. F., Hayer, A., Helenius, A., & Koumoutsakos, P. (2006). Simulations of (an)isotropic diffusion on curved biological surfaces. *Biophysical Journal, 90*(3), 878–885. doi:10.1529/biophysj.105.073809

Sbalzarini, I. F., Mezzacasa, A., Helenius, A., & Koumoutsakos, P. (2005). Effects of organelle shape on fluorescence recovery after photobleaching. *Biophysical Journal, 89*(3), 1482–1492. doi:10.1529/biophysj.104.057885

Sbalzarini, I. F., Walther, J. H., Bergdorf, M., Hieber, S. E., Kotsalis, E. M., & Koumoutsakos, P. (2006). PPM – a highly efficient parallel particle-mesh library for the simulation of continuum systems. *Journal of Computational Physics, 215*(2), 566–588. doi:10.1016/j.jcp.2005.11.017

Sbalzarini, I. F., Walther, J. H., Polasek, B., Chatelain, P., Bergdorf, M., & Hieber, S. E. (2006). *A software framework for the portable parallelization of particle-mesh simulations, LNCS, 4128,* 730–739.

Sethian, J. A. (1999). *Level set methods and fast marching methods.* Cambridge, UK: Cambridge University Press.

Thakur, R., Bordawekar, R., Choudhary, A., Ponnusamy, R., & Singh, T. (1994). PASSION runtime library for parallel I/O. In *Proceedings of the IEEE scalable parallel libraries conference* (pp. 119-128). Washington, DC: IEEE.

Thakur, R., Gropp, W., & Lusk, E. (1999). Data sieving and collective I/O in ROMIO. In *Proceedings of the 7th symposium on the frontiers of massively parallel computation* (pp. 182-189).

Turkiyyah, G., Reed, D., & Yang, J. (1996). Fast vortex methods for predicting wind-induced pressures on buildings. *Journal of Wind Engineering and Industrial Aerodynamics, 58,* 51–79. doi:10.1016/0167-6105(95)00020-R

Verlet, L. (1967). Computer experiments on classical fluids. I. Thermodynamical properties of Lennard-Jones molecules. *Physical Review, 159*(1), 98–103. doi:10.1103/PhysRev.159.98

Vizing, V. G. (1964). On an estimate of the chromatic class of a p-graph. *Diskret. Analiz, 3,* 25–30.

Voronenko, Y. (2008). *Library generation for linear transforms.* Unpublished doctoral dissertation, Carnegie Mellon University, Pittsburgh, PA.

Walther, J. H., & Sbalzarini, I. F. (2009). Large-scale parallel discrete element simulations of granular flow. *Engineering Computations, 26*(6), 688–697. doi:10.1108/02644400910975478

Wray, A. A. (1988). *A manual of the vectoral language (Internal report)*. Moffett Field, CA: NASA Ames Research Center.

Zheng, G., Shi, L., & Kale, L. V. (2004). FTC-Charm++: An in-memory checkpoint-based fault tolerant runtime for Charm++ and MPI. In *Proceedings of the IEEE conference on cluster computing* (pp. 93-103).

## ENDNOTE

[1] On the Intel Nehalem architecture, the ratio is one order of magnitude if only 1 or 2 cores of the processor are used in a pipelined way.

*This work was previously published in International Journal of Distributed Systems and Technologies, Volume 1, Issue 2, edited by Nik Bessis, pp. 40-56, copyright 2010 by IGI Publishing (an imprint of IGI Global).*

# Chapter 11
# A Simulator for Large–Scale Parallel Computer Architectures

**Curtis L. Janssen**
*Sandia National Laboratories, USA*

**Ali Pinar**
*Sandia National Laboratories, USA*

**Helgi Adalsteinsson**
*Sandia National Laboratories, USA*

**David A. Evensky**
*Sandia National Laboratories, USA*

**Scott Cranford**
*Sandia National Laboratories, USA*

**Jackson Mayo**
*Sandia National Laboratories, USA*

**Joseph P. Kenny**
*Sandia National Laboratories, USA*

## ABSTRACT

*Efficient design of hardware and software for large-scale parallel execution requires detailed understanding of the interactions between the application, computer, and network. The authors have developed a macro-scale simulator (SST/macro) that permits the coarse-grained study of distributed-memory applications. In the presented work, applications using the Message Passing Interface (MPI) are simulated; however, the simulator is designed to allow inclusion of other programming models. The simulator is driven from either a trace file or a skeleton application. Trace files can be either a standard format (Open Trace Format) or a more detailed custom format (DUMPI). The simulator architecture is modular, allowing it to easily be extended with additional network models, trace file formats, and more detailed processor models. This chapter describes the design of the simulator, provides performance results, and presents studies showing how application performance is affected by machine characteristics.*

DOI: 10.4018/978-1-4666-0906-8.ch011

# INTRODUCTION

The degree of parallelism that must be exposed to efficiently utilize modern large-scale parallel computing systems is intimidating. Because individual processor performance gains are currently achieved primarily through multiple cores on a chip and multiple threads of execution in a core, the rate at which parallelism must be exposed by an application will increase as a function of overall machine performance relative to historical trends. This results in greater design complexity for both machine architects and application software developers. The use of simulation, however, can aid both in their efforts to obtain high utilization from future computing platforms.

Simulation is already used extensively in the design of computing systems for both functional verification and timing estimation. As an example of the range of capabilities available, including just a few examples of open-source timing simulators, there are processor simulators (Binkert et al., 2006; M5Sim), memory simulators (Jacob; Wang et al., 2005), and network simulators ns-3 (ns-3).

Several simulators have been developed to generate performance estimates for high-performance computing architectures. These range from high-fidelity and computationally expensive simulators for measuring performance between two nodes (Rodrigues et al., 2003; Underwood, Levenhagen, & Rodrigues, 2007) to lower-fidelity and lower-cost simulators that can estimate performance on large-scale machines. These lower-fidelity simulators use a variety of approaches to generate the application's processor and network workload including tracing, direct execution, and the use of skeleton applications. Additionally, the flow of data through the network is modeled with varying fidelity. In the present chapter we are concerned with lower-fidelity and lower-cost simulation techniques to enable simulation at very large scales, and we will briefly discuss these simulator variants in more detail, giving examples

of simulators supporting each capability before turning to a detailed description of our simulator in Section 2.

When an application is traced, the full program is run in order to collect information about how it executes. The resulting data is output into a trace file, which contains data such as the time spent in computation and the amount of data sent and received by each node. This trace file is read by the simulator, allowing it to replay the run, adjusting the simulated times to account for differences between the simulated machine and that which was used to collect the traces (Zheng, Wilmarth, Jagadishprasad, & Kale, 2005). In the case of Message Passing Interface (MPI) (Message Passing Interface Forum, 2008) traces, events that are higher level than simple sends and receives are recorded, such as all-to-all broadcast or all-to-one reduce. These network events along with associated parameters are logged without the details of the underlying messages that are used to implement the operation. It is the responsibility of the simulator to either convert these higher-level operations into the low-level messages that implement the operation or to provide an appropriate timing model that does not require simulation of the low-level messages.

In the direct execution approach the full application is run on each node (Prakash et al., 2000; Riesen, 2006; Zheng et al., 2005). This is different from normal benchmarking because, instead of real time, a virtual time is used to determine the execution time. The virtual time is computed by using a network model to estimate communication times. The contribution to the virtual time due to processor execution can be determined simply by using the measured real time for non-communication work or by using a processor model. This model can be informed by measurements of actual application processor utilization or more detailed processor simulations.

The third approach to generating the machine's workload does not use a full application. Instead, a so-called skeleton application is used that provides enough information to the simulator for it to model both computation and communication. This takes advantage of the fact that the computations needed to determine program flow are a small subset of the total number of computations needed by typical high-performance computing applications. The skeleton application can be constructed in a variety of ways. An application programmer could directly program a skeleton application, giving the programmer the opportunity to experiment with different algorithms before having to write the full application. Existing applications can be skeletonized by replacing portions of the code doing computation with calls that instruct the simulator to account for the time implicitly (Susukita et al., 2008). Skeleton applications can also be constructed using automated analysis tools, for example, using compiler analysis techniques to abstract away portions of the application (Adve, Bagrodia, Deelman, & Sakellariou, 2002). Skeleton applications have the advantage of capturing the essence of the application in sufficient detail to enable reasonably accurate simulation while being much less expensive than running the application.

Various approaches are also taken to model the network layer. These range from relatively simple models that only consider endpoint congestion (Prakash et al., 2000) to accurate models that treat the flow of data through the network in detail (Benveniste & Heidelberger, 1995; Petrini & Vannesch, 1997; Zheng et al., 2005). In endpoint congestion models the only network bottlenecks are the nodes. If two messages arrive simultaneously at a node, only one at a time can be received, and the delay in reception of the second message is determined from simple network performance characteristics such as the latency and bandwidth. This model does not reflect the fact that internal to the network fabric there can be contention for resources. Detailed network models are aware of the machine's network topology and use this information, along with other details such as routing algorithms, to estimate message arrival times.

Both approaches are useful in that the endpoint congestion model provides an inexpensive way to obtain an optimistic performance estimate while the more detailed models take into account the impact on performance of machine topology and process layout effects.

In the present work we describe a macro-scale simulator for estimating the performance of large-scale parallel machines. The goals of the simulator are to assist in system design and application development. The simulator is modular, permitting multiple computation and communication models to be employed. This will allow the study of architectures at a variety of fidelities so we can trade off the computational cost of doing a simulation against the accuracy of the result. The simulator will be distributed under an open-source license to maximize its usefulness to the high-performance computing community. We focus on an extremely lightweight implementation, rather than enabling parallelism in the simulator itself. Parallelism can be easily introduced when performing independent simulations of architecture variants. We also provide a detailed MPI model that converts the high-level MPI events into the necessary communication operations. Because the MPI capability is implemented to be modular, it is simple to investigate the relative performance of various MPI algorithms. The simulator is designed to allow the use of alternative programming models, as well.

Our work is done in the context of a larger project to develop a parallel multi-scale simulator that permits users of the simulator to select the desired level of fidelity for each component of the machine. This larger project is an outgrowth of the Structural Simulation Toolkit (SST) (Rodrigues et al., 2003; Underwood et al., 2007) and the macro-scale components described herein will be referred to as SST/macro to distinguish them from the existing micro-scale SST components.

## THE MACROSCALE SIMULATOR

The execution of an application on a parallel machine can be represented as a collection of computation and communication events. These events have complex but known dependencies; for example, a synchronization event must occur in all parallel tasks before any task can move forward. We model the execution of these events using a discrete event simulator. Using models to determine the duration of these computation and communication events, the simulator determines event completion times. Thus, the message timing of applications is determined, allowing the efficiency and scalability of applications to be examined.

We avoid the synchronization overheads incurred by parallel discrete event simulation and implement an extremely lightweight simulator within a single kernel thread. Application tasks are modeled using lightweight threads, allowing the simulator to maintain the complex states of numbers of tasks ranging into the millions. Application task threads use a well-defined interface layer to generate simulation events, reproducing the coarse-grained communication and computation loads of real applications. This lightweight implementation allows us to simulate up to 200,000 MPI send/receive pairs per second on a single workstation, with a memory footprint that scales linearly with the number of peers.

Figure 1 illustrates the high-level design of the simulator. The process layer supports two

*Figure 1. Application threads create communication and compute kernels and push them down to the interface layer. The interface layer schedules events on the discrete event simulator, possibly using calls to servers. Callbacks are made to the process layer via request objects when events complete.*

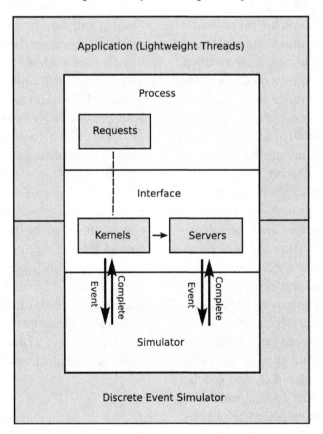

execution modes, skeleton application and trace-driven, using lightweight threads. Task threads create communication and compute kernels which are parameterized with data for a particular communication operation or compute block. Kernels for MPI operations, for instance, require the arguments to the MPI call, while compute kernels require a description of the CPU instructions to be simulated. Tasks interact with the simulator back-end by pushing kernels down to the interface layer. The interface layer coordinates interaction with network and CPU models and handles the scheduling of resulting events on the simulator back end. The interface layer includes servers, such as *mpiserver* which manages interaction with the network model in MPI contexts. When kernels are completed, the process layer receives callbacks via request objects.

SST/macro is implemented in C++, allowing a flexible, modular design that provides opportunities for modification and extension. The inheritance diagram provided in Figure 2 highlights the flexibility of our design in the context of kernel objects. As specified by the *kernel* base class, all kernels have *start()* and *complete()* methods and maintain a list of event handlers, which require notification of the kernel's completion. These are the only methods required by the simulator to incorporate kernels as discrete events. The various specializations of the kernel class

handle the specific requirements of particular operations by defining the *start()* and *complete()* methods. While calling *start()* on an *mpisendengine* kernel results in a call to *mpiserver::send()*, invoking a network model to determine delays, a call to *start()* on a *computekernel* results in a call to the node model associated with the task, invoking a processor model. By encapsulating implementation details behind well-defined interfaces, modules within the simulator can easily be replaced; for example, alternate programming models could be simulated by replacing the MPI interface layer with an interface layer supporting a different parallelization model.

## THE MPI MODEL

The Message Passing Interface (MPI) (Message Passing Interface Forum, 2008) provides a standard interface for programming distributed memory parallel machines in a portable and efficient manner. The MPI interface currently consists of over 200 function calls providing a rich set of communication primitives. Two of the most common sets of primitives include those for point-to-point communication and those for collective communication. Point-to-point operations are available for a variety of modes, including buffered, synchronous (will only complete after

*Figure 2. Inheritance diagram for kernel objects. Kernel specializations handle the specific requirements of particular operations while providing a uniform interface to the discrete event simulator*

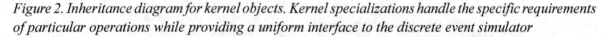
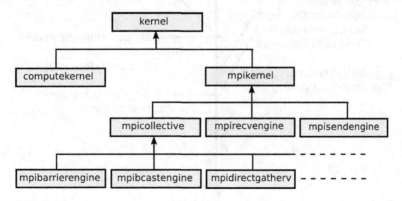

the matching receive is posted), and ready (the matching receive must be posted before the send) modes. For each of these send modes, as well as the receive calls, there are blocking (which have completed when they return) and non-blocking (a separate call is used to check for completion) versions. In addition to these point-to-point calls, collective operations that involve groups of processors are commonly employed. These include such operations as all-to-all broadcast, all-to-one reduce, all-to-one gather, and so on. Both the point-to-point and collective operations are typically implemented using a relatively small set of point-to-point communication primitives which are specific to a particular networking technology.

Skeleton applications and MPI trace files typically provide information about only MPI calls and their associated argument lists. This means that no information is available to the simulator about the low-level point-to-point messages that a particular MPI library uses to implement an operation. The timings due to the low-level op-

erations must be modeled by the simulator, and this presents us with the opportunity to implement a variety of models, at varying levels of fidelity, to represent the MPI operations. At the low-fidelity, low-cost end, MPI collectives can be treated without consideration of the low-level MPI implementation. An analytic or empirical performance model could be used to determine when each process will complete the operation, and a single simulator event to continue execution of all processes at the appropriate virtual time would be inserted into the event queue. A higher-fidelity approach, which is implemented in SST/macro, is to have the simulator schedule events needed for all of the low-level data transfers in the same way an MPI implementation would. If this is done while also using a network model that includes congestion effects, then the effect of congestion on the collective operation time is estimated by the simulator. In this way, the effects of changes in the MPI implementation can be studied using the simulator.

*Figure 3. A timeline for the interaction of two lightweight application threads with the discrete event simulator for MPI send/receive operations and computation*

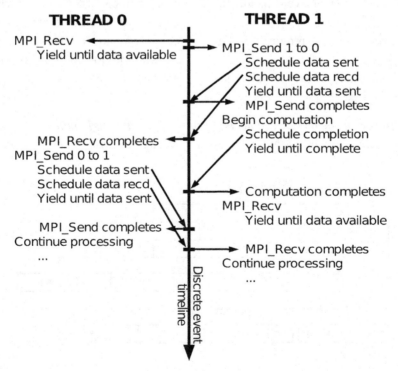

Lightweight application threads perform MPI operations through calls to the interface layer, resulting in determination of completion times for the required events by the network model and the scheduling of these events with the discrete event simulator. A timeline detailing the chronology of events scheduled by two lightweight application threads performing typical operations is shown in Figure 3. When an MPI send or receive operation is performed, the thread yields until the appropriate event is executed by the simulator indicating that enough simulation time has elapsed for the data to have been sent or received. Likewise with computation, the application trace or CPU model determines when a computation operation completes and schedules a completion event with the simulator. The application thread performing the computation yields until this completion event is triggered.

A simplified class collaboration diagram for the SST/macro MPI components is shown in Figure 4. Application threads that utilize MPI are instances of classes inheriting from the *mpiapp* class, which in turn inherits from the simulator's generic class for threads, *thread*. Three such MPI applications are shown in the figure: *mpipingpong* (a simple ping-pong skeleton application), *minimd*

(a skeleton molecular dynamics application which is discussed in Section 2), and *mpitrace* (a trace file reader, which is discussed in Section 2). Each MPI application object references an *mpiapi* object, which provides the MPI application programming interface. The *mpiapi* object uses an *mpistrategy* object to simulate MPI communication by building the appropriate *kernel* objects (shown in Figure 2). The *mpistrategy* object has a collection of strategies specialized for particular operations. For example, implementations of the *MPI_Barrier* function are specializations of the *mpibarrierstrategy* abstract base type. Specialized implementations of barrier strategies can be provided, or the provided *mpicorebarrier* specialization can be used. This specialization can provide a high-fidelity barrier implementation typical of many actual MPI implementations or it can perform a low-fidelity barrier that requires minimal processor time to simulate. These low-fidelity collective operations are currently only used to synchronize the nodes after *MPI_Init* is called. Otherwise, the high-fidelity MPI core operations are used in the results presented herein.

*Figure 4. Collaboration diagram for MPI components. Solid lines indicate inheritance (is-a relationships) and dashed lines indicate containment (has-a relationships).*

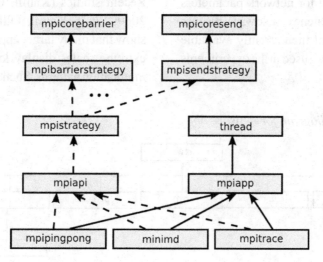

## THE NETWORK MODEL

As the next generation ultra scale systems increasingly rely on higher concurrencies, the effect of the interconnection network on the overall system performance becomes even more important, especially for applications with intense communication loads. Consequently, there has been renewed interest in interconnect design in the computer architecture community with many new ideas and promising results being reported. It is important to predict the performance of these proposed interconnect ideas on modern high-performance computing applications. We believe our simulator will be instrumental in this respect, as the software framework allows easy integration of new methods to enable experiments with proposed techniques on large scale, real world applications.

In keeping with the focus on modularity in the simulator design, the network system is designed as a separate module in order to provide the flexibility required to support a rich set of techniques. Moreover, the network can be simulated in arbitrary detail, which allows trading off between fidelity and runtime of simulations. For example, the network could simply be a latency-based model, which assigns a pre-specified delay to each message, or a cycle-level model that captures the finer details of a router. The general framework can support any topology, routing algorithm, etc., and can be easily tuned for network parameters such as bandwidth and latency. Below, we discuss the basic components of the currently available network system, which we used in the experiments described in Section 3.

## TOPOLOGY AND ROUTING

Within SST/macro, an instance of the network object is defined by its topological description (i.e., the connections between routers/processors) and a routing method to compute a path for a message between two processors. As illustrated in Figure 5, we can currently support torus, fat-tree, hypercube, Clos, and gamma topologies, detailed descriptions of which can be found in (Dally & Towles, 2004). The *product* object in this figure enables producing tori of different dimensions. To define a new interconnect, the user needs to provide a method to build the interconnect topology and a routing method to compute a path for a message between two processors. The system will take care of the details of congestion as we will explain in the next section.

The current network module is designed for maximum runtime efficiency. The routing algorithms are static (i.e., messages between two processors always follow the same path, regardless of network status) and follow the shortest path on the network. Bandwidth is allocated on all links in the message path for the entire time required to transmit all of the data.

## CONGESTION MODELING

Recent studies (Kamil, Oliker, Pinar, & Shalf, 2009; Shalf, Kamil, Oliker, & Skinner, 2005) show that many target applications that can reach extreme scales display local but irregular communication patterns. Such applications commonly

*Figure 5. Inheritance diagram for network objects*

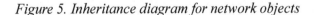
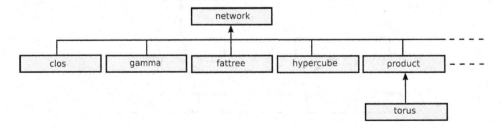

suffer from network congestion due to hot spots in the network; thus, modeling congestion is crucial for the accuracy of a network simulator.

From a modeling perspective, irregular communication patterns pose the biggest challenge, as the network congestion cannot be predicted a priori. Different parts of the network can be congested at different times, and the congestion depends not only on network features, such as topology, bandwidth, and routing algorithm, but also on processor features, as they determine when the messages are injected into the system. Thus, for such irregular applications, detailed simulation that accounts for the routes of messages and congestion on individual network components is essential.

As a general-purpose tool, SST/macro can use multiple approaches to model networks. The *full* interconnect object corresponds to the fully connected interconnect, which provides a congestion-free network. The time required for a message to arrive at its destination depends only on the size of the message. The *sharedcircuit* interconnect object, on the other hand, is designed to model congestion on a link-by-link basis by modeling the communication between each pair of nodes as a continuous flow of data. Each flow has bandwidth allocated to it in such a way that the sum of the bandwidth of all flows passing through a given network link does not surpass the bandwidth of the link. In our current implementation, the oldest active flow receives all the bandwidth it can use. The next oldest flow is allocated any remaining bandwidth it can use, and so on. In this way, network congestion can be modeled efficiently while still obtaining reasonable accuracy as will be shown in Section 3.

## TRACE FILE DRIVEN SIMULATION

SST/macro is able to generate network traffic and processor workloads using trace files that record MPI calls and the time spent performing computation between MPI calls. Currently, two trace formats can be processed: Open Trace Format (OTF) (Knupfer, Brendel, Brunst, Mix, & Nagel, 2006) and DUMPI. The *mpitrace* class (see Figure 4) reads the trace file using the *parser* abstract base class which has specializations for both file formats. Additional formats can be added easily by providing additional *parser* specializations. Different trace formats provide differing levels of detail about the MPI call signature, and this impacts the accuracy of the simulator.

Open Trace Format traces are collected by linking the target application with the VampirTrace library (VampirTrace). VampirTrace uses the PMPI interface to intercept MPI calls, and it records trace information in OTF formatted trace files. VampirTrace writes a binary file for each process. The OTF standard provides an interface specification for reading and writing OTF trace files. The binary files can be read by the *otfdump* utility provided with the VampirTrace library. This utility produces ASCII encoded files, which the simulator uses as input.

The DUMPI format is a custom MPI trace file format, recorded in binary, which has been developed as part of the SST/macro simulator. Like OTF, DUMPI files are obtained by linking the application with a library that uses the PMPI interface to intercept MPI calls. The DUMPI format records more information than OTF, including the full signature of all MPI-1 and MPI-2 subroutine calls. With this additional detail we are able to more accurately simulate an application. The DUMPI format also records return values and MPI request information. This allows error checking and permits us to match immediate mode MPI operations with the MPI operations that complete them. In addition, DUMPI allows individual functions to be profiled instead of the entire program. Processor hardware performance counter information can also be stored in DUMPI files using the Performance Application Programming Interface (PAPI). This allows information such as cache misses and floating point operations to be logged. Such data is recorded both within and between MPI calls. This information will be used by the simulator in more detailed processor models, as they are made available.

## SKELETON APPLICATIONS

Trace files are generated with specific application input and parallel task configuration, yielding a detailed profile of one particular run. Through the manipulation of parameters used to model the hardware and swapping in different messaging models and strategies, trace-driven simulation can contribute significantly to performance optimization and hardware design at parallelism scales on the same order as that used to generate the trace. However, the challenge of optimizing codes or designing hardware for extreme scales requires simulation capabilities long before hardware is actually available for trace file generation. Additionally, many distributed-memory codes have branch statements that are dependent on which a set of requests was matched at a given stage. These execution details cannot be adequately captured in trace-driven execution, since the trace file reader cannot retroactively redirect control flow in the application.

Direct execution is an elegant strategy for generating traces at large scales on more readily available hardware, but the requirement of running the full application hampers parameter studies and limits the scale that is ultimately achievable. Though skeletonizing an existing application requires a greater programmer effort than trace-driven simulation or direct execution, driving the simulator from a skeleton application provides an immensely powerful approach to evaluate efficiency and scalability at extreme scales and to experiment with code reorganization or high-level refactoring without having to rewrite the numerical part of an application. This is further facilitated by the reduction in code size that happens when the bulk of computation is removed.

As a basic parallel application, consider a simple ping-pong between pairwise ranks in a parallel system (rank 0 exchanges data with rank 1, rank 2 with rank 3, etc.). The implementation of this program on the simulator, given in Figure 6, looks almost identical to the native MPI implementation, except for differences in the syntax of MPI calls. Building on this basic skeleton application, it is easy to test the effects of varying network topology, hardware layout (e.g., processors per node), indexing strategies for node allocation, etc. Using a contention-free network model, *mpipingpong*

*Figure 6. Main run loop for a pairwise-exchange MPI ping-pong skeleton application*

```
void mpipingpong::run() {
  this->mpi_->init();
  mpicomm world = this->mpi_->comm_world();
  mpitype type = mpitype::mpi_double;
  int rank = world.rank().id;
  int size = world.size().id;
  if(! ((size % 2) && (rank+1 >= size))) {
    // With an odd number of nodes, rank (size-1) sits out
    mpiid peer(rank ^ 1); // partner nodes 0<=>1, 2<=>3, etc.
    mpiapi::const_mpistatus_t stat;
    for(int half_cycle = 0; half_cycle < 2*niter; ++half_cycle) {
      if((half_cycle + rank) & 1)
        mpi_->send(count_, type, peer, mpitag(0), world);
      else
        mpi_->recv(count_, type, peer, mpitag(0), world, stat);
    }
  }
  mpi_->finalize();
}
```

has been run with up to 16M nodes on a single workstation processor with a memory footprint of roughly 4KiB for each MPI peer.

A more significant application is the skeletonization of miniMD, a molecular dynamics micro-application from the Mantevo project (Mantevo). The full miniMD application is reasonably small, at 1830 source lines of code, and the skeleton application is one-quarter the size at 456 lines. Most of the key computations in miniMD get collapsed down to simple *compute(...)* calls, while all MPI calls and control logic relevant to execution patterns are retained. The skeleton version of the time integrator in miniMD (Figure 7) provides an example of how this mixture of pre-evaluated timing information and original program logic can be used to drive the simulator.

The two calls to *env->compute(...)* simulate the actual time integration in miniMD. The interpolated time values for these calls come from a parametric evaluation of miniMD performance, but they could just as well be obtained from detailed microprocessor simulations, runs on emulator systems such as QEMU, or constitutive performance models. These time values can also be scaled or have noise added to them to study the effects of load imbalance or rogue OS noise. This skeletonization effort is being used as a development platform for analyzing and instrumenting more significant application codes.

## RESULTS

In this section we present performance results for our simulator, both in terms of the ability of the simulator to reproduce measured machine performance and in terms of the computational expense of running the simulator. We also use the simulator to determine the sensitivity of application runtimes to changes in machine characteristics in order to demonstrate the power of simulation in understanding application performance.

### Experimental Setup

Performance studies were carried out on two separate platforms. Parallel studies of AMG2006 (Henson & Yang, 2002) were performed on Sandia's RedStorm Qualification (RSQ) machine, which consists of 32 dual processor compute nodes and 48 quad processor compute nodes. These are

*Figure 7. Time integrator from the skeletonized miniMD application*

```
void minimd::integrate::run(shared_ptr<atom> atm,
    shared_ptr<force> frc,
    shared_ptr<neighbor> nbr, shared_ptr<comm> cmm,
    shared_ptr<thermo> thm, shared_ptr<timer> tmr)
{
    mpiid rank = mpi_->comm_world().rank();
    for(int n = 0; n < this->ntimes; ++n) {
        env_->compute(interpolator->get("integrate::run", 0));
        if((n+1) % nbr->every) {
            cmm->communicate(atm);
        }
        else {
            cmm->exchange(atm);
            cmm->borders(atm);
            nbr->build(atm);
        }
        frc->compute(atm, nbr);
        env_->compute(interpolator->get("integrate::run", 1));
        if(thm->nstat)
            thm->compute(n+1, atm, nbr, frc);
    }
}
```

respectively based on 2.4 GHz dual-core AMD Opteron and 2.2 GHz quad-core AMD Opteron processors. RSQ consists of a single cabinet; in this case the interconnect is reduced to a 2D mesh of dimension 4x24. The mesh is wrapped in the larger dimension. The link bidirectional bandwidth of the mesh is 9.6 GB/s and the bandwidth of the HyperTransport (HT) that connects the router chip to the processor is 3.2 GB/s in each direction. Parameters for use in the simulation of AMG on RSQ were determined by running MPI benchmarks on the system. The simulator models the bidirectional links in RSQ as a pair of unidirectional links, thus only data for unidirectional bandwidths were collected. The communication bandwidth between nodes on an otherwise idle network is limited by the HT link between the processor and the router chip, and the measured unidirectional bandwidth was in this case 1823 MB/s. When two pairs of nodes communicate and the network traffic for each of these pairs is routed over a single router-router network link, the measured aggregate unidirectional bandwidth over the shared router-router link was 3245 MB/s. The nearest neighbor latency was measured at 4.44 µs. We also measured the bandwidth and latency for MPI communication between a pair of processes on the same node to be 6115 MB/s and 2.8 µs, respectively. These results were obtained using only the quad-core nodes when the machine was otherwise idle.

For applications, we used the *mpipingpong* skeleton application described in Section 2 and the AMG2006 benchmark (Henson & Yang, 2002). AMG2006 is a parallel implementation of the Algebraic Multi-Grid method. It was developed at Lawrence Livermore National Laboratory, and is part of the Sequoia benchmark suite (ASC Sequoia Benchmark Codes). The code is written in ISO standard C using MPI for parallelization. The algebraic multi-grid method is commonly used to solve sparse systems of linear equations, especially those that arise in applications of finite element methods. The dominant computational kernel is sparse matrix vector multiplication; thus, the memory bandwidth is the main factor that determines performance. For parallelization, each processor is assigned a portion of the finite elements (sub-domain) and the associated variables/equations in the sparse matrix. Communication is required to exchange boundary information between sub-domains. The average MPI message size for these non-collective calls is around 2-10 KB. Collective calls dominate the total communication time, as they take around 90% of the total MPI time. More detailed information about AMG2006 can be found at (AMG benchmark summary).

## Validation of the Simulator

The simulator was validated on results from a range of AMG configurations using the latencies and bandwidths measured for RSQ above. The ranks were laid out along the nodes of the mesh, traversing the shorter dimension first. We used processor counts of powers of 2 from 8 to 128. These were run using 1 processor per node (ppn), 2ppn, and 4ppn. Two logical grid decompositions were used, a 1D decomposition and a 3D decomposition. Traces were collected using the lightweight DUMPI library. Figure 8 shows the measured simulated wall-time versus the measured elapsed wall-time with the simulation driven from these DUMPI traces.

## Capabilities of the Simulator

We begin highlighting the capabilities of SST/macro by describing two sets of benchmark simulations of the *mpipingpong* skeleton application. The first is used to measure how much processor time the simulator itself requires, and the second illustrates how the simulator can be used to study machine performance. Using a contention-free network model to focus on the process layer

*Figure 8. Comparison of simulated and observed runtimes for the AMG2006 program for a variety of node counts and decompositions*

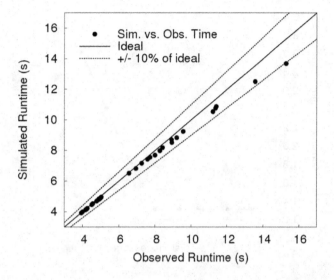

performance, simulations were performed with up to $2^{20}$ peers. Figure 9 demonstrates the high performance context switching that our light-weight thread-based process implementation can achieve. An MPI ping/pong send/receive pair can be simulated in about 5 μs of time. Nearly 1,000 processors can be simulated before the third level cache no longer holds the simulator's data, at which point walltimes begin to increase significantly. After the third level cache size is exceeded, the cost of simulating a send/receive pair levels off to around 10.5 μs. Figure 10 illustrates the results of simulations using a fat-tree network with 4 levels and a radix of 24. The effects of traffic congestion

*Figure 9. Performance of mpipingpong simulations using a contention-free network model with up to $2^{20}$ peers sending a total of 4M messages. The step in the performance curve corresponds to the point at which the program and its data no longer fit into third level cache.*

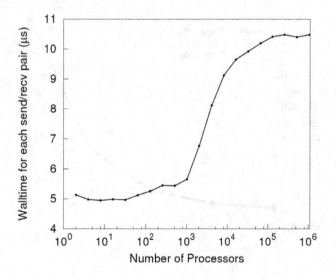

*Figure 10. Traffic congestion in mpipingpong simulations with random MPI rank assignment on a fat-tree network (4 levels, radix 24). Each node sends $65536/n_{proc}$ messages.*

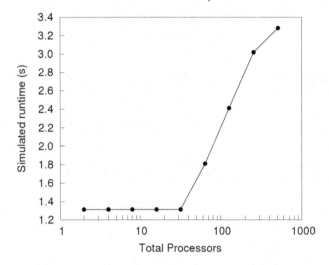

on the performance of the *mpipingpong* application are very clearly observed as the number of nodes surpasses 12, which is the number of nodes connected to a single radix 24 crossbar in the fat-tree.

The modular and high performance infrastructure, and growing collection of hardware and software modeling capabilities provided by SST/macro create a powerful platform for exploring hardware and software design. We present here the results of several parametric studies which demonstrate this ability to develop insights by rapidly performing simulations spanning design spaces. The following parameter studies were performed using AMG traces and simulator parameters as described above. Figures 11 and 12 respectively illustrate the sensitivity of simulated

*Figure 11. Studies of the sensitivity to network latency of trace-driven AMG simulations using 128 nodes with a single processor per node. Time is measured as latency is varied holding the bandwidth constant at 1 GB/s.*

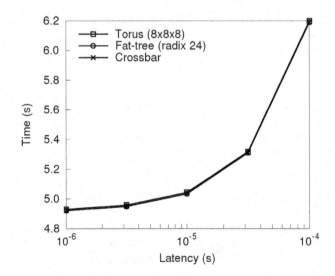

*Figure 12. Studies of the sensitivity to network bandwidth of trace-driven AMG simulations using 128 nodes with a single processor per node. Time is measured as bandwidth is varied holding the latency constant at 3 μs.*

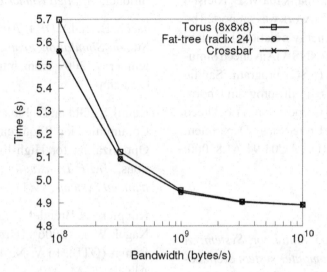

AMG execution times to latency and bandwidth variations. The AMG simulation was done using DUMPI traces collected using 128 processors of RSQ. Varying only latency and holding all other parameters constant, we see that for latencies on the order of 10 μs the predicted runtimes are fairly insensitive to changes in the latency. Reducing latencies even further produces very little benefit in runtime, while at latencies of 100 μs performance the runtimes begin to increase sharply. Varying network bandwidth while holding the latency constant, we find that at 1 GB/s or greater bandwidth, little performance variation is seen in the AMG runtimes, and all of the network topologies perform similarly. When the bandwidth falls significantly lower than 1 GB/s, runtimes significantly increase, and variation is observed among the network topologies, with the torus topology giving slightly longer execution times than fat-tree or crossbar topologies.

These initial parameter studies focus on network characteristics. However, as more processor and messaging models become available within SST/macro, these types of sensitivity studies will be possible for a wide range of hardware and software parameters.

## CONCLUSION

We have described SST/macro, a macro-scale simulator for the coarse-grained simulation of applications running on large-scale parallel computers. The simulator is designed to assist in the development of computing architectures and applications, and has a flexible architecture allowing treatment of different hardware and software components at various fidelities. Our implementation is extremely lightweight, enabling large-scale systems to be simulated on a single processor. We also provide a flexible approach to modeling MPI that can be used to easily investigate the effect on performance of changes to the MPI library and do not preclude the investigation of alternative programming models. The simulator can be driven through trace files collected by running applications on an existing machine or by skeleton applications which provide enough information for the simulator to predict the corresponding applications' execution times. We have found that the simulator reproduces actual runtimes with an error that is typically less than 10%.

## ACKNOWLEDGMENT

The authors would like to thank Ida M. B. Nielsen for helpful comments. This work was supported by the US Department of Energy's National Nuclear Security Administration (NNSA) Advanced Simulation and Computing (ASC) program. Sandia National Laboratories is a multi-program laboratory operated by Sandia Corporation, a Lockheed Martin Company, for the United States Department of Energy under contract DE-AC04-94-AL85000.

## REFERENCES

M5Sim. (n.d.). *The M5 Simulator System: A modular platform for computer system architecture research.* Retrieved September 9, 2009 from http://www.m5sim.org

Adve, V. S., Bagrodia, R., Deelman, E., & Sakellariou, R. (2002). Compiler-Optimized Simulation of Large-Scale Applications on High Performance Architectures. *Journal of Parallel and Distributed Computing, 62*(3), 393–426. doi:10.1006/jpdc.2001.1800

AMG benchmark summary. (n.d.). Retrieved September 11, 2009 from https://asc.llnl.gov/sequoia/benchmarks/ AMG_summary_v1.0.pdf

Benveniste, C., & Heidelberger, P. (1995). *Parallel simulation of the IBM SP2 interconnection network.* Paper presented at the 1995 Winter Simulation Conference, New York, NY.

Binkert, N. L., Dreslinski, R. G., Hsu, L. R., Lim, K. T., Saidi, A. G., & Reinhardt, S. K. (2006). The M5 Simulator: Modeling Networked Systems. *IEEE Micro, 26*(4), 52–60. doi:10.1109/MM.2006.82

Dally, W., & Towles, B. (2004). *Principles and Practices of Interconnection Networks.* San Francisco: Morgan Kaufmann.

Henson, V. E., & Yang, U. M. (2002). BoomerAMG: A Parallel Algebraic Multigrid Solver and Preconditioner. *Applied Numerical Mathematics, 41.*

Jacob, B. (n.d.). *DRAMsim: A Detailed Memory-System Simulation Framework.* Retrieved September 9, 2009 from http://www.ece.umd.edu/dramsim/

Kamil, S., Oliker, L., Pinar, A., & Shalf, J. (2009). Communication Requirements and Interconnect Optimization for High-End Scientific Applications. *IEEE Transactions on Parallel and Distributed Systems, 99*(1).

Knupfer, A., Brendel, R., Brunst, H., Mix, H., & Nagel, W. E. (2006). Introducing the open trace format (OTF). In V. N. Alexandrov, G. D. van Albada, P. M. A. Sloot, & J. Dongarra (Eds.), *Proceedings, Part II Computational Science-ICCS 2006, 6th International Conference* (LNCS 3992).

Mantevo. (n.d.). Retrieved September 9, 2009 from https://software.sandia.gov/mantevo/

Message Passing Interface Forum. (2008). *MPI: A Message-Passing Interface Standard: Version 2.1.* Retrieved September 9, 2009 from http://www.mpi-forum.org

ns-3. (n.d.). *The ns-3 network simulator.* Retrieved September 9, 2009 from http://www.nsnam.org/

PAPI. (n.d.). Retrieved September 9, 2009 from http://icl.cs.utk.edu/papi/

Petrini, F., & Vannesch, M. (1997). SMART: A simulator of massive architectures and topologies. In *Proceedings of the Euro-PDS* (pp. 185-191).

Prakash, S., Deelman, E., & Bagrodia, R. (2000). Asynchronous parallel simulation of parallel programs. *IEEE Transactions on Software Engineering, 26*(5), 385–400. doi:10.1109/32.846297

Riesen, R. (2006). A Hybrid MPI Simulator. In *Proceedings of the IEEE International Conference on Cluster Computing (CLUSTER'06).*

Rodrigues, A., Murphy, R., Kogge, P., Brockman, J., Brightwell, R., & Underwood, K. (2003). *Implications of a PIM architectural model for MPI*. Paper presented at the IEEE International Conference on Cluster Computing, Los A Lamitos, CA, USA.

Sequoia Benchmark Codes, A. S. C. (n.d.). Retrieved September 11, 2009 from https://asc.llnl.gov/sequoia/benchmarks/

Shalf, J., Kamil, S., Oliker, L., & Skinner, D. (Artist) (2005). *Analyzing Ultra-Scale Application Communication Requirements for a Reconfigurable Hybrid Interconnect*.

Susukita, R., Ando, H., Aoyagi, M., Honda, H., Inadomi, Y., Inoue, K., et al. (2008). *Performance prediction of large-scale parallel system and application using macro-level simulation*. Paper presented at the SC '08: Proceedings of the 2008 ACM/IEEE conference on Supercomputing, Piscataway, NJ, USA.

Underwood, K., Levenhagen, M., & Rodrigues, A. (2007). *Simulating Red Storm: challenges and successes in building a system simulation*. Paper presented at the 2007 IEEE International Parallel and Distributed Processing Symposium (IEEE Cat. No.07TH8938), Piscataway, NJ, USA.

VampirTrace. (n.d.). Retrieved September 9, 2009 from http://www.tu-dresden.de/zih/vampirtrace

Wang, D., Ganesh, B., Tuaycharoen, N., Baynes, K., Jaleel, A., & Jacob, B. (2005). DRAMsim: a memory system simulator. *SIGARCH Comput. Archit. News*, *33*(4), 100–107. doi:10.1145/1105734.1105748

Zheng, G., Wilmarth, T., Jagadishprasad, P., & Kale, L. (2005). Simulation-based performance prediction for large parallel machines. *International Journal of Parallel Programming*, *33*(2-3), 183–207. doi:10.1007/s10766-005-3582-6

*This work was previously published in International Journal of Distributed Systems and Technologies, Volume 1, Issue 2, edited by Nik Bessis, pp. 57-73, copyright 2010 by IGI Publishing (an imprint of IGI Global).*

# Chapter 12
# The Red Storm Architecture and Early Experiences with Multi-Core Processors

**James L. Tomkins**
*Sandia National Laboratories, USA*

**Ron Brightwell**
*Sandia National Laboratories, USA*

**William J. Camp**
*Sandia National Laboratories, USA*

**Sudip Dosanjh**
*Sandia National Laboratories, USA*

**Suzanne M. Kelly**
*Sandia National Laboratories, USA*

**Paul T. Lin**
*Sandia National Laboratories, USA*

**Courtenay T. Vaughan**
*Sandia National Laboratories USA*

**John Levesque**
*Cray Inc., USA*

**Vinod Tipparaju**
*Oak Ridge National Laboratory, USA*

## ABSTRACT

*The Red Storm architecture, which was conceived by Sandia National Laboratories and implemented by Cray, Inc., has become the basis for most successful line of commercial supercomputers in history. The success of the Red Storm architecture is due largely to the ability to effectively and efficiently solve a wide range of science and engineering problems. The Cray XT series of machines that embody the Red Storm architecture have allowed for unprecedented scaling and performance of parallel applications spanning many areas of scientific computing. This chapter describes the fundamental characteristics of the architecture and its implementation that have enabled this success, even through successive generations of hardware and software.*

DOI: 10.4018/978-1-4666-0906-8.ch012

## INTRODUCTION

In 2001, the U.S. Department of Energy's National Nuclear Security Administration (NNSA) commissioned Sandia National Laboratories (Sandia) to obtain new computational capability to address mission needs for very high-end computation. After a Request For Information (RFI) failed to provide proposed architectures that met the application scalability and cost requirements for the new system, Sandia issued a Request For Proposals (RFQ) that essentially prescribed in detail the architecture for a new massively parallel computer, dubbed Red Storm. Sandia received proposals from two potential suppliers, but neither proposal met the requirements as laid out in the Statement Of Work (SOW). However, one of the proposers, Cray, Inc., indicated a willingness to engineer a system to Sandia's architectural specifications and within the cost envelope. Subsequently, Sandia awarded the development contract to Cray, and Sandia and Cray then jointly produced the Red Storm supercomputer system–going from architectural specification to first hardware deployment in approximately 30 months. This extremely short development time was largely enabled by the simple design for scalability and for scalable manufacturability promulgated by Sandia in the architectural specifications.

As part of the contract, Cray was required to develop a commercial product based on the Red Storm architecture. In 2005, Cray introduced the XT3 supercomputing system. Subsequent versions (XT4 and XT5) have been widely deployed in the high-performance computing market; and in 2008, the Cray XT product line became the most successful supercomputer in history with over one thousand cabinets sold. Although national security was a key target, the Red Storm architecture has proven to be effective at solving a wide range of science and engineering problems. These applications include climate change, fusion, material science, structural response, nanomaterials, biology, catalysis, combustion and astrophysics. This chapter describes the fundamental characteristics of the Red Storm architecture and its implementation that have enabled this success, even through successive generations of hardware and software.

We previously described our approach to the Red Storm architecture prior to its development (Brightwell et al., 2005). In this chapter, we summarize the key points of our approach and provide a retrospective now that the architecture has been widely deployed. The rest of this chapter is organized as follows. In the next section, we discuss the history of massively parallel processing (MPP) systems that influenced the development of the Red Storm architecture and enumerate the key characteristics instrumental in its success. In the following section, we describe the hardware components of the architecture and the evolution of the Red Storm machine at Sandia. Following that, the software environment is presented, with a focus on the important factors that enabled scalability and performance across successive generations of hardware. We continue with a discussion of the Cray XT product line, and then provide several examples of application performance on the Sandia Red Storm system and Cray XT systems at Oak Ridge National Laboratory. The final section summarizes the major contributions of this chapter.

## RED STORM ARCHITECTURE

### Experience and Influences

The Red Storm architecture grew out of the experience gained during Sandia's long history of using and operating large-scale parallel computers. Sandia's experience began with the first 1024-processor nCUBE-10 computer system in 1987. It continued with a 16 thousand-processor Thinking Machines CM2, two 1024-processor nCUBE2s, a 128-processor Intel iPSC/2, and a 128-processor Intel iPSC/860. All of these first-generation machines used hypercube network fabric topologies. In the fall of 1993, Sandia acquired a 3600+ processor Intel Paragon, which was the first large Sandia machine with a mesh network topology. In early 1997, Sandia took delivery of the first of the DOE ASCI machines, the ASCI Red machine (Mattson, Scott, & Wheat, 1996), which had over 9500 processors in its full configuration. Like the Paragon, the ASCI Red system was built by Intel and also had a mesh topology.

In the mid-nineties, Cray Research created the T3D and T3E architectures that also were mesh/torus machines. Although Sandia did not obtain a T3D or T3E, a number of Sandia staff were involved in those projects and were favorably influenced by their success.

In the late 1990s, Sandia began designing and building a series of large-scale commodity clusters called CPlant™. Unlike other clusters at that time, which were largely single-user machines, CPlant was designed to be a "virtual supercomputer," that is, to provide a multi-user system environment equivalent to that provided by purpose-built supercomputers. The largest of these clusters had over 2500 processors. Like the Paragon and ASCI Red, the CPlant™ clusters had a mesh network topology. During the intervening period, there have been dramatic changes in computing technology. However, the basic characteristics that made for good overall system performance have remained the same. These are a communication network that provides balance in its computation to communication ratio, a highly scalable and low overhead operating system and system software, an integrated system design, and a level of reliability that makes it possible to accomplish significant work between interrupts.

Issues with then-state-of-the-technology HPC systems have been active discussion topics throughout the past thirteen SOS Workshops on Distributed Supercomputing(Thirteenth SOS Workshop on Distributed Supercomputing, 2009). While difficult to enumerate the impact, conferences such as these always provide experience and data to the development of the next generation of systems.

## KEY ARCHITECTURAL CHARACTERISTICS

An important design goal was the ability to execute a single application effectively across the entire machine. This form of computing is termed capability computing and is in contrast to clusters that may execute hundreds of different applications at any time. Capability computing places severe demands on system balance and reliability. Careful consideration must be given to processing speed, memory bandwidth, interconnect bandwidth and latency, and I/O to ensure that no part of the system is a bottleneck to data movement. Red Storm was intended to provide excellent performance at the full scale of the machine on a broad set of complex science and engineering applications. The architectural characteristics presented below were intended to produce a system that would meet this overall goal.

*A tightly-coupled single system and a true MPP:* A single system providing a single system view to users and to system managers: It was designed from its inception to be a single system. As a result, custom packaging and Reliability, Availability, and Serviceability (RAS) features are incorporated into the design. The design is also simplified in that it leaves out unneeded components. This is different from a cluster, which is typically built by more loosely integrating separate commodity or server computer systems.

*Balanced system performance:* The performance of processors, memory systems, interconnect, and I/O needs to be balanced and provide good overall system performance on a broad set of complex scientific and engineering application codes. The application codes need to achieve good parallel efficiency at the full scale of the machine. The relative balance that can be achieved is strongly influenced by available technology and cost considerations.

*Usability*: The functionality of system hardware and software must meet the needs of users for very large-scale MPP computing. Red Storm was not intended to encompass meeting the needs of word processing or web browsing or other similar desktop computing applications, or even using non-scalable connection-based structures such as UNIX sockets.

*Scalability*: System hardware, software, and performance must scale appropriately from a single cabinet system to a system with thousands of nodes. The physical system size and component part count need to scale linearly with the computational power of the system. There is no inherent scalability limit for the Red Storm architecture. However, the SeaStar (Brightwell, Hudson, Pedretti, & Underwood, 2006) network router table has an address limit of 32 thousand nodes; and, obviously, relative efficiency for fixed-sized problems or problems that are highly non-local will decrease at very large scales on any realistic interconnect.

*Reliability*: For many NNSA mission-critical applications, the required Mean Time Between Interrupts (MTBI) for a single application executing across the entire machine does not decrease and in fact often increases with system memory size. At the same time, the native failure rate scales with the number of parts in the system. In fact, without aggressive reliability approaches involving redundancy of critical components, elimination of high-failure rate parts (e.g., rotating storage), and extreme measures to protect logic and state within the node and the interconnect network, it would not be possible to meet MTBI goals. For Red Storm, a period of at least 50 hours MTBI was specified. Sandia application codes may run for a hundred or more hours on a single problem. For these kinds of applications, the measure of a supercomputer's reliability is MTBI of the application code and not percent availability of the machine.

*Upgradeability*: Upgradeability was designed into the architecture. When the contract awarded to Cray, it provided for an upgrade path of at least a factor of three in performance. Red Storm and the Cray XT have proven to be highly upgradeable. Most Cray XT machines have been upgraded at least once and many have had multiple upgrades. Red Storm has had two major upgrades.

*Red/Black switching*: Sandia needs to have the ability to switch major portions of its large capability supercomputers between different levels of classification. Red/Black switching provides this capability. Major sections up to all of the compute nodes of the machine can be moved between different levels of classification. Red/Black switching is a unique Red Storm capability that has not been implemented on any other Cray XT system.

*Space, power, cooling*. Leading-edge capability supercomputers are very large, and require a significant amount of power and cooling. Dense packaging and careful design can substantially reduce the system physical size and the power and cooling needed to operate it. This is major benefit that is achieved by custom packaging design and packaging.

*Price/performance*: Excellent performance per dollar is possible through the use of high-volume commodity parts where feasible. By using high-volume processors and memory parts, it was possible to keep the price close to the cost of a commodity cluster and still meet the requirements for a true capability system.

*Three-dimensional mesh/torus interconnect*: The Red Storm architecture has a three dimensional mesh/torus network topology.

This architectural characteristic is driven by physical scalability and upgradeability requirements. The part counts and cabling in mesh interconnects, unlike those in fat-trees and other large switch based interconnects, grow linearly with the number of nodes. As the system size increases, the complexity of a mesh interconnect does not increase; however, the number of hops to get from one end of the mesh to the other does increase. Also, using a mesh interconnect made Red/Black switching practical.

*Functional hardware and software partitioning:* Red Storm has three functional hardware and software partitions: (1) service and I/O (SIO) nodes, (2) compute nodes, and (3) RAS and system management. Functional hardware and software partitioning provides the ability to use simpler components and system software for the compute nodes. It also provides for a robust RAS and system management system that does not interfere with the computing capability.

## RED STORM HARDWARE

### Cabinet Hardware

The fundamental building block for Red Storm is a cabinet, which includes the cooling, power supplies, CPU boards, card cages, and backplanes. It was known at the outset that cabinet design was an area where a custom solution was needed. Two CPU boards, one for compute nodes and one for service and SIO nodes, and a backplane board had to be designed and built. In addition, several small boards had to be designed and built for the I/O, interconnect, and for the voltage regulator modules (VRMs). The custom cabinet design was essential to building in RAS features and component monitoring. Using a single, very high reliability fan to provide for the cabinet cooling

is an example of one of the advantages enabled by a custom design.

Each original cabinet was designed to have up to 24 CPU modules. There are two types of CPU modules, compute modules and SIO modules. Compute modules have four nodes and SIO modules have two nodes. The SIO modules also have two PCI-X (later systems have PCI-e) busses for each node. All modules have four SeaStar interconnect chips and the same interface to the backplane. On the SIO modules, two of the SeaStar chips are not connected to a node; however, by putting four SeaStar chips on each module, the mesh interconnect is the same for all boards, and the CPU boards are interchangeable in the mesh. The SIO modules provide the interface to file systems, for users to login, and for moving data on and off of the machine. An SIO node also acts as the boot node for the system.

A system consists of at least one cabinet, a system management workstation, and a root file system (normally a RAID). Most systems have many cabinets, several systems have over a hundred cabinets, and one XT system has over 200 cabinets. The system at Sandia has 155 CPU cabinets and 40 cabinets used for Red/

*Figure 1. Front of red storm cabinet*

Black switching. Cabinets are connected to each other through high-speed interconnect cables. All cabinets are connected to the system management workstation through a separate Ethernet network. Figure 1 and Figure 2 show some early Red Storm cabinets from the front and back.

In Figure 1, the picture of the front of the Red Storm cabinets also shows the overhead cable trays for the Y-direction (across rows) of the mesh interconnect. The picture of the back of the cabinets shows how cables are connected to the backplane and how they are routed between cabinets in the X-direction (along a row). The Z-direction cables are hard to see in the picture, however, there are some in the right cabinet of the back picture. Not all of the cables are connected in this picture.

## Compute Node Hardware

The AMD Opteron processor was chosen for the system for three primary reasons. First, the Opteron was designed with a HyperTransport (HT) interface that provided a high-bandwidth low-latency path into the processor that could be used for a high-performance custom interconnect. Use of HT provided a great deal of licensable intellectual property and collaterals that would simplify and

reduce the risk in fabric development. Second, the Opteron was designed with an integrated memory controller, which, based on pre-production testing, provided excellent performance on Sandia's application codes. Lastly, by using a high volume commodity processor, the cost of processors and memory would be minimized. This was in fact validated by performance analyses that showed that the Intel and AMD x86 commodity processors provided the best cost-performance across the set of applications most important to Sandia.

## Interconnect Hardware

At the outset of the project Sandia knew that a high performance, custom interconnect would be needed to meet the performance and scalability goals. None of the commercially available interconnects could meet the performance requirements in the Red Storm specification. The interconnect specifications were based on scaling studies on the existing ASCI machines (ASCI Red, ASCI Blue Mountain, ASCI White) in 2001 and on Sandia's CPlant™ cluster. See Table 1 for some of the Red Storm specifications.

*Figure 2. Back of red storm cabinet*

## Initial Configuration and Upgrades

Cray began delivering the original Red Storm system in the fall of 2004 and completed the delivery in first part of 2005. The original system had 10368 compute nodes and 512 SIO nodes in 124 CPU cabinets. It had two SIO node partitions, one on each end of the system and Red/Black switch cabinets (see Figure 3). The system was configured in a three-dimensional mesh with a torus in the Z-direction only. System configuration details are given in Table 1.

In the third quarter of 2006, Sandia's system was upgraded by adding a fifth row of cabinets and by replacing all of the processors with dual-core Opterons. The system then had total of 155 CPU cabinets with 12,960 compute nodes and 640 service and I/O nodes. The system layout was the same as in Figure 3, except for the addition of the fifth row of cabinets. System configuration details are given in Table 1.

Sandia's system went through a second major upgrade in the third quarter of 2008. The 65 cabinets in the center section were upgraded to quad-core Opteron processors. The memory configuration in the rest of the machine was changed to provide 2 GB of memory per core for each compute node throughout the whole machine,

*Table 1. Red storm configurations*

| Metric | Year | | |
|---|---|---|---|
| | **2005** | **2006** | **2008** |
| System Theoretical Peak Performance (TF) | 43.52 | 130.56 | 290.3 |
| HPL Performance (TF) | 36.19 | 101.4 | 204.2 |
| CPU Cabinets | 124 | 155 | 155 |
| Red/Black Switches | 16 | 20 | 20 |
| Total Nodes<br>Compute Nodes<br>Service & I/O Nodes | 10,880<br>10,368<br>256+256 | 13,600<br>12,960<br>320+ 320 | 13,600<br>12,960<br>320+320 |
| Total Number of Cores<br>Compute Node Cores<br>Service & I/O Node Cores | 10,880<br>10,368<br>256+256 | 27,200<br>25,920<br>640+640 | 39,680<br>38,400<br>640+640 |
| Compute Node Topology (X, Y, Z) | 27x16x24 | 27x20x24 | 27x20x24 |
| Total System Memory (TB)<br>Compute Node Memory (TB)<br>Service & I/O Node Memory (TB) | 33.4<br>30.4<br>3.0 | 39.19<br>35.44<br>3.75 | 78.75<br>75.0<br>3.75 |
| Aggregate Memory Bandwidth (TB/s) | 58.0 | 78.1 | 126.3 |
| Compute Node Memory Bandwidth (GB/s) | | | |
| DDR 333<br>DDR 400<br>DDR2 800 | 5.33<br>6.4 | 5.33<br>6.4 | 6.4<br>12.8 |
| Interconnect Performance | | | |
| Bi-Section B/W (X, Y, Z) (TB/s)<br>Bi-Directional Link Bandwidth (GB/s)<br>MPI Nearest Node Latency (μs) | 3.7, 6.2, 8.3<br>9.6<br>~5 | 4.6, 6.2, 10.4<br>9.6<br>~5 | 4.6, 6.2, 10.4<br>9.6<br>~5 |
| Disk Storage (TB) | 170+170 | 170+170 | 1500+700 |
| Parallel File System Bandwidth (GB/s) | 50 + 50 | 50 + 50 | 100 + 70 |
| External I/O Bandwidth (GB/s) | 25 + 25 | 25 + 25 | 25 + 25 |
| Power (MW) | ~1.8 | ~2.3 | ~2.5 |

*Figure 3. Original red storm system cabinet layout*

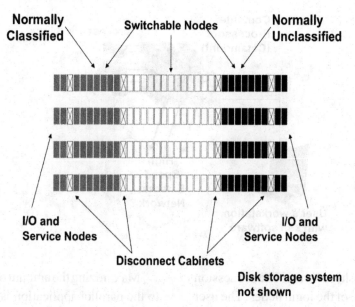

and over 2 PB of disk storage was added to the file system. The current system has a mix of dual-core and quad-core compute nodes, which required modifications to the system software to support. These changes required most of the compute node modules to be removed and modified or replaced. However, there was no change in the cabinet layout. As for the first two Red Storm configurations, the details are given in Table 1. These two upgrades have allowed researchers to make important assessments of the performance of multi-core architectures at large scale and – more importantly – to meet critical NNSA mission goals.

## RED STORM SOFTWARE

Like the hardware, the system software design relies on functional partitioning to achieve the architectural goals of a single system MPP, high performance, usability, reliability, and scalability. Sets of nodes are designated to perform specific tasks, with each set running system software best suited for the specialized function. Most of the nodes are in the compute partition and use the compute modules described in the previous section, which have four nodes per module. Compute nodes run a lightweight kernel operating system called Catamount (Kelly & Brightwell, 2005), which is a third-generation lightweight kernel that Sandia and the University of New Mexico developed and deployed on Sandia's Intel Paragon and the ASCI Red systems. The SIO partition provides access to the compute partition as well as performing services for jobs executing in the compute partition. The service nodes run Linux and pre-configured sets of nodes provide the interactive development, job launch, file I/O, and high-speed access to external services. Figure 4 depicts the key functional partitions.

The underlying RAS system that provides system management and health monitoring is not shown in the diagram. There is one RAS processor on each module that runs a real-time version of Linux. Cray developed the custom management and monitoring software that runs on the RAS system.

To the user, the functional partitions appear as one single system. The typical user accesses Red Storm via a local workstation running a version

*Figure 4. Functional partitions of red storm nodes*

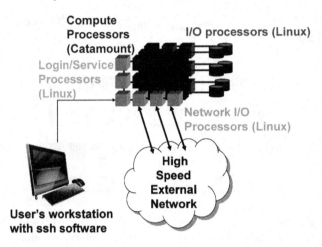

of the secure shell (ssh) software. The ssh session is established on one of the login nodes. The user performs job setup tasks, such as compilation and problem input creation. Once ready, the user submits the job script, specifying the number of processors needed for the parallel application. When sufficient compute nodes are available, the job script runs on a service node and the application binary is fanned out in a logarithmic fashion onto the assigned compute nodes. These nodes are dedicated to this job only. The application instances on each compute processor core perform independent computation and when necessary, pass messages to each other over the tightly-coupled mesh network. File I/O flows between the compute processors and the I/O nodes. The TotalView debugger and performance monitoring tools are available, should the user require them to diagnose a problem. When the application completes, the user can review the results from the login node. If desired, the user can direct that the files be sent over the external network for post processing or archival storage. Numerous service nodes and thousands of compute nodes were likely used to assist in this typical usage scenario. However, to the user, who simply "ssh'd to redstorm.sandia.gov", the system appeared as one, very powerful, desktop computer.

Maximizing the amount of CPU time delivered to the parallel application is critical to achieving high performance. Catamount is a minimal operating system, designed to initialize hardware resources and turn over those resources to a single, running application. This approach ensures that the application is given the maximum amount of CPU time. It also ensures that the operating system introduces very little noise into the rate of application progress. Studies have shown that parallel application scalability can be significantly impacted by operating system noise (Ferreira, Brightwell, & Bridges, 2008; Petrini, Kerbyson, & Pakin, 2003). Finally, since Catamount is small in size, it is much easier to make reliable.

The SIO partition uses SUSE Linux as the base operating system distribution. This general-purpose OS was selected as more functions and features are needed to provide user services and support for the compute partition. All SIO nodes use the same kernel version for simplicity of maintenance and operation. However, user level services and daemons are minimized to only the set required for the node function. For example, the nodes providing the I/O service run the Lustre (Donovan et al., 2003) parallel file system, but other services such as mail and cron are not enabled.

One critical software component used by all nodes in the system is the networking software that runs over the tightly coupled mesh. It plays a critical role in achieving high performance and scalability and is described in the next section.

## PORTALS NETWORKING SOFTWARE

The Portals (Brightwell, Riesen, Lawry, & Maccabe, 2002) network programming interface was initially developed by Sandia and the University of New Mexico as an integral part of the lightweight operating systems designed for MPP systems in the early 1990s(Shuler et al., 1995). There are several fundamental design features of Portals that differentiate it from other low-level network programming interfaces developed for high-performance network hardware.

Since the target platform for Portals is MPPs, high performance is obviously a key requirement. As such, Portals was designed specifically to achieve low latency and high bandwidth for MPI-based network transfers. Unlike other programming interfaces with similar performance goals, Portals was also designed for applications with tens of thousands of communicating endpoints. This requirement places additional burden on the interface to provide and maintain high-performance while scaling network resources appropriately. Portals provide mechanisms needed to ensure that networking resources are independent of the size of the parallel job or the number of communicating processes. Examples of such mechanisms include a connectionless communication model and flexible buffering semantics that efficiently support one-sided remote read/write operations as well as traditional two-sided send/receive message passing capability.

Most network programming interfaces for high-performance computing provide a set of function calls for establishing communication and moving data. Typically, there are a few op-tions associated with these operations that allow for some flexibility in how the capabilities of the underlying network transport are used to meet the semantics of the next higher layer in the network stack. In contrast, Portals is based on the concept of protocol building blocks. These blocks can be assembled to better match the needs and semantics of the higher-level data movement layer.

One of the primary motivations for this approach is the need for a process in an MPP to use the network for several different functions simultaneously. An application process uses the network not only for high-performance data movement libraries like MPI (MPI Forum, 1994), but also for file I/O and remote procedure calls. In addition, other system services and processes rely on network communications as well. For example, the parallel runtime system used for job launching and parallel file system both rely on network services. Portals was designed to provide the features and capabilities needed by all of these networking layers.

This flexibility has allowed for implementations of several application-level libraries, including multiple MPI libraries (Brightwell, 2005), Cray SHMEM (Cray Research Inc.), ARMCI (Tipparaju, Kot, Nieplocha, Bruggencate, & Chrisochoides, 2007), and GASNet (Bonachea, Hargrove, Welcome, & Yelick, 2009), as well as several system-level services, including the Lustre filesystem (Donovan et al., 2003), PDIO (N.T.B. Stone & Porter, 2006), and even TCP/IP. Portals has provided the necessary functionality to enable these higher-level network applications and services and has been effective at delivering the performance provided by the underlying SeaStar network hardware.

One of the main concerns in developing the Portals API and the associated reference implementation was not to restrict how and where message processing could be done. Early versions of Portals were restricted to running inside the operating system with direct access to the memory of an application process. This situation was ideal for custom MPP systems where the network interface was integrated into the memory bus, but was highly inefficient for cluster systems where the network interface was attached to the I/O bus. Portals was designed to allow an implementation to perform message process activities in the best way for a given system. In the case of an intelligent or programmable network interface, such as the Cray SeaStar (Brightwell et al., 2006), an implementation of Portals can perform message processing activities on the network interface. Alternatively, for those networks that have limited or no programmability, message processing can be implemented in kernel-space or user-space as appropriate.

Because nearly all services depend upon a functioning network layer, the initial implementation of Portals for the SeaStar was interrupt-driven. When a message arrives at a node, the SeaStar interrupts the host processor, and the operating system processes the message header and programs the SeaStar to deliver the data to its destination. This interrupt-driven implementation, while initially low-performance, allowed development to proceed on other parts of the system. Eventually, the interrupt-driven path became sufficiently optimized and robust that it became the production implementation. Sandia also implemented a slightly higher-performance implementation of Portals where all message processing activities were offloaded to the embedded processor on the SeaStar. The Portals API and implementation for the SeaStar allows a process to use both of these paths simultaneously if desired.

Another key to the success of Portals was the ability to implement it efficiently in both Linux and a lightweight kernel. Although there are optimizations that can be leveraged in a lightweight kernel environment, these are not overly restrictive. Providing the opportunity for optimization in a lightweight kernel environment does not hamper the implementation in a more full-featured operating system like Linux.

With the emergence of multi-core processors, it became necessary to support an alternative implementation of Portals message processing for intra-node messages. Since the interrupt-driven implementation relied on the operating system to process messages, it was relatively straightforward to add an optimization path that used memory-to-memory copies to transfer intra-node Portals messages. As the number of cores per node increased, it also became clear that interrupts and Portals processing could be handled on the particular core containing the destination process. The flexibility of the implementation and the accompanying semantics allowed for this relatively straightforward optimization as well. At least initially, the ability to optimize at the Portals layer provided the ability to continue to run existing codes without requiring significant modifications to applications or underlying communication libraries.

## CRAY XT

The Cray XT product line differs slightly from the Red Storm system at Sandia. In this section we touch on the differences in hardware and software and describe the evolution of the Cray XT systems and Cray Supercomputing Center of Excellence at Oak Ridge National Laboratory.

As mentioned previously, Red Storm is the only system with red/black switch cabinets. The Cray XT network is a three-dimensional torus in all directions. The software on the Cray XT is also slightly different than Red Storm. The Cray XT product runs a lightweight Linux operating system on compute nodes rather than a lightweight kernel. Cray calls this software the Cray Linux Environment.

Shortly after the installation at Sandia, other organizations began porting and optimizing applications for future generations of the Cray XT line. One of those organizations was Oak Ridge National Laboratory (ORNL), funded by the US

DoE Office of Science. An interesting caveat of the ORNL work was that a group of Cray specialists, called the Cray Supercomputing Center of Excellence (COE), were designated to assist Office of Science Researchers in porting and optimizing applications. The idea behind the CoE was to form collaborations with the DoE researchers to better understand how the applications should be structured to fully utilize the XT system and to identify improvements to the XT software that would facilitate application scalability. In addition to the Cray CoE, ORNL staffed a group of computer specialists, who possess domain expertise in the various science disciplines of interest, to work with the researchers. An important collaboration grew consisting of the Office of Science researcher, the ORNL Scientific Application group and the Cray Center of Excellence that was able to identify bottlenecks in the XT system, to be addressed by the Cray development group, as well as issues with the important applications, which could be addressed by the code application groups. Over the past four years, XT deployments at ORNL have grown from an initial Cray XT3 system with a peak performance of 26 teraFLOPS to the largest Cray XT5 system deployed, called Jaguar, which has a peak performance of 1.38 petaFLOPS.

## APPLICATION PERFORMANCE

In this section, we discuss performance results for several applications on the Red Storm system at Sandia as well as a large Cray XT system installed at Oak Ridge National Laboratory.

## Application Performance on Multi-Core Processors

### Shock Hydrodynamics

Sandia has been using several applications to track the performance of the Red Storm system through its various hardware and software upgrades. One of these applications, CTH, is an explicit, three-dimensional, multi-material shock hydrodynamics code developed at Sandia. CTH is designed to model a large variety of two- and three-dimensional problems involving high-speed hydrodynamic flow and the dynamic deformation of solid materials, and includes several equations of state and material strength models (Hertel et al., 1993). Figure 5 shows the performance of CTH version 7.1 with a weak scaling, flat mesh Shaped Charge problem taken after various upgrades to Red Storm. The single-core results are with the original 2.0 GHz Opteron processors with OS version 1.3.21 and PGI compiler version 6.1.3. The first dual-core results were taken after the dual-core upgrade, using 2.4 GHz dual-core processors with 333 MHz memory, OS version 1.4.22, and PGI version 6.1.3. The second dual-core results were taken after the quad-core upgrade after the memory on the dual-core processors was upgraded to 400 MHz, using OS version 2.0.62.1 and PGI version 7.1.4. The quad-core results are with 2.2 GHz quad core processors, OS version 2.0.61, and PGI version 7.1.4.

The results show that, after the dual-core upgrade, CTH was from 11% to 18% slower on the dual-core processors when compared to using single-core processors while using twice as many sockets. This data for CTH is consistent with that of most other applications, which ran about 85% as fast on 2500 dual-core nodes compared to 5000 single-core nodes, which represents a 70% increase of capability of the machine on a per-node basis.

Due to the memory speed upgrade that occurred during the quad-core upgrade, the dual-core results sped up by 9-21%. This somewhat surprising result indicates that memory performance was not the only influence, since the memory performance increase was 20%. The end result is that the upgraded dual-core results are within a few percent of the single-core results, except for a few outstanding points.

The quad cores compare well to the upgraded dual cores, with the times falling within 3%,

*Figure 5. CTH scaling performance*

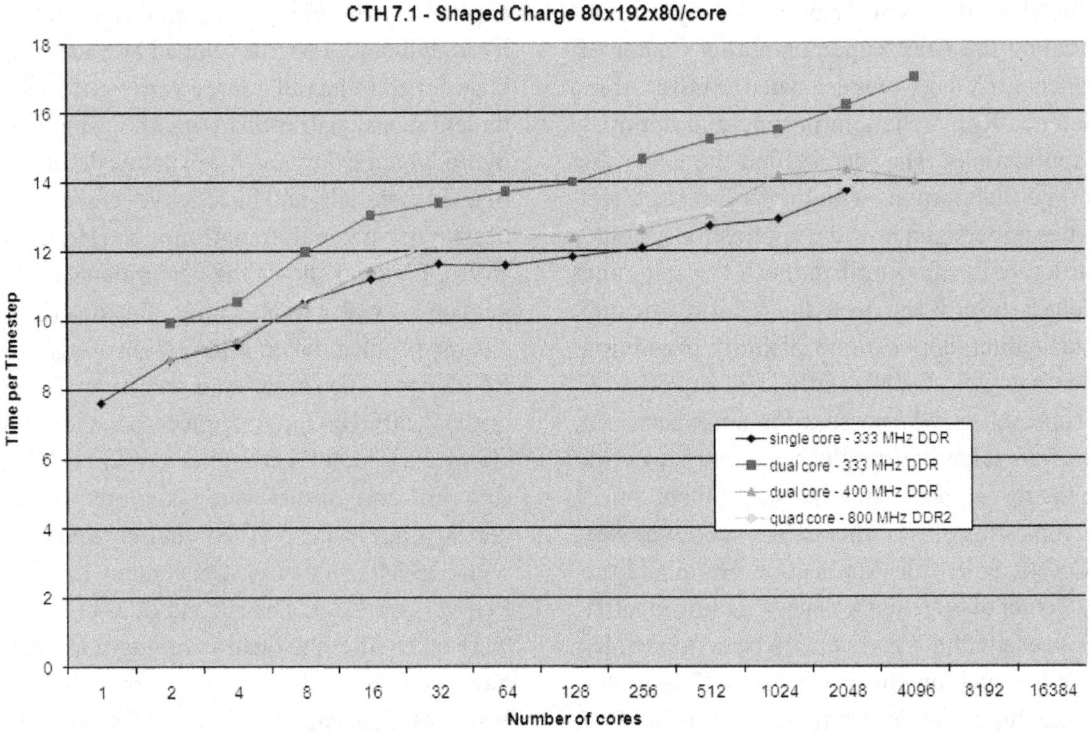

except for a few data points. This is a slightly better result than the milestone report (Vaughan, 2008), which concluded that the quad cores were about 11% slower than the dual cores on several applications running on thousands of cores. After two upgrades, CTH runs from 1% to 7% slower on the quad cores than the single cores, which means that each quad core is equivalent to at least 3.7 single core nodes.

## Semiconductor Device Modeling

The Charon semiconductor device simulator was developed to provide high fidelity simulations of devices in radiation environments (Hennigan, Hoekstra, Castro, Fixel, & Shadid, 2007). Charon models semiconductor devices by the drift-diffusion equations, which consists of a Poisson equation for the electrostatic potential plus two convection-diffusion-reaction equations for the electron and hole concentrations. Each defect

species adds an additional transport equation. The system of equations is discretized in space by a stabilized finite element method on an unstructured mesh, and solved with a fully-coupled implicit Newton-Krylov method (Hennigan et al., 2007; Lin et al., 2009). The large number of defect species (e.g., 30-40) involved in these simulations rapidly leads to a very large number of degrees of freedom (DOF). High fidelity solutions require solutions of very large linear systems. Therefore, improving the scalability of the solvers is critical. One of the key factors in reducing the solution time and improving the scalability of the linear solver is the pre-conditioner. Red Storm has been a critical resource for evaluating and improving algorithms for the linear solvers work at Sandia, particularly for work involving multi-grid pre-conditioners (Gee, Siefert, Hu, Tuminaro, & Sala, 2006; Lin, et al., 2009; Lin, Shadid, Tuminaro, & Sala). These solver improvements impact many other application codes.

*Figure 6. Reduction in solve time for BJT test case due to multi-grid pre-conditioner*

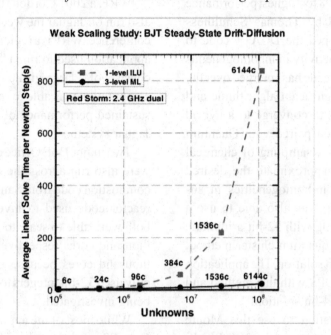

Figure 6 shows a weak scaling study for a steady-state drift-diffusion solution of a 2D bipolar junction transistor (BJT). The average linear solve time per Newton step is plotted against the total number of DOFs. The problem is scaled up to 110 million DOF and run on 6144 cores of the 2.4-GHz dual-core processors. For the 110 million DOF case on 6144 cores, the multigrid preconditioner is 35 times faster than the one-level preconditioner. This 6144-core calculation on 3072 dual-core nodes was also performed on 1536 quad-core nodes (half the nodes). The ratio of the dual-core time to the quad-core time was 0.91, so the simulation took about 10% longer on the quad-core nodes. To demonstrate that application codes can successfully run to completion at full-scale on Red Storm, this problem was run on 38,360 cores with a combination of dual-core and quad-core processors.

To demonstrate that Red Storm can be used for large science runs, a steady-state drift-diffusion solution was performed for a larger 2D BJT. The direct-to-steady-state solution for a one billion DOF problem was obtained in under one hour on 24,600 cores using the quad-core nodes. This calculation required eleven Newton steps, each Newton step requiring an average of 291 Krylov iterations per step. The linear solve time took about 90% of the total run time during a Newton step.

## SCIENCE APPLICATIONS ON JAGUAR

With the installation of the 1.38 petaFLOPS system in the fourth quarter of 2008, eight of the major applications used by the HPC community were able to scale to the full size of the machine. The work required to make the applications ready for running at scale cannot be overlooked. On all of these applications, code teams worked many months to enable the applications to scale over 100 thousand cores.

In order to scale to the full size of the 150 thousand-core Jaguar system, two applications required algorithmic changes. One of these applications, the DCA++ code, won the prestigious

Gordon Bell prize in 2008 for highest performance achieved. A team led by Thomas Schulthess (CSCS/ORNL) developed the DCA++ code to investigate superconductivity in inhomogeneous materials. The DCA++ code has emerged over the last two years, with significant algorithmic and programmatic changes to converge to a hybrid quantum cluster method paired with Quantum Monte Carlo that uses a sampling of chemical impurities/disorder to approximate the desired physics of nanoscale in-homogeneities in superconductors. DCA++ was also able to use a stochastic solver running with 32-bit arithmetic that is embedded in a quantum cluster method, which iterates to a 64-bit solution. The application achieved 1.34 petaFLOPS with this method and 720 teraFLOPS with 64-bit solution.

The second application to use this Monte Carlo sampling technique was the WL-LSMS application, which investigates magnetism for high density disk drives. This particular application was able to achieve a sustained performance of 1.05 petaFLOPS in 64-bit precision, the first real application to achieve that mark.

Both of these applications are material codes that make heavy use of DGEMM/ZGEMM based dense linear algebra. Two other applications that have run across the entire Jaguar system were selected because they were Gordon Bell finalists in 2008. One of those efforts, LS3DF, also a materials code looking at materials to be used in solar energy system, was ported from the IBM BG/P to Jaguar within a few days and was able to achieve 442 teraFLOPS, twice the performance of BG/P. This code team, lead by Lin Wang Wang of UCB won the 2008 Gordon Bell prize for elegance. The second Gordon Bell finalist was a group from UCSD, lead by Laura Carrington. This application was ported from the Ranger system at University of Texas, which is a commodity cluster from Sun with Opteron nodes and an InfiniBand interconnect, in one week and was able to increase performance by a factor of five over the Ranger.

WRF, a 2007 Gordon finalist application, was also run on Jaguar the week prior to the SC 2008 conference. WRF is a regional weather forecasting application used to run a "Nature Study," which consists of a large girdle grid of the globe. This computation was able to reach an unprecedented sustained performance of 50 teraFLOPS on the Jaguar system.

Two major DoE Office of science applications were also run across the entire system. S3D, a combustion code from Sandia, and GTC, a fusion reactor code used to investigate ITER design, both were able to scale to 144 thousand and 121 thousand cores respectively. GTC failed at 142 thousand cores because the application design only used 32-bit integers to represent the particles being investigated.

While most of the applications that run on the Cray XT system are based on the MPI programming model, a few use variants of the Global Address Space (GAS) programming model. This alternative model is being considered to help achieve productivity on these large, complex machines. A GAS model provides an abstraction that allows users to access the remote memory of other processors, in the spirit of shared memory programming to simplify development of distributed memory codes. By virtue of the abstraction they provide, partitioned GAS languages like Unified Parallel C (UPC), Co-Array Fortran (CAF), and GAS libraries such as the Global Arrays Toolkit (Nieplocha, et al., 2006) have the unique ability to expose features such as low overhead communication or global address space support in the underlying system -- lack of these features results in poor performance.

The primary consideration for the Red Storm architecture was MPI, so there was little hardware support for the GAS model. As mentioned above, Portals was designed to support a scalable MPI implementation; however; despite the lack of explicit support for GAS languages and libraries, recent experience in porting the NWChem computational Chemistry package (Kendall et al., 2000)

*Figure 7. CCSD(T) performance on Cray XT*

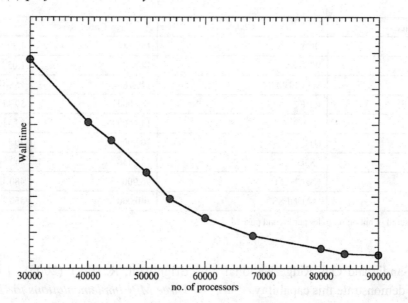

and the Global Arrays toolkit used by NWChem on Jaguar lead to a few interesting discoveries regarding the GAS features of the system. GAS features required by the Global Arrays library that were not directly available in hardware on the XT, such as support for one-sided atomic accumulate operation and one-sided strided data transfer, could be efficiently implemented in software (in this case, the ARMCI one-sided communication library (Nieplocha et al., 2006) used in Global Arrays) and performance and unprecedented scalability was delivered to NWChem application.

The scaling of the parallel implementation of the CCSD(T) module in NWChem to 92 thousand cores can be seen in Figure 7. NWChem achieved a sustained performance of 475 teraFLOPS, which is the largest run this code has ever made. Strong scalability of a GAS model (Global Arrays) ultimately enabled the scaling of a real scientific application, NWChem, thus demonstrating the ability of the Red Storm architecture to run and scale applications written in the GAS model.

Finally, MADNESS, a numerical framework for computing with multi-resolution methods used by applications including chemistry, atomic/ molecular physics, solid state, and nuclear physics, was developed by a team lead by Robert Harrison of ORNL has also run beyond 100 thousand cores with sustained performance greater than 50%. The following table lists several of the application codes that have run on a significant portion of the Jaguar machine at ORNL.

## SUMMARY

The Red Storm architecture developed by Sandia National Laboratories and implemented by Cray, Inc., has resulted in the most successful line of large-scale supercomputers in history. This chapter has summarized key points of the architecture that have enabled this success. We have discussed several important properties that allow a wide spectrum of applications to achieve unprecedented levels of performance and scalability. In particular, we have examined features of the architecture and the implementation that allowed for effective use of multi-core processors, and we have presented performance results from several applications

*Table 2. Application scaling on jaguar*

| Science | Code | Cores | Perf |
|---|---|---|---|
| Materials | DCA++ | 150,144 | 1.3 PF |
| Materials | WL-LSMS | 149,580 | 1.05 PF |
| Seismology | SPECFEM3D | 149,784 | 165 TF |
| Weather | WRF | 150,000 | 50 TF |
| Combustion | S3D | 144,000 | 83 TF |
| Fusion | GTC | 102,000 | 20 * |
| Materials | LS3DF | 147,456 | 442 TF |
| Chemistry | NWCHEM | 96,000 | 480 TF |
| Chemistry | MADNESS | 140,000 | 550 TF |

*Performance measured in billion particles per second pushed.

on systems at Sandia and Oak Ridge National Laboratory that demonstrate this capability.

## ACKNOWLEDGMENT

Sandia is a multi-program laboratory operated by Sandia Corporation, a Lockheed Martin Company, for the United States Department of Energy's National Nuclear Security Administration under contract DE-AC04-94AL85000. Parts of this research used resources of the National Center for Computational Sciences at Oak Ridge National Laboratory, which is supported by the Office of Science of the United States Department of Energy under contract DE-AC05-00OR22725.

## REFERENCES

Bonachea, D., Hargrove, P., Welcome, M., & Yelick, K. (2009, May). *Porting GASNet to Portals: Partitioned Global Address Space (PGAS) Language Support for the Cray XT.* Paper presented at the Cray User Group Conference, Atlanta, Georgia.

Brightwell, R. (Ed.). (2005). *A Comparison of Three MPI Implementations for Red Storm (Vol. 3666).* Sorrento, Italy: Springer.

Brightwell, R., Camp, W., Cole, B., DeBenedictis, E., Leland, R., & Tomkins, J. (2005). Architectural Specification for Massively Parallel Computers - An Experience and Measurement-Based Approach. *Concurrency and Computation, 17*(10), 1271–1316. doi:10.1002/cpe.893

Brightwell, R., Hudson, T., Pedretti, K., & Underwood, K. D. (2006). Cray's SeaStar Interconnect: Balanced Bandwidth for Scalable Performance. *IEEE Micro,* (May/June).

Brightwell, R., Riesen, R., Lawry, B., & Maccabe, A. B. (2002). *Portals 3.0: Protocol Building Blocks for Low Overhead Communication.* Paper presented at the 2002 Workshop on Communication Architecture for Clusters.

Cray Research Inc. (n.d.). *SHMEM Technical Note for C, SG-2516.*

Donovan, S., Huizenga, G., Hutton, A. J., Ross, C. C., Petersen, M. K., & Schwan, P. (2003, July 2003). *Lustre: Building a File System for 1,000-node Clusters.* Paper presented at the Ottawa Linux Symposium, Ottawa, Canada.

Ferreira, K., Brightwell, R., & Bridges, P. (2008, November). *Characterizing Application Sensitivity to OS Interference Using Kernel-Level Noise Injection.* Paper presented at the ACM/IEEE International Conference on High-Performance Computing, Networking, Storage, and Analysis (SC'08), Austin, Texas.

MPI Forum. (1994). MPI: A Message-Passing Interface Standard. *International Journal of Supercomputer Applications and High Performance Computing, 8.*

Gee, M. W., Siefert, C. M., Hu, J. J., Tuminaro, R. S., & Sala, M. G. (2006). *ML 5.0 Smoothed Aggregation User's Guide (No. SAND2006-2649).* USA: Sandia National Laboratories.

Hennigan, G. L., Hoekstra, R. J., Castro, J. P., Fixel, D. A., & Shadid, J. N. (2007). *Simulation of Neutron Radiation Damage in Silicon Semiconductor Devices (No. SAND2007-7157).* USA: Sandia National Laboratories.

Hertel, E. S., Bell, R. L., Elrick, M. G., Farnsworth, A. V., Kerley, G. I., McGlaun, J. M., et al. (1993, July). *CTH: A Software Family for Multi-Dimensional Shock Physics Analysis.* Paper presented at the 19th International Symposium on Shock Waves, Marseille, France.

Kelly, S., & Brightwell, R. (2005, May). *Software Architecture of the Lightweight Kernel, Catamount.* Paper presented at the Cray User Group Conference, Albuquerque, New Mexico.

Kendall, R. A., Apr\`a, E., Bernholdt, D. E., Bylaska, E. J., Dupuis, M., & Fann, G. I., et al. (2000). High performance computational chemistry: An overview of NWChem a distributed parallel application. *Computer Physics Communications, 128*(1-2), 260–283. doi:10.1016/S0010-4655(00)00065-5

Lin, P. T., Shadid, J. N., Sala, M., Tuminaro, R. S., Hennigan, G. L., & Hoekstra, R. J. (2009). Performance of a Parallel Algebraic Multilevel Preconditioner for Stabilized Finit Element Semiconductor Device Modeling. *Journal of Computational Physics, 228*(17), 6250–6267. doi:10.1016/j.jcp.2009.05.024

Lin, P. T., Shadid, J. N., Tuminaro, R. S., & Sala, M. G. (n.d.). Performance of a Petrov-Galerkin Algebraic Multilevel Preconditioner for Finite Element Modeling of the Semiconductor Device Drift-Diffusion Equations. *International Journal for Numerical Methods in Engineering.*

Mattson, T. G., Scott, D., & Wheat, S. R. (1996, April). *A TeraFLOP Supercomputer in 1996: The ASCI TFLOP System.* Paper presented at the International Parallel Processing Symposium, Honolulu, HI.

Nieplocha, J., Palmer, B., Tipparaju, V., Krishnan, M., Trease, H., & Apra, E. (2006). Advances, Applications and Performance of the Global Arrays Shared Memory Programming Toolkit. *International Journal of High Performance Computing Applications, 20*(2), 203–231. doi:10.1177/1094342006064503

Petrini, F., Kerbyson, D. J., & Pakin, S. (2003, November). *The Case of the Missing Supercomputer Performance: Identifying and Eliminating the Performance Variability on the ASCI Q Machine.* Paper presented at the ACM/IEEE Conference on High Performance Networking and Computing, Phoenix, AZ.

Shuler, L., Jong, C., Riesen, R., Dresser, D. W. v., Maccabe, A. B., Fisk, L. A., et al. (1995, 1995). *The Puma Operating System for Massively Parallel Computers.* Paper presented at the Intel Supercomputer Users' Group, Albuquerque, NM.

SOS Workshop on Distributed Supercomputing. (2009). Retrieved from http://www.cs.sandia.gov/Conferences/SOS13/

Stone, N. T. B., Gill, D. B. B., Johanson, B., Marsteller, J., Nowoczynski, P., Porter, D., et al. (2006, June). *PDIO: HIgh-Performance Remote File I/O for Portals-Enabled Compute Nodes.* Paper presented at the International Conference on Parallel and Distributed Processing Techniques and Applications, Las Vegas, Nevada.

Tipparaju, V., Kot, A., Nieplocha, J., Bruggencate, M. t., & Chrisochoides, N. (2007, March). *Evaluation of Remote Memory Access Communication on the Cray XT3.* Paper presented at the Workshop on Communication Architectures for Clusters, Long Beach, California.

Vaughan, C. (2008). *Level II ASC Milestone 3159 Red Storm 284 TeraFLOPS Upgrade Final Report* (No. SAND2008-7937P). Sandia National Laboratories, USA.

*This work was previously published in International Journal of Distributed Systems and Technologies, Volume 1, Issue 2, edited by Nik Bessis, pp. 74-93, copyright 2010 by IGI Publishing (an imprint of IGI Global).*

# Chapter 13
# The Sicilian Grid Infrastructure for High Performance Computing

**Carmelo Marcello Iacono-Manno**
*Consorzio COMETA, Italy*

**Marco Fargetta**
*Consorzio COMETA, Italy*

**Roberto Barbera**
*Consorzio COMETA, Italy, and Università di Catania, Italy*

**Alberto Falzone**
*NICE srl, Italy*

**Giuseppe Andronico**
*Istituto Nazionale di Fisica Nucleare, Italy*

**Salvatore Monforte**
*Istituto Nazionale di Fisica Nucleare, Italy*

**Annamaria Muoio**
*Consorzio COMETA, Italy*

**Riccardo Bruno**
*Consorzio COMETA, Italy*

**Pietro Di Primo**
*Consorzio COMETA, Italy*

**Salvatore Orlando**
*Istituto Nazionale di Astro-Fisica, Palermo*

**Emanuele Leggio**
*Consorzio COMETA, Italy*

**Alessandro Lombardo**
*Consorzio COMETA, Italy*

**Gianluca Passaro**
*Consorzio COMETA, Italy*

**Gianmarco De Francisci-Morales**
*Consorzio COMETA, Italy, and Università degli Studi di Catania, Catania*

**Simona Blandino**
*Consorzio COMETA, Italy, and Università degli Studi di Catania, Catania*

## ABSTRACT

*The conjugation of High Performance Computing (HPC) and Grid paradigm with applications based on commercial software is one among the major challenges of today e-Infrastructures. Several research communities from either industry or academia need to run high parallel applications based on licensed*

DOI: 10.4018/978-1-4666-0906-8.ch013

*software over hundreds of CPU cores; a satisfactory fulfillment of such requests is one of the keys for the penetration of this computing paradigm into the industry world and sustainability of Grid infrastructures. This problem has been tackled in the context of the PI2S2 project that created a regional e-Infrastructure in Sicily, the first in Italy over a regional area. Present chapter will describe the features added in order to integrate an HPC facility into the PI2S2 Grid infrastructure, the adoption of the InifiniBand low-latency net connection, the gLite middleware extended to support MPI/MPI2 jobs, the newly developed license server and the specific scheduling policy adopted. Moreover, it will show the results of some relevant use cases belonging to Computer Fluid-Dynamics (Fluent, OpenFOAM), Chemistry (GAMESS), Astro-Physics (Flash) and Bio-Informatics (ClustalW)).*

## INTRODUCTION

The growing demand for parallel programming and High Performance Computing (HPC) poses a question: Grids (Foster & al., 2001) try to maximize the overall infrastructure exploitation instead of the performance of each single application running on them; in fact, the quality policies address the performance of the whole infrastructure over long periods, instead of the performance of each single run. For instance, a typical quality parameter for Grids is the total number of jobs run over a month. Grid users usually have a different point of view and they decide among the various computing solutions (proprietary cluster, buying time on a supercomputer, etc.) having in mind the time performance of their own applications as the most relevant parameter to be evaluated and traded-off with the expensiveness of the candidate solution. Bridging the gap between Grid and HPC may result in a great advantage for Grids as the business of massive parallel applications can bring novel resources and foster infrastructures' sustainability. Some technical aspects of running HPC programs on Grids have been described in a recent paper (Orlando & al., 2008). Obviously the hardware equipment is the basic factor driving the application performance. The usual choice during the building of a Grid infrastructure is to have more processors instead of the fastest ones, in order to run more jobs simultaneously. This is one of the differences (probably the most important one) between an HPC cluster dedicated (often tailed) on a single application and a general-purpose Grid infrastructure. Nevertheless, as it happens for many technologies, adaptability and procedure standardization can largely compensate for the use of commercial components and architectures instead of customized ones. For instance, sharing resources allows more processors compared to the average dedicated clusters and this feature may be exploited to enhance the performances for well-scalable applications.

Having in mind the above considerations, the strategic importance of such HPC applications comes from the growing demand about this specific computing paradigm arising from both academic institutions and private enterprises. Small/medium size companies may take advantage of the Grid infrastructures to run HPC programs otherwise too much expensive for either hardware costs or lack of human expertise. Acting as a reliable, standardized and reasonably fast HPC facility, a Grid infrastructure can sensitively enlarge the range of its users. This is easier to happen for a regional Grid whose Virtual Organization (VO) usually gathers all the institutions acting on the same area, resulting in a more versatile and multi-disciplinary community compared to the international VOs that are often devoted to a single discipline. The following sections describe the efforts that the Sicilian Grid infrastructure is producing to fully support to HPC applications. Section 2 briefly describes the Sicilian Grid infrastructure, its characteristics and purposes. Section 3 illustrates the adopted scheduling policy and the newly developed license server. Section 4 treats middleware modifications and general porting procedure. Section 5 outlines some use cases testifying the wideness and variety of impacted fields also reporting about the results of preliminary tests. Finally, Section 6 draws some conclusions.

## THE PI2S2 PROJECT AND THE SICILIAN GRID INFRASTRUCTURE

The PI2S2 project (Barbera, 2007) aims at providing Sicily with a Virtual Laboratory running a computational Grid for scientific and industrial applications. The COMETA Consortium (Falzone, 2007), is a partnership among the Sicilian Universities of Catania, Messina and Palermo, the National Research Institutes for Nuclear Physics (INFN), Astro-Physics (INAF), Geo-Physics and Volcanogy (INGV) and the SCIRE Consortium. The COMETA Consortium (Barbera, 2006) developed the PI2S2 project and currently manages the infrastructure. The adopted standards rank it at a very high technology level to become an open, general purpose, on-demand facility for distributed computation and massive data storage (the first one on a regional scale in Italy). The Sicilian infrastructure is connected to the international computational Grids (See Figure 1) in order to improve both the level of scientific collaboration between the Sicilian Universities and Research Institutes and their counterparts in the rest of the world, and enhance the competitiveness of local Small and Medium Enterprises.

The main sites of this infrastructure are located at the Universities of Catania, Messina and Palermo and the INAF and INFN sites in Catania. During 2008, the PI2S2 infrastructure reached the overall amount of 2000 cores and 300 TB of data storage capacity, so becoming one among the most important computing centers of Italy.

The adoption of the InfiniBand low-latency network layer since the very beginning of the project testifies about the consideration towards HPC applications. InfiniBand is a low latency connection designed to improve the communication efficiency over the local networks connecting the Worker Nodes of each site. The peculiarity of this connection is that the optimization focuses on the latency time of little data packets. In fact, in the usual nets, the overall data throughput is the most relevant parameter. This difference is connected with parallel programs that have to exchange very frequent little data burst instead of distanced large packages. Latency on the InfiniBand net drops to a few microseconds, from 10 to 100 times better than the usual value over the Ethernet. The applications need to be compiled and linked to the specific libraries in order to use the InfiniBand layer for their node-to-node communications. Thus a Grid expert usually assists the user of a parallel InfiniBand application in the porting procedure. The InfiniBand net layer is reserved for applications in the sense that no Grid services use it for its communications.

PI2S2 infrastructure currently runs many applications belonging to several disciplines ranging from Astro-Physics to Chemistry, from Nuclear Physics to Bioinformatics. Particularly significant applications are those related to Civil Defense, such as the simulations about volcanic ashes or lava flow paths. Although most applications belong to academia, some Fluid-Dynamic applications aim at the development of industrial products. Thus, the PI2S2 infrastructure is a production facility opened to industry. The adopted middleware is gLite3.1. Many extensions have been added to the standard software in order to better support the user applications. This is particularly true for parallel HPC applications. The availability of a large data storage capacity is another key

*Figure 1. The Sicilian grid infrastructure*

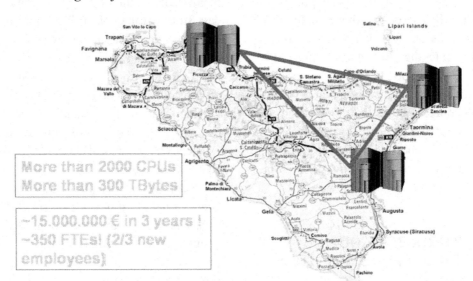

opportunity that is currently being explored as well as HPC. Genius web portal (Falzone, 2007) designed for non-expert users, gives access to the infrastructure from a wide variety of devices such as personal computers (either desktops or notebooks), palmtops, mobile phones and so on.

Some future projects concern the COMETA infrastructure beyond the end of the PI2S2 project scheduled for February 2009. Among them, a relevant one is about linking the 4 sites located in the Catania Campus by the InfiniBand net layer. The site-to-site distances are within the specifications and the overall amount of available cores will range towards one thousand. The challenging aspect of the project is how to manage this super-site, as each component site must preserve its operational and legal autonomy: a simple merging is not feasible as each site belongs to a different institution. On the other hand, with current middleware, a single parallel application cannot run over more than a site, so merging is necessary unless the middleware is modified. Such a modification addresses a very general issue and cannot be tackled by a single VO, requiring a common effort of all the Grid community at its higher

levels, so the idea is to use this super-site only for a few special applications requiring such a large amount of cores. Dedicated connections among the 3 cities are also under consideration, but the target is not related to parallel applications. The dedicated connections are intended to keep faster and more secure the communications amongst the infrastructure's services.

gLite middleware adopts the Message Passing Interface (MPI) libraries (Pacheco, 2008) as the standard communication tool among the cooperating simultaneous processes. The only supported version is MPICH. The updated MPI2 code is supported as well. Next sections describe how MPI applications can run on the Grid infrastructure and some of them have been actually deployed on it. Scheduling, license server and middleware modifications will be the main subjects.

## Scheduling Policy and License Server

The coexistence of several heterogeneous jobs running on the same infrastructure is a major difference between Grids and dedicated clusters. The advantage of having more resources is worthy only if they are effectively shared among the various users whose requirements may be very different. HPC jobs may last for several days, so a queuing time up to one or two days may be acceptable as it is far lower than execution time. On the other hand, short jobs lasting up to a few hours are usually privileged in order to start their execution as soon as possible. PI2S2 sites have different queues for jobs of different durations with increasing priority for shorter jobs, but the situation is more complex due to the variety of requirements to be satisfied. For instance, emergency jobs, related to volcanic surveillance and Civil Defence need absolute priority, so these jobs perform pre-emption on the running cores interrupting the execution of short ones. Pre-emption can be very negative for the emptied job in the case the incoming job is very long. Emergency jobs are not very long, so pre-emption is acceptable. HPC jobs need from tens to hundreds cores; the more resources needed the more they have to wait before they are available. According to the usual policy, they starts only if there are no shorter jobs queued and there are enough free resources. This situation can cause long queuing times for MPI jobs when many short jobs compete with them for resource allocation. As the duration of the MPI jobs can be very long, pre-emption is not feasible; the short pre-empted jobs may remain interrupted for days. Currently, the policy adopted for HPC jobs is resource reservation. When scheduled, an HPC job begins to collect and reserve unloaded cores up to needed amount. This policy is reasonably effective as the number of HPC jobs is far lower compared to the number of short jobs, so the resource turn-over is fast enough to avoid the reserved cores being idle for a sensibly long period. An on-line automatic control, avoiding monopolistic resource allocation, completes the described basic mechanism.

Another important modification of the standard situation is the creation of queues dedicated to single applications. This is due to the need of authorizing a strictly restricted group of users to access the license server or a privileged scheduling policy. For instance, HPC users have a dedicated group into the COMETA VO and their jobs have a special scheduling as above described.

Many HPC programs require a software license. Together with many legal issues, the use of such programs on a distributed infrastructure raises the technical problem of making the license available to all the working nodes. Currently many licenses are either "username-locked", i.e. connected to the user name, or "node-locked", i.e. connected to the physical net address of the executing processor. None of these solutions fits the distributed environment of Grid infrastructures where a possibly unique license must be shared for all the executions that may run on different and geographically distant sites. Thus a license server providing the so-called "floating" licenses allows each user to contact the license server asking for the authorization that is granted up to the stated number of simultaneous users. On job completion, the client packet releases the used license items, keeping them available to another user. Comparing to a cluster sharing a private net, Grid infrastructures add a further difficulty, because licenses must be delivered on a public net to the remote execution sites.

FlexLM is a free software package allowing the management of such "floating" licenses from a single server, although the tool is replicated on other two servers for redundancy reasons. In the usual scheme, the user writes the address and port of the license server on a configuration file or an environment variable to be read by the executable that contacts the server to authorize the run. Up to this point, every user of the Virtual Organization who is able to submit jobs on the infrastructure, can use the licensed software simply by addressing the server license. Site administrators can arrange a first filter by setting the execution permissions on the executable file of the package, but this only works when the file is statically stored on the infrastructure. In fact, VO members may still run their unauthorized software asking for the license to the license server bringing their own executables. To avoid this, the Grid License Manager (GridLM) developed by the Catania Grid support group, associates license granting to the identity of each single user. More precisely, execution permission is granted if the user belongs to an authorized group inside the VO, so the user must be authenticated on the infrastructure also specifying the specific user group. For instance, in order to use a commercial SW ('example_sw') on the COMETA infrastructure, the authentication command becomes:

```
voms-proxy-init --voms cometa:/come-
ta/example_sw.
```

Moreover, the user must add a line with the specific tag describing the commercial SW to the Job Description Language (JDL). Also thanks to the encrypted communications, this mechanism is both enough secure and flexible to be used over a public network between the distant sites of the COMETA infrastructure.

Currently the GridLM tool is undergoing a further development in order to associate the license also to the proxies that are delegated by the user credentials when a job is submitted. This will allow the starting of the production step for many applications that are currently being tested. The adoption of robot certificates, i.e. an authentication method linked to the application more than a single user, will also have a positive impact on these applications that are described later on.

## MPI Modifications to gLite Middleware

At present time, the standard version of the adopted middleware gLite3.1, only supports the MPICH version of MPI. The parallel applications using other communication systems (LAM, OpenMPI)

have to be modified and recompiled using the MPICH libraries. EGEE community has shown interest about the integration of other MPI versions into the middleware.

HPC requires the full exploitation of the worker nodes and communication capabilities. HPC applications are intrinsically more complicated than other job types and reach the highest performances only if all the involved nodes are dedicated to them, so the most important applications require to run on reserved executing nodes. Moreover, many other HPC applications are adapted from the shared memory paradigm, i.e. the execution is optimized for a few multi-core processors with a huge memory available on the same board. This standard is widely diffused in the industry world where workstations with multi-processor motherboards are normally used to run licensed software for simulation and design purposes. Many of these applications have been adapted to a distributed environment but their communication efficiency drops when the core number is increased to more than a few tens. Even some applications originally designed to run on a distributed environment often show their best performances when they minimize net communication, using all the cores of the same processor. The concentration of job execution on the lowest number of physical processors is a winning strategy in order to enhance software performance. This consideration only fails in a few cases, for two basic reasons: 1) either the application requires more memory than the available amount on a single physical processor, or 2) the communication is so fast that it competes with local processing. The situation 1) is rather probable. In this case, the only advantage of using sparse cores is that the distribution over different processors averages the overall amount of required memory per core with the other jobs that are usually less pretentious. However, the advantage is actually vanished by the increased overload of net communication. The situation 2) is rather uneven. Although on our infrastructure, either of the two may occur, they have not been observed so far, so this "Granularity" issue has been the first major modification to the standard middleware. A new JDL tag has been added to select how many cores of the same physical processor have to be used by the job. Performance improvement resulted in a rough 3 factor for an application that has been built on shared memory systems (GROMACS). Lower figures were detected for other applications. Obviously, performance improvement must be evaluated for each single case, due to its dependency on software implementation especially about the communication over the net.

An MPI (Gropp, 2006) program is a current FORTRAN or C code including some calls to MPI library functions that allow information exchange among the cooperating nodes running the MPI program and the synchronization of the execution flow. Usually a master node starts the processes on the other (slave) nodes by establishing some remote connections. On the Sicilian Grid this procedure is based on the use of Script Secure Shell (SSH) and requires an initial setup for the necessary key exchange.

In order to provide instruments to satisfy the requirements of HPC applications, many patches have been developed for the LCG-2 Resource Broker (RB), Workload Management System (WMS), User Interface (UI) and Computing Element (CE). These patched components support new tag types for MPI flavours in addition to the existent MPICH one:

- MPICH2 for MPI2;
- MVAPICH for M PI with InfiniBand native libraries;
- MVAPICH2 for MPI2 with InfiniBand native libraries.

In the MPI implementations currently deployed on the PI2S2 infrastructure, it is required that the cooperating nodes running a MPI program are tightly connected each other, in order to ensure

enough low latency for the node-to-node communication. Based on this assumption, current middleware does not support geographic distribution of MPI jobs on nodes belonging to different Grid sites, although some studies have been targeting the problem (Turala, 2005). Despite the above limitation, the number of available processor ranges from several tens into the hundreds for many sites, so running a MPI application on a Grid infrastructure leads to a sensitive performance improvement.

Moreover, all PI2S2 Grid sites are equipped with the InfiniBand 4x low-latency network connection, so High Performance Computing (HPC) applications requiring fine grain parallelism run in a proper HW/SW environment.

The usual procedure in order to port a MPI application to the Grid is to recompile it using the Portland Group C/Fortran, gcc or Intel compiler, including the libraries of one among the several supported MPI flavors (MPICH, MPICH2, MVAPICH, MVAPICH2 corresponding to the combination of MPI and MPI2 codes over a GigaBit or InfiniBand communication layer). The extension to the gLite3.1 middleware version essentially consists in a wrapper, able to collect the needed information from the Local Job Scheduler (usually LSF). Two special scripts ("mpi.pre.sh" and "mpi.post.sh") have been introduced to be sourced before and after the execution of the MPI program in order to respectively prepare the execution environment and collect final results. The following code in Box 1 illustrates a modified JDL file:

Note the new tags and the pre- and post-processing scripts. It is the user that usually provides these two scripts as they have to match the specific needs of each application. Nevertheless, the middleware modifications greatly simplify the user's work, as the wrapper cares about file copying on the slave nodes and environment settings. An open issue is the execution of pre- and post-processing scripts on the slave nodes. In fact, the

*Box 1.*

```
Type = "Job";
JobType = "MPICH";
MPIType = "MPICH_pgi706";
NodeNumber = 12;
Executable = "mergesort-mpi1-pgi";
#Arguments = "12";
StdOutput = "mpi.out";
StdError = "mpi.err";
InputSandbox = {"mergesort-mpi1-pgi","mpi.pre.sh","mpi.post.sh"};
OutputSandbox = {"mpi.err","mpi.out"};
```

mpi.pre.sh and mpi.post.sh only run on the master node. The MPI session on the slave node is opened directly by the user code by the MPI_Init instruction, so it is only after this command that a script can be launched to act in the actual session where the MPI program will run on the slave node. This means that only by inserting a script into the user code, it can set the proper environment on the slave node. This approach is not recommendable because it is far better for debugging to keep application and middleware codes well separated. In fact, in case of error occurrence during job execution, having two clearly distinct software levels is very desirable in order to lead to a fast recovery. The adopted alternative approach is then to statically modify the .bashrc script executed at every start of the remote session which, on its turn, implies that a there must be a dedicated user profile tailed on the single application. Summarily, we create a new dedicated queue, together with a new group users enabled to access it. These new profiles include the configuration script, so when the MPI_Init will start a new session on a slave node for these novel users, it will run the configuration script. This technique is rather complicated, but it is feasible provided that only a very few applications do require it. A similar technique is adopted when the job requires a specific library that cannot be installed statically

as it is incompatible with a part of the middleware. If the user still wants to run the job renouncing to part of the middleware, a new dedicate queue with a particular user profile allows a dynamic installation of the desired library without any permanent interferences with the installed middleware.

The described approach is the standard one when the application is totally open and modifiable. Nevertheless, other approaches are preferable for standard software packages where any modifications or even recompilation is difficult for technical and/or legal reasons. A common situation happens when the MPI package to be gridified, has its own wrapper or it is closed, in the sense that the source code is not available for modification. Portability is nevertheless possible, but the usual submission mechanism has to be by-passed. What we do then, is to submit a test MPI application that reserves the same number of cores required by the "actual" MPI application and proofs the status of the infrastructure. After the test code terminates its execution, the mpi.post.sh launches the "actual" MPI application. On one hand, running a test application immediately before the production run is very useful in case of failure in order to diagnose whether the error is due to the infrastructure or the application. On the other hand, by-passing the common submission mechanism requires a great caution by the user, as he/she might be tempted to use more resources than allowed, with no communication to the middleware. The result could be that a worker node runs more process than the middleware is aware of. In order to avoid such a security degradation, this submission mechanism is only allowed to a few selected users, qualified as HPC users. They use a dedicated queue with a peculiar scheduling policy as described before. Common users cannot reserve more than a core per single job, as opening new sessions on other cores is prohibited to them.

The complexity of MPI jobs pushed the development of other software tools that are not specifically connected to MPI, i.e. that can be adopted for any kinds of jobs. For instance, long durations of MPI jobs require a constant monitoring of the job evolution. The gLite3.1 middleware offers the Perusal job technique, i.e. during the job execution, some selected files are copied at regular intervals from the working directory to another one where the user can inspect them. As the request of running long duration and MPI jobs started well before the adoption of this middleware version, we developed a similar "watchdog" (Bruno, 2008) mechanism since the time when the PI2S2 infrastructure ran with the LCG middleware. A special version of the mpi.pre.sh has been introduced in order to include this important monitoring activity. By modifying the supplied open script code, the user can adapt the monitoring tool to the specific needs of his/her application, gaining a greater flexibility compared to the perusal file technique. This is the reason why this approach has survived to the adoption of gLite3.1. Another tool has been recently added to further increase the level of control over job execution. This "VisualGrid" tool (Iacono-Manno, 2009) allows the user to save the image files produced during the job execution and create a quasi-live video that can be used for either job execution monitoring or demonstration purpose. Finally, the lack of

recursive commands in the standard middleware for file up/download to/from the catalogue, was detected during the development of the scripts for an MPI applications. This led to the extension of the standard middleware commands as described on the PI2S2 wiki (Bruno, 2007).

Similarly to all the applications to be "gridified", i.e. modified in order to run on a Grid infrastructure, MPI applications require the definition of a strategy ("computational schema") in order to fully exploit the Grid's opportunities. For instance, the way data are moved from/to their storage devices, greatly impacts the overall performance. This is particularly true for MPI programs that often have the more strict time constraints amongst Grid programs, being very similar to real-time applications as for some Civil Defence simulations. The usual choice for MPI applications, that are intrinsically more complex compared to the average of other Grid programs, is to install them statically the SW package, having them available on each node of the infrastructure as a shared part of the file system. Thus the execution time is reduced, as the code is immediately available for execution with no need for long data transfers; on the other hand, some work overhead is paid in case of SW updating, due to security reasons that prevent common user to access sensitive areas of the file systems and require the intervention of a Software Manager.

The following use cases illustrate a wide range of different HPC situations and the related solutions.

## USE CASES

FLASH (Fryxel & al., 2000) is a 3D astrophysical hydrodynamic code for supercomputers; it is widely used in current astrophysical research due to its modularity that allows to easily add more physics, more complex meshes and customized

*Figure 2. Speed-up vs. number of cores*

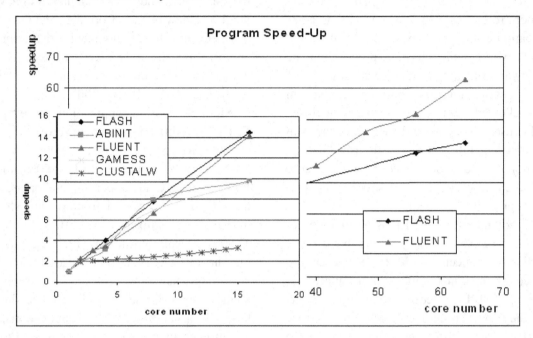

solvers. Production started during the last September and the number of the submitted jobs (each usually a few days long) have gone into the hundreds. Figure 2 shows performance enhancement vs. the number of cores and the diagram indicates a good behavior up to 64 cores.

FLUENT (ANSYS, 2008) is a commercial package currently used in Computer Fluid Dynamics (CFD) mainly for flow modeling and heat and mass transfer simulations. This application has been deployed and tested on the various sites of the infrastructure and it begun its production since late 2008. This application shows a good scalability with an increasing number of cores as reported by the following Figure 2.

ABINIT (Gonze, 2009) is a package whose main program allows one to find the total energy, charge density and electronic structure of systems made of electrons and nuclei (molecules and periodic solids) within Density Functional Theory. It has been tested on the PI2S2 infrastructure on up to a few tens of cores.

GAMESS (Gordon, 2009) is a program for ab-initio molecular quantum chemistry. GAMESS can compute molecular wavefunctions including many effects and corrections. It has been running on the Sicilian Grid Infrastructure since 2007.

ClustalW-MPI (Lombardo, 2008) is a parallel implementation of ClustalW, a general purpose multiple sequence alignment program for DNA and proteins; it produces biologically meaningful multiple sequence alignments of divergent sequences. It has been implemented on the Sicilian Grid as a part of the ViralPack package (Lombardo, 2008), a Genius-integrated application for virology studies by the PI2S2 infrastructure.

The diagrams show a good speed-up improvement for all the tested applications. However only two of them (FLASH, FLUENT) have been extensively proofed up to a massive amount of cores as they are specifically built to run on many cores and have been tested on various infrastructures. Recent tests for FLUENT on the PI2S2 infrastructure have reached 176 cores. Other programs (GAMESS, ABINIT) have been deployed on a limited number

*Figure 3. Workstation speed-up comparison*

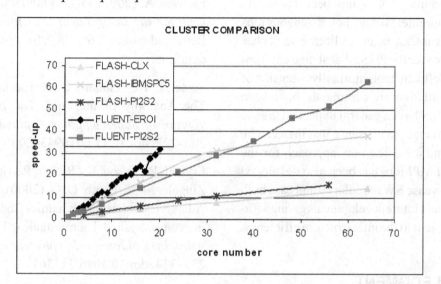

of cores because they did not scale well on a high number of cores or simply because users were satisfied by the reached performance. The close-up of Figure 2 shows the behaviors of the above applications with an increasing number of cores.

The collected results have also been used to compare Grid to other clusters' efficiency. Figure 3 shows the comparison between the PI2S2 clusters and other HPC platforms. Each diagram referring to a program (FLASH or FLUENT) is directly comparable with the other similar ones. Results show that the performance of the PI2S2 infrastructure is at least comparable to other clusters (CLX, IBMSPC5, EROI) with a similar hardware and number of cores. In the FLUENT case, the availability of more processors is effective in compensating the performance gap between the top-level processors of dedicated cluster and shared Grid infrastructure facility.

As a description of the work-in-progress we briefly report about OpenFOAM (OpenCFD, 2009), that is an open-source simulation environment widely used in CFD as an equation solver. Differently from other tools, the OpenFOAM user can manipulate the code and even write his/her own solvers. OpenFOAM has been the most difficult porting case ever, due to the peculiar directory structure and the need for appropriate script sourcing on all the nodes. Currently, the 64-bit OpenFOAM-1.4.1 version runs on the Gigabit net layer on up to 16 cores. Porting to InfiniBand is still under development.

## CONCLUSION AND FUTURE DEVELOPMENTS

Grid is being used as an HPC environment, despite of initial difficulties, running several MPI programs on the Sicilian Grid infrastructure. Many applications are performing their advanced tests and some of them have started their production with encouraging results.

The increasing demand for MPI applications is pushing forward a reorganization of the middleware in order to offer a wider and tighter support to this important class of applications. New wrappers have been added in order to match the combination of different network layers (TCP/IP, InfiniBand), compilers and MPI flavours. A specific scheduling policy has been chosen to fulfill the requirements of the heterogeneous jobs running on the infrastructure. A license server has been developed for the PI2S2 distributed environment. Other software tools, normally extension of the standard middleware commands, have been developed. They have a general impact on the use of the infrastructure in the sense that they can be used by all the jobs. The new approach for the integration of MPI jobs has been also developed in order to increase SW modularity and ease both maintenance and future developments giving a further enhancement to the infrastructure efficiency.

## ACKNOWLEDGMENT

The PI2S2 Project has been funded by the Italian Minister of Research and University.

## REFERENCES

ANSYS Co. (2008). *Fluent.* Retrieved on February, 4th, 2009 from http://www.fluent.com/

Barbera, R. (2006). *COnsorzio Multi-Ente per la promozione e l'adozione di Tecnologie di calcolo Avanzato.* Retrieved January 16th, 2009, from http://www.consorzio-cometa.it/

Barbera, R. (2007). *Progetto per l'Implementazione e lo Sviluppo di una e-Infrastruttura in Sicilia basata sul paradigma Grid.* Retrieved January 16th, 2009, from http://www.pi2s2.it/

Bruno, R. (2007). Recursive Catalog Interaction with lcg-rec-* Tools. *PI2S2 Wiki Pages.* Retrieved on January, 29th, 2009, from https://grid.ct.infn.it/twiki/bin/view/ PI2S2/CatalogUpDownload

Bruno, R. (2008). The WatchDog Utility. *PI2S2 Wiki Pages.* Retrieved on January, 29th, 2009, from https://grid.ct.infn.it/twiki/ bin/view/PI2S2/ WatchdogUtility

Falzone, A. (2007). *Grid Enabled web eNvironment for site Independent User job Submission.* Retrieved January 16th, 2009, from https://genius.ct.infn.it

Foster, I., Kesselmann, C., & Tuecke, S. (2001). The Anatomy of the Grid. *The International Journal of Supercomputer Applications, 15*(3), 200–222. doi:10.1177/109434200101500302

Fryxell, B., Olson, K., Ricker, P., Timmes, F. X., Zingale, M., & Lamb, D. Q. (2000). FLASH: An Adaptive Mesh Hydrodynamics Code for Modeling Astrophysical Thermonuclear Flashes. *The Astrophysical Journal. Supplement Series, 131*(1), 273–334. doi:10.1086/317361

Gonze, X., & al., (2009). *Abinit.* Retrieved on February, 4th, 2009, from http://www.abinit.org/

Gordon, M. (2009). *GAMESS.* Retrieved on February, 4th, 2009, from http://www.msg.chem.iastate.edu/GAMESS/

Gropp, W. (2006). *The Message Passing Interface (MPI) standard.* Retrieved January 27th, 2009, from http://www.mcs.anl.gov/ research/ projects/mpi/

Iacono-Manno, C. M. (2009). The VisualGrid Tool. *PI2S2 Wiki Pages.* Retrieved on February 2nd, 2009 from https://grid.ct.infn.it/twiki/ bin/ view/PI2S2/VisualGrid

Li, K. B. (2003). Multiple ClustalW-MPI: ClustalW analysis using distributed and parallel computing. *Bioinformatics (Oxford, England), 19*(12), 1585–1586. doi:10.1093/bioinformatics/btg192

Lombardo, A., Muoio, A., Iacono-Manno, C. M., Lanzalone, G., & Barbera, R. (2008). *ViralPack.* Retrieved on February, 4th, 2009, from http://documents.ct.infn.it/record/ 170/files/posternapoli.pdf?version=1

OpenCFD. (2009). *The Open Source CFD Toolbox*. Retrieved on February, 4th, 2009, from http://www.opencfd.co.uk/ openfoam/

Orlando, S. Peres., G., Reale, F., Bocchino, F., & Sacco, G. (2008), High Performance Computing on the COMETA Grid Infrastructure, In *Proceedings of the Grid Open Days at the University of Palermo* (pp.181-185), Catania: Consorzio COMETA

Pacheco, P. (2008). *Parallel Programming with MPI*. Retrieved January 27th, 2009, from http://www.cs.usfca.edu/mpi/

Turala, M. (2005). *The CrossGrid Project*. Retrieved on January, 28th, 2009, from http://www.eu-crossgrid.org/project.htm

*This work was previously published in International Journal of Distributed Systems and Technologies, Volume 1, Issue 1, edited by Nik Bessis, pp. 40-54, copyright 2010 by IGI Publishing (an imprint of IGI Global).*

# Section 3
# High Performance Distributed Systems and Applications

# Chapter 14
# Credential Management Enforcement and Secure Data Storage in gLite

**Francesco Tusa**
*Università degli Studi di Messina, Italy*

**Massimo Villari**
*Università degli Studi di Messina, Italy*

**Antonio Puliafito**
*Università degli Studi di Messina, Italy*

## ABSTRACT

*This chapter describes new security solutions for Grid middleware, and specifically faces the issues related to the management of users' and servers' credentials, together with storing and secure data transmission in the Grid. Our work, built on Grid Security Infrastructure (GSI), provides new capabilities (i.e. smart card Grid access, and strong security file storage XML-based) to be used on top of different Grid middlewares, with a low level of changes. This work is currently implemented on gLite and accomplishes the access to Grid resources in a uniform and transparent way. These improvements enable the Grid computing toward the new processing model known as business services.*

## INTRODUCTION

In the last years, a huge amount of scientific computations has been performed on the Grid, thus addressing the always increasing demand for computational and storage power, and offering an infrastructure available to the scientists 24 hours-a-day. The geographically spread resources

of Grid can be virtually exploited as a traditional computing system by means of a specific middleware that hides much of the complexity, giving the user impression that all the resources are available as a coherent computer center (Foster, Kesselman, & Tuecke, 2001).

Both gLite (The Enabling Grids for E-sciencE project: http://www.eu-egee.org/, 2009) and Globus (Foster & Kesselman, 1998) grid middlewares refer to the Grid Security Infrastructure (GSI)

DOI: 10.4018/978-1-4666-0906-8.ch014

(Foster, Kesselman, Tsudik, & Tuecke, 1998) for enabling secure authentication and communication over an insecure network. GSI is based on public key encryption (Brincat, 2001), X.509 certificates (Housley, Ford, Polk, & Solo, 1999) and the SSL (Secure Sockets Layer) communication protocol (Dierks & Allen, 1999). According to the GSI specifications, a user needs to have a trusted X.509 certificate in order to be authenticated on the Grid. The certificate must by issued by a Certification Authority (CA) (Weise, 2001).

When originally thought, the Grid was a mean to share resources among academic partners based on trusting. The current security infrastructure, exactly matches the scientists' requirements in terms of authentication needs to access the grid computational resources. Nowadays the Grid is emerging as a valid support also for commercial applications. As evidence, the European Commission (EC) is also trying to move toward the use of grid resources in business context. EC has funded a "Business Experiments in Grid Technologies" (BEinGRID: http://www.beingrid.eu/, 2009) project, to foster the adoption of the so-defined Next Generation Grid technologies by the accomplishment of several business experiments.

However, to be the Grid recognized as a key enabling technology for commercial applications, it is necessary to guarantee better services in terms of QoS, accountability (S-Sicilia Project. Bringing commercial applications to the Grid: http://ssicilia.unime.it/, 2009) and security. We focus on this latter aspect, proposing both an encrypted file storage and a user credential management system, based on smart card devices and crypto-tokens. This chapter aims to build an additional security layer on top of the existing security infrastructure: the integrations involve accounting mechanisms on the User Interface[1] (UI), storage encryption on the Storage Elements[2] (SE) and data computing on the Worker Nodes[3] (CE).

According to the existing authentication mechanisms of gLite, both the user X.509 certificate (i.e. the RSA public key together with the related

user identity) and the related RSA private key are stored on the UI home directory on two different files: the first one contains the public key and the related user credentials while the second one holds the user private key. Both files are encoded using the Privacy Enhancement for Internet Electronic Mail (PEM) format (Linn, 1993). Thus, the user private key plays a crucial role and the fact it is stored on the file system implies that it could be potentially stolen and then employed by insider attackers (e.g. malicious system administrator). According to the traditional GSI authentication model, in order to gain access to a grid resource, a user has to employ his own RSA key-pair for generating a temporary proxy certificate (Tuecke, Welch, Engert, Pearlman, & Thompson, 2004). Once this latter is generated, it has to be digitally signed (Brincat, 2001) through the RSA private key associated to the user himself.

This is the first security issue we intend to address, proposing and implementing a new solution for storing and using the RSA private key in a more secure way than the existing one: a new credential management system has been developed exploiting smart cards to store and interact with the user's RSA key-pair. By means of the introduced tweaks, all the cryptographic operations involving the key-pair (mainly the private key) can be directly performed on the smart card, supplied with an ad hoc micro-processor, exploiting the user private key it stores (as detailed in Section "Architecture"). In order to implement the previously described features, the voms-proxy-init software module of the UI has been modified: the source code involved in the proxy certificate generation has been integrated with a new component to allow the interaction with the smart card device.

We also present an innovative solution for storing data in a secure way into the Grid, validated through a performance analysis of the costs, comparing the job execution time with and without security features. Our contribution points out specifically on how to provide a data encryption solution for the grid SEs, since the default middleware implementations are based on a traditional, not encrypted storage systems. Some recent works are trying to address the same security issues, proposing cryptographic algorithms and "key-stores" for holding the symmetric keys involved on the secure data management (as described from Blanchet, Mollon, & Deléage, 2006; Montagnat et al., 2006, in the Section "Related Works"). We think key-stores could represent a weak ring of the proposed security solutions: if an attacker gains full access on key-stores he could simultaneously access all data those keys encrypted. Instead of using the key-store, we propose an XML data encapsulation to keep both encrypted data and metadata (i.e. the owner of a X.509 certificate, the associated encrypted symmetric key and other useful information) related to a specific sequence of user data (e.g. the input data for a job that has to be executed on the computational grid).

The key value of our solution is related to the minimum level of changes needed at the middleware layer: differently from the above key-store based approach, it is not necessary to integrate a new centralized entity in the architecture (which could be a vulnerable point of failure), since all the necessary functional elements are stored within the self-contained XML wrapper. This allows a strong environment independence and interoperability (as described by Nagaratnam et al., 2002). Moreover the Grid entities are not really aware of the security structures created on top of the existing GSI.

A further security improvement is also achieved partitioning the "secret" user data into several disjointed subsets called chunks (each associated to a different XML wrapper stored on the Grid SE). Each chunk represents a sub-part of the whole file. While the owner is aware of the subdivision schema, a potential attacker is not (this implies that the correct fragmentation order has to be kept by the file's owner in order to have information properly reconstructed). Furthermore, since the data each chunk contains is stored by means of a

different symmetric key, if an attacker knows the key of a single chunk, the whole file security could be still preserved. This is the main advantage of our data security solution vs. the key-store one.

As detailed in Section "Conclusions", in order to integrate such new security mechanisms on top of the existing GSI, two dynamic libraries have been developed: the first one (libgscrypt) exploits the PKCS#11 standard interface (RSA Laboratories, 2007) to interact with OpenSC (Smart card driver for Open Source Operating Systems: http://www.opensc-project.org/opensc/, 2009) and thus the cryptographic device. It enables the beginning/termination of the smart card communication sessions; the execution of both digital sign and RSA encoding/decoding operations on a byte sequence; data conversion from/to BASE64 (Freed & Borenstein, 1996). The second library (libsgxml), linked against the Grid File Access Library[4] (GFAL) to interact with the grid SEs, instead provides a set of procedures involving the XML wrapper creation and management.

Finally, as already stated, the jobs on the Grid require security credentials throughout their run for accessing secure Grid resources. We underline, as well reported in (Kouril & Basney, 2005), that the delegating long-lived credentials to long-running jobs brings an increased risk that a credential will be compromised and misused. While many researchers have proposed more solutions based on MyProxy (Novotny, Tuecke, & Welch, 2001) online credential repository, we present an innovative solution where new families of jobs are used: idle job (see Section "Architecture"). Thus represents a workaround, it allows to us a long life cycle of the jobs, and determines a new technique for delegating issues.

This chapter is organized as follows: Section "Related" briefly explores some of the security solutions presented in literature, involving both grid accounting management and encrypted storage: benefits and drawbacks are highlighted. Section "Architecture" reports a description of the whole middleware architecture, pointing out our new developed features and their integration within the existing grid infrastructure. Section "System Implementation" describes some of the issues which have been addressed during the work implementation: smart card interaction under Linux, software libraries implementation and encrypted data job execution. Statistical measurement of the proposed solution is evaluated in Section "Performance Analysis". Section "Conclusions" ends the chapter.

## RELATED WORK

The Grid Security Infrastructure (GSI) (Foster et al., 1998) enables secure authentication and communication over an open network. GSI is based on public key encryption mechanisms, X.509 certificates and on the Secure Sockets Layer (SSL) communication protocol, with extensions for single sign-on and delegation. This delegation is performed through the X.509 Proxy Certificates that allow to delegate users' privileges to another entity.

Many researchers are trying to remove the complexity of Grid authorization mechanism with X.509 certificates, providing a middleware (i.e. Grid Portals based on standard Web technologies) for an automatic delegation with the X.509 Proxy Certificates. The solutions provided do not use any distributed approach, furthermore they made a strong and heavy changes of Grid infrastructure. In our opinion, it is necessary to address more Grid security lacks with a low level of integration. The architecture we have proposed has these guidelines and it can be seen as set of security improvements easily applicable in heterogeneous contexts and Grid inter-domains.

Often the Grid Portals do not integrate cleanly with existing Grid security systems such as the GSI. The authors in (Novotny et al., 2001) have solved this problem using an online credentials repository system, called MyProxy. MyProxy allows Grid Portals to use the GSI to interact with

Grid resources in a secure way. The drawback of MyProxy is represented by the centralized credential management that raises significant security concerns as the central server is an attractive target. For instance, it can be vulnerable to denial of service attack. Moreover, all the solutions reported just below, manage the Grid access with users' credentials login and password based. This type of access has been chosen in order to simplify the use of the Grid also by people not aware of information systems. These constrains in terms of centralized services and password-based access systems represent a weakness of the whole Grid security system, since they are not particular suitable in a Business context.

A typical example of using of MyProxy server is given in (Ionescu, Nae, & Gherega, 2007). This represents a Grid-based e-learning platform that uses a standard Web browser to access the e-learning and Grid resources through a Grid Portal. The system offers a standard web security protocol stack, and it does not support any kind of delegation. The authors have solved this problem by integration of the Grid authentication mechanisms with the capabilities of Web servers using MyProxy server. The architecture provides an articulate solution for the problem of credentials management and delegation for trusted access of users to the e-learning resources, including Grid services: a centralized model with many more new entities.

The system that suffers of the same issues of MyProxy is represented by the Securely Available Credentials Protocol (SACRED) (Arsenault & Farrell, 2001). It is a credential storage and retrieval system, and it formalizes a secure XML based protocol that allows the systems access with login and password. It does not perform any form of delegation and it is centralized repository as well as MyProxy. Its operation is also transparent inside one CA domain but does not address inter-domain use of credentials. It disallows X.509 proxy delegation as defined in GSI.

The work in (Jana, Chaudhuri, Datta, & Bhaumik, 2005) uses dynamic user credential management with the dynamic token generation for the communication session. That scheme makes the grid environment more secure and less hack-proneness. The dynamic token generated forms parts of the private key, while user id of the client provides the public key in terms of PKI (Public Key Infrastructure). They do not provide any distributed approach. Even such infrastructure does not present any fault-tolerance system and it can be vulnerable to the DoD attacks (Jana, Chaudhuri, Datta, & Bhaumik, 2006). The same authors explore the on-demand service needs of ubiquitous computing requiring a common interoperable platform with security standards. They propose an interoperable model with solution to security issues particularly single sign-on, delegation of access rights, integration with various local authentication schemes, trust and privacy, but they do not address any issue concerning the Scalability and Reliability of the system proposed.

CredEx (Vecchio, Humphrey, Basney, & Nagaratnam, 2005) is a credential exchange system. The users are responsible for mappings between the credentials they posses, which we believe is not a good idea. Another problem is that choosing the least privilege credential for a given operation would involve multiple calls to the service and would require the user to knowing which aliases to retrieve.

Abawajy, 2008, describes the architecture of a scalable, secure and reliable on-line credential management service called SafeBox for InterGrid computing platform. SafeBox provides InterGrid users with secure mechanism for storing one or multiple credentials. The user can access with login and password on need. The certificates can be obtained by providing the user password. The author highlight that they solve the issues about the fault-tolerance services, but the architecture shows a meaningful modification of the basic infrastructure (InterGrid) also introducing an articulate credential exchange protocol.

Many other works exist about security in Grid Computing. Secure grid storage systems have been specifically analyzed by some recent research works. The work (Montagnat et al., 2006) refers to biomedical data management on the computational grids (such as EGEE) and works by encrypting the files and storing them on normal Storage Elements. The sensitive information is the encryption key, which is stored in a service, called the Hydra key-store. The name Hydra depends on the partitioning schema of the keys which are split and distributed to at least three key-stores, thus even if one does not work, the key can be reconstructed from the active two key-stores. There is also a safety reason: no key can be reconstructed from the content of one single service, i.e. if one of the key servers gets compromised, the hacker cannot decrypt the files.

The article (Blanchet et al., 2006) describes another solution for granting confidentiality of data used in biomedical applications running on the EGEE grid. This kind of applications use data provided from UI or public FTP/HTTP servers to be executed. The proposed solution assumes that the encrypted storage system has to be developed in order to be completely transparent for biomedical applications. The keys used for the encryption are not revealed to the users and stored in a decentralized way avoiding possible system failures (the approach is based on the Shamir secret sharing). Each file is encrypted using a different AES key stored in the distributed "key-store". The transfer of the keys between the servers and the client is very important, consequently an encrypted and mutual authenticated connection in used. For granting the transparency of the solution, specific software has been employed for catching all the process input/output calls (of the job on the Worker Node) and translating them in equivalent remote calls. In this way an on-fly decryption on the Worker Node is allowed (higher security and better performance).

As previously introduced, both the works (Blanchet et al., 2006; Montagnat et al., 2006) modify the standard middleware architecture introducing a new centralized entity for cryptographic key management (i.e. the key-stores). Differently from those works, our solution tries to minimize the changes needed at the middleware layer including all the necessary storage security elements within a self-contained XML wrapper.

File system performance is another critical aspect to be considered. The previous discussed work (Blanchet et al., 2006) also provides a section dedicated to the system performance which is analyzed by means of a comparison among different remote file access method using the developed storage solution and the usual grid commands. A graphical representation shows how

long (seconds) the file transfer lasts in the different test measurement scenarios. Our performance analysis is also based on statistical considerations: each of the time measurements is obtained using a series of experiments in order to minimize the variability factor the grid introduces on job execution (due to network congestion and variable users' job workload). Furthermore, unlike (Blanchet et al., 2006), our graphs deeply describe the internal timing related to the different operations a job performs when it is executed on encrypted input data (i.e. I/O time, decrypting time, etc.).

In (Feichtinger & Peters, 2005) the authors describe an efficient method to access authorization in distributed (Grid) storage systems. Client applications obtain "access tokens" from an organization's file catalogue upon the execution of a file name execution request. Whenever a client application tries to access the requested files, the token is transparently passed to the target storage system. Thus the storage service can decide on the authorization of a request without itself having to contact the authorization service. The authors tested the performance of the proposed solution by measuring the time for executing a copy command of 1-byte files from server to client machines. The time includes the secure retrieving of the authorization envelope from the catalogue

service, the related decoding and finally the time for copying operation. The measurements were performed for 20 and 100 clients: a comparison is made among the process with GSI authentication and that without GSI authentication. Differently from our work, the performance analysis this work proposes is thus based on the evaluation of different approaches on user authentication.

Finally, as well as in our vision, the last work (Ko, Kim, Lee, Choi, & Kim, 2008) shows that the XML wrapper offers a high scalability and allows to manage efficiently large number of users and great amounts of data. Moreover, the authors highlighted that XML data release fits well in a dynamic environments, where a new approach to specify access control policies, an authorization model and encrypt the specific portions of XML data using users' keys are preferred.

## ARCHITECTURE

This work aims to provide a set of new security mechanisms for the gLite grid middleware, exploiting the existing GSI. First aspect we managed refers to a new accounting mechanism, based on the use of smart card devices for interacting with the user's RSA key-pair. As depicted in Figure 1, such tweak involves the UI component (depicted on the left upper side of the image) and it is explained in Section "Using smart cards for managing users' credentials and accessing grid resources". The second security aspect we analyzed involves both the SEs and CEs (represented on the right and bottom side of the picture), modified in order to provide encrypted permanent storage and secure data communication while jobs are executed. These new added features are instead explained in Subsection "Encrypted File System": Paragraph "XML wrapper" shows the structure and the employment of the XML wrapper previously introduced, while Paragraph "Secure data transfer and computation" illustrates the logical flow of operations involved in the execution of a

*Figure 1. Representation of a grid computing scenario for executing a pool of jobs on different XML chunks. The depicted environment is simplified since it assumes that all the jobs are queued up to the same Computing Element (CE).*

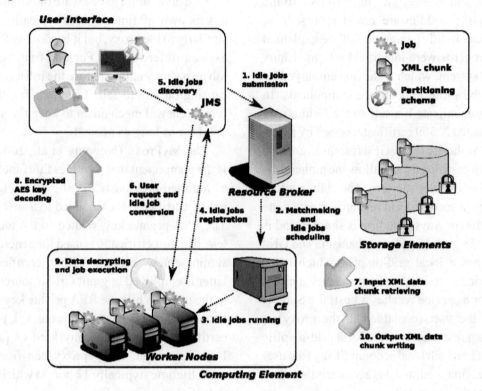

job on a set of encrypted data. This current section, also provides a short introduction on smart card technology.

## Using Smart Cards for Managing Users' Credentials and Accessing Grid Resources

Smart cards (as well USB crypto-tokens) have recently placed an important role in Information Technology. In fact, they can be easily used for practical applications in our workday life. A smart card is a hardware device whose dimensions are similar to a credit card. It can be used for storing and processing data with a high level of security. The core of a smart card is composed of a set of electronic circuits such as memories and microprocessors. The smart card technology guarantees two levels of security, the user has to

prove something that he has (i.e. smart card) and also something that he knows (i.e. private Personal Identify Number - PIN): two-factor authentication (T-FA). Furthermore, this type of devices takes the advantages of using ad hoc processors, designed to perform RSA and DSA operations in an efficient way. Microprocessor smart cards are able to generate RSA key pairs on board, avoiding the risk of extracting the private key from its internal memory. Since the private key cannot be extracted from the card, the device could be used as support for developing information system with a high level of security. USB crypto-token represents a device easy to use, look like USB pen drive and it is a small hardware derived by the merging of a smart card with an USB card reader. The idea this work is describing is based on the use of microprocessor smart cards.

Since gLite security infrastructure needs the execution of complex cryptographic algorithms, in our opinion, to integrate smart cards into the existing Grid middleware could represent an added value. In this paragraph will be explained how smart cards were integrated into the Linux operating system, which is the one employed by many of the gLite middleware components. In order to authenticate himself to the Grid a user needs a trusted X.509 certificate, issued by a Certification Authority (CA). Grid resources are also issued with certificates that allow the authentication to other users or services. The authorization of a user on a specific Grid resource can be done in two different ways. The first is simpler, and is based on the grid-mapfile mechanism. The Grid resource has a local grid-mapfile which maps user certificates to local accounts. When a user's request for a service reaches a host, the Subject Name of the user (contained in the proxy) is checked against what is in the local grid-mapfile to find out to which local account (if any) the user certificate is mapped, and this account is then used to perform the requested operation.

The second way relies on the Virtual Organisation Membership Service (VOMS) which allows a more detailed definition of user privileges. With this system the information is presented to services via an extension to the proxy. At the time the proxy is created, one or more VOMS servers are contacted, and they return a mini certificate known as Attribute Certificate (AC) which is signed by the VO and contains information about group membership and any associated roles within the VO.

To create a VOMS proxy the ACs are embedded in a standard proxy, and the whole thing is signed with the private key of the parent certificate. Services can then decode the VOMS information and use it as required, e.g. a user may only be allowed to do something if he has a particular role from a specific VO. One consequence of this method is that VOMS attributes can only be used with a proxy, they cannot be attached to a CA-issued certificate.

One other thing to be aware of is that each AC has its own lifetime. This is typically 12 hours similarly to the proxy, but it is possible for ACs to expire at different times. For long-running jobs, the job proxy may expire before the job has finished, causing the job to fail. To avoid this, there is a proxy renewal mechanism to keep the job proxy valid for as long as needed.

The MyProxy (Novotny et al., 2001) server is the component that provides this functionality, as reported previously. As shown in Figure 2, a public certificate is associated to a specific user. The RSA private key, related to the identity attested in the certificate, is used for generating and signing a new temporary proxy certificate. This latter is employed to grant Grid resources access to the users. While the RSA private key (in PEM encoded form) is password protected, the proxy certificate doesn't need any kind of password. For this reason, every proxy certificate has a short lifetime (typically 12 hours) which reduces potential security risks.

Our new approach to obtain the encoded version of the hash, included within the proxy certificate for granting trust, is instead based on a more secure smart card interaction: once the hash is computed, it is sent as an input data to the smart card, which will directly perform the RSA encoding on that data (by means of the private key it stores). Such approach presents several advantages: first, since the private key can never be extracted from the device, it will be impossible to steal such secret key or to have multiple copies of it; second, all the cryptographic operations involving the RSA user's private key (e.g. the sign) will be safely performed on the smart card itself exploiting the ad-hoc chip it provides. This new set of features introduce a valid countermeasure against the inside attackers, since the user's private key is stored on a specific crypto-device instead than in the user's home directory.

*Figure 2. Certificate chain for proxy generation*

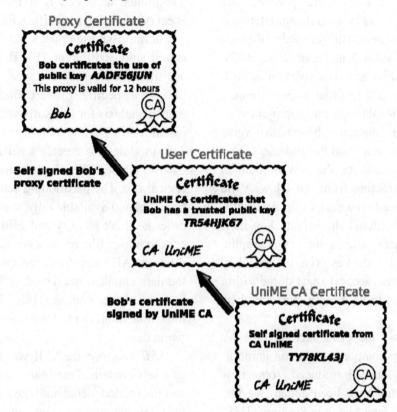

## Encrypted File System

This section intends to describe the security storage system developed on top of the gLite grid middleware. The architectural integrations are mainly based on the employment of asymmetric RSA and symmetric AES cryptographic algorithms, in order to increase data integrity and confidentiality on the file storage system. As reported above, the work has been developed to enforce the security of the Grid SEs, encoding data by means of cryptographic symmetric algorithms, in order to allow a specific user or a group of them (i.e. the file data owners) to retrieve the pieces of information stored on the SEs (through a software layer built on GFAL).

According to our idea, the symmetric AES key (the size for such key using the plain format is 256 bits) is stored on the SE together with the encrypted data. Since the symmetric key has to be kept secret, it is encoded using the owner's RSA public key[5] (the size for the encrypted key is 2048 bits). Following this method, a user who can access the AES key, can also access the corresponding encrypted file. In order to retrieve the AES key, a file owner has to employ his own private key which is stored on the UI (in the user's home directory or on a crypto-token device).

Our approach for data storing is mainly based on the XML wrapper used as a self-contained medium for storing data file and the related metadata. This method focuses on the employment of the standard defined by the World Wide Web Consortium (W3C, within the particular XML recommendation model provided in XML encryption: http://www.w3.org/TR/xmlenc-core/, 2009), for encrypting data and representing the result in XML: the result of encrypting data is an XML Encryption element which contains or references the ciphered data. This kind of approach matches the requirements of interoperability for heterogeneous systems in several computational distributed scenarios (such those based on the web services, as described in (Nagaratnam et al., 2002).

As shown in Figure 1, our solution is built upon the existing GSI in order to provide new security capabilities through the employment of cryptographic algorithms, involving both the grid middleware components and the grid users, who are responsible to manage the new introduced mechanisms, interacting from the UI with the RSA key-pair stored on a smart card or crypto-token (in order to avoid the private key theft risks). This scenario allows the cryptographic operations involving the keys (i.e. the AES key decoding for granting access to data stored within an XML wrapper) to be directly performed by the smart card.

Figure 1 shows the gLite architecture. We remark that many components remain unmodified but, as previously introduced, some new functional elements have been added: we just introduced a new Java Message Service[6] (JMS) daemon, installed on the UI and implemented by means of Apache ActiveMQ to pursue the idle job submission mechanism.

Finally, using smart cards even for the servers (i.e. SEs or WNs with public/private key-pair) it is possible to prevent any fraudulent off-line attack perpetrated by malicious system administrators who can not gain direct access to the private key to perform file decryption. For off-line attack we mean the capability of the system administrator to perform the file decrypting without neither monitoring nor event registrations (i.e. data logs). In a business context, such the one we are describing, each Grid element could be equipped with a reader and a smart card were the certificate, to grant the credential, will be stored. With this improvement, the RSA private key of user and server can be preserved from most of potential security lacks.

In order to strengthen the security mechanisms of the solution, the user data is also divided into different parts called chunks. Each chunk stores a disjointed set of data from the user file, which is encrypted using a specific AES symmetric key. Furthermore, these chunks have to be sent and stored among different SEs. Before the chunks are transmitted, they are generated on the UI through a specific software module (the performance analysis for this software module will be discussed in section "Performance Analysis"). This module also creates a partitioning schema used for reassembling the data chunks into a single logical file. The partitioning schema requires to be secret and available only to the file owner. In order to break security and gain illegitimate access to a user file, an attacker has to rustle each different AES key from the chunks' set. Once the data chunk is decrypted, information has to be correctly reassembled: this job implies to test the whole number of chunks permutation, in the worst case.

*XML wrapper:* the XML wrapper is employed as a self-contained medium for storing data file and the related metadata: when a user logged on the UI wants to store his own reserved data on the Grid, he has to run a specific software module in order to proceed. Such module will be responsible of data subdivision and encryption, using different XML wrappers and chunks spread among different SEs. Figure 3 depicts the internal structure of an XML chunk which could be stored on a grid SE. As the Figure shows, the set of nodes of a chunk includes: the *owners definition* (a list of X.509 certificates encoded in PEM form), a *list of AES symmetric keys* (each associated to a different owner and encrypted with the related owner's public key), finally the *ciphered data* (encrypted by means of the included AES symmetric key), stored inside the XML node through a BASE-64 encapsulation mechanism (as specified in (Freed & Borenstein, 1996). The set of data is associated to a SHA-1 digest in order to verify its correctness (and prevent errors during data computing).

The first two elements of the described structure can be named chunk metadata; the last one instead represents the real data of the chunk. The

*Figure 3. Graphical representation of the XML chunk logical structure: together with the node which contains the encrypted data and the attributes, the key node and certificates node are shown. The public key of each certificate is employed to protect the AES key stored in the key node: data owner can access the chunk encrypted AES key using the own RSA private one (using the smart card on the UI).*

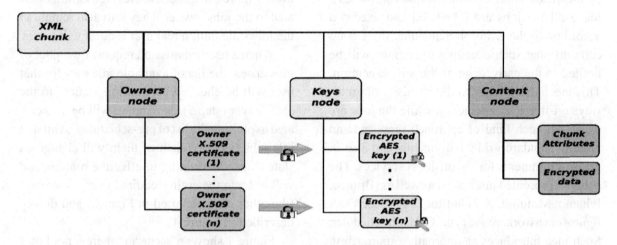

whole chunk is digitally signed following the recommendation model provided in (XML sign: http://www.w3.org/TR/xmlenccore/, 2009), in order to prevent metadata (and data) tampering perpetrated by malicious users.

As will be detailed in the following paragraph "Secure data transfer and computation", a job that has to access reserved data must obtain a clear version of the AES key associated to the encoded data. The XML wrapper contains one (or more, according to the number of chunk's owners) encrypted version of such key (ciphered through the public RSA key of the owner): in order to perform the job operations, the owner (of both the job and the chunk) has to employ his RSA private key (which is stored on the cryptographic device on the UI) for retrieving the plain version of the AES key concerning his own data.

*Secure data transfer and computation:* as Figure 1 shows, when a user needs to execute a job on his own reserved grid data, he has to submit a specific request to the Resource Broker[7] (RB) (step 1). Our security improvement on the existing architecture, also grants data protection while the jobs are executed: each job will process

its own set of data which has been protected using a specific AES symmetric key. Since the jobs are spread among different WNs (even different WNs of different Computing Elements[8] (CE)), an attacker won't be able to gain access to the whole sets of data while it is processed on the Grid: in order to break our security system, each dataset has to be "sniffed" and decoded using the specific key related to that chunk. When initial user data have been mapped on a high number of chunks, the probability of such event is very low.

Even if the attacker retrieves all the fragmented data, their right sequence has to be reconstructed (in the same way as the one registered in the partitioning schema on the UI). Since this information is reserved (the partitioning schema is protected in order to grant access to only the data owner), the potential threat has to test all the possible combinations in order to obtain the original data sequence (which requires as much time as the number of chunks).

According to the job execution model we propose, for a certain grid user, many jobs (which perform the same set of operation, e.g. a software system simulation) could run in the same time, each taking as input different data chunks: anyway, for each of those jobs (pool of jobs), the first task to execute refers to the AES key decrypting by means of smart card interaction (on the UI). Since all the jobs are scheduled and executed according to the Grid Job Scheduler, there is no certainty that such decoding operations will be limited to the early stage of the jobs execution. This mechanism leads to the requisite of an always on-line user interaction while the jobs are executed: such kind of approach represents an issue in standard grid environments and also in grid environments for the business services. The solution presented just below, as well as (Bruneo, Iellamo, Minutoli, & Puliafito, 2009) described, figures out a workaround of the Grid Job Scheduler. Such idea introduces an alternative approach to the traditional job scheduling mechanisms: a JMS daemon running on a public server (i.e. the UI in our case) should be instantiated in order to implement the idle job scheduling tweak. This latter will be useful to provide a new different approach to manage jobs submission and retrieving phases.

Our new job submission idea is based on the concept of job reservation. A particular job family (called idle job) was created. Such jobs, once submitted, have a fixed idle lifetime during which they wait for the task to be accomplished. The concept consists into submitting these jobs in an asynchronous way to the Grid before the arrival of a real users' request (as represented in Figure 1, step 1). According to our approach, each user could submit the own set of idle jobs which will be later used: by means of the smart card based credential management, in the early stage of such process, the user will employ the cryptographic device to generate the temporary proxy certificate and send his submission request to the RB. Once such submission phase ends, the smart card can be extracted from the reader. The idle jobs will be thus scheduled according to the traditional grid approach (step 2 in the Figure), that is the RB will select the best CE to which to queue up each submitted job.

When such idle jobs will change its state from scheduled to running (step 3 in the Figure) they will register themselves to the JMS server (step 4 in the Figure), in a specific message topic associated to the jobs' owner. They will also remain in the idle state until a real user request will occur.

When a user submission request for a pool of jobs arises, the list of available idle jobs for that user will be checked performing a query to the JMS server (step 5). A mapping will be thus created exploiting the list of pre-scheduled, available idle jobs (step 6): each of them will change its state from idle running to effective running and will execute the entire required user's operation (the other steps reported in Figure 1 and deeply described in Figure 4).

Figure 1 shows a scenario where a pool of 3 jobs has been submitted. Each job will also access a different data chunk (each chunk is mapped on a different SE). Once the jobs are sent to the CEs, they can be moved and executed on the different WNs (step 3). The scenario depicted is simplified since only one CE is shown.

Differently from the traditional approach, the required interactions with the user on the UI will be performed within the time slot related to the early running phase of the jobs set. Since all the selected jobs are pre-scheduled they will be practically executed at the same time (on the available WNs): the user interaction time will thus be related (and limited) to the execution time of the slower job. As above mentioned, the communication between such components takes place using modules and daemons based on the JMS protocol.

A mandatory requirement for the job execution is related to data retrieving: each job will communicate with the pertaining SE (by means of the set of functions available in our developed library) in order to retrieve the associated XML wrapper (step 7). The same set of functions will be later employed for writing output results (exploiting the XML wrapper container).

*Figure 4. Sequence Diagram for explaining the sequence of steps involved in the job execution using the proposed secure system XML storage: the sequence number is referred to the logical steps of the Figure 1.*

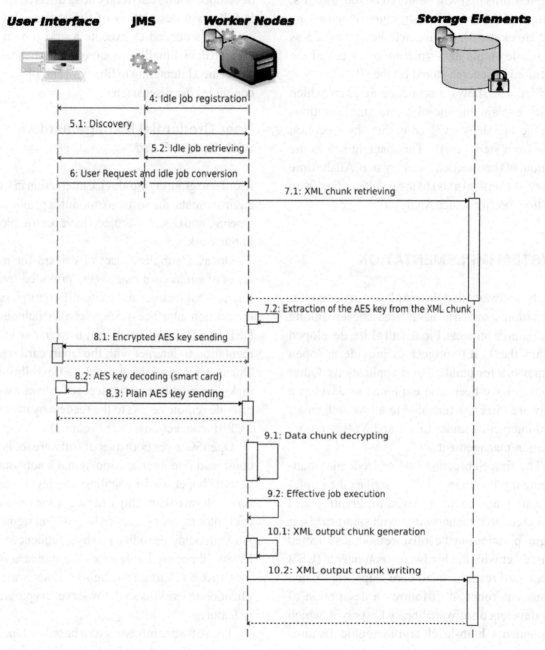

Once the XML wrapper has been retrieved from each SE, the related AES key has to be extracted in order to access the related data. Since the AES key is encrypted by means of his owner's RSA public key, a mechanism to interact with the UI has to be used for retrieving a plain version of such key (step 8).

When the AES key has been retrieved by the job, the preliminary environment configuration will terminate and the effective job execution will begin (step 9). Each job will perform its own set of operations and obtain a sequence of output results that will be stored on the grid SEs, using the XML container structure. When all the jobs are executed, the user will be able to access the whole output data structure by means of the partitioning schema stored on the UI.

Figure 4 shows a sequence diagram which clearly explains the idle job submission operations and the sub-steps involved in the jobs execution flow from step 7 to 10. The diagram shows the amount of time needed for every step. All the time intervals (vertical axis) fit the result coming from Section "Performance Analysis".

## SYSTEM IMPLEMENTATION

All the software modules employed in our implementation's scenario have been chosen among open source projects. First of all gLite, developed within the EGEE project to provide an open framework for building grid applications. Other projects have been also exploited to develop a software infrastructure able to allow both smart card interaction under Linux and XML wrapper creation/management.

The first Subsection ("User credential management with smart card") describes the implementation approach employed for granting grid user credential management with smart cards. It begins pointing out the software modules selected to interact with the hardware components (USB smart card readers, smart card chips, etc...), in a Linux environment. It follows a description of our developed software library libsgcrypt, which implements high-level cryptographic features interacting with hardware. Finally a report of the changes performed on the middleware components (i.e. voms-proxy-init), for integrating the features provided by libsgcrypt, concludes the discussion.

The second Subsection ("Secure data management XML-based: how to encrypt, decrypt and use data") describes the implementation details related to our encrypted storage system, based

on the XML wrapper idea: the set of procedures developed within our library libsgxml is analyzed. It follows a description of the logical flow of operations needed to execute a grid job on encrypted data. Finally a report on how such task is performed interacting to libsgxml and libsgcrypt, concludes the discussion.

## User Credential Management with Smart Card

In order to grant crypto-device interaction in Linux environments, the software modules provided by OpenSC and OpenCT projects have been exploited in our work.

OpenCT supplies a set of drivers for many types of smart card reader (i.e. provided by different manufacturer and with different physical connection interfaces). Such set also includes the USB CCID compliant driver, used in our implementation to interact with the smart card reader. OpenCT allows a high level of flexibility also making available specific pieces of software which provide remote access to the readers by means of TCP/IP connections. (See Figure 5)

OpenSC gives both a set of software tools (i.e. command line interface tools) and a software library (libopensc) for enabling low-level interaction with smart card chips, to pursue the execution of cryptographic operations (e.g. digital signature, RSA encoding/decoding) on byte sequences. The library libopensc implements the standard interface PKCS#11 to allow high-level software application to exploits such low-level cryptographic features.

The software infrastructure based on OpenCT and OpenSC is depicted in Figure IV-A. Together with the above mentioned open source projects, in the highest layer of the stack, user-level applications are also represented: these latter do not directly interact with libopensc through the PKCS#11 interface; this task is accomplished by means of an additional layer implemented by our library libsgcrypt. Differently from libopensc,

*Figure 5. Layered stack for interacting with smart card in Linux environments*

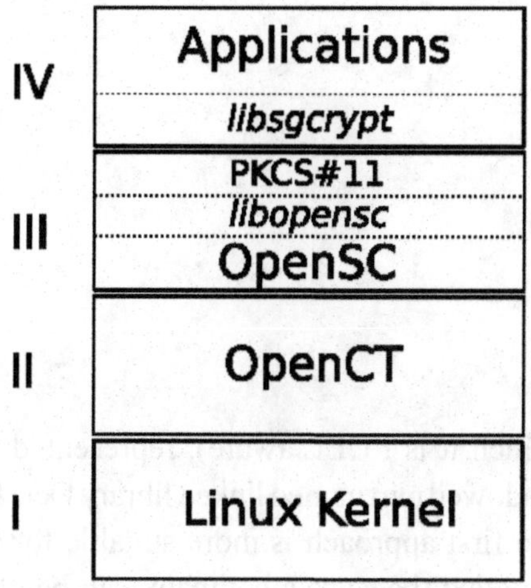

libgscrypt allows a high hardware abstraction: it is built on top of the PKCS#11 interface to implement a set of high-level logical procedures and perform cryptographic operations through the smart card. Such set of features provided by libsgcrypt includes:

- int initialize_libcrypt(const char *pin, bool debug) to initialize the communication between the smart card, the reader driver and the Operating System
- libcrypt_sign(const unsigned char *in, const unsigned int in size, unsigned char **out, unsigned int *out size) to perform digital sign operations, that is to perform data encoding exploiting the RSA private key the smart card stores
- libcrypt getCertificateX509(unsigned char **certificate, int *certificate size, bool intoFile, const char *filename) to retrieve from the smart card the user X.509 certificate
- libcrypt chunk_encrypt(const unsigned char *in, const unsigned int size in, unsigned char **out, unsigned int *size out, unsigned char **key) to encrypt user data that has to be encapsulated within the

XML wrapper (there is also a similar function which allows data decrypting)

In order to allow smart card interaction in the voms-proxy-init software tool, a set of tweaks has been applied on its source code. For accomplishing our new grid credential management, some parts of the existing source code have been removed and some other parts have been integrated exploiting libsgcrypt.

To achieve the proxy certificate generation, the tool voms-proxy-init also needs to access the user RSA public key (associated to the user's X.509 certificate). In our new implementation, since this latter is stored on the smart card (instead of the UI file system), during each user session, it has to be extracted and written to a temporary file: such task is accomplished invoking the function libcrypt_getCertificateX509. Right now, a method to retrieve user credentials has been developed and a preliminary version of the proxy certificate can be created. The third logical step involved on the voms-proxy-init tweak, is also the main one: once this first version of the proxy certificate has been generated, it is necessary to perform the digital signature operation: in the original voms-proxy-init implementation, the function used to perform such task is located in the sslutils.c file of the source code, and is named proxy sign. Such procedure has been modified removing all the references to the old RSA user's private key (such the second prototype parameter).

Furthermore, the original procedure to perform digital signature operation (based on OpenSSL crypto API) has been replaced with our new one, grounded on the libcrypt sign function (implemented in our library libsgcrypt).

## Secure Data Management XML-Based: How to Encrypt, Decrypt and Use Data

In a business context, companies require a high security level of data storage. Data often represent

*Box 1.*

```
proxy_sign(X509 * user_cert,
// PRIVATE_KEY reference
X509_REQ * req,
X509 ** new_cert,
int seconds,
STACK_OF(X509_EXTENSION) * extensions,
int limited_proxy,
int proxyver)
```

their real core business; thereby they have to be encrypted when stored on the SEs, to ensure both confidentiality and privacy. This task can be performed exploiting the set of functions implemented by libsgcrypt: in order to allow jobs execution, data have to be decrypted, processed, and stored in an encrypted way again. In our implementation, a user that wishes to submit jobs and to perform the processing on his data, can choose among different approaches (showed in Figure 6):

The job is seen as a black box, i.e. the source code is not available or not modifiable.

The job can include a piece of source code with decryption/encryption capabilities.

In Figure 6(a) two new jobs have been introduced: $J_{DEC}$ which receives as input a sequence of encrypted data and provides as output a set of plain data; $J_{ENC}$ which performs the vice versa operation; $J_1$ is a whichever user submitted job that can only take plain data as input. In Figure 6(a), data at the beginning are encrypted, the job $J_{DEC}$ provides the decryption, and then it transfers plain data to $J_1$. This job is NOT aware that data were originally encrypted. $J_1$ receives plain data through a common Linux Pipe ("|"); the job retrieves data from the standard I/O and writes the output results again to the standard I/O. At the end, the job $J_{ENC}$ performs the encryption of the results.

Figure 6(b) shows a single rectangle (the job $J_2$), in which the job owns all the security features to perform the decryption and encryption of data

(on which it is FULL aware), represented from the shadowed part named linked library Dec(Enc).

The first approach is more suitable for business context, because a company can benefit of our security features without having to modify her processes. However this technique presents a weakness, that is, it is possible to intercept plain data at the pipe level. The second approach is more invasive, as it requires modifications of the source code but it offers better performance in terms of processing time and data security.

Looking at the Figure 6, keeping in mind what has been previously exposed regarding the jobs $J_{DEC}$, $J_{ENC}$ and $J_2$, input/output data streams for these jobs are based on the XML wrapper container. The internal structure of an XML wrapper comprises: the owners definition list, the encrypted AES keys list and the ciphered user data. In order to create and manage such wrappers, we have implemented a set of procedures, grouped within the libsgxml library. To perform encrypting/decrypting operations on data stored within the XML wrappers, it is also needed to exploit the features included in the libsgcrypt library.

When the jobs $J_{DEC}$ or $J_2$ are performing input operations on encrypted data, they have to invoke the following functions from the two libraries:

- getContentTag(const char *content, const unsigned int content size, const char *tag, char ** out, int *out size) to get data content from an XML element

*Figure 6. Data flow from the left side to the right side: the job is NOT aware of data decryption/encryption (a). The job is FULL aware of data decryption/encryption (b)*

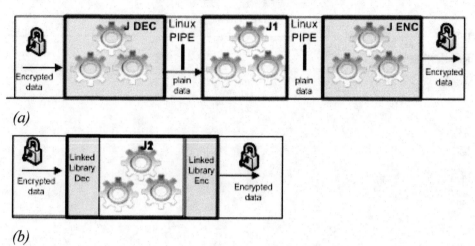

*(a)*

*(b)*

- unsigned char *libcrypt_unBase64(const unsigned char *in, const unsigned int in size) to decode encrypted data from BASE64 to byte stream
- initialize_libcrypt
- libcrypt_chunk_decrypt.

When $J_{ENC}$ or $J_2$ are performing output operations on plain data they will produce an encrypted data sequence. In order to generate output XML wrapper, the procedures to invoke from the two libraries are:

- int initialize_libsgxml(const char *filename, const bool debug) to begin the creation of an XML wrapper
- bool createElement(const char *name) to create a XML wrapper element
- bool generateChunkKey(const unsigned char *id, const unsigned char *name, const unsigned char *key) to fill the key field of a XML wrapper element
- bool generateChunkFile(const unsigned char *nameFile, const unsigned char *date, const unsigned long int size, const unsigned char *chunk) to fill the file field of an XML wrapper element

- bool generateChunkOwner(const unsigned char *id, const unsigned char *name, const unsigned char *certificate) to fill the owner field of an XML wrapper element
- initialize_libcrypt
- libcrypt_chunk_encrypt
- unsigned char *libcrypt toBase64(const unsigned char *in, const unsigned int in size) to encode encrypted data to BASE64 before including them within the XML wrapper.

Next section provides an in depth analysis comparing job execution on both plain and encrypted data (using the job implementation reported in Figure 6(b)) in order to measure the time overhead of our security solution.

## PERFORMANCE EVALUATION

In this section we assess a series of experimental tests carried on a scenario similar to the one of Figure 1, in order to analyze the performance of the developed security system. (See Figure 7)

In a preliminary phase we generated a random set of data files whose dimensions are 1MB,

*Figure 7. Comparison between the execution time of Pdj and Edj for different data size with 95% confidence interval.*

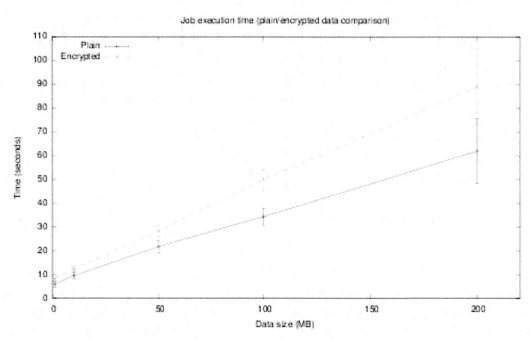

10MB, 50MB, 100MB and 200MB. For each of these files we executed the encrypting algorithm and the XML encapsulation using a software tool running on the UI. Such program allows a user to manage XML wrapper also interacting with smart card devices. Once the above mentioned task ends, a set of encrypted XML chunks is obtained. The XML chunk data encapsulation increases the data size of a variable factor between 30-40% (due to the MIME conversion). Since, to reduce data size, another step is required, that is a file compression with GZIP. This determines a really small increasing of original data size (< 2%), but it introduces a CPU overloading. Figure 8(b) gives estimation oh the load.

The analysis we have performed is based on the comparison of the execution time for two types of jobs:

A job which retrieves and accesses (i.e. bufferies) a set of data stored on a grid SE (using GFAL).

A job which retrieves and accesses an encrypted XML chunk stored on a grid SE (according to the flow described in the diagram of Figure 4).

The two kinds of jobs allow us to analyze the impact of our security solution on the traditional job execution, pointing out the time overhead related to the execution of the cryptographic operations. Both jobs have been designed for retrieving a set of data without executing further operations on it.

In brief, the two types of jobs are now defined plain data job ($P_{dj}$) and encrypted data job ($E_{dj}$). Figure 6 (top side) helps to understand the meaning of $P_{dj}$ and $E_{dj}$:

$$P_{dj} = J_1$$
$$E_{dj} = J_{ENC} + J_1$$

Using this approach, the measured time is independent from the task of the job. Data are accessed from the SE (in our test all the jobs are submitted to the same CE and data are stored on the same SE) for both $P_{dj}$ and $E_{dj}$.

When an encrypted data job has to be executed, three different phases are involved: the first one (Figure 8(a)) refers to the job I/O operation, that is the necessary time to retrieve the input data from the grid SEs (such task has to be performed

*Figure 8. Timings comparison of the three different phases involving job execution: plain/encrypted data jobs for I/O operations (a); plain/encrypted data jobs for CPU operations (b); Timings for AES key decoding involving encrypted data jobs execution (c)*

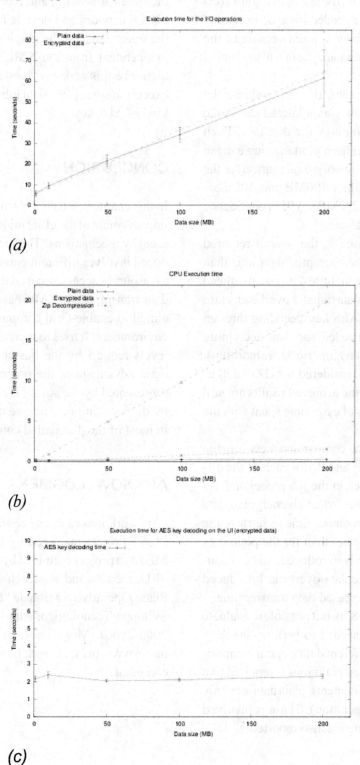

*(a)*

*(b)*

*(c)*

also for plain data jobs); the second one (Figure 8(b)) refers to the effective CPU time needed to accomplish the job task; the last one (Figure 8(c)) finally shows the time needed for a job to contact the UI in order to obtain a plain version of the AES key (such task obviously refers to encrypted data jobs only).

For all of such graphs, the x-axis shows the different data sizes, the y-axis instead shows the different execution timings for that task. Each point of the graph has been plotted using a mean value over a distribution of 50 measures (for the sizes 1MB, 10MB, 50MB, 100MB) and 100 measures (for the size of 200MB). A 95% confidence interval has been evaluated.

As shown in Figure 7, the overall required time is greater for the encrypted data jobs than for the plain ones due to: little data size overhead which also implies a data transfer overhead; extra time needed for the AES key decoding through the UI; extra time needed for data decrypting operation (using the asymmetric AES algorithm); extra time has to be considered for GZIP deflating phase. However the achieved results are still encouraging in terms of extra time spent with the new procedures.

Figure 8 shows a comparison between the execution times of $E_{dj}$ and $P_{dj}$ for each of the different phases involved in the job processing. As depicted in Figure 8(a), when an encrypted data job is executed, the required time to retrieve the input data is a bit greater than for the plain data job case. As previously introduced, this is a consequence of the little data overhead introduced which leads to an increased data transfer time.

Looking at figure 8(b), is it possible to evaluate the amount of time needed to perform the AES decoding task for different data sizes: a comparison between encrypted/plain jobs is reported (we remark that in our experiments, plain data jobs only perform buffering operation). Timings involved in GZIP data deflating are also reported.

Figure 8(c) finally depicts the time needed to retrieve a plain version of the AES key (i.e. the time for sending and receiving the AES key via the network and decode it on the UI through the smart card): as the graph shows, such time is independent from the XML wrapper size. Furthermore this task involves only encrypted job execution since plain data jobs do not require any kind of AES key.

## CONCLUSION

In this chapter we have presented an architectural improvement of the gLite middleware concerning security mechanisms. The security system introduced involves different parts of the Grid as well as resources access, secure data storing and secure data transmission, XML-based. Our solution is aimed to enable Grid computing in commercial environment. It tries to increase the Grid security levels request by the business companies. The main advantage of the proposed architecture is represented by the strong level of flexibility and by the low "impact" degree of changes required in most of the distributed computing platforms.

## ACKNOWLEDGMENT

This work makes use of results produced by the PI2S2 Project managed by the Consorzio CO-META, a project cofunded by the Italian Ministry of University and Research (MIUR) within the Piano Operativo Nazionale "Ricerca Scientifica, Sviluppo Tecnologico, Alta Formazione" (PON 2000-2006). More information is available at http://www.pi2s2.it and http://www.consorzio-cometa.it.

# REFERENCES

Abawajy, J. H. (2008). An Online Credential Management Service for Intergrid Computing. *Asia-Pacific Conference on Services Computing* (pp. 101-106).

Arsenault, A., & Farrell, S. (2001). *Securely available credentials* (Tech. Rep. RFC3157). Available from http://www.ietf.org/rfc/rfc3157.txt

BEinGRID. http://www.beingrid.eu/. (2009).

Blanchet, C., Mollon, R., & Deléage, G. (2006, April). Building an Encrypted File System on the EGEE Grid: Application to Protein Sequence Analysis. In I. C. Society (Ed.), *Proceedings of the first international conference on availability, reliability and security (ARES)* (pp. 965 - 973).

Brincat, K. (2001, April). On the Use of RSA as a Secret Key Cryptosystem. *Designs, Codes and Cryptography, 22,* 317–329. doi:10.1023/A:1008354524654

Bruneo, D., Iellamo, G., Minutoli, G., & Puliafito, A. (2009). Gridvideo: A practical example of non-scientific application on the Grid. *IEEE Transactions on Knowledge and Data Engineering, 21*(5), 666–680. doi:10.1109/TKDE.2008.191

Dierks, T., & Allen, C. (1999). *The Transport Layer Security (TLS) Protocol* (Tech. Rep. RFC2246). Available from http://www.ietf.org/rfc/rfc2246.txt

Feichtinger, D., & Peters, A. J. (2005, November). Authorization of Data Access in Distributed Storage Systems. *In The 6ᵗʰ IEEE/ACM international workshop on grid computing* (pp. 172-178).

Foster, I., & Kesselman, C. (1998, July). The Globus Project: a status report. In *IPPS/SPDP '98 Heterogeneous computing workshop proceedings* (pp. 4-18).

Foster, I., Kesselman, C., Tsudik, G., & Tuecke, S. (1998, November). A Security Architecture for Computational Grids. In A. Press (Ed.), *5ᵗʰ ACM conference on computer and communications security* (pp. 83-92).

Foster, I., Kesselman, C., & Tuecke, S. (2001). The Anatomy of the Grid: Enabling Scalable Virtual Organizations. *The International Journal of Supercomputer Applications, 15*(3).

Freed, N., & Borenstein, N. (1996). *MIME: Multipurpose Internet Mail Extensions* (Tech. Rep. RFC2045). Available from http://www.ietf.org/rfc/rfc2045.txt

Housley, R., Ford, W., Polk, W., & Solo, D. (1999). *Internet X.509 Public Key Infrastructure Certificate and CRL Profile* (Tech. Rep. RFC2459). Available from http://www.ietf.org/rfc/rfc2459.txt

Ionescu, F., Nae, V., & Gherega, A. (2007). Credentials Management for Authentication in a Grid-Based R-Learning Platform. *International Symposium on Parallel and Distributed Computing. ISPDC '07.* (pp. 16).

Jana, D., Chaudhuri, A., Datta, A., & Bhaumik, B. (2005, Nov.). Dynamic user credential management in grid environment. *TENCON 2005 IEEE Region 10* (pp. 1-6).

Jana, D., Chaudhuri, A., Datta, A., & Bhaumik, B. (2006). Interoperability and Security issues of Grid Services for Ubiquitous Computing. *ACS/IEEE International Conference on Computer Systems and Applications,* (pp. 1114-1117).

Ko, H. J., Kim, K. I., Lee, E. J., Choi, W. G., & Kim, U. M. (2008). An effective XML data Release in Dynamic Environments. *International Conference on Hybrid Information Technology,* (pp. 182-189).

Kouril, D., & Basney, J. (2005). A Credential Renewal Service for Long-Running jobs. *6ᵗʰ IEEE/ACM International Workshop on Grid Computing,* (pp. 63-68).

Laboratories, R. S. A. (2007). *PKCS#11: Cryptographic Token Interface Standard* (Tech. Rep.). Available from ftp://ftp.rsasecurity.com/pub/pkcs/pkcs-11/ v2-20/pkcs-11v2-20a3.pdf

Linn, J. (1993). Privacy Enhancement for Internet Electronic Mail: Message Encryption and Authentication Procedures (Tech. Rep. RFC1421). Available from http://www.ietf.org/rfc/rfc1421.txt

Montagnat, J., Jouvenot, D., Pera, C., Frohner, A., Kunszt, P., Koblitz, B., et al. (2006). *Implementation of a Medical Data Manager on top of gLite services* (Tech. Rep.). Available from http://cdsweb.cern.ch/ search.py?p=EGEE-TR-2006-002

Nagaratnam, N., Janson, P., Dayka, J., Nadalin, A., Siebenlist, F., Welch, V., et al. (2002, July). *The Security Architecture for Open Grid Services* (Tech. Rep.). Available from www.cs.virginia.edu/~humphrey/ogsa-sec-wg/OGSA-SecArch-v1-07192002.pdf

Novotny, J., Tuecke, S., & Welch, V. (2001). An Online Credential Repository for the Grid: Myproxy. *Tenth International Symposium on High-Performance Distributed Computing (HPDC-10),* (pp. 104-111).

S-sicilia Project. Bringing commercial applications to the Grid: http://s-sicilia.unime.it/. (2009).

Smart card driver for Open Source Operating Systems: http://www.opensc-project.org/opensc/. (2009).

The Enabling Grids for E-sciencE project. http://www.eu-egee.org/. (2009).

Tuecke, S., Welch, V., Engert, D., Pearlman, L., & Thompson, M. (2004). *Internet X.509 Public Key Infrastructure (PKI) Proxy Certificate Profile* (Tech. Rep. RFC3820). Available from http://www.ietf.org/rfc/rfc3820.txt

Vecchio, D. D., Humphrey, M., Basney, J., & Nagaratnam, N. (2005). Credex: User-centric credential management for grid and web services. *IEEE International Conference on Web Services,* (pp. 149-156).

Weise, J. (2001, August). Public Key Infrastructure Overview. *Sun BluePrints OnLine.* Available from http://www.sun.com/blueprints/0801/publickey.pdf

XML encryption: http://www.w3.org/tr/xmlenc-core/. (2009).

XML sign: http://www.w3.org/tr/xmlenc-core/. (2009).

## ENDNOTES

[1]    This middleware component provides a set of user programs and tools for interacting with the grid

[2]    This is the gLite middleware component that provides uniform access to data storage resources

[3]    This is the gLite middleware component where the users' jobs are executed

[4]    It allows the interaction with the Storage Elements in a POSIX-like way

[5]    According to the GSI implementation each grid user has it own X.509 certificate, issued by a trusted Certification Authority, associated to a RSA key-pair. In the current GSI implementation, the key-pair is stored using a PEM encoding (Linn, 1993) in the user's home directory on the UI

6    ActiveMQ is an open sourced implementation of JMS 1.1 as part of the J2EE 1.4 specification.

7    This is the core of the computational grid which manage the job scheduling mechanisms

8    This is as a queue for the jobs

*This work was previously published in International Journal of Distributed Systems and Technologies, Volume 1, Issue 1, edited by Nik Bessis, pp. 76-97, copyright 2010 by IGI Publishing (an imprint of IGI Global).*

# Chapter 15
# A Grid–Aware Emergency Response Model (G–AERM) for Disaster Management

**Eleana Asimakopoulou**
*University of Bedfordshire, UK*

**Chimay J Anumba**
*Loughborough University, UK*

**Dino Bouchlaghem**
*The Pennsylvania State University, USA*

## ABSTRACT

*The emergency management community is working toward developments associated with the reduction of losses in lives, property and the environment caused by natural disasters. However, several limitations with the particular collaborative nature of current Information and Communication Technology (ICT) in use have been reported. In particular, how emergency management stakeholders within an ICT environment can bring together all their resources in a collaborative and timely manner so as to improve the effectiveness and efficiency of emergency response tasks. With this in mind, the authors describe the Grid-Aware Emergency Response Model (G-AERM) to make the best of functionality offered by emerging ICT to support intelligence in decision making toward a more effective and efficient emergency response management.*

## INTRODUCTION

Research studies over the last fifty years suggest that the number of losses caused by natural catastrophes is becoming increasingly significant. It is not only that the public is growing ever more

aware of natural disasters due to increased general knowledge and the expansion of mass media, but also that the number of natural catastrophes is constantly increasing (Burton et al., 1978; Bryant, 1991; Lekkas, 2000). Some of the factors responsible for this development include the increase in the world's population and the density of population within an area and the emergence of

DOI: 10.4018/978-1-4666-0906-8.ch015

settlement in areas that were previously uninhabited. Apart from human losses, natural disasters cause damage to buildings, infrastructure, and everyday activities.

As natural disasters are considered a threat and of great risk to people, property and the environment, specific bodies have been funded at international, national, regional and local level, in order to prevent, organize, analyze, plan, make decisions, and finally assign available resources to mitigate, prepare for, respond to, and recover from all effects of disasters (Trim, 2003; Shaw et al., 2004). These bodies act under the relevant policies and in line with the principles of the emergency management discipline. In particular, several international bodies, such as the North Atlantic Treaty Organization, the United Nations and the European Union have recognized the great problem related to the losses to humanity caused by the occurrence of natural disasters. Therefore, they have funded relevant departments responsible for the application of emergency management operations, as well as for the improvement of the relevant processes through further research into natural disasters and investigation of the current and future needs of humanity (European Commission, 2000).

The authorities involved in emergency management use a range of information and communication technologies (ICT) in order to assess the disastrous situation caused by the occurrence of an extreme natural phenomenon and to respond to it. Science has improved the equipment used to detect, sense, measure and store the characteristics of natural phenomena. At the same time, people witness rapid progress in the telecommunications sector everyday. The following section discusses the limitations of the current ICT used by the emergency management authorities, with particular reference to those used during the emergency response operations. In particular, it is focused on the communication between relevant parties and on the technological support which the decision makers, operational units and victims have available during an emergency response operation.

## LIMITATIONS OF THE CURRENT ICT IN USE IN EMERGENCY RESPONSE MANAGEMENT

The area of emergency response is characterized by distributed operations that are of a multidisciplinary and interdisciplinary nature. Emergency management authorities are required to cooperate in order to plan, control, coordinate, take appropriate decisions and provide with an effective and efficient response to an emergency situation caused by the occurrence of a natural disaster. On this basis, a number of processes – distributed in nature – take place during the response phase. To achieve the effective and efficient management of the response operations, a number of resources owned by each relevant authority are made available for disposition. Resources – like their owners – may be distributed and/or multidisciplinary in nature.

During such operations, information management becomes crucial. Emergency management stakeholders – as decision makers – require continuous access to various distributed resources in order to plan, make appropriate decisions, and allocate resources for particular tasks. Although supporting ICT and relevant available collaborative computer-based systems would be adequate to support the requirements, there is the 'hazards and disaster research informatics problem' (NRS, 2006). Various limitations of ICT were confirmed when various emergency management stakeholders from UK and Greece interviewed. They stressed the need for bringing together all their resources in a collaborative and timely manner. They state that there is not any particular concern with individual ICT; however they are clearly dissatisfied with the collaborative nature of these distinct ICT. It is important to note that a range of ICT is used throughout the response operations.

These are owned by different dispersed organizations, and they are distributed and heterogeneous in nature. Amongst other limitations, it is inefficient for emergency managers to leave their bases in order to meet at the operation's centre in order to manage the situation in a collaborative way. It is time-consuming, whilst the incompatibility of ICT limits them in having access to their own data stores and to communicate directly with their operational units. Incompatibilities between ICT also have caused communication of inaccurate information between senders and receivers and delays in collecting information, communicating decisions and plans of action. Overall, ICT incompatibilities have caused lack of the right information in time, which in turn may result in not taking into account an unknown to decision makers available resource. Moreover, it has been found that there are situations where a computational resource is required to run complex what-if scenarios and simulations in order to assist decision makers in taking a more informed decision. These clearly demonstrate an incomplete collaborative approach. Table 1 summarized the current ICT limitations during emergency response operations

These limitations clearly suggest that there is the need for a computerized, real time system able to support emergency management decision makers in making more informed decisions. In this system, each one of the resources could report the completion of the task, its availability, problems it may have and in general, its status at any time would prove beneficial for the whole emergency response operation. This is because emergency management stakeholders would have access to more up-to-date information about the situation, which would enable them to assess the situation in a more informed way (Asimakopoulou et al., 2008). That is to say, the approach would lead them to identify a better solution based on dynamic and accurate information in a timely manner.

## THE EMERGENCY RESPONSE MODEL (ERM)

Using Soft Systems Methodology (SSM) for the integration of current processes in disaster response operations and current ICT limitations led to the production of a set of requirements for emergency management stakeholders to respond appropriately in an emergency situation. These are illustrated in Table 2.

The produced Emergency Response Model (ERM) stands as a system owned, managed and operated by the emergency management and other directly involved authorities when a natural

*Table 1. Current ICT limitations during emergency response operations*

| Current ICT Limitations during Emergency Response Operations |
| --- |
| Gathering of stakeholders to a centralised place is time consuming |
| Centralised store of important information |
| Gathering of stakeholders to a centralised place limits access to individuals' centralised resources/data |
| Non-timely exact information about the phenomenon |
| Not exact information about available resources |
| No real-time pictures |
| Failing of telephone networks |
| Overloaded telephone networks |
| Possible computer network failure |
| Incompatibility of computerised means of communication |

*Table 2. The Set of requirements for the Emergency Response Model*

| Set of Requirements for the Emergency Response Model |
| --- |
| 1. Emergency management authorities' stakeholders to work remotely and collaboratively in order to plan, control, coordinate and communicate relevant actions in a more effective and efficient way; |
| 2. Stakeholders to receive dynamically the most up-to-date information about the current situation (upon request); |
| 3. Stakeholders to dynamically the most up-to-date information in relation to what resource is available to use (upon request) |
| 4. Stakeholders to work in an environment that is free of any ICT compatibility problems; |
| 5. ICT resources to dynamically collect and store the most up-to-date information about the current situation; |
| 6. ICT resources to dynamically assess and allocate incomplete jobs to other available resources if they become unavailable; |
| 7. ICT resources to interoperate in a compatible way; |
| 8. All resources to dynamical and collaboratively work in an environment as defined by the set of policies. |

disaster occurs, to assist the collaborative nature of the emergency response and rescue operations, by improving the effectiveness and the efficiency in terms of controlling, coordinating and communicating the emergency management procedures and the relevant resources. In particular, the ERM suggests the collaborative and dynamic provision and use of all currently available resources and instrumentation in order to dynamically collect all data relevant to the situation concerned. In turn, data should be dynamically stored and collaboratively and collectively assessed and, if required, to dynamically alert relevant resources including stakeholders about the situation concerned. Individual and/or collaborative resources as decision makers should be able to collectively access as much as possible from relevant and accurate collected dynamic data in order to collaboratively and collectively assess data and make an informed decision that should be dynamically forwarded and allocated to an appropriate and available collaborative operational unit(s) and/or other collaborative resource(s) as specified in the job plan. Following this, the operational unit(s) and/or other resource(s) have to take collaborative action(s) and run the allocated job(s) and finally, to dynamically report job(s)' completion, failure or the need for additional resource(s). In the event of the need for external resource(s), the system should dynami-cally alert relevant decision maker(s) to allow external resource(s) to collaboratively join. Finally, for all these functions to run smoothly and according to the bodies of law, the codes of practice, the quality of service, the ethicality and other issues including environmental and humanitarian concerns, a set of pre-defined and/or dynamically generated policies as required appropriately should be embedded. The ERM is illustrated in Figure 1.

Overall, it is believed that the ERM will facilitate emergency management stakeholders with an up-to-date picture of what is available and what is known so that emergency management decision makers increase their possibilities in identifying a better solution in order to control the situation. It is also able to interact with relevant instrumentation, governmental bodies – that are able to amend policies – and external experts, such as structural engineers, whose expert advice is considered important in cases like the occurrences of strong earthquakes in urban areas. Clearly, the proposed approach of the ERM to facilitate emergency management stakeholders with an up-to-date picture of what is currently available about the situation concerned will increase possibilities for a better solution to be encountered. The forms in which the model's activities appear and operate should support the distributed nature of emergency response management to further support

*Figure 1. The Emergency Response Model (Asimakopoulou, 2008)*

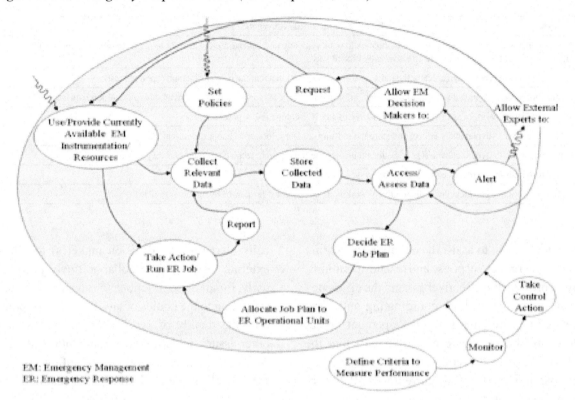

EM: Emergency Management
ER: Emergency Response

current practice, in terms of effectiveness and efficiency.

## THE TECHNOLOGICAL APPROACH

Latest developments in networking and resource integration have resulted in the Grid technology concept. This refers to an infrastructure and set of protocols to enable the integrated and collaborative use of distributed heterogeneous resources including high-end computers, networks, databases, and scientific instruments owned and managed by multiple organizations, referred to as Virtual Organizations (VO) (Foster & Kesselman, 2004). Grid technology is able to allocate and re-schedule resources dynamically in real-time according to the availability of optimal solution paths and computational resources. It is possible and useful to employ it within the emergency response

management domain. During response operations, stakeholders need to work collaboratively to make informed decisions based on multiple dispersed resources; increase their understanding about the situation by knowing as much as possible in relation to what is distributed available at a given timeframe; and run complex and intensive application problem-solving scenarios in parallel. The proposed approach allows multiple distributed owners to form VOs to share, integrate and virtualize their numerous heterogeneous resources and expertise in a dynamic fashion that are governed by differing policies. It is therefore believed that the deployment of a Grid infrastructure on top of the existing resources of relevant authorities could assist in tackling ICT related incompatibility problems and foster collaboration in an improved manner by utilizing a multidimensional approach.

## THE GRID-AWARE EMERGENCY RESPONSE MODEL (G-AERM)

This section introduces the G-AERM that has been resulted from the convergence of a set of technical requirements based on Grid technology as the underlying framework to strengthen the ERM as shown in Figure 1.

In particular, pairing the activities of the ERM with Grid technology will enable 'a Grid-aware model that is owned, managed and operated by a VO that is dynamically formed by emergency management and other directly involved authorities when a natural disaster occurs. It is believed that the VO will improve the effectiveness and the efficiency of emergency response operations in terms of controlling, coordinating and communicating the emergency management procedures and the relevant resources, by allowing utilization of parallel distributed power processing to run complex tasks; providing seamless integrated access to assess what is currently available and known and relevant to the emergency from multiple dispersed resources; and finally, by assisting the collaborative nature of the emergency response and rescue operations' (Asimakopoulou, 2008).

Therefore, we suggest 'a Grid-Aware Emergency Response Model (G-AERM) in the form of a VO to support the collaborative and dynamic provision and use of all currently available resources and instrumentation in order to dynamically integrate and seamlessly collect and store all data relevant to the emergency. In turn, the VO should allow the collaborative and collective assessment of this data, and if required to dynamically alert relevant registered and authorized resources and instrumentation including emergency management stakeholders about the emergency. Individual and/or collaborative resources, such as decision makers (as members of the VO) should be able to collectively access as much as possible integrated data from various relevant resources in order to collaboratively and collectively assess data and make an informed decision. This should

then be forwarded and allocated dynamically to an appropriate and available collaborative operational unit(s) and/or other collaborative resource(s) as specified in the produced ER job plan. Following this, the operational unit(s) and/ or other resource(s) have to take collaborative action(s) and run the allocated job(s) and finally, to dynamically report job(s) completion, failure or the need for additional resource(s). In the event of the need for external resource(s), the VO should dynamically alert relevant decision maker(s) to allow external resource(s) to collaboratively join the VO. Finally, for all these functions to run smoothly and according to the bodies of law, the codes of practice, the quality of service, the ethicality and other issues including environmental and humanitarian concerns, a set of pre-defined and/or dynamically generated policies as required appropriately should be embedded within the VO' (Asimakopoulou, 2008).

Clearly, a number of distributed resources and instrumentation generate a continuous flow of information in various forms. Such distributed and heterogeneous resources include, but are not limited to, instrumentation, such as telephone units, satellites, cameras, sensors, computers, databases and application software. The Grid layer will enable the emergency response management team to make real-time intelligent decisions and act accordingly by assessing multiple dispersed resources. For example, the G-AERM will enable the utilization of these distributed and heterogeneous resources by feeding (manually or by pushing dynamically to) the VO members with relevant information in a more integrated form, as it may be required by an emergency management stakeholder. This will serve as a combined method of an oral and/or text messaging report, which are received by a member of an operational unit using a mobile phone. The Grid layer may also convert and save information, such as combined reports and associated images in a format that can be used (retrieved) for future reference if required.

Further to these, the G-AERM will alert stakeholders of situations requiring urgent attention. It will also foster team working and collaboration between dispersed decision makers as VO members whose decisions may be dependent on each other's interactions. Resource integration at that level will support decision makers since it will allow them to view satellite images of the affected area, observe seismic activity, forecast, simulate and run what-if scenarios using other members' data modelling and mining tools, collaborate with (internal and external) experts and other authorities. Overall, the G-AERM approach as a whole will assist VO members to request and access as much information as is required and possible to acquire about a particular instance from different sources, and therefore to allow them to have a holistic view of the current situation. In turn, these will assist decision makers to prioritize and ultimately make more informed decisions, which will be disseminated to available rescue teams who will then take care of the operational tasks. The latter will be able to receive better-described ER job plans, push more meaningful reports and request more resources if required. Similarly, VO members would benefit from the use of each others' spare computational capacity to run highly intensive operations (Asimakopoulou, 2009).

However, for the VO environment to operate within the G-AERM environment, emergency management authorities, such as Fire and Rescue Service, Health and Ambulance Service, Emergency Management Section and Police department need to set a number of policies. To achieve this, stakeholders will be required to register their services using the "set of policies" activity. These policies will identify the quality of service to which each VO member will function. Such quality of service will also include information related to authorization levels. Authorities wishing to utilize expertise from external parties will also be required to seek and set up an agreed policy with the invited party. External resources may include, but not be limited to, structural and mechanical engineers, meteorologists, geologists, military or other, non-human resources.

Figure 2 illustrates the aforementioned types of interactions between VO members when using the G-AERM. It also shows the main interactions between emergency response managers, operational unit leaders, external experts, data sources, model sources, data mining, computers and other instrumentation, such as satellites.

## THE G-AERM ARCHITECTURE

Details of the G-AERM architecture, which could be used as the basis for a real-world application (Newman and Lamming, 1995), are presented in this section. A number of technical aspects associated with the G-AERM architecture, including the outline architecture of the G-AERM illustrating the main Grid standards and services available to the emergency response management VO members and the detailed architecture of the G-AERM illustrating a deeper understanding of how Grid-based functions and resource interactions – as these have been described in the G-AERM – support each activity of the ERM for the benefit of the emergency response management VO members.

### The Outline Architecture of the G-AERM

A real world application based on the G-AERM should facilitate access to either individuals or members of the VO formed. These members required to gain access to the G-AERM via a secure authentication mechanism, which will check the user's credentials. Checking will be performed using the user's credentials across a proxy database, which will hold the user's log-in details. It is expected that users have registered their log-in details prior to their first attempt to use the system. They should be able to register their details and log-in via the Grid Services Portal Interface (GSPI). The latter should preferably be

*Figure 2. VO Members' Interactions when using the G-AERM*

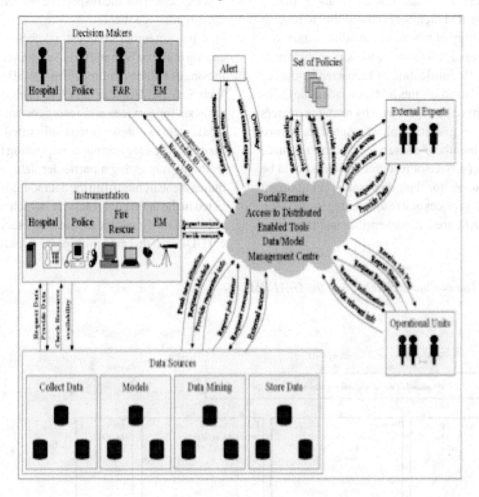

accessible via a Web browser, which supports a Graphical User Interface (GUI).

Once emergency management stakeholders are authenticated to the GSPI, they should have access to a number of services (access and assess data, resources, est.) – as detailed in the ERM and G-AERM – via the embedded Grid functionality. Authenticated members are able to register their owned resources including, but not limited to, their data sources, expertise profiles, collaboration tools, computers and other ICT (Asimakopoulou, 2009). Registrations of these resources require some semantic tagging using XML-based metadata descriptions in the form of WSDL documents. These metadata descriptions will then be forwarded to a central database (proxy database), which should act as a "yellow pages directory". The latter is also known as a UDDI service and it is to be used by others to identify, locate and use these resources. There may be a possibility that those members (service or resource providers) have already made descriptions of their owned resources to their local UDDI. In such instances, members still have to register their resources to the main G-AERM's UDDI directory, which will then communicate with the local UDDI to identify, locate and give access to others interested in using them. Finally, the G-AERM should facilitate members with a wizard assisting them to semantically tag and register their resources.

Another service that should be made available to the G-AERM members is the ability to request the availability of resources including data, models, mining and collaborative tools, computational power, etc. Identification of requested resources should be based on the XML metadata descriptions that have been provided by resource owners during the registration phase. Again, a wizard assisting members as service and/or resource requestors (service or resource seeker) should be made available for their disposal. It is important to note that services and resources registered with the G-AERM are external entities and therefore,

it is expected that the respective owners autonomously manage them.

Upon a member's request, a Web Server broadcasting multiple Web and Grid Services compatible messages will be required. The GWSB (Grid and Web Services Broadcaster) will enable multiple requests for services and resources based on the XML metadata descriptions submitted by a VO member when registering or requesting them. For example, requesting a particular data service requires the searching of all the data sources that have listed in the main UDDI service, which will the be able to identify and locate the listed service in local UDDIs, if there are multiple results. Assuming

*Figure 3. The outline architecture of the G-AERM*

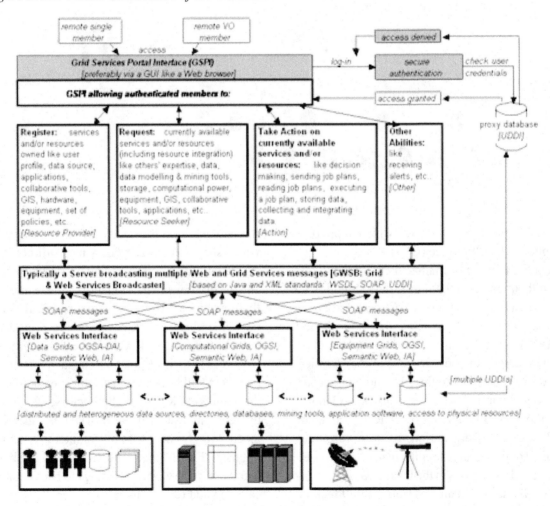

that the member, as a requestor, is authenticated to access the requested data items, access will be provided via means of a virtualized data source (Asimakopoulou, 2009). Figure 3 illustrates the outline architecture of the G-AERM.

## THE DETAILED ARCHITECTURE OF THE G-AERM

This section describes the detailed architecture of the G-AERM, which can be used as the specification framework for the development of real-world G-AERM applications. It is expected that decision makers will broadly follow current emergency management processes. The expectation is that the VO will consist of single or multiple VO users, who will access the collaborative environment either as decision makers, invited external experts or operational unit leaders. Figure 4 details the G-AERM architecture, the components of which are described next.

### Secure Access to the Grid Services Portal Interface (GSPI)

VO members are required to access the Grid Services Portal Interface (GSPI) using the Secure Authorization service. To gain access to the GSPI, perspective users need to apply for a certificate in order to be allowed to sign-on. This allows them to utilize single sign-on (SSO) so they will not be required to undertake multiple sign-on when accessing distributed services belonging to different owners.

As can be seen in the Connectivity Layer, the Grid system utilizes the Grid Security Infrastructure (GSI), which allows reliable and secure access to resources using Public Key Infrastructure (PKI), Secure Socket Layer (SSL) and X509 certificates. Based on their authentication, the VO member(s) will have access only to services, which are registered to their account. These services are located in the Grid Customized Applications Layer and are

described in the Grid Services database system, which recalls resource authentication via the "set of policies" service. For example, an emergency manager decision maker has the right to "access" a number of resources in order to "assess" them and "decide a relevant ER job plan". This is accessible by the emergency response operational units.

When external expertise is required, the relevant leader is provided with the ability to amend or set up a policy at an appropriate level as required, in order for the invited external resource to join the VO environment. Similarly, leaders can amend or set up policies following the organization hierarchy.

### Grid Services Portal Interface (GSPI)

This is located in the Grid Customized Applications Layer and its underlying specification relies on the Open Grid Services Infrastructure (OGSI), Open Grid Services Architecture (OGSA) and the Data, Access and Integration Services (DAIS) specification framework. In particular, a number of Application Programming Interfaces (APIs) have to be in place in order to provide access to the required services, such as access to dispersed data sources, model sources, mining tools, collaborative environments, application software, computational power and instrumentation. These APIs can be programmed using various languages, such as C++, Java, Python and XML.

### Collective Layer (OGSA-DAI and Grid Services Broker)

As mentioned earlier, it is expected that a number of resources will be available via the GSPI for decision makers to individually and/or collaboratively take them into consideration in order to produce an emergency response job plan together. In this respect, a Service Provider as a decision maker or else will need to register their resources/services to the resource directory (UDDI) and specify the policy in which the registered resource/service will

*Figure 4. The detailed architecture of the G-AERM*

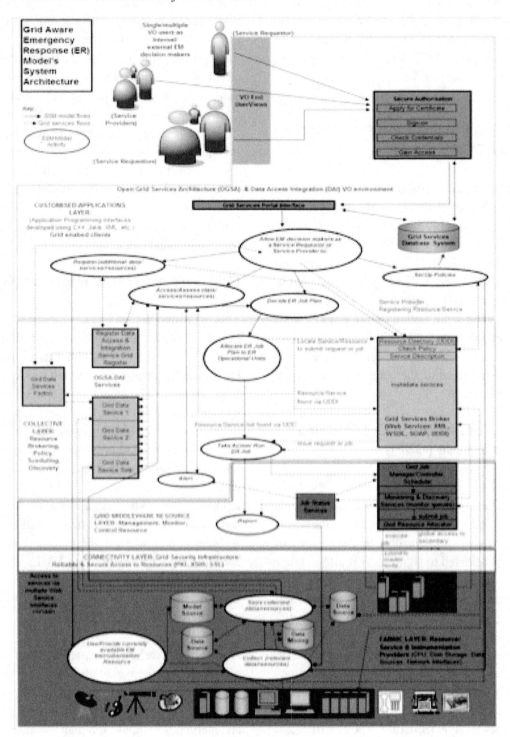

be used by others. This will enable other parties to locate registered resources/services.

In particular, to register resources/services, the Service Providers will be required to describe their resources/services using the Web Services Description Language (WSDL) in order to define how the service is to be used by others. Registered services/resources can be found using the Grid Services Broker, which includes registered services/resources metadata services (XML), which are connected to a Service Requestor using the Simple Object Access Protocol (SOAP). The Grid Services Broker is located in the Collective Layer.

On the other hand, an individual or a group of EM decision makers as Service Requestors will need to "access" a number of appropriate and relevant resources/services including data sources, model sources, data mining, decision support applications, processing power and other physical resources in order to "assess" the current situation and "decide the best possible ER job plan". As detailed in Bessis (2009), the following list specifies the exact steps and the Grid technicalities required for an individual Service Requestor to request access to appropriate data/resource services using the OGSA-DAI specification framework, which operates under the Web Services Resource Framework (WSRF):

- EM decision maker as a Service Requestor will need to request the Data Access and Integration Service Grid Register (DAISGR) for the source of data about a particular instance like X;
- The DAISGR will return a handler to the Service Requestor;
- The DAISGR will send a request to the Grid Data Services Factory (GDSF) to access the relevant data sets that are registered with it;
- The GDSF will create a Grid Data Service (GDS) to manage access to relevant data sets;

- The GDSF will return a handler of the GDS to the EM decision maker;
- EM decision maker as a Service Requestor will perform the query to the respective GDS using a database language such as Structured Query Language (SQL);
- The GDS will interact with the available dataset(s);
- The GDS will return the query results in a XML format to the Service Requestor.

In the event that the GDSF has identified more than one of the data sets (for example, GDS 1: Grid Data Service 1, GDS 2: Grid Data Service 2, etc.) that contain the relevant information, the EM decision maker, as a Service Requestor, will either select a particular GDS (for example, GDS1) based on his preference(s) or request for data to be integrated into the GDS sink. That is to say, a GDS sink will handle the communications between the EM decision maker and the multiple GDSs (GDS1, GDS2, etc.), which will further interact with their respective data source sets in order to return query results in a XML format to the EM decision maker.

Following the process described above, an EM decision maker will be able to "assess" data related resources (using emergency response operation current practices and conventional methods) in order to "decide an ER job plan", which will be "allocated" to the respective "ER operational unit" which will take care in "taking action and run the ER job", alongside the instrumentation/resources allocated to this job.

The Grid Services Broker, described earlier, enables the Semantic Web functionality via the use of Intelligent Agents to identify and locate both data and other types of resources. These may include data harvesting or a requirement for processing power to, for example, run highly intensive application jobs, such as a simulation to forecast the optimum (shortest) time to safely evacuate a number of trapped people and suggest the optimum evacuation route.

To achieve this, the Grid Services Broker operating under the WSRF needs to locate appropriate services/resources required to undertake action as specified. The Grid Services Broker will check resource availability through its UDDI directory, the service description and the policies, using XML-based metadata descriptions. If the job is issued to human-related resources and these resources are found, the Grid Services Broker will issue the request to "run the ER job" by the relevant human-related operational unit.

If the job is issued to a computer-based resource, to run a simulation scenario and these computer based resources are found, the Grid Services Broker will issue a request to "run the ER job" via the Grid Job Manager, which will act as a non-human actor. The Grid Job Manager is located in the Grid Middleware Resource Layer and it takes responsibility of controlling, managing, monitoring and scheduling (computationally related) issued jobs.

If resources are not found to satisfy the policy requirements or not found at all through the UDDI directory, the Grid Services Broker will "alert" decision makers to take appropriate action, such as to negotiate policy requirements and/or seek alternative resources.

## Grid Middleware Resource Layer

Once a computational related job is issued to the Grid Job Manager via the "take action/run ER job" and the Grid Services Broker, the Grid Job Manager needs to check its scheduler and its job queues in order to discover the resource (for example, a cluster) and ultimately submit the ER job via the Grid Resource Allocator. Once the resource is found, the Grid Resource Allocator sends the job to the resource in order to execute the job. Initially, the job will be sent to the Master node, which co-ordinates and spread sub-job tasks to the cooperating slave nodes. If a sub-job is interrupted for any reason, the Grid Manager will order it to retry job completion for a predefined

number of times. The Grid Monitor Services will alert the Grid Manager (for example, the cluster master node) in the event that the retry has been unsuccessful. In such a case, the embedded Grid Services fault tolerance will request the Grid Manager to firstly save the partially completed work to a secondary storage and secondly, to alongside the Grid Resource Allocator, to identify and issue an alternate path to execute the remaining sub-jobs. Once the job is completed, the Monitoring Services, which are located at the Grid Job Manager, informs the Job Status Services, which further notifies the "Report" system activity, which will be stored to the data sources of the 'Collect' activity. The Job Status Services will concurrently inform the Grid Job Manager that resources are available for future use via the Monitoring and Discovery Services. If a job has not been completed, or has failed because no resources have been found available at the specified time, the Grid Controller will keep the job in the Monitor Queues and will attempt to identify alternate solutions for a predefined number of times. In the case that the process is unsuccessful because of the expiration of the numbers of attempts or because of policies specified in the job plan, the Job Status Services will raise an "alert".

## Fabric Layer: Resource/Service and Instrumentation Providers

This layer consists of the currently available EM distributed and potentially incompatible instrumentation/resources owned by different authorities, such as the GSCP, EMS, Police, Fire and Rescue, and Health and Ambulance Services. Their instrumentation/resources include, but are not limited to, VHF radios, mobile phones, landlines, vehicles (police, cars, ambulances, etc.), aircraft, satellites, computers, clusters, campus Grids, data, earth observation systems, weather stations, seismographs, geographical information systems, satellite phones, pagers, TV channels, military equipment, radio stations, data sources, model sources, data mining tools, etc. It is expected that human-related resources, such as operational units and external experts will be notified about their duties via the appropriate ICT equipment as mentioned above.

These instrumentation/resources – depending on their physical nature – will be registered in the G-AERM's Data Grids, Computational Grids or Equipment Grids so they can be accessed accordingly. These will then feed the "collect data" activity with appropriate information about the natural phenomenon and the current situation. These types of information are then stored in database or model-base management systems via the "store collected data" activity. This activity functions as the gateway for the OGSI, OGSA-DAI Services Specification and the Grid Services Broker to locate and make instrumentation/resources available to the decision makers via the "access/assess data" activity in order to "decide ER job plan".

## Implications of Embedding the G-AERM into the Real World

Findings from the evaluation exercise with six emergency management stakeholders and five grid technology experts clearly demonstrate that the G-AERM overcomes all the ICT limitations they currently face, adopts the processes of emergency response management and addresses all their requirements as shown in Table 1. All participants in this evaluation exercise were fully satisfied with the proposed G-AERM and that its capacity to clearly stand and strengthen their current practice during emergency response operations in a far more collaborative, effective and efficient manner if a G-AERM application was available. Figure 5 demonstrates the strength, weaknesses, opportunities and threats of the G-AERM, as these have been resulted from the evaluation exercise.

Embedding the G-AERM into the real world enables various individuals and/or collective resources to make a more than currently informed decision by increasing the opportunities for a

better solution to be encountered. It will allow them to know more about the concerned situation by running complex and intensive what if scenarios and/or other problem-solving scenarios in parallel; but most importantly, by providing them with seamless integrated access to assess what is currently available and relevant from multiple dispersed resources; and by allowing them to work in a collaborative manner. Clearly the Grid potentially increases the size and complexity of the problem spaces that can realistically be addressed not only by emergency management scenarios, but by all types of interdisciplinary type of enquiries, which an organization may wish to address.

Another very important implication of embedding the G-AERM in the real world is that there is the need for some of the ICT methods currently used by emergency management stakeholders to be able to work in a Grid environment. Apparently, the G-AERM requires the use of electronic based resources to take full advantage of this approach. It is important to note that the G-AERM assumes that the emergency management authorities have access to a number of instruments and that any related data needed to be accessed and assessed shall be stored in electronic form. Currently there is data that is article based, such as maps, materials specifications, building, engineering plans and town plans. However, there is much activity in developing relevant middleware and this is considered as achievable by Grid technology experts.

## CONCLUSION

This chapter introduced Grid technology as a method to allow emergency management stakeholders to improve their practices. That is planning, controlling, coordinating and communicating emergency management procedures and relevant resources. In particular, the chapter illustrated the conflicts and ICT limitations, which emergency management stakeholders face during emergency

*Figure 5. SWOT analysis of the evaluation exercises of the G-AERM*

| Strengths | Weaknesses |
|---|---|
| • First time that a single model accommodating all processes required to manage emergency response operations | • OGSI has been replaced by WSRF |
| • Designed for planning, controlling, coordinating, collaborating and communicating actions between emergency management stakeholders | • Means of communication (like VHF) are not yet integrated with Grid environment |
| • Architecture diagram is correct and technologically feasible | • Cancellation of physical meeting between emergency management stakeholders during decision making may become a norm |
| • Support for creating and sustaining VOs | • On demand alteration of governmental policies should be in line with government's procedures |
| • Support for emergency managers to collaborate remotely | • Installation of cameras for real time images in areas with difficult access (i.e. forests, sea) |
| • Tools supporting objective information sharing between involved bodies | • Not all data is currently in digital format |
| • Use of APIs can provide remote access to a number of collaborative tools | |
| • Industry security standards adopted | |
| • GSI, by using PKI, SSL and X509 certificates allows secure access to the registered resources | |
| • Service Providers can register and make available their resources/services to a UDDI by using the latest developments in Web Services | |
| • Service Seekers can be made aware of the most relevant and available resources/services by using the latest developments in Grid Services | |
| • Automatic expert identification | |
| • Support to run simulations towards decision making | |
| • Expansion of decision making search space | |
| • Time efficient (especially in areas with difficult access) | |
| • Real time information and feedback | |
| • Error handling leading to fewer erroneous decisions | |
| • Enabling more informed decisions | |
| • On demand alteration of policies | |
| • Support for fault tolerance (Grid-FT) | |
| • Web Services and OGSA-DAI are suitable technologies for developing proposed services | |
| • Overcomes all current ICT limitations | |
| **Opportunities** | **Threats** |
| • Grid-based applications are in their infancy and such a complex concept that has yet not been implemented will advance parties involved when developing applications | • Will governmental bodies commit setting relevant policies in the speed that emergency management stakeholders may require? |
| • Digitalisation of data currently handled by relevant bodies | • Potential performance issues where Web Services are being employed |
| • Scale of G-AERM will challenge and advance collaborative practice | • Infrastructure supporting real world applications need to be kept up-to-date with new technological developments |
| • Collaborative practice between governmental bodies to enable G-AERM application development | • Availability of operational unit to provide the system with feedback during operation |
| • Development of pre-defined and/or dynamically generated policies as required | • Political decisions of governments towards real world manifestations |
| • Building of Grid infrastructure in relevant bodies in order to accommodate G-AERM | • Policies for sharing information between relevant bodies |
| • Relevant people will learn more as they will receive training of how to operate a G-AERM based application | |
| • G-AERM and its application may be utilised as a method to train staff using real world recorded past cases | |
| • Number of supporting activities that strengthen and extend current good practice | |

response operations. To overcome such problems, we discussed the integration of Grid technology in the field of emergency response management, as the most appropriate way to address the set of problems, requirements and issues that emergency management stakeholders face during such opera-

tions. This has been done via the development and successful evaluation of the G-AERM for natural disasters. The G-AERM supports the collaborative and dynamic provision and use of all currently available resources and instrumentation to dynamically integrate and seamlessly collect access and assess collected and stored data from multiple distributed ICT sources in order to decide and issue an appropriate emergency response job plan to relevant operational units. The approach adopted in the G-AERM architecture allowed stakeholders to identify and select choices from a far larger range of resources available. In turn, this may increase the possibilities for emergency management decision makers to take and issue more informed decisions of a collaborative nature towards the accomplishment of issued tasks in a far more effective and efficient way.

## REFERENCES

Asimakopoulou, E. (2008). *A Grid-Aware Emergency Response Model for Natural Disasters*. Unpublished doctoral dissertation, Loughborough University, UK.

Asimakopoulou, E. (2009). Using Grid Technology for Maximizing Collaborative Emergency Response Decision Making. In Bessis, N. (Ed.), *Grid Technology for Maximizing Collaborative Decision Management and Support: Advancing Effective Virtual Organizations*. Hershey, PA: IGI Publishing. doi:10.4018/978-1-60566-364-7.ch013

Bessis, N. (2009). Model Architecture for a User tailored Data Push Service in Data Grids. In Bessis, N. (Ed.), *Grid Technology for Maximizing Collaborative Decision Management and Support: Advancing Effective Virtual Organizations*. Hershey, PA: IGI Publishing. doi:10.4018/978-1-60566-364-7.ch012

Bryant, E. A. (1991). *Natural Hazards*. Cambridge, UK: Cambridge University Press.

Burton, I., Kates, R. W., & White, G. F. (1978). *The Environment as Hazard*. New York: Oxford University Pres.

European Commission. (2000). *Vade - mecum of Civil Protection in the European Union*. Luxembourg: Office for Official Publications of the European Communities.

Foster, I., & Kesselman, C. (2004). *The Grid 2: Blueprint for a new computing infrastructure*. San Francisco, CA: Morgan Kaufmann Publishers.

Lekkas, E. L. (2000). *Natural and Technological Catastrophes*. Greece: Access Pre-Press.

National Research Council (NRC). (2006). *Facing Hazards and Disasters: Understanding Human Dimensions*. Washington, DC: National Academy Press.

Newman, W. M., & Lamming, M. G. (1995). *Interactive System Design*. Reading, MA: Addison-Wesley.

Shaw, R. (2001). Don't Panic: Behaviour in Major Incidents. *Disaster Prevention and Management, 10*(1).

Trim, P. R. F. (2003). Disaster Management and the Role of the Intelligence and Security Services. *Disaster Prevention and Management, 12*(1).

*This work was previously published in International Journal of Distributed Systems and Technologies, Volume 1, Issue 3, edited by Nik Bessis, pp. 40-55, copyright 2010 by IGI Publishing (an imprint of IGI Global).*

# Chapter 16
# A Mathematical Analysis of a Disaster Management Data-Grid Push Service

**Nik Bessis**
*University of Bedfordshire, UK*

**Antony Brown**
*University of Bedfordshire, UK*

**Eleana Asimakopoulou**
*University of Bedfordshire, UK*

## ABSTRACT

*Much work is under way within the Grid technology community on issues associated with the development of services fostering the integration and exploitation of multiple autonomous, distributed data sources through a seamless and flexible virtualized interface. These developments involve fluid and dynamic, ad hoc based interactions between dispersed service providers and consumers. However, several obstacles arise in the design and implementation of such services. In this chapter, the authors examine a notable obstacle, namely how to keep service consumers informed of relevant changes about data committed in multiple and distributed service provider levels, and most importantly, when these changes can affect others' well-being. To achieve this, the authors use aggregated case scenarios to demonstrate the need for a data-Grid push service in a disaster management situation. In this regard, the chapter describes in detail the service architecture, as well as its mathematical analysis for keeping interested stakeholders informed automatically about relevant and critical data changes.*

## INTRODUCTION

Data integration has long been discussed in other literature reviews. Many concerns have been encountered, as most of the datasets addressed by individual applications are very often heterogeneous and geographically distributed. Hence, the ability to make data stores interoperable remains a crucial factor for the development of these types of systems (Wohrer et al., 2004). Clearly, one of the challenges for such facilitation is that of data integration; these challenges have been widely discussed (Calvanese et al., 1998; Reinoso et al., 2008). Moreover, Foster et al. (2001) explain that

DOI: 10.4018/978-1-4666-0906-8.ch016

the combination of large dataset size, geographic distribution of users and resources, and computationally intensive analysis results in complex and stringent performance demands that, until recently, have not been satisfied by any existing computational and data management infrastructure. Recent advances in computer networking and digital resource integration resulted in the concept of Grid technology. In particular, Grid computing addresses the issue of collaboration, data and resource sharing (Kodeboyina, 2004). It has been described as the infrastructure and set of protocols to enable the integrated, collaborative use of distributed heterogeneous resources including high-end computers, networks, databases, and scientific instruments owned and managed by multiple organizations, referred to as Virtual Organizations (Foster, 2002). A Virtual Organization (VO) is formed when different organizations come together to share resources and collaborate in order to achieve a common goal (Foster et al., 2002).

The need to integrate databases into the Grid has also been recognized (Nieto-Santisteban, 2004) in order to support science and business database applications (Antonioletti et al., 2005). Significant effort has gone into defining requirements, protocols and implementing the OGSA-DAIS (Open Grid Services Architecture – Data, Access and Integration Services) specification as the means for users to develop relevant data Grids to conveniently control the sharing, accessing and management of large amounts of distributed data in Grid environments (Antonioletti et al., 2005; Atkinson et al., 2003). Ideally, OGSA-DAIS as a data integration specification aims to allow users to specify 'what' information is needed without having to provide detailed instructions on 'how' or 'from where' to obtain the information (Reinoso Castillo et al., 2004).

On the other hand, working with obsolete data yields to an information gap that in turn may well compromise decision-making. Bessis (2009) and Bessis and Asimakopoulou (2008) explain that it

is value creation for collaborators to automatically stay informed of data that may change over time. Repeatedly searching data sources for the latest relevant information on a specific topic of interest can be both time-consuming and frustrating. A set of technologies collectively referred to as 'Push', 'NetCasting' or 'WebCasting' was introduced in late 90s. This set of technologies allowed the automation of search and retrieval functions. Ten years on, Web Services have overtaken most of Push technology functionality and become a standard supporting recent developments in Grid computing with state-of-the-art technology for data and resource integration.

However, if a Grid is a system to enable flexible, secure, coordinated resource sharing among dynamic collections of individuals, institutions and resources (Foster, 2002) then it should be all about designing a dynamic service that is inherent in a VO (Weishaupl & Schikuta, 2004). That is to say, updates within a distributed data environment are much more frequent and can happen from within any data source in the network. Hence, there is a need for updates to be migrated to other sites in the network so that all the copies of the latest, relevant and up-to-date data are synchronized and communicated to maintain a consistency and homogeneity across the VO. Several authors have highlighted the need from different viewpoints, including Foster (2002), Bessis (2003), Magowan (2003), Raman (2003), Watson (2003), and Venugopal et al. (2005). On this basis, OGSA-DAIS as a data integration specification should ideally address the ability to allow users to specify 'what' information is needed without having to provide detailed instructions on 'how' or 'from where' to obtain the information, as well as to automatically 'keep' users 'informed' of latest, relevant, specific changes about data in a single or multiple autonomous distributed database(s) and/or data source(s) that are registered within the VO. The requirement is widely regarded as a highly important service for individual and collaborative decision-making, as it will sustain competitive advantage and maintain consistency and homogeneity across an organizational setting. Moreover, fresh data are also particularly important in parallel and dynamic environments where opportunistic and extreme types of critical decisions are required. In turn, latest developments in the Grid technology area, discussed in Bessis and Chauhan (2008), have resulted in producing data Grid services to automatically push to the users the latest, relevant, specific changes about data that are registered within the Grid application which they (users) have access to. Our motivation here is to push this further and describe such a data-Grid push service for assisting decision making in disaster management situations.

With this in mind, the contributions of our chapter are to: i) provide an overview of Pull-Push models; ii) present a background work including aggregative case scenarios, describing the need for such a data-Grid push service in disaster management situations; iii) use the aggregative case scenarios to offer a mathematical analysis for the

data-Grid push service itself and iv) discuss the data-Grid push service architecture in the form of sequence diagrams.

## OVERVIEW OF DATA PUSH TECHNOLOGY AND RELATED SERVICES

In general, there are two generic models, namely the Pull and Push models, for a client to retrieve data from a data source. The distinction between the generic Pull and the Push models is shown in Figure 1. In the Pull model, a web client (W-C) needs to initiate a search by specifying search parameters. The web server (W-S) receives the client's request and it performs a data query to the database server (DB-S). If there are any retrieved data, these are made available to the web client via the web server. In this model, web clients are always required to initiate the search function in order to retrieve data.

*Figure 1. Sequence diagrams of generic pull and push models*

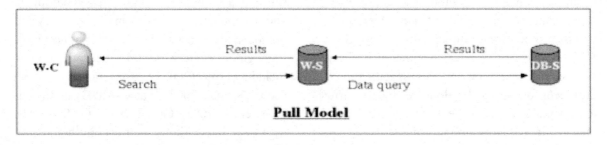

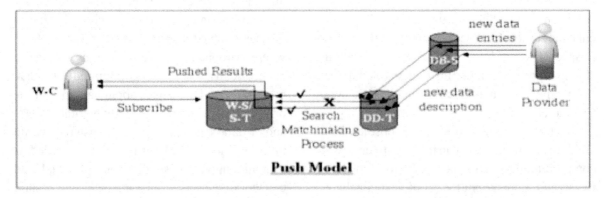

In the Push model, a web client (W-C) needs to subscribe by specifying a set of parameters and the period in which they wish to keep informed of any new and/or data updates occurring at the data source level, as relevant to the specified parameters. These parameters are stored as a new record in the subscriber's table (S-T) that is located in the web server (W-S). The Push approach as discussed in Bessis (2003) suggests that every time a data provider commits a new data entry in the database server (DB-S), a data description record (with reference to the new data entry) is generated and stored in a Data Description Table (DD-T). Once a record is stored in the DD-T, a trigger will cause an automatic search between the records stored in the DD-T and subscriber's table (S-T) to identify relevant matches. If there are any retrieved data, these are pushed to the client via the web server. In this model, web clients are required to subscribe once and are not required to initiate the search function every time new data are committed within a data source.

Overall, Push can streamline the delivery of user tailored, specific information to a variety of users via Internet or a web browser. There are various technologies including Web 2.0, AJAX, WS-Notification and/or WS-Eventing supporting the development of pure or feel a-like push mechanisms. For example, RSS (Really Simple Syndication) feed technology is mainly a push feel a-like mechanism that is used to publish frequently updated content containing either a summary of content from an associated web site or the full text in an automated manner. The user subscribes to a feed by entering the feed's link into the reader or by clicking an RSS icon in a browser, which in turn it initiates the subscription request. The main difference is that Push transactions can be based on a user's specific information preferences. Whenever such new content matching a user's specific preference(s) is made available on one of those sites, the server would automatically push that information to the subscriber. Technically speaking, RSS are pulled by the user. That is to say,

it is the users who request the server periodically for new content; the server itself does not send information to the client without their request. These continual requests have many disadvantages and again technically speaking they are bandwidth inefficient. In contrast, a Push service residing at the server side would automatically inform subscribers as soon as only relevant – with regard to the user's tailored, specific request – content has been updated.

It is also well known that decisions are not merely single actions but they are dependant on parts or results of other decisions. In brief, user tailored Push technology enables a decision maker to specify a set of parameters into a subscriber form and as those conditions match specific parts of the newly updated and/or created content, such information are 'pushed' to the subscribed decision maker. It is therefore the viewpoint that user tailored Push technology addresses data consistency, which it is an important property as it determines how 'relevant', 'accurate' and 'fresh' the data is.

Updates within a distributed environment are more frequent compared to a centralized one and therefore, these specific updates must be also checked about their consistency first prior to a potential further action like a two or a three commit protocol when they have to be migrated to other sites in the network. It must be stressed that a two or a three commit protocol may not be an appropriate action since synchronization over a data Grid refers to the data synchronization in the virtualized table layer and not in the actual data source layer. If however, it is required this will then enable all the copies of the data to be consistently synchronized and provide the homogeneous status that may be critically required by a VO and its individual members. Within a Grid environment, virtualization services can use the Grid notification service to know about schema related changes (important for federated query processing) and state related changes (important for identifying failures of data source, which may have an impact on the processing of many virtualization services). However, it is evident that the Grid notification service is limited and overall there is a feeling that data Grids and P2P networks generally do not provide strong consistency guarantees because of the overhead of maintaining locks on huge volumes of data and the ad hoc nature of the network respectively (Venugopal et al., 2005).

## BACKGROUND

Overall, phenomena such as earthquakes, hurricanes, storms, landslides, forest fires, heavy snow and others take place daily and are considered as natural phenomena. Abramovitz (1999) points out that 'floods, storms and other events are a vital part of nature, restoring soil fertility and shaping the landscape' and thus, 'natural phenomena are normal and essential planetary actions' (Asimakopoulou et al., 2005). However, when they appear in some extreme forms they may cause large-scale changes into the shape and anatomy of the earth and thus, 'natural phenomena have periodically decimated the population of the planet' (Mitra, 2001). It is therefore clear that an extreme natural phenomenon may be characterized as catastrophic and hazardous by the scope of people in relation to their lives, property, as well as their environment. For example, an earthquake occurring in an inhabited area, such as a magnitude 7.2 of Richter earthquake in Los Angeles will cause disruption to the normal life of the community.

An important feature of hazard is that it has the 'notion of probability, or a likelihood of occurring. A hazard is a threat, not the actual event. Any hazard can manifest itself in an actual harmful event. In other words, if it can be measured in terms of real damage or harm it is no longer a hazard but has become an event, disaster or catastrophe. Every specific hazard magnitude is attached to a usually empirically derived return period, which is site-specific' (Thywissen, 2006). The return period of a magnitude 7.2 of Richter earthquake is different for Los Angeles compared to an earthquake occurring in the Pacific Ocean. Further to this, 'seismic risk consists of the components seismic hazard, seismic vulnerability, and value of elements at risk (both, in human and economic terms)' (Wahlström et al., 2004). This is evident as there are over a million earthquakes each year; however most of these are insignificant. About 3,000 of these produce noticeable effects (e.g., tremors, ground shaking) and finally, about 20 each year cause major damage and destruction (Parvez, 2009). In order to quantify hazards, each magnitude is tied to a specific return period or its inverse, frequency. The latter ensemble is the magnitude-frequency relationship of a particular hazard and it is always an inherent characteris-

*Table 1. Relationship between earthquake magnitude and effect (adapted from Louie, 1996)*

| Magnitude (Richter scale) | Earthquake effects | Events' frequency per year |
|---|---|---|
| ≤2.4 | Usually not felt, but can be recorded by seismograph | 900,000 |
| ≥2.5-5.4≤ | Often felt, but only causes minor damage. | 30,000 |
| ≥5.5-6.0≤ | Slight damage to buildings and other structures. | 500 |
| ≥6.1-6.9≤ | May cause a lot of damage in very populated areas. | 100 |
| ≥7.0-7.9≤ | Major earthquake. Serious damage. | 20 |
| ≥8.0 | Great earthquake. Can totally destroy communities near the epicenter. | 0.1-0.2 |

tic of a specific locality or region (Thywissen, 2006). Table 1 depicts the relationship between the magnitude scale, effect and event frequency.

Although each earthquake has a magnitude value, its effects vary greatly according to distance, ground conditions, construction standards, and other factors (Louie, 1996). Therefore, it is important to identify the earthquake's intensity criteria, which is defined as the 'measure of an earthquake's destructive power (size and strength)' (GEO 101-02 Introduction to Geology, 2006). This is measured by the Modified Mercalli Intensity scale, which qualitatively links earthquake power to its effect on buildings. The earthquake intensity depends on a number of criteria including amount of energy released by the earthquake; duration of shaking; distance from the epicenter; focal depth of earthquake; type of rock and degree of consolidation; population density; type of building construction; and earthquake magnitude.

For the purpose of this chapter three of the aforementioned criteria are taken into consideration. These are the earthquake magnitude, the population density and the type of building construction, with the latter including the building resistance.

## Earthquake Magnitude

The term earthquake magnitude is defined as the 'quantitative measure of the energy released by an earthquake at its source' (GEO 101-02 Introduction to Geology, 2006) and it is measured by

the Richter scale magnitude. The magnitude is determined by the measurement of the size of the seismic waves and the distance from epicenter (GEO 101-02 Introduction to Geology, 2006).

## Population Density

The term population density is defined by 'the total population size of a country or area divided by its surface area, measured in square kilometers' (United Nations, 2008).

## Type of Building Construction

The term type of building construction refers to the magnitude of earthquake the affected building can afford, as this is defined by the seismic regulations of the area. Further to this, the building resistance refers to whether the building follows the current regulation (which may differs from years to years and areas to areas), or it is an older construction. Table 2 exemplifies this.

## Aggregative Case Scenarios (ACS)

It is important to note that the purpose of this chapter is not to demonstrate what parameters should be used for alerting disaster management services. It is about demonstrating the notion of our data-Grid push service and its functionality with combining a number of criteria and parameters values, which if they have been assessed in isolation disaster management services and other

*Table 2. Building constructions and their resistance*

| HR: High resistance | Current regulation, buildings that have no experience of a number of earthquakes in the past |
|---|---|
| MR: Moderate resistance | Current regulation, buildings that have experienced a number of earthquakes in the past |
| LR: Low resistance | Previous regulation, buildings that have experience of a number of earthquakes in the past. |
| NR: No resistance | No regulation existence, very old buildings that have or have not experienced a number of earthquakes |

*Table 3. Criteria and data values for Aggregative Case Scenarios (ACS)*

| ACS | Event | Population, density area | Earthquake magnitude (Richter scale) | Type of building consideration | Building resistance | Level of alert to be produced |
|-----|-------|--------------------------|--------------------------------------|-------------------------------|---------------------|-------------------------------|
| ACS1 | $E_1$ | x1 (LOW) | ≥5.5-6.0≥ | b1, ≥ 8.0 | LR | LOW (check) |
| | $E_2$ | x2 (HIGH) | ≥5.5-6.0≥ | b2≥10.0 | HR | NO Alert |
| | $E_3$ | x2 (HIGH) | ≥5.5-6.0≥ | b3 no regulation | NR | HIGH |
| ACS2 | $E_4$ | x1 (LOW) | ≥6.1-6.9≥ | b4≥6 | LR | HIGH |
| | $E_5$ | x2 (HIGH) | ≥6.1-6.9≥ | b5≥8 | MR | LOW (Check) |
| | $E_6$ | x2 (HIGH) | ≥6.1-6.9≥ | b6≥8 | LR | MEDIUM |
| ACS3 | $E_7$ | x1 (LOW) | ≥7.0-7.9≥ | b7 no regulation | NR | HIGH |
| | $E_8$ | x2 (HIGH) | ≥7.0-7.9≥ | b8≥10 | HR | NO Alert |
| | $E_9$ | x2 (HIGH) | ≥7.0-7.9≥ | b9≥8 | MR | MEDIUM |

interested parties may have not been alerted appropriately. In other words, assessment of isolated values could yield to misleading alerts, which in turn, may result to human losses.

Table 3 describes three different aggregative case scenarios (ACS) of earthquakes affecting a wide area x, which consists of smaller areas such as x1 and x2.

*ACS1:* An earthquake of a magnitude between 5.5 and 6.0 of the Richter scale occurs in an area x. There are three building types, b1, b2 and b3 in this area. The first type of buildings, b1 (area x1, a low-density populated area) refers to low resistant buildings as they have been constructed using previous seismic construction regulation and their resistance are up to 8.0 of the Richter scale. These buildings have also experienced a number of earthquakes during their lifetime. Let's assume that the combination of these attributes lead to a low level alert. A second type of buildings, b2 are located in area x2 that is a highly populated area. These buildings have been constructed under the current seismic regulations (up to 10.0 of the Richer scale), and thus, they refer to as high resistant buildings. Again, let's assume that

there should be no alerting situation in this case. Finally, in the highly populated area x2, there are few old buildings, b3, which have been constructed without following any building regulation. These buildings may have experienced a number of earthquakes over the years. In brief, these buildings refer to as a no resistant buildings and the expectation is that an earthquake must cause a highly alerting situation for them. Our expectation is that the disaster management team will prioritise their rescue activities based on the level of alert produced.

*ACS2:* An earthquake of a magnitude between 6.1 and 6.9 of the Richter scale occurs in an area x. There are three building types, b4, b5 and b6 in this area. The first type of buildings, b4 (area x1, that is a low-density populated area) refers to low resistant buildings as they have been constructed using previous seismic construction regulation and their resistance are up to 6.0 of the Richter scale. These buildings have experienced a number of earthquakes during their lifetime. Let's assume that the combination of these attributes lead to a high level alert. A second type of buildings, b5 are located in area x2 that is a highly populated area. These buildings have been constructed using the current seismic construction regulation (up to 8.0 of the Richter scale), and thus, they refer to as moderate resistant buildings. In turn, let's assume that there should be a low-level alerting situation in this case. Finally, in the highly populated area x2, there is a third type of buildings, b6, which have been constructed using previous building regulations. These buildings may have experienced a number of earthquakes over the years. In brief, these buildings refer to as low resistant buildings and the expectation is that an earthquake must cause a medium alerting situation for them. Again, our expectation is that the disaster management team will prioritise their rescue activities based on the level of alert produced.

*ACS3:* An earthquake of a magnitude between 7.0 and 7.9 of the Richter scale occurs in an area x. There are three building types, b7, b8 and b9. The first type of buildings, b7 (area x1, a that is a low-density populated area) refers to no resistant buildings as they have been constructed with using no seismic construction regulation and thus, the combination of these attributes must lead to a high level alert. A second type of buildings, b8 are located in area x2 that is a highly populated area. These buildings are built under the current seismic regulations (up to 10.0 of the Richer scale), and thus, they refer to as high resistant buildings. We assume that there should be no alerting situation in this case. Finally, in the highly populated area x2, there is another type of buildings, b9, which have been constructed using previous building regulation and their resistance are up to 8.0 of the Richter scale. These buildings refer to as moderate resistant buildings and the expectation is that an earthquake must cause a medium alerting situation for them. Once again, our expectation is that the disaster management team will prioritize

their rescue activities based on the level of alert produced.

Similarly, various aggregative case scenarios (ACS) can be produced when incorporating various criteria and when assessing them with different data values.

## A MATHEMATICAL ANALYSIS OF THE DISASTER MANAGEMENT DATA-GRID PUSH SERVICE

A continuous request for data consists of several elements: the initial search terms, $W$, defines the scope of the data of interest to the requester. It consists of a series of search terms combined with 'and', 'or' and 'not' operators. The duration of subscription $l$, defining the length of timeframe of the request. These two elements can define the basic data request.

$$D = S_1 \cup S_2 \cup S_3 \cup \ldots \cup S_m$$

where $S_1$, $S_2$, $S_{3, \ldots,}$ $S_m$ are data sources, available on to the grid and descriptions of changes to the data are stored in datastore $D$. With no temporal component:

$$Req_w(D) = Pd$$

where $Pd$ is the pushable data to be sent to the client. The data pushed is the data available that matches the request. Taking time into account,

at time $t$, if $t < t_0 + l$, $Req_{w,l}(D_t) = Pd_t$

where $t_0$ is the time the request was created. Here, if the request is still valid, then the current data to be pushed, $Pd_t$, will be the data from the current dataset, $D_t$, that satisfies the request. In order to send only the updates of the data to the subscriber, we define the data Push, $P_t$, as the difference between the current pushable data and the previously pushed data.

$$P_t = Pd_t/Pd_{t-1}$$

The frequency of update of the data sources related to the request will determine the frequency of the Pushes sent to the client. For static or periodically updated data, this should not cause any problems. However, in the case of continuously updated data (or new data generation) will be pushed continuously to the client, potentially overloading the client ability to deal with it (either in terms of processing time or in bandwidth). Therefore, the data needs to be pushed periodically, aggregating the continuous changes into discrete periods, $T_0, T_1... T_0+l$, each period will have a default length, $k$.

At time $t$, if $(t < t_0+l)$ and$(t = gk, g \in N)$
$$Req_{w,l,f}(D_t) = Pd_t$$

$$P_{Tq} = Pd_t/Pd_{t-k}$$

The client should be able to specify the maximum frequency of Pushes they receive, by adding a frequency value to the request. This frequency length would replace the default length.

At time $t$, if $(t < t_0+l)$ and$(t = gf, g \in N)$
$$Req_{w,l,f}(D_t) = Pd_t$$

$$P_{Tq} = Pd_t/Pd_{t-f}$$

Thus, pushes are sent (at most) every $f$ time units, each push containing any changes to the requested data that have happened since the last push. This ensures that the client is sent updates at a rate that can be dealt with usefully. However, this means that there is a delay between changes in data and results being pushed to the client. In emergency situations, such delays would be highly undesirable.

In many situations, the client may want to specify a series, $C$, of 1 to n criteria, $C_1, C_2. C_n$, where criteria define a situation in the data that would trigger an immediate push. If such criteria

are attached to a request, each time the data relating to that request is checked against the criteria. If any of the criteria are matched, a push is sent to the client.

At time $t$, if $(t < t_0+l)$ and $((Req_C (D_t) \neq \{\})$ or $(t = gf, g \in N))$ $Req_{w,l,f,C}(D_t) = Pd_t$

$$P_{Tq} = Pd_t - Pd_{t-f}$$

This enables the client to override their own specified frequency for their request if certain conditions exist in the data. The criteria $C$, need to be determined by the client as part of their data request.

## Exemplifying the Data-Grid Push Service using ACS1

Using the above earthquake data scenario, we will assume that the disaster management team (DMT) coordinator is responsible for a geographic area $x$ and so their request will be for the data they require that occurs in their area. The search term for their data requests, $W$, specifies the data of interest to the DMT (see Table 3 for details)

*W = population density, earthquake magnitude, type of building construction, building resistance, location = x*

The duration of their request will be 100 time units, and the maximum frequency of updates will be 5 time units.

*l = 100, f = 5*

Alert criteria are formulated to produce pushes of data in situations where alerts need to be issued. High alerts should be issued when an area is hit by an earthquake, which exceeds the maximum tolerances for buildings within that area, for example when:

$C_1$ = *earthquake magnitude > type of building construction, alert(High)*

Medium alerts should be issued if moderate resistance buildings are hit by earthquakes very close to their maximum tolerances (within 1.0 point) or if low resistance buildings are hit by earthquakes close to their maximum tolerance (within 2.0 points).

$C_2$ = *(0 > Earthquake magnitude – type of building construction ≤ 1) and Building Resistance = MR, alert(Medium)*

$C_3$ = *(0 > Earthquake magnitude – type of building construction ≤ 2) and Building Resistance = LR, alert(Medium)*

Low alerts should be issued if low or moderate resistance buildings are subjected to earthquakes within 3 points of their maximum tolerances.

$C_4$ = *(0 > Earthquake magnitude – type of building construction ≤ 3) and Building Resistance = LR or MR, alert(Low)*

Once this request is activated, for a period of 100 time units, every 5 time units any changes in the data about earthquakes in this area will be pushed to the client. This allows ongoing evaluation of the situation. In the event that the data matches situations specified in the criteria, a push will instantly be sent, regardless of the frequency of the request. This allows for rapid, targeted response in the event that the need arises.

In ACS1, we have 3 events, $E_1$, $E_2$ and $E_3$ (see Table 3).

Specifically, at $t$=0, the DMT issue the request $Req_{w,100,4,C}(D)$, where $C = \{C_1, C_2, C_3, C_4\}$. The initial push of data, $P_{T0}$, is generated, containing all of the initial data related to the search, $W$. No events occur (and so no data changes), at $t$=5 a new push is generated containing any updates since the last

push, $P_{T1}$ = $dP_5/dP_0$. However, in this case the push is empty, so no push is sent.

At $t$ = 10, E1 occurs. A push is already scheduled to be generated at this time, so $P_{T2}$ = $dP_{10}/dP_5$ contains the data relating to E1 and is pushed to the DMT.

At $t$ = 12, E2 occurs. E2 does not contain data matching any of the criteria in $C$ (it is a situation that produces no alert) and a push is not scheduled to happen at this time. So, the data for E2 is added to the datastore D but not sent to the DMT.

AT $t$ = 15, the next push is sent. $P_{T3}$ = $dP_{15}/dP_{10}$ contains the data relating to E2 and is pushed to the DMT.

At $t$ = 16, E3 happens. E3 contains data that matches criteria $C_1$ (i.e. a high alert situation) and a new Push, $P_{T4}$ = $dP_{16}/dP_{15}$ is generated and sent to the DMT, including the data relevant to the alert situation.

In this way, regular updates of the situation of interest are pushed to the DMT at a rate they can handle, but vital information is sent immediately. In addition, the alert criteria allow for selection of combination of multiple criteria, which on their own would not be important. This ability for the client to formulate their own alert situations and add them to their basic search makes the push technique suitable for use in situations such as disaster management.

## THE ARCHITECTURE AND IMPLEMENTATION FOR A DATA-GRID PUSH SERVICE

Relevant architectures and the implementation of such a data-Grid push service have been extensively discussed in Bessis and Chauhan (2008) and in Bessis (2009). The implementation of such a dynamic service incorporates the combination of Web Services standards (XML, SOAP, UDDI and WSDL) and open source technologies. Specifically, technologies used included JAVA 1.5.0._06, JACARTA TOMCAT 1.6.5, Apache ANT 1.6.5,

*Figure 2. Process model architecture for a user tailored "Data Push" in a Data Grid (Bessis, 2009)*

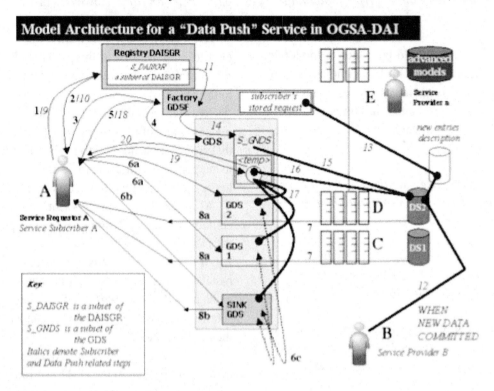

MySQL 4.0, MySQL Control Centre 0.9.4-beta, Apache AXIS 1.1 in TOMCAT, OGSA-DAI 2.1 and OGSA-DAI WSI 2.1.

The following – as shown also in Figure 2 – lists the steps required for "Service Requestor A" to interact with appropriate data services:

- Action 1: "Service Requestor A" has to request the Data Access and Integration Service Grid Register (DAISGR) for a source of data about X;
- Action 2: Register returns a handle to "Service Requestor A";
- Action 3: "Service Requestor A" sends a request to the Factory (GDSF) to access the relevant data sets that are registered with it;
- Action 4: Factory creates a Grid Data Service (GDS) to manage access to relevant data sets;

- Action 5: Factory returns a handle of the GDS to "Service Requestor A";
- Action 6a: "Service Requestor A" performs the query to the respective GDS using a database language;
- Action 7: The GDS interacts with the dataset(s);
- Action 8a: The GDS returns query results in a XML format to "Service Requestor A".

Finally assume that new data – that is of critical importance and of interest for "Service Requestor A" – committed in a database available from "Service Provider B". With this in mind, let's assume that "Service Requestor A" subscribes his interest to the data-Grid push service so they can be informed automatically of forthcoming – and only relevant– entries. Let's now assume that at a later stage, "Service Provider B" updates data stored in their database. Our approach suggests that if such entries are of interest to the subscriber, the data-Grid push service should automatically inform "Service Requestor A" of them. The following, also shown in Figure 2, lists the steps required for "Service Requestor A" to keep informed automatically of specific changes committed in dispersed heterogeneous databases:

- Action 9: "Service Requestor A" as a "Service Request Subscriber" has to request subscription to the Subscribe_Data Access and Integration Service Grid Register (S_DAISGR) – a service that is a subset of the Data Access and Integration Service Grid Register (DAISGR) – for a source of specific new/updated data about X where xi = x1;
- Action 10: S_DAISGR returns a handle to "Service Request Subscriber A";
- Action 11: S_DAISGR sends a request to the Factory (GDSF) to access the relevant data sets that are registered with it;
- Action 12: "Service Provider B" commits new data and (metadata) descriptions about new data entries are automatically generated;
- Action 13: When new data has been committed within any dataset registered to the GDSF, a trigger will cause an automatic search between the records storing new data description and subscribers' parameters (also stored in the GDSF) to identify relevant matches (check whether xi = x1 or else):
- If no matches (i.e. xi ≠ x1) found GDSF does nothing (i.e. not return a handle).
- Action 14: If matches found (i.e. xi = x1) GDSF creates a Subscriber_Grid Notification Data Service (S_GNDS) to manage access to relevant data sets;
- Action 15: The S_GNDS interacts with the dataset(s) to pull out matches;
- Action 16: The S_GNDS creates a temporary table <Temp> to store pulled matches;

- Action 17: The trigger attached to the <Temp> automatically runs a search facility to select any differences with previous GDS including the GDS Sink;
- If no differences found GDSF does not return a handle to the "Subscriber A" and deletes S_GNDS' <Temp> contents automatically.
- Action 18: If differences found GDSF returns a handle of the S_GNDS to the "Subscriber A";
- Action 19: "Service Request Subscriber A" performs the query to the <Temp> using a database language;
- Action 20: The <Temp> returns query results in a XML format to the "Subscriber A".

## CONCLUSION

The chapter has endorsed the logic that data and resource integration using concepts and practices associated with data-Grid push services could support disaster managers in making informed decisions within their VO as well as produce automatically different levels of alerts. We adopted the view that the combination of a number of criteria and parameters values, which they continuously and may unpredictably change in time could be assessed and dealt in a more efficient manner.

We described these using a number of aggregative case scenarios as well as model them mathematically. Finally, we presented and illustrated the model architecture, which its real-world implementation has extended current functionality offered by the OGSA-DAIS specification to keep interested decision makers informed automatically about relevant up-to-date data.

# REFERENCES

Anand, P. (2002). *Foundations of Rational Choice Under Risk*. Oxford, UK: Oxford University Press.

Antonioletti, M., Atkinson, M. P., Baxter, R., Borley, A., Chue Hong, N. P., & Collins, B. (2005). The design and implementation of Grid database services in OGSA-DAI. *Concurrency and Computation*, *7*(2-4), 357–376. doi:10.1002/cpe.939

Arthur, W. B. (1991). Designing Economic Agents that Act like Human Agents: A Behavioral Approach to Bounded Rationality. *The American Economic Review*, *81*(2), 353–359.

Asimakopoulou, E., Anumba, C. J., Bouchlaghem, D., & Sagun, A. (2006, August). *Use of ICT during the response phase in emergency management in Greece and the United Kingdom*. Paper presented at the International Disaster Reduction Conference (IDRC), Davos, Switzerland.

Atkinson, M., Dialani, V., Guy, L., Narang, I., Paton, N., Pearson, P., et al. (2003). *Grid database access and integration: requirements and functionalities*. Retrieved August 17, 2008, from http://www.ggf.org/documents/GFD.13.pdf

Baker, M., Buyya, R., & Laforenza, D. (2002). *Grids and Grid technologies for wide-area distributed computing*. New York: John Wiley & Sons, Inc.

Bessis, N. (2003). Towards a homogeneous status of communicated research. In *Proceedings of the Sixth International Conference on the Next Steps: Electronic Theses and Dissertations Worldwide*, Berlin. Retrieved August 17, 2008, from http://edoc.hu-berlin.de/conferences/ etd2003/bessis-nik/PDF/index.pdf

Bessis, N. (Ed.). (2009). *Model architecture for a user tailored data push service in data grids. Grid Technology for Maximizing Collaborative Decision Management and Support: Advancing Effective Virtual Organizations* (pp. 236–256). Hershey, PA: IGI Global.

Bessis, N., & Asimakopoulou, E. (2008, July). *The development of a personalized and dynamic driven RSS specification for the built environment*. Paper presented at the IADIS International Conference on Web Based Communities, Amsterdam.

Bessis, N., & Asimakopoulou, E. (2008, August 25-29). Towards a grid aware forest fire evacuation warning system. In *Proceedings of the Int. Disaster Reduction Conference*, Davos, Switzerland.

Bessis, N., & Chauhan, J. (2008, April). *The design and implementation of a Grid database consistency service in OGSA-DAI*. Paper presented at the IADIS International Conference on Information Systems, Algarve, Portugal.

Bessis, N., French, T., Burakova-Lorgnier, M., & Huang, W. (2007). Using Grid technology for data sharing to support intelligence in decision making. In Xu, M. (Ed.), *Managing Strategic Intelligence: Techniques and Technologies* (pp. 179–202). Hershey, PA: IGI Global.

Calvanese, D., Giacomo, G., & Lenzerini, M. (1998, August). *Information integration: conceptual modelling and reasoning support*. Paper presented at the third Conference on Cooperative Information Systems, New York.

Clemen, R. (1996). *Making Hard Decisions: An Introduction to Decision Analysis* (2nd ed.). Belmont, CA: Duxbury Press.

Duhan, S., Levy, M., & Powell, P. (2001). Information systems strategies in knowledge-based SMEs: the role of core competencies. *European Journal of Information Systems*, *1*(10), 25–40. doi:10.1057/palgrave.ejis.3000379

Foster, I. (2002). What is the Grid? a three point checklist. *Grid Today*, *1*(6). Retrieved August 17, 2008, from http://www.Gridtoday.com/02/0722/100136.html

Foster, I., Kesselman, C., Nick, N. M., & Tuecke, S. (2002). The physiology of the Grid: an open Grid services architecture for distributed systems integration. *Globus.* Retrieved August 17, 2008, from http://www.globus.org/alliance/publications /papers/ogsa.pdf

Foster, I., Kesselman, C., & Tuecke, S. (2001). The anatomy of the Grid: enabling scalable virtual organisations. *The International Journal of Supercomputer Applications, 15*(3), 200–222. doi:10.1177/109434200101500302

GEO 101-02 Introduction to Geology. (2006). *GEO.101-02.* Retrieved December 15, 2009, from http://www.geo.ua.edu/intro03/quakes.html

Kodeboyina, D., & Plale, B. (2004). *Experiences with OGSA-DAI: portlet access and benchmark.* Retrieved August 17, 2008, from http://www-unix.mcs.anl.gov/~keahey/DBGS/DBGS_files/ dbgs_papers/kodeboyina.pdf

Levy, A. (2002). Logic-based techniques in data integration. In Minker, J. (Ed.), *Logic Based Artificial Intelligence* (pp. 575–595). Norwell, MA: Kluwer Academic Publishers.

Louie, J. N. (1996). *What is Richter Magnitude?* Retrieved December 15, 2009, from http://www. seismo.unr.edu/ftp/pub/ louie/class/100/magnitude.html

Magowan, J. (2003, April). *A view on relational data on the Grid.* Paper presented at the International Parallel and Distributed Processing Symposium, Nice, France.

Nieto-Santisteban, M. A., Gray, J., Szalay, A. S., Annis, J., Thakar, A. R., & O'Mullane, W. J. (2004). *When database systems meet the Grid (Tech. Rep.).* Microsoft Corporation, Microsoft Research.

Parvez, I. A. (2009). *Earthquake Parameters.* Retrieved December 15, 2009, from http://www. cmmacs.ernet.in/ cmmacs/pdf/parvez_lec2.pdf

Pratali, P. (2003). The strategic management of technological innovations in the small to medium enterprise. *European Journal of Innovation Management, 6*(1), 18–31. doi:10.1108/14601060310456300

Raman, V., Narang, I., Crone, C., Haas, L., Malaika, S., Mukai, T., et al. (2003). *Data access and management services on Grid. Global Grid Forum.* Retrieved August 17, 2008, from http://61.136.61.58:81/gate/big5/ www.cs.man. ac.uk/Grid-db/papers/dams.pdf

Reinoso Castillo, J. A., Silvescu, A., Caragea, D., Pathak, J., & Honavar, V. G. (2008). *Information extraction and integration from heterogeneous, distributed, autonomous information sources – a federated ontology – driven query-centric approach.* Paper presented at IEEE International Conference on Information Integration and Reuse. Retrieved August 17, 2008, from http://www. cs.iastate.edu/ ~honavar/Papers/indusfinal.pdf

Simon, H. (1977). *The new science of management decision.* Englewood Cliffs, NJ: Prentice Hall.

Thywisswen, K. (2006). *Components of Risk. A Comparative Glossary.* Tokyo, Japan: United Nations University. Retrieved December 15, 2009, from http://www.unisdr.org/eng/library/ Literature/9985.pdf

Ullman, J. (1997, January). *Information integration using logical views.* Paper presented at the Sixth International Conference on Database Theory, Troy, MI.

United Nations. (2008). *Demographic dynamics and sustainability.* Rerteived December 15, 2009, from http://www.un.org/esa/sustdev/natlinfo/ indicators/indisd /english/chapt5e.htm

Venugopal, S., Buyya, R., & Ramamohanarao, K. (2005). *A taxonomy of data Grids for distributed data sharing management and processing.* Retrieved August 17, 2008, from http://arxiv.org/ abs/cs.DC/0506034

Wahlström, R., Tyagunov, S., Grünthal, G., Stempniewski, L., Zschau, J., & Müller, M. (2004). Seismic Risk analysis for Germany: Methodology and preliminary results. In Malzahn, D., & Plapp, T. (Eds.), *Disasters and Society, Hazard Assessment to Risk Reduction* (pp. 83–90). Berlin: Logos Verlag.

Watson, P. (2002). *Databases and the Grid* (Tech. Rep.). Retrieved August 17, 2008, from http://www.cs.ncl.ac.uk/research/ pubs/books/ papers/185.pdf

Weishaupl, T., & Schikuta, E. (2004). *Dynamic service evolution for open languages in the Grid and service oriented architecture*. Paper presented at the Fifth International Workshop on Grid Computing, Pittsburgh, PA.

Wohrer, A., Brezany, P., & Janciak, I. (2004). *Virtalisation of heterogeneous data sources for Grid information systems*. Retrieved August 17, 2008, from http://www.par.univie.ac.at/publications/ other/inst_rep_2002-2004.pdf

*This work was previously published in International Journal of Distributed Systems and Technologies, Volume 1, Issue 3, edited by Nik Bessis, pp. 56-70, copyright 2010 by IGI Publishing (an imprint of IGI Global).*

# Chapter 17
# Service and Management Oriented Traffic Information Grid

**Yu Fang**
*Tongji University, China*

**Dong Liang Zhang**
*Tongji University, China*

**Chun Gang Yan**
*Tongji University, China*

**Hong Zhong Chen**
*Tongji University, China*

**Changjun Jiang**
*Tongji University, China*

## ABSTRACT

*Traffic information service plays an important role in one's daily life. However, traffic information processing is very complicated because of its dynamic, cooperative and distributed features. This chapter presents the Service and Monitoring Oriented Traffic Information Grid. In this system, it is a remarkable characteristic to provide real-time, dynamic information services for travelers and traffic managers by grid technology. The system provides travelers with services of optimized route scheme, bus arrival prediction based on real-time route status, and route status forecast. For traffic managers, the system can provide vehicle tracing, traffic monitoring, history data analysis, and decision making on traffic control strategy. In this regard, key research includes large multi-source traffic data integration, route status forecast, and optimum dynamic travel scheme implementation based on massive GPS data.*

DOI: 10.4018/978-1-4666-0906-8.ch017

# INTRODUCTION

With the aim of making all resources in Internet overall connected and shared, grid (Foster, Kesselman, & Tuecke, 2001; Foster, Kesselman, Nick, & Tuecke, 2002) became a research focus after Internet and Web. To promote the computation performance, grid tries to make the most of the resources, including supercomputers, storage devices, network, software, information, knowledge, scientific instruments and others.

In USA, grid researchers are focused on computing grid and data grid, such as TeraGrid (TeraGrid, 2000) and GIG (Global Information Grid). In Europe, grid project, including DataGrid (DataGrid, 2004), e-Learning (E-Learning Centre, 1994), and e-Culture, emphasize grid application. In other countries, such as Japan, India, Singapore, South Korea, and so on, some grid programs have been established.

China has also enhanced investment to grid research and applications. At present, some key projects have been supported, e.g., National Grid by 863-program, ChinaGrid project by Ministry of Education (MoE), Network Computing by NSFC, and Shanghai Grid by Shanghai Municipality (ChinaGrid, 2003).

Information Service Grid (ISG) intends to share data, knowledge, software and other kinds of information in Internet. Because these information resources are distributed, dynamic and heterogeneous, ISG provides autonomic, QoS assuring, scalable and dynamic information services for virtual organizations.

Researchers have applied ISG to Intelligent Transportation Systems (ITS) (Zhang, Zhi, Zeng, & Jiang, 2004). Road construction in China is the fastest in the world. However, the traffic capacity of road network cannot match the increasing of traffic flows, and traffic jams are becoming more and more serious in large cities. Government has realized that only construction cannot deal with the transportation problems. Advanced information technologies are required to increase efficiency of the transportation management. Actually, some big cities, like Shanghai City Transportation Management Bureau (SCTMB) has attempted to improve work efficiency and management level by information technology. SCTMB, and its subordinate administrative offices and companies, have already developed some management systems for taxi, bus, truck, etc., respectively. But the main disadvantages of these systems are: 1) these systems are isolated and transportation data cannot be shared and utilized efficiently; 2) transportation management systems cannot support the exact, real-time and dynamic information services. Therefore it is urgent to integrate all isolated systems and develop an overall information service system, a statistic analysis system, a real-time monitoring system, and an assistant decision making system.

At the end of 2003, we began to cooperate with Shanghai City Traffic Information Center (SCTIC) to establish a transportation information service platform based on Grid. SCTIC provides us with historical and real-time GPS data and implements traffic information services on-demand and information release. The grid nodes of Tongji University and Shanghai Supercomputing Center provide computing support. In August 2004, we developed the prototype system version 2.0 (Jiang, Zhang et al., 2005) of Traffic Information Grid (TIG) based on the version 1.0 (Zhang, Zhi, Zeng, & Jiang, 2004; Jiang, Zeng et al., 2003). In 2006, we develop the model system version 3.0 of TIG under the support of National Develop and Reform Commission of China. In this system, besides real-time GPS data, real-time sensors data and video data are also provided by SCTIC. And the aim of the system is not only provide traffic information, but also for traffic monitoring.

The rest of the chapter is organized as follow: First, we introduce the architecture of TIG, and describe the network topology and system architecture of it. Next, we present several key technologies of traffic information grid. After that, we show the implementation results of our traffic

*Figure 1. TIG network topology*

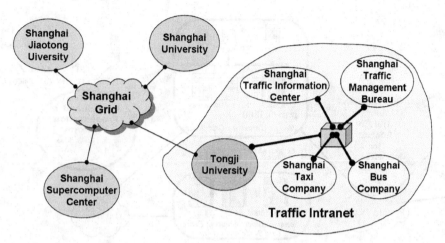

information service platform. Finally, conclusions are drawn.

## ARCHITECTURE OF TRAFFIC INFORMATION GRID

In the following paragraph, attention will be given to the architecture design of Traffic Information Grid (TIG). Since TIG is built on the existent ITS and the necessary IT resources of all kinds that can be provided, the discussion about its architecture design will be divided into two parts. The first part introduces the IT resources that can be used to build TIG, as well as network topology that focuses on the organization of these physical resources. The second part focuses on the software architecture design of TIG, which mainly describes how to organize components and functions of all kinds in the software system based on hierarchically logical layers.

### IT Resources and Network Topology

In topological Graph of network structure, TIG includes two kinds of network nodes (Shown in Figure 1). One is Traffic Intranet (sometimes called SPTN, Shanghai Private Traffic Network),

the other is Shanghai Grid. In the traffic Intranet, different traffic departments are connected to each other via 100M-network. The Intranet not only is the source of all kinds of traffic data, but also provides a platform of traffic information on-demand and publication for TIG. Both Shanghai Grid nodes, which provide enough computation and storage resources for TIG, and Tongji University Grid node, a platform for traffic data-processing and information service computing, have been connected with the Traffic Intranet via 1000M network. Thus Tongji University, as a core Grid node, can integrate the Traffic Intranet and Shanghai Grid together into a whole part, and forms the TIG at last (Figure 1).

TIG provides traffic information management and services and traffic decision-making for corresponding traffic travelers, managers and decision-makers by taking advantage of information Grid technology. Shanghai Traffic Information Management Center authorizes all Grid nodes in Shanghai Grid to persist and process massive traffic date gathered from different traffic departments. Here, Tongji University Grid node acts as traffic information Grid Schedule portal of TIG. The processed traffic information will be publicized as corresponding traffic services. And traffic services consumers can demand them via all

*Figure 2. TIG run-time framework*

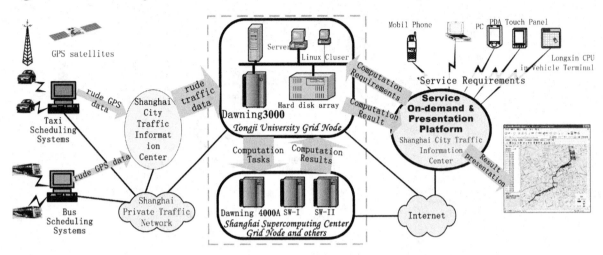

kinds of information terminals, such as PDA, Cell Phones, PC, In-Vehicle terminals, etc (Figure 2).

Based on the network structure discussed above, the following implementation scheme is adopted for TIG. In the scheme, the system consists of three parts: (1) real time traffic data acquisition; (2) the platform of services on demand and information releasing; and (3) the center of traffic data processing and service supporting. The implementation scheme is shown in Figure 2.

Firstly, original real-time traffic data, which are acquired by GPS on taxis and buses, are integrated into uniform data in SCTIC. And then the formatted data are delivered to the grid node in Tongji University through SPTN. Secondly, the platform of traffic services on demand and information release accepts service requirements from in-vehicle terminal, mobile phones, PDAs and PCs, and transforms them into computation tasks in Tongji Grid Node. Then the computation results from grid nodes are displayed for users through corresponding graphical user interface. Finally, as the center of traffic data processing and service supporting, the grid node in Tongji University processes the computing requirements from the platform of services on demand.

## System Architecture

The aim of Traffic Grid Application Platform is to integrate dynamically available computation and storage resources together, and provide enough and reliable computation and storage capability for traffic information services processing, e.g., traffic flow simulation and route status prediction, so that TIG can provide highly-performed, timely and enriched traffic information services for all kind of clients. To realize the prospective aim, The Service Grid technology is introduced into the TIG. Taking advantage of the conception and implementation technique of Open Grid Service Architecture, the Traffic Grid Application Platform is constructed based on four-layer architecture.

*Grid resource layer:* This layer is to provide a mechanism and implementation technique for collection, virtualization, assembling of all kinds of available computation and storage resources. In Shanghai Grid, there are various computation resources, such as "DAWN 3000" high performance super computer in Tongji University Grid node, "DAWN 4000A" high performance super computer in Shanghai Super Computer Center Grid node, "ZIQIANG" high performance super computer in Shanghai University Grid node and many Linux and Windows clusters which each Shanghai Grid node has. To integrate these heterogeneous computation resources together smoothly and seamlessly, first of all they should be virtualized into corresponding computation services with unified interface. Meanwhile, Shanghai Grid provides enough storage resources for TIG which includes storage resources, e.g., all kinds of DBMS (Database Management System), SAN (Storage Area Network), and etc. These heterogeneous data storage resources also should be virtualized into a unified access interface for all kinds of data providers so that they can storage data into these storage spaces transparently. For the above goal, Grid infrastructure is installed into the corresponding Grid nodes so that these resources can be virtualized and assembled in resource layer. Consequently, a virtual organization is founded, which provides computation and storage services for corresponding traffic applications.

*Grid service support layer:* In order to use Gird resource's more effectively and transparently, there must be some management mechanism and technology for resources scheduling and management. This layer focuses on task scheduling, resource management, data management, and other Grid Support services. Task Scheduling service assigns computing tasks to corresponding Grid nodes based on some assignment policies. Resource Management service takes charge of monitoring and controlling resources, so that the whole system can run with high reliability. Data Management supports accessing heterogeneous databases and transferring massive traffic data. Other Grid services include authority and security service for Gird resources, and so on.

*Function and service providing layer:* This layer composes of traffic application services. Some are for traveler service e.g., optimum travel scheme and bus arrival prediction, others are for management and monitoring e.g., real-time taxi tracing, history data evaluation and hybrid traffic flow parallel simulation.

*Presentation layer:* Traffic Information presentation Layer provides rich traffic information publication ways and technologies, so that users can access the information provided by TIG in anytime, anywhere. Various terminators, such as mobile phone, telephone, computer, PDA, and mobile TV can have easy access to TIG. The interfaces include settled clients such as PCs and touch screens, and mobile terminals such PDAs and smart phones. Using PCs or mobile devices, users can easily get traffic information services and monitoring services by B/S or C/S mode.

## KEY TECHNOLOGIES OF TRAFFIC INFORMATION GRID

### Dynamic Traffic Grid Task Scheduler

Traffic applications of all kinds in TIG can use resources in Shanghai Grid to process and store traffic data. Here, with responsibility for allocating suitable resources to corresponding traffic tasks, task scheduler plays a very important role in constructing high performance traffic Grid platform.

There are two kinds of task schedulers which are static scheduler and dynamic scheduler. Static scheduler consumes fewer resources than dynamic scheduler, but cannot achieve high performance because it cannot obtain dynamic information in run time. On the contrary, dynamic scheduler does. Dynamic scheduler can be divided into two kinds of processing types: on-line type and batch type. On-line type assigns task one by one. And batch type gives an optimal schedule in batch tasks, which can make a better match between task and resources. If ratio of tasks arrival is low, and computing resources are enough, on-line type is a good choice; if not, batch type should be a good choice. In TIG, traffic computing tasks are much more than computing resources from Shanghai Grid, therefore, batch type is a pretty good choice for Traffic grid Task Scheduler.

In TIG, traffic Grid task scheduler, wrapped as Grid services, is deployed in Tongji University Grid node and provides unified access interface for all kind of traffic Grid clients. When some client requests some computation service, the service will create a task firstly. And then task scheduler module will request the current Grid nodes and submit the task to the according Grid node. Finally, the computation service returns the result to the user.

There are two modules included in dynamic traffic Grid scheduler component, which are traffic resource management module, and task schedule module.

Traffic resource management module puts focus on monitoring, management and allocation of all kinds of resources. What the module does is to manage all kinds of local computation and storage resources and register these resources

into resources information registry of MDS. This module also manages authority and security of resources. Resource allocation component is to allocate an available resource for a specified resource requester, which is based on allocation policies for according resources. Before allocating a resource to a requester, the allocation component will query schedule service provided by task schedule module. The schedule service returns suitable resource references to the requester according to requester parameters and dynamic schedule information. In this way the productivity of the whole traffic Grid application platform can be guaranteed.

Dynamic task Grid scheduler module includes four parts: (1) task receiver;(2)task scheduler;(3) task manager;(4)task pool. The working process of task schedule module includes six steps as follows.

1. Task receiver listens to requester;
2. Put task into task pool, if task pool is available when task receiver receives task from client;
3. Task scheduler fetches one task based on scheduling policy and task priority;
4. Task scheduler sends task to task manager;

*Figure 3. Logical structure of dynamic task Gird scheduler*

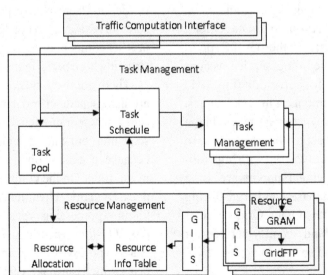

*Table 1. Size of GPS data (Acquisition frequency: 10 seconds; each message: 70 bytes)*

| Year | Vehicle type | Number of vehicles | Traffic (KB/s) | Data size per day (GB) | Data size per year (TB) |
|------|--------------|--------------------|-----------------|------------------------|--------------------------|
| 2004 | Bus | 3,000 | 20.5 | 1.690 | 0.602 |
|      | Taxi | 5,000 | 34.2 | 2.816 | 1.044 |
|      | Special vehicle | 1,000 | 6.8 | 0.563 | 0.201 |
|      | Total | 9,000 | 61.5 | 5.069 | 1.807 |
| 2005 | Bus | 7,000 | 47.9 | 3.943 | 1.405 |
|      | Taxi | 20,000 | 136.7 | 11.265 | 4.015 |
|      | Special vehicle | 3,400 | 23.2 | 1.915 | 0.683 |
|      | Total | 30,400 | 207.8 | 17.123 | 6.103 |
| 2006 | Bus | 8,000 | 54.7 | 4.506 | 1.606 |
|      | Taxi | 30,000 | 205.1 | 16.898 | 6.023 |
|      | Special vehicle | 4,000 | 27.3 | 2.253 | 0.803 |
|      | Total | 42,000 | 287.1 | 23.657 | 8.432 |

*Table 2. Size of loop sensor data (Acquisition frequency: 20 seconds; each message: 75 bytes)*

| Year | Vehicle type | Number of vehicles | Traffic (KB/s) | Data size per day (GB) | Data size per year (TB) |
|------|--------------|--------------------|-----------------|------------------------|--------------------------|
| 2006 | High Speed | 1600 | 5.6 | 0.48 | 0.172 |
|      | Normal | 2000 | 7.0 | 0.64 | 0.23 |
|      | Total | 2600 | 12.6 | 1.12 | 0.402 |

5.  Task manager finds a suitable computation Grid node, and sends the task to the node
6.  Task manager listens to the node until the task is finished, and sends back the result to the client.

Figure 3 shows the logical structure of dynamic task Gird scheduler based on Gram and MDS of Globus Toolkit 2. Here traffic computation interface plays a role as task receiver.

## Multi-Source Data Integration

In Shanghai, some distributed and autonomous information systems produce massive traffic data every year as shown in Table 1 and Table 2. So how to integrate these heterogeneous data is important.

In TIG, GPS data is first rectified to the road because of the excursion of signal (Shi, Zhang,

Fang, & Jiang, 2003). Then the data can be used in computing of route status.

We use the method of curve fitting to integrate multi-source data. The longitude and the latitude in a piece of GPS data are mapped onto a road segment id by deviation correcting. And the direction is transformed to two directions of a road segment as 0 or 1. So a GPS record is presented as road segment id, direction, velocity, and time.

The road situation in a direction of a road segment for a day is presented as the relationship of velocity and time, that is $v = f(t)$, where $v$ is velocity of vehicles and it is a function of time $t$. Given n data points $(t_i, v_i), i = 0, 1, ..., n-1$, we can use the least square method to complete data fitting. The approximating polynomial with degree $m - 1$ is:

$$f(t) = \sum_{i=1}^{m-1} a_i t^i, (m \le n).$$

To determine above polynomial, we construct a new polynomial which is linearly composed of orthogonal polynomials $P_i(t)$, i.e.,

$$f(t) = \sum_{i=1}^{m-1} C_i P_i(t),$$

where $\{P_i(t)\}$ is constructed with Gram-Schmidt method (Wang & Qu, 1998) by

$$P_0(t) = 1,$$

$$P_1(t) = 1 - \alpha_1,$$

$$P_i(t) = (t - \alpha_i)P_{i-1}(t) - \beta_{i-1}P_{i-2}(t), i = 2, 3, ..., m-1$$

Let

$$d_i = \sum_{j=0}^{n-1} p^2(t_j), i = 0, 1, ..., m-1,$$

then according to Gram-Schmidt theorem, we can get

$$\alpha_{i+1} = \frac{1}{d_i} \sum_{j=0}^{n-1} t_j P^2(t_j)$$

and $\beta_i = d_i / d_{i-1}, i = 0, 1, ..., m-2$. And the polynomials in $\{P_i(t)\}$ are orthogonal with each other. Using the least-square method, we can get

$$C_i = \frac{1}{d_i} \sum_{j=0}^{n-1} v_i P(t_j), i = 0, 1, ..., m-1.$$

In fact, curve fitting with an approximating polynomial is to work out $C_i$. And a time-velocity model of road situation comes out correspondingly, i.e.,

$$v = f(t) = \sum_{i=0}^{m-1} a_i t^i, (m \le n).$$

## Route Status Forecasting Based on Massive Traffic Information

Route status forecast is the foundation of the ravel scheme service. The quality of the forecasting will influence the result of dynamic travel scheme directly. However, urban transportation is such a complex huge system that a lot of factors impact it, such as routes, vehicles, persons, weather, temperature, time, accidents, etc. Factually, we use GPS data to reflect the road status. The road status is divided into three levels in our system:

SA: v > 30km/h;

SB: 15km/h ≤ v ≤ 30km/h;

SC: v < 15km/h.

Here, v is the velocity from the GPS data. Since there are about 25,000 route segments and 14,000 intersections in Shanghai, sufficient GPS data are necessary to road status forecasting. So, the calculation efficiency based on the forecasting models is very important. The neural network models (Yang, 1999) are used here. We select 16 main road segments and corresponding GPS data of 30 days. The data are separated into two groups. One is for learning and the other for verification. Table 3 shows the difference between the serial computation and parallel computation. Obviously, parallel computation can make forecasting faster.

Anyway, to shorten processing time and improve the forecasting precision, parallel comput-

*Table 3. Comparison of calculation time between single CPU and multi CPUs*

| CPU Number | Cost(minutes) | Speedup ratio |
|---|---|---|
| 1 | 80.431 | |
| 2 | 41.248 | 1.95 |
| 3 | 30.453 | 2.641 |
| 4 | 20.392 | 3.944 |
| 8 | 9.314 | 8.635 |
| 16 | 5.968 | 13.477 |

ing with high performance computers are needed for modeling route status forecasting based on massive data.

## Optimum Dynamic Travel Scheme

Nowadays many traffic information systems have been taking effect, such as parking guidance, route status notification, bus transfer, etc. These service systems can only inform end users of known data by rote, whereas what users really need is an intelligent system that can help them making selection of travel scheme based on real-time status. Generally, Optimum Dynamic Travel Scheme is one of the top-ranking services for travelers and administrators. Drivers can reach the destination in minimum time with the service. On the other hand, as to administrators, this service can reduce jams with global dynamic route guidance. In or-

der to implement the Optimum Dynamic Travel Scheme service, a dynamic route network model and an efficient dynamic route searching model are established. The search time must be less than 30 seconds. Furthermore, the implementation of Optimum Dynamic Travel Scheme must take into account the global balance of route guidance to avoid new traffic jams resulting from leading too many vehicles to some routes. So we must calculate the path in parallel (Gendreau, Laporte, & Semet, 2001; Hribar, Taylor, & Boyce, 2001; Gendreau, Guertin, Potvin, & Taillard, 1999; Tremblay & lorian, 2001). The following experiment in Table 4 verifies this idea. In this experiment, we use the computers in the grid node of Tongji University. An optimum dynamic path from Tongji University (located at the intersection of Siping Rd. and Zhangwu Rd.) to Shanghai Jiaotong University

*Table 4. Testing results on Dawning3000 and PC cluster*

| CPU Number | Cost(minutes) | Speedup ratio |
|---|---|---|
| 1 | 32.065 | |
| 2 | 20.961 | 1.529 |
| 3 | 12.808 | 2.502 |
| 4 | 11.457 | 2.797 |
| 8 | 6.399 | 5.009 |
| 10 | 5.128 | 6.251 |
| 12 | 4.416 | 7.259 |
| 16 | 3.455 | 9.408 |

(located at the intersection of Huashan Rd. and Guangyuan Rd.) is searched.

## Regional Hybrid Traffic Flow Simulation

Due to lacking in computing resources and real time requirement of traffic services, many useful traffic simulations can never be carried out under traditional IT technologies. The "as is" traffic flow simulation can only simulate traffic status in one cross, instead of traffic status with a region or a global area. As a matter of fact, this kind of traditional traffic flow simulation is meaningless for actual traffic flow control.

Nowadays, traffic simulation technology, which has been applied systematically and quantificationally into traffic schedule, traffic management and other traffic services, shows great superiority and extensive applicability. However, the simulation with high fidelity cannot be realized without a mass of mighty computation power. For example, the success of dynamic travel scheme depends on the precise simulation of total urban traffic status. High performance computation resources assembled by Grid technology provide necessary and powerful computing capability to simulate accurately status of ten thousands of route segments geographically distributed in Shanghai, which has totally never been achieved by traditional methods.

After establishment of traffic grid application platform, a regional hybrid traffic flow simulation system is developed for co-simulation of multi-region and huge route network, visualized micro- and macro- simulation, simulation and experiment for hybrid traffic flow, verification and evaluation for kinds of traffic models in Shanghai city. Based on the region traffic flow, we can perform many traffic services, such as the Optimum Dynamic Travel Scheme service, the Route Status Forecasting service, and so on.

## Inter-Vehicle Communication Networks

Inter-vehicle communication (IVC) networks are an instantiation of a mobile ad hoc network (MA-NET), however, have its unique characteristics and challenges such as rapid topology changes, frequent fragmentation, small effective network diameter, predictable topology changes, etc.

To further improve the routing performance in the IVC network, the RH-GPSR routing protocol is adopted that introduces the road topology and heuristic search-based mobility prediction scheme into GPSR by utilizing one of the characteristics of IVC networks, Predictable Topology Changes. Each router in RH-GPSR maintains two history samples $(x_1, y_1, t_1)$ and $(x_2, y_2, t_2)$ for every neighbor node, which denote the previous location and beacon time for this neighbor node and the same information found in the last beacon packet for the same neighbor, respectively. The thinking behind RH-GPSR is to estimate the location of neighbor nodes in the current time based on the history information and the route topology. The mobility prediction scheme in RH-GPSR is described as follows:

Step 1: Compute the distance L the neighbor node has moved from location $(x_1, y_1)$ to $(x_2, y_2)$ by a modified well-known graph search algorithm A* (Chen & Jiang, 2006), since it is a valid assumption that the node moves always along the shortest path.

Step 2: Determine the average velocity v of this node using the distance–time formula:

$$v = \frac{L}{t_2 - t_1}$$

Step 3: Estimate the current location based on v, the route topology and the current time.

In RH-GPSR, when a node is ready to forward a packet, firstly, it estimates the current location of each neighbor node using the proposed mobility prediction scheme; secondly, the packet will be forwarded to the neighbor node that is within the transmission range and has the closest distance from the estimated location to the destination node. More details of RH-GPSR are described in (Chen & Jiang, 2006).

## IMPLEMENTATION RESULTS

One obvious new feature is that TIG supports multiple presentation ways respectively for different kinds of traffic clients. Here, service oriented technologies give great contribution to it. Web Services make it available that all traffic services defined with WSDL provide unified access interfaces. No matter on what client platform, traffic services can be accessed smoothly and seamlessly. Some examples of running result on mobile terminals are shown in Figure 4.

Users who use PC or some powerful in-vehicle terminals which can connect to Internet through wide-band network, have access to traffic services via IE (Shown in Figure 4 a, b) with the help of web explorer installed in these terminals ahead of time.

Users, who use some terminals which have access to Internet only through narrowband network, have access to a Java-based interactive interface (Shown in Figure 4 c) which is independent of software operation system and hardware platform. Users, who use PDA, have access to a specified application (Shown in Figure 4 d) based on Windows Mobile SDK. Because the backend services are all implemented based on service oriented architecture, no matter what these presentation modes are, these client applications have access to the same traffic information services.

Also TIG provides real-time information service for public traffic information. An example is bus arrival prediction. For bus No. 72, TIG provides real-time bus position information for the digital bulletin boards at the bus stations (See Figure 4 e). Besides traffic information service for public, TIG also provides some model application on traffic monitoring and controlling. For traffic management, real-time taxis tracing is quite useful, and one can trace a taxi by its registered number (See Figure 4 f).

## CONCLUSION

TIG is a distributed, heterogeneous, dynamic, autonomic and cooperative (Du, Chen, & Liu, 2002) system. It helps to resolve complex urban traffic problems which cannot be resolved efficiently by traditional techniques to enhance throughput and productivity of urban traffic. At the same time, it can demonstrate grid techniques and Traffic Application Grid, driving the development of grid application techniques.

There are naturally differences between this system and ordinary ITS system. Existing ITSs can only provide static traffic information service or dynamic information without further processing. But our system has characteristics as follows.

1. Intelligent traffic information service and management obtain the support of information grid for the first time.
2. This system makes the creative application of data grid technology to flowing-car data to reflect traffic status of the whole city.
3. This system implements multi-source dynamic data (e.g., GPS data, loop sensor data) acquisition, amalgamation, management and modeling.
4. This system supports dynamic travel scheme and route status forecasting of main route segment, and provides dynamic traffic information service for public on terminals such as PC, in-vehicle terminal, mobile phone, PDA. etc.

*Figure 4. Implementation results of information service provided by TIG*

(a). a view of real-time route status

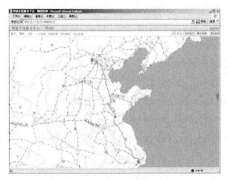

(b). Long distance (shanghai to Beijing) navigation

(c). Information service for in-vehicle terminal

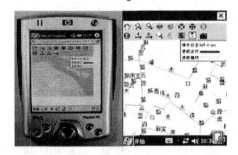

(d). Information service for PDAs

(e). Bus arrival prediction service of TIG

(f). Tracing of a taxi in TIG

## ACKNOWLEDGEMENT

This work is supported by National High Technology Research and Development Program ("863"Program) of China (2009AA011906-6) and Suporting Program (2009BAK43B37), National Defense Basic Research Program (A1420080182).

## REFERENCES

Chen, L., & Jiang, C. J. (2006). Geographic routing with road topology and heuristic search based mobility prediction. In *Proceedings of the International Conference on Sensing, Computing and Automation*, Chong Qing, China (pp. 3214-3218).

*ChinaGrid project*. (2003). Retrieved from http://www.chinagrid.net

Du, Z. H., Chen, Y., & Liu, P. (2002). *Grid Computing*. Beijing, China: Tsinghua University Press.

*E-learning Centre*. (1994). Retrieved from http://www.e-learningcentre.co.uk/

Foster, I., Kesselman, C., Nick, J., & Tuecke, S. (2002). Grid services for distributed system integration. *Computer*, *35*(6), 37–46. doi:10.1109/MC.2002.1009167

Foster, I., Kesselman, C., & Tuecke, S. (2001). The anatomy of the grid: Enabling scalable virtual organizations. *The International Journal of Supercomputer Applications*, *15*(3), 200–222. doi:10.1177/109434200101500302

Gendreau, M., Guertin, F., Potvin, Y., & Taillard, E. (1999). Parallel tabu search for real-time vehicle routing and dispatching. *Transportation Science*, *33*(4), 381–390. doi:10.1287/trsc.33.4.381

Gendreau, M., Laporte, G., & Semet, F. (2001). A dynamic model and parallel tabu search heuristic for real-time ambulance relocation. *Parallel Computing*, *27*(12), 1641–1653. doi:10.1016/S0167-8191(01)00103-X

Gong, Y. L., Dong, F. P., Li, W., & Xu, Z. W. (2003). VEGA infrastructure for resource discovery in grids. *Journal of Computer Science and Technology*, *18*(4), 413–422. doi:10.1007/BF02948915

Hribar, R., Taylor, E., & Boyce, E. (2001). Implementing parallel shortest path for parallel transportation application. *Parallel Computing*, *27*(12), 1537–1568. doi:10.1016/S0167-8191(01)00105-3

Jiang, C. J., & Zeng, G. S., et al. (2003). Research on traffic information grids. *Journal of Computer Research and Development*, *40*(12), 1676–1681.

Jiang, C. J., & Zhang, Z. H., et al. (2005). Urban Traffic Information Service Application Grid. *Journal of Computer Science and Technology*, *20*(1), 134–140. doi:10.1007/s11390-005-0015-3

Shi, Y. Q., Zhang, Z. H., Fang, Y., & Jiang, C. J. (2003). Build city traffic information service system based on grid platform. In *Proceedings of the 2003 IEEE Intelligent Transportation Systems*, Shanghai, China (Vol. 1, pp. 278-282).

*The DataGrid project*. (2004). Retrieved from http://eu-datagrid.web.cern.ch/ eu-datagrid/

*The TeraGrid project*. (2000). Retrieved from http://www.teragrid.org

Tremblay, N., & Iorian, M. (2001). Temporal shortest paths: Parallel computing implementa-tions. *Parallel Computing*, *27*(12), 569–1609. doi:10.1016/S0167-8191(01)00107-7

Wang, D. H., & Qu, D. Y. (1998). A study of a real-time dynamic prediction method for traffic volume. *China Journal of Highway and Transport*, *11*, 102–107.

Yang, Z. S. (1999). *The Theory and Model of Inducement System of City traffic Flow*. Beijing, China: People Traffic Press.

Zhang, Z. H., Zhi, Q., Zeng, G. S., & Jiang, C. J. (2004). In M. L. Li (Ed.), *The Architecture of Traffic Information Grid* (LNCS 3032, pp. 209-212). New York: Springer Verlag.

*This work was previously published in International Journal of Distributed Systems and Technologies, Volume 1, Issue 4, edited by Nik Bessis, pp. 14-26, copyright 2010 by IGI Publishing (an imprint of IGI Global).*

# Chapter 18
# Mining Environmental Data in the ADMIRE Project Using New Advanced Methods and Tools

**Ondrej Habala**
*The Slovak Academy of Sciences, Slovakia*

**Martin Šeleng**
*The Slovak Academy of Sciences, Slovakia*

**Viet Tran**
*The Slovak Academy of Sciences, Slovakia*

**Branislav Šimo**
*The Slovak Academy of Sciences, Slovakia*

**Ladislav Hluchý**
*The Slovak Academy of Sciences, Slovakia*

## ABSTRACT

*The project Advanced Data Mining and Integration Research for Europe (ADMIRE) is designing new methods and tools for comfortable mining and integration of large, distributed data sets. One of the prospective application domains for such methods and tools is the environmental applications domain, which often uses various data sets from different vendors where data mining is becoming increasingly popular and more computer power becomes available. The authors present a set of experimental environmental scenarios, and the application of ADMIRE technology in these scenarios. The scenarios try to predict meteorological and hydrological phenomena which currently cannot or are not predicted by using data mining of distributed data sets from several providers in Slovakia. The scenarios have been designed by environmental experts and apart from being used as the testing grounds for the ADMIRE technology; results are of particular interest to experts who have designed them.*

DOI: 10.4018/978-1-4666-0906-8.ch018

## INTRODUCTION

We present our work in the project ADMIRE, where we use advanced data mining and data integration technologies to run an environmental application, which uses data mining instead of standard physical modeling to perform experiments and obtain environmental predictions.

The chapter starts with description of the project ADMIRE, its vision and goals, and motivation and goals specific to our work in the project. Then we describe the history and current status of the environmental application. The core of the chapter then presents our approach to the integration of data from distributed resources. We have developed a prototype of data integration engine that allows users to specify data integration process in form of a workflow of reusable processing elements.

## THE EU ICT PROJECT ADMIRE

The project ADMIRE (Advanced Data Mining and Integration Research for Europe (ADMIRE)) is a 7th FP EU ICT project which aims to deliver a consistent and easy-to-use technology for extracting information and knowledge from distributed data sources. The project is motivated by the difficulty of extracting meaningful information by mining combinations of data from multiple heterogeneous and distributed resources. It will also provide an abstract view of data mining and integration, which will give users and developers the power to cope with complexity and heterogeneity of services, data and processes. One of main goals of the project is to develop a language that serves as a canonical representation of the data integration and mining processes.

The work presented in this chapter concentrates on using the ADMIRE technology and platform in order to bring new methods of data integration, exchange, and use to the environmental management domain, specifically in Slovakia. In the current situation, we often see environmental ap-

plications that are either using only in-house data, or use external data obtained as a static package, which over time looses accuracy simply by not being updated with new information, measurements, and corrections. An establishment of a new data-transfer contract between a provider and a user of an environmental data set is usually a cumbersome process, taking sometimes months, making some environmental data use scenarios outright impossible, since in the time it would take to obtain the data, the scenario would lose its purpose. While this situation may be alleviated by a rapid move of the data providers and data consumers in Slovakia towards the INSPIRE-prescribed web services technology (INSPIRE, 2007), we currently see almost no such efforts (and this situation is not specific to Slovakia). Only at the end of 2009 a law actually prescribing the creation of INSPIRE-compliant national infrastructure for environmental data has been passed, and it is probable that its implementation will take more than two years.

While the ADMIRE platform does not follow the INSPIRE-related directives in existence so far, the components of the applications are web services, and so surely follow the general spirit of INSPIRE. By engaging Slovak environmental management institutions (Slovak Hydro-meteorological Institute, Slovak Water Enterprise, Institute of Hydrology of the Slovak Academy of Sciences, and others) in preparing and evaluating experimental scenarios for environmental data integration and data mining, we try to achieve two goals. The first is to test the ADMIRE platform on a real application, with real and critical end-users. This goal serves the project itself. The other goal is to introduce the end-users to state-of-the-art data integration technologies, capable of negotiating and delivering environmental data on-line, without the usual delays and tedious preparation. This effort may prepare the foundation for later deployment of production web services for environmental data access, transfer, processing and visualization, as is foreseen in INSPIRE.

The rest of this chapter describes the Flood Forecasting Simulation Cascade (FFSC), the actual suite of data, services, and scenarios, which tries to do environmental data integration and data mining using data and processing services (such as custom meteorological or hydrological models) distributed across organizational boundaries.

## Flood Forecasting Simulation Cascade

The Flood Forecasting Simulation Cascade is a SOA-based environmental application, developed within several past FP5 and FP6 projects (K-Wf Grid), (CROSSGRID), (MEDIGRID). The application's development started in 1999 in the 5th FP project ANFAS (ANFAS). In ANFAS, it was mainly one hydraulic model (FESWMS). It then continued with a more complex scenario in 5th FP project CrossGrid, turned SOA in 6th FP projects K-Wf Grid and MEDIgRID, and finally extended the domain to environmental risk management in ADMIRE.

The application is now comprised of a set of environmental scenarios, with the necessary data and code to deploy and execute them. The scenarios have been chosen and prepared in cooperation with leading hydro-meteorological experts in Slovakia, working mainly for the Slovak Hydrometeorological Institute (SHMI), Slovak Water Enterprise (SWE), and the Institute of Hydrology of the Slovak Academy of Sciences (IH SAS). We have gathered also other scenarios from other sources, but in the end decided to use the ones presented below, because they promise to be the source of new information for both the environmental domain community, as well as for the data mining community in ADMIRE.

Together with the scenarios, we have gathered a substantial amount of historical data. SWE has provided 10 years of historical data containing the discharge, water temperature, and other parameters of the Vah Cascade of waterworks (15 waterworks installations and reservoirs in the west of Slovakia). SHMI has provided 9 years of basic meteorological data (precipitation, temperature, wind) computed by a meteorological model and stored in a set of GRIB (Gridded Binary) files, hydrological data for one of the scenarios, and also partial historical record from their nationwide network of meteorological data. They have also provided several years of stored weather radar data, necessary for one of the scenarios. The programs used by the application are in the context of ADMIRE described in Data Mining and Integration Language (DMIL) (Atkinson, 2009). The processes described in DMIL perform data extraction, transformation, integration, cleaning and checking. Additionally, in some scenarios we try to predict future values of some hydrometeorological variables; if necessary, we use a standard meteorological model to predict weather data for these cases.

## Environmental Scenarios of ADMIRE

In this chapter we present the suite of environmental scenarios, which we use to test the data mining and integration capabilities of the ADMIRE system. The scenarios are part of the Flood Forecasting and Simulation Cascade application, which has been in the meantime expanded beyond the borders of flood prediction into a broader environmental domain.

There are three scenarios, which are in the process of being implemented and deployed in the ADMIRE testbed. These scenarios have been selected from more than a dozen of candidates provided by hydro-meteorological, water management, and pedagogical experts in Slovakia. The main criterion for their selection was their suitability for data mining application. The scenarios are named ORAVA, RADAR, and SVP, and they are in different stages of completion, with ORAVA being the most mature one, and SVP only in the beginning stages of its implementation.

*Figure 1. The target area of the Orava data mining scenario. The blue area in the eastern part is the Orava reservoir. Below it is a much smaller reservoir (Tvrdosin), which may be actually considered part of the Orava reservoir. The red dots in the map are the places where hydrological measurement stations are located, and from which historical observations are available.*

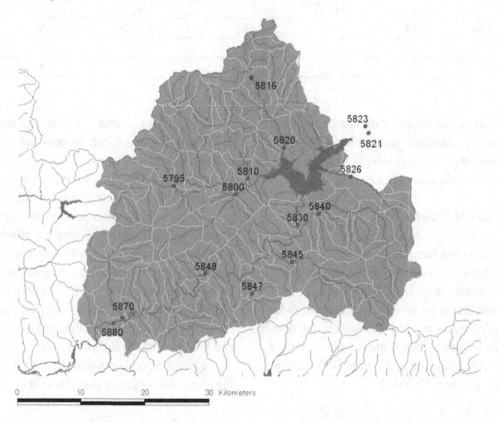

## The ORAVA Scenario

The scenario named ORAVA has been designed by the Hydrological Service division of the Slovak Hydrometeorological Institute, Bratislava, Slovakia. Its goal is to predict the water discharge wave and temperature propagation below the Orava reservoir, one of the largest water reservoirs in Slovakia.

The pilot area covered by the scenario (see Figure 1) lies in the north of Slovakia, and covers a relatively small area, well suitable for the properties of testing ADMIRE technology in a scientifically interesting, but not too difficult setting.

The data, which has been selected for data mining, and which we expect to influence the scenario's target variables – the discharge wave propagation, and temperature propagation in the outflow from the reservoir to river Orava – is depicted in Table 1.

For predictors in this scenario, we have selected rainfall and air temperature, the discharge volume of the Orava reservoir and the temperature of water in the Orava reservoir. Our target variables are the water height and water temperature measured at a hydrological station below the reservoir. As can be seen in Figure 1, the station directly below the reservoir is no.5830, followed by 5848 and 5880.

If we run the data mining process in time T, we can expect to have at hand all data from sensors up to this time (first three data lines in Table 1).

*Table 1. Overview of the main predictors and target variables in the Orava data mining scenario*

| Time | Rainfall | $Temp_{Air}$ | Discharge | $Temp_{Reservoir}$ | $Height_{Station}$ | $Temp_{Station}$ |
|------|----------|--------------|-----------|--------------------|--------------------|------------------|
| T-2 | $R_{T-2}$ | $F_{T-2}$ | $D_{T-2}$ | $E_{T-2}$ | $X_{T-2}$ | $Y_{T-2}$ |
| T-1 | $R_{T-1}$ | $F_{T-1}$ | $D_{T-1}$ | $E_{T-1}$ | $X_{T-1}$ | $Y_{T-1}$ |
| T | R | $F_T$ | $D_T$ | $E_T$ | $X_T$ | $Y_T$ |
| T+1 | $R_{T+1}$ | $F_{T+1}$ | $D_{T+1}$ | | $X_{T+1}$ | $Y_{T+1}$ |
| T+2 | $R_{T+2}$ | $F_{T+2}$ | $D_{T+2}$ | | $X_{T+2}$ | $Y_{T+2}$ |

Future rainfall and temperature can be obtained by running a standard meteorological model. Future discharge of the reservoir is given in the manipulation schedule of the reservoir.

## The RADAR Scenario

This scenario has been designed in cooperation with the Slovak Hydrometeorological Institute. The aim of this scenario is to create a short-term rainfall prediction by mining a database of radar images in connection with historical rainfall data, measured by precipitation measurement station network consisting of more than 600 stations covering the whole Slovakia.

The scenario consists of 2 stages (see Figure 2). In the first stage, we process the raw radar measurements and produce a series of motion vectors for areas with higher water vapor density (meaning higher *potential precipitation*). These motion vectors are then used in a data mining process together with real weather observations made by automated meteorological measurement stations. Since we are able to predict motion vectors for a limited time (up to one hour) into the future, we can thus create a very short-term, but detailed and accurate weather prediction which can help predict local flash floods.

Figure 2 also shows that it is our theory that the prediction of future precipitation motion vec-

*Figure 2. The processing of data in the RADAR scenario is performed in two stages – first we recompute the radar imagery to motion vectors, and then we perform data mining on the motion vectors and the weather data measured by local meteorological measurement stations.*

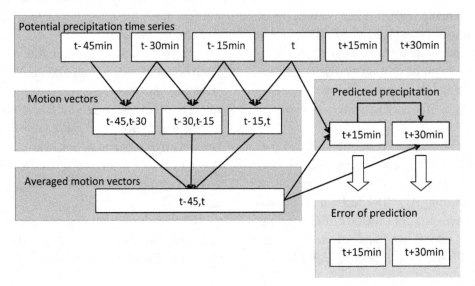

tors can be improved by calculating the error of prediction, and using it in future motion vector generation.

## The SVP Scenario

This scenario, which is still in the design phase, is the most complex of all scenarios expected to be deployed in the context of ADMIRE. It uses the statistical approach to do what the FFSC application did before ADMIRE – predict floods. The reasons why we decided to perform this experiments are mainly the complexity of simulation of floods by physical models when taking into account more of the relevant variables, and the graceful degradation of results of the data mining approach when facing incomplete data – in contrast to the physical modeling approach, which usually cannot be even tried without having all the necessary data.

For predicting floods, we have been equipped with 10 years of historical data from the Vah cascade of waterworks by the Slovak Water Enterprise, 9 years of meteorological data (precipitation, temperature, wind) computed by the ALADIN model at SHMI, hydrological data from the river Vah, again by SHMI, and additionally with measured soil capacity for water retention, courtesy of our partner Institute of Hydrology of the Slovak Academy of Sciences. We base our efforts on the theory, that the amount of precipitation, which actually reaches the river basin and contributes to the water level of the river is influenced by actual precipitation and its short-term history, water retention capacity of the soil, and to lesser extent by the evapo-transpiration effect.

## Integration of Distributed Environmental Data Sources

In this section, we discuss the data integration engine designed for the environmental data integration and mining. It is motivated by the scenarios described in previous section. We first describe

requirements that we took into account and then we present our approach to environmental data integration. In the discussion, we give examples mainly from Orava scenario; the first scenario implemented using our data integration engine.

In Orava river management scenario, the data from three different sources are used. The data are owned and maintained by different organizations. To allow the data mining operations proposed for this scenario, the data from those different sources must be integrated first. Furthermore, the data are kept in different formats. In the case of Orava scenario, two data sets are stored in relational database (waterworks data, water stations measurements) and one is kept in binary files (precipitation data are stored in GRIB files – binary file format for meteorological data). From technical point of view, we must be able to work with the heterogeneous data stored in distributed, autonomous resources. In our work, we have considered so far the data in the form of lists of tuples.

In the following, we use the term data resource to denote a service providing access to data, with a single point of interaction. We use the term processing resource to denote a service capable of performing operations on the input lists of tuples. Data resource can have capabilities of a processing resource.

Atomic units used for data access and transformations are called processing elements (PE), and are actually OGSA-DAI (Antonioletti et al., 2005; Karasavvas et al., 2005) process elements. Following types of processing elements are needed:

- Data retrieval PEs – operations able to retrieve the data from different, heterogeneous data sources. Data retrieval PEs is executed at data resources. This class of PEs is also responsible for transforming raw data sets to the form of tuples.
- Data transfer PE – able to transfer list of tuples between distinct processing resources.
- Data transformation PE – operations that transform input list of tuples. These PEs

can perform data transformation on per tuple basis, or can be used to aggregate tuples in the input lists.

- Data integration PEs – given input lists of tuples, data integration operations combine the tuples from input lists into a coherent form.

An operation has one or more inputs and one or more outputs. Inputs can be either literals or list of tuples and a outputs are list of tuples. Operations can be chained to form a data integration workflow – an oriented graph, where nodes are operations and edges are connection of inputs and outputs of the operations.

The term Application Processing Element (APE) will denote a data integration workflow that can be executed at a single resource. APE is a composition of atomic operations that provides functionality required by a data integration task. For example, in Orava scenario we use the precipitation data from GRIB files. The GRIB reader processing element extracts the data from GRIB files; it has two inputs – the first is a list of GRIB files and the second is a list of indexes in GRIB value arrays. The GRIB reader activity outputs all the values at input indexes from all the input files. We use an operation that queries the GRIB metadata database to determinate GRIB files of interest and another operation that transform given geo-coordinates in WGS84 to the indexes consumed by GRIB reader activity. This small workflow of three operations forms a single APE that provides precipitation data for given time period and geo-coordinates. The idea behind APE is to provide data integration blocks that can be executed at a single processing or data resource and can be reused for in multiple data integration tasks. Similarly to atomic PE, the inputs of APE can be literals or list of tuples and outputs are list of tuples.

The goal of our proposed data integration engine is to provide means of executing data integration tasks that are composed of multiple APEs and can integrate the data from distributed, autonomous and possibly heterogeneous data resources. Our data integration engine is designed to run the data integration tasks, given the input parameters and the APE workflow specification.

APE workflow specification is composed of four components: definition of APEs instances, mapping between inputs and outputs of connected APEs, mapping between the definition of integration task parameters and the parameter inputs of APEs in workflow and the definition of the result output.

In alignment with ADMIRE project vision, the APEs are specified in Data Mining and Integration Language (DMIL) (Atkinson, 2009) that is being developed within the project. The goal of DMIL is to be a canonical representation of data integration process, described in an implementation independent manner. The APE instance is specified by the DMIL description of the process that should be executed, the specification of the data/processing resource it should be executed at and APE instance identifier that is unique within the APE workflow specification. Figure 3 depicts the APEs workflow of the Orava river management scenario.

In our view, the main advantage of proposed data integration engine is that user can specify sub-workflows that are executed on a separate data resources and the engine automatically connects the results of APEs executed on distributed resources. This helps to deal with the complexity of the distributed data integration.

## Preliminary Results

Table 2 shows the details of the data integration process and the inputs of the data mining (model training) in the ORAVA scenario. For this purpose we usually use data for one year.

As we can see the data is sometimes sparse and inputs cannot be used to predict the last value of the water temperature at the hydrological measurement station under the Orava reservoir

*Figure 3. The data integration process of the Orava scenario, which loads historical data from several (organizationally distributed) databases, processes, cleans, repairs the data – acting as part of the CRISP-DM process – and then feeds it into the actual prediction model training.*

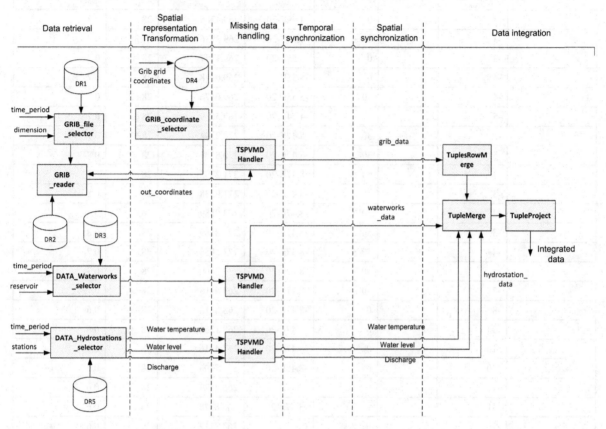

(number 5830 in Figure 1). First we can review the rainfall at the Orava reservoir (*Rainfall_Orava* column). It has been established by consultation that if there is no data recorded, no rainfall was measured, so we can replace the missing values by "0" value (*ReplaceMissingValues* filter). Second problem which we need to deal with is the rainfall measured at the station (*Rainfall_Station* column). Values such as a -1.0E-20 are only noise from the database from which it was retrieved, so we have to add another filter to deal with this noise (*ZeroEpsilon* filter). *ZeroEpsilon* filter converts all values lower than any epsilon value to the "0"value. Also if we compare these three columns: *Air_Temperature_Orava*, *Air_Temperature_Station* and *Water_Temperature_Station* we can see that these three columns doesn't have

the same scale. The *Air_Temperature_Station* column is in Kelvins, but the other two are in degrees of Celsius. So another filter we had to develop in our ORAVA scenario is *Kelvin2Celsius*, which uses a simple mathematical expression to convert Kelvins to degrees Celsius. The final problem we had to solve in our scenario is the missing values in the *Water_Temperature_Orava* column. In this case we can't use simply *ReplaceMissingValues* filter as we don't know which values to put in the table. The measurement of the water temperature in the Orava basin is done only in 24 hours interval (one value a day, as opposed to hourly periodicity for other inputs). If we look at the data in this column, we can see that the value is not changing rapidly in one day interval, because of the significant amount of

*Table 2. Sample of the raw input data of ORAVA scenario*

| Water_temp Orava | Air_temp Orava | Rainfall Orava | Outflow Orava | Rainfall Station | Air_temp Station | Flow Station | Water_temp Station |
|---|---|---|---|---|---|---|---|
| | -3 | | 0 | -4.79E-20 | 269.4385 | 28 | 0.7 |
| | -3 | | 0 | -1.94E-20 | 269.2736 | 27.37 | 0.7 |
| | -3 | | 0 | -5.55E-20 | 269.1447 | 28 | 0.7 |
| | -4 | | 0 | -5.55E-20 | 269.0278 | 28 | 0.7 |
| 1 | -4 | | 30 | -5.55E-20 | 269.0476 | 28.62 | 0.7 |
| | -5 | | 30 | -4.24E-20 | 269.5059 | 28.62 | 0.7 |
| | -5 | | 30 | -8.47E-20 | 270.2394 | 28.62 | 0.7 |
| | -5 | | 30 | -8.47E-20 | 270.8507 | 28 | 0.7 |
| | -3 | | 50 | -8.47E-20 | 271.2792 | 28 | 0.7 |
| | -3 | | 50 | -8.47E-20 | 271.9238 | 28 | 0.8 |
| | -2 | | 50 | -8.47E-20 | 272.0889 | 28.62 | 0.8 |
| | -3 | | 50 | -8.47E-20 | 271.8189 | 28 | 0.8 |
| | -4 | | 50 | -8.47E-20 | 271.2053 | 28 | 0.7 |
| | -5 | | 50 | -8.47E-20 | 270.3569 | 28 | 0.7 |
| | -7 | | 50 | -8.47E-20 | 269.6116 | 28 | 0.7 |
| | -8 | | 0 | -8.47E-20 | 268.8618 | 28 | 0.6 |
| | -9 | | 0 | -8.47E-20 | 268.1252 | 28 | 0.6 |
| | -10 | | 0 | -8.47E-20 | 267.4316 | 28 | 0.6 |
| | -10 | | 0 | -8.47E-20 | 266.7706 | 28 | 0.6 |
| | -11 | | 0 | -8.47E-20 | 266.2573 | 28 | 0.6 |
| | -11 | | 0 | -8.47E-20 | 265.8878 | 28 | 0.6 |
| | -11 | | 0 | 0 | 268.7712 | 29.25 | 0.6 |
| | -11 | | 0 | -4.24E-20 | 268.3068 | 29.25 | 0.7 |
| | -12 | | 0 | -4.24E-20 | 267.8816 | 29.25 | 0.7 |
| | -12 | | 0 | -4.24E-20 | 267.5674 | 28.62 | 0.7 |
| | -13 | | 45 | -8.47E-20 | 267.2082 | 28.62 | 0.7 |
| | -13 | | 45 | -8.47E-20 | 266.7314 | 29.25 | 0.7 |
| | -14 | | 45 | -8.47E-20 | 266.2274 | 29.25 | 0.7 |
| 0,9 | -14 | | 40 | -8.47E-20 | 265.8981 | 29.25 | 0.7 |
| | -15 | | 40 | -8.47E-20 | 266.6896 | 29.25 | 0.7 |
| | -14 | | 40 | -8.47E-20 | 268.0646 | 29.25 | 0.7 |

water in the basin, and its considerable thermal storage capacity, which is only little affected by daily changes in air temperature. So we have decided to use linear interpolation for filling in the missing hourly water temperature values. We have developed new *LinearTrend* filter which replaces missing values from start point to the end point by adding only computed delta following linear function. In Table 3 we can see all the changes made to our integrated data. We have also discovered from the data, that the date and time has no significance to our scenario so we

*Table 3. Sample of the integrated and preprocessed ORAVA scenario data*

| Water_temp Orava | Air_temp Orava | Rainfall Orava | Outflow Orava | Rainfall Station | Air_temp Station | Flow Station | Water_temp Station |
|---|---|---|---|---|---|---|---|
| 1.0 | -3.0 | 0.0 | 0.0 | 0.0 | -2.71152 | 28.0 | 0.7 |
| 1.0 | -3.0 | 0.0 | 0.0 | 0.0 | -2.8764 | 27.37 | 0.7 |
| 1.0 | -3.0 | 0.0 | 0.0 | 0.0 | -3.00535 | 28.0 | 0.7 |
| 1.0 | -4.0 | 0.0 | 0.0 | 0.0 | -3.12223 | 28.0 | 0.7 |
| 1.0 | -4.0 | 0.0 | 30.0 | 0.0 | -3.1024 | 28.62 | 0.7 |
| 0.995833 | -5.0 | 0.0 | 30.0 | 0.0 | -2.64408 | 28.62 | 0.7 |
| 0.991667 | -5.0 | 0.0 | 30.0 | 0.0 | -1.91062 | 28.62 | 0.7 |
| 0.9875 | -5.0 | 0.0 | 30.0 | 0.0 | -1.29926 | 28.0 | 0.7 |
| 0.983333 | -3.0 | 0.0 | 50.0 | 0.0 | -0.87076 | 28.0 | 0.7 |
| 0.979167 | -3.0 | 0.0 | 50.0 | 0.0 | -0.22617 | 28.0 | 0.8 |
| 0.975 | -2.0 | 0.0 | 50.0 | 0.0 | -0.06113 | 28.62 | 0.8 |
| 0.970833 | -3.0 | 0.0 | 50.0 | 0.0 | -0.33115 | 28.0 | 0.8 |
| 0.966667 | -4.0 | 0.0 | 50.0 | 0.0 | -0.94468 | 28.0 | 0.7 |
| 0.9625 | -5.0 | 0.0 | 50.0 | 0.0 | -1.79313 | 28.0 | 0.7 |
| 0.958333 | -7.0 | 0.0 | 50.0 | 0.0 | -2.53837 | 28.0 | 0.7 |
| 0.954167 | -8.0 | 0.0 | 0.0 | 0.0 | -3.2882 | 28.0 | 0.6 |
| 0.95 | -9.0 | 0.0 | 0.0 | 0.0 | -4.0248 | 28.0 | 0.6 |
| 0.945833 | -10.0 | 0.0 | 0.0 | 0.0 | -4.71842 | 28.0 | 0.6 |
| 0.941667 | -10.0 | 0.0 | 0.0 | 0.0 | -5.37943 | 28.0 | 0.6 |
| 0.9375 | -11.0 | 0.0 | 0.0 | 0.0 | -5.89274 | 28.0 | 0.6 |
| 0.933333 | -11.0 | 0.0 | 0.0 | 0.0 | -6.26224 | 28.0 | 0.6 |
| 0.929167 | -11.0 | 0.0 | 0.0 | 0.0 | -3.37876 | 29.25 | 0.6 |
| 0.925 | -11.0 | 0.0 | 0.0 | 0.0 | -3.84318 | 29.25 | 0.7 |
| 0.920833 | -12.0 | 0.0 | 0.0 | 0.0 | -4.26844 | 29.25 | 0.7 |
| 0.916667 | -12.0 | 0.0 | 0.0 | 0.0 | -4.58262 | 28.62 | 0.7 |
| 0.9125 | -13.0 | 0.0 | 45.0 | 0.0 | -4.9418 | 28.62 | 0.7 |
| 0.908333 | -13.0 | 0.0 | 45.0 | 0.0 | -5.41865 | 29.25 | 0.7 |
| 0.904167 | -14.0 | 0.0 | 45.0 | 0.0 | -5.92264 | 29.25 | 0.7 |
| 0.9 | -14.0 | 0.0 | 40.0 | 0.0 | -6.25193 | 29.25 | 0.7 |
| 0.9 | -15.0 | 0.0 | 40.0 | 0.0 | -5.46036 | 29.25 | 0.7 |
| 0.9 | -14.0 | 0.0 | 40.0 | 0.0 | -4.08536 | 29.25 | 0.7 |

have decided to remove these two columns (it was necessary only in the for data integration phase for data values identification).

After this data preparation phase we can approach the data mining phase. From our view the easiest model to use and to fulfill our needs is a linear regression classifier/model. We use our set of 8760 rows to train the model and also to evaluate it using 10-fold cross-validation. The output function we have received from the training is:

*Table 4. Sample of the actual (validation) and predicted data*

| Sample no. | Validation data | Predicted data | Error |
|---|---|---|---|
| 1 | 11.6 | 13.071 | 1.471 |
| 2 | 15.2 | 14.335 | -0.865 |
| 3 | 6.4 | 7.614 | 1.214 |
| 4 | 0.7 | 2.284 | 1.584 |
| 5 | 11.7 | 10.948 | -0.752 |
| 6 | 14.3 | 16.526 | 2.226 |
| 7 | 15.6 | 12.891 | -2.709 |
| 8 | 15.7 | 12.838 | -2.862 |
| 9 | 0.8 | 1.752 | 0.952 |
| 10 | 15.8 | 15.188 | -0.612 |
| 11 | 15.4 | 16.553 | 1.153 |
| 12 | 14.9 | 12.795 | -2.105 |
| 13 | 15.4 | 15.66 | 0.26 |
| 14 | 0.7 | 2.318 | 1.618 |
| 15 | 15 | 12.628 | -2.372 |
| 16 | 14.8 | 16.692 | 1.892 |
| 17 | 10.1 | 8.53 | -1.57 |
| 18 | 7.6 | 8.311 | 0.711 |
| 19 | 12.9 | 13.699 | 0.799 |
| 20 | 10.3 | 7.39 | -2.91 |

*Table 5. Some parameters of the trained data mining model of the ORAVA scenario*

| Correlation coefficient | 0.9639 | |
|---|---|---|
| Class complexity | order 0 | 60957.772 bits | 6.9586 bits/instance |
| Class complexity | scheme | 71405.9701 bits | 8.1514 bits/instance |
| Complexity improvement (Sf) | -10448.1981 bits | -1.1927 bits/instance |
| Mean absolute error | 1.1791 | |
| Root mean squared error | 1.4607 | |
| Relative absolute error | 23.8739% | |
| Root relative squared error | 26.609% | |
| Total Number of Instances | 8760 | |

$Water\_temp_{station}$

$$= 0.6473 \times Water\_temp_{Orava} + 0.0239 \times Air\_temp_{Orava} - 0.0359$$
$$\times Rainfall_{Orava} - 0.0055 \times Outflow_{Orava} - 0.0418 \times Rainfall_{station}$$
$$+ 0.0117 \times Air\_temp_{station} - 0.0503 \times Flow_{station} + 2.4324$$

Table 4 shows an example of a few predicted and actual (validation) values of the model. Table 5 then shows the parameters of the trained model. We can see that the correlation coefficient is high and mean absolute and root mean squared errors are relatively low, so we conclude that our model is well trained for the data we have, and we can use it for predictions.

## CONCLUSION

In this chapter, we have presented preliminary results of our ongoing work on the data integration engine for environmental data that is being developed in the scope of ADMIRE project. We have first described four scenarios dealing with the integration and mining of environmental data. The main challenge is that the environmental data required by scenarios are maintained and provided by different organizations and are often in different formats. Our work concentrated on providing a platform that would allow integration of data from distributed, heterogeneous resources. Our results allow users to construct reusable application processing elements specified in DMIL (Atkinson, 2009) (language for data mining and integration, which is being designed within the project) and the engine executes them transparently on distributed data resources.

The data mining process has several inputs, which are used as the model's predictors. Among them is the accumulated rainfall over the target area, the air temperature in the target area (one or more spatially differentiated time series may be used, depending on availability), the discharge of the principal up-stream water reservoir, and the temperature of the water in the reservoir. Historical data is used for training of the model; data from physical weather modeling is then used to obtain the predicted water level and water temperature at the target point in the river.

The date and time columns have been removed in this sample for the sake of readability of the actual data.

## ACKNOWLEDGMENTS

This work is supported by projects ADMIRE FP7-215024, APVV DO7RP-0006-08, DMM VMSP-P-0048-09, RECLER ITMS: 26240220029, SMART ITMS: 26240120005, SMART II ITMS: 26240120029, VEGA No. 2/0211/09.

## REFERENCES

ADMIRE. (n.d.). *EU FP7 ICT project: Advanced Data Mining and Integration Research for Europe (ADMIRE), 2008-2011. Grant agreement no. 215024.* Retrieved November 2009, from http://www.admire-project.eu

ANFAS. (n.d.). *EU FP5 IST RTD project: datA fusioN for Flood Analysis and decision Support (2000-03).* IST-1999-11676.

Antonioletti, M., Atkinson, M. P., Baxter, R., Borley, A., Chue Hong, N. P., & Collins, B. (2005). The Design and Implementation of Grid Database Services in OGSA-DAI. *Concurrency and Computation, 17*(2/4), 357–376. doi:10.1002/cpe.939

Atkinson, M., et al. (n.d.). ADMIRE White Paper. *Motivation, Strategy, Overview and Impact, 9.*

CROSSGRID. (n.d.). *EU FP5 IST RTD project: Development of Grid Environment for Interactive Applications (2002-05) IST-2001-32243.* Retrieved April 2009, from http://www.eu-crossgrid.org

Directive 2007/2/EC of the European Parliament and of the Council of (2007, March). *Establishing an Infrastructure for Spatial Information in the European Community (INSPIRE).* Retrieved from January 2010, from http://eurlex.europa.eu/JOHtml.do? uri=OJ:L:2007:108:SOM:EN:HTML

*Finite Element Surface Water Modeling System (FESWMS)* (n.d.). Retrieved November 2009, from http://smig.usgs.gov/SMIC/ modelpages/feswms.html

K-Wf Grid. (n.d.). *EU FP6 RTD IST project: Knowledge-based Workow System for Grid Applications (2004-2007) FP6-511385*. Retrieved August 2008, from http://www.kwfgrid.eu

Karasavvas, K., Antonioletti, M., Atkinson, M. P., Chue Hong, N. P., Sugden, T., Hume, A. C., et al. (2005). *Introduction to OGSA-DAI Services* (LNCS 3458, pp. 1-12). ISBN 978-3-540-25810-0

*MEDIGRID. (n.d.)*. EU FP6 RTD Sust.Dev. project: Mediterranean Grid of Multi-Risk Data and Models (2004-2006) GOCE-CT-2003-004044, call FP6-2003-Global-2.

*This work was previously published in International Journal of Distributed Systems and Technologies, Volume 1, Issue 4, edited by Nik Bessis, pp. 1-13, copyright 2010 by IGI Publishing (an imprint of IGI Global).*

# Chapter 19

# Collaborative e-Learning and ICT Tools to Develop SME Managers:
## An Italian Case

**Genoveffa (Jeni) Giambona**
*University of Reading, UK*

**David W. Birchall**
*University of Reading, UK*

## ABSTRACT

*Small and medium-sized enterprises (SMEs) create a dynamic and successful European economy. Existing skill deficiencies in sales, management and administrative staff are adversely affecting competitiveness in almost a third of those small firms surveyed (Bolden, 2001, 2007). Additionally, attending face-to-face and classroom-based development courses is problematic for time-poor SME managers. Thanks to the development of new technologies online learning is becoming commonplace due to wireless and mobile devices, together with the Internet boom, are providing the infrastructure necessary to support the development of new learning forms. Collaborative learning, especially as represented by an action learning approach, would seem ideal for SME managers. But can collaborative learning be adopted as a blanket approach in the case of SME managers? Or should one first take into account the contextual influences on learning, networking and collaboration?*

## BACKGROUND

Small and medium-sized enterprises (SMEs) have a vital role in creating a dynamic and successful European economy. However, faced with the ever-increasing and overwhelming legislative,

political and competitive demands, SMEs have to respond by accelerating their rate of learning and adaptability to equip them to compete in the digital economy. Research shows that involvement in competence development activities has a positive effect on individual SMEs' competitiveness and performance (Observatory of European

DOI: 10.4018/978-1-4666-0906-8.ch019

SMEs, 2003). Research has also identified that existing skill deficiencies in sales, management and administrative staff were adversely affective competitiveness in almost a third of those small firms surveyed (Bolden, 2007, 2001). Moreover, research by Smallbone (1998) and Smallbone and Rogut (2005) reported that increasing competition and internalisation of markets are major concerns for small businesses, especially those in the new EU member states. Indeed, the factors believed to be the most important for the future survival and growth of the firm are still the capabilities and skills of the owner in adapting the organisation to change. Hence attention should be directed towards helping these companies survive and find new ways to innovate and deal with change (Bolden, 2007). Attending face-to-face and classroom-based development courses is nevertheless problematic for time-poor SME managers. However, thanks to the rapid development of new technologies online learning is becoming more and more commonplace. Indeed, wireless and mobile devices, together with the booming of the Internet, are providing the infrastructure necessary to support the development of new learning forms.

Life in the real world implies constant interacting and networking with other people and it is hard to deny that there is a social dimension to learning as well (Vygotsky, 1978; Lave & Wenger, 1991). For many SME managers there is a clear argument for membership of an inter-organisational learning community (possibly described as a group or team) for several compelling reasons. First, many SME organisations do not have more than one general manager and the only option available to individual managers to gain the preferred level of socialisation in the learning process is to look outside the organisation. SME managers, as indicated earlier, tend to be focused on immediate problem solving, so it is often essential to extend their perspectives on issues confronting them and to have their assumptions challenged by outsider views. Since their statements and actions are open to immediate interpretation and could provoke

reactions in ways which would limit the opportunities for learning, managers may not feel able to expose either their full thinking to a small group within their own organisation or ideas whilst at a formative stage (Birchall & Giambona, 2007).

Hence, collaborative learning, especially as represented by an action learning approach where real-life business challenges are discussed and experiences shared, would seem ideal for SME managers. In particular, it is widely assumed that:

1. Action learning sets are particularly useful for chief executives in small companies faced with complex policy decisions;

2. Executives find it difficult to discuss the situation, float ideas and seek feedback within their own organisation;

3. Executives want their actions to be based on objective thinking which has been submitted to the scrutiny of an informed peer group;

4. Executives need to know that all the feasible options have been generated and evaluated.

The bottom line of all this seems to be that other executives operating at a similar level must have found themselves in similar situations and will be useful advisers, consultants and confidants. Hence, networks will be very useful and a collaborative approach will aid the learning process.

But is this really true? Can collaborative learning be adopted as a blanket approach in the case of SME managers? Or should we first take into account what the contextual influences on learning, networking and collaboration are?

In this chapter the authors will first of all focus on collaborative and networked learning and its benefits as seen for SME managers. Then, the outcomes of two focus groups held in Italy with SME managers, intermediaries and providers of e-learning will be presented. The Italian focus groups were part of the research carried out for ADAPT, a pan-European EU-funded project led by Henley Management College which is seeking to refine e-learning principles and how they should be adapted to different contexts and cultures. The role of context in e-learning programme delivery will also be analysed. The chapter will end with a series of conclusions, recommendations and implications for further research.

This chapter fits in very well with the mission of the Journal as it deals with the integration of theory and practice in applied technologies for SME management development.

## COLLABORATIVE LEARNING: WHAT IS IT?

Learning within a team has a long tradition in the UK. Experiential team learning may be seen as having its origins in the work of Bion with returning POWs in the 1940s and later at the *Tavistock Institute of Human Relations* (Bion, 1968). Outdoor education based on teamwork had its UK origins with the establishment of the Outward Bound School in North Wales to prepare naval cadets for the rigours of wartime service (Walsh & Golins, 1976). The syndicate method for management development was pioneered at the then Administrative Staff College at Henley using group-based learning as the vehicle, not only for mastery of subject matter, but also experimentation with management behaviours (Rapaport et al., 2001). Much of this early work was focused on behavioural change, building on self-awareness resulting from peer feedback. The process was normally supported by an expert facilitator (Bolden, 2001). The experience was intended as transformational and as preparation for coping with new challenges and experiences in the workplace. These experiences were believed important in the development of management capability. The term 'Action Learning' was coined by Revans in the 1960s (Revans, 1983) to describe a process whereby managers developed through working in teams to tackle real organisational problems, seeking both new knowledge and insights on an 'as needed' basis rather than as

a prescribed curriculum devised by the teacher. It took the management development process from the classroom and back to the workplace (Pedler et al., 2005).

*Collaborative learning*, as a term, has its origins in software systems to support collaborative work. It has subsequently been described as: '*a particularly important kind of social activity, the collaborative construction of new problem solving knowledge. Collaboration is a process by which individuals negotiate and share meanings relevant to the problem-solving task at hand.... Collaboration is a coordinated, synchronous activity that is the result of a continued attempt to construct and maintain a shared conception of a problem*' (Dillenbourg, 1996).

An important distinction between earlier team-based approaches and collaborative e-learning is the use of Computer Mediated Communications (CMC) technology to support interaction. But the adoption of CMC for delivery, in itself, does not automatically lead to collaborative learning. Group learning can also take the rather different form of *cooperative learning* which is seen as the division of a task between a group of learners with each responsible for a portion of the total activity rather than mutual engagement in joint problem solving (Dillinbourg, 1996).

The potential application of CMC systems designed for workflow management for educational provision was soon recognised. 'The loneliness of the long distance learner' was seen as being overcome if computer mediated communication enabled the learner to establish relationships with peers and then to keep in touch. Workflow systems, such as Lotus Notes, could become the backbone of the learning process by utilising the workflow process tools to form Learner Management Systems. Access to programmed materials and information resources could provide the knowledge base for learners. However, much early development of applications appears to have been driven more by technical specialists than pedagogic experts and was focused on acquiring and testing of knowledge rather than the 'deeper' learning that could result from team-based, experiential learning.

Exceptions to this are evident, however, for example, networked learning. Here the emphasis has been less on the transfer of prescribed knowledge from the teacher to the learner and more on self-directed learning within a team with members having a degree of collective responsibility for the learning of other team members (Hodgson & Watland, 2004). They define networked management learning as 'learning by managers that is supported by ICT used to connect learners with, in particular, other people (learners, teachers/tutors, mentors, librarians, technical assistants, etc.) as well as to learning resources and information of various kinds and types...... It is based on a social constructionist view that assumes that learning emerges from relational dialogue with and/or through others in learning communities..... the processes involved in collaborative/ networked learning as joining a knowledge community and becoming able to converse in the language of that community.' They further quote Leidner and Jarvenpaa (1995) – 'In the domain of business education, decision-making skills including analytical and problem-solving skills and communication skill are seen as critical. We might therefore speculate that methods requiring interaction and student involvement would be preferred over traditional methods. Thus, the informating up or transforming with the corresponding collaborative or constructivist models might be ways to improve the quality of business education. In contrast, co-operative learning may well support a transmission or instructionalist paradigm (Hodgson & Watland, 2004) rather than an emphasis on the social dimensions of cognition (Arbaugh & Benbunan-Fich, 2006).

So what then are the underlying assumptions about learning within a team? They include:

1. The challenge from peers leads to a deeper understanding and learning as a result of the articulation of ideas and their scrutiny and testing. This fits with the notion of the resolution of socio-cognitive conflict and appropriation (Dillingbourg, 1996)

2. Experienced managers have considerable tacit knowledge which, if explicated, can contribute to the learning of others (Moon et al., 2005)

3. The sharing of experiences by peers can provide a broader context for the learner in which to embed the topic or theme and as a result increase the connectivity to the 'real world' and through establishing relevance, subsequent application and embedding of the learning. (based on principles applying to Revans' action learning; Revans, 1982)

4. Learners will be willing to step outside their comfort zone and experiment with new behaviours in a 'safe' environment (Moon et al., 2005)

5. Peers will offer support and motivation thereby increasing the likelihood of learner engagement in the learning process.

6. Working within an 'engaged' team can lead to the generation of new insights and ideas and on to new knowledge development.

7. Peers, by giving a broader perspective on the learner's issues and challenges being faced, can assist in developing a more strategic perspective for the learner.

8. Members develop skills in presenting ideas and concepts, advocacy, challenge, criticising constructively and also coping personally with criticism.

9. Generally the 'bar is raised' for learners and all are challenged to develop their understanding to a higher plane than if each worked in isolation with the knowledge base.

10. Immersion in the process leads to rich learning.

Moving on from the underlying assumptions about the impact of team-based learning, there are further assumptions about the conditions required to provide the experience and engage the learner: -

1. A shared task owned by the team members with agreement covering expectations for the outputs
2. Processes and methods of working will be the subject of a 'psychological' contract agreed amongst members and important in trust development (8).
3. Teams will be self-regulating
4. Evaluation of the performance of the learners will be based on an assessment of the group's outputs
5. There will be diversity of background in the team's composition such that there will be challenge of ideas and differences in insights.
6. There will be facilitation of the process in order to encourage reflection on team performance and learning as well as regular reviews of the psychological contract.
7. Where the task is to be undertaken in a virtual environment the technology infrastructure will be 'fit of purpose' and will support the preferred working styles of members

Learning in a virtual environment can have side-benefits for participants who shouldn't be either overlooked or under-estimated. As work in organisations becomes more and more 'virtual', competency in virtual working has greater significance for individuals. More over, leadership competence in these environments is becoming essential for managers. New insights about self-awareness and the behaviours of others can result from the learning process if this aspect is built into the regular review of learning. The various elements in the group problem-solving process were well articulated by McGrath and Hollinshead (1994). From their model one would suggest that certain tasks are more difficult to achieve virtually than others (resolving conflicts of interest or of power). Mastery in the more complex areas is desirable to the prospective virtual team leader and, if not mastery, recognition that means other than virtual working are necessary to achieve the desired outcomes in relation to these aspects of teamwork.

So how is the effectiveness of collaborative learning evaluated? On programmes of study with a formal examination procedure, achievement of learner outcomes is often assumed to be an indication of the efficacy of the approach. This appears often to be based on a test of knowledge acquired in the case of a formal written examination or of task achievement e.g. a group report providing a 'solution' to a case exercise along with the analysis. But in the case of experiential learning, as pointed out earlier, the objective is greater personal insight and if appropriate behaviour modification as a result. Both are areas which present difficulty to evaluators. In the case of manager development it might be argued that the ultimate test is whether or not the individual is a more effective manager in the workplace as a result of the intervention. The embedding of learning into managerial behaviours can be tested (Kirwan & Birchall, 2006) but approaches are not without criticism. Much evaluation has to take into consideration the practicality and costs of data collection, as well and the reliability of the data in enhancing understanding of the mechanisms at play in determining the performance change.

Prior research leaves many issues in relation to collaborative learning identified but unresolved (Hodgson & Watland, 2004). The authors suggest that a useful starting point in improving our understanding of the nature and impact of collaborative learning is the definition and validation of design principles as the basis of ensuring sound and appropriate pedagogic design. Making design assumptions explicit and mapping their application can then form the basis for subsequent evaluation with the aim of explaining the mechanisms at work i.e. what works, in what circumstances and how.

## RESEARCH METHODOLOGY

Based on the 'systematic review' approach advocated among others by Pawson (2006), the first step involved in the research was a review and analysis of the summative evaluation of EnSEL, a pan-European e-learning programme based on virtual action learning delivered, among other countries, in Italy as well. Also, available documents, like for example minutes of Steering Committee Meetings, were examined. The purpose of the review was to identify what, according to the final evaluation study, were the areas that affected collaborative e-learning.

However, the summative evaluation study presented a pooling of outcomes which were not tailored to the single countries taking part in the programme but were recommendations applying to all the countries participating in the programme.

As our aim was to see 'what works, for whom and in what circumstances' (Pawson, 2006; Pawson & Tilley, 1997) we tested the set of principles in two focus groups with Italian representatives of SMEs, intermediaries and providers in order to find out whether theory, i.e. the theory according to the meta-analytic approach as represented in the evaluation study, corresponded to the reality of whether SME managers in Italy really think they benefit from a collaborative learning approach and whether they agreed that the areas identified in the evaluation study really are the ones which can 'make or break' a collaborative e-learning programme.

## FOCUS GROUPS OUTCOMES

### Purpose of the Focus Groups

The aim of the Focus Groups was to inform and consult with SMEs, trainers, intermediaries and providers in order to understand how e-learning deliveries do not necessarily fit all needs. A further aim was to understand how e-learning

programmes can be adapted to meet specific SME needs. The participants in the focus groups were 11 in total and they represented a cross-section of SMEs, trainers and providers. The meetings were facilitated under the guidance of an experienced EU-accredited facilitator

First of all, all participants started a discussion on issues concerning e-learning in their specific work environment, talking also about the challenges they faced and the opportunities they were given.

After discussing their specific issues, each Group was asked to comment on the outcomes, as captured on clipboards, of the other Group's discussion. At the end of the workshop, both Groups convened again in a plenary so that overall conclusions could be drawn.

### Plenary

The plenary discussion started around the following question: 'What does e-learning mean to you? What differences are there in terms of our understanding of the term?' There was agreement on the fact that e-learning is a 'tool embedded in a context'—that is to say, specific forms of e-learning vary depending on the context of delivery. All participants agreed also on the fact that, as one of them put it, 'the focal point must be users and their specific needs. So users must be provided with the right methodologies which can allow them to get what they need.' Hence, the impossibility, according to the participants, of giving a single definition of what e-learning is. Moreover, e-learning was seen as a means of social learning which, as one participant pointed out, 'must also take into account the cultural diversity of SMEs.' Hence, dialogue and communication during the learning process was seen as paramount.

The discussion also led to an analysis of how collaborative e-learning programmes really are and of how true the belief that e-learning is cheaper that traditional delivery. One of the providers attending the focus groups suggested that 'a collaborative approach makes costs soar... e-learning is cheaper only when it replicates the top-down and transmissive approach of traditional learning.' Recognition of resource constraints of course, impacts on the view of e-learning as social learning.

Possibly, because of the assumption that e-learning is more effective when it is approached as a means of social learning, participants also questioned the effectiveness of e-learning as a standalone means of delivery – it was felt that face-to-face sessions, which allow users to establish a personal relationship, are necessary.

## Discussions of Group 1

As mentioned earlier, this group discussed the following specific issues relating to e-learning:

- Learner engagement;
- Real-life situations and authentic activities;
- The use of stories.

The discussion started around the issue of collaborative learning and *learner engagement*. It is always a challenge for training providers to attract and engage SME managers in training and development programmes. Of course, the engagement of learners is closely linked to their motivation and, as a participant stressed:

*Strong motivation is needed which, in the case of the SMEs I'm involved in, is strongly contextualised. And when I talk about context, I specifically refer to the single business' context and culture, not even the sector, but the single SME: its history, management, internal equilibrium, territory, relationship with the unions. So when we go and design an e-learning course, all these things must be taken into account to tailor a programme which responds to the client's specific needs.*

It seems clear that a tailored course which targets the specific needs of the group and which bears in mind the specific contextual factors as specified above has more chance of motivating and keeping learners engaged. In other words, the perceived value of the course must be as clear as possible to the SME managers 'attending' it. This is more important than any types of methodological approach.

Moreover, participants seemed to agree that face-to-face sessions are important to create a climate of trust and a higher emotional involvement. Thanks to these pre-conditions, managers might feel more motivated and see the value of the learning journey to their business and also open up more easily to 'learning in a team'.

The issue of *real-life business situations and authentic activities* is closely linked to the first two and all participants agreed that it is indeed very important in terms of motivation and perceived value. As mentioned, SMEs want to see a practical and immediate return on business when they invest time and money in learning activities; also, they want to have a clear understanding of what the value of the development initiative is. The link between real-life situations, motivation, engagement and perceived value seems well-reflected in what a provider said: 'We attract managers by offering... things that are perceived as being necessary to their job.' However, real-life situations can make it easier to transfer the knowledge gained to the business. Moreover, when sharing real challenges in a learning group, the other members of the group can realise that they might have the same problems and that there is a gap they need to address. It follows that e-learning initiatives should also provide applied knowledge relevant to real-life business experiences and present authentic information.

The *use of stories* is linked to that of real-life situations: it is quite evident that stories can play a vital role in working on real-life situations and, hence, in aiding sharing and collaboration. In the words of a participant, 'a simple story can convey a complex idea by actively involving listeners in co-creating that idea.'

Participants also agreed that 'case studies are sometimes impersonal' while personal stories are much more effective in relating a case and in getting people involved and motivated. Stories were seen as an excellent vehicle for learning as they are more interesting than more traditional, drier forms of communication. They were also seen as memorable messages which tend to stick with the listener and get passed on from team to team down the years.

Moreover, the incentive of using stories might be seen in their potential to offer the possibility of getting real solutions to real problems.

## The Second Group's Discussion

They discussed the following specific issues relating to e-learning:

- Role of the facilitator;
- Blended approach;
- Creating and sustaining networks.

The *role of the facilitator* was indeed seen as quite important especially when talking about e-learning as a form of social and collaborative learning, participants thought of the role of the facilitator as crucial... So facilitators could create a relationship with the target audience even before the design of the course has started.

As one participant summed up:

*Facilitators must be good active listeners. Also, they must change an environment characterised by a fear of sharing information. Managers must realise that sharing information can have advantages, that being in a network can be important to the business. In other words, sharing ideas and information can lead to positive results for the business.*

Another participant made a distinction:

*If we are talking about a collaborative model, the role of the facilitator is strategic, in the sense that it is the facilitator that 'guides' the process and checks on timings, rhythm and keeps the social interaction alive. If, on the contrary, we are talking about a more 'transmissive' model, the facilitator has just a marginal role.*

So it seems that the role of the facilitator is linked to the learning model. But it seemed clear from the discussion that managers in Italy are believed not ready for a collaborative approach to e-learning for two reasons: firstly, in Italy managers are less inclined to share information as they think that by giving up what they know they also give up competitive advantage; second, there is a cultural factor as well, already as children, from primary school, people are not used to learning in a collaborative way.

One of the participants pointed out that:

*At school, the layout of the classroom itself tells you that it is not made for collaborative learning. It is made for a top-down approach: there is a teacher who talks and who is the repository of knowledge and there is somebody who listens in a more or less reactive or productive way; the concept is always that something is being transmitted.*

Facilitators could 'educate' managers to the advantages of a more collaborative approach to learning. However, one participant stressed that 'we should wonder whether managers and leaders [in Italy] are more suitable to a top-down approach... although I don't think that managers are naturally inclined towards social processes, I still think that the role of the facilitator is important [in making them more so].'

The issue of *blended learning* was definitely linked to previous discussions about e-learning as social learning and learning as social interaction. It was recognised that nowadays blended learning is the most widespread approach to e-learning delivery. Then, it was stressed that:

*When SMEs are involved, it is difficult not to include some bits of traditional educational approaches which take place in the classroom... there must be a form of physical presence because I think it gives learning a more immediate emotional effect. Face-to-face gives the chance to clarify situations that are almost impossible to solve through technology alone.*

Going back to the e-learning as a social learning issue, it was pointed out that only face-to-face encounters give the chance to learners to express themselves emotionally, something which our knowledgeable informants saw as vital to the learning process, especially in a collaborative context. In the words of one participant:

*Face-to-face sessions are invaluable in collaborative learning because they help create trust, and without trust nothing can really be achieved online. I think that we cannot have online collaborative learning that doesn't include some face-to-face sessions: it is thanks to face-to-face that we can create a collaborative environment that can then be continued in the online part of the course. When communicating online, we don't have a coffee break: indeed, it is during these informal chats that we often find solutions to a lot of issues.*

However, it was also pointed out that one of the historical issues with SME managers is lack of time so that spending many days in a classroom is not feasible for them. There was hence agreement on the fact that blended learning is important because SME managers and leaders still want to do part of the learning journey online because it is any time, any place: face-to-face sessions are important to create a climate of trust and a higher emotional involvement. Thanks to these pre-conditions, managers might then feel more motivated and see more the value of the learning journey to their business. So, it is good to start with

face-to-face to then move online where, possibly, the exchange of experiences will become easier.

One participant effectively summed up the common agreement that *'We talk about face-to-face, online and self-directed learning. We must realise that each of these contributes in its on way to the learning experience. Being able to 'blend' the different environments is what makes blended learning effective.'*

The issue of *creating and sustaining networks* was seen as directly linked to the social and collaborative aspects of learning and e-learning in particular. Networks were seen as potential 'learning hubs', hence their importance: *'A community that can work together and that is still there after a few years and that, in inverted commas, has a life of its own, is the result of a successful learning journey.'* However, there was common agreement on the fact that creating and sustaining them is extremely difficult, especially in the context of Italian SME managers as it would be difficult for them to understand the advantages of being part of a network made up of peers with whom to share information. This is well summed up by the following statement: *'we must not forget that managers might not want to be "collaborative" because they often think that owning information, and not sharing it, is strategically important. Persuading them that the opposite is true is very difficult.'*

It was recognised that *'the concept of "community" is a very difficult one in any case as 'it implies an idea of a non-hierarchical society, of a society which is "networked"... a society which doesn't reflect the one we live in... the concept of "communities" seems to imply a process of spontaneous aggregation and, as all spontaneous aggregations, it is difficult to manage or govern.'*

Communities are the result of a learning process, of a series of steps. Clearly there cannot be a community without a good facilitator, a collaborative process and various technologies that are targeted to different needs.

## CONCLUSIONS

From the focus group discussions, the main points identified by SMEs operating in the Italy are outlined below. These can be used to inform future training providers of SMEs on how to address these specific e-learning needs.

It was clear that for our Italian knowledgeable informants e-learning has a value if approached as a means of social learning. This socio-cultural approach must also take into account the cultural diversity of SMEs, where by cultural diversity the specific organisational culture is meant.

The major points which came out of the focus groups seem to be the following:

- Make sure that engagement is achieved by making it immediately clear what the value of the course is to the business. No one denies that doing online activities are convenient, interesting and that it fits in with a lack of time at work. However, the truth is that most of these courses are never finished. So, the question is: what gives the feeling that we are not doing something which is as important and as useful as learning in the classroom? So the users' perceived value is very important. Perhaps one of the answers could be shared responsibility: learners and teacher should work out together a teaching and learning process so that there can be shared understanding. The learning process should be shared and agreed upon by all those involved in the process – only in this way can the real needs of the target audience be met and possibly learner's engagement achieved;
- Pay attention to the learning environment, which should be interactive and easy to use. However, the online platform and the technological tools used need to be tailored to the target audience. Italian SME managers do not seem to think that 'flashy' technology is that important. Even when the activities are the most technologically advanced, the real point to bear in mind is how much value-added they carry in the eyes of the users;
- Both collaborative tools and dialogue are fundamental in the learning process.
- Social interaction was seen as vital in the learning process as it allows learners a shared understanding of the knowledge necessary to develop collaborative learning.
- The importance of the role of the facilitator in the e-learning process was agreed upon by everyone, especially when we are talking about group learning and the facilitation of a more collaborative approach.
- The context where the learning process takes place has the utmost importance: forgetting the context and using a 'one-size-fits-all' approach will almost certainly lead to the failure of the e-learning programme. Context is an important variable in every learning process, but often this variable is forgotten. This is the reason why sometimes there is the risk of using an approach which is not appropriate to the specific context and, hence, ineffective. A needs analysis exercise could be carried out by facilitators even before the course is designed. The latter could then work on the planning of the course, especially from a pedagogical perspective, so that it is properly directed to the target audience.

However, the main thing which seemed to come out of the focus groups is that Italian SME managers do not seem to be ready, as yet, for a collaborative, action learning approach where the individual's business problems and knowledge are shared with the other members of the learning group. The sentence 'knowledge equals competitive advantage' was often used during the discussion, implying that giving out knowledge to other members of a learning group seems very improbable as far as Italian managers are concerned.

It seems that Italian SMEs must first be educated to the advantages of a collaborative approach to learning. To this end, it seems important that the design of each project should not forget to allow time to build relationships because we know that trust is an important variable that makes collaboration possible. Also, learning and the retention of what is learnt happen more easily when social relationships are established among the learners. So, every learning course should include these types of spaces/activities. However, all this should happen in a simple, intuitive way. Social interaction makes the construction of knowledge possible.

The role of the facilitator and that of critical reflection are seen as important, especially in educating Italian SME managers to e-learning programmes which are less transmissive and more collaborative. Also, facilitators can allow learners to analyse, reshape and systematically 'position' what has been learnt.

We feel that the above conclusions and recommendations are important points to bear in mind when dealing with the integration of theory and practice in applied technologies for SME management and leadership development.

## ACKNOWLEDGMENT

The authors would like to thank the ADAPT partners for their contributions to the project that prompted this chapter.

## REFERENCES

Arbaugh, J. B., & Benbunan-Fich, R. (2006). An Investigation of Epistemological and Social Dimensions of Teaching in Online Learning Environment. *Academy of Management Learning & Education*, 5(4), 435–447.

Bion, W. R. (1968). *Experiences in groups*. London: Tavistock.

Birchall, D. W., & Giambona, G. (2007). SME manager development in virtual learning communities and the role of trust: A conceptual study. *Human Resource Development International*, 10(2), 187–202. doi:10.1080/13678860701347164

Bolden, R. (2001). *Leadership Development in Small and Medium Sized Enterprises: Final Report (Tech. Rep.)*. Mardon Hill, UK: University of Exeter, Centre for Leadership Studies.

Bolden, R. (2007). Leadership development in SMEs: designing a customised solution. *GITAM Journal of Management*, 5(3), 40–53.

Dillenbourg, P. (1996). What do you mean by "collaborative learning"? In Dillenbourg, P. (Ed.), *Collaborative learning: Cognitive and computational approaches*. Amsterdam, The Netherlands: Pergamon.

Hodgson, V., & Watland, P. (2004). Researching Networked Management Learning. *Management Learning*, 35(2), 99–116. doi:10.1177/1350507604043027

Kirwan, C., & Birchall, D. (2006). Transfer of learning from management development programmes: testing the Holton model. *International Journal of Training and Development*, 10(4), 252–268.

Lave, J., & Wenger, E. (1991). *Situated Learning: Legitimate Peripheral Participation*. New York: Cambridge University Press.

Leidner, D., & Jarvenpaa, S. E. (1995). The Use of Information Technology to Enhance Management School Education: A Theoretical View. *Management Information Systems Quarterly*, 19(2), 13–25.

McGrath, J. E., & Hollingshead, A. B. (1994). *Groups Interacting with Technology*. Thousand Oaks, CA: Sage.

Moon, S., Birchall, D., Williams, S., & Vrasidas, C. (2005). Developing design principles for an e-learning programme for SME managers to support accelerated learning at the workplace. *Journal of Workplace Learning, 17*(5-6), 370–375. doi:10.1108/13665620510606788

Observatory of European SMEs. (2003). *Competence Development in SMEs* (Tech. Rep. No. 1).

Pawson, R. (2006). *Evidence-Based Policy: A Realist Perspective*. London: Sage.

Pawson, R., & Tilley, N. (1997). *Realistic Evaluation*. New York: Sage.

Pedler, M., Burgoyne, J. G., & Brooks, C. (2005). What has Action Learning learned to become? *Action Learning Research and Practice, 2*(1), 49–68.

Rapaport, R. N., Life, E. A., & Brodie, M. B. (2001). *Mid-Career Development: Research Perspectives on a Developmental Community for Senior Administrators*. London: Routledge.

Revans, R. (1983). *A. B. C. of Action Learning*. London: Lemos & Crane.

Revans, R. W. (1982). *The Origins and Growth of Action Learning*. Bromley, UK: Chartwell-Bratt.

Smallbone, D. (1998). Internationalisation of markets and SME development: Some results from an international comparative study. *Economics and Organisations, 1*(6), 13–25.

Smallbone, D., & Rogut, A. (2005). The challenge facing SMEs in the EU's new member states. *The International Entrepreneurship and Management Journal, 1*(2), 219–240. doi:10.1007/s11365-005-1130-x

Vygotsky, L. S. (1978). *Mind in Society: The Development of Higher Psychological Processes*. Cambridge, MA: Harvard University Press.

Walsh, V., & Golins, G. L. (1976). *The exploration of the Outward Bound process*. Denver, CO: Colorado Outward Bound School.

*This work was previously published in International Journal of Distributed Systems and Technologies, Volume 1, Issue 3, edited by Nik Bessis, pp. 71-82, copyright 2010 by IGI Publishing (an imprint of IGI Global).*

# Chapter 20
# Sketch Based Video Annotation and Organization System in Distributed Teaching Environment

**Jia Chen**
*Chinese Academy of Sciences & the Graduate University of Chinese Academy of Sciences, China*

**Cui-xia Ma**
*Chinese Academy of Sciences, China*

**Hong-an Wang**
*Chinese Academy of Sciences, China*

**Hai-yan Yang**
*Chinese Academy of Sciences and the Graduate University of Chinese Academy of Sciences, China*

**Dong-xing Teng**
*Chinese Academy of Sciences, China*

## ABSTRACT

*As the use of instructional video is becoming a key component of e-learning, there is an increasing need for a distributed system which supports collaborative video annotation and organization. In this chapter, the authors construct a distributed environment on the top of NaradaBrokering to support collaborative operations on video material when users are located in different places. The concept of video annotation is enriched, making it a powerful media to improve the instructional video organizing and viewing. With panorama based and interpolation based methods, all related users can annotate or organize videos simultaneously. With these annotations, a video organization structure is consequently built through linking them with other video clips or annotations. Finally, an informal user study was conducted and result shows that this system improves the efficiency of video organizing and viewing and enhances user's participating into the design process with good user experience.*

DOI: 10.4018/978-1-4666-0906-8.ch020

## INTRODUCTION

Video materials have already been widely used in teaching environment and playing an active role in delivering lecture information to learners. However, most of the existing video delivery systems generally aim to improve the process of teacher's one-way information delivery to the learners but fail to support interactive participation of both teacher and students. Thanks to the continuous increase of network brand width, this situation may be changed by applying a distributed architecture which provides an environment in which the teachers and students can comment and manipulate video materials simultaneously.

To construct a good performance video system, exploring what the teachers and students want for such system is a great help. For teachers, authoring video materials is always a time-consuming work, especially for those who have not professional computer skills, mastering the professional authoring tools such as Adobe Premiere is still a challenging task. The professional software generally provides a series of video authoring functions such as fade in/out video effect or video transitions, however, these functions may not meet the special education needs in class. In general, an ideal video system in teachers' expectation should be: (1) Easy to make comments on video materials (2) Easy to change video play sequence. For students, they are more interested in how to express their opinions or their attitude on the video. Generally, they want a video system in which they can freely add annotations and share them with their classmates and teachers. And after class when they want to trace back what they annotated in class, the system should easily locate that position.

Our system aims to provide (1) A distributed architecture which support collaborative operations in different geological locations(2) An interactive environment provided to teachers with the ability of organizing video clips effectively and conveniently; (3) A method enabling teachers to impose extra information into the video content freely; (4) An interactive communication mode between teachers and students during teaching process which support group's collaborative work on the video materials. In this chapter, we present a distributed architecture and a sketch based interface for facilitating the interactively instructional video organizing and viewing with integrating sketching annotations into video clips. Sketching annotation are collaboratively added into video clips based on different video-related context, such as panorama or situation of video objects, which addresses the needs of teachers and students who teach or learn better through natural and flexible interactive methods. Our system is mainly used in the following application scenarios:

- Collaborative video annotation. Teachers and students collaboratively add annotation in the video and by exchanging their annotation they can have an experience similar to the classic classroom discussions
- Organizing archived video. Teachers apply our system to prepare for their lecture materials
- Dynamic modification of the viewing sequence of organized video clips. As the lecture delivery is an interactive process which may vary a lot according to different feedback from students.

## RELATED WORK

There has been a lot of research work related with video organizing and viewing. Zhang (2002) proposed a hierarchy structure and a process scheme for organizing video data to facilitate the indexing. Zhu (2004) introduced InsightVideo, a video analysis and retrieval system, which joined video content hierarchy, hierarchical browsing and retrieval for efficient video access (Zhu, 2004). In order to improve the efficiency and interaction of the traditional video viewing process, a number of projects related to interactive video have been provided. Since early development of hypertext systems, videos have been taken as part of hypertext research in projects such as Aspen Movie Map described by Lippman (1980). And Sawhney (1997) introduced a generic framework to structure and dynamically present a new form of video- and text-based media called hypervideo. Shipman (2008) proposed a hypervideo system called Hyper-Hitchcock, which dealt with so-called detail-on-demand video, namely only one link at any given time. All the projects above focus on the linkability of video clips, but concern little about providing an efficient and intuitive way to build these links.

Distributed teaching system has been a research hotspot for years. Simon (2003) constructs a distributed architecture and used a Tablet PC-based presentation system in an undergraduate computer architecture class. Bouras (2001) explores e-learning based on a multi-user distributed virtual reality environment. This system extends virtual reality project with distributed features and allows students and staff to meet in social shared spaces and engage in on-line real-time seminars and tutorials. And most of the existing video annotation or organization systems work independently and have no information exchange with other end machines. VideoAnnEx (Lin, 2003), a system developed by IBM in order to assists authors in the task of annotating video sequences with MPEG-7 metadata. VideoAnnEx segment video sequence input into smaller units called video shots. Each shot in the video sequence can be annotated with static scene descriptions, key object descriptions, event descriptions, and other lexicon sets (Smith, 2001). The annotated descriptions are associated with each video shot and stored as MPEG-7 descriptions in an output XML file. VideoAnnEx can also open MPEG-7 files in order to display the annotations for the corresponding video sequence (Adams, 2002). The difference between VideoAnnEx and our system lies on that VideoAnnEx is a stand alone video annotation

system using MPEG-7 metadata framework, while our system is a distributed collaborative video annotation system with a series of sketch based methods to insert annotations into video material as additional information. Another related work is Microsoft's MRAS system which aims to support annotation of multimedia content about a lecture asynchronously. A user can share a lecture along with the comments with other students or teachers. Users add their own annotations and upload them to the annotation server. The MRAS system focuses on users' asynchronous on-demand training, not like live synchronous online discussing and annotation in our system. Classroom 2000 project captures much of the rich interaction during a typical university lecture including all aspects of a lecture in classroom—audio, video, blackboards, etc. All activities are captured and recorded with timestamps, later students can access the 'lecture' by replaying the recorded video, audio and slides etc. iVas system can associate archived digital video clips with various text annotations and impression annotations using the client server architecture, The system analyzes video content to acquire cut/shot information and color histograms. Then it automatically generates a web document that allows the users to edit the annotations. It's also a stand alone system. SMAT system is a collaborative annotation system which allows users to collaboratively add annotation to multimedia contents such as archived video clips using text, whiteboard. eSports (Zhai, 2005) design a collaborative and synchronous video annotation platform which is used in Internet scale cross-platform grid computing environment. The platform facilitates computer supported cooperative work in distance sport coaching and other education settings. eSports allows collaboratively annotating not only archived video clips but also live video capture. Our system provides not only video annotation methods but also ways to organize the structure of videos which determines the sequence of video playing.

*Figure 1. System architecture*

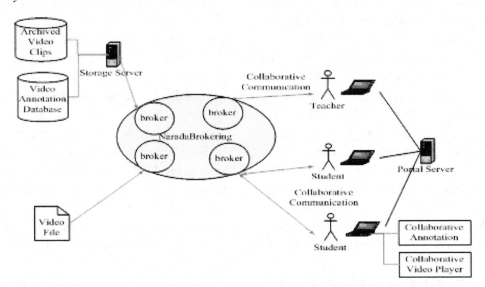

## Overview of Sketch Based Distributed Collaborative Design

To make our system easy to extend, we apply a component based design on the top of Narada Brokering. Figure 1 shows the architecture of our system. Our system takes video files as input and save them into the storage server, and in the process of upload, the system does some preprocessing work such as video analysis as well to speed up the following operations. Data stored in storage server includes archived video files, video annotation database and video structure database. Every annotation and video structure generated by user input will be stored in these databases. Portal server serves to facilitate the collaborative work of both teachers and students.

User roles in our system include teacher and student. The teacher role's main operation is video organization, video playing and video annotation. The role of student has a lower authority than teacher. a student can play videos and make annotations on them but is not permitted to organize video structures.

## Sketch-Based Collaborative Video Annotation

In general, *video annotations* are input through assigning different forms of captioning or keywords to a digital video (Qi, 2007). The purpose of existing video annotation systems is mostly for better indexing and faster searching. Therefore, a typical video annotation system always tries to make the form of annotations as simple as possible.

We extend the concept of video annotation which leads to acting as the index of video content and imposing extra information into the video to facilitate learners' understanding. Video annotation can be any form of sketch drawing, such like text, graphics, or symbol, etc. Furthermore, these sketching annotations can be linked with other video clips or video annotations to implement the creation of hypervideo. In Figure 2, a typical user interface for sketching video annotations is shown.

To achieve the video annotations, we provide two methods in the chapter. One is panorama-based annotation making, in which sketching annotation is inputted based on video-related context, such as the beginning and ending frames of it. The other is interpolation based annotation

*Figure 2. Typical interface for sketching video annotations, Sketching annotations are listed on the right column*

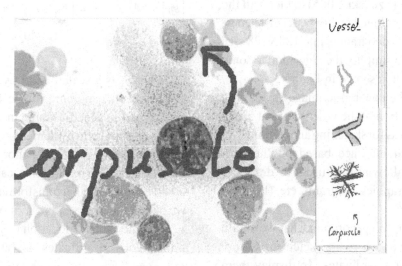

which needs some human input to determine the trajectory of annotations. The mixture of these two methods meets the needs from all kinds of video and experiments have proven that it may greatly improve authoring efficiency.

## Panorama-Based Annotation

Most of existing video applications provide users an access to video content through video timeline, and in order to change video content, video authors have to spend a lot of time editing all related frames. To avoid the time-consuming work, we proposed a novel panorama-based annotation method based on computer vision and sketch-based interface technology.

First, before generating a video panoramic image, we use a similar method as described in (Sawhney, 1997) to evaluate a video shot whether or not suitable to be the source of a video panoramic image taking into account factors such as field of view, color and image quality. Then with the images taken from the shot, we implement the SIFT feature extraction method (Lowe, 2004) to match

*Figure 3. Generating panoramic image*

**(a)9ᵗʰframe(b)55ᵗʰframe(c)80ᵗʰframe(d)90ᵗʰframe**

**(e) panorama result image**

successive frame images and feature-based image stitching method (Szeliski, 2005) to blend all the video frame images together. For better efficiency, we resample the video frames into 128X128 size images in order to simplify the algorithm to some degree. The result is shown in Figure 3.

We can use the panoramic image as not only a good interpretation of the video shot but also a background canvas for sketching annotations. We provide a sketch interface based on the panoramic image, allowing the users to draw explanatory text, graphics, diagrams, etc, (Figure 3 a).

Using sketches on panorama, what we obtain is just the positions where the sketch strokes are on the panoramic coordinates. To display them correctly on corresponding video frames, we still need to get the geometrical relationship between specific frame's local coordinates and the panoramic global coordinates. During the process of generating panorama, we apply *affined projection* to represent the relationship between video frames and panoramic images, namely

$$\begin{pmatrix} sx \\ sy \\ s \end{pmatrix} = A \begin{pmatrix} x' \\ y' \\ 1 \end{pmatrix}, A = \begin{pmatrix} h_{11} & h_{12} & h_{13} \\ h_{21} & h_{22} & h_{23} \\ h_{31} & h_{32} & 1 \end{pmatrix}$$

Where s is a scalar, and (x,y) is the position of a pixel in panorama image I, (x', y') is its counterpart in specific frame image I', and hij is a homography matrix elements which have been calculated in the stage of panorama generation. Projecting sketch onto frames can be taken as an inverse process of that transformation. Therefore, we obtain the inverse matrix of A, denoted as A':

And the sketch's location (x',y') in a specific frame's local coordinates can be obtained as:

$$A' = \begin{pmatrix} h'_{11} & h'_{12} & h'_{13} \\ h'_{21} & h'_{22} & h'_{23} \\ h'_{31} & h'_{32} & h'_{33} \end{pmatrix}$$

*Figure 4. Sketching annotations on Panoramic image and its playing*

**(a) Sketching annotation on panoramic image**

**(b) Comparison between original frame and annotated frame**

**(c) The annotation moves along with the video object's movement**

$$\begin{pmatrix} x^{'} \\ y^{'} \\ 1 \end{pmatrix} = A^{'} \begin{pmatrix} sx \\ sy \\ s \end{pmatrix}$$

Figure 4 compares the original frame images with result images which clearly show that while user draw a sketching annotation only once on the panorama, the method can correctly project it to proper frames and on proper positions.

## Collaborative Interpolation-Based Active Annotation

Not all video shots can generate a panoramic image, and we need a supplement for panorama based method. For those videos which fail to generate panoramic images, we propose an interpolation-based method receiving user input to determine the sketch's trajectory and interpolating the path to make the annotations' movement smooth.

For example, if user points out the location of sketch on ith and jth frame (i<j), then for mth frame where i<m<j. we can use linear interpolation to obtain the location of sketch on mth frame as:

$$x_m = x_i + \frac{(x_j - x_i) \times (m - i)}{j - i}$$
$$y_m = y_i + \frac{(y_j - y_i) \times (m - i)}{j - i}$$

Figure 5 shows the real trajectory of video object and the interpolated trajectory of active annotation. Due to the linear interpolation we applied on the annotation, it may be not accurately in accordance to the video object's real moving trajectory. We have considered applying more complicated interpolation to fit the trajectory of annotation. However, as the linear interpolation is good enough for education purpose use and the more complicated interpolation will need more user input, we choose linear interpolation in the end. And the later user study shows the usage of the video annotation is not affected by the inaccuracy of its trajectory.

Some example results are shown in Figure 5, although it need more user input, interpolation based method can achieve an effect as good as panorama based method and it can be applied to a wider range of videos.

## Collaborative Sketch Interaction Event

The message event, which supports collaborative work, is implemented by extending the client end protocal. Figure 6 shows the XML description of sketch event. User C sends sketch message to User A and B, and the message contains the sketch's current position and time information.

*Figure 5. The real trajectory of video object and the interpolated trajectory of active annotation*

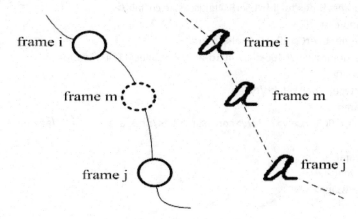

*Figure 6. Example results of interpolation based annotations*

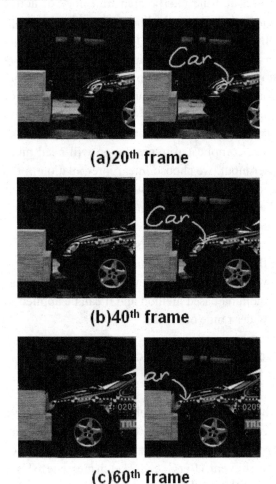

**(a)20ᵗʰ frame**

**(b)40ᵗʰ frame**

**(c)60ᵗʰ frame**

To avoid call blocking which may occur in the client end, multi process and message callback is adopted in this chapter. First, we implement the user interface and message transmission with different process so that the process of sending/receiving message and user interface will not interrupt each other. When receiving iq information section which need callback, the system ensure the operation's fluency by Windows message response methods. As shown in Figure 7, the user's operation has to go through the stages of generation, transmission, collision detection, collision deliver/receive, execution.

As both the transmission and execution of user operations are time consuming tasks, we apply multi-process handling method to separate interface processing, data transmission from operation execution to ensure the fluency of interface handling.

As shown in Figure 8, remote site directly sends data to data execution process after receiving operation command, and then the data execution process will modify the original digital ink document. The entire process of operation handling has no interruption with the user interface process, and the user interface process will reflect the change of current document when it is rendered next time.

*Figure 7. XML description of sketch event*

```
<message from='initiator@10.0.0.4/iel' to='userA@10.0.0.4/iel' type='normal'>
<addresses xmlns='http://iel.iscas.ac.cn/protocol/address'>
<address type='to' jid='UserA@iel.iscas.ac.cn/lab' />
<address type='to' jid='UserB@iel.iscas.ac.cn/lab'/>
</addresses>
<UserId>UserC@10.0.0.4/iel</UserId>
<SessionId>3587b40c-dea7-401d-a5c7-536b4ec4f184</SessionId>
<Event>
   <type>NewSketch</type>
<params>
    <x>965</x><y>732</y><pressure>3.2</pressure><angle></angle><time></time>
</params>
</Event>
</message>
```

*Figure 8. Process of operation handling*

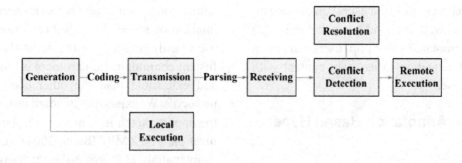

## CONTENT ORIENTED COLLABORATIVE VIDEO ORGANIZATION

### Direct Manipulation of Sketch Annotation

*Direct manipulation* involves continuous representation of objects of interest, and rapid, incremental actions and feedback (Beaudouin-Lafon, 2000). What the teachers really care about when applying videos is how to arrange video contents and how to integrate them together instead of but not how to switch from different complicated window or master powerful rendering tools. In the chapter, we attempt to build an environment in which users can intuitively manipulate both video node and video connections. Our efforts to achieve this goal include:

1.  A totally manipulation on video clips allowing users to drag-and-drop, create, modify and delete the video clips.
2.  Manipulation on video links which allow users to change the directions of links.
3.  An informal ink-based interface to provide users flexibility of making the video structure in any form as they want according to their own teaching styles and preferences.

### Representation of Video Clip and Its Sketching Annotation

Abstract of a video clip is usually described using a static thumbnail image or a short playback. We proposed a novel sketching annotation based representation, and every video clip is represented by a video node which is surrounded by a series of annotations arranged according to the sequence of their occurrence (Figure 9). The benefit lies

*Figure 9. Operation handling mode*

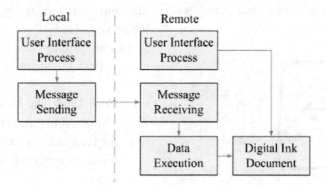

in: (1) As every annotation in the chapter stands for a video content unit, the users can operate on video clips as well as on video content units; (2) For a well annotated video clip, users can get an overall understanding to its main content with only a glimpse.

## Sketching Annotation Based Hyper Video

*Hypervideo*, as a kind of interactive video, contains embedded user clickable anchors allowing navigation between video and other hypermedia element (Sawhney, 1997). In the chapter we link sketching annotation with each other to implement the hypervideo interactively without data copying or any change in the original video file, as shown in Figure 10. By linking annotations and video clips together, we obtain a video structure as shown in Figure 10 d and convert the video from a linear medium into a non-linear one.

## Sketching Event Based Communication and Collaboration Model

In order to keep the sketching annotation in different end machines in accordance, our system should support instant communication, multipoint communication, asynchronous calls and decentration.

*Figure 10. Representation of video node and its sketching annotations*

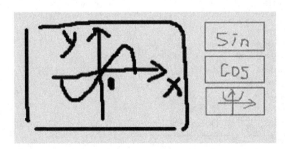

In the collaborative video annotation and organization system, there is a strict need for communication speed. And a fast response can make users easily get access to the status of other users. Instant communication protocol is more flexible and extensible than the other communication protocols. We extend the standard instant protocol to support sketch information's instant communication. The XMPP (Saint, 2004) we use in our chapter apply TCP protocol in the transport layer, and XML presentation mode in the presentation layer. Through deploying communication server, the system can ensure that different sites' effective connection. Every session of XMPP begins with <stream>,and during the session XMPP can send three types of information: *Presence*, which is used to represent users' status (online, busy et al); *Message*, which issued to transmit common information that needs not feedback of receiving end; *User information quest*, which need feedback from receiving end.

In our system, every user operation will be broadcast to the other users in the same work space, there the low level communication system need to transfer the local message to other site, which needs a one-to-many communication support. This chapter extends the server end to multi-point broadcast user message to other users. Figure 11 shows an example of XML description of multi-point communication. From the figure, we can see that through adding add addresses information section into the message, the system can realize multi point broadcasting at one time, without the need to send the same information to different users repeatedly, which greatly relieve the server's load.

In our system, there are two communication modes: Push mode and Answer mode.

- *Push Mode:* the local site actively send information to other sites if there is no needs for feedback. In most instances, data transmissions apply this kind of communication mode

*Figure 11. Links between annotations and video clips*

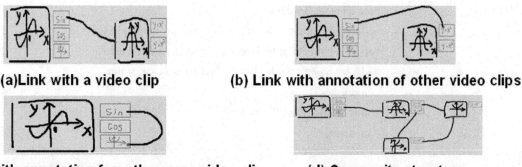

**(a)Link with a video clip**     **(b) Link with annotation of other video clips**

**(c) Link with annotation from the same video clip**     **(d) Composite structure**

- *Answer Mode:* the local site send request to other sites and the other sites return feedback. As there are some other tasks for the system to deal with, we adopt Asynchronous Call way to transform data. In this mode, the calling party goes on to process other tasks without waiting for called party's feedback, until the call returns.

In the traditional Client / Server architecture, all the interaction operations must be processed in the server side. This classic mode is stable however leads to lack of flexibility (For example, in order to share a document, the system has to upload it to the work space server) and hard to extend or deploy. Taking into account the distributed nature of distance learning system, decentration in a proper degree (For example, user's personal information is saved in the local machine) can greatly relieve the load of server.

In the collaborative environment, data sharing between different users are implemented through distributed methods. When user initiates a session, the successive participants will receive the initiator's data information, and then process following interactions. Decentration can offer users ability to edit documents in the off-line status while the traditional methods need the users keep on line all the time. This mechanism supports both synchronous and asynchronous operations, while avoiding extra data server.

## IMPLEMENTATION AND USER STUDY

We implement the system according to the methods described above, and the system user interface consists of a video organization designer and a video player. Figure 12 shows the interface of video organization designer. This designer is used by teachers to arrange a series of geography class videos. The top left view is video organization view and the top right view is video files list in which video files are represented by annotations. The bottom left view is a player for video preview and bottom right one is for panorama based annotating.

Figure 13 is the main interface of video player which consists of a video playing view, a video structure display and a sketch notepad which can be applied similar as a whiteboard.

An informal user study was conducted to test the usability of the system. 12 participants were invited to operate the system, including 8 females and 4 males with the age between 18 and 30, and observation was drawn during the process (Figure 14). Their feedback was as below:

*About Sketching Annotation:* the video sketching annotation tool is easy to use and panorama

*Figure 12. XML description example of multi point broadcasting*

```
<message to='10.0.0.4'>
<addresses xmlns='http://iel.iscas.ac.cn/protocol/address'>
<address type='to' jid=' UserA@iel.iscas.ac.cn /Work' />
<address type='cc' jid=' UserB@iel.iscas.ac.cn /Home' />
</addresses>
<body>Hello, world!</body>
</message>
```

*Figure 13. Screenshot of video organization designer*

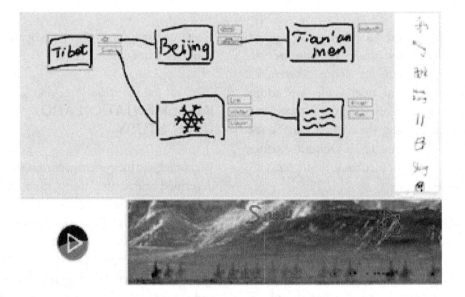

*Figure 14. Screenshot of video player*

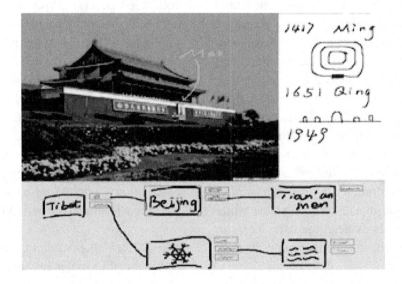

based and interpolation based methods can meet the needs of different video materials and different use purposes. Participants claim that with the system they gain a better understanding of the lecture structure especially when the video materials have relationship between each other.

*About Sketching Annotation Based Video Organization:* The video organization designer provides an easy way to arrange video content which is hard to achieve using traditional systems. Participants reflect that they were deeply impressed that with the system it takes them no more than ten minutes to prepare a standard 45-minute class.

*About Collaborative Annotation:* Participant claims that the system has a good performance that it can give real time feedback for user's operation command. And the collaborative work on video data greatly improves their communication efficiency.

## CONCLUSION

This chapter presents a distributed video annotation and organization system in which teachers and students can collaboratively edit sketch annotations, organize video clips, and exchange video comments. The main contributions of our system are: First, we provide a sketch based interface which supports synchronous collaborative video annotation. Second, the video annotation can be played back synchronously with the original stream, and the annotations can be taken as assistant tool for discussion between teachers and students. Third, it supports fast collaborative video organization and different users can work collaboratively to change the video playing sequence. Fourth, we proposed a novel method to organize video content using sketching annotation which can greatly improve instructors' efficiency and flexibility in video organization. And the panorama-based and interpolation-based active

annotation making make it possible to impose active additional information into video frames, which can be a powerful supplement to the video content. We apply sketch-based interface in the whole application to enhance the communication between instructors and learners. An informal user study proved that our system can be well accepted by teachers and students.

Possible future directions may be to attempt to apply multi-modal interaction technologies such as voice recognition, gesture recognition to improve interactivity. And it may be helpful to combine it with network based video delivery system which support online learning and have more target audience.

## ACKNOWLEDGMENT

This work was supported by National Key Basic Research and Development Program under Grant No. 2006CB303105 and by National Natural Science Foundation of China under GrantNo.60703079.

## REFERENCES

Abowd, G. D. (1999). Classroom 2000: An Experiment with the Instrumentation of a Living Educational Environment. *IBM Systems Journal, 38*(4), 508–530. doi:10.1147/sj.384.0508

Abowd, G. D., Gauger, M., & Lachenmann, A. (2003). The Family Video Archive: an annotation and browsing environment for home movies. In *Proceedings of the 5th ACM SIGMM Intl Workshop on Multimedia Information Retrieval* (pp. 1-8).

Adams, W. H., Lin, C. Y., Iyengar, G., Tseng, B. L., & Smith, J. R. (2002). *IBM Multimodal Annotation Tool. IBM Alphaworks*. IBM.

Bargeron, D., Gupta, A., Grudin, J., & Sanocki, E. (1999). Annotations for Streaming Video on the Web: System Design and usage studies. In *Proceedings of the ACM 8th Conference on World Wide Web.*

Bargeron, D., Gupta, A., Grudin, J., Sanocki, E., & Li, F. (2001). Asynchronous Collaboration Around Multimedia and its Application to On-Demand Training. In *Proceedings of the 34th Hawaii International Conference on System Sciences (HICSS-34).*

Beaudouin-Lafon, M. (2000). Instrumental Interaction: An interaction model for designing post-WIMP user interfaces. In *Proceedings of the ACM Conference on Human Factors in Computing Systems* (pp. 446-453). New York: ACM Press.

Bouras, C., & Philopoulos, A. (1998). Distributed virtual reality environments over web for distance education. In *Proceedings of EDEN Conference* (pp. 481-484).

Bouras, C., Philopoulos, A., & Tsiatsos, T. (2001). e-Learning through Distributed Virtual Environments. *Journal of Network and Computer Applications.*

Lin, C. Y., Tseng, B. L., & Smith, J. R. (2003). VideoAnnEx: IBM MPEG-7 Annotation Tool for Multimedia Indexing and Concept Learning. In *Proceedings of the IEEE Intl. Conf. on Multimedia and Expo (ICME)*, Baltimore.

Lippman, A. (1980). Movie-maps: An application of the optical videodisc to computer graphics. In *Proceedings of the ACM SIGGRAPH Computer Graphics* (pp. 32-42).

Liu, F., Hu, Y., & Gleicher, M. L. (2008). Discovering panoramas in web videos. In *Proceeding of the 16th ACM international Conference on Multimedia* (pp. 329-338). New York: ACM.

Liu, Y. J., Ma, C. X., & Zhang, D. L. (2009). *EasyToy: A Plush Toy Design System Using Editable Sketching Curves.* IEEE Computer Graphics and Applications.

Lowe, D. G. (2004). Distinctive Image Features from Scale-Invariant Keypoints. *International Journal of Computer Vision, 60*(2), 91–110. doi:10.1023/B:VISI.0000029664.99615.94

Qi, G., Hua, X., Rui, Y., Tang, J., Mei, T., & Zhang, H. (2007). Correlative multi-label video annotation. In *Proceedings of the 15th international Conference on Multimedia.*

Saint-Andre, P. (2004). *Extensible Messaging and Presence Protocol (XMPP): Core. RFC 3920.*

Sawhney, N., Balcom, D., & Smith, I. (1997). Authoring and Navigating Video in Space and Time. In *Proceedings of IEEE MultiMedia* (pp. 30-39).

Shipman, F., Girgensohn, A., & Wilcox, L. (2008). Authoring, viewing, and generating hypervideo: An overview of Hyper-Hitchcock. In *Proceedings of the ACM Trans. Multimedia Comput. Commun. Applications* (Vol. 5, No. 2, pp. 1-19).

Simon, B., Anderson, R., & Wolfman, S. (2003). Activating computer architecture with Classroom Presenter. In *Proceedings of the WCAE 2003.*

Smith, J. R., Srinivasan, S., Amir, A., Basu, S., Iyengar, G., Lin, C. Y., et al. (2001). Intergrating Features, Models, and Semantics for TREC Video Retrieval. In *Proceedings of the NIST TREC-10 Text Retrieval Conference.*

Steves, M. P., Ranganathan, M., & Morse, E. L. (n.d.). SMAT: Synchronous Multimedia and Annotation Tool. In *Proceedings of the International Conference on System Science.*

Szeliski, R. (2005). *Image alignment and stitching: A tutorial* (Tech. Rep. No. MSR-TR-2004-92). Microsoft Research.

Xia, S., Sun, D., Sun, C., Chen, D., & Shen, H. F. (2004). Leveraging single-user applications for multi-user collaboration: the coword approach. In *Proceedings of the 2004 ACM conference on Computer supported cooperative work.*

Zhang, D., Zhou, L., Briggs, R. O., & Nunamaker, J. F. (2006). Instructional video in e-learning: assessing the impact of interactive video on learning effectiveness. *Information & Management*, 15–27. doi:10.1016/j.im.2005.01.004

Zhang, Y. J., & Lu, H. B. (2002). A hierarchical organization scheme for video data. *Pattern Recognition*, 2381–2387. doi:10.1016/S0031-3203(01)00189-3

Zhu, X., Elmagarmid, A. K., Xue, X., Wu, L., & Catlin, A. (2004). *InsightVide: Towards Hierarchical Video Content Organization for Efficient Browsing, Summarization, and Retrieval*. IEEE Trans. Multimedia.

*This work was previously published in International Journal of Distributed Systems and Technologies, Volume 1, Issue 4, edited by Nik Bessis, pp. 27-41, copyright 2010 by IGI Publishing (an imprint of IGI Global).*

# Chapter 21
# OBIRE:
## Ontology Based Bibliographic Information Retrieval in P2P Networks

**Xiangyu Liu**
*Brunel University, UK*

**Maozhen Li**
*Brunel University, UK*

**Yang Liu**
*Brunel University, UK*

**Man Qi**
*Canterbury Christ Church University, UK*

## ABSTRACT

*It has been widely recognized that bibliographic information plays an increasingly important role for scientific research. Peer-to-peer (P2P) networks provide an effective environment for people belonging to a community to share various resources on the Internet. This chapter presents OBIRE, an ontology based P2P network for bibliographic information retrieval. For a user query, OBIRE computes the degree of matches to indicate the similarity of a published record to the query. When searching for information, users can incorporate their domain knowledge into their queries which guides OBIRE to discover the bibliographic records that are of most interest of users. In addition, fuzzy logic based user recommendations are used to compute the trustiness of a set of keywords used by a bibliographic record which assists users in selecting bibliographic records. OBIRE is evaluated from the aspects of precision and recall, and experimental results show the effectiveness of OBIRE in bibliographic information retrieval.*

## INTRODUCTION

The past few years have witnessed a rapid development of peer-to-peer (P2P) networks for users belonging to a community to share various resources over the Internet (Milojicic et al., 2002). P2P networks usually organize peer nodes in a decentralized way to enhance reliability in resource sharing. Resources can be arbitrarily distributed into peer nodes without a structure, or they can be distributed following certain structures such as

DOI: 10.4018/978-1-4666-0906-8.ch021

Distributed Hash Tables (DHTs). DHT based P2P networks such as Chord (Stoica et al., 2002), Pastry (Rowstron & Druschel, 2001), CAN (Ratnasamy et al., 2001) have shown enhanced scalability in routing lookup messages for locating resources with a guaranteed number of hops.

It has been widely recognized by the research community that bibliographic information plays an increasingly important role for scientific research. The salient features of P2P networks make them a good candidate for scalable and reliable bibliographic information sharing wherein peer researchers can effectively exchange bibliographic information to promote research. However, two challenging issues have to be deal with when applying P2P technologies for bibliographic information retrieval – the support of range queries and the integration of peer expertise knowledge in queries.

Although DHT structured P2P networks can achieve high scalability in routing lookup messages, they only support exact matches of resources using single hash keys. Based on DHTs, some works are available that support range queries in P2P networks. For example, SWORD (Oppenheimer et al., 2004) supports multi-attribute range queries to locate suitable peer nodes. In SWORD, each DHT is used to manage a resource attribute. A query is routed by identifying its preferred attribute and using the corresponding DHT. Similarly, Building on Chord, MAAN (Cai et al., 2004) also uses multiple DHTs to manage range queries. Mercury (Bharambe, Agrawal, & Seshan, 2004) is another example that supports range queries over multi-attributes. Like SWORD and MAAN, Mercury maintains a separate logical overlay for each attribute albeit it does not employ DHTs. Maintaining a DHT or logical overlay for each resource attribute involves updating each of them when a resource advertisement is received. As the number of attributes of resources increases, the update traffic would also increase heavily.

On the other hand, when searching for bibliographic information in a P2P network, users would expect to receive a list of bibliographic records that maximally satisfies their requirements. To meet this end, the expert knowledge of users in a particular research domain needs to be reflected in a P2P network guiding the system to retrieval the information that is most relevant to a user query. With the development of Semantic Web (Berners-Lee, Hendler, & Lassila, 2001), ontologies have been widely used for knowledge representation. Knowledge related to a research domain can be represented in the form of ontologies which can be considered as global ontologies. The expert knowledge of users can be considered as user ontologies. It is still a challenging task for P2P networks to automatically merge global ontologies with user ontologies so that users can be maximally satisfied when searching for bibliographic information (Kalfoglou & Schorlemmer, 2003).

This chapter presents OBIRE, an ontology based P2P network for bibliographic information retrieval. A novelty of OBIRE lies in its capability to merge global ontologies with user ontologies to maximally satisfy users in their queries. OBIRE supports three types of matches – keyword exact matches, matches with semantics, and matches with merged ontologies. In addition, fuzzy logic based user recommendations are used to compute the trustiness of a set of keywords used by a publication which assists users in selecting bibliographic records. Experimental results show the performance of OBIRE in bibliographic information retrieval from the aspects of the three types of matches it supports.

The remainder of the chapter is organized as follows: we present OBIRE with a focus on matchmaking of bibliographic records, ontology merging, and fuzzy logic based user recommendations. Next, the chapter evaluates the performance of OBIRE. After that, we discuss some related work from the aspects of bibliographic information retrieval and ontology merging. Finally, we conclude the chapter and point out some future work.

*Figure 1. OBIRE components*

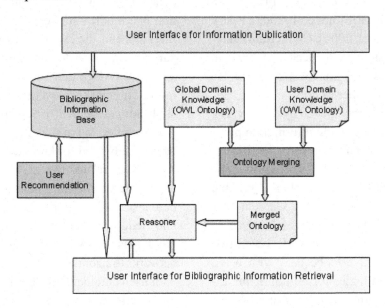

## OBIRE

OBIRE adopts a super-peer structure to manage peers that can be further grouped based on their research interests. Figure 1 shows the components of OBIRE. Peers publish bibliographic records to a bibliographic information base (BIB). Each super-peer nodes manages one BIB and super-peers exchanges bibliographic records periodically. For a research domain, OBIRE maintains an ontology representing global domain knowledge. When searching for bibliographic information, peers can incorporate their domain knowledge in the form of ontologies to the system to guide OBIRE to discover bibliographic records that are most relevant. This is achieved by using the ontology merging component to merge two ontologies which represent global domain knowledge and user domain knowledge respectively. OWL (Web Ontology Language, http://www.w3.org/TR/owl-features) is used for ontology definitions.

For a user query, OBIRE matches the keywords used in the query with the keywords used by published bibliographic records. OBIRE supports three query matching modes - keyword exact matching, semantic matching, and matching with merged ontologies. For semantic matching, OBIRE uses its reasoner to infer the semantic distance between a user query keyword ($K_q$) and a keyword of a publication ($K_p$) based on the OWL ontology definition which represents global domain knowledge. A degree of match (to be presented) is computed which reflects the semantic distance between $K_q$ and $K_p$. For matching with merged ontology, a match degree of $K_q$ to $K_p$ is computed based on an OWL ontology which is merged from the OWL ontology for global domain knowledge and an OWL ontology for user domain knowledge. For a user query, OBIRE returns a list of bibliographic records of which each comes with a degree of match to the query. In addition, the user recommendation component of OBIRE computes the trustiness of the keywords associated with a bibliographic record based on user feedback. The OBIRE prototype is implemented with Java programming language, and the Jena Ontology API (http://jena.sourceforge.net/ontology) is used to implement the reasoner component. Figure 2 shows a snapshot of OBIRE.

*Figure 2. A snapshot of OBIRE*

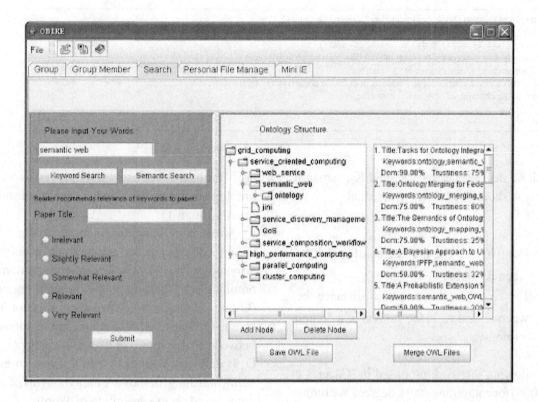

## Degree of Match

The degree of match between a user query keyword $(K_q)$ and a keyword of a publication $(K_p)$ represents the semantic distance of the two in the context of an ontology definition. We define the following semantic relationships between $K_q$ and $K_p$ based on the work proposed by Paolucci et al. (2002):

- *exact* match, $K_q$ and $K_p$ are equivalent or $K_p$ is a subclass of $K_p$.
- *plug-in* match, $K_p$ subsumes $K_q$.
- *subsume* match, $K_q$ subsumes $K_p$.
- *nomatch*, no subsumption between $K_q$ and $K_p$.

For each match, a numerical degree is computed so that the semantic relationship between $K_q$ and $K_p$ can be quantified. Tsetsos et al. (2006) use fuzzy sets theory to evaluate service matchmaking. The relationships between the properties of advertised services and the properties of service queries are mapped to fuzzy linguistic variables, e.g., *exact* is mapped to *very relevant*, and *plugin* is mapped to *relevant*. In their work, linear trapezoidal membership functions are assumed for capturing the vagueness of the various linguistic terms. The preliminary results show the effectiveness of the fuzzy linguistic approach in quantifying match degrees for service matchmaking. However, one major concern with the approach is that the mapping from a semantic relationship to a fuzzy variable does not consider the semantic distances of the properties involved. For example, two *plugin* matches with different semantic distances are mapped to the same fuzzy variable which is *irrelevant*. To increase the accuracy in assigning

*Algorithm 1. Ontology merging*

> **Input:** Global Domain Ontology $O_1$ and User Domain Ontology $O_2$
> **Output:** Merged Ontology $O_1$
> 1: add a root node to both $O_1$ and $O_2$ to correlate $O_1$ and $O_2$ ;
> 2: **for** each node $n_i$ (except for the root) in $O_2$ following a breadth-first order
> 3: **if** $n_i$ is equivalent to any node $m_j$ in $O_1$, continue;
> 4: **else if** $n_i$ is a direct subclass of any node $m_j$ in $O_1$ in the context of $O_2$, then
> 5: add $n_i$ to the children set of $m_j$ in $O_1$, continue;
> 7: **end if**;
> 8: **end for**;

matching degrees between $K_q$ and $K_p$, semantic distances should be taken into account.

Let

- $Dom(K_q, K_P)$ be the degree of match between $K_q$ and $K_p$.
- $\| K_q, K_p \|$ be the semantic distance between $K_q$ and $K_p$ in the context of a domain ontology.

Following the work proposed in (Caceres et al., 2006) for computing match degrees, we further define $Dom(K_q, K_P)$ as follows:

Each bibliographic record has a number of keywords in its publication. For a user

$$Dom(K_q, K_p) = \begin{cases} 1 & \text{if } K_q \text{ and } K_p \text{ are } exact \text{ match} \\ \frac{1}{2} + \frac{1}{e^{(\|K_q, K_p\|-1)}} & \text{if } K_q \text{ and } K_p \text{ are } plugin \text{ match } \| K_q, K_p \| \geq 2 \\ \frac{1}{2 \times e^{(\|K_q, K_p\|-1)}} & \text{if } K_q \text{ and } K_p \text{ are } subsume \text{ match } \| K_q, K_p \| \geq 1 \end{cases}$$

query keyword $K_q$, the similarity degree of match of $K_q$ to a bibliographic record with a number of keywords can be computed using formula (2):

$$SDom(K_q, P(K_p)) = \sum_{i=1}^{n} Dom(K_q, K_{pi}) \Big/ n, \qquad K_{pi} \in P(K_p)$$
(2)

## Ontology Merging

To facilitate the incorporation of user domain knowledge into the system to guide OBIRE to discover bibliographic information records that

are of the interests of users, a simple yet automatic ontology merging algorithm is developed shown in (Algorithm 1).

An ontology is organized as a tree structure. The "thing" concept is added as a common root node in an ontology (line 1). In order to merge user domain ontology ($O_2$) with the global domain ontology ($O_1$), the algorithm relocates every concept from $O_2$ into $O_1$ (lines 3-5). The equivalent relationship between a concept $C_1$ in $O_1$ and a concept $C_2$ in $O_2$ is defined as either $C_1$ and $C_2$ have an exact string matching, or they are the synonyms of each other based on the definition of WordNet(http://wordnet.princeton.edu).

## User Recommendation with Fuzzy Logic

Each bibliographic record has a number of keywords associated with it. Through the user interface of OBIRE, users can make a recommendation to OBIRE about the relevance of the keywords used by a publication. A fuzzy logic based recommendation is proposed which defines five linguistic terms - "*irrelevant*", "*slightly relevant*", "*somewhat relevant*", "*relevant*", and "*very relevant*". According to (Dombi & Gera, 2005), a generalized cut function can be defined as follow:

$$[x]_{a,b} = \left[\frac{x-a}{b-a}\right] = \begin{cases} 0 & \text{if } x \leq a \\ \frac{x-a}{b-a} & \text{if } a < x < b \\ 1 & \text{if } b \leq x \end{cases}$$
(3)

where a, b are real numbers and a<b.

All nilpotent operators are constructed using the cut function. The formula of the nilpotent conjunction is $C(x, y) = [x+y-1]$, where $x, y \in [0, 1]$. Having considered that the generalized cut function can be used to describe piecewise liner membership functions, and trapezoidal shaped membership functions are used to represent fuzzy sets (Deerwester, Dumais, Furnas, Landauer, & Harshman, 1990), we propose a trapezoidal membership function using the conjunction of the two generalized cut functions:

$$C([X]a,b,1 - [X]c,d) = [[X]a,b + 1 - [X]c,d - 1] = [[X]a,b - [X]c,d] \qquad (4)$$

where a, b,c,d are real numbers and $a<b\leq c<d$.

For each linguistic term, the range of $x$ can be computed using equation (3) and (4). For a user recommendation on a bibliographic record, OBIRE generates a random number within the range of $x$ of the recommended term to indicate the degree of relevance of the keywords to the publication. For a publication with a number of recommendations, an average value is computed to indicate the degree of relevance of the keywords used. Figure 3 shows the membership functions of the aforementioned terms.

## OBIRE EVALUATION

The performance of OBIRE was evaluated from the aspects of precision and recall which are standard measures that have been used in information retrieval for measuring the accuracy of a search method or a search engine (Rijsbergen, 1979). Precision $P$ is defined as the percentage of the number of retrieved and relevant bibliographic information records over the total number of retrieved records. Recall $R$ is defined as the percentage of the number of retrieved and relevant records over the number of total relevant records. Let $RT$ represent the set of retrieved records, and

*Figure 3. Relevance assessment*

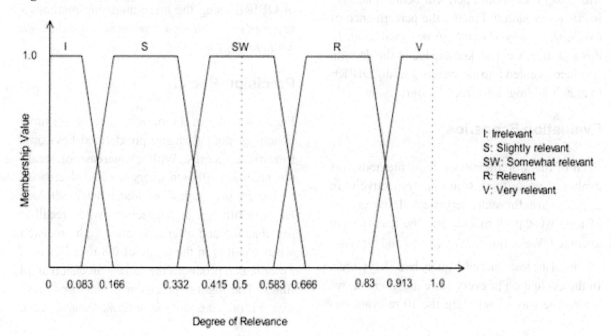

*RL* represent the set of relevant records. Precision and recall can be computed as follows:

$$P = \frac{|RT \cap RL|}{|RT|}, \; R = \frac{|RT \cap RL|}{|RL|}$$

## Evaluation Methods

We used three matching methods to evaluate the performance of OBIRE – *keyword-based exact match, semantic match,* and *match with ontology merging.* Firstly, we evaluated *keywords based exact match* to retrieve bibliographic information of interest. Due to the fact that keyword-match searches will often produce a large number of hits of which many are irrelevant, we expected that keyword-match should produce the worst results among the three methods. Secondly, we evaluated *match with semantics* by which information is retrieved based on a global domain ontology. Ontology represents the domain knowledge of a specific research area. There should be more relevant results returned for each retrieval so that the value of $|RT \cap RL|$ increases. Hence, *match with semantics* should perform better than *keywords exact match.* Finally, the performance of *match with merged ontology* was evaluated. In this test, user's expert knowledge in the domain was incorporated into the system guiding OBIRE to match bibliographic records of relevant.

## Evaluation Scenarios

Each of the aforementioned three methods was evaluated using three scenarios respectively. In each scenario for each query method, five groups of tests were performance and the results were averaged. We defined $|RT|_{max} = 50$ and $|RL|_{total} = 10$ in all the tests, and each query had 5 keywords. In the evaluation of every matching method, we varied the way of selecting the 10 relevant tar-

geted records and the 5 keywords in each scenario. Specifically:

- In the first scenario, we used 5 pre-defined keywords to retrieve pre-defined 10 relevant records;
- In the second scenario we randomly selected 10 records as targeted relevant records, and randomly selected 5 keywords from the set of keywords used by the selected 10 records;
- In the third scenario, we randomly selected 10 records as targeted relevant records, and randomly select the 5 keywords from the set of keywords used by the 50 records.

In all the above scenarios for each matching method, if the total number of retrieved and relevant records was less than 10 (the number of targeted relevant records), then we randomly select records one by one from the rest of the set of records.

## Evaluation Results

In this section, we present our evaluation results of OBIRE using the three matching methods - *keyword exact match, semantic match* and *match with ontology merging.*

## Precision-Recall

Figure 4 a shows the performance of the three matching methods using pre-defined keywords to retrieve records. With an increase of recall, the precision of each query method decreases. However, the method of *match with ontology merging* offers a high precision when recall is less than 0.5 and offers a relative high precision when recall is in the range of 0.8 to1. *Keyword exact match* produces the lowest precision at all times. The highest precision of *keyword exact match* is only 0.6, but *semantic match* and *match*

*Figure 4. Precision-recall of OBIRE*

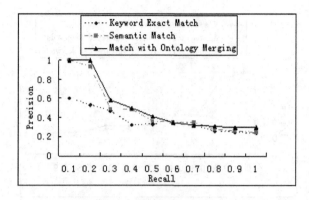

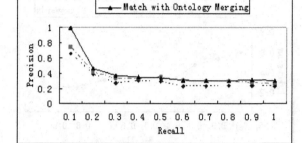

(a) the first scenario

(b) the second scenario

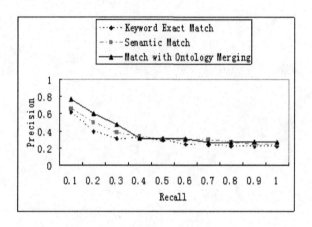

(c) the third scenario

*with ontology merging* can reach a precision of 1 when their recalls are low.

Figure 4 b shows the performance of the three matching methods in the second scenario where the 10 relevant records were randomly selected, and the 5 query keywords were selected from the set of keywords used by the 10 records. Figure 4(c) shows the performance of the three matching methods in the third scenario where the 10 relevant records were randomly selected, and the 5 query keywords were randomly selected from the whole set of keywords. From Figure 4(b) and Figure 4(c) we observe that the performance of each of the three matching methods is slightly better in

the second scenario than that in the third scenario. We also observe that *semantic match* and *match with ontology merging* perform similarly when recall is in the range of 0.5 to 0.8. The performance of *match with ontology merging* depends on the quality of the merged ontology.

For the three matching methods, we also compared their performance in the three scenarios respectively which is shown in Figure 5. The three matching methods perform best when pre-defined keywords are used. As bibliographic records were randomly selected in both the second scenario and the third scenario, each of the three matching methods performs similarly in these two scenarios.

*Figure 5. Precision-recall of each matching method*

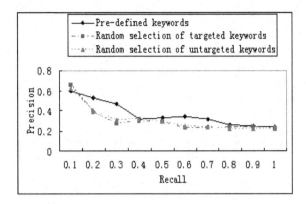

(a) keyword exact match

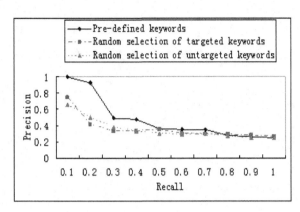

(b) semantic match

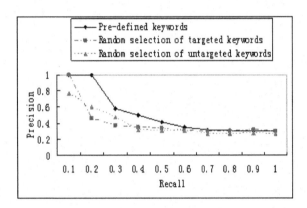

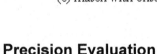

(c) match with ontology merging

## Precision Evaluation

We also evaluated the performance of the three matching methods in terms of precision in retrieval of bibliographic records. Figure 6 a, b, and c shows the evaluation results of the three methods respectively. In the three scenarios, *semantic match* performs better than *keyword exact match*. However, the performance of *match with ontology merging* is close to that of *semantic match*. For example, in the first scenario as shown in Figure 6 a, *match with ontology merging* performs better than *semantic match* when the number of retrieved records is less than 10. When the number of retrieved records is in the range of 15 and 30, *semantic match* outperforms *match with ontology*

*merging*. The explanation is that more records will be returned by the system using a merged ontology which defines more relationships of keywords compared with the case of *semantic match*. As a result, the number of targeted relevant records increases, but the number of records irrelevant to the targets may also increase.

It should be pointed that, in the three scenarios, *match with ontology merging* retrieved the least number of records for the 10 targeted records compared with other two matching methods respectively. For example, *match with ontology merging* retrieved no more than 40 records for the 10 targets, while *semantic match* retrieved around 45 records and keyword exact match retrieved almost 50 records for the 10 target records.

*Figure 6. Precision of OBIRE*

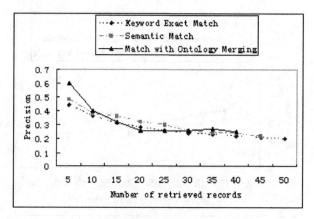

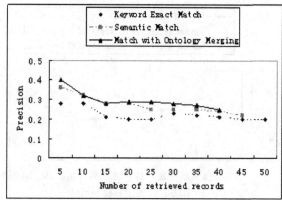

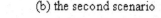

(a) the first scenario

(b) the second scenario

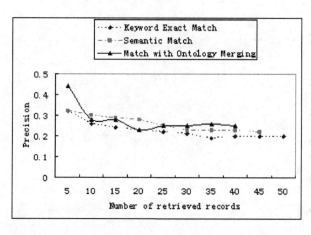

(c) the third scenario

We also evaluated the performance of each matching method in the three scenarios, and the results are plotted in Figure 7 a, b, and c respectively. As we expected, the three matching methods perform better in the first scenario using pre-defined targeted records and keywords than in other two scenarios. It is worth noting that the performance of each matching method is quite stable in the three scenarios, especially when the number of retrieved and retuned records is in the range of 30 - 40. This observation reflects a stable performance of OBIRE in bibliographic information retrieval.

## Recall Evaluation

We compared the performance of recall of the three matching methods in the three scenarios, and the results are plotted in Figure 8 a, b, and c respectively. We observe that in the three scenarios, *match with ontology merging* retrieved the least number of records to achieve of recall of 1. The method of *keyword exact match* performs worst in this aspect, e.g., it needs to retrieve almost 50 records to achieve a recall of 1. We also evaluated the performance of each matching method in the three scenarios. The results are plotted in Figure 9 a, b, and c respectively. We also observe that

*Figure 7. Precision of each matching method*

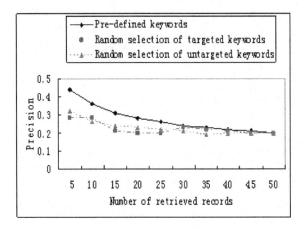

(a) keyword exact match

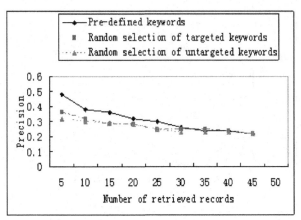

(b) semantic match

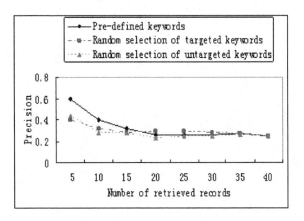

(c) match with ontology merging

performance of the three matching methods in the aspect of recall is stable which further reflects the stable performance of OBIRE.

## Related Work

In this section, we discuss some related work to OBIRE from the aspects of bibliographic information retrieval and ontology merging.

## Bibliographic Information Retrieval

ShaRef (Wilde et al., 2008) is an XML-based system for users to share bibliographic information and to collaborate. A central repository is used for collecting publication data which can be either traditional bibliographic data (books, journal articles or conference papers) or it can be data about Web resources on a particular topic. A user logs in the system as a member of one or more groups, and is assigned with the permissions to access a list of shared bibliographic records.

Bibster et al. (2004) utilizes ontologies in the P2P bibliographic sharing systems. Each peer Bibster could import their own bibliographic metadata into a local RDF (http://www.w3.org/RDF) repository in which the bibliographic metadata consist of two common ontologies - ACM Topic Hierarchy and SWRC (Semantic Web for Research Communities, http://ontoware.org/projects/swrc).

*Figure 8. Recall of OBIRE*

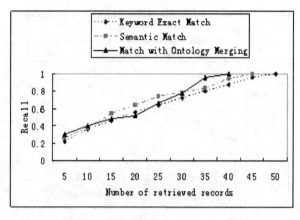

(a) the first scenario

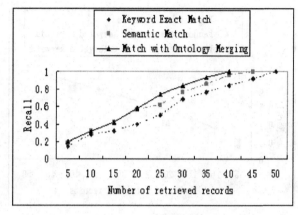

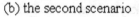

(b) the second scenario

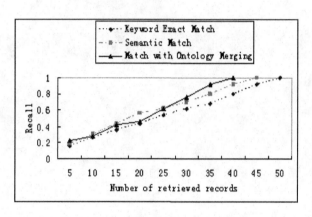

(c) the third scenario

Queries are translated into the RDF query language (SeRQL) for retrieving bibliographic metadata. Bibster automatically formulates queries in terms of two ontologies - using SWRC if a query has fields such as authors, publication types, or using ACM Topic Hierarchy if a query has fields which are specific to Computer Science terms. A matching function determines how closely the semantic content of a query matches the expertise model of each peer. The expertise model describes which concepts from the ACM ontology a peer can answer the query. For a user query, Bibster returns bibliographic details including titles, publish years and authors. In Bibster, peers use a shared ontology to advertise semantic descriptions of

their expertise through which a semantic overlay is built. User queries are routed in the semantic overlay from one peer to another depending on the expertise a peer has.

SemreX (Jin & Chen, 2008), a similar system to Bibster, is also a bibliographic information sharing system using P2P paradigms. In SemreX, bibliographic information is represented in the format of PDF including journals, proceedings, technical reports. Each file belongs to a special directory when it is made sharable. Since some researchers may have more than one research interests, papers are stored in different directories based on their topics. Similar to Bibster, SemreX uses ACM Topic Hierarchy to categorize files.

*Figure 9. Recall of each matching method*

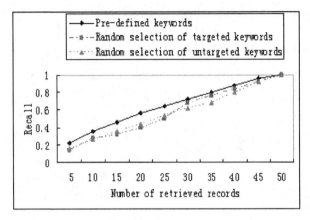

(a) keyword exact match

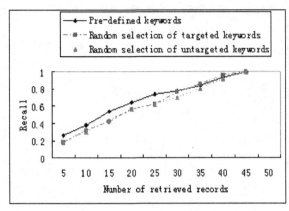

(b) semantic match

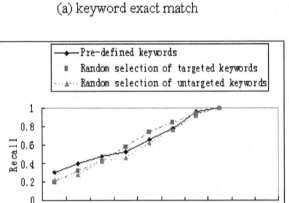

(c) match with ontology merging

For a user query, papers belonging to a specific topic will be retrieved based on the ACM ontology. SemreX has a semantic overlay to classify literature documents using Latent Semantic Indexing (LSI) (Deerwesteet et al., 1990) and Support Vector Machine (SVM) (Burges, 1998).

Both Bibster and SemreX use ACM Topics to facilitate bibliographic information retrieval. However, it is not desirable to have a single global ontology that suits all the users in queries. Expert knowledge of peers (i.e., user ontologies) should be incorporated into system ontologies guiding a system to discover bibliographic records that

are most relevant to a user query which entails ontology merging.

## Ontology Merging

Ontology merging processes two source ontologies with conceptually divarications and returns a merged ontology (Stumme & Maedche, 2001). Ontology merging is performed by taking the union of the terms and the axioms defining them. The goal of ontology merging is to create a single coherent ontology that includes the information from all the source ontologies. Instance-based and schema-based merging approaches are widely used for ontology merging.

## Instance Based Merging

Instance-based merging mainly exploits machine learning techniques to uncover the semantic relations between concepts. FCA- MERGE (Stumme & Maedche, 2001) is a typical instance-based method to merge application-specific of the given source ontologies. It adopts bottom-up approach which offers a global structural description of the merging process. For the source ontologies, it extracts instances from a given set of domain-specific text documents by applying natural language processing techniques. The extracted instances are analyzed by using mathematically founded techniques taken from Formal Concept Analysis to derive a lattice of concepts as a structural result of FCA–MERGE. Finally, ontology engineer creates the concepts and relations of the merged ontology from the concepts lattice. This method depends on the availability of instance data. Therefore, it does not work on cases where there is an insignificant number of instances or no instance at all.

## Schema Based Merging

Schema-based merging only considers the schema information, but not instance data. It consists of two approaches - linguistic matching which considers the name similarity between names of schema and structural matching which compares combinations of elements that appear together in a schema.

Cupid (Madhavan et al., 2001) combines both linguistic and structural matching techniques. The interconnected elements of a given schema are processed as a schema tree. For linguistic matching, individual schema elements are matched based on their names, data types, and domains using a pre-compiled dictionary to identify short-terms, acronyms and synonyms between each pair of elements. Structural matching of schema elements is performed based on the similarity of their contexts or vicinities. At the end of each phase, a similarity coefficient between 0 and 1 is calculated. Linguistic similarity coefficient means the similarity of two elements in different source schemas, and structural similarity is a measure of the similarity of the contexts in which the elements occur in the two schemas. Combining with two coefficients, a similarity coefficient of node called weighted similarity is calculated by a formula. Finally, a mapping is created by choosing pairs of schema elements with maximal weighted similarity.

PROMPT (Noy & Musen, 2000) provides a semi-automatic approach to ontology merging. It starts with the linguistic matching for the initial comparison, but process of merging depends on the structure of the ontology. The underlying ontological structures of the Protégé-2000 (http://protege.stanford.edu) are used to inform a set of heuristics for identifying further matches between ontologies. At the beginning of merging, an initial list of matches is created by PROMPT based on class names. Users select one of the PROMPT suggestions from the list or use an ontology-editing environment to specify the desired operations directly. PROMPT executes additional changes with its type of operation, and generates a list of suggestions for the user based on the structure of the ontology around the arguments to the last operation that helps to find possible solutions for some diversity. However, user's intervention plays a key role in the merging process.

OBIRE processes two source ontologies as trees, and checks the position of every node in one source and tries to relocate it in another source based on ontology definitions. The whole merging process is performed automatically.

## CONCLUSION

In this chapter, we have presented OBIRE, a P2P network for bibliographic information retrieval.

OBIRE supports *keyword based exact matches*, *matches with semantics*, and *matches with ontology merging*. User domain knowledge can be incorporated into the system which guides OBIRE to discover the bibliographic records that are most relevant to user queries. OBIRE has been evaluated from the aspects of precision and recall, and the evaluation results showed that at most cases *matches with ontology merging* produces the best results, and *keyword based exact matches* produces the worst results.

OBIRE supports ontology merging to unify two ontologies with conceptually divarications in a particular research domain. However, the merging algorithm only focuses on linguistic matches during the merging process without addressing uncertainties of concepts of ontologies. Future work includes the application of Bayesian networks (Pan, Ding, Yu, & Peng, 2005) for improved work on ontology merging.

# REFERENCES

Berners-Lee, T., Hendler, J., & Lassila, O. (2001). The semantic web. *Scientific American, 284*(5), 34–43. doi:10.1038/scientificamerican0501-34

Bharambe, R., Agrawal, M., & Seshan, S. (2004). Mercury: supporting scalable multi-attribute range queries. In *Proceedings of the ACM SIGCOMM Conference on Applications, Technologies, Architectures, and Protocols for Computer Communication* (pp. 353-366).

Burges, J. C. (1998). A tutorial on support vector machines for pattern recognition. *Data Mining and Knowledge Discovery, 2*(2), 121–167. doi:10.1023/A:1009715923555

Caceres, C., Fernandez, A., Ossowski, S., & Vasirani, M. (2006). Agent-based semantic service discovery for healthcare: an organizational approach. *IEEE Intelligent Systems, 21*(6), 11–20. doi:10.1109/MIS.2006.107

Cai, M., Frank, M., Chen, J., & Szekely, P. (2004). MAAN: a multi-attribute addressable network for grid information services. *Journal of Grid Computing, 2*(1), 3–14. doi:10.1007/s10723-004-1184-y

Deerwester, M. S., Dumais, S., Furnas, G., Landauer, T., & Harshman, R. (1990). Indexing by latent semantic analysis. *Journal of the American Society for Information Science American Society for Information Science, 41*(6), 391–407. doi:10.1002/(SICI)1097-4571(199009)41:6<391::AID-ASI1>3.0.CO;2-9

Dombi, J., & Gera, Z. (2005). The approximation of piecewise linear membership functions and Łukasiewicz operators. *Fuzzy Sets and Systems, 154*(2), 275–286. doi:10.1016/j.fss.2005.02.016

Haase, P., et al. (2004). Bibster- A semantic-based bibliographic peer-to-peer system. In *Proceedings of the Third International Semantic Web Conference* (pp. 122-136).

Jin, H., & Chen, H. (2008). SemreX: Efficient search in a semantic overlay for literature retrieval. *Future Generation Computer Systems, 24*, 475–488. doi:10.1016/j.future.2007.07.008

Kalfoglou, Y., & Schorlemmer, M. (2003). Ontology mapping: the state of the art. *The Knowledge Engineering Review, 18*(1), 1–31. doi:10.1017/S0269888903000651

Madhavan, J., Bernstein, P. A., & Rahm, E. (2001). Generic schema matching with cupid. In *Proceedings of the 27th VLDB Conference*.

Milojicic, T. S., et al. (2002). *Peer-to-peer computing* (Tech. Rep. HPL-2002-57). HP Labs.

Noy, N. F., & Musen, M. A. (2000). PROMPT: algorithm and tool for automated ontology merging and alignment. In *Proceedings of the AAAI/IAAI* (pp. 450-455).

Oppenheimer, D., Albrecht, J., Patterson, D., & Vahdatm, A. (2004). Distributed resource discovery on Planetlab with SWORD. In *Proceedings of the 1st workshop on Real, Large Distributed Systems*.

Pan, R., Ding, Z., Yu, Y., & Peng, Y. (2005). A bayesian network approach to ontology mapping. In *Proceedings of the 4th International Semantic Web Conference (ISWC'05)* (pp. 563-577).

Paolucci, M., Kawamura, T., Payne, T., & Sycara, K. (2002). Semantic matching of web service capabilities. *In Proceedings of the 1st Int'l Semantic Web Conference (ISWC)* (pp. 333-347).

Ratnasamy, S., Francis, P., Handley, M., Karp, R. M., & Shenker, S. (2001). A scalable content-addressable network. In *Proceedings of the SIGCOMM* (pp. 161-172).

Rowstron, A., & Druschel, P. (2001). Pastry: scalable, distributed object location and routing for large-scale peer-to-peer systems. In *Proceedings of the IFIP/ACM Int'l Conference on Distributed Systems Platforms (Middleware)* (pp. 329-350).

Stoica, I. (2002). Chord: a scalable peer-to-peer lookup protocol for Internet applications. *IEEE Transactions on Networks, 11*(1), 17–32. doi:10.1109/TNET.2002.808407

Stumme, G., & Maedche, A. (2001). Ontology merging for federated ontologies on the semantic web. In *Proceedings of the International Workshop for Foundations of Models for Information Integration (FMII-2001)*, Italy.

Tsetsos, V., Anagnostopoulos, C., & Hadjiefthymiades, S. (2006). On the evaluation of semantic web service matchmaking systems. In *Proceedings of the 4th IEEE European Conference on Web Services (ECOWS)* (pp. 255-264).

van Rijsbergen, A. (1979). *Information Retrieval*. London: Butterworths.

Wilde, E., Anand, S., Bucheler, T., Nabholz, N., & Zimmermann, P. (2008). Collaboration support for bibliographic data. *International Journal of Web Based Communities, 4*(1), 98–109. doi:10.1504/IJWBC.2008.016493

*This work was previously published in International Journal of Distributed Systems and Technologies, Volume 1, Issue 4, edited by Nik Bessis, pp. 58-73, copyright 2010 by IGI Publishing (an imprint of IGI Global).*

# Compilation of References

Abawajy, J. H. (2008). An Online Credential Management Service for Intergrid Computing. *Asia-Pacific Conference on Services Computing* (pp. 101-106).

Abowd, G. D., Gauger, M., & Lachenmann, A. (2003). The Family Video Archive: an annotation and browsing environment for home movies. In *Proceedings of the 5th ACM SIGMM Intl Workshop on Multimedia Information Retrieval* (pp. 1-8).

Abowd, G. D. (1999). Classroom 2000: An Experiment with the Instrumentation of a Living Educational Environment. *IBM Systems Journal, 38*(4), 508–530. doi:10.1147/sj.384.0508

Adam, C. (2005). *From Web Services to SOA and everything in between: The journey begins.* Retrieved March 20, 2009, from http://www.webservices.org

Adams, W. H., Lin, C. Y., Iyengar, G., Tseng, B. L., & Smith, J. R. (2002). *IBM Multimodal Annotation Tool. IBM Alphaworks.* IBM.

ADMIRE. (n.d.). *EU FP7 ICT project: Advanced Data Mining and Integration Research for Europe (ADMIRE), 2008-2011. Grant agreement no. 215024.* Retrieved November 2009, from http://www.admire-project.eu

Adve, V. S., Bagrodia, R., Deelman, E., & Sakellariou, R. (2002). Compiler-Optimized Simulation of Large-Scale Applications on High Performance Architectures. *Journal of Parallel and Distributed Computing, 62*(3), 393–426. doi:10.1006/jpdc.2001.1800

AMG benchmark summary. (n.d.). Retrieved September 11, 2009 from https://asc.llnl.gov/sequoia/benchmarks/AMG_summary_v1.0.pdf

Amir, Y., & Wool, A. (1998). Optimal availability quorum systems: Theory and Practice. *Information Processing Letters, 65*(5), 223–228. doi:10.1016/S0020-0190(98)00017-9

Anand, P. (2002). *Foundations of Rational Choice Under Risk.* Oxford, UK: Oxford University Press.

Andrieux, A., Czajkowski, K., Dan, A., Keahey, K., Ludwig, H., & Pruyne, J. (2004). *Web Services Agreement Specification (WS-Agreement) (Tech. Rep.).* Muncie, IN: Open Grid Forum.

ANFAS. (n.d.). *EU FP5 IST RTD project: datA fusioN for Flood Analysis and decision Support (2000-03).* IST-1999-11676.

Angskun, T., Fagg, G. E., Bosilca, G., Pjesivac-Grbovic, J., & Dongarra, J. J. (2006). Scalable fault tolerant protocol for parallel runtime environments. In *Proceedings of the Euro PVM/MPI* (p. ICL-UT-06-12).

Anjomshoaa, A., Brisard, F., Drescher, M., Fellows, D., Ly, A., & Mc-Gough, S. (2005). *Job submission description language (JSDL) specification (Tech. Rep.).* Muncie, IN: Open Grid Forum.

ANSYS Co. (2008). *Fluent.* Retrieved on February, 4th, 2009 from http://www.fluent.com/

Antonioletti, M., Atkinson, M. P., Baxter, R., Borley, A., Chue Hong, N. P., & Collins, B. (2005). The Design and Implementation of Grid Database Services in OGSA-DAI. *Concurrency and Computation, 17*(2/4), 357–376. doi:10.1002/cpe.939

Arbaugh, J. B., & Benbunan-Fich, R. (2006). An Investigation of Epistemological and Social Dimensions of Teaching in Online Learning Environment. *Academy of Management Learning & Education, 5*(4), 435–447.

Arsenault, A., & Farrell, S. (2001). *Securely available credentials* (Tech. Rep. RFC3157). Available from http://www.ietf.org/rfc/rfc3157.txt

Arthur, W. B. (1991). Designing Economic Agents that Act like Human Agents: A Behavioral Approach to Bounded Rationality. *The American Economic Review*, *81*(2), 353–359.

Asanovic, K., Bodik, R., Catanzaro, B. C., Gebis, J. J., Husbands, P., Keutzer, K., et al. (2006). *The landscape of parallel computing research: A view from Berkeley* (Tech. Rep. No. UCB/EECS-2006-183). University of California at Berkeley, Berkeley, CA.

Asimakopoulou, E. (2008). *A Grid-Aware Emergency Response Model for Natural Disasters*. Unpublished doctoral dissertation, Loughborough University, UK.

Asimakopoulou, E., Anumba, C. J., Bouchlaghem, D., & Sagun, A. (2006, August). *Use of ICT during the response phase in emergency management in Greece and the United Kingdom*. Paper presented at the International Disaster Reduction Conference (IDRC), Davos, Switzerland.

Asimakopoulou, E. (2009). Using Grid Technology for Maximizing Collaborative Emergency Response Decision Making. In Bessis, N. (Ed.), *Grid Technology for Maximizing Collaborative Decision Management and Support: Advancing Effective Virtual Organizations*. Hershey, PA: IGI Publishing. doi:10.4018/978-1-60566-364-7.ch013

Atkinson, M., Dialani, V., Guy, L., Narang, I., Paton, N., Pearson, P., et al. (2003). *Grid database access and integration: requirements and functionalities*. Retrieved August 17, 2008, from http://www.ggf.org/documents/GFD.13.pdf

Atkinson, M., et al. (n.d.). ADMIRE White Paper. *Motivation, Strategy, Overview and Impact, 9*.

Aumueller, D., Do, H. H., Massmann, S., & Rahm, E. (2005). Schema and ontology matching with coma++. In *Acm sigmod* (pp. 906-908).

*Avaki Corporation Home Page*. Retrieved September 3, 2009, from http://www.avaki.com

Aziz, A., & Mitchell, S. (2007). *An introduction to JavaScript Object Notation (JSON) in JavaScript and .NET*. Retrieved March 20, 2009, from http://msdn.microsoft.com/en-us/library/bb299886.aspx

Baker, M., Buyya, R., & Laforenza, D. (2002). *Grids and Grid technologies for wide-area distributed computing*. New York: John Wiley & Sons, Inc.

Barbera, R. (2006). *COnsorzio Multi-Ente per la promozione e l'adozione di Tecnologie di calcolo Avanzato*. Retrieved January 16th, 2009, from http://www.consorzio-cometa.it/

Barbera, R. (2007). *Progetto per l'Implementazione e lo Sviluppo di una e-Infrastruttura in Sicilia basata sul paradigma Grid*. Retrieved January 16th, 2009, from http://www.pi2s2.it/

Bargeron, D., Gupta, A., Grudin, J., & Sanocki, E. (1999). Annotations for Streaming Video on the Web: System Design and usage studies. In *Proceedings of the ACM 8th Conference on World Wide Web*.

Bargeron, D., Gupta, A., Grudin, J., Sanocki, E., & Li, F. (2001). Asynchronous Collaboration Around Multimedia and its Application to On-Demand Training. In *Proceedings of the 34th Hawaii International Conference on System Sciences (HICSS-34)*.

Barreto, J., & Ferreira, P. (2004). *Optimistic consistency with version vector weighted voting* (Tech. Rep. No. RT/004/2004). Lisboa, Portugal: Distributed Systems Group.

Beaudouin-Lafon, M. (2000). Instrumental Interaction: An interaction model for designing post-WIMP user interfaces. In *Proceedings of the ACM Conference on Human Factors in Computing Systems* (pp. 446-453). New York: ACM Press.

Beck, M., Dongarra, J. J., Fagg, G. E., Geist, G. A., Gray, P., & Kohl, J. (1999). HARNESS: A next generation distributed virtual machine. *Future Generation Computer Systems*, *15*, 571–582. doi:10.1016/S0167-739X(99)00010-2

BEinGRID. http://www.beingrid.eu/. (2009).

Belalem, G., & Slimani, Y. (2007). A Hybrid Approach to Replica Management in Data Grids. [IJWGS]. *International Journal of Web and Grid Services*, *3*(1), 2–16. doi:10.1504/IJWGS.2007.012634

Bell, W. H., Cameron, G. D., Capozza, L., Millar, A. P., Stockinger, K., & Zini, F. (2003). Optorsim: A grid simulator for studying dynamic data replication strategies. *International Journal of High Performance Computing Applications, 17*(4), 403–416. doi:10.1177/10943420030174005

Benkner, S., & Engelbrecht, G. (2006). A Generic QoS Infrastructure for Grid Web Services. *AICT-ICIW: Proceedings of the Advanced Int'l Conference on Telecommunications and Int'l Conference on Internet and Web Applications and Services* (p. 141). Washington, DC: IEEE Computer Society

Benveniste, C., & Heidelberger, P. (1995). *Parallel simulation of the IBM SP2 interconnection network.* Paper presented at the 1995 Winter Simulation Conference, New York, NY.

Berkovsky, S., Eytani, Y., & Gal, A. (2005, September 19-22). Measuring the Relative Performance of Schema Matchers. In *Proceedings of the 2005 IEEE/WIC/ACM International Conference on Web Intelligence* (WI'05) (pp. 366-371), Compiegne, France.

Berners-Lee, T., Hendler, J., & Lassila, O. (2001). The semantic web. *Scientific American, 284*(5), 34–43. doi:10.1038/scientificamerican0501-34

Bernstein, P. A., Melnik, S., Petropoulos, M., & Quix, C. (2004). Industrial-Strength Schema Matching. In *ACM SIGMOD Record* (pp. 38-43).

Bessis, N. (2003). Towards a homogeneous status of communicated research. In *Proceedings of the Sixth International Conference on the Next Steps: Electronic Theses and Dissertations Worldwide*, Berlin. Retrieved August 17, 2008, from http://edoc.hu-berlin.de/conferences/ etd2003/bessis-nik/PDF/index.pdf

Bessis, N., & Asimakopoulou, E. (2008, August 25-29). Towards a grid aware forest fire evacuation warning system. In *Proceedings of the Int. Disaster Reduction Conference*, Davos, Switzerland.

Bessis, N., & Asimakopoulou, E. (2008, July). *The development of a personalized and dynamic driven RSS specification for the built environment.* Paper presented at the IADIS International Conference on Web Based Communities, Amsterdam.

Bessis, N., & Chauhan, J. (2008, April). *The design and implementation of a Grid database consistency service in OGSA-DAI.* Paper presented at the IADIS International Conference on Information Systems, Algarve, Portugal.

Bessis, N. (2009). Model Architecture for a User tailored Data Push Service in Data Grids. In Bessis, N. (Ed.), *Grid Technology for Maximizing Collaborative Decision Management and Support: Advancing Effective Virtual Organizations*. Hershey, PA: IGI Publishing. doi:10.4018/978-1-60566-364-7.ch012

Bessis, N. (Ed.). (2009). *Model architecture for a user tailored data push service in data grids. Grid Technology for Maximizing Collaborative Decision Management and Support: Advancing Effective Virtual Organizations* (pp. 236–256). Hershey, PA: IGI Global.

Bessis, N., French, T., Burakova-Lorgnier, M., & Huang, W. (2007). Using Grid technology for data sharing to support intelligence in decision making. In Xu, M. (Ed.), *Managing Strategic Intelligence: Techniques and Technologies* (pp. 179–202). Hershey, PA: IGI Global.

Bharambe, R., Agrawal, M., & Seshan, S. (2004). Mercury: supporting scalable multi-attribute range queries. In *Proceedings of the ACM SIGCOMM Conference on Applications, Technologies, Architectures, and Protocols for Computer Communication* (pp. 353-366).

Bhatele, A., & Kale, L. V. (2008). Application-specific topology-aware mapping for three dimensional topologies. In *Proceedings of the IEEE international symposium on parallel and distributed processing* (pp. 1-8).

Binkert, N. L., Dreslinski, R. G., Hsu, L. R., Lim, K. T., Saidi, A. G., & Reinhardt, S. K. (2006). The M5 Simulator: Modeling Networked Systems. *IEEE Micro, 26*(4), 52–60. doi:10.1109/MM.2006.82

Bion, W. R. (1968). *Experiences in groups.* London: Tavistock.

Birchall, D. W., & Giambona, G. (2007). SME manager development in virtual learning communities and the role of trust: A conceptual study. *Human Resource Development International, 10*(2), 187–202. doi:10.1080/13678860701347164

*BitTorrent Home Page.* (n.d.). Retrieved August 21, 2009, from http://www.bittorrent.com/

Blanchet, C., Mollon, R., & Deléage, G. (2006, April). Building an Encrypted File System on the EGEE Grid: Application to Protein Sequence Analysis. In I. C. Society (Ed.), *Proceedings of the first international conference on availability, reliability and security (ARES)* (pp. 965-973).

Bocciarelli, P., D'Ambrogio, A., & Angelaccio, M. (2007). QShare: QoS-Enabled Description and Discovery of Services in SOA-Based P2P Applications. In *Proceedings of the 16th IEEE International Workshop on Enabling Technologies: Infrastructures for Collaborative Enterprises* (pp. 159-166). Washington, DC: IEEE Press.

Bolden, R. (2001). *Leadership Development in Small and Medium Sized Enterprises: Final Report (Tech. Rep.)*. Mardon Hill, UK: University of Exeter, Centre for Leadership Studies.

Bolden, R. (2007). Leadership development in SMEs: designing a customised solution. *GITAM Journal of Management, 5*(3), 40–53.

Bonabeau, E., Dorigo, M., & Theraulaz, G. (1999). *Swarm intelligence: from natural to artificial systems.* New York: Oxford University Press.

Bonachea, D., Hargrove, P., Welcome, M., & Yelick, K. (2009, May). *Porting GASNet to Portals: Partitioned Global Address Space (PGAS) Language Support for the Cray XT.* Paper presented at the Cray User Group Conference, Atlanta, Georgia.

Bonomi, E., Flück, M., George, P., Gruber, R., Herbin, R., & Perronnet, A. (1989). Astrid: Structured finite element and finite volume programs adapted to parallel vectorcomputers. *Computer Physics Reports, 11,* 81–116. doi:10.1016/0167-7977(89)90019-1

Bouras, C., & Philopoulos, A. (1998). Distributed virtual reality environments over web for distance education. In *Proceedings of EDEN Conference* (pp. 481-484).

Bouras, C., Philopoulos, A., & Tsiatsos, T. (2001). e-Learning through Distributed Virtual Environments. *Journal of Network and Computer Applications.*

Bradford, J. P., & Fortes, J. (1998). Performance and memory access characterization of data mining applications. *WWC: Proceedings of the Workload Characterization: Methodology and Case Studies* (p. 49). Washington, DC: IEEE Computer Society.

Brandt, J., Gentile, A., & Mayo, J. P'ebay, P., Roe, D., Thompson, D., & Wong, M. (2009). Methodologies for advance warning of compute cluster problems via statistical analysis: a case study. In *Proceedings of the 2009 workshop on Resiliency in high performance (Resilience '09)* (pages 7-14). New York: ACM.

Brightwell, R., Hudson, T., Pedretti, K., & Underwood, K. D. (2006). Cray's SeaStar Interconnect: Balanced Bandwidth for Scalable Performance. *IEEE Micro,* (May/June).

Brightwell, R., Riesen, R., Lawry, B., & Maccabe, A. B. (2002). *Portals 3.0: Protocol Building Blocks for Low Overhead Communication.* Paper presented at the 2002 Workshop on Communication Architecture for Clusters.

Brightwell, R. (Ed.). (2005). *A Comparison of Three MPI Implementations for Red Storm (Vol. 3666).* Sorrento, Italy: Springer.

Brightwell, R., Camp, W., Cole, B., DeBenedictis, E., Leland, R., & Tomkins, J. (2005). Architectural Specification for Massively Parallel Computers - An Experience and Measurement-Based Approach. *Concurrency and Computation, 17*(10), 1271–1316. doi:10.1002/cpe.893

Brightwell, R., Hudson, T., Pedretti, K., & Underwood, K. D. (2006). SeaStar Interconnect: Balanced Bandwidth for Scalable Performance. *IEEE Micro, 26*(2).

Brincat, K. (2001, April). On the Use of RSA as a Secret Key Cryptosystem. *Designs, Codes and Cryptography, 22,* 317–329. doi:10.1023/A:1008354524654

Brocco, A., Frapolli, F., & Hirsbrunner, B. (2008, September). BlatAnt: Bounding Networks' Diameter with a Collaborative Distributed Algorithm. In *Proceedings of the Sixth International Conference on Ant Colony Optimization and Swarm Intelligence*, Bruxelles, Belgium. New York: Springer.

Brocco, A., Frapolli, F., & Hirsbrunner, B. (2009, April). Bounded Diameter Overlay Construction: A Self Organized Approach. In *Proceedings of the IEEE Swarm Intelligence Symposium*, Nashville, TN. Washington, DC: IEEE.

Brocco, A., Hirsbrunner, B., & Courant, M. (2007, April). Solenopsis: A Framework for the Development of Ant Algorithms. In *Proceedings of the Swarm Intelligence Symposium*, Honolulu, HI (pp. 316-323). Washington, DC: IEEE.

Bronevetsky, G. (2009). Communication-sensitive static dataflow for parallel message passing applications. In *Proceedings of the International symposium on code generation and optimization (CGO)* (pp. 1-12).

Brown, J. L., Goudy, S., Heroux, M. A., Huang, S. S., & Wen, Z. (2006). An evolutionary path towards virtual shared memory with random access. In *Proceedings of the eighteenth annual ACM symposium on Parallelism in algorithms and architectures (SPAA '06)* (page 117). New York: ACM.

Brown, K. H., Summers, R. M., Glass, M. W., Gullerud, A. S., Heinstein, M. W., & Jones, R. E. (2001). *ACME Algorithms for Contact in a Multiphysics Environment API Version 1.0* (Sand Report SAND2001-3318).

Bruneo, D., Iellamo, G., Minutoli, G., & Puliafito, A. (2009). Gridvideo: A practical example of non-scientific application on the Grid. *IEEE Transactions on Knowledge and Data Engineering*, *21*(5), 666–680. doi:10.1109/TKDE.2008.191

Bruno, R. (2007). Recursive Catalog Interaction with lcg-rec-* Tools. *PI2S2 Wiki Pages*. Retrieved on January, 29th, 2009, from https://grid.ct.infn.it/twiki/bin/view/PI2S2/CatalogUpDownload

Bruno, R. (2008). The WatchDog Utility. *PI2S2 Wiki Pages*. Retrieved on January, 29th, 2009, from https://grid.ct.infn.it/twiki/ bin/view/PI2S2/WatchdogUtility

Bryant, E. A. (1991). *Natural Hazards*. Cambridge, UK: Cambridge University Press.

Burges, J. C. (1998). A tutorial on support vector machines for pattern recognition. *Data Mining and Knowledge Discovery*, *2*(2), 121–167. doi:10.1023/A:1009715923555

Burton, I., Kates, R. W., & White, G. F. (1978). *The Environment as Hazard*. New York: Oxford University Pres.

Buyya, R., & Murshed, M. (2002). GridSim: a toolkit for the modeling and simulation of distributed resource management and scheduling for Grid computing. *Concurrency and Computation*, *14*(13-15), 1175–1220. doi:10.1002/cpe.710

Caceres, C., Fernandez, A., Ossowski, S., & Vasirani, M. (2006). Agent-based semantic service discovery for healthcare: an organizational approach. *IEEE Intelligent Systems*, *21*(6), 11–20. doi:10.1109/MIS.2006.107

Cai, M., Frank, M., Chen, J., & Szekely, P. (2004). MAAN: a multi-attribute addressable network for grid information services. *Journal of Grid Computing*, *2*(1), 3–14. doi:10.1007/s10723-004-1184-y

Cai, Z., & Lin, X. (2008). QCast: A QoS-Aware Peer-to-Peer Streaming System with DHT-Based Multicast. *Lecture Notes in Computer Science*, *5036*, 287–295. doi:10.1007/978-3-540-68083-3_29

Calvanese, D., Giacomo, G., & Lenzerini, M. (1998, August). *Information integration: conceptual modelling and reasoning support*. Paper presented at the third Conference on Cooperative Information Systems, New York.

Camacho, D., Aler, R., Castro, C., & Molina, J. M. (2002). Performance evaluation of ZEUS, JADE, and SkeletonAgent framework. *2002 IEEE Systems, Man, and Cybernetics Conference*, *4*(6). IEEE.

Camp, W. J., & Tomkins, J. L. (2002). Thor'sHammer: The First Version of the Red Storm MPP Architecture. In *Proceedings of the Supercomputing 2002 Conf. High Performance Networking and Computing*.

Carriero, N., & Gelernter, D. (1989). Linda in context. *Communications of the ACM*, *32*(4), 444–458. doi:10.1145/63334.63337

Chang, R.-S., & Chang, J.-S. (2006). Adaptable Replica Consistency Service for Data Grids. In *Proceedings of the Third International Conference on Information Technology: New Generations (ITNG'06)*, Las Vegas, NV (pp. 646-651).

Chappell, D. (2004). *Enterprise Service Bus*. USA: O'Reilly Press.

Chapple, S. R., & Clarke, L. J. (1994). The parallel utilities library. In *Proceedings of the IEEE scalable parallel libraries conference* (pp. 21-30).

Chatelain, P., Curioni, A., Bergdorf, M., Rossinelli, D., Andreoni, W., & Koumoutsakos, P. (2008a). Billion vortex particle direct numerical simulations of aircraft wakes. *Computer Methods in Applied Mechanics and Engineering*, *197*, 1296–1304. doi:10.1016/j.cma.2007.11.016

Chen, L., & Jiang, C. J. (2006). Geographic routing with road topology and heuristic search based mobility prediction. In *Proceedings of the International Conference on Sensing, Computing and Automation*, Chong Qing, China (pp. 3214-3218).

Chen, Y., Iyer, S., Liu, X., Milojicic, D., & Sahai, A. (2007). SLA Decomposition: Translating Service Level Objectives to System Level Thresholds. *International Conference on Autonomic Computing: Proceedings of the Fourth International Conference on Autonomic Computing* (p. 3). Washington, DC: IEEE Computer Society.

Chen-Chan Chang, K., He, B., & Zhang, Z. (2005). Toward Large Scale Integration: Building a MetaQuerier over Databases on the Web. In *Proceedings of the Second Conference on Innovative Data Systems Research* (CIDR) Asilomar, Ca. (pp. 44-55).

*ChinaGrid project*. (2003). Retrieved from http://www.chinagrid.net

Chukmol, U., Rifaieh, R., & Benharkat, A. (2005). EXSMAL: EDI/XML semi-automatic Schema Matching Algorithm. In the *7th International IEEE Conference on E-Commerce Technology (CEC)* (pp. 422-425).

Clabby Analytics. (2004). *The grid report*. Retrieved July 3, 2008, from http://www-03.ibm.com/grid/pdf/Clabby_Grid_Report_2004_Edition.pdf

Clemen, R. (1996). *Making Hard Decisions: An Introduction to Decision Analysis* (2nd ed.). Belmont, CA: Duxbury Press.

Cohen, W., Ravikumar, P., & Fienberg, S. E. (2003) A Comparison of String Distance Metrics for Name-Matching Tasks. In: Proceedings of *IJCAI-03 Workshop on Information Integration on the Web* (pp. 73-78).

Colella, P. (2004). *Defining software requirements for scientific computing*. Presentation slides.

*Condor Project Home Page*. (n.d.). Retrieved August 24, 2009, from http://www.cs.wisc.edu/condor/

Consortium, U. P. C. (2005). *UPC language specifications* (Vol. 2) (Tech Rep. No. LBNL-59208). Berkeley, California: Lawrence Berkeley National Laboratory.

*CoolStreaming Home Page*. (n.d.). Retrieved September 15, 2009 from http://www.coolstreaming.us

COPE. Corporate-Scale Resources Context-Sensitive Performance Modeling, EPSRC Project GR/L59610/01.

Cray Research Inc. (n.d.). *SHMEM Technical Note for C, SG-2516*.

Crockford, D. (2006). *RFC 4627, The application/json media type for JavaScript Object Notation (JSON)*. Retrieved March 20, 2009, from http://www.faqs.org/ftp/rfc/ pdf/rfc4627.txt.pdf

CROSSGRID. (n.d.). *EU FP5 IST RTD project: Development of Grid Environment for Interactive Applications (2002-05) IST-2001-32243*. Retrieved April 2009, from http://www.eu-crossgrid.org

Czezowski, A., & Christen, P. (2002). *Performance Analysis of KDD Applications using Hardware Event Counters*. Retrieved May 15, 2009, from http://datamining.anu.edu.au/ talks/2002/cap2002-kdd.ps.gz

Dally, W., & Towles, B. (2004). *Principles and Practices of Interconnection Networks*. San Francisco: Morgan Kaufmann.

Daly, J. (2006). A Higher Order Estimate of the Optimum Checkpoint Interval for Restart Dumps. *Future Generation Computer Systems*, 303–312.

Deerwester, M. S., Dumais, S., Furnas, G., Landauer, T., & Harshman, R. (1990). Indexing by latent semantic analysis. *Journal of the American Society for Information Science American Society for Information Science*, *41*(6), 391–407. doi:10.1002/(SICI)1097-4571(199009)41:6<391::AID-ASI1>3.0.CO;2-9

Department Of Energy. (2007). Annual Energy Review 2007. *Energy Information Administration*. Retrieved June 16, 2009 from www.dramexchange.com

Department of Energy. (2007). *Modeling and Simulation at the Exascale for Energy and the Environment*. Washington, DC: Office of Science. Retrieved from http://www.mcs.anl.gov/~insley/ E3/E3-draft-2007-08-09.pdf

Di Caro, G., & Dorigo, M. (1998). AntNet: Distributed stigmergetic control for communications networks. *Journal of Artificial Intelligence Research*, *9*(2), 317–365.

Di Stefano, A., Morana, G., & Zito, D. (2009). P2P Strategy for QoS Discovery and SLA Negotiation in Grid Environment. *Future Generation Computer Systems*, *25*(8), 862–875. doi:10.1016/j.future.2009.03.001

Dierks, T., & Allen, C. (1999). *The Transport Layer Security (TLS) Protocol* (Tech. Rep. RFC2246). Available from http://www.ietf.org/rfc/rfc2246.txt

Dillenbourg, P. (1996). What do you mean by "collaborative learning"? In Dillenbourg, P. (Ed.), *Collaborative learning: Cognitive and computational approaches*. Amsterdam, The Netherlands: Pergamon.

Directive 2007/2/EC of the European Parliament and of the Council of (2007, March). *Establishing an Infrastructure for Spatial Information in the European Community (INSPIRE)*. Retrieved from January 2010, from http://eurlex.europa.eu/JOHtml.do?uri=OJ:L:2007:108:SOM:EN:HTML

Djordjevic, G. L., & Tosic, M. B. (1996). A heuristic for scheduling task graphs with communication delays onto multiprocessors. *Parallel Computing*, *22*, 1197–1214. doi:10.1016/S0167-8191(96)00041-5

Do, H. H., Melnik, S., & Rahm, E. (2002). Comparison of schema Matching Evaluations. In *GI-Workshop Web and Databases*. (pp 221-237), Erfurt, Germany.

Dombi, J., & Gera, Z. (2005). The approximation of piecewise linear membership functions and Łukasiewicz operators. *Fuzzy Sets and Systems*, *154*(2), 275–286. doi:10.1016/j.fss.2005.02.016

Domenici, A., Donno, F., Pucciani, G., Stockinger, H., & Stockinger, K. (2004). Replica consistency in a data grid. *Nuclear Instruments & Methods in Physics Research. Section A, Accelerators, Spectrometers, Detectors and Associated Equipment*, *534*, 24–28. doi:10.1016/j.nima.2004.07.052

Donovan, S., Huizenga, G., Hutton, A. J., Ross, C. C., Petersen, M. K., & Schwan, P. (2003, July 2003). *Lustre: Building a File System for 1,000-node Clusters*. Paper presented at the Ottawa Linux Symposium, Ottawa, Canada.

Duhan, S., Levy, M., & Powell, P. (2001). Information systems strategies in knowledge-based SMEs: the role of core competencies. *European Journal of Information Systems*, *1*(10), 25–40. doi:10.1057/palgrave.ejis.3000379

Durand, D., Jain, R., & Tseytlin, D. (2003). Parallel I/O scheduling using randomized, distributed edge coloring algorithms. *Journal of Parallel and Distributed Computing*, *63*, 611–618. doi:10.1016/S0743-7315(03)00015-7

Du, Z. H., Chen, Y., & Liu, P. (2002). *Grid Computing*. Beijing, China: Tsinghua University Press.

Ehrig, M., & Staab, S. (2004). QOM-Quick Ontology Mapping. In *Proceedings of the Third International Semantic Web Conference (ISWC)* (pp. 683-697). Hiroshima, Japan.

*E-learning Centre*. (1994). Retrieved from http://www.e-learningcentre.co.uk/

Elnozahy, E. N. M., Alvisi, L., Wang, Y.-M., & Johnson, D. B. (2002). A survey of rollback-recovery protocols in message-passing systems. *ACM Computing Surveys*, *34*(3), 375–408. doi:10.1145/568522.568525

Erradi, A., Padmanabhuni, S., & Varadharajan, N. (2006). Differential QoS support in Web Services management. *IEEE Intentional Conference on Web Services* (pp. 781-788). Chicago: IEEE Computer Society.

European Commission. (2000). *Vade - mecum of Civil Protection in the European Union*. Luxembourg: Office for Official Publications of the European Communities.

Exchange, D. R. A. M. (2009). Retrieved June 16, 2009 from http://www.dramexchange.com

*Facebook Home Page*. (n.d.). Retrieved August 28, 2009, from http://www.facebook.com

Fagg, G. E., Gabriel, E., Bosilca, G., Angskun, T., Chen, Z., Pjesivac-Grbovic, J., et al. (2004). Extending the MPI specification for process fault tolerance on high performance computing systems. In *Proceedings of the international supercomputing conference (ISC2004)*.

Falzone, A. (2007). *Grid Enabled web eNvironment for site Independent User job Submission*. Retrieved January 16th, 2009, from https://genius.ct.infn.it

Fatahalian, K., Knight, T. J., Houston, M., Erez, M., Horn, D. R., Leem, L., et al. (2006). Sequoia: Programming the memory hierarchy. In *Proceedings of the SC06 conference on high performance networking and computing* (p. 83). Washington, DC: ACM/IEEE.

Feichtinger, D., & Peters, A. J. (2005, November). Authorization of Data Access in Distributed Storage Systems. *In The 6th IEEE/ACM international workshop on grid computing* (pp. 172-178).

Feldman, M. (2008). ORNL's "Jaguar" Leaps Past Petaflop. *HPCWire.* Retrieved July 5, 2009 from http://www.hpcwire.com/blogs/ ORNLs_Jaguar_Leaps_Past_Petaflop_34282109.html

Ferreira, K., Brightwell, R., & Bridges, P. (2008). *Characterizing Application Sensitivity to OS Interference Using Kernel-Level Noise Injection.* Paper presented at the International Conference for High Performance Computing, Networking, Storage, and Analysis (SC'08), Austin, TX.

Ferreira, K., Brightwell, R., & Bridges, P. (2008, November). *Characterizing Application Sensitivity to OS Interference Using Kernel-Level Noise Injection.* Paper presented at the ACM/IEEE International Conference on High-Performance Computing, Networking, Storage, and Analysis (SC'08), Austin, Texas.

*Finite Element Surface Water Modeling System (FESWMS)* (n.d.). Retrieved November 2009, from http://smig.usgs.gov/SMIC/ modelpages/feswms.html

Floros, N., Meacham, K., Papay, J., & Surridge, M. (1999). Predictive Resource Management for Unitary Meta-Applications. *Future Generation Computer Systems,* *15*(5-6), 723–734. doi:10.1016/S0167-739X(99)00022-9

Foster, I. (2002). What is the Grid? a three point checklist. *Grid Today, 1*(6). Retrieved August 17, 2008, from http://www.Gridtoday.com/ 02/0722/100136.html

Foster, I., & Kesselman, C. (1998, July). The Globus Project: a status report. In *IPPS/SPDP '98 Heterogeneous computing workshop proceedings* (pp. 4-18).

Foster, I., & Kesselman, C. (Eds.). (2000). *The grid: Blueprint for a new computing infrastructure.* San Francisco: Morgan Kaufmann Publishers.

Foster, I., Jennings, N., & Kesselman, C. (2004). Brian meets brawn: Why grid and agents need each other. *3rd International Joint Conference on Autonomous Agent and Multi-agent Systems (AAMAS'04)* (pp. 8-15). New York: ACM Press.

Foster, I., Kesselman, C., Nick, N. M., & Tuecke, S. (2002). The physiology of the Grid: an open Grid services architecture for distributed systems integration. *Globus.* Retrieved August 17, 2008, from http://www.globus.org/ alliance/ publications /papers/ogsa.pdf

Foster, I., Kesselman, C., Tsudik, G., & Tuecke, S. (1998, November). A Security Architecture for Computational Grids. In A. Press (Ed.), *5th ACM conference on computer and communications security* (pp. 83-92).

Foster, I., & Kesselman, C. (1997). Globus: a Metacomputing Infrastructure Toolkit. *International Journal of High Performance Computing Applications, 11*(2), 115. doi:10.1177/109434209701100205

Foster, I., & Kesselman, C. (2004). *The Grid 2: Blueprint for a new computing infrastructure.* San Francisco, CA: Morgan Kaufmann Publishers.

Foster, I., Kesselman, C., Nick, J., & Tuecke, S. (2002). Grid services for distributed system integration. *Computer, 35*(6), 37–46. doi:10.1109/MC.2002.1009167

Foster, I., Kesselman, C., & Tuecke, S. (2001). The anatomy of the Grid: enabling scalable virtual organisations. *The International Journal of Supercomputer Applications, 15*(3), 200–222. doi:10.1177/109434200101500302

Foster, I., & Kesselmann, C. (2004). *The Grid 2: Blueprint for a New Computing Infrastructure.* Dordrecht, The Netherlands: Elsevier.

Foster, I., Kesselmann, C., & Tuecke, S. (2001). The Anatomy of the Grid. *The International Journal of Supercomputer Applications, 15*(3), 200–222. doi:10.1177/109434200101500302

Freed, N., & Borenstein, N. (1996). *MIME: Multipurpose Internet Mail Extensions* (Tech. Rep. RFC2045). Available from http://www.ietf.org/rfc/rfc2045.txt

Fryxell, B., Olson, K., Ricker, P., Timmes, F. X., Zingale, M., & Lamb, D. Q. (2000). FLASH: An Adaptive Mesh Hydrodynamics Code for Modeling Astrophysical Thermonuclear Flashes. *The Astrophysical Journal. Supplement Series, 131*(1), 273–334. doi:10.1086/317361

Gallis, M. A., Torczynski, J. R., & Rader, D. J. (2004). Molecular gas dynamics observations of Chapman-Enskog behavior and departures there from in nonequilibrium gases. *Physical Review E: Statistical, Nonlinear, and Soft Matter Physics, 69*, 042201. doi:10.1103/PhysRevE.69.042201

Gao, X., Yu, Z., & Shin, Y. (2006). The Lagrangian Algorithm Implement of QoS-Aware Service Composition on P2P Networks. In *Proceedings of the IEEE Asia-Pacific Conference on Services Computing* (pp. 356-361). Washington, DC: IEEE Press.

Garmany, J., & Freeman, R. (2004). Multi-master replication conflict avoidance and resolution. *Select Journal, independent Oracle Users Group, 11*(4), 9-15.

Gaspary, L. P., Barcellos, M. P., Detsch, A., & Antunes, R. S. (2007). Flexible Security in Peer-to-Peer Applications: Enabling New Opportunities Beyond File Sharing. *Computer Networks, 51*(17), 4797–4815. doi:10.1016/j.comnet.2007.07.005

Gee, M. W., Siefert, C. M., Hu, J. J., Tuminaro, R. S., & Sala, M. G. (2006). *ML 5.0 Smoothed Aggregation User's Guide (No. SAND2006-2649)*. USA: Sandia National Laboratories.

Gendreau, M., Guertin, F., Potvin, Y., & Taillard, E. (1999). Parallel tabu search for real-time vehicle routing and dispatching. *Transportation Science, 33*(4), 381–390. doi:10.1287/trsc.33.4.381

Gendreau, M., Laporte, G., & Semet, F. (2001). A dynamic model and parallel tabu search heuristic for real-time ambulance relocation. *Parallel Computing, 27*(12), 1641–1653. doi:10.1016/S0167-8191(01)00103-X

GEO 101-02 Introduction to Geology. (2006). *GEO.101-02*. Retrieved December 15, 2009, from http://www.geo.ua.edu/intro03/quakes.html

*Gnutella Protocol Specification*. (n.d.). Retrieved September 1, 2009, from http://rfc-gnutella.sourceforge.net/

Goel, S., Sharda, H., & Taniar, D. (2005). Replica Synchronisation in Grid Database. *Int. Journal Web and Grid Services, 1*(1), 87–115. doi:10.1504/IJWGS.2005.007551

Gong, Y. L., Dong, F. P., Li, W., & Xu, Z. W. (2003). VEGA infrastructure for resource discovery in grids. *Journal of Computer Science and Technology, 18*(4), 413–422. doi:10.1007/BF02948915

Gonze, X., & al., (2009). *Abinit*. Retrieved on February, 4th, 2009, from http://www.abinit.org/

Goodale, T., Jha, S., Kaiser, H., Kielmann, T., Kleijer, P., & Laszewski, G., von, et al. (2006). SAGA: A Simple API for Grid Applications. High-level application programming on the Grid. *Computational Methods in Science and Technology, 12*(1), 7–20.

Gordon, M. (2009). *GAMESS*. Retrieved on February, 4th, 2009, from http://www.msg.chem.iastate.edu/GAMESS/

Gray, J., Helland, P., O'Neil, P. E., & Shasha, D. (1996). The Dangers of Replication and a Solution. In *Proceedings of the 1996 ACM SIGMOD International Conference on Management of Data*, Montreal, Quebec (pp. 173-182).

Greengard, L., & Gropp, W. D. (1990). A parallel version of the fast multipole method. *Computers & Mathematics with Applications (Oxford, England), 20*(7), 63–71. doi:10.1016/0898-1221(90)90349-O

GRIA. Grid Resources for Industrial Applications. Retrieved May 15, 2009, from www.gria.org

*Groove HomePage*. Retrieved September 5, 2009, from http://office.microsoft.com/ en-us/groove/FX100487641033.aspx

Gropp, W. (2006). *The Message Passing Interface (MPI) standard*. Retrieved January 27th, 2009, from http://www.mcs.anl.gov/ research/projects/mpi/

Gruber, R., & Keller, V. (2009). *HPC @ GreenIT*. Berlin, Germany: Springer.

Gummadi, K. P., Dunn, R. J., Saroiu, S., Gribble, S. D., Levy, H. M., & Zahorjan, J. (2003). Measurement, Modeling and Analysis of Peer-to-Peer File-sharing Workload. *ACM SIGOPS Operating Systems Review, 37*(5), 314–329. doi:10.1145/1165389.945475

Gupta, A., & Awasthi, L. K. (2007). P4P: Ensuring Fault Tolerance for Cycle-Stealing P2P Applications. In *Proceedings of the International Conference on Grid Computing and Applications* (pp. 151-155). Las Vegas, NV: CSREA Press.

Gupta, A., & Awasthi, L. K. (2008). Secure Thyself: Securing Individual Peers in Collaborative Peer-to-Peer Environments. In *Proceedings of the International Conference on Grid Computing and Applications* (pp. 140-146). Las Vegas, NV: CSREA Press.

Gupta, R., Manion, T. R., Rao, R. T., & Singhal, S. K. (2008). Peer-to-Peer Authentication and Authorization. *United States Patent: 7350074.*

Gupta, A., & Awasthi, L. K. (2007). Peer Enterprises: Possibilities, Challenges and Some Ideas Towards Their Realization. *Lecture Notes in Computer Science, 4806*(2), 1011–1020. doi:10.1007/978-3-540-76890-6_27

Gupta, A., & Awasthi, L. K. (in press). IndNet: towards a peer-to-peer community network connecting the information technology industry and academia in India. *International Journal of Networking and Virtual Organizations.*

Gupta, A., & Awasthi, L. K. (in press). PArch: A Cross-Organizational Peer-to-Peer Framework Supporting Aggregation and Exchange of Storage for Efficient Email Archival. *International Journal of Business Information Systems.*

Gupta, R., Sekhri, V., & Somani, A. K. (2006). CompuP2P: An Architecture for Internet Computing Using Peer-to-Peer Networks. *IEEE Transactions on Parallel and Distributed Systems, 17*(11), 1306–1320. doi:10.1109/TPDS.2006.149

Haase, P., et al. (2004). Bibster- A semantic-based bibliographic peer-to-peer system. In *Proceedings of the Third International Semantic Web Conference* (pp. 122-136).

Hack, J., & Bierly, E. (2007, November 6-7). *Computational and Informational Technology Rate Limiters to the Advancement of Climate Change Science.* Paper presented to the DOE Advanced Scientific Computing Research Advisory Committee. Retrieved from http://www.sc.doe.gov/ascr/ ASCAC/presentationpage1107.html

Han, J., & Kamber, M. (2006). *Data Mining: Concepts and Techniques.* Morgan Kaufmann

Hasselmeyer, P., Koller, B., Schubert, L., & Wieder, P. (2006). Towards SLA-Supported Resource Management. *Lecture Notes in Computer Science: Vol. 4208 High Performance* [Munich, Germany: Springer Berlin / Heidelberg]. *Computer Communications,* 743–752.

He, B., & Chen-Chan Chang, K. (2003). Statistical Schema Matching across Web Query Interfaces. In Proceedings of the *ACM SIGMOD International Conference on Management of Data* (pp. 217-228), San Diego, California.

He, B., & Chen-chuan Chang, K.(2006). Automatic Complex Schema Matching Across Web Query Interfaces: A Correlation Mining Approach. In *ACM Transactions on Database Systems* (*TODS*) (pp. 346-395). New York: ACM Press.

He, B., Chen-Chan Chang, K., & Han, J. (2004). Discovering complex matchings across Web Query Interfaces: A Correlation Mining Approach. In Proceedings of the *Tenth ACM SIGKDD International Conference on Knowledge Discovery and Data Mining (KDD)* (pp. 148-157). New York, NY: ACM Press.

He, H., Meng, W., Yu, C., & Wu, Z. (2005). WISE-Integrator: A System for Extracting and Integrating Complex Web Search Interfaces of the Deep Web. In *Proceedings of the 31st International Conference on Very Large Data Bases (VLDB)* (pp. 1314-1317), Trondheim, Norway.

He, Z., Peng, C., & Mok, A. (2006). A Performance Estimation Tool for Video Applications. *RTAS Proceedings of the 12th IEEE Real-Time and Embedded Technology and Applications Symposium* (pp. 267-276). Washington, DC: IEEE Computer Society.

Heermann, P. (1998). Production Visualization for the ASCI One TeraFLOPS machine. In [Washington, DC: IEEE.]. *Proceedings of the Visualization, 98,* 459–462.

Hemmert, S., Underwood, K., & Rodrigues, A. (2007). An Architecture to Perform NIC Based MPI Matching. In *Proceedings of the 2006 International Conference on Cluster Computing (Cluster 2007).*

Hennigan, G. L., Hoekstra, R. J., Castro, J. P., Fixel, D. A., & Shadid, J. N. (2007). *Simulation of Neutron Radiation Damage in Silicon Semiconductor Devices (No. SAND2007-7157).* USA: Sandia National Laboratories.

Henson, V. E., & Yang, U. M. (2002). BoomerAMG: A Parallel Algebraic Multigrid Solver and Preconditioner. *Applied Numerical Mathematics, 41*.

Heroux, M. (2003). *Trilinos Home Page*. Retrieved from http://trilinos.sandia.gov

Heroux, M. (2009). *Mantevo Home Page*. Retrieved from http://software.sandia.gov/mantevo

Heroux, M., et al. (2009). Improving Application Performance via Mini-applications (Tech. Rep. No. SAND2009-5574). Sandia National Laboratories, USA.

Heroux, M. A., Bartlett, R. A., & Howle, V. E. (2005). An overview of the Trilinos project. *ACM Transactions on Mathematical Software, 31*(3), 397–423. doi:10.1145/1089014.1089021

Hertel, E. S., Jr., Bell, R. L., Elrick, M. G., Farnsworth, A. V., Kerley, G. I., McGlaun, J. M., et al. (1993). CTH: A Software Family for Multi-Dimensional Shock Physics Analysis. In *Proceedings of the 19th International Symposium on Shock Waves 1, 274ff,* Université de Provence, Provence, France.

Hey, T., Papay, J., & Surridge, M. (2005). The Role of Performance Engineering Techniques in the Context of the Grid. *Concurrency and Computation: Practice and Experience, 17*(2-4).), 297-316.

Hieber, S. E., & Koumoutsakos, P. (2008). An immersed boundary method for smoothed particle hydrodynamics of self-propelled swimmers. *Journal of Computational Physics, 227,* 8636–8654. doi:10.1016/j.jcp.2008.06.017

Hockney, R. W., & Eastwood, J. W. (1988). *Computer simulation using particles*. London: Institute of Physics Publishing.

Hodgson, V., & Watland, P. (2004). Researching Networked Management Learning. *Management Learning, 35*(2), 99–116. doi:10.1177/1350507604043027

Housley, R., Ford, W., Polk, W., & Solo, D. (1999). *Internet X.509 Public Key Infrastructure Certificate and CRL Profile* (Tech. Rep. RFC2459). Available from http://www.ietf.org/rfc/rfc2459.txt

Hribar, R., Taylor, E., & Boyce, E. (2001). Implementing parallel shortest path for parallel transportation application. *Parallel Computing, 27*(12), 1537–1568. doi:10.1016/S0167-8191(01)00105-3

Hu, W., & Qu, Y. (2006). Block Matching for Ontologies. In Proceedings of the *5th International Semantic Web Conference (ISWC).* (pp. 300-313), Athens, GA, USA.

Huang, C. (2004). *System support for checkpoint/restart of Charm++ and AMPI applications*. Unpublished Master thesis, University of Illinois, Illinois.

Huang, Y., Brocco, A., Courant, M., Hirsbrunner, B., & Kuonen, P. (2009). MaGate Simulator: a simulation environment for a decentralized grid scheduler. In *Proceedings of the International Conference on Advanced Parallel Processing Technologies (APPT'09),* Rapperswil, Switzerland. New York: Springer.

Huang, Y., Brocco, A., Kuonen, P., Courant, M., & Hirsbrunner, B. (2008). SmartGRID: A Fully Decentralized Grid Schedul- ing Framework Supported by Swarm Intelligence. In *Proceedings of the Seventh International Conference on Grid and Cooperative Computing (GCC '08),* China (LNCS 4967pp. 160-168). Washington, DC: IEEE Computer Society.

Huang, C., Lawlor, O., & Kale, L. V. (2004). *Adaptive MPI. LNCS, 2958,* 306–322.

Hughes, D., Warren, I., & Coulson, G. (2004). Improving QoS for Peer-to-Peer Applications Through Adaptation. In *Proceedings of the IEEE International Workshop on Future Trends in Distributed Computing Systems* (pp. 178-183). Washington, DC: IEEE Press.

Hu, W., Zhao, Y., & Qu, Y. (2008). Matching large ontologies: A divide-and-conquer approach. *Journal of Data Knowledge Engineering, 67,* 140–160. doi:10.1016/j.datak.2008.06.003

Iacono-Manno, C. M. (2009). The VisualGrid Tool. *PI2S2 Wiki Pages*. Retrieved on February 2nd, 2009 from https://grid.ct.infn.it/twiki/ bin/view/PI2S2/VisualGrid

ICKnowledge LLC. (2009, June). *IC Cost Model 0904a.*

*Instant Messenger Home Page*. (n.d.). Retrieved September 10, 2009, from http://www.aim.com

Ionescu, F., Nae, V., & Gherega, A. (2007). Credentials Management for Authentication in a Grid-Based R-Learning Platform. *International Symposium on Parallel and Distributed Computing. ISPDC '07.* (pp. 16).

ITRS International Roadmap Committee. (2007). *International Technology Roadmap for Semiconductors.*

*Jabber Home Page.* (n.d.). Retrieved September 7, 2009, from http://www.jabber.org

Jacob, B. (2009). DRAMSim: University of Maryland Memory-System Simulation Framework. *University of Maryland Memory-Systems Research.* Retrieved June 19, 2009 from http://www.ece.umd.edu/dramsim/#version2

Jacob, B. (n.d.). *DRAMsim: A Detailed Memory-System Simulation Framework.* Retrieved September 9, 2009 from http://www.ece.umd.edu/dramsim/

Jana, D., Chaudhuri, A., Datta, A., & Bhaumik, B. (2005, Nov.). Dynamic user credential management in grid environment. *TENCON 2005 IEEE Region 10* (pp. 1-6).

Jarvis, S. A., Spooner, D. P., Keung, H. N., Cao, J., Saini, S., & Nudd, G. R. (2006). Performance prediction and its use in parallel and distributed computing systems. *Future Generation Computer Systems, 22*(7), 745–754. doi:10.1016/j.future.2006.02.008

Jennings, N. R. (2001). An agent-based approach for building complex software systems. *Communications of the ACM, 44*(4), 35–41. doi:10.1145/367211.367250

Jiang, C. J., & Zeng, G. S., et al. (2003). Research on traffic information grids. *Journal of Computer Research and Development, 40*(12), 1676–1681.

Jiang, C. J., & Zhang, Z. H., et al. (2005). Urban Traffic Information Service Application Grid. *Journal of Computer Science and Technology, 20*(1), 134–140. doi:10.1007/s11390-005-0015-3

Jin, H., & Chen, H. (2008). SemreX: Efficient search in a semantic overlay for literature retrieval. *Future Generation Computer Systems, 24*, 475–488. doi:10.1016/j.future.2007.07.008

*JXTA Home Page.* (n.d.). Retrieved August 29, 2009, from http://www.sun.com/jxta

Kahle, J. (2005). The Cell Processor Architecture. In *Proceedings of the 38th Annual IEEE/ACM International Symposium or Microarchitcture.* Washington, DC: IEEE Computer Society.

Kale, L. V., Bhandarkar, M., Jagathesan, N., Krishnan, S., & Yelon, J. (1996). Converse: an interoperable framework for parallel programming. In *Proceedings of the IEEE international parallel processing symposium (IPPS)* (pp. 212-217).

Kale, L. V., Bohm, E., Mendes, C. L., Wilmarth, T., & Zheng, G. (2007). Programming Petascale Applications with Charm++ and AMPI. In *Proceedings of the Petascale computing: Algorithms and applications.* New York: CRC Press.

Kalfoglou, Y., & Schorlemmer, M. (2003). Ontology mapping: the state of the art. *The Knowledge Engineering Review, 18*(1), 1–31. doi:10.1017/S0269888903000651

Kamil, S., Oliker, L., Pinar, A., & Shalf, J. (2009). Communication Requirements and Interconnect Optimization for High-End Scientific Applications. *IEEE Transactions on Parallel and Distributed Systems, 99*(1).

Kamwar, S. D., Schlosser, M. T., & Garcia-Molina, H. (2003). The EigenTrust Algorithm for Reputation Management in P2P Networks. In *Proceedings of the 12th International Conference on World Wide Web* (pp. 640-651).

Karasavvas, K., Antonioletti, M., Atkinson, M. P., Chue Hong, N. P., Sugden, T., Hume, A. C., et al. (2005). *Introduction to OGSA-DAI Services* (LNCS 3458, pp. 1-12). ISBN 978-3-540-25810-0

Karypis, G., & Kumar, V. (1998a). A fast and high quality multilevel scheme for partitioning irregular graphs. *SIAM Journal on Scientific Computing, 20*(1), 359–392. doi:10.1137/S1064827595287997

Karypis, G., & Kumar, V. (1998b). Multilevel k-way partitioning scheme for irregular graphs. *Journal of Parallel and Distributed Computing, 48*, 96–129. doi:10.1006/jpdc.1997.1404

KaZaA Home Page. (n.d.). Retrieved September 5, 2009, from http://www.kazaa.com/us/index.htm

Keiter, E. R., Mei, T., Russo, T. V., Rankin, E. L., Pawlowski, R. P., Schiek, R. L., et al. (2008). *Xyce Parallel Electronic Simulator: Users' Guide, Version 4.1* (Tech. Rep. No. SAND2008-6461). Sandia National Laboratories, USA.

Kelly, S., & Brightwell, R. (2005, May). *Software Architecture of the Lightweight Kernel, Catamount.* Paper presented at the Cray User Group Conference, Albuquerque, New Mexico.

Kelly, W., & Mason, R. (2005). G2-P2P: A Fully Decentralized Fault-Tolerant Cycle Stealing Framework. In *Proceedings of the Australian Workshop on Grid Computing and e-Research* (pp. 33-39).

Kemme, B. (2000). *Database Replication for Clusters of Workstations.* Unpublished doctoral dissertation, Swiss Federal Institute of Technology Zurich, Germany.

Kendall, R. A., Apr\`a, E., Bernholdt, D. E., Bylaska, E. J., Dupuis, M., & Fann, G. I., et al. (2000). High performance computational chemistry: An overview of NWChem a distributed parallel application. *Computer Physics Communications, 128*(1-2), 260–283. doi:10.1016/S0010-4655(00)00065-5

Keyes, D., Kritz, A., & Tang, W. (2007, November). *Fusion Simulation Project (FSP): Workshop Report.* Paper presented at the DOE Advanced Scientific Computing Research Advisory Committee (ASCAC) meeting.

Kim, J., Dally, W. J., & Abts, D. (2007). Flattened butterfly: a cost-efficient topology for high-radix networks. In *Proceedings of the 34th Annual International Symposium on Computer Architecture* (pp.126-137).

Kim, J., Dally, W. J., Scott, S., & Abts, D. (2008). Technolgy-driven, highly-scalable, Dragonfly topology. In *Proceedings of the 35th Annual International Symposium on Computer Architecture* (pp.77-88).

Kim, S. (2001). An O(N) level set method for Eikonal equations. *SIAM Journal on Scientific Computing, 22*(6), 2178–2193. doi:10.1137/S1064827500367130

Kirwan, C., & Birchall, D. (2006). Transfer of learning from management development programmes: testing the Holton model. *International Journal of Training and Development, 10*(4), 252–268.

Knupfer, A., Brendel, R., Brunst, H., Mix, H., & Nagel, W. E. (2006). Introducing the open trace format (OTF). In V. N. Alexandrov, G. D. van Albada, P. M. A. Sloot, & J. Dongarra (Eds.), *Proceedings, Part II Computational Science-ICCS 2006, 6th International Conference* (LNCS 3992).

Ko, H. J., Kim, K. I., Lee, E. J., Choi, W. G., & Kim, U. M. (2008). An effective XML data Release in Dynamic Environments. *International Conference on Hybrid Information Technology,* (pp. 182-189).

Kodeboyina, D., & Plale, B. (2004). *Experiences with OGSA-DAI: portlet access and benchmark.* Retrieved August 17, 2008, from http://www-unix.mcs.anl.gov/~keahey/DBGS/DBGS_files/ dbgs_papers/kodeboyina.pdf

Kogge, P. (2008). *ExaScale Computing Study: Technology Challenges in Achieving Exascale Systems (Tech. Rep.).* Notre Dame, IN: University of Notre Dame, Department of Computer Science.

Konigs, A. (2005). Model transformation with triple graph grammars. *Model Transformations in Practice Workshop, Part of ACM/IEEE 8th International Conference on Model Driven Engineering Languages and Systems (MoDELS 2005),* Jamaica.

Koteras, R., & Gullerud, A. S. (2003, April). *Presto User's Guide Version 1.05* (JSand Report SAND2003-1089).

Kouril, D., & Basney, J. (2005). A Credential Renewal Service for Long-Running jobs. *6th IEEE/ACM International Workshop on Grid Computing,* (pp. 63-68).

Kraiss, A., Schoen, F., Weikum, G., & Deppisch, U. (2001) Towards response time guarantees for e-service middleware, In C. Jensen, C., et al. (Eds.), *Extending Database Technology: Vol. 2287 Archive Proceedings of the 8th International Conference on Extending Database Technology: Advances in Database Technology* (pp. 58–63), London, UK: Springer-Verlag.

Kuenning, G. H., Bagrodia, R., Gay, R. G., Popek, G. J., Reiher, P. L., & Wang, A.-I. (1998). Measuring the Quality of Service of Optimistic Replication. In *Proceedings of the Workshops on Object-Oriented Technology (ECOOP '98),* Brussels, Belgium (pp. 319-320).

K-WfGrid. (n.d.). *EU FP6 RTD IST project: Knowledge-based Workow System for Grid Applications (2004-2007) FP6-511385*. Retrieved August 2008, from http://www.kwfgrid.eu

Laboratories, R. S. A. (2007). *PKCS#11: Cryptographic Token Interface Standard* (Tech. Rep.). Available from ftp://ftp.rsasecurity.com/pub/pkcs/pkcs-11/ v2-20/pkcs-11v2-20a3.pdf

Laudon, J. (2007). *UltraSPARC T1: A 32-threaded CMP for Servers*. Paper presented at the Berkeley CMP.

Lave, J., & Wenger, E. (1991). *Situated Learning: Legitimate Peripheral Participation*. New York: Cambridge University Press.

Lee, J. W., & Asanovic, K. (2006). METERG: Measurement-Based End-to-End Performance Estimation Technique in QoS-Capable Multiprocessors. *RTAS Proceedings of the 12th IEEE Real-Time and Embedded Technology and Applications Symposium* (pp. 135-147). Washington, DC: IEEE Computer Society.

Lee, K., Jeon, J., Lee, W., Jeong, S., & Park, S. (2003). *QoS for Web Services: Requirements and possible approaches*. Retrieved March 20, 2009, from W3C: http://www.w3c.or.kr/ kr-office/TR/2003/ws-qos/

Leidner, D., & Jarvenpaa, S. E. (1995). The Use of Information Technology to Enhance Management School Education: A Theoretical View. *Management Information Systems Quarterly, 19*(2), 13–25.

Lekkas, E. L. (2000). *Natural and Technological Catastrophes*. Greece: Access Pre-Press.

Levy, A. (2002). Logic-based techniques in data integration. In Minker, J. (Ed.), *Logic Based Artificial Intelligence* (pp. 575–595). Norwell, MA: Kluwer Academic Publishers.

Liang, J., & Nahrstedt, K. (2006). RandPeer: Membership Management for QoS Sensitive Peer-to-Peer Applications. In *Proceedings of the 25th IEEE International Conference on Computer Communications* (pp. 1-10). Washington, DC: IEEE Press.

Li, K. B. (2003). Multiple ClustalW-MPI: ClustalW analysis using distributed and parallel computing. [Oxford: Oxford University Press.]. *Bioinformatics (Oxford, England), 19*(12), 1585–1586. doi:10.1093/bioinformatics/btg192

*LimeWire Home Page*. (n.d.). Retrieved September 7, 2009, from http://www.limewire.com

Lin, C. Y., Tseng, B. L., & Smith, J. R. (2003). VideoAnnEx: IBM MPEG-7 Annotation Tool for Multimedia Indexing and Concept Learning. In *Proceedings of the IEEE Intl. Conf. on Multimedia and Expo (ICME)*, Baltimore.

Linn, J. (1993). Privacy Enhancement for Internet Electronic Mail: Message Encryption and Authentication Procedures (Tech. Rep. RFC1421). Available from http://www.ietf.org/rfc/rfc1421.txt

Linnolahti, J. (2004). QoS Routing for P2P Networking (HUT T-110.551). *Seminar on Internetworking*.

Lin, P. T., Shadid, J. N., Sala, M., Tuminaro, R. S., Hennigan, G. L., & Hoekstra, R. J. (2009). Performance of a Parallel Algebraic Multilevel Preconditioner for Stabilized Finit Element Semiconductor Device Modeling. *Journal of Computational Physics, 228*(17), 6250–6267. doi:10.1016/j.jcp.2009.05.024

Lin, P. T., Shadid, J. N., Tuminaro, R. S., & Sala, M. G. (n.d.). Performance of a Petrov-Galerkin Algebraic Multilevel Preconditioner for Finite Element Modeling of the Semiconductor Device Drift-Diffusion Equations. *International Journal for Numerical Methods in Engineering*.

Lippman, A. (1980). Movie-maps: An application of the optical videodisc to computer graphics. In *Proceedings of the ACM SIGGRAPH Computer Graphics* (pp. 32-42).

Liu, F., Hu, Y., & Gleicher, M. L. (2008). Discovering panoramas in web videos. In *Proceeding of the 16th ACM international Conference on Multimedia* (pp. 329-338). New York: ACM.

Liu, Y. J., Ma, C. X., & Zhang, D. L. (2009). *EasyToy: A Plush Toy Design System Using Editable Sketching Curves*. IEEE Computer Graphics and Applications.

*LiveStation Home Page*. (n.d.). Retrieved August 28, 2009, from http://www.livestation.com

Li, Z., & Mohapatra, P. (2004). QRON: QoS-Aware Routing in Overlay Networks. *IEEE Journal on Selected Areas in Communications, 22*(1), 29–40. doi:10.1109/JSAC.2003.818782

Lombardo, A., Muoio, A., Iacono-Manno, C. M., Lanzalone, G., & Barbera, R. (2008). *ViralPack*. Retrieved on February, 4th, 2009, from http://documents.ct.infn.it/record/ 170/files/posternapoli.pdf?version=1

Louie, J. N. (1996). *What is Richter Magnitude?* Retrieved December 15, 2009, from http://www.seismo.unr.edu/ftp/pub/ louie/class/100/magnitude.html

Lowe, D. G. (2004). Distinctive Image Features from Scale-Invariant Keypoints. *International Journal of Computer Vision, 60*(2), 91–110. doi:10.1023/B:VISI.0000029664.99615.94

Lu, J., Wang, S., & Wang, J. (2005). An experiment on the Matching and Reuse of XML Schemas. In Proceedings of the *5th International Conference on Web engineering (ICWE)* (pp. 273-284), Sydney, Australia.

M5Sim. (n.d.). *The M5 Simulator System: A modular platform for computer system architecture research.* Retrieved September 9, 2009 from http://www.m5sim.org

Madhavan, J., Bernstein, P.A., & Rahm, E. (2001). Generic schema matching with cupid. In *Proceedings of the 27th VLDB Conference*.

Madhavan, J., Bernstein, P. A., & Rahm, E. (2001, September 11-14). Generic schema matching with cupid. In *Proceedings of 27th International Conference on Very Large Data Bases* (pp. 49-58), Roma, Italy.

Magowan, J. (2003, April). *A view on relational data on the Grid.* Paper presented at the International Parallel and Distributed Processing Symposium, Nice, France.

Mann, R. (2007, September). *BioEnergy Science Center: A DOE Bioenergy Research Center.* Paper presented at the 2007 Fall Creek Falls Workshop, Nashville, Tennessee. Retrieved from http://www.iter.org

Mantevo. (n.d.). Retrieved September 9, 2009 from https://software.sandia.gov/mantevo/

Marculescu, R., & Nandi, A. (2001). Probabilistic application modeling for system-level performance analysis. In W. Nebel, W., & A. Jerraya, A., (Eds.), *Design, Automation, and Test in Europe: Proceedings of the conference on Design, automation and test in Europe* (pp. 572–579). Piscataway, NJ: IEEE Press

Marculescu, R., Pedram, M., & Henkel, J. (2004) Distributed Multimedia System Design: A Holistic Perspective., *Design, Automation, and Test in Europe: Vol. 2 Proceedings of the conference on Design, automation and test in Europe* (pp. 21342). Washington, DC: IEEE Computer Society.

Marti, S., & Garcia-Molina, H. (2006). Taxonomy of Trust: Categorizing P2P Reputation Systems. *Computer Networks. Special Issue on Trust and Reputation in Peer-to-Peer Systems, 50*(4), 472–484.

Mattson, T. G., Scott, D., & Wheat, S. R. (1996, April). *A TeraFLOP Supercomputer in 1996: The ASCI TFLOP System.* Paper presented at the International Parallel Processing Symposium, Honolulu, HI.

McGrath, J. E., & Hollingshead, A. B. (1994). *Groups Interacting with Technology.* Thousand Oaks, CA: Sage.

McLaughlin, B. (2002). *Building Java enterprise applications.* O'Reilly Press.

Meacham, K., Floros, N., & Surridge, M. (1998). Industrial Stochastic Simulations on a European Meta-Computer. In Pritchard, D., & Reeve, J.S., (Eds.), *Lecture Notes In Computer Science: Vol. 1470 Proceedings of the 4th International Euro-Par Conference on Parallel Processing* (pp. 1131-1139). London, UK: Springer-Verlag

*MEDIGRID. ( n.d. ).* EU FP6 RTD Sust.Dev. project: Mediterranean Grid of Multi-Risk Data and Models (2004-2006) GOCE-CT-2003-004044, call FP6-2003-Global-2.

Melnik, S., Garcia-Molina, G., & Rahm, E. (2002). Imilarity Flooding: A Versatile Graph Matching Algorithm and Its Application to Schema Matching. In *Proceedings of the 18th International Conference on Data Engineering* (pp. 117-128), San Jose, CA.

Menasce, D. A. (2002). QoS issues in Web Services. *IEEE Internet Computing, 6*(6), 72–75. doi:10.1109/MIC.2002.1067740

Mendling, J., & Hafner, M. (2007). From WS-CDL choreography to BPEL process orchestration. [JEIM]. *Journal of Enterprise Information Management, 21*(5), 525–542. doi:10.1108/17410390810904274

Meo, M., & Milan, F. (2008). QoS Content Management for P2P file-sharing applications. *Future Generation Computer Systems, 24*(3), 213–221. doi:10.1016/j.future.2007.07.002

Message Passing Interface Forum. (2008). *MPI: A message-passing interface standard, version 2.1*. Stuttgart, Germany: High-Performance Computing Center Stuttgart.

Message Passing Interface Forum. (2008). *MPI: A Message-Passing Interface Standard: Version 2.1*. Retrieved September 9, 2009 from http://www.mpi-forum.org

Michlmayr, E. (2006). Ant Algorithms for Search in Unstructured Peer-to-Peer Networks. In *Proceedings of the 22nd International Conference on Data Engineering Workshops (ICDE2006)* (p. 142). Washington, DC: IEEE Computer Society.

Micron technology. (2007). *Calculating Memory System Power for DDR3*. Boisie, ID.

Milojicic, D., Kalogeraki, V., Lukose, R. M., Nagaraja, K., Pruyne, J., Richard, B., et al. (2002). *Peer-to-peer Computing* (Tech. Rep. No. HPL-2002-57 20020315). HP Labs Research Library, Technical Publications Department.

Milojicic, T. S., et al. (2002). *Peer-to-peer computing* (Tech. Rep. HPL-2002-57). HP Labs.

MIPS Technologies, Inc. (2007). *MIPS64® 5Kc® Processor Core Data Sheet*.

Moab Grid Suite. (2009). *Cluster Resource Inc*. Retrieved from http://www.clusterresources. com/pages/products/moab-grid- suite.php

Molecular Dynamics Simulator, L. A. M. M. P. S. (2009). Retrieved from http://lammps.sandia.gov/index.html

Montagnat, J., Jouvenot, D., Pera, C., Frohner, A., Kunszt, P., Koblitz, B., et al. (2006). *Implementation of a Medical Data Manager on top of gLite services* (Tech. Rep.). Available from http://cdsweb.cern.ch/ search.py?p=EGEE-TR-2006-002

Moon, B., & Saltz, J. (1994). Adaptive runtime support for direct simulation Monte Carlo methods on distributed memory architectures. In *Proceedings of the IEEE scalable high-performance computing conference* (pp. 176–183). Washington, DC: IEEE.

Moon, S., Birchall, D., Williams, S., & Vrasidas, C. (2005). Developing design principles for an e-learning programme for SME managers to support accelerated learning at the workplace. *Journal of Workplace Learning, 17*(5-6), 370–375. doi:10.1108/13665620510606788

MPI Forum. (1994). MPI: A Message-Passing Interface Standard. *International Journal of Supercomputer Applications and High Performance Computing, 8*.

Murphy, R. C. (2007, September 27-29). On the Effects of Memory Latency and Bandwidth on Supercomputer Application Performance. In *Proceedings Of the IEEE Internaional Symposium on Workload Characterization 2007 (IISWC07)*.

Murphy, R., Rodrigues, A., Kogge, P., & Underwood, K. (2009). *The Implications of Working Set Analysis on Supercomputing Memory Hierarchy Design*. Paper presented at the International Conference on Supercomputing, Cambridge, UK.

Murphy, R. C., & Kogge, P. M. (2007, July). On the Memory Access Patterns of Supercomputer Applications: Benchmark Selection and Its Implications. *IEEE Transactions on Computers, 56*(7), 937–945. doi:10.1109/TC.2007.1039

Nagaratnam, N., Janson, P., Dayka, J., Nadalin, A., Siebenlist, F., Welch, V., et al. (2002, July). *The Security Architecture for Open Grid Services* (Tech. Rep.). Available from www.cs.virginia.edu/~humphrey/ogsa-sec-wg/OGSA-SecArch-v1-07192002.pdf

National Research Council (NRC). (2006). *Facing Hazards and Disasters: Understanding Human Dimensions*. Washington, DC: National Academy Press.

Nemati, A. G., & Takizawa, M. (2008). Application Level QoS for Multi-Media Peer-to-Peer Networks. *In Proceedings of the International Conference on Advanced Information Networking and Applications* (pp. 319-324).

Newman, W. M., & Lamming, M. G. (1995). *Interactive System Design*. Reading, MA: Addison-Wesley.

Nieplocha, J., Palmer, B., Tipparaju, V., Krishnan, M., Trease, H., & Apra, E. (2006). Advances, Applications and Performance of the Global Arrays Shared Memory Programming Toolkit. *International Journal of High Performance Computing Applications, 20*(2), 203–231. doi:10.1177/1094342006064503

Nieto-Santisteban, M. A., Gray, J., Szalay, A. S., Annis, J., Thakar, A. R., & O'Mullane, W. J. (2004). *When database systems meet the Grid (Tech. Rep.)*. Microsoft Corporation, Microsoft Research.

Novotny, J., Tuecke, S., & Welch, V. (2001). An Online Credential Repository for the Grid: Myproxy. *Tenth International Symposium on High-Performance Distributed Computing (HPDC-10),* (pp. 104-111).

Noy, N. F., & Musen, M. A. (2000). PROMPT: algorithm and tool for automated ontology merging and alignment. In *Proceedings of the AAAI/IAAI* (pp. 450-455).

ns-3. (n.d.). *The ns-3 network simulator*. Retrieved September 9, 2009 from http://www.nsnam.org/

Numrich, R. W., & Heroux, M. A. (2009). A performance model with a fixed point for a molecular dynamics kernel. In *Proceedings International Supercomputing Conference '09.*

Observatory of European SMEs. (2003). *Competence Development in SMEs* (Tech. Rep. No. 1).

*OceanStore Home Page.* (n.d.). Retrieved September 2, 2009, from http://oceanstore.cs.berkeley.edu/

Oldfield, R. A., Arunagiri, S., Teller, P. J., Seelam, S., Riesen, R., Varela, M. R., & Roth, P. C. (2007, September). Modeling the impact of checkpoints on next-generation systems. In *Proceedings of the 24th IEEE Conference on Mass Storage Systems and Technologies*, San Diego, CA.

Oliner, A., & Stearley, J. (2007, June). What supercomputers say: A study of five system logs. In *Proceedings of the 37th Annual IEEE/IFIP International Conference on Dependable Systems and Networks*, Edinburgh, UK (pp. 575-584). Washington, DC: IEEE Computer Society Press.

OpenCFD. (2009). *The Open Source CFD Toolbox*. Retrieved on February, 4th, 2009, from http://www.opencfd.co.uk/ openfoam/

Oppenheimer, D., Albrecht, J., Patterson, D., & Vahdatm, A. (2004). Distributed resource discovery on Planetlab with SWORD. In *Proceedings of the 1st workshop on Real, Large Distributed Systems.*

Orlando, S. Peres., G., Reale, F., Bocchino, F., & Sacco, G. (2008), High Performance Computing on the CO-META Grid Infrastructure, In *Proceedings of the Grid Open Days at the University of Palermo* (pp.181-185), Catania: Consorzio COMETA

Orlando, S., Palmerini, P., Perego, R., & Silvestri, F. (2002). Adaptive and Resource-Aware Mining of Frequent Itemsets. *ICDM: Proceedings of the 2002 IEEE International Conference on Data Mining* (pp. 338-345). Washington, DC: IEEE Computer Society.

Pacheco, P. (2008). *Parallel Programming with MPI*. Retrieved January 27th, 2009, from http://www.cs.usfca.edu/mpi/

Pacitti, E., Minet, P., & Simon, E. (1999). Fast Algorithms for Maintaining Replica Consistency in Lazy Master Replicated Databases. In *Proceedings of the Int. Conf. on Very Large Databases*, Edinburgh, UK.

Palmerini, P., Orlando, S., & Perego, R. (2004). Statistical Properties of Transactional Databases. *Symposium on Applied Computing: Proceedings of the 2004 ACM symposium on Applied computing* (pp. 515-519). New York: ACM

Pan, R., Ding, Z., Yu, Y., & Peng, Y. (2005). A bayesian network approach to ontology mapping. In *Proceedings of the 4th International Semantic Web Conference (ISWC '05)* (pp. 563-577).

Paolucci, M., Kawamura, T., Payne, T., & Sycara, K. (2002). Semantic matching of web service capabilities. In *Proceedings of the 1st Int'l Semantic Web Conference (ISWC)* (pp. 333-347).

Papazoglou, M. P. (2003). Service-oriented computing: Concepts, characteristics and directions. *4th International Conference on Web Information Systems Engineering (WISE 2003)* (pp. 3-12). Rome: IEEE Computer Society.

PAPI. (n.d.). Retrieved September 9, 2009 from http://icl.cs.utk.edu/papi/

Park, J. S., An, G., & Chandra, D. (2007). Trusted P2P Computing Environments With Role-Based Access Control. *Information Security, IET, 1*(1), 27–35. doi:10.1049/iet-ifs:20060084

Parvez, I. A. (2009). *Earthquake Parameters*. Retrieved December 15, 2009, from http://www.cmmacs.ernet.in/cmmacs/pdf/parvez_lec2.pdf

Pathan, M., & Buyya, R. (2009). Architecture and performance models for QoS-driven effective peering of content delivery networks. *Multiagent and Grid Systems, 5*(2), 165–195.

Pawson, R. (2006). *Evidence-Based Policy: A Realist Perspective*. London: Sage.

Pawson, R., & Tilley, N. (1997). *Realistic Evaluation*. New York: Sage.

Payne, T. R. (2008). Web Services from an Agent perspective. *IEEE Intelligent Systems, 23*(2), 12–14. doi:10.1109/MIS.2008.37

Pedler, M., Burgoyne, J. G., & Brooks, C. (2005). What has Action Learning learned to become? *Action Learning Research and Practice, 2*(1), 49–68.

Pei, J., Hong, J., & Bell, D. A. (2006a). A Novel Clustering-based Approach to Schema Matching. In Proceedings of the 4th *International Conference on Advances in Information Systems (ADVIS)* (pp. 60-69), Izmir, Turkey.

Peltz, C. (2003). Web Services orchestration and choreography. *Web Services Journal, 03*(07), 30–35.

Perego, R., Orlando, S., & Palmerini, P. (2001). Enhancing the Apriori Algorithm for Frequent Set Counting. In G. Goos, J. Hartmanis, & J. van Leeuwen (Eds.). ), *Lecture Notes In Computer Science: Vol. 2114 Proceedings of Third International Conference on Data Warehousing and Knowledge Discovery* (pp 71-82). Springer Berlin / Heidelberg

Petrini, F., & Vannesch, M. (1997). SMART: A simulator of massive architectures and topologies. In *Proceedings of the Euro-PDS* (pp. 185-191).

Petrini, F., Kerbyson, D. J., & Pakin, S. (2003, November). *The Case of the Missing Supercomputer Performance: Identifying and Eliminating the Performance Variability on the ASCI Q Machine.* Paper presented at the ACM/IEEE Conference on High Performance Networking and Computing, Phoenix, AZ.

Petrini, F., Kerbyson, D., & Pakin, S. (2003). *The Case of the Missing Supercomputer Performance: Achieving Optimal performance on the 8,192 Processors of ASCI Q.* Washington, DC: IEEE.

Petriu, D., Amer, H., Majumdar, S., & Abdull-Fatah, I. (2000) Using analytic models for predicting middleware performance., In M. Woodside, M. et al. (Ed.), *Workshop on Software and Performance: Proceedings of the 2nd international workshop on Software and performance* (pp. 189-194), New York: ACM Ping, W. An Introduction to Artificial Neural Networks. Lecture Notes. Retrieved May 15, 2009, from http://www.physiol.net/study/resource/pdf/An%20Introduction%20to% 20Artificial%20Neural%20Networks.ppt

Prakash, S., Deelman, E., & Bagrodia, R. (2000). Asynchronous parallel simulation of parallel programs. *IEEE Transactions on Software Engineering, 26*(5), 385–400. doi:10.1109/32.846297

Pratali, P. (2003). The strategic management of technological innovations in the small to medium enterprise. *European Journal of Innovation Management, 6*(1), 18–31. doi:10.1108/14601060310456300

Püschel, M., Moura, J. M. F., Johnson, J. R., Padua, D., Veloso, M. M., & Singer, B. W. (2005). SPIRAL: Code generation for DSP transforms. *Proceedings of the IEEE, 93*(2), 232–275. doi:10.1109/JPROC.2004.840306

Qi, G., Hua, X., Rui, Y., Tang, J., Mei, T., & Zhang, H. (2007). Correlative multi-label video annotation. In *Proceedings of the 15th international Conference on Multimedia.*

Qthreads. (2009). *Sandia National Laboratories: Qthreads.* Retrieved from http://www.cs.sandia.gov/qthreads

Rahm, E., & Bernstein, P. A. (2001). A survey of approaches to automatic schema matching. In *The International Journal on Very Large Data Bases.*

Rahm, E., Do, H. H., & Maßmann, S. (2004). Matching Large XML Schemas. In *SIGMOD Record* (pp. 26-31). New York, NY: ACM Press.

Rajasekhar, S., Khalil, I., & Tari, Z. (2006). Probabilistic QoS Routing in WiFi P2P Networks. In *Proceedings of the 20th International Conference on Advanced Information Networking and Applications* (pp. 811-816).

Raman, V., Narang, I., Crone, C., Haas, L., Malaika, S., Mukai, T., et al. (2003). *Data access and management services on Grid. Global Grid Forum.* Retrieved August 17, 2008, from http://61.136.61.58:81/gate/big5/ www. cs.man.ac.uk/Grid-db/papers/dams.pdf

Ranganathan, K., & Foster, I. (2001). Identifying dynamic replication strategies for a high performance data grid. In []. New York: Springer.]. *Proceedings of the Grid: Second International Workshop, 2242,* 75–86.

Rapaport, R. N., Life, E. A., & Brodie, M. B. (2001). *Mid-Career Development: Research Perspectives on a Developmental Community for Senior Administrators.* London: Routledge.

Ratnasamy, S., Francis, P., Handley, M., Karp, R. M., & Shenker, S. (2001). A scalable content-addressable network. In *Proceedings of the SIGCOMM* (pp. 161-172).

Reinoso Castillo, J. A., Silvescu, A., Caragea, D., Pathak, J., & Honavar, V. G. (2008). *Information extraction and integration from heterogeneous, distributed, autonomous information sources – a federated ontology – driven query-centric approach.* Paper presented at IEEE International Conference on Information Integration and Reuse. Retrieved August 17, 2008, from http://www.cs.iastate. edu/ ~honavar/Papers/indusfinal.pdf

Revans, R. (1983). *A. B. C. of Action Learning.* London: Lemos & Crane.

Revans, R. W. (1982). *The Origins and Growth of Action Learning.* Bromley, UK: Chartwell-Bratt.

Riesen, R. (2006). A Hybrid MPI Simulator. In *Proceedings of the IEEE International Conference on Cluster Computing (CLUSTER'06).*

Ripeanu, M., & Foster, I. (2001). Peer-to-peer architecture case study: Gnutella network. In *Proceedings of the First Conference on Peer-to-peer Computing,* Sweden (pp. 99-100). Washington, DC: IEEE Computer Press.

Ripeanu, M., Iamnitchi, A., Foster, I., & Rogers, A. (2007). *In Search of Simplicity: A Self-Organizing Group Communication Overlay* (Tech. Rep. No. TR-2007-05). Vancouver, Canada: University of British Columbia.

Risse, T., Wombacher, A., Surridge, M., Taylor, S., & Aberer, K. (2001). Online Scheduling in Distributed Message Converter Systems. In Gonzalez, T., (Ed.), *Parallel and distributed computing and systems: proceedings of the IASTED international conference* (pp. 177-184), California: ACTA Press.

Rodrigues, A., Murphy, R., Kogge, P., Brockman, J., Brightwell, R., & Underwood, K. (2003). *Implications of a PIM architectural model for MPI.* Paper presented at the IEEE International Conference on Cluster Computing, Los ALamitos, CA, USA.

Rodrigues, L., & Raynal, M. (2003). Atomic Broadcast in Asynchronous Crash-Recovery Distributed Systems and its use in Quorum-Based Replication. *IEEE Transactions on Knowledge and Data Engineering, 15*(5), 1206–1217. doi:10.1109/TKDE.2003.1232273

Roitman, H., & Gal, A. (2006). Ontobuilder: Fully automatic extraction and consolidation of ontologies from web sources using sequence semantics. In *EDBT workshops* (pp. 573-576).

Rowstron, A., & Druschel, P. (2001). Pastry: scalable, distributed object location and routing for large-scale peer-to-peer systems. In *Proceedings of the IFIP/ACM Int'l Conference on Distributed Systems Platforms (Middleware)* (pp. 329-350).

Rupnow, K., Rodrigues, A., Underwood, K., & Compton, K. (2006). Scientific Applications vs. SPEC-FP: A Comparison of Program Behavior. In *Proceedings of the International Conference on Supercomputing.*

Saint-Andre, P. (2004). *Extensible Messaging and Presence Protocol (XMPP): Core. RFC 3920.*

Saito, Y., & Shapiro, M. (2005). Optimistic Replication. *ACM Computing Surveys, 37*(1), 42–81. doi:10.1145/1057977.1057980

Sawhney, N., Balcom, D., & Smith, I. (1997). Authoring and Navigating Video in Space and Time. In *Proceedings of IEEE MultiMedia* (pp. 30-39).

Sbalzarini, I. F., Hayer, A., Helenius, A., & Koumoutsakos, P. (2006). Simulations of (an)isotropic diffusion on curved biological surfaces. *Biophysical Journal, 90*(3), 878–885. doi:10.1529/biophysj.105.073809

Sbalzarini, I. F., Mezzacasa, A., Helenius, A., & Koumoutsakos, P. (2005). Effects of organelle shape on fluorescence recovery after photobleaching. *Biophysical Journal, 89*(3), 1482–1492. doi:10.1529/biophysj.104.057885

Sbalzarini, I. F., Walther, J. H., Bergdorf, M., Hieber, S. E., Kotsalis, E. M., & Koumoutsakos, P. (2006). PPM – a highly efficient parallel particle-mesh library for the simulation of continuum systems. *Journal of Computational Physics, 215*(2), 566–588. doi:10.1016/j.jcp.2005.11.017

Sbalzarini, I. F., Walther, J. H., Polasek, B., Chatelain, P., Bergdorf, M., & Hieber, S. E. (2006). *A software framework for the portable parallelization of particle-mesh simulations. LNCS, 4128*, 730–739.

Schmid, S., & Wattenhofer, R. (2007). Structuring Unstructured Peer-to-Pee Networks. In *Proceedings of the 14th Annual IEEE International Conference on High Performance Computing (HiPC)*, Goa, India. Washington, DC: IEEE Press.

Schoonderwoerd, R., Holland, O., Bruten, J., & Rothkrantz, L. (1997). Ant-based load balancing in telecommunications networks. *Adaptive Behavior, 5*(2), 169. doi:10.1177/105971239700500203

Schopf, J. (2003). *Ten actions when superscheduling: A grid scheduling architecture.* Paper presented at the Workshop on Scheduling Architecture, Tokyo.

*Secure Linux Home Page.* (n.d.). Retrieved September 15, 2009, from http://www.nsa.gov/research/ selinux/index.shtml

Sequoia Benchmark Codes, A. S. C. (n.d.). Retrieved September 11, 2009 from https://asc.llnl.gov/sequoia/benchmarks/

Sethian, J. A. (1999). *Level set methods and fast marching methods.* Cambridge, UK: Cambridge University Press.

SETI@Home Project Home Page. (n.d.). Retrieved August 28, 2009, from http://setiathome.berkeley.edu

Shalf, J., Kamil, S., Oliker, L., & Skinner, D. (Artist) (2005). *Analyzing Ultra-Scale Application Communication Requirements for a Reconfigurable Hybrid Interconnect.*

Shaw, R. (2001). Don't Panic: Behaviour in Major Incidents. *Disaster Prevention and Management, 10*(1).

Shen, K. (2004). Structure management for scalable overlay service construction. In *Proceedings of the First Symposium on Networked Systems Design and Implementation (NSDI'04)* (pp. 21-21). Berkeley, CA: USENIX Association.

Shi, Y. Q., Zhang, Z. H., Fang, Y., & Jiang, C. J. (2003). Build city traffic information service system based on grid platform. In *Proceedings of the 2003 IEEE Intelligent Transportation Systems,* Shanghai, China (Vol. 1, pp. 278-282).

Shipman, F., Girgensohn, A., & Wilcox, L. (2008). Authoring, viewing, and generating hypervideo: An overview of Hyper-Hitchcock. In *Proceedings of the ACM Trans. Multimedia Comput. Commun. Applications* (Vol. 5, No. 2, pp. 1-19).

Shiva, S. (2005). *Advanced Computer Architectures* (p. 7). Boca Raton, FL: CRC Press.

Shudo, K., Tanaka, Y., & Sekiguchi, S. (2005). P3: P2P-Based Middleware Enabling Transfer and Aggregation of Computational Resources. In *Proceedings of the IEEE International Symposium on Cluster Computing and the Grid*(pp. 259-266). Washington, DC: IEEE Press.

Shuler, L., Jong, C., Riesen, R., Dresser, D. W. v., Maccabe, A. B., Fisk, L. A., et al. (1995, 1995). *The Puma Operating System for Massively Parallel Computers.* Paper presented at the Intel Supercomputer Users' Group, Albuquerque, NM.

Shvaiko, P., & Euzenat, J. (2005). A Survey of Schema-based Matching approaches. *Journal on Data Semantics IV, 3730*, 146–171. doi:10.1007/11603412_5

Simon, B., Anderson, R., & Wolfman, S. (2003). Activating computer architecture withClassroom Presenter. In *Proceedings of the WCAE2003.*

Simon, H., Zacharia, T., Stevens, R., et al. (2007). *Modeling and Simulation at the Exascale for Energy and the Environment* (Tech. Rep.). Department of Energy. Retrieved from http://www.sc.doe.gov/ascr/ ProgramDocuments/ TownHall.pdf

Simon, H. (1977). *The new science of management decision.* Englewood Cliffs, NJ: Prentice Hall.

Singh, A., & Liu, L. (2003). TrustMe: Anonymous Management of Trust Relationships in Decentralized P2P Systems. In *Proceedings of the Third International Conference on Peer-to-Peer Computing* (pp. 142-149). Washington, DC: IEEE Press.

Smallbone, D. (1998). Internationalisation of markets and SME development: Some results from an international comparative study. *Economics and Organisations, 1*(6), 13–25.

Smallbone, D., & Rogut, A. (2005). The challenge facing SMEs in the EU's new member states. *The International Entrepreneurship and Management Journal, 1*(2), 219–240. doi:10.1007/s11365-005-1130-x

Smart card driver for Open Source Operating Systems: http://www.opensc-project.org/opensc/. (2009).

Smiljanic, M., Keulen, M., & Jonker, W. (2006). Using Element Clustering to Increase the Efficiency of XML Schema Matching. In *Proceedings of the 22nd International Conference on Data Engineering Workshops (ICDE Workshops).*

Smith, J. R., Srinivasan, S., Amir, A., Basu, S., Iyengar, G., Lin, C. Y., et al. (2001). Intergrating Features, Models, and Semantics for TREC Video Retrieval. In *Proceedings of the NIST TREC-10 Text Retrieval Conference.*

SOS Workshop on Distributed Supercomputing. (2009). Retrieved from http://www.cs.sandia.gov/ Conferences/ SOS13/

S-sicilia Project. Bringing commercial applications to the Grid: http://s-sicilia.unime.it/. (2009).

Steves, M. P., Ranganathan, M., & Morse, E. L. (n.d.). SMAT: Synchronous Multimedia and Annotation Tool. In. *Proceedings of the International Conference on System Science.*

Stoica, I. (2002). Chord: a scalable peer-to-peer lookup protocol for Internet applications. *IEEE Transactions on Networks, 11*(1), 17–32. doi:10.1109/TNET.2002.808407

Stone, N. T. B., Gill, D. B. B., Johanson, B., Marsteller, J., Nowoczynski, P., Porter, D., et al. (2006, June). *PDIO: HIgh-Performance Remote File I/O for Portals-Enabled Compute Nodes.* Paper presented at the International Conference on Parallel and Distributed Processing Techniques and Applications, Las Vegas, Nevada.

Strube, A., Rexachs, D., & Luque, E. (2008). Software probes: Towards a quick method for machine characterization and application performance prediction. *Proceedings of the 2008 International Symposium on Parallel and Distributed Computing* (pp. 23-30). Washington, DC: IEEE Computer Society

Stumme, G., & Maedche, A. (2001). Ontology merging for federated ontologies on the semantic web. In *Proceedings of the International Workshop for Foundations of Models for Information Integration (FMII-2001),* Italy.

Su, W., Wang, J., & Lochovsky, F. (2006). Holistic Query Interface Matching using Parallel Schema Matching. In *Proceedings of the 22nd International Conference on Data Engineering (ICDE),* Atlanta, GA.

Surana, S., Godfrey, B., Lakshminarayanan, K., Karp, R., & Stoica, I. (2006). Load balancing in dynamic structured peer-to-peer systems. *Performance Evaluation, 63*(3), 217–240. doi:10.1016/j.peva.2005.01.003

Surridge, M., Taylor, S., De Roure, D., & Zaluska, E. (2005). Experiences with GRIA-Industrial Applications on a Web Services Grid. In *E-SCIENCE: Proceedings of the First International Conference on e-Science and Grid Computing* (pp. 98-105). Washington, DC: IEEE Computer Society. TAPAS, Trusted and QoS-Aware Provision of Application Services. Retrieved May 15, 2009, from http://tapas.sourceforge.net

Susukita, R., Ando, H., Aoyagi, M., Honda, H., Inadomi, Y., Inoue, K., et al. (2008). *Performance prediction of large-scale parallel system and application using macro-level simulation.* Paper presented at the SC '08: Proceedings of the 2008 ACM/IEEE conference on Supercomputing, Piscataway, NJ, USA.

Szeliski, R. (2005). *Image alignment and stitching: A tutorial* (Tech. Rep. No. MSR-TR-2004-92). Microsoft Research.

Termier, A., Rousset, M.-A., & Sebag, M. (2004). DRY-ADE: a new approach for discovering closed frequent trees in heterogeneous tree databases. In *Proceedings of the 4th IEEE International Conference on Data Mining* (ICDM) (pp. 543-546).

*TerraNet Home Page*. (n.d.) Retrieved August 29, 2009, from http://www.terranet.se

Thakur, R., Bordawekar, R., Choudhary, A., Ponnusamy, R., & Singh, T. (1994). PASSION runtime library for parallel I/O. In *Proceedings of the IEEE scalable parallel libraries conference* (pp. 119-128). Washington, DC: IEEE.

Thakur, R., Gropp, W., & Lusk, E. (1999). Data sieving and collective I/O in ROMIO. In *Proceedings of the 7th symposium on the frontiers of massively parallel computation* (pp. 182-189).

*The DataGrid project*. (2004). Retrieved from http://eu-datagrid.web.cern.ch/ eu-datagrid/

The Enabling Grids for E-sciencE project. http://www.eu-egee.org/. (2009).

*The TeraGrid project*. (2000). Retrieved from http://www.teragrid.org

Thoziyoor, S., Ahn, J. H., Muralimanohar, N., & Jouppi, N. (2008). *Cacti 5.1*. HP Labs.

Thywisswen, K. (2006). *Components of Risk. A Comparative Glossary*. Tokyo, Japan: United Nations University. Retrieved December 15, 2009, from http://www.unisdr.org/eng/library/ Literature/9985.pdf

Tipparaju, V., Kot, A., Nieplocha, J., Bruggencate, M. t., & Chrisochoides, N. (2007, March). *Evaluation of Remote Memory Access Communication on the Cray XT3*. Paper presented at the Workshop on Communication Architectures for Clusters, Long Beach, California.

Tonellotto, N., Wieder, P., & Yahyapour, R. (2005). A proposal for a generic grid scheduling architecture. In *Proceedings of the Integrated Research in Grid Computing Workshop*, Greece (pp. 337-346). New York: Springer.

Tremblay, N., & Iorian, M. (2001). Temporal shortest paths: Parallel computing implementa -tions. *Parallel Computing, 27*(12), 569–1609. doi:10.1016/S0167-8191(01)00107-7

Trim, P. R. F. (2003). Disaster Management and the Role of the Intelligence and Security Services. *Disaster Prevention and Management, 12*(1).

Troger, P., Rajic, H., Haas, A., & Domagalski, P. (2007). Standardization of an API for Distributed Resource Management Systems. In *Proceedings of the Seventh IEEE International Symposium on Cluster Computing and the Grid (CCGRID '07)* (pp. 619-626). Washington, DC: IEEE Computer Society.

Tsetsos, V., Anagnostopoulos, C., & Hadjiefthymiades, S. (2006). On the evaluation of semantic web service matchmaking systems. In *Proceedings of the 4th IEEE European Conference on Web Services (ECOWS)* (pp. 255-264).

Tuecke, S., Welch, V., Engert, D., Pearlman, L., & Thompson, M. (2004). *Internet X.509 Public Key Infrastructure (PKI) Proxy Certificate Profile* (Tech. Rep. RFC3820). Available from http://www.ietf.org/rfc/rfc3820.txt

Turala, M. (2005). *The CrossGrid Project*. Retrieved on January, 28th, 2009, from http://www.eu-crossgrid.org/project.htm

Turkiyyah, G., Reed, D., & Yang, J. (1996). Fast vortex methods for predicting wind-induced pressures on buildings. *Journal of Wind Engineering and Industrial Aerodynamics, 58*, 51–79. doi:10.1016/0167-6105(95)00020-R

*TVU Networks Home Page*. Retrieved August 25, 2009, from http://www.tvunetworks.com

Ullman, J. (1997, January). *Information integration using logical views*. Paper presented at the Sixth International Conference on Database Theory, Troy, MI.

Underwood, K., Levenhagen, M., & Rodrigues, A. (2007). *Simulating Red Storm: challenges and successes in building a system simulation*. Paper presented at the 2007 IEEE International Parallel and Distributed Processing Symposium (IEEE Cat. No.07TH8938), Piscataway, NJ, USA.

United Nations. (2008). *Demographic dynamics and sustainability*. Rerteived December 15, 2009, from http://www.un.org/esa/sustdev/natlinfo/ indicators/indisd / english/chapt5e.htm

VampirTrace. (n.d.). Retrieved September 9, 2009 from http://www.tu-dresden.de/zih/vampirtrace

van Rijsbergen, A. (1979). *Information Retrieval*. London: Butterworths.

Vaughan, C. (2008). *Level II ASC Milestone 3159 Red Storm 284 TeraFLOPS Upgrade Final Report* (No. SAND2008-7937P). Sandia National Laboratories, USA.

Vazhkudai, S., Schopf, J. M., & Foster, I. (2002). Predicting the performance of wide area data transfers. *Proceedings of the 16th International Parallel and Distributed Processing Symposium* (pp. 34-43). Washington, DC: IEEE Computer Society. Wikipedia. *Subsets of e-business applications*. Retrieved May 15, 2009, from http://en.wikipedia.org/wiki/E-business#Subsets

Vecchio, D. D., Humphrey, M., Basney, J., & Nagaratnam, N. (2005). Credex: User-centric credential management for grid and web services. *IEEE International Conference on Web Services,* (pp. 149-156).

Venugopal, S., Buyya, R., & Ramamohanarao, K. (2005). *A taxonomy of data Grids for distributed data sharing management and processing*. Retrieved August 17, 2008, from http://arxiv.org/abs/cs.DC/0506034

Verlet, L. (1967). Computer experiments on classical fluids. I. Thermodynamical properties of Lennard-Jones molecules. *Physical Review, 159*(1), 98–103. doi:10.1103/PhysRev.159.98

Vizing, V. G. (1964). On an estimate of the chromatic class of a p-graph. *Diskret. Analiz, 3*, 25–30.

Voronenko, Y. (2008). *Library generation for linear transforms*. Unpublished doctoral dissertation, Carnegie Mellon University, Pittsburgh, PA.

Vygotsky, L. S. (1978). *Mind in Society: The Development of Higher Psychological Processes*. Cambridge, MA: Harvard University Press.

Wahlström, R., Tyagunov, S., Grünthal, G., Stempniewski, L., Zschau, J., & Müller, M. (2004). Seismic Risk analysis for Germany: Methodology and preliminary results. In Malzahn, D., & Plapp, T. (Eds.), *Disasters and Society, Hazard Assessment to Risk Reduction* (pp. 83–90). Berlin: Logos Verlag.

Waldrich, O., Wieder, P., & Ziegler, W. (2006). A meta-scheduling service for co-allocating arbitrary types of resources. *Lecture Notes in Computer Science, 3911*, 782. doi:10.1007/11752578_94

Walsh, V., & Golins, G. L. (1976). *The exploration of the Outward Bound process*. Denver, CO: Colorado Outward Bound School.

Walther, J. H., & Sbalzarini, I. F. (2009). Large-scale parallel discrete element simulations of granular flow. *Engineering Computations, 26*(6), 688–697. doi:10.1108/02644400910975478

Wang, C., Hong, M., Pei, J., Zhou, H., Wang, W., & Shi, B. (2004). Efficient Pattern-Growth methods for Frequent Tree Pattern Mining. In *8th Pacific-Asia Conference, on Advances in Knowledge Discovery and Data Mining (PAKDD)*. LNCS, 3056, (pp. 441-451), Springer, Sydney, Australia.

Wang, Z., Wang, Y., Zhang, S., Shen, G., & Du, T. (2006). Matching Large Scale Ontology Effectively. In Proceedings of the *First Asian Semantic Web Conference (ASWC)* (pp. 99-106), Beijing, China.

Wang, D. H., & Qu, D. Y. (1998). A study of a real-time dynamic prediction method for traffic volume. *China Journal of Highway and Transport, 11*, 102–107.

Wang, D., Ganesh, B., Tuaycharoen, N., Baynes, K., Jaleel, A., & Jacob, B. (2005). DRAMsim: a memory system simulator. *SIGARCH Comput. Archit. News, 33*(4), 100–107. doi:10.1145/1105734.1105748

Watson, P. (2002). *Databases and the Grid* (Tech. Rep.). Retrieved August 17, 2008, from http://www.cs.ncl.ac.uk/research/ pubs/books/papers/185.pdf

Watts, M. (2009). *Microphotonic Circuits, Networks, and Sensors*. Center For Integrated Photonic Systems Annual Meeting: Massachusetts Institute of Technology.

Watts, J., & Taylor, S. (1998). A practical approach to dynamic load balancing. *IEEE Transactions on Parallel and Distributed Systems, 9*(3), 235–248. doi:10.1109/71.674316

Weber, I., Haller, J., & Mulle, J. A. (2008). Automated derivation of executable business processes from choreographies in virtual organisations. *International Journal of Business Process Integration and Management, 3*(2), 85–95. doi:10.1504/IJBPIM.2008.020972

Weigand, G. (2007, November). *Energy Assurance and High Performance Computing*. Paper presented at Supercomputing 2007 ORNL booth.

Weise, J. (2001, August). Public Key Infrastructure Overview. *Sun BluePrints OnLine*. Available from http://www.sun.com/blueprints/0801/publickey.pdf

Weishaupl, T., & Schikuta, E. (2004). *Dynamic service evolution for open languages in the Grid and service oriented architecture*. Paper presented at the Fifth International Workshop on Grid Computing, Pittsburgh, PA.

Wilde, E., Anand, S., Bucheler, T., Nabholz, N., & Zimmermann, P. (2008). Collaboration support for bibliographic data. *International Journal of Web Based Communities, 4*(1), 98–109. doi:10.1504/IJWBC.2008.016493

Wohrer, A., Brezany, P., & Janciak, I. (2004). *Virtualisation of heterogeneous data sources for Grid information systems*. Retrieved August 17, 2008, from http://www.par.univie.ac.at/publications/ other/inst_rep_2002-2004.pdf

Wolski, R., Spring, N., & Hayes, J. (1999). The Network Weather Service: A Distributed Resource Performance Forecasting Service for Metacomputing. *Future Generation Computer Systems, 15*(5-6), 757–768. doi:10.1016/S0167-739X(99)00025-4

Woodside, C. M., & Menascé, D. A. (2006). Guest Editors' Introduction: Application-Level QoS. *IEEE Internet Computing, 10*(3), 13–15. doi:10.1109/MIC.2006.49

Wray, A. A. (1988). *A manual of the vectoral language (Internal report)*. Moffett Field, CA: NASA Ames Research Center.

Xia, S., Sun, D., Sun, C., Chen, D., & Shen, H. F. (2004). Leveraging single-user applications for multi-user collaboration: the coword approach. In *Proceedings of the 2004 ACM conference on Computer supported cooperative work.*

Xiaohui, W., Zhaohui, D., Shutao, Y., Chang, H., & Huizhen, L. (2006). CSF4: A WSRF compliant metascheduler. In *Proceedings of the 2006 World Congress in Computer Science, Computer Engineering, and Applied Computing (GCA)* (Vol. 6, pp. 61-67). Las Vegas, NV: Bentham Science.

XML encryption: http://www.w3.org/tr/xmlenc-core/. (2009).

XML sign: http://www.w3.org/tr/xmlenc-core/. (2009).

Xu, R., & Wunsch, D. (2005). Survey of Clustering Algorithms. *Neural Networks, IEEE Transactions* (pp. 645-678).

Xu, J., Li, B., & Lee, D. (2002). Placement Problems for Transparent Data Replication Proxy Services. *IEEE Journal on Selected Areas in Communications, 20*(7), 1383–1398. doi:10.1109/JSAC.2002.802068

Yang, Z. S. (1999). *The Theory and Model of Inducement System of City traffic Flow*. Beijing, China: People Traffic Press.

Yu, H., & Vahdat, A. (2001). The Costs and Limits of Availability for Replicated Services. In *Proceedings of the Eighteenth ACM Symposium on Operating Systems Principles (SOSP '01)* (pp. 29-42). New York: ACM.

Zhang, Z. H., Zhi, Q., Zeng, G. S., & Jiang, C. J. (2004). In M. L. Li (Ed.), *The Architecture of Traffic Information Grid* (LNCS 3032, pp. 209-212). New York: Springer Verlag.

Zhang, D., Zhou, L., Briggs, R. O., & Nunamaker, J. F. (2006). Instructional video in e-learning: assessing the impact of interactive video on learning effectiveness. *Information & Management*, 15–27. doi:10.1016/j.im.2005.01.004

Zhang, Y. J., & Lu, H. B. (2002). A hierarchical organization scheme for video data. *Pattern Recognition*, 2381–2387. doi:10.1016/S0031-3203(01)00189-3

Zhao, X., Liu, E., & Clapworthy, G. J. (2008). Service-oriented digital libraries: A Web Services approach. *3rd International Conference on Internet and Web Applications and Services (ICIW2008)* (pp. 608-613). Athens: IEEE Computer Society.

Zhao, X., Liu, E., Clapworthy, G. J., Quadrani, P., Testi, D., & Viceconti, M. *(2008). Using Web Services for distributed medical visualisation.* 5th Intenational Conference on Medical Visualisation (MediVis08) *(pp. 57-62).* London: IEEE Computer Society.

Zheng, G., Shi, L., & Kale, L. V. (2004). FTC-Charm++: An in-memory checkpoint-based fault tolerant runtime for Charm++ and MPI. In *Proceedings of the IEEE conference on cluster computing* (pp. 93-103).

Zheng, G., Wilmarth, T., Jagadishprasad, P., & Kale, L. (2005). Simulation-based performance prediction for large parallel machines. *International Journal of Parallel Programming, 33*(2-3), 183–207. doi:10.1007/s10766-005-3582-6

Zhoun, W., Wang, L., & Jia, W. (2004). An Analysis of Update Ordering in Distributed replication systems. *Future Generation Computer Systems, 20*(4), 565–590. doi:10.1016/S0167-739X(03)00174-2

Zhu, X., Elmagarmid, A. K., Xue, X., Wu, L., & Catlin, A. (2004). *InsightVide: Towards Hierarchical Video Content Organization for Efficient Browsing, Summarization, and Retrieval.* IEEE Trans. Multimedia.

Zhu, X., Luo, J., & Song, A. (2008). A Grid Information Services Architecture Based on Structured P2P Systems. *Lecture Notes in Computer Science, 5236,* 374–383. doi:10.1007/978-3-540-92719-8_34

# About the Contributors

**Nik Bessis** is currently a Head of Distributed and Intelligent Systems (DISYS) research group, a Professor and a Chair of Computer Science in the School of Computing and Mathematics at University of Derby, UK. He is also an academic member in the Department of Computer Science and Technology at University of Bedfordshire (UK). He obtained a BA (1991) from the TEI of Athens, Greece and completed his MA (1995) and PhD (2002) at De Montfort University (Leicester, UK). His research interest is the analysis, research, and delivery of user-led developments with regard to trust, data integration, annotation, and data push methods and services in distributed environments. These have a particular focus on the study and use of next generation and Grid technologies methods for the benefit of various virtual organizational settings. He is involved in and leading a number of funded research and commercial projects in these areas. Prof. Bessis has published over 120 papers, won 2 best paper awards and is the editor of several books and the Editor-in-Chief of the *International Journal of Distributed Systems and Technologies* (IJDST). In addition, Prof. Bessis is a regular reviewer and has served several times as a keynote speaker (CISIS-2010; ICADIWT-2010; IARIA-2010; WCST-2011), conferences/workshops/track chair (EIDWT-2011/12; 3PGCIC-2011/12; IADIS-2010/11/12; CISIS-2011/12; IMIS-2012; AINA-2011/12; PARELEC-2011; INCoS-2010/11/12), associate editor, session chair, and scientific program committee member.

\* \* \*

**Helgi Adalsteinsson** is a Principal Member of the Technical Staff in the Scalable Computing R&D department at Sandia National Laboratories in Livermore, CA. He is involved in a host of research efforts on novel application domains, algorithms and programming models for numerically intensive computing.

**Ken Alvin** received his B.S. in Aerospace Engineering from Iowa State University in 1983, and his M.S. and Ph.D. from University of Colorado in Boulder in 1990 and 1993, respectively. From 1983 to 1989 he was a space structures dynamics engineer for Harris Corporation. He joined Sandia National Laboratories in 1994 as a structural dynamics researcher, developing algorithms for inverse problems, sensitivity analysis, and transient response of structural and solid mechanics. He helped develop the massively parallel structural dynamics code, Salinas, which won a Gordon Bell Award in 2002, and managed the Computational Solid Mechanics and Structural Dynamics Department at Sandia from 2002 to 2006. From 2006 to 2007, he was a detailee to the federal office of DOE/NNSA's Advanced Simulation and Computing (ASC) Program in Washington D.C., leading the effort to develop a national code strategy for the ASC Program. For the last two years he has managed the Applied Mathematics and Applications

Department and served as the deputy program director for the ASC program at Sandia, and as national security code applications representative to the Alliance for Computing at Extreme Scales (ACES) and the Institute for Advanced Architectures (IAA).

**Youssef Amghar** is professor in the field of information systems at the University of Lyon. His field of teaching concern project management, databases and development processes. His is an active member of SOC team. His current research interests include business process, services, interoperability of applications and legal documents modeling. He is author of several papers related to these research activities and managed some projects about decisions support and elearning.

**Giuseppe Andronico** was born in Catania (Italy) in January 1965. He graduated in Physics "cum laude" at the University of Catania in 1991 and since 1995 he holds a Ph. D. in Physics from the same University. Since March 2001 he is technologist at the INFN Sezione di Catania. Since his graduation his main research activity has been done in the realm of theoretical physics. He has been involved in lattice field theory simulations. Since late 1999 he has been interested in grid computing participating to several initiatives: European DataGRID, InfnGrid, EGEE. In these initiatives he has been involved in developing code, in operations, in training and in dissemination activities. More recently he has been involved in some European funded projects: in EELA and EUMEDGRID he has been involved as WP manager, in EUChinaGRID he has been involved as Technical Manager, in EGEE-II and then in EGEE-III.

**Chimay J Anumba** graduated at 18 with a First Class Honours (Summa Cum Laude) degree in Building from the University of Jos, Nigeria. He worked briefly as a construction site engineer and as a design engineer before undertaking postgraduate research in Civil Engineering (Computer-Aided Engineering) at the University of Leeds, UK. On completion of his PhD in 1989, he joined Curtins Consulting Engineers plc, and was involved in a wide range of civil and structural engineering projects as an Engineer/Senior Engineer. This was followed by a period as a Senior Lecturer and Reader in Computer-Aided Engineering at the University of Teesside, UK. In 1998 he joined Loughborough University, UK, as Reader in Computer-Integrated Construction and subsequently became Founding Director of the university-wide Centre for Innovative and Collaborative Engineering (1999) and Professor of Construction Engineering & Informatics (2000). He is a past Chair of the European Group for Intelligent Computing in Engineering and was recently on the governing Council of the Institution of Civil Engineers (ICE). Professor Anumba's research work has received support with a total value of over £15m ($30m) and he has successfully supervised over 31 doctoral candidates and 15 postdoctoral researchers. He has more than 400 publications in his field, undertakes advisory/consultancy work for the UK Government and several firms, and is Co-Editor of the Journal of Information Technology in Construction (ITCon). He has won several awards for his work, including an Engineering Foresight Award from the Royal Academy of Engineering. Visiting Professor/Scholar appointments include Massachusetts Institute of Technology (MIT), USA; Stanford University, USA; Hanyang University, Korea; Hong Kong Polytechnic University; Universiti Teknologi Malaysia (UTM); Chongqing University, China; UTHM (Malaysia); University of Florida, USA; and Covenant University (Nigeria). In recognition of his substantial and sustained original contributions to the field of Construction Engineering and Informatics, Professor Anumba was awarded the higher doctorate degree of Doctor of Science, DSc, by Loughborough University in July

2006. In January 2007, he was also awarded an Honorary Doctorate by Delft University of Technology in The Netherlands for outstanding scientific contributions to Building and Construction Engineering.

**Eleana Asimakopoulou** has a first degree (University of Luton, UK) and an MA (University of Westminster, UK) in Architecture and a PhD (Loughborough University, UK) in managing natural disasters using Grid technology. Dr Asimakopoulou is currently a visiting lecturer at the Department of Computer Science and Technology at the University of Bedfordshire. Eleana is the editor of a book and a regular reviewer in several international conferences and journals. Her research interests include emergency management, response and planning for disasters, business continuity, construction and risk management, and also advanced ICT methods (such as grid and other forms of applicable collaborative technologies) for disaster management.

**Lalit K. Awasthi** is the professor of Computer Science and Engineering at the National Institute of Technology, Hamirpur. His research interests include fault-tolerance in distributed systems, mobile computing and P2P networks/computation. He has over 50 research papers published at various international forums. He completed his M.Tech from IIT Delhi and PhD from IIT Roorkee.

**Roberto Barbera** was born in Catania (Italy) in October 1963. He graduated in physics "cum laude" at the University of Catania in 1986 and since 1990 he holds a PhD in physics from the same University. Since 2005 he is associate professor at the Department of Physics and Astronomy of the Catania University. Since his graduation his main research activity has been done in the realm of experimental nuclear and particle physics. He has been involved in many experiments in France, Russia, United States and Sweden to study nuclear matter properties in heavy ion collisions at intermediate energies. He is author of more than 100 scientific papers published on international journals and more than 150 proceedings of international conferences. He is also referee of prestigious reviews in the field of Grid computing such as *Journal of Grid Computing and Future Generation Computer Systems*. Since 1997 he is involved in the NA57 Experiment at CERN SPS and in the ALICE Experiment at CERN LHC. Within ALICE, he has been the coordinator of the Off-line software of the Inner Tracking System detector and member of the Off-line Board. Since 1999 he is interested in Grid computing. He is a member of the Executive Board of the Italian INFN Grid Project (grid.infn.it). At Italian level, he is the Chief Technical Officer of the Consorzio COMETA and the Director of two big Grid Projects (TriGrid VL and PI2S2) funded by the Sicilian Regional Government and by the Ministry of University and Research, respectively. At European level, he is the Technical Coordinator of the EC funded EELA-2 Project and has several responsibilities in other EC Grid Projects such as EGEE-III, EUAsiaGrid, and EU-IndiaGrid. Since 2002 he is the responsible of the GENIUS grid portal project and, in 2004, he created the international GILDA grid infrastructure for training and dissemination that he coordinates since the beginning. Since the birth of GILDA he has been the organizer of/teacher in more than 350 Grid training events (tutorials, schools, and even university courses) around the world.

**Brian Barrett** is a computer scientist with the Scalable System Software group at Sandia National Laboratories. He received his Ph.D. in Computer Science from Indiana University. His research efforts are on the development of scalable high performance networks for next-generation HPC machines, as well as the communication libraries to support application development. Prior to joining Sandia National

Laboratories, Barrett was a founding member of the Open MPI project, both while at Indiana University and with the Advanced Computing Laboratory at Los Alamos National Laboratory, developing the Open MPI implementation of the MPI standard. He has also worked on a scalable communication subsystem for discrete event simulators while at the Information Sciences Institute.

**Radjaa Behidji** is a graduate from University of Oran (Es Senia), Algeria, where she received her Master's degree in Computer Science (June 2009) from Faculty of Sciences, University of Oran, Algeria. Her research interests are replication and consistency strategies, data grid and load balancing.

**Ghalem Belalem** graduated from University of Oran, Algeria, where he received PhD degree in computer science in 2007. He is now a research fellow of management of replicas in data grid. His current research interests are distributed systems, grid computing, data grid, cloud computing, placement of replicas and consistency in large scale systems.

**Naima Belayachi** is a graduate from University of Oran (Es Senia), Algeria, where she received her Master's degree in Computer Science (June 2009) from Faculty of Sciences, University of Oran, Algeria. Her research interests are replication and consistency strategies, multi-agents systems and decision-making systems.

**Aïcha-Nabila Benharkat** is associate professor at the Computer Science Department (INSA de LYON) since 1992. In this role, she worked on the Integration of heterogeneous databases using Description Logics. Currently, her research interests include the interoperability domain, schema matching techniques in small and large scale, business process as well as the interoperability in service oriented information system and quality and Web services discovery. Aïcha-Nabila BENHARKAT participated to the organisation of scientific events (the international conference. She is member of several conference program committees.

**David W. Birchall** research interests are in the area of management learning and innovation practices in organisations. He has particular expertise in the development of systems to support remote learners. David has consulted and lectured throughout the world on aspects of innovation, technology and organisation capabilities, organisational learning and knowledge management. His latest book – Capabilities for Strategic Advantage: Leading Through Technological Innovation, co-authored with George Tovstiga – was published in May 2005 by Palgrave.

**Simona Blandino** was born in Ragusa (RG), Italy on July 15th 1982. She received both Bachelor's and Master's degree (cum laude) in Computer Engineering from the University of Catania respectively in 2004 and 2008. From 2007 she has been working for COMETA Consortium on Grid Computing.

**Dino Bouchlaghem** is a qualified architect with a PhD in Environmental Design from the University of Manchester Institute of Science and Technology. He joined Loughborough University as a lecturer in 1994 and he became a professor in 2003. Dino is Editor-in-Chief, International Journal of Architectural Engineering and Design Management Member, International Council for Building Research Studies and Documentation (CIB). His research interests include Computer Aided Building Design: Thermal Modelling and Simulation, 3D visualisation and VR Design Management: IT support for the Design

Process, Construction Briefing, Information Management Process and Product Modelling in Concurrent Engineering Knowledge Management for sustainable Construction The Management of Visual Resources in Learning and Teaching.

**Ron Brightwell** received his BS in mathematics in 1991 and his MS in computer science in 1994 from Mississippi State University. He joined Sandia National Laboratories in 1995 and is currently Technical Manager of the Scalable System Software Department. He has authored more than 55 refereed journal and conference publications. His research interests include high-performance, scalable communication interfaces and protocols for system area networks, operating systems for massively parallel processing machines, and parallel program performance analysis libraries and tools. He is a Senior Member of the IEEE and the ACM.

**Amos Brocco** born October 7. 1981, got a Msc. in Computer Science (major) / Mathematics (minor) from the University of Fribourg (Switzerland) in 2005. Since the end of 2005 he is working as Ph.D. student with the Pervasive and Artificial Intelligence research group at the University of Fribourg. His research interests are in the area of distributed swarm intelligence, adaptive network algorithms and bio-inspired techniques in general.

**Antony Brown** has been a member of staff at the University of Bedfordshire for 8 years, lecturing in computer science with a speciality in system modelling, databases and internet technologies. He was awarded his PhD by the University of Bedfordshire in 2008 for his thesis on 'Multilevel modelling and prediction of melanoma incidence'. Dr Brown also runs a web development company specializing in advising and developing academic projects. He also has a keen interest in computer gaming and cinema.

**Riccardo Bruno** was born in Catania the 3rd December 1969 and graduated in computer science in May 1999, he started to work as researcher for the University of Catania from April 1999. In April 2000 he joined the LHS Company as software consultant for the BSCS billing system sold to telephony mobile companies belonging to the EMEA countries. He joined the INFN in Catania the 1st January 2006 as responsible of the activity WP 5.2 (Dissemination of Advanced Knowledge Activities) of the EUMEDGRID project, finished on February 2008. From March 2008 he is involved as responsible of the activity NA2.3 (Training) of the EELA-2 project.

**William J. Camp** is director emeritus of Computing, Computation, Information and Mathematics at Sandia National Laboratories and is currently Chief Supercomputing Architect and leader of exascale computing technology planning efforts at Intel Corporation. Bill received a BEE/NE from Manhattan College and a PhD in mathematical and computational physics from Cornell University. He has been involved in high performance computing for nearly 40 years, as a user, R&D leader, and architect. He has been associated with a succession of highly scalable MPP computers: the nCUBE-10, nCUBE-2, the Intel Paragon, the Intel Tflops, the Cray T3D, T3E, and XT3. With his Sandia colleagues in the Cplant project, he pioneered the development of large scalable linux clusters as true supercomputers. In 1988, he founded and led the Massively Parallel Computing Research Lab at Sandia. On leave from Sandia, he worked in the mid-90's on the T3D and T3E projects at Cray Research. In 1996, Bill returned to Sandia and became director of CCIM. In 2001--2005 at Sandia, he and Jim Tomkins architected the Red Storm/ Cray XT3 supercomputer for which they received two patents.

**Jia Chen**, male, is currently a master candidate in Intelligence Engineering Lab at Institute of Software, Chinese Academy of Sciences. He was born in 1984, and in 2007 he obtained his bachelor degree from Beihang University major in software engineering. His research interests include information visualization, computer vision and human computer interaction. In the past, he has done a series of work on Chinese form inks processing and oil drilling visualization. Recently, he is working on sketch based video summary generation and video organization in distributed environment. Cuixia Ma, female, born in 1975, is currently an Associate Research Fellow in Intelligence Engineering Lab at Institute of Software, Chinese Academy of Sciences. Her research interests include Human Computer Interaction Technologies, Sketch based human interface.

**Gordon Clapworthy** is Professor of Computer Graphics at the University of Bedfordshire (UK). He has a BSc (Class 1) in mathematics and a PhD in Aeronautical Engineering from the University of London, and an MSc (dist.) in computer science from City University (London). He has been involved in 19 European projects, coordinating 8 of them.

**Michele Courant** graduated in 1982 and received her PhD Degree in Computer Science in 1987 from the IRISA at the University of Rennes (France). She is currently a senior researcher at the Department of Informatics at the University of Fribourg, co-leader of the Pervasive and Artificial Intelligence Research Group. Her research activities aims at providing concepts, middleware and methodologies, for facilitating the design of adaptive systems made of heterogeneous interconnected entities.

**Hong Zhong Chen** received his M.S. from the Department of Computer Science and Technology, Tongji University, Shanghai, China, in 1981. He worked in Computer Department, Ruhr University, Germany as a visiting scholar form 1985 to 1986. Now he is a professor in Computer Science and Technology in Tongji University. His main research focus on: Supporting Technology of System Software, operating system, grid computing, etc. In recent years, he has published more than 20 papers in journals and conference proceedings.

**Scott Cranford** received the MS degree in Electrical Engineering from University of Colorado in Boulder in 2003. He is a Senior Member of the Technical Staff in the Scalable Computing R&D department at Sandia National Laboratories in Livermore, CA. His research interests include performance analysis, probabilistic modeling and parallel computing.

**Pietro Di Primo** was born in Catania during 1972. He scored a master's degree as a telecommunication engineer at the Catania University during 2004 and a higher level master on ICT during 2005. He worked as an ICT consultant for ACSE Co. in Milan. Since 2007 he joined the Grid team at the Catania Section of the National Institute for Nuclear Physics.

**Douglas Doerfler** obtained his MSEE from Kansas State University in 1985. He joined Sandia National Laboratories in Albuquerque, NM after graduation. At Sandia he has had a variety of assignments that include the development and deployment of perimeter security systems and airborne, real-time automatic target recognition systems. His most recent work has been researching scalable computer architectures, focusing on the performance and architectural tradeoffs of high performance processors and high-speed interconnects. He is also participates in defining the technical requirements and the procurement of high-performance computing platforms for Sandia and the NNSA's ASC program.

**Sudip Dosanjh** heads computer science research at Sandia National Laboratories. He is a Co-Director of the Institute for Advanced Architectures and Algorithms (IAA) and the Alliance for Computing at the Extreme Scale (ACES). The IAA, a collaboration with Oak Ridge National Laboratory, has a goal of enabling Exascale computing in the next decade through the co-design of architectures and algorithms. ACES, a collaboration with Los Alamos National Laboratory, is developing and deploying a 2010 production capability Petaflops supercomputer. A preliminary architecture for Trinity, a 2014 trans-petaflops system, is also being created. He received his Ph.D. from U.C. Berkeley in 1986 and has published over three-dozen articles on computational science and massively parallel computing.

**Marcus Epperson** is a Technical Staff member at Sandia National Laboratories in Albuquerque, New Mexico, USA. He is a lead system designer and integrator for large-scale capacity HPC systems, and a system software engineer. He received a Bachelors degree in Computer Science from New Mexico Tech in 2001.

**David A. Evensky** was granted a Ph.D. in Chemical Physics from the University of Illinois in 1993. He is currently a Principal Member of Technical Staff at Sandia National Laboratories at the Livermore California site. His research interests include high performance computing and its application to scientific problems.

**Alberto Falzone** is an IT consultant for NICE srl, Cortanze (AT) Italy, since June 2000. An exclusively knowledge base about distributed computing based on LSF tool, which NICE is vendor since 1996, and JOB management, was built during the customers assistance activity in the first period. He takes care the scientific customers mainly, as INFN Istituto Nazionale di Fisica Nucleare, ENEA (the Italian Environment and Energy Agency), CRS4 in Cagliari and others, with support activities for their clusters in LAN or WAN. Teaching activities about LSF was held in SNS (Scuola Normale Superiore) in Pisa for customer's system administrators. Support in R&D about EnginFrame as web portal infrastructure, developed from NICE srl, he has trusted within the same scientific context. Since January 2001 he started to develop the GENIUS portal, as NICE partner, powered by EnginFrame, working in collaboration with Roberto Barbera, as INFN partner. He does maintain the supervision of GENIUS Portal development planned for HEP experiments, with significative results for CMS in INFN Padova site, Italy. Since october 2002 he started a mutual collaboration with Science Academy of Prague, Intitute of Physics, Czech Republic, where GENIUS has been installed. Since 2006 he supported the installation of all sites in COMETA Consortium, taking care about HPC layers on every cluster and specific customizations to enable HPC features within gLite environment on the PI2S2 insfrastructure. Other research interest areas, as IT consultant, are security infrastructures development, firewalling and internet routing, bioinformatics.

**Yu Fang** received her Ph.D. degree from the Department of Computer Science and Technology, Tongji University, Shanghai, China, in 2006. Since 2006 she is an associate Professor of Tongji University. During her four years in the Key Laboratory for Embedded System and Service Computing of Chinese

Ministry of Education, she anticipated various national and international research projects centered on mobile information service and mobile network, especially in Intelligent Transport System (ITS) application and mobile navigation. Her research focuses on: Data model, organization and service for mobile navigation, traffic data acquisition and transformation based on self-organized vehicle network, perception-based navigation with self-organized vehicle network and sensor network, well-understood navigation service on mobile devices, etc.

**Marco Fargetta** graduated in Computer Engineering at the University of Catania in 2002 with a thesis on a new Java extension for Computational Reflection. Since 2006 he holds a Ph.D. in Computer Engineering from the same University with a thesis titled "A Model for Automatically Supporting Advanced Reservation, Allocation and Pricing in a Grid Environment". Afterwards he has worked in Grid projects at national (i.e. TriGrid VL and PI2S2 founded by the Sicily Region) and international (i.e. ICEAGE founded by the EU) level. Actually he is working at INFN (Istituto Nazionale di Fisica Nucleare) in the context of the EU founded EUAsiaGrid Project.

**Al Geist** is a Corporate Research Fellow at Oak Ridge National Laboratory. He is the Chief Technology Officer of the Leadership Computing Facility and also leads a 30 member Computer Science Research Group. He is one of the original developers of PVM (Parallel Virtual Machine), which became a worldwide de facto standard for heterogeneous distributed computing. He was actively involved in the design of the Message Passing Interface (MPI-1 and MPI-2) standard.

**Genoveffa (Jeni) Giambona** research interests are in the area of leadership development, management learning, virtual teams and trust. She also researches meta-evaluation and the study of how learning mechanisms work in different contexts and cultures. She leads an EU sponsored project on the meta-evaluation of e-learning programmes. Jeni also has an interest in the application of realist synthesis, narrative analysis and discourse analysis.

**Ankur Gupta** is the professor of Computer Science and Engineering at the Model Institute of Engineering and Technology, Jammu, India. His research interests include network management, P2P networks/computing and software engineering. He has over 20 research papers published in International Conferences and Journals, besides two patents pending at the US Patents and Trademarks Office and a defensive publication to his name. He has over 7 years of software development experience with Hewlett-Packard. He is a recipient of the AICTE (All India Council for Technical Education) Career Award for Young Teachers.

**Ondrej Habala** is a researcher at the Institute of Informatics of the Slovak Academy of Sciences since 2001, when he received his MSc in software engineering from the Slovak University of Technology. He was born in 1977 and computers are his main interest since 1991. He specializes in data and metadata management, environmental applications of distributed computing and grid computing. He is the author and co-author of numerous scientific papers in the field of grid computing and environmental applications of computer technologies.

**Scott Hemmert** received a BS in Physics and German from Brigham Young University in 1996. He also receive his PhD in electrical engineering from Brigham Young University in 2003. Since then he has been working for Sandia National Laboratories where he is a Senior Member of Technical Staff. His current research interests include network interface architectures for accelerating messaging protocols and the implications of using accelerators in high performance computing.

**Michael Heroux** is a Distinguished Member of the Technical Staff at Sandia National Laboratories, working on new algorithm development, and robust parallel implementation of solver components for problems of interest to Sandia and the broader scientific and engineering community. He leads development of the Trilinos Project, an effort to provide state of the art solution methods in a state of the art software framework. He leads the Mantevo project, which is focused on the development of Open Source, portable micro-applications and micro-drivers for scientific and engineering applications. Michael Heroux received a Ph.D. in Mathematics from Colorado State University in 1989.

**Beat Hirsbrunner** is full professor and leader of the Pervasive and Artificial Intelligence research group at the University of Fribourg. He holds a diploma and PhD in theoretical physics from ETHZ Zurich and University of Lausanne. He has been postdoc, visiting researcher and professor at the universities of Rennes and Berkeley, EPFL Lausanne, and IBM Research Labs San José. He has conducted research works on topics of parallel, distributed and pervasive computing, coordination languages, and human-computer interaction. He has been involved in several Swiss, European and US research projects. He served as dean of the Faculty of science of the University of Fribourg, and is since 2001 member of the swiss NSF council and vice-president of SARIT.

**Ladislav Hluchý** is the director of the Institute of Informatics of the Slovak Academy of Sciences. He has received a MSc in 1975, and PhD. in 1986. Since 1985 he leads the Departement of Parallel and Distributed Computing, and since 1992 he is the director of the Institute. He is the editor-in-chief of the Computing and Informatics journal, member of IEEE and other professional societies, and supervisor of numerous BsC., MsC. and PhD. theses.

**Ye Huang** obtained his Master degree from Chongqing University (China) in 2007. Since end of 2007, he is doing his Ph.D at the University of Fribourg (Switzerland), and working on the project SmartGRID, which is funded by Hasler Foundation, and collaborated with Grid and Ubiquitous Computing Group, University of Applied Sciences Western Switzerland. His research interests concern grid and distributed systems, service oriented interoperation and negotiation.

**Carmelo Marcello Iacono-Manno**, after cum laude physics graduation during 1990, worked at the Laboratorio Nazionale del Sud, Istituto Nazionale di Fisica Nucleare (INFN), on Data Acquisition and Control Systems developing sequential and parallel C codes for the readout programs and electronic device control. He also developed an off-line application for off-line data analysis based on a neural network simulation. After PhD graduation in 2003, he joined the Grid team at the INFN Catania Section, collaborating to the Trigrid and PI2S2 projects as an application supporter focusing on parallel and massive calculus. He helped porting many applications onto the Grid, covering various fields such as Computer Fluid-Dynamics (Fluent, OpenFOAM), Chemistry (GROMACS, GAMESS), Nuclear Physics (CoMD-II, ISOSPIN). He also contributed to the development of tools for middleware extension (VisualGrid, watchdog, recursive catalogue command) and cared about some of the editorial activities of the Consorzio COMETA (Proceedings of the Grid Open Days at the University of Palermo).

**Curtis V. Janssen** received his BS in Chemistry from the University of Illinois at Urbana-Champaign and his PhD in Theoretical Chemistry from the University of California at Berkeley. He is currently a Distinguished Member of Technical Staff at Sandia National Laboratories in Livermore, CA. He is the lead architect and programmer for the Massively Parallel Quantum Chemistry program, which serves as a testbed for new programming methodologies, new algorithms, and new quantum chemistry methods. Dr. Janssen's interest span the various technologies required for high performance scientific computation, including areas such as parallel programming models, performance analysis, machine architecture, and software development techniques.

**Changjun Jiang** received his Ph.D. degree in Control theory from Institute of Automation Chinese Academy of Sciences. He is the Distinguished Professor and PhD administrator of Computer Science in Tongji University. His research interests include Network Computing, Parallel Processing, Grid computing, Petri Nets and ITS. He has presided above 30 Foundation Items of National High-tech R&D Program, National Basic Research Program of China and National Key Technologies R&D Program etc. He has published more than 118 journal and conference papers in "Science of China", "IEEE Transactions on Robotics & Automation", "IEEE Transactions on Fuzzy Systems", and other respected journals both at home and abroad, over 40 of which are indexed by SCI and EI.

**Suzanne M. Kelly** is a distinguished member of technical staff at Sandia National Laboratories. Suzanne holds a BS in computer science from the University of Michigan and an MS in computer science from Boston University. Suzanne has worked on projects related to system-level software and information systems. In her current assignment, she has oversight responsibility for the system software on the Red Storm computer. Her previous assignment was leading the operating system team for the MPP, ASCI Red. Prior to her six-year sojourn in information systems for nuclear defense technologies, she worked on various high-performance computing file archive systems.

**Joseph P. Kenny** received a Ph.D. in chemistry from the University of Georgia in 2003. He is a Senior Member of the Technical Staff in the Scalable Computing R&D department at Sandia National Laboratories in Livermore, CA. His research focuses on development approaches and performance for scientific software.

**Doug Kothe** is the director of science for the National Center for Computational Sciences (NCCS) at Oark Ridge National Laboratory, responsible for guiding the multidisciplinary research teams using the center's leadership computing systems. Doug has more than 20 years of experience in computational science research. Before joining the NCCS, Doug was deputy program director for Theoretical and Computational Programs in the Advanced Simulation and Computing (ASC) Program at Los Alamos National Laboratory (LANL). Doug received his B.S. in chemical engineering from the University of Missouri–Columbia and his M.S. and Ph.D. in nuclear engineering from Purdue University. He is the author of more than 60 refereed publications and has written more than a half-million lines of source code.

**Pierre Kuonen** obtained a Master degree in electrical engineering from the Swiss Federal Institute of Technology (EPFL) in 1982. After six year of experience in industry he joined the Computer Science Theory Laboratory at EPFL in 1988 and started working in the field of parallel and distributed computing. He received his Ph.D degree from EPFL in 1993. Since 1994 he steadily worked in the field of parallel and distributed computing. First at EPFL where he founded and managed the GRIP (Parallel Computing Research Group) then at the University of Applied Science of Valais. Since 2003 he is full professor at the University of Applied Science of Fribourg in the Information and Communication technologies department (TIC) where he is leading the GRID & Ubiquitous Computing Group. Besides is teaching activities he continues to actively participate to national or international research projects. Pierre Kuonen is author or co-author of more than 50 scientific publications.

**Dimosthenis Kyriazis** received the diploma from the Dept. of Electrical and Computer Engineering of the National Technical University of Athens, Athens, Greece in 2001, the MS degree in techno-economic systems (MBA) co-organized by the Electrical and Computer Engineering Dept - NTUA, Economic Sciences Dept - National Kapodistrian University of Athens, Industrial Management Dept - University of Piraeus and his PhD from the Electrical and Computer Engineering Department of the National Technical University of Athens in 2007. He is currently a researcher in the Telecommunication Laboratory of the Institute of Communication and Computer Systems (ICCS). Before joining the ICCS he has worked in the private sector as Telecom Software Engineer. He has participated in numerous EU / National funded projects (such as NextGRID, Akogrimo, BEinGRID, HPC-Europa, GRIA, Memphis, Fidis, etc). His research interests include Grid computing, scheduling, Quality of Service provision and workflow management in heterogeneous systems and service oriented architectures.

**Emanuele Leggio** was born in Ragusa, Italy in 1978. He receveid the Master Degree in mechanical engineering from Catania University in 2007. He worked for Consortium SCIRE, Numidia s.r.l., Honor Center of Italian Universities (H2CU) in the field of Computational Fluid Dynamics (CFD) and GRID computing. On 2008 he joined the GRID team at INFN Catania section developing CFD modelling of Marmore Waterfalls and developed Fluent-GRID environment. He is from November 2008 a PhD student in innovative technologies for sustainable mobility at the University of Rome "Tor Vergata".

**John M. Levesque** is the director of Cray's Supercomputing Center of Excellence based at Oak Ridge National Laboratory (ORNL). The CoE assists the DoE's Office of Science researchers in porting and optimizing their applications to the Cray systems at ORNL. Mr. Levesque is in Cray's Chief Technology Office in charge of application performance. Levesque has been at Cray Inc since 2001. Prior to joining Cray, Levesque had a similar role at IBM Research as the director of the Advanced Computing Technology Center (ACTC) based in Yorktown Heights. Prior to joining IBM, Levesque was the President of Applied Parallel Research, a company founded by Levesque to develop parallel programming software. Levesque has been in High Performance computing since 1968 having worked at Sandia Laboratories, Air Force Weapons Laboratory, R&D Associates, Pacific Sierra Research on systems ranging from the Star 100-Cyber 205, Illiac IV, all the Crays, IBM SP, Thinking Machines CM, Intel Paragon, nCube, etc. Levesque is a world renowned lecturer on Optimization of Fortran application and author of the book "Guidebook to Fortran on Supercomputers".

**Maozhen Li** is a Senior Lecturer in the School of Engineering and Design at Brunel University, United Kingdom. He received the PhD from Institute of Software, Chinese Academy of Sciences in 1997. He joined Brunel University as a full-time lecturer in 2002. His research interests are in the areas of grid computing, intelligent systems, P2P computing, semantic web, information retrieval, content based image retrieval. He has over 70 scientific publications in these areas. He authored *"The Grid: Core Technologies"*, a well-recognized textbook on grid computing which was published by Wiley in 2005. He has served as an IPC member for over 30 IEEE conferences. He is on editorial boards of the International Journal of Grid and High Performance Computing, the International Journal of Distributed Systems and Technologies, and the International Journal on Advances in Internet Technology.

**Paul T. Lin** received his BS in Aerospace Engineering from the University of Michigan and his MS and PhD in Mechanical and Aerospace Engineering from Princeton University. He is currently a member of the technical staff at Sandia National Laboratories. His research interests include high performance computing, scalable linear solvers, preconditioners, multigrid methods, and algorithms for multicore processors.

**Enjie Liu** is a Senior Lecturer in Computing at the University of Bedfordshire (UK). She has a BSc in computer science from Southwest University in China and a PhD in telecommunications from Queen Mary, University of London. She has been involved in one previous European project and is currently participating in 4 EPSRC/European projects.

**Xiangyu Liu** is an MPhil student in the School of Engineering and Design at Brunel University. His research interests include peer-to-peer computing, information retrieval, semantic web.

**Yang Liu** is a PhD student in the School of Engineering and Design at Brunel University. His research interests include peer-to-peer computing, information retrieval, semantic web, distributed and parallel computing.

**Alessandro Lombardo** is a molecular biologist with a PhD in phytosanitary technologies on biotechnological applications in plant pathology at the University of Catania. He is member of the steering committee of the italian technological platform "IT-Plants for the future", member of the scientific committee, challenge conversion, of the italian technological platform "Biofuels Italy". Since 2005 he is responsible of the laboratory of biotechnology, genomic analysis and varietal correspondence (Science and Technology Park of Sicily) and since 2008 responsible of the laboratory of phytopathology (Science and Technology Park of Sicily). He was involved in several Interregional, national and regional projects. He is author of about 25 scientific papers published in international refereed journals and presented in national and international congress and 1 patent. His main research areas are the development of expression vectors for plants, yeasts and bacteria, bioinformatic applied on plant viruses, variety correspondence, molecular characterization of plants, yeasts and viruses.

**Jackson Mayo** received the Ph.D. degree in physics from Princeton University in 2005. He is a Senior Member of Technical Staff in the Visualization & Scientific Computing Department at Sandia National Laboratories in Livermore, CA. His research interests include application of methods from theoretical physics to complex, nonlinear, and statistical phenomena in science and engineering.

**Salvatore Monforte** graduated in computer sciences at the University of Catania in 1991 and got his PhD in electronic engineering, computer science and telecommunications in 2002. From 1999 to 2000 he has been working within the Ipp-hurray Research Group of the Polytechnic Institute of Porto School of Engineering (Isep-ipp) studying the Worst Case Response Time scheduling in R-Fieldbus real-time systems. Since 2000 has been collaborating within the National Institute of Nuclear Physics (INFN) as IT specialist for "DataGRID", EGEE, EGEE-II, EGEE-III EU projects as member of Workload Management System Package WP1/JRA1 group, developing gLite EGEE Grid middleware since 2000. He has a more than 5 years experience in programming and Web programming languages, grid computing, computers networks. He is author of more than 20 papers published on international peer-reviewed journals.

**Gianmarco De Francisci Morales** was born in Caltagirone (CT), Italy on July 7th 1983. He received both his Bachelor's and Master's degree in Computer Engineering (cum laude) from the University of Catania respectively in 2004 and 2008. From 2007 he has been working for COMETA Consortium on Grid Computing. He is currently a PhD student in computer science and engineering at IMT Institute for Advanced Studies Lucca.

**Annamaria Muoio** was born in Cava de' Tirreni on 15 august of 1971. In 1998 she graduated in nuclear physics. She joined the TriGrid and PI2S2 projects in 2005, porting applications on the Sicilian Grid; in particular, she focused on multi-disciplinary scientific and industrial applications accessible via a web gateway (Genius). She implemented applications for the CHIMERA multidetector, the ISOSPIN experiment, the CoMD-II (Constrained Molecular Dynamics) model the ViralPack project, an industrial project carried out for the Clean Room, for pollution calculation. Dr. Muoio also taught during many tutorials both in Italy and abroad and participated as a Grid expert to various schools.

**Richard Murphy** is a computer architect in the scalable computer architecture department at Sandia National Laboratories. He received his Ph.D. in computer engineering at the University of Notre Dame. His research interests include computer architecture, with a focus on memory systems and Processing-In-Memory, VLSI, and massively parallel architectures, programming languages, and runtime systems. He spent 2000 to 2002 at Sun Microsystems leading projects in hardware resource management and dynamic configuration.

**Jeff Nichols** is currently the Associate Laboratory Director (Interim) of ORNL's Computing and Computational Sciences Directorate where he provides scientific and management oversight for the divisions and programs within the Directorate. Prior to joining ORNL, Jeff was the Deputy Director of the Environmental Molecular Sciences Laboratory at Pacific Northwest National Laboratory (PNNL). Jeff joined PNNL as a Staff Scientist in 1993 and later became Technical Group Leader of the High Performance Computational Chemistry group. Jeff Nichols has a Ph.D. in Theoretical Physical Chemistry from Texas A&M University.

**Jeff Ogden** is serving as a Hewlett-Packard High Performance Computing Expert currently engaged at Sandia National Laboratories (SNL). He has been in this position since 2001. His prior industry experience includes Intel Corporation, Honeywell Defense and Lockheed Martin Information Systems. He has served in a variety of roles including technical lead, HPC systems design and engineering, software engineering, and embedded systems engineering. Jeff is the founder and lead developer of the Cbench open source project (http://cbench.sourceforge.net) used extensively to scalably benchmark and test HPC systems at SNL. He has a Masters of Science in Computer Engineering from The University of New Mexico.

**Ron Oldfield** is a senior member of the technical staff at Sandia National Laboratories in Albuquerque, NM. He received the B.Sc. in computer science from the University of New Mexico in 1993. From 1993 to 1997, he worked in the computational sciences department of Sandia National Laboratories, where he specialized in seismic research and parallel I/O. His work on the Salvo Seismic Imaging project led to an R&D 100 award in 1998. From 1997 to 2003 he attended graduate school at Dartmouth College and received his Ph.D. in June 2003. In September of 2003, he returned to Sandia to work in the Scalable System Software department. He currently leads projects in scalable I/O, resilience, and informatics. His research interests include parallel and distributed computing, parallel I/O, resilience, performance modeling, and scalable informatics.

**Salvatore Orlando** is research astronomer at the INAF-Osservatorio Astronomico di Palermo since the end of 1999. He graduated in Physics "cum Laude" at the University of Palermo in 1993 and since 1997 he holds a PhD in physics from the same University. In 1995, he was research fellow at the Dept. of Astronomy and Astrophysics, the University of Chicago (USA), and in 1997-1999, research fellow at the European Space Agency (ESA) - Solar System Division (Noordwijk, The Netherlands). Since his graduation his main research activity has been performed in the realm of optically thin astrophysical plasmas, more specifically solar and stellar coronae, supernova remnants. He has developed and applied hydrodynamic and magnetohydrodynamic parallel numerical models on High Performance Computing (HPC) systems, and Grid/HPC infrastructures. He is author of about 50 scientific articles on refereed international journals (first author of about 20), and of several invited presentations at international meetings. He is scientific coordinator of PHOENIX, an European program for the transfer of knowledge on young stellar objects (2006-2010), and member of the scientific and technical board in the framework of the COMETA-CILEA agreement for HPC and Grid technologies.

**Gianluca Passaro** has been working as a technician for the Consorzio COMETA since 2005. He deals with the configuration and maintenance of the net and various services (mail, virtual machines). He also supports the deployment of the applications focusing on HPC.

**Ali Pinar** received his PhD degree in 2001 in computer science from University of Illinois at Urbana-Champaign and his B.S. and M.S. degrees in 1994 and 1996, respectively, in Computer Engineering from Bilkent University, Turkey. He is a member of the Information and Decision Sciences Department at Sandia National Laboratories. Before joining Sandia, he was with the High Performance Computing Research Department at Lawrence Berkeley National Laboratory. His research is on combinatorial problems arising in algorithms and applications of scientific computing, with emphasis on parallel computing, sparse matrix computations, computational problems in electric power systems, graph data mining, and interconnection network design. Dr. Pinar is a member of SIAM and its activity groups in Supercomputing, Computational Science and Engineering, and Optimization; IEEE Computer Society; and ACM. He is also elected to serve as the secretary of the SIAM activity group in Supercomputing for the 2008—2009 term.

**Nikolaos Psimogiannos** is a PhD Candidate in the University of the Aegean, Department of Information and Communication Systems Engineering. He received his Diploma from the Department of Electrical and Computer Engineering of the National Technical University of Athens (NTUA), Greece, in 2003 and his MS degree in Techno-Economic Systems (MBA) co-organized by the Electrical and Computer Engineering Department - NTUA, Economic Sciences Department - National Kapodistrian University of Athens, Industrial Management Department - University of Piraeus, in 2006. In 2003, he joined the Telecommunication Laboratory of the Institute of Communication and Computer Systems (ICCS), as a researcher. He has participated in several projects funded by the EU and National Agencies. His research interests are in the area of Communication Networks (Wireless Broadband Networks, Cellular, Wireless Sensor Networks, Ad-hoc Networks, WLANs, IMS, Mesh Networks).

**Antonio Puliafito** is a full professor of computer engineering at the University of Messina, Italy. His interests include parallel and distributed systems, networking, wireless and GRID computing. He is currently the director of the RFIDLab, a research lab on RFID and wireless, the vice-president of the Consorzio Cometa whose aim is to enhance and exploit high performance computing. He is actively working in grid computing and virtualization in the projects TriGrid VL, PI2S2 and RESERVOIR.

**Mahesh Rajan** is a Distinguished Member of the Technical Staff at Sandia National Laboratory in Albuquerque, New Mexico, USA. His main interests are in parallel and distributed programming performance analysis, tuning, and modeling. He provides user support of scientific applications for large capability class High Performance Computing (HPC) systems like Red Storm and for large HPC capacity clusters. He obtained a Ph.D degree in Engineering Science and Mechanics from Virginia Tech in 1981.

**Arun Rodrigues** joined the Sandia National Labs in June 2006 after receiving his PhD from the University of Notre Dame, working under Peter Kogge on programming models and architectural tradeoffs in Processors-In-Memory. Working in the Scalable Computer Architecture Group, he is involved in the specification and procurement of next-generation capability class supercomputers. His research interests are in architectural simulation, advanced memory systems, and network acceleration. Arun is currently the lead developer of the Structural Simulation Toolkit (SST), a system simulation framework for exploring novel HPC architectures.

**Ivo F. Sbalzarini** completed his MSc in Mechanical Engineering with majors in Control and Computational Science at ETH Zurich. He then did his PhD in Computer Science at ETH Zurich under the supervision of Prof. Petros Koumoutsakos. He received the Willi Studer Prize for his graduation thesis and the international Chorafas Science Award for his PhD dissertation. Dr. Sbalzarini was invited Professor at École Normale Supérieure (Paris, France) and Group Leader at the Mediterranean Institute for Life Sciences (Split, Croatia). Currently, he is Assistant Professor of Computational Science at ETH Zurich. Ivo Sbalzarini is a member of the governing board of the Technical Society of Zurich (TGZ), a member of the Swiss Institute of Bioinformatics (SIB), and served in the Federal Project Group "Swiss National Strategic Plan for High Performance Computing and Networking". Dr. Sbalzarini is one of the core developers of the PPM Library.

**Martin Šeleng** is a researcher at Institute of Informatics, Slovak Academy of Sciences. In 1999 he obtained his MSc degree in mathematics and computer science at the Faculty of Mathematics and Physics at the Commius University in Bratislava. He worked previously at the Faculty of Economy and Informatics at the Economic University as a researcher and a teacher in the field of mathematics, statistics and computer science. He received his PhD. in statistics from the University of Economics in Bratislava in 2009. He has extensive experience in e-mail communication-related system development and information system evaluation. He has been employed at the Institute since 2006. He is the author and co-author of several scientific papers and participated/participates in the K-Wf Grid, Commius and Admire European projects and in several national projects. He teaches information retrieval at the Faculty of Informatics and Information Technologies at Slovak University of Technology in Bratislava. His research interests include data mining, email communication and large scale information processing.

**Sana Sellami** is a PhD candidate at the INSA of Lyon (National Institute of Applied Sciences Lyon France). She received her Master degree from Computer Science from INSA of Lyon in 2006 and Engineering degree from INSAT, Tunisia in 2006. Her main research interests are related to Large scale XML schemas matching domain,

**Fabrizio Silvestri** is currently a Researcher at ISTI - CNR in Pisa. He received his PhD from the Computer Science Department of the University of Pisa in 2004. His research interests are mainly focused on Web information retrieval with particular focus on efficiency related problems like caching, collection partitioning, distributed IR in general. In his professional activities Silvestri is member of the program committee of many of the most important conferences in IR as well as organizer and, currently, member of the steering committee, of the workshop Large Scale and Distributed Systems for Information Retrieval (LSDS-IR). He has more than 40 publications on the field of efficiency in IR. In particular, in these last years his main research focus is on query log analysis for performance enhancement of Web search engines. In the topic of the tutorial, Silvestri has written recently a survey paper for the journal *Foundations and Trends in Information Retrieval*, and has given a keynote speech at the LA-Web 2008 conference with a talk entitled "Past Searches Teach Everything: Including the Future.

**Branislav Šimo** is a researcher at the Institute of Informatics of the Slovak Academy of Sciences since 2001, when he received his MSc in software engineering from the Slovak University of Technology. He specializes in collaborative user interfaces, distributed and grid computing and process workflow management technologies. He is the author and co-author of numerous scientific publications, and active participant in development of research prototypes in the context of EU and national-scale research projects.

**Dongxing Teng**, male, is an Associate Research Fellow in Intelligence Engineering Lab at Institute of Software, Chinese Academy of Sciences. He was born in 1973, and obtained his Ph.D degree from Tsinghua University in 2001. His research interests include information visualization technologies, Business Intelligence and Human computer Interaction.

**Vinod Tipparaju** is a Research Staff Member in the Future Technologies Group at the Oak Ridge National Laboratory. He is one of the main developers of Global Arrays toolkit and the ARMCI communication library. His research interests include Programming Models for High Performance Computing, Network Interconnects and Collective Communication Algorithms.

**James L. Tomkins** has over thirty years of experience in high performance computing. He spent the first twenty years as a computer code developer. Of these, the first 15 years involved developing simulation codes for nuclear reactor safety and the next five involved research into making scientific and engineering applications scale for Massively Parallel Processors (MPPs). In early 1995, James became the project leader for the ASCI Red computer project. (ASCI Red was the first of the big ASCI machines and a joint development project between Sandia National Laboratories and Intel.) As a result of the ASCI Red work, he began working on developing a new supercomputer system architecture. This architecture became the Red Storm architecture and, through a joint development-contract with Cray, the Cray XT architecture. In late December of 2008, James retired from Sandia National Laboratories as a Senior Scientist/Engineer and is now doing limited consulting in supercomputer architectures. He has a Bachelor's Degree in Physics from the University of Northern Iowa and a Master of Science Degree in Nuclear Engineering from the University of Illinois.

**Viet Tran** is a researcher at the Institute of Informatics of the Slovak Academy of Sciences since 1995, when he received his MSc from the Slovak University of Technology, and holds a PhD. diploma since 2003 in Applied Informatics. He is experienced in distributed and parallel processing, tool and application development. He has participated in several EU-funded projects including ANFAS, CROSSGRID, EGEE, ADMIRE, DEGREE. He was also the leader of Slovak national projects VEGA-2/6103/27 and APVV INTAP. His main research interests are in distributed and parallel computing technologies, cluster computing, grid computing, data management and environmental applications. The current focus of his research is in cloud computing. He also provides training and support for grid applications for users in Slovakia as well as users in Earth Science and Astrophysics. He is the author and co-author of more than 70 publications.

**Konstantinos Tserpes** is research associate in the Telecommunication Laboratory of the Institute of Communication and Computer Systems (ICCS), Athens, Greece. He graduated from the Computer Engineering and Informatics department, University of Patras, Greece. In 2006 he received his MBA in Techno-Economical Systems. He acquired his PhD in the area of service oriented architectures with a focus on quality aspects from the school of Electrical and Computer Engineers of the National Technical University of Athens (NTUA) in 2008. He has been involved in several EU (NextGRID, AkoGRIMO, HPC-Europa, EchoGRID, CHALLENGERS, etc) and National funded (HellasGRID, USNES) projects and his research interests are revolving around service oriented computing and its application and business extensions.

**Francesco Tusa** was born in Messina on Feb 5th 1983. He received the Laurea Degree in Computer Engineering from the University of Messina, Italy, in 2007. He's currently attending his PhD in advanced technologies for information engineering at the University of Messina. His research interests are in the areas of security for distributed computing, such as Grid and Cloud environments.

**Man Qi** is a Senior Lecturer in Department of Computing at Canterbury Christ Church University, UK. She was a Research Fellow in Dept. of Computer Science at University of Bath, UK from Jan. 2001 to Oct. 2003. Her research interests are in the areas of Computer Graphics, Computer Animation, Multimedia and Grid Computing Applications

**Theodora A. Varvarigou** received the BTech degree from the National Technical University of Athens, Athens, Greece in 1988, the MS degrees in electrical engineering (1989) and in computer science (1991) from Stanford University, Stanford, California in 1989 and the PhD degree from Stanford University as well in 1991. She worked at AT&T Bell Labs, Holmdel, New Jersey between 1991 and 1995. Between 1995 and 1997 she worked as an assistant professor at the Technical University of Crete, Chania, Greece. Since 1997 she was elected as an assistant professor while since 2007 she is a professor at the National Technical University of Athens, and Director of the Postgraduate Course "Engineering Economics Systems". Prof. Varvarigou has great experience in the area of semantic web technologies, scheduling over distributed platforms, embedded systems and grid computing. In this area, she has published more than 150 papers in leading journals and conferences. She has participated and coordinated several EU funded projects, related to subject of the IRMOS project such as POLYMNIA, Akogrimo, NextGRID, BEinGRID, Memphis, MKBEEM, MARIDES, CHALLENGERS, FIDIS, and other.

**Courtenay Vaughan** obtained his Ph.D in Applied Mathematics from the University of Virginia in 1989. He joined Sandia National Laboratories in Albuquerque, NM after graduation working in the field of parallel computing. He has worked on benchmarking, testing, and performance analysis and modeling of applications on parallel computers.

**Jeffrey Vetter** is a computer scientist in the Computer Science and Mathematics Division (CSM) of Oak Ridge National Laboratory (ORNL), where he leads the Future Technologies Group and directs the Experimental Computing Laboratory. Dr. Vetter is also a Joint Professor in the College of Computing at the Georgia Institute of Technology, where he earlier earned his PhD. He joined ORNL in 2003, after four years at Lawrence Livermore National Laboratory. Vetter's interests span several areas of high-end computing (HEC) -- encompassing architectures, system software, and tools for performance and correctness analysis of applications.

**Massimo Villari** received the Laurea degree in 1999 in electronic engineering, University of Messina Italy. Since 2000 he was PhD student in advanced technologies for information engineering and in 2003 he received his PhD. In the 2002 he was in a stage next Cisco Systems and he was involved on MPEG4IP and NEMO projects. In 2003/2004/2005 was professor of the matters Computer Science, Lab of CS, Elaboration Systems and Database. Since 2006 he is an assistant professor at the University of Messina. He is currently a member of directive council of Centre on Information Technologies Development and their Applications next University of Messina. He is actively working as Security Designer in cloud computing and virtualization in the European Project RESERVOIR.

**Hongan Wang**, male, born in 1963, is currently a Research Fellow in Intelligence Engineering Lab at Institute of Software, Chinese Academy of Sciences. His research interests include human interface and real time database.

**Tao Wang** is a research assistant at the University of Bedfordshire (UK). He has a BSc in computer science from University of Ulster and an MSc in telecommunication and Internet systems from the University of Ulster (N. Ireland, UK). He is currently working on 2 European projects.

**Belabbes Yagoubi** graduated from University of Oran, Algeria, where he received PhD degree in computer science in 2007. He is currently leading a research team on the management of resources in grids. His main research interests are in the grid computing, distributed systems, load balancing and resource management challenges in Grids.

**Chun Gang Yan**, Professor of Tongji University, received her Ph.D. degree from the Department of Computer Science and Technology, Tongji University, Shanghai, China, in 2006. Her current research interests include Petri Net theory, concurrent model and algorithms. In recent years, she has published more than 10 papers in journals and conference proceedings.

**Haiyan Yang**, female, is currently a Ph.D candidate in Intelligence Engineering Lab at Institute of Software, Chinese Academy of Sciences. Her research interests include Human Computer Interaction Technologies, Sketch based human interface.

**Dong Liang Zhang**, Postdoctoral of Tongji University, received his Ph.D. degree from the Department of Computer Science and Technology, Tongji University, Shanghai, China, in 2009. His current research interests include large scale traffic flow simulation and load balancing on parallel computing. In recent years, he has published more than 10 papers in journals and conference proceedings.

**Xia Zhao** is a research assistant at the University of Bedfordshire (UK). She has a BSc in computer science & education from Liaoning Normal University (Dalian, China) and an MSc (dist) in Software Engineering for the e-Economy from the University of Leicester (Leicester, UK). She is currently working on 2 European projects.

# Index